MW01131507

Pioneers and Professions

There are many pioneers in all profession. We read about Madame Curie, Sir Isaac Newton; and many others; but in surveying we like to refer to Lewis and Clark and a few others; but actually they were essentially cartographers. I guess one could consider cartography as part of surveying, but we cannot name a true surveyor. When we define Pioneer, I consider it as a person who "breaks new ground" a phrase that came along from the pioneers of the western expansion of America. When the Pioneer, while pulling a plough, because he had no horse, would physically pull the plough into prairie soil breaking it for receiving the seeds of life. This in my opinion what Curt Brown was "A pioneer of Surveying" in that he took an area of surveying that transcended the manual manipulation of instruments and formed and expanded a new area of surveying, namely the law. Curt never intended surveyors to be lawyers, but what he did intended that surveyors understand the law so that they could better understand their place in the profession, in placing boundary lines on the ground that would meet the needs of the courts and the clients. From humble articles he started writing as aids to surveyors to his now famous textbooks, of which I have the pleasure and honor of being selected to carry on his tradition, Curt wanted surveyors to "understand the law" and apply the law, but to let the lawyers practice the law.

I first met Curt in 1965 when he was President of ACSM. His first book had just been published. I was 35 years old and liked the law. We became instant friends. We spent many hours discussing cases and philosophies. Although we were distant by miles, we occupied the same house of realizing, that to have a full rounded surveyors, we must develop a group on young men and women who understand our full potential is not in our abilities to manipulate instruments but in our abilities to place the law on an equal footing with technology. Thus in my opinion Curt was as much of a pioneer as were those many surveyors who trudged the open prairies and woods placing their millions of monuments as tribute to their work. Curt has influenced many young men and women to express their full potential in the legal aspects of surveying. Is that what a pioneer does?

– Walter Robillard
    Co-Author, *Boundary Control and Legal Principles*
    Co-Author, *Evidence and Procedures for Boundary Location*

****

Remembrances of Curtis M. Brown

If there ever was a figure in the land surveying arena who deserved to be chronicled, it is without a doubt Curtis Brown, a real pioneer in bringing rules of law and proper procedure to the profession. Mike Pallamary has done a remarkable job in helping to continue his legacy.

Mr. Brown did great service to the profession with his many writings and lectures, and by doing so created an awareness among professionals. Mike Pallamary has also done a great service to the profession by re-introducing these contributions and making them available to today's surveyor. I was particularly taken by comments from a variety of knowledgeable surveyors on particular issues.

– Donald A. Wilson, LLS, PLS, RPF
  Co-Author, *Boundary Control and Legal Principles*
  Co-Author, *Evidence and Procedures for Boundary Location*

****

Curtis Maitland Brown's work is well known to surveyors. Although he was not an attorney and had no authority to define rules of law, his writings have been used for decades as the most authoritative statement of boundary law in print. My teachings began in the mid-1970's and I found my legal training to be in conflict with Curt's conclusions. Accordingly, at a "Meet the Authors" conference at the University of Florida, I invited Curt to appear with me as my guest at a series of three three-day seminars to debate our opinions about the surveyor's duty and obligation as regards ownership.

As always, Curt was very gracious and accepted my invitation. We appeared together in Houston, Texas, Reno, Nevada, and Corvallis, Oregon. After several days of vigorous debate and input from surveyors in attendance, Curt and I concluded that surveyors actually do render opinions of ownership, regardless of their disclaimers. I was always impressed with Curt's integrity, character, and willingness to accept new ideas. He is sorely missed in our profession.

My sincere thanks to Mike Pallamary for compiling this work and tracing Curt's thoughts and ideas.

– Ted Madson
  Director, LSS Seminars

****

Additional Titles by Michael J. Pallamary

The History of San Diego Land Surveying Experiences
(with Curtis M. Brown)

Advanced Land Descriptions
(with Roy Minnick and Paul Cuomo)

Lay of the Land – The History of Land Surveying in San Diego County

THE CURT BROWN CHRONICLES

THE WRITINGS AND LECTURES OF CURTIS M. BROWN, PROFESSIONAL LAND SURVEYOR

Michael J. Pallamary, PLS

Edited By: Michael J. Pallamary, PLS
Assistant Editor: Gregory P. Hopkins, PLS
Book and Cover Design Concept: Michael J. Pallamary, PLS

authorHOUSE®

AuthorHouse™
1663 Liberty Drive
Bloomington, IN 47403
www.authorhouse.com
Phone: 1-800-839-8640

www.pallamaryandassociates.com
www.tiepoints.com

Cover Image: James Pascoe's 1870 Official Map of the Pueblo of San Diego, California

First published by AuthorHouse   3/9/2011

ISBN: 978-1-4520-9051-1 (dj)
ISBN: 978-1-4520-9052-8 (sc)
ISBN: 978-1-4520-9053-5 (e)

Printed in the United States of America

This book is printed on acid-free paper.

Certain stock imagery © Thinkstock.

To Maureen, Michael, Justin, Elizabeth, Paige, and Bostyn.

Thank you for your love and support.

"Professional stature cannot be attained by self-proclamation. The lazy say, 'give me the prize without the training, the wages without work, the reward without the quest, heaven without probation, a profession's prestige without a profession's skill.' If the land surveyor is to have professional standing, that standing must be earned and bestowed upon him by others."

– Curtis M. Brown
Professional Land Surveyor
San Diego, California

In Loving Memory of
Paul Anthony Cuomo
California Land Surveyor

1937 – 2008

"The purpose of this publication is to perpetuate
the works of the most prolific and influential
Land Surveyor of the 20th century."

Paul Anthony Cuomo, PLS
Comments on the preparation of
The Curt Brown Chronicles

IN MEMORIAM

As many Professional Land Surveyors would agree, there are not enough words to express the land surveying community's appreciation to the late Paul Cuomo. Ever since I met Paul in the early '80's, while we served as officers and members of the California Land Surveyors Association (CLSA), we have enjoyed a bond that goes far beyond that enjoyed by most people. In addition to our friendship, Paul has been one of the driving forces in my professional life. Thanks to him, we began this project and as a result of our mutual interest in the works of Curt Brown, I have been able to complete this work. Accordingly, this homage is intended to serve as a token of my appreciation to Paul along with our mutually inspired intention to honor the late Curtis M. Brown. Together and apart, both men were giants in the profession.

Although Paul and I spent considerable time presenting various seminars and lectures, my fondest memories go back to 1988 when Paul served as incoming President of CLSA. Always a man of ambition, he took great pride in organizing the annual state conference being held in Anaheim, California. Paul worked night and day to put on a world class event. He accomplished this by garnering the participation of several of the profession's finest luminaries, Curt Brown, Walt Robillard, Charles Moffitt, and Ben Bucker. It is not surprising that one of my favorite memories is of the evening when Paul hosted a dinner with these fine gentlemen. The repartee and conversation was decidedly priceless. If nothing else, if one did not take an interest in land surveying after that meeting, there would simply be no hope for the profession.

Paul began his surveying career in 1958 with the California Division of Highways (CALTRANS). He received his license to practice land surveying in 1973 and that year started teaching boundary classes at Santa Ana Junior College. He left Caltrans in 1980 and joined the Orange County Surveyor's Office as Deputy County Surveyor. In 1985, Paul founded Pacific Land Seminars and began offering exam preparation workshops for the California Land Surveyor in Training (LSIT) and Professional Land Surveyor exams. He also founded Paul Cuomo Press, Inc. Paul "retired" in 1993 to become a consultant in the boundary and mapping fields and to focus more on surveying education.

Paul was the founder and past chairman of the California Foundation for Land Surveying Education. He was a major supporter of California State Polytechnic University Pomona's (Cal Poly Pomona) efforts to obtain ABET accreditation for their 4-year Surveying option program. As a result of the Foundations efforts, over $100,000 in scholarships have been awarded to surveying students at Cal Poly Pomona and California State University at Fresno. In addition to funding scholarships, the foundation also provided over $50,000 in equipment donations to the Fresno, Pomona, Santiago Canyon Community College, and San Jacinto Community College surveying programs.

Paul co-authored the university textbook "Advanced Land Descriptions" with the author, Michael Pallamary and the late Roy Minnick. He also authored "Surveying Principles for Civil Engineers." Paul has been an Expert Examiner for the California State Board of Registration for Professional Engineers and Land Surveyors and he held the office of president at both the local and state level for CLSA. Through Pacific Land Seminars, Paul presented classes, seminars, and workshops across the United States. As an educator and mentor over the past four decades, Paul's devotion to the advancement of surveying education has touched thousands of lives and careers.

1988 California Land Surveyors Conference
Anaheim, California
Walt Robillard, Curt Brown, Michael Pallamary, Paul Cuomo,
Frank Moffitt, Ben Buckner

Paul made many other important and largely unheralded contributions to the land surveying profession. To most, Paul will be remembered as a friend, educator, and mentor to the many men and women who came in contact with him. Beginning in the mid 1970's, Paul developed a passion and devotion to the advancement of land surveying education. His commitment lasted four decades. Through his many classes, seminars, and workshops throughout the country, Paul shaped the careers of literally thousands of individuals. Following many years of unselfish contributions to the land surveying profession, my dear friend Paul Cuomo passed away on December 2, 2008.

ACKNOWLEDGMENTS

Many of the articles published herein first appeared in The American Congress on Surveying and Mapping's (ACSM) journals and magazines. It is therefore with great appreciation that I thank that organization for permitting me to share these valuable works. I would also like to extend my personal gratitude to ACSM Executive Director Curtis W. Sumner for his support of this endeavor.

I remain forever honored by the support and friendship bestowed upon me by Curt's widow, Thelma. Her confidence in me and the merits of this project are revered with the greatest of honor and appreciation. I am also pleased to have Curt's son Patrick as a friend. He has been very supportive of this project and I am grateful for his counsel and support of my efforts.

As with all things worthy and of value in my life, I am perpetually indebted to my wife Maureen. A woman of extraordinary beauty and patience, she has tolerated my early morning efforts and late night research. She has been kind enough to accept my insomnia fueled devotion to completing this work. In many ways, she has made a greater contribution to the surveying profession than I alone could have made.

I am also delighted to express my love and gratitude to Peggy Cuomo, Paul's loving wife. She has continually supported this project and as with Maureen, she has been patient as we worked our way through many hours of research and work. As with my own humble successes, a good woman stood behind Paul. I am also grateful to the support and friendship of Tony and Tom Cuomo, Paul and Peggy's sons. They have both made valuable contributions to this work and without their help, this book would not have been possible.

My son Justin has also assisted in this work by his regular contributions to these research efforts. His prescient vision of the evolution of the surveying profession is of great value and he will undoubtedly continue to make advancements on behalf of the profession.

As with previous works, I find myself returning to a core of individuals who had a great influence upon me, oftentimes without their knowledge. I would be remiss if I failed to acknowledge the invaluable influence Chuck Safford had upon me. It is because of Chuck's talent as an educator that I first became interested in the surveying profession to the degree I have immersed myself. It is also through Chuck that I was able to meet Curt.

Although no longer with us and undoubtedly surveying greener pastures, three more unique men have guided me in my earlier days. Their impact has been very influential and I often think of them whenever I am challenged to make a difficult decision in everyday life and in my work. To the late Don Nasland, PLS, and PE, I thank you for sharing with me the importance of honesty and ethics, two subjects on which Curt similarly placed high value. It is not surprising that Don and Curt worked together over the years on many important subjects.

To the late Harlan Dye, PLS, I thank you for teaching me the importance of humility and conducting oneself with a professional demeanor, two attributes also embraced by Curt. It is no surprise to know that these two giants in the profession were co-workers.

My appreciation for those who have supported me must extend to the late Ivan Nolan, PLS. Ivan inspired me to take my technical skills seriously and to apply myself in the pursuit of this important surveying trait. He has set the bar high and I am always reminded of his support over the years.

In addition to these exceptional men of inspiration, I would be remiss if I failed to acknowledge the support and influence of others whose paths I have crossed and those who continue to make contributions where they can. I am grateful to the distinguished members of the Land Surveyors Advisory Council on Technical Standards (LSACTS). Members Dave Ambler, Mike Butcher, Sean Englert, Greg Hopkins, Gary Hus, Casey Lynch, Robert Lee McComb, Larry Stevens, Ian Wilson and David Woolley all contributed to the completion of this work. To these individuals, I am indebted for their friendship and devotion to the Land Surveying profession. Indeed, Dave Ambler remains a model of the Professional Land Surveyor and his career is a credit to the profession. He has made a great many contributions to the practice of land surveying by virtue of his tireless efforts in advancing the cause of land surveying through participation in the community and by selfishly volunteering his time.

Mike Butcher's efforts in advancing the professional image of the Land Surveyor, combined with his prominence in the California Land Surveyor's Association, all of which is fueled by his passion for surveying excellence, continues to serve as a catalyst for the advancement of the profession and technical community.

Greg Hopkins's contributions to this work are beyond call or measure. His willingness to serve as an editor of this work and his unending support of the profession are unprecedented. Combined with his innate ability to serve the profession both in a public capacity and a private one, remain a model of professional stature reached by few people.

Gary Hus' extraordinary passion for elevating professional standards throughout the profession combined with his effectiveness as an analytical thinker have provided me with more than enough fuel to complete this work. Whenever I needed a source of motivation, I would merely look upon Gary and his efforts over the years.

Robert Lee McComb has made so many extraordinary contributions to the land surveying profession, they are too numerous to enumerate. His brilliance in the area of mathematics as well as his longstanding personal relationship with Curt Brown has provided me with some of my greatest inspirations for this week. Thank you.

Casey Lynch's goals and aspirations as a Professional Land Surveyor combined with his tenacity as a boundary survey have proved refreshing, enlightening, and inspiring. His ability and willingness to shoulder a load and his motivational demeanor have provided me with more than enough reason to put the hours needed into this work.

Larry Stevens' dedication and efforts to advance the land surveying profession are inspirational at many levels. His visions for the Professional Land Surveyor and his commitment to fulfilling these noble objectives are of such immense value, there are not enough words to recognize his efforts and contributions to this work.

Ian Wilson's critical and highly valued interpretation of land surveying principles remind me of Curt's approach to problem solving. His influence upon this work are evident and the extraodinary influence he has had upon the land surveying profession are admirable.

Dave Woolley's friendship and guidance in the development of professional land surveying standards and standards of care are a model for all, surveyor and non-surveyor alike to emulate. His recognition of the value of Curt's works and his application of these principles in his daily practice and contributions to the education of Land Surveyors cannot be overstated.

As with my earlier work, I remain indebted to my old friends in the profession. Their influence upon my life and professional career cannot be overstated. As I am unable to prioritize these individuals, I offer my thanks in no formal order of contribution or priority. I wish to thank Jack Gechter, D. K. Nasland, Mike Curren, Reggie Deck, Jack Roth, Mike Valenti, Hal Davis, Scott Fitch, Howard Dye, Bruce Hall, Steve Martin, Peter Fitzpatrick, Mike Clyburn, Beth Swersie, Stan MacIntosh, Rick McCormick, John Winn, Jim Taylor, Fred LePage, Les Carter, John Montes de Oca, Rick Brooks, Lou Hall, Bill Goodwin, Michelle Thompson, Frank Fitzpatrick, Allan Wake, E. Gary Chapman, Hans Peter Craig, Kent Whittaker, Don Wooley, Geff Dye, Bob Elliot, Doug Melchior, James Meyer, Dan Rinehart, John Butcher, Clyde Elmore,

Keith Vincent, Ken Shumaker, Ron Parker, Jeff Safford, William Snipes, Sid Xinos, Sean Pavlik, Stanley Macintosh, Sal Tecce, Dan Sparks, Rex Plummer, Pat McMichael, Pete Golding, Tim Reilly, Jim Nowlan, Rudy Pacheco, Jose Luis Gomez, Bob Meadows, Jon Blake, Rick Turner, Dave Viera, Larry Walsh, John Walters, Al Turner, Jim Algert, Armond Marois, Ron Ashman, Dan Harrison, Wayne Savoie, Bruce Marquis, Tony Nothdurft, Ryan Hunsicker, John Morris, Paul Goebel, Brian Wiseman, Peter Wiseman, Chris Ciremele, Andy Karydes, Frank Green, John Coffey, Chuck Moore, Blake Torgersen, Keith Nofield, Howard Brunner, Ross Carlson, Les Carter, Karl Cebe, Chuck Christiansen, Pat Christiansen, Glenn Odone, Lee Hennes, Phil Giurbino, Scott Fitch, Yazmin Arellano, John Grisafi, Greg Helmer, Jas Arnold, Kathy Morgan, Keith Nofield, Robert Bateman, Herm Bateman, John Pavlik, John Berggren, Joe Betit, Sam Diaz, Bob Ozibko, Scott Peters, Brian Polley, Erick Ricci, David Rick, Jill Van Houten, Steve Shelton, Richard Siegmund, Bob Wallace, Joe Yuhas, Andy Ziemniak, Daniel Hall, Clint Hale, Steve Nasland, Brian Faraci, Tom Harrington, David Grimes, Chuck Harris, Russ Forsberg, Vince Sincek, Gary Szytel, Randy Brown, Chris Royak, Jay Seymour, Paul DeSimone, Frank DeSimone, Dr. James Crossfield, Dr. Fareed Nader, and Alan Frank.

If Curt were with us today, he no doubt would have been intrigued by the wonders of the Internet and its value as a forum for the discussion and advancement of the surveying profession. I wish to extend my thanks to my able Internet allies and others who make regular contributions to the advancement of the profession including Ryan Versteeg, Evan Page, Ric Moore, Dane Ince, R. Lee Hixson, Jason Camit, S. Sean Ryan, Jim Frame, Anthony Maffia, Eric Ackerman, Steve Gardner, Dennis Hunter, David Hanrion, Ben Lund, Gregory Sebourn, Dave Lindell, and Gary O'Connor. I have also benefited from and remain motivated by others similarly devoted to the advancement of the land surveying profession. They include such luminaries as Dave Contreras, Bill Hofferber, Matthew Vernon, Rob McMillan, Todd Thomas, Terry Connors, Aaron Smith, Roger Frank, Dale Derix, Gary Lipincott, Steve Hawxhurst, Dave Murtha, David Boss, Dave Jarrell, Dave Faessel, Afshin Oskuni, Jim Casey, Eugene Cook, Lloyd Cook, Phil Danskin, Paul Buehler, Ken Brazzell, Ray Carlson, Bruce Barton, and Marc Cheves. I wish to extend a special thanks to NSPS members John Matonich and A. Wayne Harrison. Their support of my efforts is greatly appreciated and their friendship highly valued.

Last but not least, I wish to extend my thanks to Surveyor/Civil Engineer Charles Swart, an able surveyor in Montana and Texas who long ago recognized the importance of Curt and his efforts. If I missed anyone, it was not intentional.

EDITORIAL NOTES

The bulk of these lectures and writings were taken from various ACSM periodicals as well as from the personal collection of Curtis M. Brown. As is evident, a contemporary analysis of Curt's writings reveals that he principally focused on some well defined thematic issues. The subject material has therefore been categorized under a series of topics so as to present an overall theme and uniform mode of context. The extent of Curt's interest in these diverse subjects is evident by the volume of writing associated with the material at hand.

In the course of organizing and compiling Curt's writings, it became necessary to exercise discreet and judicious editing privileges in order to maintain harmony with the grammar as well as to avoid confusion whenever possible. In many of the articles, obvious liberties were taken with regards to rules of the English language. This occurred because many of these articles were extracted from an industry journal where most of the contributors knew each other and owing to their unique relationships, they occasionally adopted a more casual form of writing. In other cases, they used a very structured and mechanical style when it was necessary to make a technical or legal point.

In certain instances, italics replaced quotations and commas were discretely inserted when deemed necessary or to add clarity. As these articles were published over a large span in time, different grammatical rules were employed. And too, obvious errors were observed. In other instances, the peculiar modes of period and journal writing were retained so as to retain the flavor of the scriveners. It is hoped the reader can discern the difference. In all instances, every effort was made to preserve the spirit and import sought to be conveyed by the writers.

I have also added some color to this work by including copies of historical advertisements with the consent and permission of ACSM. My objectives are twofold. First and foremost, it is important for the reader to appreciate the technological climate of the surveying profession during Curt's era, particularly as his thinking evolved. He and his peers were involved in many of the cases that helped define the court's treatment and recognition of the rules of land surveying. Although technology has advanced considerably and new means of surveying are developing accordingly, Curt's fundamental discussions on the practice of land surveying are timeless. As one eventually learns, it does not matter how sophisticated your measuring tools are; if you are measuring to the wrong monument, the results will always be wrong. My other goal in including these ads is to provide a historical look at the evolution of land surveying technology as well as to place Curt's ideas in historical context. Considerable effort has been made to remove the moiré effect, a condition that arises when old magazine and newspaper photographs are scanned. Consequently, many of the images have been somewhat compromised.

The reader is cautioned to recognize that the articles and lectures presented in this book are as originally published. Therefore, many of the laws and citations may no longer be valid and none of the principles or cases should be accepted as dicta. In the spirit of Curt's approach to land surveying law, the reader is encouraged to investigate further.

Last but not least, when I felt it necessary, I have added clarifying notes to assist the reader in comprehending certain aspects of these articles or to elaborate on points once considered to be common knowledge within the surveying community. In some instances, the inclusion of a note was nothing more than good housekeeping. These additions are noted thus: [MP NOTE: Explanation follows.]

Thank you for indulging me and for allowing me to share the works of Curtis Maitland Brown with you.

Michael J. Pallamary, PLS
San Diego, California 2010

CONTENTS

BIOGRAPHY

CURTIS MAITLAND BROWN

PROFESSIONAL LAND SURVEYOR

By Michael J. Pallamary, PLS

In order to properly explain the importance of Curtis Brown upon the surveying profession, I must ask the reader's indulgence. My own experiences leading up to my career in land surveying are perhaps typical of other Land Surveyors. I began surveying in Boston, Massachusetts in 1971 and unbeknownst to me, Curt had retired from land surveying a few months earlier. After graduating from Boston Technical High School, where I majored in electronic engineering, I took a job with one of the country's oldest civil engineering and land surveying firms, Boston-based Whitman and Howard. I initially accepted the position of a surveyor's apprentice as a summer job, something to keep me occupied. Although I had been accepted to a local engineering college to continue my education in electronics, land surveying took me elsewhere. I never looked back.

While surveying throughout New England, I attended classes at Wentworth University where I received an educational Certificate in Land Surveying. In 1976 I relocated my wife Maureen and two sons, Michael and Justin to San Diego where I continued surveying. Two years later, I attended Mesa College to further my formal education. As luck would have it, my instructor proved to be a most inspirational man, Charles (Chuck) Safford. As a direct result of his classes and inspiration, I was introduced to Curt's *Boundary Control and Legal Principles* and *Evidence and Procedures for Boundary Control*. I immediately took to these books and as I studied them, I readily observed that the vast majority of the cases and examples cited therein were all drawn from the San Diego area. In pursuit of my

3

fascination with Curt's work, I began collecting copies of the various maps and material referenced within the books and I began following Curt's footsteps.

While attending classes, I learned that Curt lived in La Mesa, a small city located east of San Diego. I took the initiative to contact him and I was delighted when he accepted my call. Following a brief conversation, we agreed to meet and in short order we became friends. This wonderful friendship lasted until the day he passed. Over the intervening years, we spent many hours looking for old maps and ancient court cases. Although Curt's technical reputation preceded him, I came to know him for his infectious sense of humor. To this day, I can still hear his hearty laugh, as he shared one of his silly jokes with me. There were many facets to Curt.

As our friendship developed, we talked about writing a book about local history. To his credit, Curt knew his health was diminishing and he was prepared to work with me; there were clearly many more stories to tell. It was obvious that if we were to write a book, we would have to move the project along. And we did. In 1988, we published *The History of San Diego Land Surveying Experiences*. Soon thereafter, we began to receive unsolicited phone calls from other surveyors who had profited from the information found in that book. We were quickly rewarded for our efforts. Thanks to Curt, legions of Land Surveyors have learned how to deal with many of the county's problem areas and I learned something about land surveying.

Curtis Maitland Brown entered this world in Maine on December 16, 1908, the third of five children born to Ona May (Wright) and Royal Caleb Brown. He and his family relocated to San Diego in June 1909. His father was employed as a surveyor for the San Diego & Arizona Eastern Railway and for a utility company.

Curt attended San Diego State College for lower division work and later graduated from the University of California at Berkley with an engineering degree in 1932. For his work on a thesis entitled "The Gas Lift," combined with a high scholastic grade average, he was awarded honors at graduation. Curt also lettered in track, a skill that would help him in the surveying profession. A mutual friend, the noted Julian Land Surveyor, Lee McComb often tells the story of when he was out looking at some land with Curt who was well into his senior years. To listen to Lee, Curt could outrun a gazelle. Indeed, Curt could hold his own with younger surveyors who tried to keep up with him in the field.

For a short time, Curt also worked at the San Diego Natural History Museum. In 1936, he married Thelma Larkin of San Diego and two years later, their son Patrick, later to become a civil engineer, was born. In 1940, the Browns moved to Rancho Santa Fe where Curt built the first of six homes. In 1941, their second son, Thomas was born.

In 1938, before Curtis embarked in earnest on his surveying career, he and Thelma began showing purebred dogs. They began with beagles and later went on to poodles and dachshunds. They spent much of their time with their dogs, and in time Thelma began judging dogs as a noted authority. She soon became an internationally recognized dog fancier and judge. In 1954, the Browns collaborated on a book *The Art and Science of Judging Dogs.* Curt later wrote a fascinating book entitled *Canine Locomotion and Gait Analysis,* relying in large part on his extensive knowledge of engineering. Some of the more favorable regarding this book can be found throughout the dog show community and includes comments such as the following: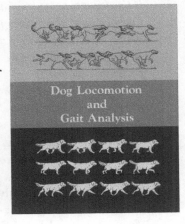

> "This is the best book on dog gaits and movement that I have ever seen . . . This book is a revelation." - Patricia Gail Burnham.

> "Curtis Brown is 'the foremost student of canine structure, function and movement in the world today.'" - Edward M. Gilbert, Jr.

> "The science of canine locomotion has come of age with the publication of this scholarly textbook." - Alfred E. Treen.

> "Breeders, exhibitors and judges will find in one place all the facts and reference necessary to understand proper gait." - Louis H. Harris.

> "To start things on the right foot I am going to commence with a splendid book - the bible of canine movement - <u>Dog Locomotion and Gait Analysis</u> by Curtis Brown. Curtis Brown is an engineer. He brings that experience to this work like a breath of fresh air! Canine movement books as well as (dare I say it) breed standards have often been little more than the compilation of generations of wives' tales, mythology and simple minded guess work."

> "I believe Brown's work is the most significant step ever made on

5

this front and – if it gets its rightful recognition – will revolutionize the way we judge and breed dogs. With that said I will try to summarize this benchmark publication."

"Brown's central theme is that a dog's function will dictate his form. If the dog is supposed to chase down foxes then he should have a body that best suits fox chasing; if he is supposed to kill vermin then he should have a body that best suits vermin killing; and so on and so on. Doesn't that make sense? Of course it does! In fact, you're probably tempted to ask "What fool wouldn't know that?" Well, the answer, incredibly enough, seems to be "Virtually everyone." Previous text books and even many breed standards are based upon an analysis of the horse, of all things! In this book Brown reveals obvious and not so obvious fundamental differences between horses and dogs." – William Kachman

In 1947, the Brown family returned to San Diego and settled in La Mesa where they remained for 47 years. In 1948, Curt obtained his license as California Licensed Land Surveyor No. 2554 whereupon he became a principal in the Surveying-Engineering firm of Daniels, Brown and Hall with offices in the Old Town section of San Diego. In 1954, the San Diego chapter of the California Council of Registered Engineers and Licensed Land Surveyors announced publication, under its sponsorship, of Curt's first book simply entitled *Boundary Control for Surveyors in California.* ACSM described this innovative treatise as follows:

THE San Diego [California] Council of Registered Engineers and Licensed Land Surveyors has recently announced publication, under its sponsorship, of a new book entitled "Boundary Control for Surveyors in California," by Curtis Maitland Brown, Licensed Land Surveyor and instructor at San Diego Vocational School and Junior College. Mr. Brown compiled the book in his capacity as chairman of the Education Committee of the Council.

This 148-page publication does not discuss the use of surveying instruments nor the mathematical details of surveying, as the title may imply, but presents the rules governing California surveyors in the establishment of boundaries as provided by statutes and the common law of the land. Statutes are quoted, court cases are summarized, and definite rules for surveying are presented. This book will be found to be an invaluable aid to surveyors in California in solving their everyday boundary survey problems.

The introduction to the book describes its purpose as follows: "Laws are but rules of conduct established by legislative action and enforced by the courts. Everyone is presumed to know these rules and, as is commonly quoted, 'Ignorance of the law is not an excuse.' It is doubtful if any man ever knew all the laws of the land, but a person can learn most of the laws pertaining to the particular field of endeavor he is engaged in. Surveying is one of those professions in which it is essential [for the practitioner in that field] to know all the rules for his conduct so that he will correctly and properly delineate the boundaries of real property during the course of his duties.

"The rules of conduct for surveyors would include (1) the statutes of the State, (2) the local ordinances, (3) the common law of the State, (4) the usual custom of fellow surveyors, and (5) a code of ethics . . .

". . . If surveyors are to maintain an honorable position in the community, it behooves them to have a better understanding of the laws of the land and better agreement among themselves . . .

"In this treatise on the laws and rules governing the conduct of surveyors, it is hoped that a more uniform standard for surveying boundaries will be obtained."

The book sells for $2.14, which includes tax and postage. It may be obtained from Curtis M. Brown, 2375 San Diego Ave., San Diego, Calif.

In the April-June 1955 edition of *Surveying and Mapping*, ACSM introduced the book:
BOUNDARY CONTROL FOR SURVEYORS IN CALIFORNIA. Written by Curtis Maitland Brown, Licensed Land Surveyor and Instructor at San Diego Vocational School and Junior College. Sponsored by the San Diego Council of Registered Engineers and Licensed Land Surveyors. Lithographed by *Frye & Smith, Ltd.*, San Diego, Calif., 1954. 150 pages. $2.00.

When ACSM and its members reviewed his book, Curt's efforts received mixed reviews. Of the varied responses, I found William Wattles' comments most intriguing. One suspects a discreet rivalry existed between the two men. At the time, Wattles, of Glendale, California was Vice President of ACSM.

****

Chase, Ltd., Photo

ACSM Board Members Participating in the 23rd Annual Congress.
Left to right, front row: Directors A. P. Bill—Massachusetts, C. M. Brown—California; Vice President S. V. Griffith—Maryland; Directors G. K. Emminizer—Maryland, D. E. Whelan—California. Back row, left to right: Directors J. S. Beazley—Florida, J. M. McAlinden—Maryland, K. S. Curtis —Indiana, and T. Dillon—Texas.

(EDITOR'S NOTE. – Mr. Brown's book has precipitated much discussion, pro and con. We present below extracts from three letters received by Secretary Dix concerning the book.)

W. C. WATTLES – Mr. Brown's book is a good brief abstract of the statutes and case citations of California, and provides a fair reference work for such matters, including the Subdivision Law and the Licensed Surveyors Act. There are numerous comments, problem diagrams, and statement explanations, which in the main are correct basic procedure.

My criticism is concerned, principally, with the academic style of recital. The "rules" laid down are basic and generally usable, but are too rigid for the subject matter. There are practically no rules which are 100 percent applicable without some qualification. This applies to the statutes and citations also; every problem requires interpretation of rules in multiple, the "majority probability" attitude; this phase is lacking in the book.

Except for collateral reference, and comparison use of comments made therein on certain procedures, the book does not appear designed to be of too great weight outside California. As a matter of fact, the text itself is specifically California.

As to chapter one, and the introduction, the above statements as to inflexibility are pertinent. The definitions are in several cases insufficient; they imply certain conditions which are not always correct. He who reads must scan between the lines for possible proper interpretation.

General California review will very probably be favorable, and rightly so up to a point, but acceptance without question or analysis will cause difficulties.

The book will be valuable in the hands of those who have the training and experience to evaluate it, but dangerous to those of lesser capacity; blind acceptance leads to pitfalls.

I have talked with others here about this book and have had similar reaction. One comment (and accepted by the author) is to the effect that there should have been more interspersing of the phrase "but the contrary may be shown."

The book is a necessary project but I feel a revision and modification should be had before ACSM can give it 100 percent support. I haven't had opportunity to discuss the book fully with Mr. Brown, but the short time I spent with him leads me to believe he would be glad to cooperate in smoothing out rough spots.

This book, although written from the viewpoint of California law, contains much useful everyday information of value to all surveyors. It is very readable, written very much to the point, and has been well illustrated.

The contents include a chapter on general legal principles which defines the terms commonly used in survey work and also emphasizes the order of importance of the elements involved in a good deed. A chapter on resurveys of subdivisions explains in some detail, and with appropriate illustrations, the techniques to be applied in re-establishing property boundaries. A similar treatise details the problems which face the surveyor in metes and bounds surveys. Other sections of the book cover such subjects as vacations, reversions, riparian owners, adverse rights, and the expert witness.

For some years, the Property Surveys Division of ACSM has been interested in developing a handbook for the practicing land surveyor. This publication meets many of the objectives set forth by the Division and might well serve as a model for similar publications in other States.

F. C. Mirgain
North Dakota Agricultural College

****

S. A. BAUER ** - My impression of the book was very much in line with the opinion of our good friend, Bill Wattles. It is a noble effort to get out such a book, as my experience with the Handbook proves, but I am inclined to agree that in the over-simplification and in the positiveness with which Mr. Brown expounds his views, the book could easily become a damaging rather than a helpful document. I feel that experienced men who know that such matters must be carefully weighed and judged will not need the book particularly, whereas the inexperienced will get the completely erroneous idea that the rules are as inflexible and rigid as Mr. Brown makes them out to be. The difficulty and charm of our very trying profession lies in the fact that no rule is absolute and there is no substitute for intensive study, investigation, and sound judgment. I think the Congress should be very careful not to promote the idea of over-simplification of a complex legal and engineering composite job.

There has been, since the war, a considerable trend in professions toward watering down in order to facilitate work. With all this talk of a "shortage of engineers," there is a growing tendency toward this watering-down process. It can only serve to debase the profession and damage the public welfare. On the other hand, efforts such as the one Mr. Brown has made should not be discouraged, but I do think that all efforts should be made to have such documents present a truer picture of the situation than the one presented.

** Past President, ACSM, Cleveland, Ohio.

****

C. R. HERR *** - So far, most, if not all, comments in regard to the book have been quite favorable. At a meeting of the executive committee of the Southern California Section of ACSM, I asked several members what their reactions were with regard to the book, and they were all of the opinion that it was quite a good and worthwhile treatise.

The book is short, but gives many references to be studied further by those in need of a particular point in question. I feel quite certain that, if every practicing surveyor in California would take time to study this book and then follow the rules and regulations as outlined, there would be a better job of surveying done by the profession as a whole.

I have ordered twelve copies for Pasadena City College to use in my class in plane surveying and hope that the boys can get a better idea of what boundary surveying means.

*** 1954 Chairman, Southern California Section, ACSM, Pasadena, Calif.

****

In a subsequent ACSM publication in early 1955, the SURVEYING AND MAPPING journal published another article entitled "Boundary Control for Surveyors in California."

Curt followed up his California work with another book, co-authored

10

by H. Frederick Landgraf, Attorney-at-Law. The work was based in large upon the material he generated while researching his previous book on California surveying.

As Curt's prominence in the surveying profession elevated, ACSM took notice and in July 1957, ACSM Chairman A. Phillips Bill appointed Curt to the organization's prestigious Property Surveys Division. He was joined by William C. Wattles. In the winter of 1957, ACSM published a review of Curt's newest book:

BOUNDARY CONTROL AND LEGAL PRINCIPLES. Curtis M. Brown. *John Wiley & Sons, Inc.*, New York, 1957. $7.50.

Boundary Control and Legal Principles is a timely contribution to much needed literature in the subject field. The development of the book from its forerunner *Boundary Control for Surveyors in California* and the background experiences of the author and his contributing associates leave little doubt that the book could well be a worthy and authoritative text for use in California and a good reference generally in the western areas of the United States - more so than in the eastern areas. Much of the text will be helpful to anyone anywhere in a general appreciation of a subject whose magnitude and complexity have been considerably over-simplified by condensation into 264 pages; a sacrifice to brevity at which your reviewer looks with alarm because the "watered down" coverage can be a dangerous hazard to the layman's or student's understanding of such a complex professional subject.

However, the author warns the reader in a brief Preface of the book's regrettable limitations and the flexibilities inherent with the law and its interpretations. In fact the book is dedicated to that authority and dean of title matters, William C. Wattles and his oft-repeated sage counsel - to most legal principles the statement "the contrary may be shown" should be added.

Thus, the *principles*, as set forth throughout the book, cannot and must not be considered rigid like a

Chase Ltd., Photo

Elmer J. Peterson (*right*) receiving the Property Surveys Division's engraved plaque for meritorious service from Curtis M. Brown, who is a Past Chairman of the Division and the incoming Vice President of ACSM. Mr. Peterson, who is the new Chairman of ACSM's Property Surveys Division, received the award for his unselfish contribution to the land surveying profession by his work on the recently published Legal Recording Study Chart "A Synopsis of State Laws to 1963 on Platting Subdivisions in the U.S.A."

geometric theorem. Whereas in geometry one may take identical conditions and apply rigid principles and always get the same result; the application of physical mechanics to principles of jurisprudence - which surveying for real property boundary determination really is - does not always give equal results even under equal conditions. With this always in mind, or the dedication slogan "the contrary may be shown" applied to every *principle*, the book can prove a valuable reference.

This reviewer practices in an area where the political jurisdiction acquires fee simple title to roads dedicated in a subdivision and acquires fee simple title to many roads by direct deeds. The book, in describing the handling of these matters (e.g., pages 58, 98, and 110) is written expressly for those areas in which the public only acquires a "public easement" over a dedicated road; thus, many of the *principles* of Chapter 6 (Locating Reversion Rights) are affected and "the contrary is true."

Instances of technical incorrectness of some statements in the text were noted. An example of this is the sentence on page 12, "Within the United States magnetic north varies from 24 degrees east of north to 22 degrees west of north, a difference of 46 degrees." The question could well be asked as to what day of what year was this true. Also, the sentence on page 12 that contains the definition of a Deflection Angle as "that of sighting on a given line and turning the angle to another line." The reviewer could call this an interior or exterior angle; a deflection angle is that obtained by sighting the prolongation of a given line and turning the angle to another line. Another sentence on page 15 could raise a question in some areas as it states, "A deed description based upon a Lambert bearing must be defined as such, otherwise true north may be implied." Unless otherwise stated, in some areas magnetic north is always assumed.

Some examples used in the text to illustrate points might have been better chosen. For example, a sentence on page 114 states: "In court cases certain things are presumed to be true until the contrary is proved; thus, if a letter is duly, written, sealed, addressed, stamped, and placed in a mail box, it is assumed to be delivered unless the contrary can be proved." It is noted here that the Post Office does a big business in "registered letters" and "return receipts" and it is generally true in court cases the sender must present proof that the letter was delivered to the addressee.

An example of a dangerous general-practice type statement is found on page 72. The sentence states, "The surveyor who is locating land from a title policy description need not devote research time to title matters other than that described or called for by the policy." In the few States in which the Torrens system is fully effective, this may be true. One needs but to note the high rates of commercial title policies to realize that they are dependent upon the individual examiner.

Generally, then, it is safe to use a title policy, but one needs to keep constant vigil, for his responsibility is not limited to such a policy.

Many of the *principles* set forth in Chapter 4, apparently apply to subdivisions that are first laid on the ground and then platted. These *principles* may not apply to subdivisions that are computed and platted and then laid on the ground. The question of "intent" versus "errors in field monumentation" takes a more complex aspect. Also, the chapter sets up many principles dealing with "proration," but the text does not state when the surveyor has the legal right to prorate without the backing of a court order or the backing of all of the affected land owners.

Caution is advised by the reviewer on the use of some of the statements (or *principles)* made in the text for the reason that they are currently under study, in various areas by various groups interested in professional conduct and practices. Examples of these questionable items in the text are: (page 89) "in the absence of an analysis showing the location of an error of closure, place the error of closure in the last course which states, thence to the point of beginning." (page 233) "To limit liability in a like manner, it is good form for the surveyor to state on his plat presented to the client 'for the exclusive use of John Doe.'"

Your reviewer would have preferred the text to delve in "Trespass Rights of Surveyors" in a more thorough manner than the short paragraph covering the subject on page 235. This paragraph does not distinguish that there are two types of trespass, civil and criminal. Many types of surveyors do enjoy criminal trespass rights; but none can enjoy civil trespass rights.

The last section of the book is entitled "Glossary of Deed Terms" and contains definitions of selected words. Brevity of the definitions as stated therein can lead the user to erroneous implications. For example, on page 259, the text notes "'And assigns' is included in deeds to take care of corporations, trustees, etc., who cannot have heirs." Your reviewer feels that this could have been better stated by noting that the words "and assigns" are included to take care of any future grantee.

Your reviewer could go on and on, citing argumentative or "contrary showings." The danger of the book to the "student" surveyor is quite apparent when one remembers that this type of surveyor is usually not in a position to know which statements or *principles* might be applied for any given condition in any given area.

The book offers a provocative challenge to the experienced surveyor who after reading the book may feel insecure until he has refreshed his knowledge of the laws covering his areas of practice. The book will be a valuable addition to the professional surveyor's library.

– *VICTOR H. GHENT, Professional Engineer and Land Surveyor*

In 1957, the California Council of Civil Engineers and Land Surveyors (CCCELS) also announced that Curt was writing a manual of instructions for the private practice of land surveying. Sponsored by CCCELS, the organization announced: "It will be intended as a guide to practitioners, setting forth the performance standards that will be accepted by the profession."

Buoyed by the success of his published works, Curt began traveling on the lecture circuit where he delivered an assortment of presentations to surveying organizations across the country. Typical of his efforts was a 1961 presentation at the Ninth Annual Convention of the CCCELS held in Sacramento. The program, entitled "Best Available Evidence," was well received.

In 1962, Curt and another ACSM associate, Winfield H. Eldridge, wrote another book, soon to become a staple in every surveyor's library. Published by John Wiley & Sons, Inc. of New York, *EVIDENCE AND PROCEDURES FOR BOUNDARY LOCATION* was 484 pages and had an immediate impact on the surveying profession. The illustrated book sold for $9.75. According to the late Walter S. Dix, writing on behalf of ACSM:

"To those who have read Curtis Brown's "Boundary Control and Legal Principles," this is the work they have been waiting for. Those who know Curtis Brown and Winfield Eldridge personally or by reputation will buy the book on merit.

"Close to 500 pages, the work is a plainly stated and cryptic assembly of facts, rules, advice, and the wisdom of experience that belongs in any library of a professional surveyor with interest in legal boundary or property line surveying.

One could elaborate on its 17 chapters, but the words "Evidence" and "Boundary Location" of the book's title should be enough to describe its contents. Besides the typical law and its pertaining precedent, Chapter 8 on "Measurements, Errors, and Computation" Chapter 15 on "Writing Descriptions," Chapter 16 on "The Surveyor in Court," and last but not least, Chapter 17 "Professional Stature," not much else should be needed to recommend the book to every serious land surveyor in the United States. In my opinion, this book will be a college textbook."

Eldridge was born on July 2, 1922 at Mt. Holly, New Jersey. He served with the U. S. Army in the Topographic Mapping Battalion for three years during World War II. He received a Bachelor of Science degree in Civil Engineering from the University of Illinois in 1958.

Prior to 1954, he was a topographic engineer with the Pacific Region of the U. S. Geological Surveys for six years. He also worked for many years with various public and private surveying companies in construction, property surveys, and forestry mapping. At the University of Illinois, Winfield served as an Instructor, Assistant Professor and Associate Professor in the Civil Engineering Department. He taught in various classes along with all phases of engineering surveying including professional courses in Property Surveying. He also managed the Summer Surveying Camp.

Keynote Address

The Honorable Stewart Lee Udall, Secretary of the Interior, U.S.A., addressed the membership of ACSM and ASP in general assembly shortly before noon Wednesday, March 18, 1964, in the Terrace Banquet Room of the Shoreham Hotel during the 1964 ACSM-ASP Convention in Washington, D. C.

Chase Ltd., Photo

ACSM officers escort United States Secretary of the Interior, Hon. Stewart L. Udall, to the General Assembly of the 1964 ACSM-ASP Convention. The speaker, Secretary Udall, *left*, with ACSM President Dix, *right*, followed by ACSM Vice President-elect Brown, *right*, and ACSM President-elect Griffith, *left*, then Secretary Udall's assistant, Charles Boatner, and next ACSM Past President Robert H. Lyddan.

In addition to working with Curt, Eldridge was the author of the ACSM publication, *Bibliography of Property Surveying Literature*. Eldridge was also a member of ASCE, ACSM, ASP, ASEE and the Canadian Institute of Surveying. As with Curt, in recognition of his efforts, ACSM recognized Professor Eldridge for his contributions to the profession in 1963, culminating in the awarding of an association plaque.

Citation to Associate Professor Winfield H. Eldridge of the University of Illinois

WHEREAS, During the 1962 Annual Meeting of the Property Surveys Division of the American Congress on Surveying and Mapping, there was duly moved, seconded, and passed a resolution requesting that the Property Surveys Division be allowed to give citations to persons who have made outstanding contributions to the Land Surveying Profession, and in particular contributions to the Property Surveys Division; and

WHEREAS, The Board of Directors of the American Congress on Surveying and Mapping did approve the Property Surveys Division resolution; and

WHEREAS, The Executive Committee of the Property Surveys Division, acting as an awards committee, did unanimously agree that the Property Surveys Division should award a citation to Professor Winfield Eldridge

(1)   For advancing the profession through his continued activities in Land Surveyor organizations;

Professor Winfield H. Eldridge (left) receives the plaque of appreciation for outstanding services to the Property Surveys Division, ACSM, from Division Chairman Curtis M. Brown during the 23rd Annual Meeting, Washington, D. C., March 26–29, 1963.

(2)   For travelling by airplane to cities throughout the State of Illinois to offer courses in Land Surveying and the legal elements thereof;

(3)   For, in particular, his literary contributions in preparing the manuscript for the yet unpublished bibliography on Land Surveying Subjects, and

(4)   For co-authoring the text Evidence and Procedures for Boundary Locations. The Property Surveys Division takes great pleasure in presenting this plaque to you, Professor Eldridge.

As ACSM's Chairman of the Legislative Committee, Curt pressed hard for education and adoption of a model law for regulating land surveying. According to Brown, ". . . laws regulating the practice of surveying in this country range from States having no laws on the subject to those in which the laws state in minutest detail what must be done, and who may do it. He urged the surveyors to regulate and discipline their own profession, through their professional societies, so that there will be no need for inhibiting and degrading statutes." As a result of Curt's ongoing efforts, he was elected to the organization's Board of Directors.

In 1964, ACSM appointed Curt to perform more important work on behalf of the association when he was put in charge of the Technical Standards Committee where he was charged with "Compiling a glossary of terms and phrases used in legal descriptions, along with their definitions, compiling a glossary of special terms and phrases used in the property surveys profession, and compiling a table of acceptable abbreviations and symbols that may be used on plats and in field notes."

During the spring of that same year, Curt took a leave of absence from Daniels, Brown & Hall so that he could serve as a visiting professor at Purdue University in Lafayette, Indiana where he taught a course on Land Surveying with an emphasis on private boundary surveys. He also prepared a course for their land surveying curriculum.

Chase, Ltd., Photo.

ACSM 25th Anniversary Meeting—Salute to ACSM Presidents, Luncheon
Presidents and terms: *Seated, left to right;* Borden 1945–47, Bauer 1950, Williams 1958, Wright 1947–49, Randall 1941–42, Higbee 1955–56. *Standing, left to right;* Barry 1961, Bestor 1959, Karo 1960, Griffith 1964, Brown 1965, Lyddan 1957. Dix 1962–63.

Curt was eventually elected president of ACSM where he served honorably in 1965 and 1966. He also served as ACSM's Chairman of the Task Committee on Education. All the while, he continued lecturing extensively across the country. Amongst his many endeavors, he returned to Purdue University where he taught an adult extension course entitled "Locating and Describing Real Property." The classes were held on Thursday evenings over a six-week period at a cost of $15.00. In accepting the position of President, Curt graciously acknowledged the importance of the prestigious post:

It is with great pleasure and humbleness that I accept the responsibilities of the office of President of the American Congress on Surveying and Mapping, and I want to thank those who voted for me.

17

Surveyors and cartographers have had a colorful past. History books point with pride to the fact that our early notables were surveyors. Recently I had the opportunity to examine the map used at the treaty of Guadalupe Hidalgo and to compare it with present day knowledge of western land forms. Within the last 140 years the accumulation of survey information startles the imagination. Surveyors have indeed had a colorful past.

However, we should not be concerned with how great we have been, but we should be concerned with what we can be. Those who sit back and rest on their laurels soon have no laurels to rest on. This is a changing world. A moment of reflection will tell us that the old village blacksmith is gone; the captains of the sailing vessels are gone; the topographer is being replaced by the camera; and the chainmen are losing ground to the electronic measuring devices.

Within the last 30 years we have seen the transit and tape decrease in importance as the camera, Electrotape, and Geodimeter have developed. It is probably true that the transit and tape surveys will not be completely eliminated, just as it is true that the horses were not completely eliminated by the automobile. The private property surveyor in the United States depends heavily upon the transit and tape to determine property lines. Even in this area, it is my expectation that in the not too distant future photogrammetric methods will be used extensively. Many of the old ways of the surveyor are gone; many more will soon be supplanted by advancing technology. If the surveyor fails to advance with the advancing technology, he will be like the village blacksmith with no place in modern society.

Introducing Our New President

Curtis M. Brown was born December 16, 1908, in Auburn, Maine. He is an honor graduate of the University of California, having received his Bachelor of Science degree in engineering in 1932.

He is a licensed land surveyor in private practice with the firm of Daniels, Brown and Hall, 2802 San Juan Street, San Diego California.

A regular contributor to SURVEYING AND MAPPING, he is well known as the author of *Boundary Control and Legal Principles;* and coauthor with Winfield Eldridge of *Evidence and Procedures for Property Surveys.*

He is well known as a speaker and lecturer on the legal aspects of surveying, and has taught courses in Land Surveying at San Diego City College. Last year he taught at the Geometronics Institute at Purdue University, and he is scheduled to teach there again this summer.

Mr. Brown has been very active in the affairs of the Property Surveys Division, ACSM, over the years and is a past chairman of that Division. He served two years as a Director of the ACSM and was on the

CURTIS M. BROWN

Board again last year as Vice President of ACSM.

He is a resident of La Mesa, California.

The man who tries to do today's job with yesterday's tools will be out of work tomorrow.

With these thoughts in mind, what is the greatest need of those who will follow the profession of surveying? The only logical answer is a better education and continuing education to meet the changing needs of the world.

We, as surveyors, must face up to the fact that surveyor education within the United States is woefully inadequate. Historically, surveyor–engineer education has been a part of civil engineering. Quoting from Professor McNair's paper, "in 1937 the average number of required semester hours of surveying courses in civil engineering curricula was 14.3. By 1948 required surveying courses averaged 11.3 semester hours. In 1958 the average was dawn to 7.7 semester hours. In 1964 the average amount of surveying required in the civil engineering curriculum is estimated to be approximately 5 semester hours."

We should not quarrel with the civil engineer's prerogative to decide for himself as to what he thinks is proper training for graduates. However, the fact remains that the deletion of surveying courses has created a void in the surveyor–engineer education within the United States. Surveyors should not bemoan the loss of standing within the civil engineering department; they should apply every effort to solve the question, "Where should surveying education be housed within the colleges of the United States?"

ACSM incoming President Earle J. Fennell presents a Presidential Service Plaque to outgoing President Curtis M. Brown.

One of the surveyor's areas of educational neglect has been geodesy. The recent accent on space travel created a need for superior students. At Ohio State University, geodesy was given a home in the geography department; today a separate department has established itself as the outstanding geodesy school within the United States.

Should the surveyors of the United States profit by this example and try to establish a separate surveying school? According to European thinking, this thought must have much merit; practically all major European universities do have separate surveyor colleges. Canada has two such curricula in universities. Could it be that the United States is out of step and the remainder of the world is correct?

Many explanations are presented for this deplorable situation. The time for offering excuses and explanations has expired; today we are interested in what can be done to correct an unacceptable situation. Our concern should be action, not further discussion. It is obvious that the education of the surveyor is deteriorating while the need is increasing. If the civil engineering department cannot adequately educate the surveyor, is it not logical to try to have a separate surveyor college established? Such a college should include geodesy, cartography, photogrammetry, and land surveying.

In some areas of surveying the fault of educational deficiencies must rest squarely upon the surveyors themselves; this is particularly true with respect to licensed surveyors. Within the United States there are only four States that have registration requirements equivalent to a college education. Most States require a high school diploma plus the passing of a written examination. After reading many licensed surveyor examinations, it can only be concluded from their simplicity that the majority of land surveyors do not need a college education to become qualified. Why should the colleges offer training where the practicing surveyors are willing to accept substandard education?

Most State laws should be changed to upgrade the educational requirements; recently this was done in both Indiana and New York. As a direct result of the Indiana law requiring the land surveyor to have the equivalent education of that obtained by a four-year curriculum in civil engineering with a major in land surveying, Purdue University added a masters program in land surveying.

In attempting to change a State law to upgrade the educational requirements of the surveyor, a technical difficulty exists; the registration law cannot say that the education shall be the equivalent of a four year curriculum in land surveying because no such curriculum exists. This is like the old argument as to which should be first, the hen or the egg. If the law is changed, colleges will meet the demand.

In some States the solution to date has been to increase the difficulty of the examination to that which could be expected of a college graduate in surveying.

This procedure is available to many boards of registration under existing State laws, and it is hoped that the right will be exercised.

Where a school of surveying is housed is immaterial; the establishment of such a school is imperative. The civil engineering departments, by their past performance, have decreased surveying education to a negligible point; it is not expected that the trend will be reversed. If it is necessary to have a surveying school created to educate surveyors adequately, let us do so.

Most surveyors proclaim themselves as being professional people. One of the essential parts of the definition of a profession is "superior education in a field of knowledge." Without a college to house the knowledge of the surveyor and without a college offering a degree in surveying, the claim of professional status appears to be reduced to mere self proclamation.

My recommendations are as follows:

(1) That the ACSM make every effort to encourage the establishment of at least one school of surveying in some university.

(2) Every State land surveyor organization actively and vigorously attempt to change the legal requirements for surveyor education to "the equivalent education that can be obtained by graduating from a four year college surveying course."

****

21

WINFIELD H. ELDRIDGE (1922–1966)

In Memoriam

*T*HE *untimely death of Vice President Winfield H. Eldridge, on March 22, 1966, marked the end of a distinguished career in surveying and mapping, and the beginning of a seemingly endless period of mourning for his family, his many friends, and the members of an indebted profession. Educator by acclaim, scholar by choice, author, lecturer, and leader, Professor Eldridge endeared himself to all who knew him and to all who benefited from his many notable contributions to the profession that he loved. It is not possible to list even a small portion of his accomplishments on this page, just as it is impossible to estimate the effect of his continuing influence, but we can take heart in the realization that the life that he lived was too filled with giving to have faded with the passing of his time, that his words shall live on, that the work that he had begun shall be continued through the lives of many admiring followers, that nothing ends but the beginning. It is with the deepest feeling of loss that we accept the harshness of this reality, finding comfort only in our knowledge that one of the enduring aspects of surveying is the perpetuation of individual accomplishments, and that, while in the years to come, they may have forgotten who set the crumbling corners of this decade, they will see in the profession the image of "Win" Eldridge, whose incomparable dedication, coupled with unique wisdom and integrity, gained for him during his lifetime an identity with the destiny of his profession. He will always be remembered, just as sincerity and devotion are remembered, for although he can no longer be the advocate of our philosophy, he is now, and he shall always be, an ideal.*

ACSM Board of Direction for March 1965–March 1966 period.
Left to Right: Director Eldridge; President Brown; Directors Stine, Laird, Hicks, Peterson, Andregg; Past President Griffith; Vice President Fennell; Directors Dayton, Pafford; and Executive Secretary Dix. Note: Directors Binyon and Darby, Treasurer Hemple, and Editor Rappleye were not present when the photograph was made.

On August 18th and 19th, 1967, Curt attended the Semi-Annual meeting of the New Mexico Section where he addressed a group of some eighty New Mexico Surveyors and their wives on the subject "Variations on Sectionalized Land Areas in the United States." Typical of the treatment he received while lecturing across the country, an article in ACSM's *Surveying and Mapping* journal described his visit.

The meeting, held at Cocina de Carlos in Albuquerque, provided an opportunity for both members and non-member surveyors from all parts of New Mexico to hear Curt Brown speak on a subject in which he is considered to be a complete authority. Members attended from Santa Fe, Artesia, Santa Rosa, Farmington, Gallup and Carlsbad in addition to the Albuquerque area. Mr. Brown's remarks were exceptionally well received, and even some of the ladies present, who admitted that they did not understand all of the technical terms he used, were nevertheless fascinated by his presentation of the subject, and understood the points he was making.

A copy of each of Mr. Brown's books, BOUNDARY CONTROL AND LEGAL PRINCIPLES, and EVIDENCE AND PROCEDURES FOR BOUNDARY LOCATION, which he wrote in collaboration with Professor Winfield Eldridge, were given as door prizes to two of the guests, and the New Mexico Section is indebted to E. S. (Stan) Holman, map and instrument dealer of Albuquerque, for donating the volumes which Mr. Brown autographed when they were presented. A copy of Victor Westphall's PUBLIC DOMAIN IN NEW MEXICO, 1854-1891 was presented to Mr. Brown by the New Mexico Section.

Upon his arrival in Albuquerque Friday morning Curt was taken to the Atomic City of Los Alamos by way of the Jemez Mountain country and was given a guided tour of the Atomic Research Center by an old acquaintance and very active ACSM member, Ben Williams, who has been in charge of surveying at the installation for many years. Following the visit to Los Alamos and return by way of historic old Santa Fe, a reception was held for Mr. Brown at the Gold Room of Fabulous Diamond Jim's at Winrock Center in Albuquerque, to which the heads of departments in Government and Private Industry concerned with surveying had been invited together with all of the members of the New Mexico Section.

On Saturday, August 19th, the day of the meeting, the officers and directors of the Section took Curt by tramway to the top of Sandia Crest near Albuquerque, where lunch was served at the Summit House Restaurant, at an elevation of over 10,000 feet, and where a meeting was held at a spot overlooking the Rio Grande valley to plan activities for the remainder of the year, the Annual Meeting and other matters. One of the highlights of the tram ride, which is the longest in North America, was passing in the tram car a rock cliff a quarter mile away on which was being supported a 30-foot banner bearing the inscription "Welcome Curt." Two members of the crew of a local surveyor had climbed to that point to dramatically emphasize that Curt was a most welcome guest of the Land of Enchantment.

****

Chase Ltd., Photo

ACSM officers at the 24th Annual Business Meeting during the ACSM-ASP Convention in Washington, D. C., March 19, 1964.
Seated, front row, left to right: Messrs. Borden, Brown, Dix, Griffith, Hemple, Evans, and Hicks.
Standing, back row, left to right: Messrs. Barry, Burroughs, Radlinski, Fennell, Landen, Darby, Emminizer, Stine, Peterson, Bill, Binyon, McAlinden, and Curtis.

Besides his extensive involvement in national surveying issues, Curt remained active in the local surveying community. In June 1968, the CCCELS reported:

A "Manual of Instructions for the Perpetuation of Survey Data" was published last September by the County Engineer Department of San Diego, headed by Dave Speer. Purpose of the Manual is: "(1) to establish recommended procedures for the preservation of survey data in compliance with state law, and (2) to provide better access to available sources of existing survey information." Curt Brown and Don Nasland of the San Diego Chapter were two of the six members on the drafting committee. The other four members represented the City Engineering Department, the County Engineering Department, and the State Division of Highways.

In 1968, John Wiley and Sons published the second edition of *BOUNDARY CONTROL AND LEGAL PRINCIPLES*. The 371 page hardcover book sold for $12.00. Curt was joined by H. Frederick Landgraf and Francois D. "Bud" Uzes. One of Curt's peers, A. Phillips Bill, a licensed surveyor and registered engineer reviewed the book on behalf of ACSM and its members.

The identification of and the resurvey of the boundaries of previously defined parcels of land involve elements both of the arts and of the sciences. The arts dominate in the analysis of the legal record of descriptive title, the evaluation of this against the record on the ground, and in the presentation of the surveyor's conclusions to his client and to the future record. Science is served in the measurements made by the resurveyor designed to make his findings more useful to the future use of the parcel of land surveyed, and in his considered efforts to make the remonumentation of the parcel more easily available and understandable to the future.

Reference material for the Land Surveyor has always been more than adequate in the scientific aspects of resurvey. However, source material available in the art of the resurveyor has been, at best, fragmentary.

Mr. Brown's definitive text BOUNDARY CONTROL AND LEGAL PRINCIPLES fills a gaping void on the reference shelf of the Land Surveyor, by its thorough treatment of the art of the Surveyor.

Your reviewer, for example, has always felt that Land Survey practice in the area of his first interest (New England) was so insular and so dependent on case law in the region that analogies would be rare to surveys in other parts of North America.

Bud Uzes
1934-2006

25

Thanks to Mr. Brown's book I find that basically the same law and the same responsibility govern the function of the re-surveyor no matter where he practices.

Subject matter is extremely well presented in a simple, logical style and the various aspects of evidence are analyzed clearly and succinctly. The text is well indexed to the drawings illustrating the various problems. I like the illustrations particularly as they simply and clearly augment the text and are not all cluttered up with a lot of extraneous material not really pertinent to the problem being discussed.

All in all, it is hard to criticize any facet of this most important contribution to the literature of our profession.

No Land Surveyor, either in practice or in training, can afford to be without this most important text!

– Phillips Bill, RLS & PE

****

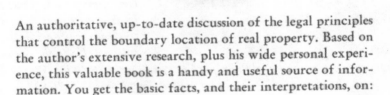

By late 1970, Curt had edged his way into retirement and in March of 1971, ACSM reported on Curt's formal departure from the surveying profession:

Past President Curtis M. Brown (left) receiving Service Citation Certificate from Secretary Dix.

Curtis M. Brown, ACSM past president, announced his retirement from active practice in November 1970. He served with distinction as ACSM's nineteenth President 1965 – March – 1966. Past President Brown has long been a leader in the profession of land surveying and included in his activities lecturing, visiting professorships, and writing. He is the author of "Boundary Control and Legal Principles" and coauthor with the late Winfield H. Eldridge of "Evidence and Procedures for Boundary Location." ACSM extends its best wishes to Curtis and Thelma Brown for a long and happy retirement, and trusts that he will continue to serve as a source of advice and counsel to the profession of surveying and mapping.

Although formally retired, Curt continued writing and in 1981, Wiley and Sons published the second edition of *Evidence and Procedures for Boundary Location*. Two of the profession's most respected and prominent men, Walter G. Robillard, and Donald A. Wilson joined him.

Don reared from southeastern New Hampshire where he had been in practice as a land boundary consultant for many years. He is both a licensed land surveyor and professional forester. In the years following publication of the revised book, Don presented seminars on a variety of topics including description interpretation, boundary evidence, surveying law, and various aspects of forensic science. Don is also a past president of both the Maine Society of Land Surveyors and the New Hampshire Land Surveyors Association.

In addition to over 200 technical publications in several disciplines, Don has been involved with the writing of 46 books. He has written two other boundary-related texts as well as researched and compiled the subject matter for seven state boundary and surveying law books. He has also testified as an expert in well over 40 boundary and title cases along with submitting verbal and written testimony to several state agencies and on numerous occasions to the State Legislature.

Don is a former faculty member of the University of Maine where he taught surveying in the School of Forestry and the Department of Civil Engineering. He is also a former faculty member at the University of New Hampshire where he continues to teach courses for the UNH Professional Development & Training Program. He is a contributing writer to Professional Surveyor Magazine and a member of the Professional Surveyor/Red Vector "Dream Team" providing on-line education for surveyors and related professionals. Presently this cooperative is offering eleven separate courses authored by Don with more currently being developed.

Walter Robillard has a diverse and impressive background in land surveying. He began his career in Mississippi as a forester on the DeSoto National Forest. He was promoted to the Regional Office in Atlanta as Regional Surveyor where he was responsible for property surveying for the 14 Southern States and Puerto Rico. In this capacity, he investigated land disputes, trespasses and various

President Brown (right) presents citation to J. Stuart Boyles.

land claims. Walt also served as a negotiator and as and expert witness as well as a technical consultant to other government agencies on various land problems. He was also placed on loan to USAID where he served as a technical consultant on property disputes and aerial photogrammetric problems to the Kingdom of Nepal and Jordan.

Walt was also active as an educator and college instructor where his duties included planning and teaching courses in aerial photogrammetry and surveying. He conducted forest management research as well as serving as a faculty advisor. His background as a teacher was also quite broad and including roles as a teaching consultant to Lockheed-Marietta Corp. of Georgia; a teaching associate for Professional Education Systems, in Eau Claire, Wis.; Adjunct Professor, New Mexico State University & Mercer University; instructor at DeKalb Technical College, Decatur, GA.; instructor at the Consulting Forester's institute and the Society of American Foresters; instructor at the Southern Technical Institute, Marietta, GA., continuing education instructor at the University of Wisconsin. Walt also taught continuing education courses on forestry, law, and surveying in all

50 states and Puerto Rico as well as producing teaching video tapes for the University of Florida. Walt is also a member of the Advisory Staff for the School of Surveying, University of Florida. He also taught in house continuing education to the Santee-Cooper Electric Corp., S.C., City of Colorado Springs, Florida Department of Transportation and Georgia Power Company.

Walt is also an attorney and in this role, he operated a private consulting and law practice. His clients included E.I. DuPont, Florida Power & Light, Florida DOT, Lockheed Corp., Georgia Power Co., Atlanta Gas Company and numerous small firms. As an attorney, Walt served as a consultant and Expert on boundary matters for major corporations, utilities, county, state & federal governmental bodies and agencies, including the U.S. Air Force. He served as an Expert Witness in land, title, riparian, and boundary matters in state and federal courts and he also testified as in expert witness in over 40 cases and in fourteen states.

The illustrated, 450-page hard cover book sold for $38.95. ACSM member James A. Thigpenn, III reviewed the book on behalf of the organization.

The second edition of the well-known text book on land surveying, originally co-authored by Curtis M. Brown and the late Winfield Eldridge, is a great deal more than a warmed-over version of the original work. Without diminishing the authority of a text enjoyed and respected for nearly 20 years, the authors have obviously reviewed every section of every chapter with a view toward the improvement of both the information and the readability of the material contained therein.

Although a substantial portion of the original publication forms the foundation of the second edition, the many additions, deletions, and revisions found throughout the later version have induced a separate character and a finely tuned statement of matters relating to the practice of land surveying. The most noticeable improvement in the new edition is the inclusion of a chapter on professional liability immediately following an enlarged chapter on unwritten transfers of land ownership, which contains most of the material formerly covered in two chapters plus some additional information. There is

Don Wilson
Professional Land Surveyor

also a new chapter on apportionment procedures for land and water boundaries, covering vacated streets, accretions, and relocations adjoining water boundaries, excess and deficiency, fractional conveyances, wills, and other proportional rights in general and in view of recognized differences in various state laws affecting such divisions.

Other chapters have been improved by the inclusion of additional pertinent information, or by restatements of the same material to give a clearer, or more complete picture to the reader. In some instances the changes amount only to a few words dropped, or added, but in other cases, such as the very important chapter on evidence, changes were noted in more than one-half of the 63 subtitled sections, varying from minor word changes to the addition of several pages of information. A similar expansion of the scope of the original material is found in the chapter dealing with professional stature, and to a lesser degree in other parts of the text. Much of the material added to the text represents the recognition of unique problems in some of the eastern states, as well as reflecting the growing interest of the members of the land surveying profession in the legal aspects of their performance.

It should suffice to say that the established respect for the original text, generated in part by the identity of its contributing co-authors, Brown and Eldridge, could not suffer in its new association with other co-authors of the ilk of Robillard and Wilson.

– JAMES A. THIGPENN, III

****

**Walt Robillard
Land Surveyor**

In addition to serving as the organization's president, Curt served ACSM's Property Surveys Division as chair of the Legislative Committee and as both Second Vice Chairman and First Vice Chairman of the Division. Curt additionally served as a part-time college instructor for various subjects, most of which focused on the legal elements of property line determination. As a partner in the firm of Daniels, Brown and Hall, Curt was in private practice for many years. Over the years, Curt appeared as a speaker at many of the annual surveyor's conventions in Utah, Wisconsin, Illinois, Michigan, Arizona, California, and Minnesota amongst others.

In 1980, Curt published a book on his family history. Entitled *The Genealogy of Caleb Browns of Epping and Candia, New Hampshire*, the book traced Curt's family roots in Old New England. Eight years later, he published another work entitled *Genealogy of John Brown of New Hampshire*. As with so many things in his life, Curt had an insatiable curiosity for all things intellectual.

As Curt found more free time, he and I began to visit various repositories and title companies researching old court cases and historical survey maps. He used to drop by my office unannounced whereupon I would cancel all of my appointments and we would head off to the library or courthouse to search for old maps and court cases. Our efforts culminated in the co-authoring of *The History of San Diego Land Surveying Experiences*. While we were working on the book, Curt's health became more and more compromised and in his zeal to see the work published, he moved forward in spite of the fact that we were in the middle of editing the work. It is with fond memory that I recall the day he showed up with a boxful of the books. The San Diego Historical Society reviewed our book in the Fall of 1990.

The Journal of San Diego History, Fall 1990, Volume 36, Number 4, ***Book Notes***

History of San Diego County Land Surveying Experiences.

By Curtis M. Brown and Michael J. Pallamary. San Diego: Privately printed, 1988. Illustrations. Index. 115 pages. $15.00. Reviewed by Howard O. Welty, San Diego Historical Society

[MP NOTE: Curt and Howard Welty were both graduates of UC Berkley. They attended school at the sane time.]

Curtis M. Brown, now in his 80s, is perhaps the dean of living land surveyors in the San Diego area. In 1984 he produced a privately printed memoir summarizing his experiences in a forty-year practice of the science and art of establishing property lines. The new work is an expansion of this in collaboration with Michael J. Pallamary, a surveyor whose hobby is researching early land history. Written primarily for the benefit of land surveyors, the book assumes the reader to be at home with offsets, tie points, and closings. It describes early boundary, public land, and subdivision surveys; traces litigation over such tracts as Middletown and Rancho Cuyamaca; and offers a wealth of anecdotes recounting Brown's

encounters with surveying problems (technical, legal, personal).
Especially illuminating is a detailed account of Brown's role in a
1966 lawsuit that settled a dispute over San Diego's pueblo land
boundaries (the Shaw-Williams controversy). A weakness of the
book is its meager editing; some ambiguous passages and misspelled
words should have been caught. (May be ordered by mail from M.
J. Pallamary, 1094 Cudahy Place, San Diego, CA 92110; $17.58,
includes tax, postage).

I still have the last batch of typo-ridden edits that were never forwarded to the publisher. I view them to this day with a smile and warm memories. Curt's zeal to publish our book, while he was still in good health, speaks volumes about our friendship and his desires. Soon after publication of the book, I coaxed Curt into speaking at a full day seminar in San Diego sponsored by the San Diego Chapter of the California Land Surveyors Association (CLSA). Held at the Mission Bay Hilton Hotel in San Diego, the room was packed. Included in the audience was the noted land use attorney, Dick Burt, a descendant of William A. Burt, inventor of the popular Burt's Solar Compass. I had the pleasure of working with Dick over the years and I was honored to consider him a friend. Curt's presentation, candid as well as comical, was one of the last time's he spoke to a room of his friends and peers. His prepared speech follows:

****

CALIFORNIA SURVEYORS TALK WITH MICHAEL PALLAMARY

SAN DIEGO, CALIFORNIA

BY CURTIS M. BROWN

1988

Mike Pallamary and I had been ruminating over past San Diego County's surveying history, and as a result we prepared a little booklet entitled *San Diego County Surveying History and Experiences*. He and many others have often asked how come that I, a non-lawyer, wrote books on the legal elements of Land Surveying? So I will give a brief explanation. I knew nothing about it and became curious. I read Clark's book on the legal elements of surveying in Michigan, mostly a treatise on the sectionalized land system. Also Hodgeman and Skelton, both good but not filling the needs for California.

Going back a bit in my background, my father, fresh from Auburn, Maine in 1908, got a job as a chainman on a San Diego County Surveyor's crew. In those days the County Surveyor was an elective post and he often did more private work than County work. If you are wondering why there were few county surveying field book records prior to about 1930, just remember the records belonged to the elected County Surveyor, a non-county employee. In 1936 San Diego County hired Earnest Childs, the last elected County Surveyor, as a full time employee, and from that time on we see the start of a better system of accumulation of San Diego County Surveyor records.

Going back a bit, in 1925, at the time I was a junior in High School, I took a commercial law class from an attorney. He assigned me the task of reporting to the class the common law of a prize fighting situation. The only instruction he gave was to go down to the County Law Library and ask the librarian how to find the information. So I did. My partial knowledge of how to do legal research then slumbered in my background until I had need for it sometime later when surveying.

After World War II I got a job as a Chief of Party for a surveyor who was just starting up. Unfortunately, I knew almost nothing about the legal elements of boundary surveys and my boss knew slightly more.

I was just as confused as the little boy was who lost his chewing gum on the henhouse floor. Each morning I was handed a bundle of maps with a minimum of instructions and was told to monument the land described in a deed. But I had one advantage, when I got in trouble I would spend the evening at the Law Library soothing my ignorance in legal books. Eventually I got enough information together to publish my first book on Boundary Control for Surveyors of California. The book was such a success that I got the notion to put out one for the entire United States. It was an immediate good seller.

**CURT BROWN AND THE AUTHOR PHOTOGRAPHED IN
1988 FOR A LOCAL NEWSPAPER ARTICLE**

PHOTOGRAPH COURTESY OF THE SAN DIEGO UNION

The subject of the legal elements of boundary location was not taught in colleges prior to about 1960; there was no suitable text available. As a result of my text, we now see many colleges offering classes in Boundary Control. In the eastern United States, where the sectionalized land system is unknown, the text was not exactly applicable, so I asked Walter Robillard and Donald Wilson to add in their thinking. Like in a nudist camp, we aired our differences. The principle difference between eastern law and western law lies in the order of importance of distance and bearing. In California, by statute law, distance when in conflict with direction is always considered as more important than direction, whereas in New England and other east coast states the reverse is generally true.

Personally I was lucky to start private surveying practice at the close of the world war; many of the old time surveyors were still alive, and I was able to find out how little they knew about the legal elements of land surveying. If any of you were around in the twenties, there was the great depression starting in 1929 and ending after the Second World War about 1947. During these 18 years almost no new Licensed Surveyors were added to the ranks; there was no need for them because of the scarcity of work. Also those that came into the profession prior to the depression were getting quite old. Bill Rumsey, John Covert, Will King, [David] Loebenstein and others were in their sunset years. At least I got to talk to them about their surveying problems and experiences. To me the saddest chapter in the history of surveying was when 5,000 plus were grandfathered in the Civil Engineer's act and given the right to practice their ignorance of surveying on the general public. I have a number of horror stories written. While I have never killed anyone, I have read several obituaries with pleasure.

One thing I forgot to mention, when I entered college I flunked the dumbbell English test twice and after taking a special course twice I passed it. When I transferred to the University of California, I had to take the test again and flunked it. After two more classes in remedial English I finally passed the test in time to graduate. My problem was in spelling. I never could and still have the same problem. You know something is wrong with your vision when you spell s—e—x as s—i—x. Now I have 15 books in print, mostly due to my excellent secretaries. They could spell, type, punctuate and never miss a period.

Of course, after a few publication successes and a fairly good practice I started to feel my oats and swelling up rather than growing. Deflation soon arrived. One day my wife and I were headed for a convention and I had a flat tire adjoining some large institution. There was this fellow looking out from a solid locked gate; obviously an inmate in an asylum. I jacked the wheel up, took off the hub cap, took off the wheel nuts and set them in the hubcap, pulled the wheel off and stepped back on the edge of the hub cap. The hubcap flew up and all the nuts went down a nearby storm drain. So I started  down the street to the nearest service station. The observer behind the gate asked where I was going. To my reply that I was going to get some more nuts, he looked at me and said "Why don't you take one nut off each of the other wheels, put on your spare tire and drive there?" I asked what he was doing locked behind a locked gate. His reply was, "I am here because I am crazy, not because I am stupid!"

So it is with Land Surveying, you can be crazy to be one, but you can never be stupid. The court records often disclose the incompetent's name in the damage award's book. As we know, surveyors are supposed to follow the footsteps of the original surveyor, but how can this be done without knowing what the old time surveyors did? This book is supposed to record past events so as to enable future surveyors to have some knowledge of what has happened in the past. Someone should write a brief history of what has happened in all counties of California.

In conclusion, I wish to point out that I was born in Maine, conclusive proof that I am a Maineack, but I hope I never get caught for being stupid.

****

I believe no discussion of Curt would be complete without additional mention of his wry sense and appreciation for humor. Typical of his view of the world was his unabashed inclusion of an amusing letter published in the otherwise staid "Comment and Discussion" column in the ACSM journal. The article, entitled **COLORFUL COMMENTS - COLORFUL MARKS - COLORFUL REMARKS** was sure to leave an impression upon the reader. It certainly left one on me.

****

CURTIS M. BROWN, San Diego, California - Irate neighbors, especially if they are teetering on the brink of sanity, create problems. When locating a disputed line, a hole was dug through asphalt coating in the street (to locate a monument) and lead and discs were set in the sidewalk area as offset markers. The usual fluorescent paint was put around the offset markers, and property corner markers set pink laths. During the survey, the neighbor had to drive around the transit and a street sweeper drove around a parked surveyor's truck. In the letter of complaint, the following was written to the surveyor's client (spelling and grammar uncorrected). The lady (?) was unable to complain about the survey, but she certainly could complain about everything else.

Dear _____,

I told you, and I thought I spoke truthfully, that I would not (couldn't) be disturbed by the surveyors. I was wrong.

Where most surveyors are content with an unobtrusive little lead mark in the concrete, this megalomaniac uses fluorescent pink paint

37

to underscore his (to his mind) virtuoso performance and definitive drawing of the property lines.

I refuse to believe that my house sits on the property line. Unfortunately, that section of sidewalk which had the lead mark is now gone. Fortunately, I'm not interested in putting up a brick wall nor in selling, so it is of little import. Neither am I impressed or convinced except in the following manner:

I am impressed with the man's imperious oafness in directing me where to drive and where to park as if I were an incompetent nincompoop, and blind to boot so that I can neither see him or his tripod. I told him I was sufficiently irritated that by parking where he did, and imperiously directing the street sweeper to avoid his instruments, the sweeper also missed my very dirty street.

No one ever accused me of being reasonable or mild-mannered and your surveyor probably will nominate me for Bitch-of-the-Year. And I guess you know I couldn't care less. And I fully intend to remove that garish phosphorescent pink crap from the walk, and its matching pink stick from my/your flowerbed.

I understand according to this mental giant I have suddenly come into possession of a manhole. How I wish I'd always wanted a manhole, and to have my house on someone's property line.

I don't care enough about it to pay for my own survey, which like yours is going to favor the person employing the surveyor. But I don't put this much credence in his line.

However, I'm not gonna fight, dispute, or worry about it. I do tell you I am prepared to ignore it, my original departure point. Lots of luck on whatever made the whole thing important to you.

(Signed) _____

P.S. If that "reference point" he claims to have located in the street adjacent to Ross's driveway is more than too unnecessary and unrevealing holes in the asphalt, I may be as blind, and about as stupid as he takes me for.

****

**CURT BROWN AND FRIENDS
1988 CLSA CONFERENCE
ANAHEIM, CALIFORNIA**

PHOTOGRAPH COURTESY OF THE AUTHOR

Curt's influence upon the legal community and American jurisprudence remains unprecedented and impressive. Over the years, as various courts across the country wrestled with complex boundary conflicts and the need for an authority to consult with in adopting its decisions, many judges and courts would rely on Curt's opinions and his work. In a Minnesota Court of Appeals decision entitled *Allen G. Potvin, et al., Respondents, vs. Timothy A. Hall, et al., Appellants, Reliastar Mortgage Corp., et al., Defendants* (C4-99-421, filed September 28, 1999 - Beltrami County District Court File No. C09863), Curt's influence can be found. The controversy involved a dispute between adjoining property owners over the location of their common boundary. Timothy and Dorothy Hall appealed the district court's order that rejected their attempt to establish the boundary line by practical location through acquiescence and instead accepted as the true boundary a line drawn by interpreting the original plat.

Their neighbors, the Potvins, hired surveyor Robert Murray to locate the south line of their lot (lot 9). Unable to locate any monuments left by the original surveyor, Murray used as a starting point a boundary line established between nearby lots 20 and 21 by court action in 1966. In that action, the Beltrami County District Court established a line of occupation and ordered the surveyor, Al Bye, to place monuments to establish the line. His work became known as the "Bye occupation line." In conducting his survey, Murray measured northward from the Bye occupation line. By relying on lines of occupation, Murray was able to describe lines that were consistent with how the residents were using the property and also consistent with the lot widths shown on the original underlying 1907 plat. The district court found that Murray's method, "though not the 'textbook approach,' established in a logical and persuasive manner the location of the boundary lines."

The court also found that the Halls failed to demonstrate, by clear and convincing evidence, a boundary by practical location through acquiescence, agreement, or estoppel between lots 9 and 10 and held that the actual boundary was the line Murray established. The Potvins conceded that the Halls had acquired, by adverse possession, that portion of lot 9 on which the Hall home is situated and the district court set a boundary four feet from the northern side of the Hall home.

The Halls appealed, contending that (1) they were only required to prove a boundary by practical location by a preponderance of the evidence, rather than by clear and convincing evidence; (2) they established a boundary by practical location; (3) surveyor Murray's attempt to locate the original boundary was inadequate; and (4) the line of adverse possession set by the district court fails to consider the Halls' reasonable use of their property. The court responded to the claim:

> *The Halls also assert error in the district court's accepting surveyor Murray's testimony to ascertain the likely placement of the originally platted boundary. They argue that Murray's testimony is not competent evidence of the true platted line and constitutes an impermissible resurvey. We agree that "[i]n any resurvey of an original survey the only authority that the surveyor has is to relocate the lines exactly as laid down by the original surveyor." Curtis M. Brown, <u>Boundary Control and Legal Principles</u> 112 (2d ed. 1969). When locating a boundary, a resurveyor is attempting to locate the line originally intended as the dividing line between two parcels of land. See generally John R. Barlow, II & Donald*

M. Von Cannon, <u>Skelton on the Legal Elements of Boundaries &</u>
<u>Adjacent Properties</u> 68-209 (2d ed. 1997)."

In another case tried in the Tennessee Court of Appeals and decided
in 2002, the appellate tribunal similarly relied on Curt's work. The case,
entitled *Stacey J. Stanley v. Daniel Ring, et al.* (Direct Appeal from the
Chancery Court for Obion County, No. 21,537 William Michael Maloan,
Chancellor, No. W2001-00950-COA-R3-CV2) concerned riparian rights
associated with a privately owned lake in a subdivision in Obion County.
The trial court found that the boundaries of lots abutting the lake extend
into the lake, and that the owners of these lots had riparian rights to limited
use of the lake as reasonable under the circumstances. In commenting on
the subject of Limited Riparian Rights, the court stated:

> *Ms. Stanley asserts that prior owners always had restricted*
> *Defendants' use of the lake, and that Mr. Clark never intended*
> *to convey any interest in the lake to Defendants' predecessors in*
> *interest. She contends that since Defendants do not own any part*
> *of the lake bed, they have no right to use the lake. The essence of*
> *her argument, as we perceive it, is that Defendants do not have*
> *riparian rights to use of the lake.*
> *The deeds conveying the lots to Defendants are silent as to any rights*
> *to use of the lake, but convey the land "with the appurtenances,*
> *estate, title, and interest thereto belonging . . . ." This Court recently*
> *addressed riparian rights inherent in such a deed in <u>The Pointe,</u>*
> *<u>LLC v. Lake Management Ass'n,</u> 50 S.W.3d 471 (Tenn. Ct. App.*
> *2000). In <u>The Pointe,</u> we stated, "it is clear that the grant of an*
> *appurtenance in a deed is meant to enhance the value and enjoyment*
> *of the property." Id. at 475. We noted that the inherent value of*
> *riparian land is derived from the accessibility and proximity of the*
> *water. Id. We further noted that when, as here, property adjacent*
> *to water is conveyed with all appurtenances, there is a presumption*
> *that the right to use and enjoyment of the water is part of the*
> *grant. Id. These riparian interests are presumed unless the terms of*
> *the grant, conveyance or deed expressly exclude them, or unless the*
> *description of the property in the deed clearly indicates that such*
> *rights are not attached to the property. Id. at 476-77. See also,*
> *<u>Curtis M. Brown, et al, Boundary Control and Legal Principles</u>*
> *199 (3rd ed 1986). Riparian water rights vest when the riparian*
> *land is acquired. 5A Richard R. Powell, <u>Powell on Real Property</u>*
> *Ch. 65 ¶ 713[3] (Patrick J. Rohan ed., 1993). These rights are*

"considered part of the package of rights in the fee." Id. They depend not on ownership of the land beneath the water, but on contact of the landowner's land with the water. Brown, supra.

More recently, a February 2003 case out of the United States District Court of Maine entitled *United States of America v. Iolanda Ponte, Trustee* (Civil No. 99-281-B-H) involved a dispute about whether an easement line was to be measured along the ground or along a leveled horizontal line. In rendering his opinion, United States District Judge D. Brock Hornby declared:

> *Maine's Law Court has said that the horizontal method is the "common" method of measuring distances, <u>Town of Union v. Strong</u>, 681 A.2d 14, 18 (Me. 1996), using as authority a 1962 text, Curtis M. Brown & Winfield H. Eldridge, <u>Evidence and Procedures for Boundary Location</u> (1962), a text that was extant at the time this easement was drafted. Another text the Law Court cites states the principle that a surveyor must consider usage at the time a particular deed description was drafted.* 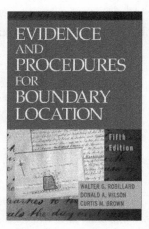 *Walter G. Robillard et al., <u>Brown's Boundary Control and Legal Principles</u> 42 (4th ed. 1995) ("The unit of measurement indicated in the description is that unit of measurement used at the time of the survey or when the description was written."). Horizontal measurement, therefore, is appropriate for this 1974 easement. There is nothing to suggest that the parties to this conservation easement had anything different in mind . . . Horizontal is not the only method. The ordinance the Law Court interpreted in <u>Strong</u> as requiring horizontal measurement for some purposes required over-the-ground measurement for other purposes. 681 A.2d at 17; <u>see also</u> Walter G. Robillard et al., <u>Brown's Boundary Control and Legal Principles</u> 45 (4th ed. 1995):*

> *In GLO [General Land Office] surveys the presumption is that all measurements are horizontal along a straight line because the law required the surveyors to perform as such. In the metes and bounds states the early measurements are presumed to be "slope"*

or "along the lay of the land." However, the contrary may always be proved. [The GLO survey] presumption has not always been in effect; in a few localities proof has been found indicating that original measurements were made along the surface . . . . [Kentucky case citation].

Although Maine was a metes-and-bounds state, see Paul G. Creteau, Maine Real Estate Law 204 (1969), horizontal measurement is the "modern" method of measurement according to the Law Court. Strong, 681 A.2d at 18 (citing Walter G. Robillard et al., Brown's Boundary Control and Legal Principles 45 (1995)). The method has been advocated since at least the late 18th century. Curtis M. Brown & Winfield H. Eldridge, Evidence and Procedures for Boundary Location 112-13 (1962); see also Robillard et al., supra, at 79 (quoting Edward Tiffin's instructions to Northwest Territory surveyors in 1815 to use horizontal measurements, not over the surface of the ground).

It is thus fitting that Curt's home state of Maine would seek his counsel in the 21st century and in the years to come, will continue to do so. Undoubtedly, his influence will continue to assist in the resolution of boundary conflicts across the United States and elsewhere. It is therefore certain that Curt's writing will continue to serve their intended purpose.

Curtis Maitland Brown died on March 4, 1993. He rests in a rustic little cemetery in Julian, California where he watches over the hills and valleys where he so freely roamed and lived life to its fullest. He rests a stone's throw from his son Patrick's engineering office.

****

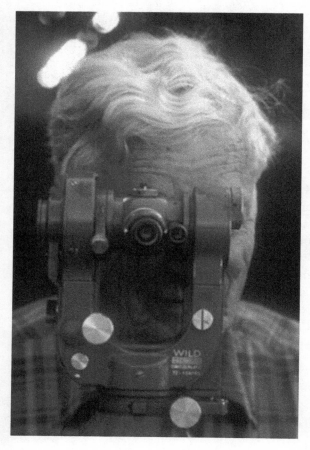

**A HUMOROUS MOMENT
WITH CURT**

**PHOTOGRAPH COURTESY
OF ROBERT LEE MCCOMB, PLS**

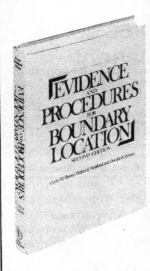

...and it all began with a Berger

Where there's a turnpike to be built—a cloverleaf to be engineered—a skyscraper to lay out—a river to bridge...chances are a Berger will be there getting it under way.

For Berger Instruments are wise in the ways of the country's leading engineers and constructors. They've been field-conditioned to meet the challenging demands of many of the major construction projects of the century.

So when you see the "signs" of *big* construction—Turner, Stone & Webster, F. H. McGraw, among others, look around—a Berger is somewhere on the scene.

Then put yourself behind the Berger and see why.

C. L. Berger & Sons, Inc., 43 Williams Street, Boston 19, Mass.

BERGER IN THE MISSILES PROGRAM: Optical alignment tooling, synchro readout devices, precision rotating mechanisms, instrumentation design and manufacturing.

THE BEST IN SIGHT IS **BERGER**

Engineering & Surveying Instruments...Made in America by American Technicians...Since 1871

AMBULATORY BOUNDARIES

THE SURVEYOR AND THE LAW

Notes on Swamp Lands, Navigable Streams, and Lakes

March 1960

Recently (Dec. 4, 1959) I was fortunate enough to be asked to speak at the Eleventh Annual Surveyors Institute at the University of Wisconsin. During the course of the program, it was informative and worthwhile to note the differences in water laws.

In the sectionalized land states, the beds of the rivers and lakes originally resided in the Federal Government. As patents to lands were issued, the new landowner, adjoining waters, was granted title to the bed of all non-navigable streams and lakes. The government retained title to the beds of navigable lakes and streams. Upon admission to the Union, title to the beds of navigable lakes and streams passed to the state. After acquiring title, a state could dispose of its rights as it saw fit.

In Wisconsin, it appears that the state has relinquished its rights in the beds of lakes to the adjoining landowner. But not so for navigable streams. Further, the State Courts of Wisconsin have taken the attitude that the remotest possibility of navigation makes a stream navigable. I believe the definition is, "a navigable stream is any stream capable of floating a log or the lightest possible boat." The test seems to be whether a canoe of the least draft (about 2 inches) is capable of floating and moving after any rain. This, in effect, means that practically any watercourse can meet this test at some time during a heavy rainy season.

The state is the sole judge as to matters between itself and its citizens and such a ruling can be enforced. However, as between the state and

un-patented land of the Federal Government, such a state rule would probably not be enforceable. In Oklahoma, the state passed a law declaring that under certain a conditions stream was navigable; hence, they owned the bed and the oil under it. But a tribe of Indians objected and the Federal Court decided that they (the courts) were the sole judge as to navigability. In this case, the stream was declared non-navigable; the Indians got the oil.

After the land has been patented by a citizen and the land is repurchased by the U. S. Government, it will undoubtedly be controlled by state laws. Since most government lands of Wisconsin are repurchased lands, the state rule of navigability will probably hold in most cases.

Apparently, in Wisconsin the object of trying to declare all possible streams navigable is for the purpose of retaining public fishing rights in the streams. Since I dearly love to fish for trout, I am highly in favor of it, even though there seems to be a tinge of unfairness to it.

In California and many western states, just the reverse is closer to the picture. Under the Spanish rule, water can be appropriated. It is far more important to use water for irrigation than it is to permit it to remain in a stream as a fish bath.

Few streams are declared navigable; the water is diverted for irrigation. In one state, I believe it is Arizona, they boast that there are no navigable streams. Of course, the fact that they have little water has something to do with it.

In Wisconsin, while the beds of lakes reside in the adjoiners, the State maintains an easement in the water for purposes of navigation and fishing. In order to create a means of access to these lakes, the platting law requires that at half-mile intervals a road shall be provided all the way to the lake. I believe this law to be reasonable and fair. In California (San Diego County), our prize asset is ocean frontage. The County has passed an ordinance requiring the dedication of a street adjoining the ocean and extending all the way to the ocean. Eventually there will no longer be private beach rights. This, of course, is confiscation without remuneration. Frankly, it is a bit sneaky but seemingly legal.

Swamplands are a special problem in Southern California. The Federal Government meandered and reserved these lands. Upon application by the State, the lands were given to the state. After the State acquired these swamplands, it sold the lands to private parties. In numerous instances, these so-called swamplands are semi-fresh lagoons adjoining the ocean. Normally the meander line of a body of water does not constitute the boundary line; the water itself is. In the case of swamplands, the land is supposed to be alternately inundated and dry. If this is so, it is non-riparian. For this reason, the boundary of swamplands is the meander line and not the water line. We must, in such cases, reestablish lost meander lines.

Swamplands had to be applied for by the State and granted to the State by the government. Any swampland not applied for and duly granted, does not come under the swamp act, and hence does not necessarily possess a meander line as a boundary line.

– CURTIS M. BROWN

DETERMINATION OF OWNERSHIP BOUNDARIES ALONG SEASHORES

CURTIS M. BROWN

CIRCA 1965

In the past the primary value of the seashore was for commerce, recreation and harvesting foods such as clams, lobsters and fish; court decisions pertained to these interests. In recent times the discovery of mineral wealth in tidal and offshore areas has led to fee title disputes and U. S. Supreme Court decisions.

In general, prior to these court cases, the upland riparian owner, with some exceptions as given below, had a fee title which extended seaward to the mean high tide line. Most coastal states believed that they had a fee title extending from the mean high tide line oceanward at least three geographical miles. The Federal Government claimed to the continental shelf. Disputes arose over oil leases issued by California in the Santa Barbara area. Both California and the Federal Government claimed fee title to the submerged lands existing between low water line and the three mile limit and both claimed benefits from oil discovered in this area.

The rule for the limits of ownership between the riparian upland owner and the State has always been that states (Texas excepted) owned below the mean high tide line. As an incident of ownership, each State had and still has the right to sell, lease or otherwise dispose of the fee title to their tide lands. In several instances this was done.

A Massachusetts colonial ordinance granted to riparian owners tidelands between the mean high tide line and the low water mark, but not more than 100 rods (1650'). New Hampshire and Maine adopted similar laws (see Reference #1). Grants made prior to the ordinance were held to extend only to the high water mark in Massachusetts and to the low water mark in Maine.

In the State of California the legislature did authorize the sale of tidelands from the mean high tide line to the low water line, and in a number of places, such as San Francisco Bay, San Diego Bay and Moro Bay, this was done.

In three Supreme Court cases, United States v California (332 US 19 in 1947), United States v Louisiana (339 US 699 in 1950), and United States v Texas (339 US 707 in 1950), the Federal Government won exclusive ownership of the fee below ordinary low water line. In the words of the court, "California is not the owner of the three-mile marginal belt along its coast, and the Federal Government rather than the State has paramount rights in the power over that belt, an incident to which is full dominion over the resources of the soil under the water area, including oil."

The Federal Government's victory was short lived. If the United States owned lands to the three mile limit, it could deed these lands to the States. By the submerged Lands Act of 1953 (Public Law 31) offshore lands were granted to the various States.

Apparently, at the time of the passage of the act, there was fear that the courts might decide that the bed of the Great Lakes belonged to the Federal Government; rights to the bed of the Great Lakes were granted to the adjoining States by this act. Also it appears that some of the congressmen were not at all pleased with the Supreme Court's ideas since the committee wrote, "The Court believed it to be in the past." Since the time of the packing of the Supreme Court during the Roosevelt Administration, many unexpected decisions have been handed down. Whether this is good or bad is not for me to say. One thing is certain, this concept of Federal fee ownership below the ordinary low water mark was the reverse of all previous expressions or expectations.

The submerged Lands Act provided among other things:

1. All rights of the Federal Government to mineral resources, fee title, etc., were quit claimed to the States for a distance of three geographical miles seaward in the Atlantic and Pacific Oceans.

2. The fee title, mineral rights, etc. in all bays and inland waters (including the Great Lakes and excepting lands acquired by the Federal Government) were quit claimed to the States.

3. Within the Gulf of Mexico, States could claim to the extent of their boundaries at the time of their admission to the Union but not more than three marine leagues (nine geographic miles).

4. The U. S. reserved lands between the three geographical mile limit and the continental shelf into itself. The United States reserved the usual rights to control commerce, navigation, national defense, etc.

5. The Act defines the three geographical mile limit as being measured from "the line of ordinary low water."

Since the passage of the act, the U. S. Supreme Court has decided that Texas and Florida, at the time of their admission to the Union, had rights to nine geographical miles, hence they could claim nine geographical miles into the Gulf of Mexico. Louisiana, Mississippi and Alabama were limited to three geographical miles.

California is contending for three geographical miles beyond the headland line of certain "historic bays" such as Monterey Bay. As yet, this decision has not been handed down though the special master has expressed his opinion.

As of the present time, the limit of demarcation between the riparian owner and the state can be in any one of several locations depending upon the general laws in force at the time of the alienation from the sovereign to the individual. These locations are:

1. Mean high water line (most States)

2. Ordinary low water line

3. Mean low water line

4. Mean lower low water line

5. One hundred rods (1650 feet) seaward of the mean high water line (Massachusetts, New Hampshire and Maine)

6. Mean Higher high water line (In Texas adjoining Spanish and Mexican land grants)

7. Meander lines (Swamp lands only)

In the State of Texas many Spanish and Mexican grants were made. Spanish law at the time of these grants was said to reserve in the sovereign all lands to the highest winter wave. As a practical matter the Texas supreme court interpreted this as "the mean of the higher high tides (See Reference #4). Thus, lands granted to private parties by the Spanish or Mexican governments within Texas did not extend seaward as far as those which were granted by the State of Texas. To my knowledge this rule has not been applied in other rancho land grant States such as parts of Alabama, Florida and California.

The early swamp land act of the United States has created difficult boundary problems for those resurveying swamp lands. In the early history of the United States, the Federal Government passed a statute law whereby the various States could apply for certain swamp and overflow lands. After these lands were acquired by the States from the Federal Government, the States could dispose of them, and they often did. Some of these so-called swamp lands adjoined the ocean. Theoretically a swamp has no definite water line limit; it is an area subject to flooding part of the year and dryness at other times. It cannot be said that a swamp has a definite water line such as a river or ocean shore; the land may be merely a bog without a standing surface pond or lake. Most States have ruled that lands acquired via the swamp lands act are not riparian and ownership is limited to the meander lines. Many of the California coastal lagoons that are permanently cut off from the ocean and were acquired via the swamp land route come under this rule (Important: The lands must have been granted to the State in compliance with the swamp lands act).

Accretion laws add confusion to the upland owners' limit of ownership. Soil attaching itself to the riparian owners land by slow and imperceptible means belongs to the riparian owner. Land gradually eroded is lost to the riparian owner. Often accretion or erosion is caused by a man made barrier. For example, if a rock jetty is built from the shore into the ocean and the offshore currents are southerly, sand is apt to deposit northerly of the jetty. In Mission Beach, California, about 100 acres of sand were added to the shore because of just such a cause. According to the Federal rule of law, accretions belong to the riparian owner regardless of the cause; according to the California rule of law, accretions caused by man made barriers belong to the State. (The Federal rule of law does not apply to fills or sudden causes.)

Since the limits of the boundary of a State's ownership now extends three geographical miles beyond the ordinary low water line, and if the same Federal rule of law for mean high tide is applied to the ordinary low water line, I suppose a State could increase its area of jurisdiction by constructing numerous jetties out from its shores, thus moving the ordinary low water line seaward by the process of accretions.

Thus far, numerous terms have been used without precise definitions. Ordinarily, legal terms are not subject to mathematical definition, and it is often times difficult to translate a court decree into an exact location on the ground. Fortunately, the courts have been precise in many shore definitions and have in general adopted meanings as proposed by the Coast and Geodetic Survey. It is easy to misunderstand tide datum definitions and thus locate lines in error.

According to the court rules of law, <u>mean high tide line</u> (also <u>ordinary high tide line</u>) is the average of all higher tides <u>at the spot being located</u>. This is a simple definition but one that is exceedingly expensive to put into effect. Most surveyors are prone to say, "I will take the average elevation for a mean high tide line as published by the USC&GS and use this value to determine a level tide line along the shore." This can be right in a few selected locations, but more often it is wrong.

The datum of the USC&GS is based upon the general adjustment of 1929 wherein sea level as observed at 26 tide stations (21 in the United States and 5 in Canada) was held fixed. This must not be confused with <u>local mean sea level</u> which is the datum referred to in court cases. While the two may be identical in a few places and may approximate one another in other places, investigations should be made to determine the differences.

In determining the local average sea level or local mean high tide line or local mean low tide, numerous considerations make this problem complex.

Tides are the result of gravitational pull of the moon and the sun. Superimposed on the predictable causes of the tide are such unpredictable factors as barometric pressure, wind velocity in one direction, land barriers, ocean currents and other items. In addition, the ocean is gradually rising at an imperceptible rate due to the melting of ice caps. Also, lands rise or fall due to various geographic causes. Taking all of the periodic factors into account, the USC&GS has concluded that an average of 18.6 years of observation is necessary to obtain a correct value for sea level. From this it can be seen that sea level varies from day to day, month to month and year to year (See page 63, reference 3).

Table of expected variation of sea level from

day to day	1 ft. or more
month to month	1 ft. or less
year to year	.1 to .2 accumulative

For any given location the error of sea level determination can be reduced by using the method of comparison (see reference 2) with the nearest tidal station that has records of 19 year tidal observations. When using this method, the probable error will be in about the following range (this varies with the distance from the tidal station and the local conditions):

1 day of observations	.25 foot error
30 days of observations	.10 foot error
365 days of observation	.05 foot error

Where the shore is flat, as in marsh lands, and where a few hundredths of a foot in elevation of the water will inundate a large area, these small errors can be significant. In steep shore conditions, 30 days of tidal observations compared with similar observations at a nearby 19 year observation station can be quite satisfactory and accurate enough for practical matters.

In summary, the line of demarcation between the upland riparian owner and the state is usually the average of all the high tides over an 18.6 year period. In some States, depending upon the laws in existence at the time of the alienation of the land from the sovereign, other legal ownership lines exist.

The correct tidal datum is that tidal datum that exists at the place the deed is written. The USC&GS 1929 datum when applied to a local spot, unless it happens to be near a control tidal observation station, is not necessarily sufficiently accurate to determine a local elevation for a specific tidal line.

The best method of determining a local datum is by the comparison method developed by the USC&GS and given in the books listed in references 2 and 3.

References

1. Brown, Curtis M.; <u>Boundary Control and Legal Principles</u>, Chapter 7, John Wiley & Sons, N. Y.

2. Kissam, Phillip; Surveying for Civil Engineers McGraw-Hill Book Co., N. Y.

3. Shalowitz, Aaron L.; Shore and Sea Boundaries, Publication 10-1, USGPO.

4. Willson, William H.; The Seashore Boundary in Texas, 12th Annual Texas Surveyors Association Short Course, 1963.

[MP NOTE: Paper on file at UCLA Map Library August 19, 1965, Record ID: 4927792, UCLA Libraries and Collections]

****

THE SURVEYOR AND THE LAW

HUGHES V. STATE OF WASHINGTON
(PERTAINING TO ACCRETIONS)

MARCH 1968

The US Supreme Court in a dispute decided an unusual case December 11, 1967, over the ownership of accretions. The Washington State rule by State Supreme Court decision is: "The upland owners' title rights extend to the point where vegetation ceases *as of the date of admission of Washington* to statehood (1889)." Thus, accretions cannot belong to the upland owner. In Louisiana, the same is true by statute law (not by court interpretation as in Washington).

Mrs. Stella Hughes owned a parcel that was patented prior to 1889 and she claimed to the mean high tide line as per Federal rule. After the state court denied her 561 feet of land between the mean high tide line and the line of vegetation, the US Supreme Court took up the matter. Two points were involved: (1) Did her land go to the high tide line; and (2) if so, did her land include accretions accumulated after statehood? The decision of the court was:

The question for decision is whether federal or state law controls the ownership of land, called accretion, gradually deposited by the ocean on adjoining upland property conveyed by the United States prior to statehood. The circumstances that give rise to the question are these. Prior to 1889, the United States, except land that had been conveyed, owned all land

58

in what is now the State of Washington to private parties. At that time owners of property bordering the ocean, such as the predecessor in title of Mrs. Stella Hughes, the petitioner here, had under the common law a right to include within their lands any accretion gradually built up by the ocean. Washington became a state in 1889, and Article 17 of the state's new constitution, as interpreted by its Supreme Court, denies the owners of ocean-front property in the state any further rights in accretion that might in the future be formed between their property and the ocean. This is a suit brought by Mrs. Hughes, the successor in title to the original federal grantee, against the State of Washington as owner of the tidelands to determine whether the right to future accretions, which existed under federal law in 1889, was abolished by that provision of the Washington Constitution. The trial court upheld Mrs. Hughes' contention that the right to accretions remained subject to federal law, and that she was the owner of the accreted lands. The State Supreme Court reversed, holding that state law controlled and that the State owned these lands. 67 Wash. 2d 799, 410 P. 2d 20 (1966). We granted certiorari. (385 US 1000) (1967). We hold that this question is governed by federal, not state, law and that under federal law Mrs. Hughes, who traces her title to a federal grant prior to statehood, is the owner of these accretions.

This brings us to the question of what the federal rule is. The state has not attempted to argue that federal law gives it title to these accretions, and it seems clear to us that it could not. A long and unbroken line of decisions of this Court establishes that the grantee of land bounded by a body of navigable water acquires a right to any natural and gradual accretion formed along the shore. In Jones v. Johnston, 18 How. 150 (1855), a dispute between two parties owning land along Lake Michigan over the ownership of soil that had gradually been deposited along the shore, this Court held that "Land gained from the sea either by alluvium or dereliction, if the same be by little and little, by small and imperceptible degrees, belongs to the owner of the land adjoining." (18 How., at 156). The Court has repeatedly reaffirmed this rule, County of St. Clair v. Lovingston, 23 Wall. 46 (1874); Jefferis v. East Oniaha Land Co., 134 US 178 (1890), and the soundness of the principle is scarcely open to question. Any other rule would leave riparian owners continually in danger of losing the access to water which is often the most valuable feature of their property, and continually vulnerable to harassing litigation challenging the location of the original water lines. While it is true that these riparian rights are to some extent insecure in any event, since they are subject to considerable control by the neighboring owner of the tideland, this is insufficient reason to leave these valuable rights at the mercy of natural phenomena which may in no way affect the interests of the tideland owner. See Stevens v. Arnold, 262 US 266, 269 - 270 (1923). We therefore hold that petitioner is entitled to the accretion that has been gradually formed along her property by the ocean.

The judgment below is reversed, and the case is remanded to the Supreme Court of Washington for further proceedings not inconsistent with this opinion.

REVERSED

As of now, it appears that US riparian land patented prior to 1889 follows the Federal rule whereas land patented after 1889 follows the state law.

– CURTIS M. BROWN

****

THE SURVEYOR'S NOTEBOOK

Optical Plummet Transit
Replaces Theodolites on Tough Jobs
at Plattsburgh Missile Base

"**As you may have guessed,** we've had some really rugged and unusual problems building the Plattsburgh (N.Y.) Missile Base," says Leigh French, Chief Field Engineer for Raymond-Kaiser-Macco-Puget Sound (A Joint Venture), contractors on the job. "No matter what unique surveying problem is involved, we have the added headache of exceptionally close tolerances—often to 1/16 or 1/32 of an inch. Needless to say, that is unusually accurate for construction work.

"In building 200-foot underground 'silos', which house Atlas F guidance systems, we first tried imported theodolites but found we couldn't get the length of focus that was required. Adolph Vaal, my instrument man on sight tube setting, was acquainted with the Gurley Optical Plummet Transit and suggested we try it. Now the theodolites are gathering dust back in the office.

"**In using the Gurley 'OP'** in this work, we often have to set up on platforms over points which are 10 to 20 feet below the instrument on the center line of the sight tube. The Gurley Shifting-Head Tripod helps us to get into alignment fast. These sight tubes must be carefully set to an angle of 49°30', so accurate vertical angles are required. The level on the telescope makes it possible to adjust and check the vertical circle verniers quickly and easily by merely leveling the telescope.

"With all the wild winds up here, we're particularly happy not to have to worry about a flapping plumb bob. Adolph Vaal tells me he feels 'safer' using the 'OP' than any other instrument he's tried; says it's 'more rugged...doesn't get out of adjustment...everything can be seen instantly.'

Leigh French (L.), Adolph Vaal on instrument platform with their Optical Plummet Transit.

One time a 70-mile-an-hour gale knocked the Gurley down and it was still in perfect adjustment. And even in 45-below-zero cold, a complete check and adjustment can be made in the field in under five minutes.

"At the moment we're working in quicksand; but we know we can count on the Gurley 'OP' to pull us out."

You, too, can count on the Gurley Optical Plummet Transit to pull you out when you have tough assignments. **Available in 21 combinations. Write for further information.**

Setting the steel in the "silo" cap.

W. & L. E. GURLEY, 530 FULTON STREET, TROY, N.Y.

Engineering and Surveying Instruments, Hydrological and Meteorological Instruments, Paper Testing Instruments, Optical Instruments, Reticle Manufacturing Facilities, Standard Weights and Measures

GURLEY Surveying and Scientific Instruments

THE SURVEYOR AND THE LAW

TIDAL BOUNDARIES -- THE BORAX CASE REVISITED

BY AARON L. SHALOWITZ, J. D.

SEPTEMBER 1968

INTRODUCTION

The March 1968 issue Of SURVEYING AND MAPPING (in this department at pp. 120-121) contained a résumé by Curtis M. Brown of the recent Supreme Court case of *Hughes v. State of Washington*, 389 U.S. 290 (Dec. 11, 1967). Being familiar with the case, I was surprised to note that in quoting the *Hughes* decision the portion dealing with the *Borax* case, *infra*, and its controlling effect on the *Hughes* case was entirely omitted. It is all the more surprising because in all the briefs and other documents filed by both litigants, including the *amicus curiae* brief filed by the United States, the *Borax* case was repeatedly cited.

Although *Borax* is a landmark case in the law of tidal boundaries, the 1965 *California* decision, *infra*, left some doubt as to the continued validity of the principle laid down in *Borax* because the Court failed to adopt the tidal datum of mean low water and adopted in effect the datum of mean lower-low water. It is therefore pertinent to examine this aspect of the *California* case and to trace the impact of *Borax* through the years on tidal boundary law as developed in state and Federal courts and in the Supreme Court of the United States.

This discussion deals with the following relevant cases in chronological order:

Borax Consolidated *v.* Los Angeles (1935)
United States *v.* California (1947)
United States *v.* Washington (1961)
United States *v.* California (1965)
Hughes *v.* State of Washington (1967)

Preliminarily, it is to be observed that under our dual system of sovereignty (state and federal) the title and rights of riparian proprietors in the soil below high-water mark of navigable waters are governed by the laws of the several states, rather than by federal law. This control extends to such attributes of ownership - commonly called riparian rights as the right to accretions to the land and rights in the tidelands themselves (lands between high and low water). Each state has dealt with such matters according to its own views of justice and policy, some retaining title to the lands, while others have recognized them as appurtenant to the upland (land above high water), and still others

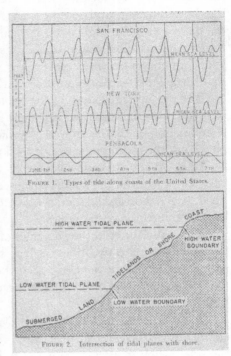

FIGURE 1. Types of tide along coasts of the United States.

FIGURE 2. Intersection of tidal planes with shore.

have granted rights therein to individuals, independent of the ownership of the uplands. This is the normal situation and Federal courts accept the interpretation of the highest court of a state as to what the state law is. However, where a situation involves a federal question, federal law applies. This was established by the Supreme Court in the *Borax* case, *infra*.

The Nature of Tidal Boundaries

Tidal boundaries, as the name implies, are boundaries associated with the rise and fall of the tide. They are referenced to tidal datums based on a particular phase of the tide, such as mean low water, mean lower-low water, and mean high water. Tidal datums as vertical reference planes for water boundaries are the most satisfactory of all datums. They possess the advantages of simplicity of definition, accuracy of determination, and certainty of recovery because they are based on recurring natural phenomena brought about by cyclical astronomic forces.

There are a number of datums which may be derived from tidal observations, the selection of the most suitable one being dependent upon the specialized purpose which the datum is to serve and the type of tide existing in a given locality. For representing the shoreline-the dividing line between land and sea-on topographic surveys and nautical charts, the datum of mean high water is used, while for depths or soundings on nautical charts a low-water datum is used (mean low water on the Atlantic and Gulf coasts and mean lower-low water on the Pacific coast) because that is the most serviceable to the mariner. [1]

The rhythmic response of the sea to the attractive forces of moon and sun, which we call the tide, is not the same everywhere. It is a continuing phenomenon but varies from day to day and from place to place. Thus, at New York the mean range is about 4.5 feet while the maximum range may be 7 feet. At the Atlantic entrance to the Panama Canal the range is less than a foot while at the Pacific entrance it averages 12.5 feet. On the other hand, at Anchorage, Alaska, a rise and fall of approximately 35 feet may be encountered on certain days.

Tides also differ in the character of the rise and fall. At New York, for example, there are two tides; a day of approximately equal range-called semidiurnal tides; at San Francisco there are two tides a day of unequal range-called mixed tides; and at Pensacola there is but one tide a day-called diurnal tides. (*See* fig. 1.)

Boundaries determined by the course of the tides involve two engineering aspects; a vertical one, predicated on the height reached by the tide during its vertical rise and fall, and constituting a tidal plane or datum, such as mean high water, mean low water, etc., and a horizontal one, related to the line where the tidal plane intersects the shore to form the tidal boundary desired, for example, mean high-water mark, mean low-water mark, etc. (*See* fig. 2.) The first is derived from tidal observations alone, and, once derived (on the basis of long-term observations), is for all practical purposes a permanent one. The second is dependent on the first, but is also affected by the natural processes of erosion and accretion, and the artificial changes made by man. A water boundary determined by tidal definition is thus not a fixed, visible mark on the ground, such as a roadway or fence, but represents a condition at the water's edge during a particular instant of the tidal cycle. [2]

Tidal boundaries are not new in American jurisprudence. The early grants, charters, and conveyances, which constitute the first links in the chains of title on which present ownerships of lands along our seacoasts are based, contain expressions such as "high-water line," "high-water mark," "the line of ordinary high water," and similar expressions pertaining to low water. Such references are at best indefinite and reflect an oversimplification of a phenomenon inherently complex and variable. Decisions interpreting such references often contain imperfections which suggest that appropriate scientific data were not always made available to the court. The *Borax* case, *infra*, established the first precise standard for the determination of the tidal boundary of "ordinary high-water mark."

BORAX CONSOLIDATED, LTD. v. LOS ANGELES

Borax Consolidated, Ltd. v. Los Angeles, 296 U.S. 10 (1935), involved the boundary between upland and tidelands on Mormon Island in the inner Los Angeles Harbor. The Borax Company owned the upland under a Federal patent and the City of Los Angeles owned the tidelands under a grant from the state, which was defined as "below the line of mean high tide of the Pacific Ocean." [3] Borax contended that the boundary is the "line of ordinary high-water" and that this has been construed by the California courts as the "line of the neap high tides." [4] This would have thrown the boundary seaward of the line claimed by the City.

The suit was instituted in a Federal district court by the City of Los Angeles to quiet title to lands it was claiming as tidelands. The court dismissed the suit, but the Court of Appeals remanded the case for a new trial and instructed the district court to ascertain as the boundary the "mean high-tide line," thus rejecting the line of "neap tides." The Borax Company appealed to the Supreme Court. In discussing this aspect of the case, the Court laid down the following important doctrine: "The question as to the extent of this federal grant, that is, as to the limit of the land conveyed, or the boundary between the upland and the tideland, is necessarily a federal question. It is a question which concerns the validity and effect of an act done by the United States; it involves the ascertainment of the essential basis of a right asserted under federal law." It therefore held that federal, rather than state, law applied.

Since federal law follows the common law of England, unless changed by statute, the Supreme Court in considering this aspect of the case adverted to the ruling of the English court in the early case of *Attorney General v. Chambers*, 4 DeG. M. & G. 206 (1854), which held "the medium tides of each quarter of the tidal period" to be the best criterion for determining the extent of the right of the Crown to the seashore or tidelands. The judges held that the same reason that excluded the highest tides of the month, the spring tides, also excluded the lowest high tides, the neaps, for both happen

as often as each other (*see* note 4 *supra*). But the Supreme Court said that in determining the limit of a federal grant neither the spring tides nor the neap tides are to be used, but a mean of all the high tides-spring, neap, and intermediate. [5]

The Court then defined more specifically how the mean of all the high tides was to be ascertained in order to achieve the requisite accuracy for delimiting the mean high-tide line. It said: "In view of the definition of the mean high tide, as given by the United States Coast and Geodetic Survey, that 'Mean high water at any place is the average height of all the high waters at that place over a considerable period of time,' and the further observation that 'from theoretical considerations of an astronomical character' there should be a 'periodic variation in the rise of water above sea level having a period of 18.6 years,' ... in order to ascertain the mean high tide line with requisite certainty in fixing the boundary of valuable tidelands, such as those here in question appear to be, 'an average of 18.6 years should be determined as near as possible'" (citing MARMER, TIDAL DATUM PLANES 76, 81, SPECIAL PUBLICATION NO. 135, U.S. COAST AND GEODETIC SURVEY (1927)).[6]

UNITED STATES v. CALIFORNIA (1947)

Twelve years later, the *Borax* decision was invoked by the United States in the case of *United States v. California*, 332 U.S. 19 (1947) - the so-called "tidelands" case-involving the tidal boundary of "ordinary low-water mark." The litigation began as an original action by the Government in the Supreme Court of the United States against the State of California in which it alleged that the State without authority was granting leases in the 3-mile marginal belt along its coast for the extraction of oil and other products therefrom. The United States moved for judgment on the basis of the State's answer, and the motion was set for hearing upon briefs filed. No documentary nor oral evidence was introduced.

In a far-reaching decision, the Supreme Court enunciated the doctrine of federal, rather than state, paramount rights in the submerged lands of the 3-mile marginal belt along its coast. This was spelled out in greater detail in the Court's decree as embracing "the lands, minerals, and other things underlying the Pacific Ocean lying seaward of the ordinary low-water mark on the coast of California, and outside of the inland waters." 332 U.S. at 804.

Following the decision, the Court named a Special Master to define with greater particularity the boundary between federal and state jurisdiction. The Court propounded three questions to the Master on which it sought recommendations. The third, which is pertinent to this discussion, was "By what criteria is the ordinary low-water mark on the coast of California to be ascertained?" (Along the California coast two low waters occur each tidal day with a marked difference in height between successive high waters and successive low waters - *see* fig. 1.)

In the briefs and oral arguments before the Special Master, it was the Government's contention that while no judicial standard had thus far been established for the term "ordinary low water," the mean of both the low waters (higher lows and lower lows} should be used rather than the mean of only the lower lows, as contended for by California. The Government based its position first on the fact that while the term "ordinary low water" is not one which the Coast and Geodetic Survey has defined and standardized for survey operations and for technical engineering use, where the word "ordinary" is used in connection with tides, it is regarded as the equivalent of the word "mean." Thus, "ordinary low-water mark" would be the same as "mean low-water mark," and this technically would be the mean of the higher lows and lower lows. (This should be kept in mind in connection with the discussion of *United States v. California* (1965) *infra*.) Secondly, where there is a variation in the height of any phase of the tide, each height having equal significance in the tidal cycle, the mean of the heights is more representative of that level than is any single height, when taken alone. [8] Finally, the Government found persuasive aid in defining "ordinary low-water mark" from the holding of the Supreme Court in the *Borax* case *supra*, defining the cognate term "ordinary high-water mark." Thus, "ordinary low water" is a different datum from "ordinary lower-low water" just as "ordinary high water" is a different datum from "ordinary higher-high water."

California's contention for the use of the mean of the lower-low waters only, was predicated primarily on the use by the Coast and Geodetic Survey of the datum of mean lower-low water for referencing soundings on its nautical charts of the Pacific coast. [9]

The Special Master reached the same conclusion as the Government, but predicated his finding on the consideration of property rights, stating that, from the point of view of a disputed real estate boundary line, there would be "no more reason to choose the mean of the lower low tides (as one interested claimant might suggest from self-interest) than to choose the mean of the higher low tides (as self-interest might likewise move the other claimant to suggest)." In the Master's view, "the middle way-the statistical mean of all the low tides over the cyclical period of approximately nineteen years-would seem to be the only choice of which neither contestant could justly complain." This he believed to be the effect of the decision in *Borax* with respect to "ordinary high-water mark." [10] The Supreme Court took no action on the Special Master's recommendations until after passage by Congress of the Submerged Lands Act of 1953. This is discussed in *United States v. California* (1965) *infra*.

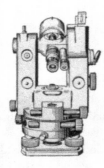

UNITED STATES v. STATE OF WASHINGTON (1961)

United States v. State of Washington, 294 F. 2d 830 (1961), was the first confrontation between the United States and a state in which the *Borax* case was directly involved. The case revolved around the ownership of accretions to littoral land along the coast of Washington to which the United States held legal title subject to a trust patent executed in 1916 to a Quinault Indian. Washington was admitted to statehood on November 11, 1889. As in the *Borax* case, the primary issue was whether federal or state law applied. If federal law, which follows the common law, then the boundary was ambulatory in nature and shifted as the forces of accretion or erosion modified the boundary line. The Government relied heavily on the principle established in *Borax*. The State of Washington contended that the boundary between tideland and upland was frozen the moment Washington became a State in 1889 and State law, which recognized the fixed boundary theory rather than the movable theory, began to apply.

The trial court held for the United States as to accretions formed prior to November 11, 1889, but for the State as to accretions formed subsequent to this date.

On appeal, the Ninth Circuit Court of Appeals reversed the trial court and held the *Borax* case to be controlling of the issues raised in the instant case, and upheld the Government's contention that federal law applies because of the underlying federal title. It said that while no question of accretion was involved in *Borax*, the principle there announced was equally applicable because accretion is an attribute of title and "the determination of the attributes of an underlying federal title, quite as much as the determination of the boundaries of the land reserved or acquired under such a title [this was the situation in *Borax*, involves the ascertainment of the essential basis of a right asserted under federal law." The court also followed Borax for determining the datum of mean high tide and the line of mean high tide (*see* text at note 6 *supra*).

The petition for a writ of certiorari by the State of Washington was denied by the Supreme Court (*United States v. State of Washington*, 369 U.S. 817 (1962)), thus finalizing the decision of the Circuit Court of Appeals.

UNITED STATES v. CALIFORNIA (1965)

United States v. California, 381 U.S. 139 (1965), was an aftermath of *United States v. California* 1947, and took cognizance of the Submerged Land, Act which Congress enacted in 1953. The purpose of the Act was to restore to the states ownership of the submerged lands seaward of their coastlines and within their respective boundaries which the Supreme Court in 1917 held the Federal Government had paramount rights in, rather than the states. While the *Borax,* case was not directly involved, overtones of it were in evidence because of the Government's contention and the recommendation of the Special Master in the 1947 *California* case.

The critical part of the Act, insofar as tidal boundaries are concerned, is Section 2(*c*), which defines "coast line" as the "line of ordinary low water along that portion of the coast which is in direct contact with the open sea and the line marking the seaward limit of inland waters." This language is similar to what the Court used in the 1947 *California* case, and in the instant case the Court's decision revolved primarily around this section.

The Court in essence accepted the Government's view that the Submerged Lands Act involved the same legal and factual situations that were considered by the Special Master in the 1947 case, and therefore it was unnecessary to name another Master. The case was derided on briefs and oral argument.

One of the important holdings of the Court-based on the legislative history of the Act was that its responsibility of giving content to the terms that Congress used was best filled by adopting the best and most workable definitions available. This it found to be provided by the 1958 Geneva Convention on the Territorial Sea and the Contiguous Zone, and the Court adopted it for purposes of the Submerged Lands Act. [11]

Except for certain modifications set out in the opinion, the Court approved the recommendations of the Special Master. One of the modifications, pertinent to this discussion, was the Court's rejection of the Special Master's interpretation of the term "ordinary low-water mark" (this corresponds to the term "line of ordinary low water" used in the Submerged Lands Act) as being the mean of all the low waters (higher lows and lower lows) and holding in effect that the average of only the lower-low tides should be used.

The main thrust of the Court's opinion is in the direction of interpreting the term "inland waters." Two-thirds of its 37-page opinion is devoted to this, whereas only two short paragraphs deal with interpreting the "line of ordinary low water." Having adopted the definitions provided by the Convention on the Territorial Sea for purposes of the Submerged Lands Act, [12] the court found no difficulty in holding that the "line of ordinary low water" in the Act and the "low-water line along the coast as marked on large-scale charts" in the Convention conform. Since the large-scale charts along the Pacific coast are based on the datum of mean lower-low water, the Court in reality foreclosed the use of any other tidal line. Its decision on this point is thus a pragmatic one and is not grounded on authority nor on a technical analysis as to why the term "line of ordinary low water" should be interpreted differently from the cognate term "line of ordinary high water," which the *Borax* case held to be based on the mean of all the high waters (higher highs and lower highs).

This pragmatic solution permits the term "line of ordinary low water" to mean one concept on the Pacific coast (mean lower-low water) and another concept on the Atlantic coast (mean low water) because the low-water line on the large-scale charts is "mean low water." But this is not to say, as has been said; that "in the technical sense, there can be more than one ordinary low water" (see, for example, "Establishing Tidal Datum Lines for Sea Boundaries" by Griffin, Jones, and McAlinden, p, 426 of this issue-Ed.). If we accept the Coast Survey's understanding of the word "ordinary," when applied to tides, as the equivalent of the word "mean" (*see* text at note 7 *supra*), then the term "ordinary low water'" becomes "mean low water"- a term of technical origin defined as "the average height of the low waters over a 19-year period." In deriving the plane of mean low water or the line of mean low water on the Atlantic coast or on the Pacific coast exactly the same tidal procedures are followed. [13]

There is one observation that should be made in connection with the Court's adoption of the Geneva Convention for purposes of the Submerged Lands Act, particularly for interpreting the term "line of ordinary low water." The use of mean lower-low water on the nautical charts of the Pacific coast and the reference to published charts in Article 3 of the Convention are both bottomed on the interest of the navigator, whereas the line originally defined by the court in *United States v. California* (1947), and subsequently adopted by Congress in the Submerged Lands Act has its origin not in navigational problems but in the common law concept of proprietary rights in the tidelands. [14]

Effect on Borax Case

When the 1965 *California* decision was and, questions arose as to the continued validity of the *Borax* decision because of the Court's holding that "the line of ordinary low water" is based on the mean of the lower-low waters only and not on the mean of all the low which would have been in consonance with the holding in *Borax* as to the cognate term "mean high water."

A careful reading of the Court's opinion will show that it contains no intent whatever to modify *Borax*. It certainly did not overrule it directly or by implication. In fact, *Borax* is not mentioned in the opinion although the Government in its brief relied on it, as did the Special Master in the 1947

California case. As stated above, the Court simply took a different approach to the problem. Only where the Submerged Lands Act is involved does the Court's approach apply. It has no wider application. That the Court had no intention of modifying *Borax* is corroborated by its statement two years later in *Hughes v. State of Washington* (1967), *infra*, that "No Subsequent case in this Court has cast doubt on the principle announced in *Borax*."

It should be noted also that the Court did not hold that the term "line of ordinary low water" is the same as the term "line of mean lower-low water." This would have been technically unsound because the two terms are based on different tidal datums each derived from different tidal values. It merely equated the term "line of ordinary low water" with the provision in Article 3 of the Geneva Convention that the baseline for measuring the territorial sea is "the low-water line along the coast as marked on large-scale charts."

HUGHES v. STATE OF WASHINGTON (1967)

Hughes v. State of Washington, 389 U.S. 290 (1967), is the most recent expression by the Supreme Court on the doctrine established in *Borax*. The case arose with the filing of a suit by Mrs. Hughes to quiet her upland title seaward to the line of mean high tide as it may exist at any given time. Petitioner is the successor in title to the original federal grantee in 1866. Washington's statehood became effective on November 11, 1889, and the question raised was whether the petitioner was entitled to the gradual and imperceptible accretions added to her land both before and after Washington's statehood.

The trial court, relying primarily on the *Borax* case and on *United States v. Washington* (1961) *supra*, upheld Mrs. Hughes' contention that federal law applies, that she was the owner, not the state, to the lands accreted to the original donation claim either prior to or subsequent to November 11, 1889, and that her boundary is the mean high tide, as expounded in *Borax*.

The Supreme Court of Washington reversed the trial court on the ground that the issue was controlled by State law, which had frozen Mrs. Hughes' boundary as of the date Washington became a State. The petitioner filed for a writ of certiorari in the Supreme Court of the United States. Following this the Court invited the Solicitor General of the United States to file an *amicus curiae* brief expressing the views of the United States. [15] Certiorari was granted.

In the Supreme Court, the State of Washington conceded that prior to statehood the petitioner Hughes was entitled to all accretions to her land in accordance with the common, or federal, law - but the moment that Washington became a State in 1889, State law came into being which modified the common law doctrine of a "movable or shifting boundary," and substituted a "fixed boundary doctrine." [16]

The question presented to the Supreme Court was therefore whether a state may alter the ambulatory boundary between its tidelands and uplands patented by the United States prior to statehood by declaring that boundary to be permanently fixed at the line of ordinary high tide on the date of admission to statehood, thereby depriving the upland owner of gradual, natural accretions occurring since that date.

The Supreme Court answered this in the negative. It said: "While the issue appears never to have been squarely presented to this Court before, we think the path to decision is indicated by our holding in *Borax Ltd. v. City of Los Angeles*, 296 U.S. 10 (1935). . . . No subsequent case in this Court has cast doubt on the principle announced in *Borax*." The Court thus held the question raised to be governed by federal, not state, law, and therefore petitioner Hughes was entitled to accretions occurring subsequent to Washington's entry into the Union.

The State argued, and the court below held, that Borax is not applicable because no question of accretions was there involved. "While this is true," the Court said, "the case did involve the question as to what rights were conveyed by the federal grant and decided that the extent of ownership under the federal grant is governed by federal law. This is as true whether doubt as to any boundary is based on a broad question as to the general definition of the shoreline or on a particularized problem relating to the ownership of accretion." *See* also *United States v. Washington* (1961) supra. The Court therefore found no significant difference between the *Borax* case and the *Hughes* case. The judgment of the Supreme Court of Washington was therefore reversed. [17]

SUMMARY

To summarize, then, reference datums determined by tidal definition, from which tidal boundaries may be established, are the most satisfactory of all datums because they are based on recurring natural phenomena brought about by cyclical astronomic forces. The principal tidal datums in use by the United States Coast and Geodetic Survey are mean high water, mean low water, and mean lower-low water. Its transcontinental leveling net is based on mean sea level.

Lands bordering the sea carry with them certain rights-termed riparian rights-such as accretions to the land. These are generally governed by state

73

law, except where there is an underlying federal title, in which case federal law controls. This was established in *Borax Consolidated, Ltd. v. Los Angeles*, 296 U.S. 10 (1935), a landmark case in the law of tidal boundaries. The case also established the first precise standard for the determination of the tidal boundary of "ordinary high-water mark" as the mean of all the high waters (higher highs and lower highs) over the cyclical period of 18.6 years.

The doctrine of *Borax* was invoked by the United States in both California cases involving ownership of submerged lands seaward of "ordinary low-water mark." In the first case, 332 U.S. 19 (1947), a Special Master named by the Supreme Court applied the rule of *Borax* to the tidal boundary of "ordinary low-water mark," although he reached his decision by a somewhat different route. In the second case, 381 U.S. 139 (1965), the Court was called upon to interpret the term "line of ordinary low water" in the Submerged Lands Act of 1953. *Borax* was not reached because the Court adopted the definitions contained in the 1958 Geneva "Convention on the Territorial Sea" for the terms used in the Act, which it held was not foreclosed by its legislative history. This resulted in accepting the term "line of ordinary low water" in the Act as the equivalent of the term "low-water line along the coast, as marked on large-scale charts" in the Convention. Applied to the California coast this is the same as using the mean of the lower-low waters only, rather than the mean of all the low waters (*see* fig. 1).

The *Borax* case was held to be dispositive, by the Ninth Circuit Court of Appeals, of the issues raised in *United States v. Washington*, 294 F. 2d 830 (1961), certiorari denied by the Supreme Court, and was applied to accretions formed both before and after Washington's entry into the Union on November 11, 1889, on the basis of the underlying federal title which the United States was holding in trust for an Indian. The State's contention that under State law the boundary between upland and tideland was frozen as of November 11, 1889, was held to be untenable.

Finally, in *Hughes v. State of Washington*, the Supreme Court came to grips for the first time with the same issue raised in *United States v. Washington* (1961) *supra*. The Court held the path to decision was indicated by its holding in the *Borax* case, of which it said "No subsequent case in this Court has cast doubt on the principle announced" here. It found no significant difference between *Borax* and *Hughes*, even though accretions were not involved in the former. But, it held, the case did decide that "the extent of ownership under the federal grant is governed by federal law. "This," the Court said, "is as true whether doubt as to any boundary is based on a broad question as to the general definition of the shoreline or on a particularized problem relating to the ownership of accretion."

There is thus an unbroken chain of cases extending over a period of 32 years in which the principles of *Borax* have been applied in State courts, in Federal lower and appellate courts, and in the Supreme Court. These establish the doctrine that riparian lands having their origin in an underlying federal title, granted either prior to or subsequent to statehood, are governed by federal, not state, law both as to boundaries between upland and tideland and as to accretions to the land. Acquisition of statehood does not alter the applicable law.

Any speculation that the 1965 *California* case, *supra*, may have cast doubt on the doctrine established in *Borax* as to the interpretation of the term "mean high water" as the "average height of all the high waters," must be dismissed on the basis of the *Hughes* case. While no judicial standard has thus far been developed for the tidal boundary of "ordinary" or "mean low water" other than the Special Master's recommendation to the Supreme Court in the 1947 *California* case (*see* text at note 10 *supra*), it is of interest that in the *Borax* case the Court said that "in order to ascertain the mean high tide line with requisite certainty in fixing the *boundary of valuable tidelands*" [emphasis added], 'an average of 18.6 years should be determined as near as possible.'" Since "tidelands" is defined as the land that is covered and uncovered by the daily rise and fall of the tide-the zone between the mean high water line and the mean low-water line along a coast-the principle, of *Borax* should apply equally, where a federal question is involved to the lower boundary of tidelands, namely, the mean low-water line.

From the point of view of long-established tidal practice, the datum of mean low water is as distinct a tidal plane from mean lower-low water, as the datum of mean high water is distinct from mean higher-high water. In each of the two situations, different tidal values are used to establish the datums.

It is also worth noting that the Court in the second *California* case did not interpret the term "line of ordinary low water" in the Submerged Lands Act to be the same as the "line of mean lower-low water." It merely held that for purposes of the Submerged Lands Act, the term "low-water line along the coast as marked on large-scale charts" conforms to the term used in the Act. It must therefore be concluded that the most that can be said for the decision on this point is that it is limited to the Submerged Lands Act only and has no wider application.

----

[1] A tidal datum is usually referred to as mean low water, mean high water, etc., but a tidal boundary is designated as line of mean low water, line of mean high water, or mean low water mark, mean high-water mark, etc.

[2] From tidal bench marks, established along the coast above the high-water mark, the elevations of which have been determined with respect to various datum planes from the tidal observations, a tidal boundary such as mean high-water mark or mean low-water mark may be established any time in the future by running spirit levels from the bench marks or by some other appropriate method.

[3] Along the Pacific coast of the United States, the mixed type of tide is the predominant one—two high waters and two low waters occur each tidal day, with marked differences between the morning and afternoon tides (*see* fig. 1).

[4] *Neap* tides are tides of decreased range occurring semimonthly as a result of the moon being in quadrature, that is, when the tidal forces of sun and moon act at right angles to each other on the waters of the earth. Tides during these periods do not rise as high nor fall as low as during the rest of the month. Contrary, *spring* tides are those of increased range occurring semimonthly as a result of the moon being new or full; that is, when sun, moon, and earth are in line and the tidal forces are acting in the same direction. Tides during these periods rise higher and fall lower than during the rest of the month.

[5] This is considered a more exact statement of the rule laid down in *Attorney General v. Chambers, supra.* For a discussion of this aspect of the *Borax* case, see SHALOWITZ, 1 SHORE AND SEA BOUNDARIES 96, PUBLICATION No. 10, U.S. COAST AND GEODETIC SURVEY (1962). This was cited and quoted with approval by the Supreme Court of New Jersey in the recent case of *Catherine O'Neill v. State Highway Department of New Jersey,* 235 A.2d 1 (Nov. 6. 1967).

[6] Because of the numerous control tide stations which the Coast and Geodetic Survey has now established along our shores based on 18.6 years of observations, intermediate tide stations may be established from much shorter series, say 1 year, and reduced to 18.6-year accuracy by comparison of simultaneous observations at the control tide station and the intermediate station. For method of comparisons, *see ibid* (1951 ed.) at 87-90.

⁷ SCHUREMAN, TIDE AND CURRENT GLOSSARY 26, SPECIAL PUBLICATION No. 228, U.S. COAST AND GEODETIC SURVEY (1949).

⁸ As applied to low water on the Pacific coast, where successive low waters fall to different levels, the mean of the two levels occurring each tidal day is more representative of the technical concept of low water than is either higher low or lower low when considered alone.

⁹ The use of this datum is for the safety and convenience of the mariner.

¹⁰ *See* Special Master's Report, reprinted as Appendix C in 1 SHALOWITZ (1962), *op. cit. supra* note 5, at 349.

¹¹ The Convention was approved by the U. S. Senate in May 1960, and ratified by the President on March 24, 1961.

¹² Article 3 of the Convention specifies that "the normal baseline for measuring the breadth of the territorial sea is the low-water line along the coast as marked on large-scale charts officially recognized by the coastal State."

¹³ Where the type of tide is predominantly diurnal (one high and one low water a day), as in the Gulf of Mexico, only the lower low-water heights are included in the average on those days when the tide becomes semidiurnal (two highs and two lows each day). This avoids the imbalance that would result from the use of both low waters. Since all low waters are used in obtaining mean values, except on the semidiurnal days, the general definition of mean low water is still applicable.

¹⁴ If the Convention on the Territorial Sea had not been available to the Court it would have been hard put to equate the term "line of ordinary low water" in the Act with the term "line of mean lower-low water" in the face of the testimony by a foremost expert on tides, by a letter from the Director of the United States Coast and Geodetic Survey, by the Special Master's recommendation on the use of the mean of all low waters, and by the Court's interpretation of ordinary or mean high water in the *Borax* case.

¹⁵ The United States in its brief recommended that certiorari be granted

on the basis of the decision in *Borax* and in *United States v. Washington* (1961) *supra*, which it said presented the very issue to be decided here.

[16] Article 17 of the Washington Constitution, as interpreted by the State Supreme Court, denies the owners of ocean-front property any further rights in accretion that might in the future be formed between their property and the ocean.

[17] In light of the above, it is difficult to reconcile Mr. Brown's concluding statement in his note on the *Hughes* case that "As of now it appears that U.S. riparian land patented prior to 1889 follows the Federal rule whereas land patented after 1889 follows the state law," with what the Supreme Court actually held. In fact, that was what the case was all about-whether accretions occurring subsequent to Washington becoming a State in 1889 were governed by federal or state law, and the Court said federal law controlled. That was also the finding of the Circuit Court of Appeals in *United States v. Washington* (1961) *supra*, and the *Borax* case itself was a post-statehood case. Mr. Brown's observation must therefore be considered an inadvertence or a misreading of the *Hughes* decision.

Dr. Shalowitz is a former Special Assistant to the Director of the U. S. Coast and Geodetic Survey and the author of the 2-volume legal technical treatise *Shore and Sea Boundaries*.

****

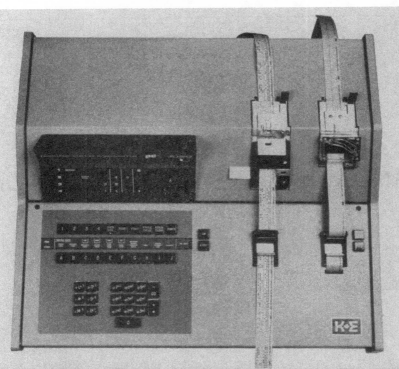

Today this gadget belongs in surveying as much as this one.

The PDS-1020 Computer is taking its place along with the transit, level, and theodolite as an everyday working tool of the surveyor. Because it's programmed to solve surveying calculations (faster by far than any calculator). Plus it's easy to learn and use. If the need is there for it to work on more sophisticated problems, we've got the programs for those too. They're part of the selling price: $24,300*. We also have a set of literature that tells the complete story. And it's yours for the asking.

*4K MEMORY, ADDITIONAL MEMORY AND OPTIONS AVAILABLE.

KEUFFEL & ESSER CO.
PHOTOGRAMMETRIC SYSTEMS DIVISION
4839 DEL RAY AVENUE, BETHESDA, MARYLAND 20014

NAME_____

FIRM_____

ADDRESS_____

CITY_____ STATE_____

CREATIVE PRODUCTS FOR THE CREATIVE ENGINEER

1867
INTO CENTURY II
1967

LAND MOVEMENTS AND BOUNDARIES

BY CURTIS M. BROWN

CONSULTING LAND SURVEYOR
SAN DIEGO, CALIFORNIA

DECEMBER 1968

The fundamental principle of Land Surveying is: "The original position of a monument, if called for, is unalterable except by reconveyance." Since this principle is a rule of law, and since most laws have exceptions depending upon the circumstances, the rule of permanence of original monument positions does have several exceptions. One example is within the sectionalized land system wherein closing corners may be adjusted to the line closed upon. Also, as a general rule for all conveyances, if an original monument interferes with a senior right, it may be used to control the direction of a line but not its legal terminus.

Within these United States, land has changed its position by forces of nature and by long continued operations of man. Withdrawal of oil in the Long Beach area of California has caused a maximum vertical settlement of 27 feet and a maximum horizontal movement of 7 feet. In the San Joaquin Valley, water removal caused sufficient land settlement to cause water canals to overflow banks. Along the San Andreas Rift sudden horizontal shifts of 22 feet occurred in the earth's crust. In the San Francisco earthquake, a sidewalk running from the front door of a house to the street was severed and displaced approximately 20 feet. Imagine walking out your front door and finding part of your sidewalk 20 feet to the north! In this earthquake, similar shifts occurred along fence lines. The question facing the land surveyor is, "Does the boundary line follow the soil or does the former absolute position control title location"?

Landslides are earth movements. During the Alaskan earthquake, the shaking caused saturated ground to change from a jelled mass to fluid. The surface soil flowed into Cook Inlet. The more usual type of slide occurs on a hillside wherein a portion of the hill, wet by rain or irrigation, slides down the hill.

Migrating land boundaries are caused by the forces of flowing water. For now, it is sufficient to mention that the usual rule for erosion and accretion is that the riparian owner loses land eroded away and gains land added by slow and imperceptible accretions.

The question to be explored is: "How does the surveyor correctly monument land boundaries after a land movement has occurred"? The problem will ultimately be resolved by court decision. But before a decision can be derived, someone must present a logical hypothesis to the court. The court does not answer questions, which are not in issue before it. Usually the surveyor is called upon to set monuments on the ground and to express his opinion. If someone objects, the matter is often appealed to the courts. Thus, the surveyor is frequently the one who collects evidence and presents a recommendation of what should be done.

The following thoughts are offered on the problems. Obviously, not all proposed solutions are founded upon court decision, since in many earth movement situations court cases are not to be found.

For a sudden rupture of the earth's surface along a distinct cleavage line, as in the San Francisco and Brawley (Imperial Valley) earthquakes, the proposed rule for locating sheared land boundaries is, "The same owner owns the same land occupied prior to the movement. Former straight lines jog at the line of cleavage." This rule presents some discomfort in the case of highway displacement, as occurred in Imperial Valley, where the road shifted about 8 feet horizontally. The right of way now jogs 8 feet at the line of cleavage. Since the road had to be patched with two triangular slivers at this point, the rule seems reasonable. It is conceivable that with a shift of a hundred feet a road right of way might be discontinuous. As an incidental result of these earthquakes, new surveyors coming into the area have been somewhat puzzled by the lack of agreement between their measurements and the record measurements.

On a sand spit, measurements were made after an earthquake and compared with accurate measurements made prior to the earthquake. The average elongation in a N 32° E direction was 1.01 feet per hundred feet. The average elongation at 90°, or S 58° E, was 0.009 foot per hundred feet. Visible ruptures or cleavage lines in the sand were not observable. However, irregular separations did occur in sidewalks, concrete paving, etc., usually at joints. This type of separation could be expected since concrete can slide on sand. For this type of earth movement the logical rule is: "Where there is elongation or compression due to earth movements and cleavage lines are not present, the elongation or shortening should be prorated between nearest original positions as determined by acceptable possession or monument evidence.

Man-caused subsidence by withdrawal of ground fluids is slow and imperceptible with time. If an area is densely built upon by streets, buildings, utilities and other man - made objects, and if fluids are withdrawn from the earth, and if horizontal shifts up to several feet occur, do ownership lines move with the earth or do they retain their absolute position? It would be an unacceptable hypothesis that the owner of a building, no matter how large or how small, would retain land in its absolute position relative to a coordinate position. Otherwise, a person owning a building today might find his building on another's land in the future. Title must shift with the surface movement. Obviously, at a distance from where the settlement is taking place, the surface will remain unchanged in position. In any area between the spot of maximum horizontal shift and the spot where no shift occurred, there would be some proportionate movement.

A suggested rule is: "Where there is gradual elongation or compression of the earth's surface caused by withdrawal of subsurface fluids, ownership lines move with the shift in surface improvements and monuments."

Along the California coastline, southwesterly of the San Andreas Rift, there is a continual movement of the land in a northerly direction. Coordinate positions of monuments on each side of the rift are in constant, though imperceptible motion. Over a long span of time, the motion becomes measurable.

During recent years, surveyors have been bombarded with the advantages of fixed coordinate zones to control property lines. The shifting of land boundaries due to earth movements is one reason why the system can never become an absolute control, although the system may be a useful tool to help control locations. In reality, the usefulness of a coordinate system stems from nearby monuments, which also shift with earth movements. It is only when new coordinate numbers are assigned to an existing monument, or when a monument is moved to its former coordinate position, that troubles ensue.

In the event of slides, it is impossible to conceive that ownership would change with the flowing of the earth's surface. In Alaska where the soil became fluid and ran into the ocean, it is probable that title follows the location as determined by bedrock. When land slides down a hill and monuments move with a slide, it is illogical that title would follow the soil of the slide. The rule suggested by this situation is: "Title location of land after a slide is determined by the title location of bedrock prior to the slide."

Ambulatory land boundaries can be caused by the forces of flowing water. This problem is discussed in another paper.

THE SURVEYOR AND THE LAW

ABOUT MEANDER LINES AND BOUNDARIES

JUNE 1971

Hugh Binyon of Florida called my attention to an interesting court case, *Bliss v. Kensey,* (233 So. 2nd 191). When surveying sectionalized lands, the original government surveyors also meandered oceans, bays, lakes, rivers and sometimes marshes. Very rarely does the present limit of private ownership match the government meander line.

Along a shoreline most surveyors do not get up the original shore meander line; they merely extend the property lines to the limits of private ownership. Normally, no problems ensue. Most people think that is how their property lines should be.

In a few cases the area between the meander line and the shoreline has been prorated the same as for accretions. Most surveyors of experience know that the original meander line of the government was inaccurately determined, and it cannot be assumed that the area between the present shoreline and the original meander line was built up by accretions.

Two situations can happen: (1) The government surveyors did in fact correctly locate the limits of private ownership and all land added in front of a property since the original survey was the result of accretions. In this situation the rules of land apportionment for accretions are clearly applicable; (2) The government surveyors did not correctly locate the limits of private ownership and a strip of land was not included between the meander line and the limits of private ownership. In this second case, opinions vary as to how the land should be apportioned.

Suppose that this situation occurred: The government surveyors failed to include a strip of upland in the area of Lot 9 (see attached figure), that is, part of the upland was mapped as being in water. In *Bliss v. Kinsey* (Florida), this was the case. Should the judge declare that the lot lines should be prolonged to the mean high water mark and thus deprive Lot 9 of frontage on the Gulf of Mexico? Or, should the judge apportion the land similar to the rules for accretions? Bliss claimed his land was determined by the prolongation of lot lines (A to B) and the dispute was over area ABC.

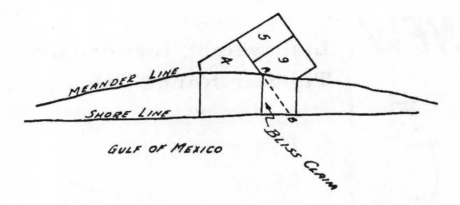

The Bliss side cited *Menasha Wooden-Ware Co. v. Lawson*, 70 Wis. 600, wherein the line was extended to the true shoreline. Also cited was *BOUNDARY CONTROL AND LEGAL PRINCIPLES* by Curtis M. Brown for the proposition that "normally the ownership of land lying between the meander and high-water mark is determined by prolonging the property line to the high-water mark."

But where the equities are wrong by following a rule, the rule is tossed out. The other side cited *Hanson v. Rice*, 88 Minn. 273 (also cited in Brown's book) wherein the opposite was held true. The judges felt that land purchasers should be able to rely at least generally upon meander lines, which indicate that certain lots consist of waterfront property. "This is not to say that meander lines be treated as boundaries, but that courts should attempt whenever possible to at least approximate the amount of shore line as indicated on a meander line when they are called upon to establish actual boundaries." In effect, Lot 9 was entitled to Gulf of Mexico frontage. I cannot quarrel with the judge's opinion.

It seems strange that land, not formed by accretions, is apportioned by the rules of accretion. The surveyor's life is anything, except dull. In three states, decisions have been made; in other states, the surveyors must await a trial.

– CURTIS M. BROWN
La Mesa, California

****

NEW

Lightweight, Inexpensive Tubular Range Poles

TubeCo high quality surveyor's Range Poles are built from sturdy welded steel tubing. Two 3' (friction fit) sections are easily assembled or disassembled — optional 3' extension available. Alternate 12" red and white markings of baked enamel assure top visibility. Easy to handle and inexpensive — will last for years.

New Tubular Survey Markers

Nothing drives into earth like a tube. TubeCo rugged survey markers are lightweight and easy to carry in special shipping case—provide permanent point of reference. Identification caps and driving mandrels available.

SPECIFICATIONS

No.	Description	Length	O.D. Dia.	Ga.	Wt. Ea.	Std. Pkg.
2308	Tubular Stake	8"	5/8"	16	4 oz.	48
2316	Tubular Stake	16"	5/8"	16	8 oz.	24
2324	Tubular Stake	24"	5/8"	16	12 oz.	24
2330	Tubular Stake	30"	5/8"	16	16 oz.	24
2300	Ident. Caps	11/16"	1"			24
2301	Ident. Caps	11/16"	1"			24
2305	Dr. Mandrel	3"	1 1/2"		18 oz.	1
2306	Dr. Mandrel	3"	1 1/2"		22 oz.	1
2310	Range Pole	6'	5/8"	16	2 lbs.	1
2310-A	Range Pole Exten.	3'	5/8"	16	12 oz.	1

For additional information send this coupon

...or write

TubeCo., Inc.

Surveying Division

1914 LaSalle Ave., Minneapolis 3, Minn.

To TUBECO., Inc.

1914 LaSalle Ave., Minneapolis, Minn.

Please send complete information on your new **TubeCo** Range Poles and Survey Markers.

NAME

FIRM

ADDRESS

CITY   STATE

THE SURVEYOR AND THE LAW

RIPARIAN BOUNDARIES

MARCH 1977

In *Oregon v. Corvallis Sand Company*, the Supreme Court of the United States on January 12, 1977, by a vote of 6 to 3, reversed a previous case *(Bonelli Cattle Co. v. Arizona*, 414 U.S. 313 in 1973) and declared that state law governs the location of riparian boundaries within a state. The case does not pertain to situations where the federal government is an adjoiner nor to cases between state boundaries.

This case involved a dispute between the State of Oregon and the Corvallis Sand Company over the ownership of two portions of lands underlying the Willamette River, which is navigable but not an interstate boundary. The first portion was within the riverbed at the time of Oregon's admission to the Union. The river by avulsion (sudden change of the river channel) changed its course to a new location in Fisher Cut. With respect to Fisher Cut lands, the trial court found that avulsion, rather than accretion, had caused the change in the channel of the river, and therefore the title to the lands remained in Corvallis Sand Company, the original owner of the land before it became a riverbed. The Oregon Court of Appeals felt bound, under Bonelli, to apply federal common law to the resolution of this property dispute. After the case got into federal courts, 26 states by *Amicus Curiae* filed opinions favoring application of state laws.

[MP NOTE: *Amicus Curiae* means "Friend of the Court"; a third party having an interest in the outcome of a case.]

After reading the Court's report and the arguments, my simplified explanation of the outcome of the case is this: Upon admission to the Union, the beds of all navigable waters were vested in the states as an absolute title. Like all other real estate, once it passed into the state, the state controls the interpretation of boundary law. It was not within the federal government's jurisdiction to regulate claims between owners (state and private or private and private).

I wish to point out that there are large variations in riparian laws from state to state. If the Bonelli case had not been reversed, many state cases would be put in jeopardy. In California on navigable rivers the mean low water line is the division line between the state and the upland owner, not the average water line per federal rule.

In the March 1968 edition of *Surveying and Mapping*, page 120, I summarized *Hughes v. State of Washington*. In this case Mrs. Stella Hughes owned a parcel that was patented prior to Washington's statehood. She claimed to the mean high tide line and the rights to accretions by federal law. By state court interpretation the Court said upland owners took to the line where vegetation ceased and had no rights to accretions. The federal court reversed the state court and gave her the rights to the mean high tide line and the rights to accretions in accordance with federal law. Is there danger that this case will be reversed? Maybe. In the Corvallis Sand Company case the issue of owning prior to statehood was not raised. It certainly appears that land acquired after statehood is subject to the Washington Court decision.

To me the message is clear. The federal courts will not take jurisdiction over any boundary cases within a state except: (1) where the federal government has owned the land prior to statehood; (2) disputes between state boundaries. In doubt are the cases where a person acquired a right prior to statehood, and the right was diminished by state laws. If a person's land is enlarged by state law, no problem can ensue; a state may give away its land if it so desires.

Author is Curtis M. Brown, L.L.S., 5075 Keeney St., La Mesa, Calif. 92041

****

DEED
INTERPRETATION

INTERPRETATION OF DEED WORDS

By Curtis M. Brown

June 1957

Curtis M. Brown of San Diego, Calif., submitted the following short paper to the Publications Committee with the suggestion that a special department be established in SURVEYING AND MAPPING for presenting material relating to the legal elements of boundary surveys. This department could receive reviews of recent or old court cases that have established important principles of surveying law. The Publications Committee and Editor would like to know if the membership of ACSM would support such a department. This would require that you be more than readers; you must also be contributors. Mr. Brown has signified his willingness to start such a department, but the committee would not want to add this department to our journal unless we are assured of adequate support.

– Editor

****

THE ENGLISH LANGUAGE contains many words that have dual or multiple meanings. Does the word *red* mean a color or a communist? Deeds (here meaning an instrument to convey real property, not a good deed by fellow man) are in writing. If words can mean two things, it can be expected that differences of opinion, as to a deed's intent, will develop. Thus, what does the word *North* mean? Is it *magnetic North*, is it *astronomical North*, or is it *North* relative to a line whose bearing is defined by other words in the deed? When the word "due" is used in conjunction with "North," does *due North* mean *astronomical North*, or does it mean *North* relative to another line?

In the final analysis, the courts resolve these questions for a particular deed, and by police power, they enforce their interpretation. If surveyors are to accurately transform deed terms into monuments upon the ground, it behooves them to study the meaning of deed terms as defined by the courts and to attempt to understand the court's thinking. The words *due* and *North* have been the subject of litigation and will be used to illustrate how courts arrive at their decisions.

North, as used by surveyors, has at least three meanings and possibly more. It may mean "in the direction of the earth's North Pole as determined by a star observation." It may mean "in the direction of the magnetic North Pole as determined by a magnetic compass at the spot of the deed." It may mean, "In a direction that is North relative to a given bearing of a line whose direction is fixed by monuments existing on the face of the earth."

Due, as defined by Webster's Dictionary (excluding meanings not applying to surveying), is "directly; exactly; as a due-East course." As used by surveyors in the early days, especially in surveying government sectionalized land, the words *true* and *due* indicated that a magnetic-North observation, as obtained from a magnetic compass, was corrected to *astronomic North*. The purpose of the term, the differentiation between magnetic and astronomical North, is no longer needed because of the abandonment of the magnetic compass as an instrument for determining property line directions. But title authors and surveyors have continued to use the terms *due* and *true* rather loosely, and often erroneously.

The following deed (*See* Figure 1) was the subject of a long-continued legal battle between Richfield Oil Corporation and Crawford, et al (249 P 2nd 600); "Beginning at a point on the SW line of said Rancho (Cuyama) at a 2-inch galvanized iron pipe 6-inches high in a mound of stones, with brass cap marked "Cuyama Rancho C-No 31', set by Gerald C. Fitzgerald, Registered Civil Engineer, and shown on map recorded in Book 26, Pages 138 and 139 of Records of Surveys, Records of Santa Barbara Co.; thence N 65° 10' 24" West along said SW line as established by said Gerald C. Fitzgerald and shown on said Records of Survey map, a distance of 2,877.60 feet; thence due North 13,295.04 to the true point of beginning; thence, due West 1320 feet; thence, due North 2640 feet; thence, due East 1320 feet; thence, due South 2640 feet to the true point of beginning, and containing eighty acres, more or less." Who would think that such an innocent looking document would be the subject of expensive litigation? The trouble arose from the interpretation of the meaning of *due North*.

One surveyor surveyed the legal description of the property by running the line 2877.60 feet along the boundary of the ranch to point A (*See* Figure 1), and then turning an angle of 65° 10' 24" at point A. The other surveyor used the same method to locate point A, but from that point, he ran a line *due North* based upon a Polaris observation. The difference between the two methods resulted in an East-West displacement of about eleven feet at point B, and this difference of eleven feet placed the location of an oil well in jeopardy.

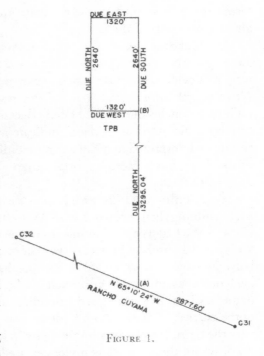

FIGURE 1.

The practice of assuming that the bearing of a given monumented line of a deed is correct, and then surveying the remainder of the deed relative to the given line, has long been an accepted custom of surveyors. But in this case the court decreed that the word due changed the basis of bearings from "North relative to a given line" to "astronomical North" as determined by a star observation.

Does this mean that every time the word *due* is used prior to the word *North* the meaning is "astronomical North as determined by a stellar observation?" Certainly not! Only in very similar cases would it be applicable.

To be valid, a deed must be in writing. In a court trial, evidence cannot be taken to exclude words from the written deed, nor can evidence be taken to include words that are not in the writings. It must be presumed that the document as written includes all of the words intended and does not omit words not written. But this does not exclude evidence taken for the purpose of explaining words that already exist within a deed. Thus, if the term *due North* is not clear in meaning, and exists in a deed, the court may take testimony from expert witnesses to explain the commonly understood meaning of the term. Such evidence is called extrinsic evidence and may be defined as evidence other than that contained in the writings. Extrinsic evidence is not accepted for the purpose of varying or contradicting the terms of the deed but to assist the court in understanding the words that already are a part of the deed.

In the above case, extrinsic evidence was admitted and many surveyors and engineers testified, some taking one side and others the opposite. The weight of evidence in this particular case precipitated the decision that *due North* meant *astronomical North*. After reviewing the case carefully, the following conclusion can be stated. Except where other terms of a deed or admissible extrinsic evidence indicate another intent, a *due North* call should be interpreted to mean an astronomical bearing. An understanding of the exception is more important than understanding the definition of due North.

Two mining men disagreed upon the meaning of a deed reading in part: "running thence North 23° 15' W, 640 feet; thence N 45° W to Devils' Canyon (11 Cal 194)." Quoting from the case, "In an action concerning a disputed boundary between two claims, depending on an agreement between parties in which the word 'North,' was used, and parole [verbal] evidence was admitted to prove that it was the custom of the locality to run boundary lines by the magnetic meridian, and that was the understanding of the parties; *Held*, that such evidence was admissible not to contradict or vary the term, but to ascertain the sense in which it was used." In a modern deed, where the compass is no longer used, the word *North* could not be *magnetic North*, but at the time of the above deed, it was proper.

The courts in each of the above cases adopted that meaning for *North* and *due North* which they believed to be the intent of the parties of the deed. No fixed rule exists that says *North* is always *astronomical North*. In older deeds in some localities, the word *North* means *magnetic North* for the simple reason that *magnetic North* was the intent at the time of the deed. In other localities, where surveys were made after the date of the abandonment of the magnetic compass, the word *North* is either *astronomical North* or "North relative to a defined line."

Ambiguous deed terms are interpreted in the light of the intent of the original parties by investigating: (1) The surrounding conditions existing at the time the deed was written, (2) The extrinsic evidence that explains the common meaning of the terms, and (3) The meaning of the ambiguous terms relative to all the other written words in the deed.

In the construction of the instrument, the intentions of the parties are to be pursued, if possible. "The only rule of much value - one which is frequently shadowed forth, but seldom, if ever, expressly stated in books - is to place ourselves as nearly as possible in the seats which were occupied by the parties at the time the instrument was executed; then, take it by its four corners, read it." (Walsh v. Hill, 38C 481.)

MORAL: If a deed is being written and *North relative to a star observation* is desired, the deed author should state *astronomical North*. If *North relative to a given line* is intended, the usage of *due North* or *true North* should be avoided. In the future, the words *due* and *true* should be restricted to the interpretation of existing records and not used in the creation of new records.

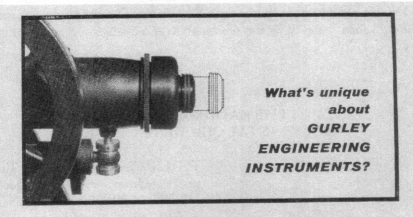

COMMENT AND DISCUSSION

MARCH 1958

The pages of SURVEYING AND MAPPING are open to a free and temperate discussion of all matters pertaining to the interests of the CONGRESS. It is the purpose of this Department to encourage comments and published material or the presentation of new ideas in an informal way.

– EDITOR

FINDING THE RADIUS OF AN EXISTING
HORIZONTAL CIRCULAR CURVE

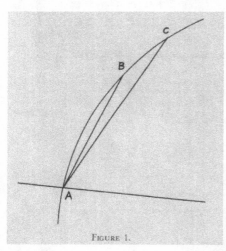

FIGURE 1.

PHILIP A. LATIMER * - The article, "Interpretation of Deed Words," SURVEYING AND MAPPING, April-June 1957, pages 159-161, is very interesting reading to me.

Beginning at point *B* the above deed reads: "due West 1320 feet; thence, due North 2640 feet; thence due East 1320 feet; thence, due South 2640 feet. . . ." Hasn't the engineer forgotten to allow for the convergence of meridians? I realize that the problem, as to point *B* being 11 feet out, is a question of the difference between the azimuth brought in from the line C 31 - C 32 and the true north.

Now, I would like to offer a suggestion as to the solution of a problem which is apt to occur more and more frequently as new highways are built on new locations.

Suppose that we are running out on the ground an old deed line which now crosses a curve of a new highway, and it is desired to ascertain the degree of curvature or the radius of curvature of the new centerline. *(See Fig. 1.)*

Lay off a chord *(AB)* of length 67.70 feet and measure the middle ordinate. The degree of curvature will then be 10 times the measured

96

middle ordinate. As a check, lay off the chord *(AC)* of length 95.75 feet and measure the middle ordinate. The degree of curvature will then be 5 times the measured middle ordinate.

EDITOR'S NOTE: - When this letter was received in July 1957, the editor became curious as to the relationship between this method and the one published in SURVEYING AND MAPPING, January-March 1956, Vol. XVI, No. 1, page 82, and undertook to experiment a bit. He kept coming up with certain small discrepancies - so small as to be of little practical importance, but disturbing nevertheless - and wrote to Mr. Latimer and requested a clue as to how the formulas had been derived.

It then developed that this is an *approximate* method, close enough for many practical purposes, to be sure, but becoming increasingly loose as the degree of curvature increases, or the radius of curvature decreases.

The derivation of the formulas** is given below. (*See* Fig. 2.)

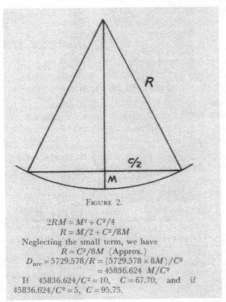

FIGURE 2.

$$2RM = M^2 + C^2/4$$
$$R = M/2 + C^2/8M$$
Neglecting the small term, we have
$$R = C^2/8M \ (\text{Approx.})$$
$$D_{arc} = 5729.578/R = (5729.578 \times 8M)/C^2$$
$$= 45836.624 \ M/C^2$$
If $45836.624/C^2 = 10, \ C = 67.70,$ and if $45836.624/C^2 = 5, \ C = 95.75.$

From figure 2 it is obvious that

$$R^2 = (R - M)^2 + (C/2)^2$$
$$= R^2 - 2RM + M^2 + C^2/4$$

* Route 2, Box 3, Edgewater, Md.

** This derivation was checked by Cecil F. Ellingwood, Coast and Geodetic Survey, who is also an instructor in Route Surveying at the U. S. Department of Agriculture Graduate School.

****

THE SURVEYOR AND THE LAW

DECEMBER 1962

Questions concerning proper procedures to be followed in locating property boundaries will be answered to the best of our ability in this department. Contributions suitable for publications in this department covering special legal problems or the results of court cases are requested. Communications should be addressed to Harold R. Brooks, Chairman, Publications Committee, ACSM, Coast and Geodetic Survey, Washington 25, D. C.

****

BRILLIANT BONER

Boners in legal descriptions may be classified as careless or brilliant. Omission of words, misspelling, and errors in grammar or punctuation are needless, careless mistakes. But upon occasion, a man, after due and careful deliberation as based upon a little knowledge, comes to a brilliant but quite erroneous conclusion. This type of error requires considerable thought and effort to achieve the obviously impossible.

The following legal description, appearing on a mortgage and supplied by W. B. Williams of Grand Rapids, Michigan, was to be surveyed by his office:

West Front Right Left 1/2, South West Front Right Left 1/4 extending Commencing at Southeast Corner thereof Thence West 439 feet, thence North 550 feet, Thence East 183 feet,

99

Thence North 769.5 feet, thence East 86 feet, Thence North to East & West line, Thence East 165 feet, Thence South to beginning & extending West 660 feet of North 875 feet. of South 2035 feet & extending Comm at Southwest corner of Section Thence East 693 feet Thence North 440 feet Thence West 420.75 feet Thence North 320 feet Thence 272.25 feet Thence South 760 feet to beginning. Section 19 (*Township and Range deleted by request*).

Is there any surveyor who could locate the property? Is it a valid mortgage? The document from which it was taken was a tax deed, abbreviated in the following form.

WFRL1/2 SWFRL1/4 ex com at SE cor thereof, th W 439 Ft., th N 550 Ft., th E 188 Ft., th N 769.5', th E 86', th N to E & W 1/4 line, th E 165 Ft., th S to beg & Ex W 660 Ft of N 875 Ft of S 2035 Ft & Ex com. at SW cor of Sec., th E 693 Ft, th N 440 Ft, th W 420.75 Ft, th N 720 Ft, th W 272.25 Ft., th S 1160 Ft to beg. Sec. 19

Obviously, the writer knew that the tax deed was an abbreviation, but he did not know the meaning of the abbreviations, nor did he have the slightest knowledge of legal description terms. But he was willing to guess. This is again proof that surveyors ought to be the ones authorized to prepare descriptions.

– CURTIS M. BROWN

----

* Neither do we!   – Editor

****

BRILLIANT BONER

MARCH 1963

L. W. MAHONE * Re: "Brilliant Boner," SURVEYING AND MAPPING, December 1962, Vol. XXII, No. 4, page 635:

There is no question but that the surveyor should prepare the description. Also, the description on the mortgage is utterly ridiculous. Whether or not this would invalidate the mortgage, I will leave to the legal profession. However, the description as contained in the tax deed (it could be better arranged) is quite understandable, and I had no trouble in plotting it. Being in Section 19, and hence on west side of township, it is natural that the SW 1/4 of section would be fractional. The notation is a little unusual but evidently, the description refers to the fractional west half of the fractional quarter. The description refers to all that is left of this tract after the exceptions have been eliminated. I do not believe I would have any trouble locating the ground, which the description covers.

* Professor, Department of Civil Engineering, University of Arkansas, Fayetteville, Arkansas.

****

THE SURVEYOR AND THE LAW

JUNE 1963

Questions concerning proper procedures to be followed in locating property boundaries will be answered to the best of our ability in this department. Contributions suitable for publication in this department - covering special legal problems or the results of court cases-are requested. Communications should be addressed to Harold R. Brooks, Chairman, Publications Committee, ACSM, Coast and Geodetic Survey, Washington 25, D. C.

LAMBERT NORTH

Under *Brilliant Boner*, December issue, apparently the abbreviations of the tax assessor are not common knowledge of all. The questionable abbreviations were: The *WFRL* means the West Fractional Lot. The *SWFRL* means the Southwest Fractional Lot. *The ex com at SE cor thereof* means Except: Commencing at the *Southeast corner thereof.* Tax abbreviations are not uniform throughout the country, but a person with experience can usually figure out the logical meanings. Tax descriptions are merely for the purpose of identifying land being taxed; they are not for the purpose of providing an accurate description of the land.

A question commonly asked arises from this situation: A deed commencing at a certain corner must be surveyed relative to "Astronomic North." Nearby the corner is a control monument whose grid coordinates are accurately known. From the control monument, a second control monument is visible, and the grid bearing is North 10° 28' 32" East between them. The correction to change "grid North" to "North" is minus 0° 28' 21" for this longitude. The bearing between the control monuments relative to "North" is then North 10° 00' 11" East. Does this line, using North 10° 00' 11" East as a bearing, form a satisfactory basis of bearing for the deed? The question is not simple to answer. Stated in another way the question is, "Are *Astronomic North* and *Geodetic North* the same at a given point?" Technically, the two are rarely identical and occasionally the difference between the two is significant.

The reason for the difference between the two directions is understood when the difference between the geoid and the spheroid of computation is explained.

The surface of the geoid is everywhere perpendicular to the pull of gravity. If for any reason the direction of pull of gravity is deflected, the geoid will have an irregular shape. For this reason the geoid is not used to compute geodetic positions (it is used for leveling).

Instruments used by surveyors depend upon the pull of gravity. A level line of sight is parallel with a bubble, said bubble being at right angles to the direction of gravity. If for any reason the pull of gravity causes a deflection in the plumb line, as, for example, by the pull of a nearby mountain mass, the level line is also deflected. Since the computation to determine astronomical direction depends upon a measured vertical angle determined relative to gravity, any deflection of the direction of pull of gravity (deflection of plumb line) will cause a change in astronomical direction.

Geodetic positions are based upon a mathematical figure (spheroid) that is made to fit, as nearly as may be, the average shape of the earth (Clark's spheroid of 1866 as used in U.S.A.). Local variation in the direction of pull of gravity does not alter the mathematical shape of the spheroid. The direction of North relative to the spheroid is not necessarily dependent upon the pull of gravity at the station; it can be computed from distant stations where the plumb line is not deflected.

The question resolves itself as to what surveyors did when they wrote deeds and made surveys; did they determine directions from astronomical observations (sun or star) or did they use geodetic directions? The answer is obvious; excluding magnetic observations, in the past astronomical bearings have practically always been determined. But there are exceptions, and in the future the exceptions will probably become more commonplace. In Alaska much of the land is being protracted as based upon geodetic monuments. Does this not imply geodetic directions? Any deed written with a State Plane Coordinate System as the basis of bearings is indirectly using geodetic directions. The positions and directions for State Plane Coordinates are derived from geodetic positions and directions.

How much difference is there between a given geodetic direction and an astronomic direction for the same point? I have been told that the average is about three seconds. But where a survey is adjoining a large mountain mass, it may be considerably more (up to about one minute).

This question of basis of bearings is always related to the written intent of the parties to a deed. Sometimes magnetic north is implied and other times "true north" or "astronomic north" is implied. Since the adoption of the State Plane Coordinate Systems, some deeds have a written intent to use grid north (mathematically related to geodetic north). In some areas the subdivision laws require the usage of State Plane Coordinates and the bearings are related mathematically to geodetic bearings.

Deeds should be on the same basis of bearings, and most surveyors are agreed that grid north, in accordance with adopted State Plane Coordinate Systems, should be the basis of bearings.

Chase Ltd., Photo
PROPERTY SURVEYS DIVISION OFFICERS
Left to right—Curtis M. Brown, Incoming Chairman; Woeber J. Reese, Outgoing Chairman; Victor H. Ghent, Secretary; and W. H. Matheny, Vice Chairman. Elmer J. Peterson, Second Vice Chairman, and Robert C. Eller, Associate Editor, were absent when the photograph was taken.

A friend returned to see what progress a sculptor was making and observed that little was done. The sculptor remarked that much was done; he had improved this place, he had changed the expression in the face, the hair was touched up, etc. The friend remarked that these were unimportant trifles. The sculptor replied that trifles made perfection, and perfection was not a trifle. The point discussed is often a trifle of only academic importance. Here are two trifles that require some thought. Who has the right answer?

1. If a person owns all the way to the center of the earth, and if there is no deflection of the plumb line, would his ownership extend in the downward direction of a plumb line located at the earth's surface?

2. If a person's rights extend "up" vertically from his surface holdings, how far is "up"? (If you want to let your imagination run wild, there are a lot of possible answers. The practical answers are much more limited).

– CURTIS M. BROWN

BRILLIANT BONER

JUNE 1963

E. H. Owens* - Author asks [1] "Is there any surveyor who could locate the property?" I would say "Yes, quite easily." He asks "Is it a valid mortgage?" Again the answer is "Yes."

As to the latter question, the obligation created by the loan is primarily evidenced by the note, not the mortgage, which is given as security in case of nonpayment. If payment is made, the mortgage will be released and be of no further effect.

If payment is not made, and it is necessary to foreclose, a court can correct the description to conform to the intention of the parties. A shrewd mortgagee would have insisted on a survey prior to the mortgage, at the expense of the mortgagor. Now, if necessary to foreclose, the mortgagee will have to pay for the survey, and if he is unable to get the mortgagor to correct the mortgage he will have the additional expense of a lawyer and court costs.

The duty of the surveyor is to interview the parties and find out their intentions and find what property was shown at the time the loan was secured; then mark it off on the ground, show the lines of possession, and finally write a correct description, which may be used in court to correct the description in the mortgage or to quiet title.

Comparing the descriptions in the mortgage and the tax deed, it is quite apparent what the intention was in each case; the tax deed, by using certain common abbreviations in which *FRL* is used as an abbreviation of fractional, is readily understood by any surveyor or title man accustomed to work in lands subdivided by the public land survey. Because of the fact that a tax title is an involuntary conveyance, it is subject to attack by the former owner on the ground of inadequacy of description and other matters.

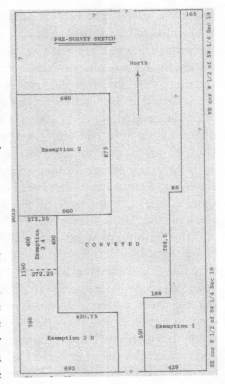

Section No. 19 is always fractional, the shortage being thrown into the West ½ of S. W. ¼ and West ½ of the N.W. ¼. A sketch is enclosed showing a presurvey location of the property; the tax deed covers the tract marked "Conveyed"; the mortgage covers the tract marked "Conveyed" and also the tract marked "3 A." Without a copy of the original government plat and a resurvey, it is impossible to determine whether exception 1 adjoins or overlaps exception 3.

The tax deed description if written out in full would read, "The west fractional ½ of the southwest fractional ¼ of Sec. 19, (insert Twp. & Range) etc," the rest of the description being perfectly obvious.

The survey investigation should reveal whether tract 3 A was intentionally included in the mortgage. This description was possibly copied or imitated from an earlier tax record description not excepting tract 3 A.

The survey investigation should reveal whether tract 3 A was intentionally included in the mortgage. This description was possible copied or imitated from an earlier tax record description not excepting tract 3 A.

A further search of the record and an investigation as to whether tract 3 A was secured by some other conveyance and is or is not in possession of mortgagor must be made by surveyor before writing a corrected description.

These descriptions are written in the gobble-de-gook known as "Legal Descriptions" in the public land survey States. These descriptions are based upon certain untrue assumptions as follows; the face of the earth is a perfect plane surface in which all north-south lines are parallel and at right angles to the east-west lines which are assumed to be straight lines instead of curved parallels of latitude; the boundary between two tracts is assumed to be a line instead of a portion of a vertical plane which cuts the surface in an undulating line due to differences of level and curvature; the mathematical relationships such as "closure" are figured as though the earth were a perfect plane; all section and subdivision of section lines are assumed to be north-south or east-west although each has its own direction, and these directions frequently vary as much as four or five degrees from true courses. These assumptions are very convenient for lawyers, courts, and plane surveyors, but mother earth refuses to go along with the assumptions. Consequently in central United States an error of about one foot to the mile exists between the plane assumption and the spherical earth upon which the described tract is to be staked. This is about a one part in 5,000 discrepancy.

The "Minimum Standard Detail Requirements for Land Title Surveys" jointly established and adopted by ATA and ACSM in 1962, provides that the title insurance company shall furnish the surveyor the record description of the property (all of which is based upon the assumption that the earth is a flat plane surface) and that the surveyor shall locate the corners within a tolerance of 0.02 foot in business districts and 0.04 foot in residential districts. This is unattainable unless a flat earth can be supplied upon which the tract can be staked. If a title company guarantees all the tracts in a "square mile," the discrepancy of about one foot must show up somewhere in the descriptions and that is 50 times the tolerance of 0.02 foot or 25 times the tolerance of 0.04 foot. If an accuracy in excess of one part in 5,000 is necessary, we must first revise the method of describing land to conform to the actual shape of the earth.

In the problem with which we started, the outside boundaries of the half quarter section are, according to custom, assumed to be north-south and east-west. In exception 1, north is taken to be parallel to the east line of the half-quarter and east and west to be parallel to the south line of the half-quarter; in exceptions 2 and 3, north is taken to mean parallel to the west line and east and west parallel to the south line of the half-quarter section. Exceptions 1 and 3 therefore, could not exactly adjoin unless the east and west lines of the half quarter are exactly parallel, a condition which very rarely exists.

In interpreting and correcting the description in the mortgage, it is obvious that *FRL* meant front-right-left to the neophyte who wrote it, "ex" stood for extending instead of except, and several other omissions were made. A correction is obviously necessary to make the instrument a valid notice to the public, and the task of the surveyor is to write a correct description, in accordance with the desire and intention of the parties, which may be used in a voluntary correction or by a forced correction by a court at the request of one of the parties. This should also be so written that it may be used in a quiet title action, if necessary, against the former owner from whom the property was taken by the tax title.

* Kansas City, Mo.
1 SURVEYING AND MAPPING, December 1962, Vol. 22, No. 4, page 608.

The Surveyor's Notebook

Reporting on Unusual Surveying Problems and Their Solutions
Notekeeper: W. & L. E. Gurley, America's Oldest Engineering Instrument Maker

How would you solve this one?

A survey party preparing a highway location study at West Stockbridge and Stockbridge, Mass., faced the problem of getting initial lines between stakes separated by heavy timber. With no time for trial and error, J. R. Kelly, Chief of Party, suspended meteorological balloons—sometimes as high as 250 feet—over the far stakes. Pointing a Gurley Transit toward the balloons gave initial direction...close enough to cut through and obtain a line with minimum labor. Whenever a sight is impossible and cutting difficult, Kelly recommends a captive pilot balloon about 6 feet in diameter, filled with gas and guyed over the station point.

Transit Found Practical for "Checking In" on Precise Traverse Points—The special traverse on this study for a continuation of the Berkshire Thruway lay between two sections of a geodetic survey begun in the 1930's, but never completed. Field time was limited, but Kelly's party quickly established coordinates with the Gurley Transit, rather than with a theodolite usually used for tying in on a previously run precise traverse.

William J. Goggins, Survey Supervisor for the Commonwealth of Massachusetts, reports that error was negligible. His program calls for a relocation of Highway 102 —starting at the New York state line and running east to Stockbridge, eventually connecting into U. S. Highway 20 near Lee. Goggins' party had to run a 700-foot line over one mountain through which a tunnel is planned. "Check in" error was negligible, even though a 150-foot rise was encountered in the relatively short distance.

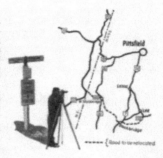

Gurley Transit's Reversion Level "Invaluable Aid"

In taping the line, the survey party used "slant measurements," taking also the difference in elevation between points. For this work, Goggins found the reversion-type level vial on the Gurley telescope "invaluable...easily read at all times." Checking the bubble in the Gurley reversion vial requires two readings only—one direct, and one reversed. Goggins says, "I am glad to have the Gurley Transit at this time...work will be very accurate...error practically eliminated."

Take a tip from William Goggins' notebook...Learn about versatile Gurley Transits. Bulletin 50 gives all details. Write for it today.

SURVEYORS: We welcome letters on your unusual solutions of surveying problems for future pages in The Surveyor's Notebook

© 1957 W. & L. E. GURLEY

EDUCATION

WHAT SHOULD BE THE EDUCATION FOR LAND SURVEYING?

PAPER DELIVERED AT THE FOURTH NATIONAL SURVEYING TEACHERS CONFERENCE

NACES, WASHINGTON

CURTIS M. BROWN, SURVEYOR
LA MESA, CALIFORNIA

AUGUST 1957

The subject of land surveying if taken in a broad sense would include photogrammetry, geodetic surveying, mine surveying, planning and route surveys, and even hydrographic surveys. In a narrow sense many of us think of property line surveyor as being the land surveyor. Since my primary interest is with the property line surveyor, many of my early remarks will be directed at his problems.

Historically the property line surveyor has been a part of civil engineering. But as civil engineering has become more complex, surveying has been pushed to one side to make room for newer subjects. The thinking of many engineers is illustrated by a recent incident that happened to a fellow surveyor. When applying for associate membership in the American Society of Civil Engineers he was asked by one of the membership committee what work he was doing. To his reply that he was a land surveyor, the remark was made, "I know that you are a land surveyor. I mean what have you done in engineering?" The attitude of many engineers is that surveying is not engineering, that it is sub-professional work to be handled by technicians. But is it? Too many of us think of the land surveyor as being the technician who operates a transit and only knows how to measure, not what to measure.

I think of boundary surveying as including many technical levels and also a professional level. We must distinguish among the chainman, instrument man, technician, and the professional surveyor. The doctors have laboratory assistants who are called technicians, not doctors. Unfortunately, the professional surveyor has many assistants who are often thought of and are considered by many to be surveyors.

Many people have attempted to define the word "profession." Like all good words it has been overworked and extended to apply to such words as "professional boxer" and "professional soldier." A similar situation exists with the word "engineer" as adopted by the A. F. of L. in their "operating engineers" union. The better term would have been "engine operators," since that is what they are.

When I speak of the professions I mean the higher sense, such as lawyer, clergy, doctors, and educators. To be a professional man certain requisites are often present, among them:

(1) Superior knowledge in his field;
(2) Ability to express learned opinions;
(3) Remuneration for his services;
(4) Liability for errors.

Thus the attorney listens to his client, gathers all available facts, and from his superior knowledge of law expresses an opinion on what to do. For his effort, he collects a fee. And upon occasions he can be held liable for his mistakes. The doctor makes measurements, observations and tests on his patient, and from these observations, combined with his superior knowledge of medicine, he expresses an opinion on the type of treatment to be followed. A fee is charged. And for neglect in his duties he can be held liable.

The property surveyor is given a deed and told to mark it on the ground. He makes measurements, observations and sets markers in accordance with his opinion, and he charges a fee. The only correct location for a boundary line is in that position that a court of competent jurisdiction will uphold. Thus in setting his property marks the surveyor is giving his opinion of where he thinks the court would uphold him. It takes superior knowledge to know where and how to set property lines. And if the surveyor fails to set his boundaries in that position that a reasonably prudent surveyor would, he must pay the damages. He is a professional man.

Let us contrast the professional surveyor with the average surveyor as the engineer knows him. On highway work the engineer in charge has surveyors who make measurements to determine the shape of the ground. They are merely measuring the ground as it exists and recording the facts, as they are. To be sure, the surveyor must have superior ability in knowing how to use instruments and how to make measurements, but this is purely technical. He does not design the road nor does he utilize his measurements. Again the engineer may tell the surveyor to grade stake a road in accordance with a given plan. Since no design or judgment is involved, it is a purely technical matter. To the average engineer the surveyor is a technician who carries out his orders. And often he is just that. But the engineers frequently overlook the fact that there is a professional surveyor's level.

When we ask "What Should be the Education for the Land Surveyor?" do we mean the technician or the professional surveyor? I visualize three distinct levels of training. They are:

Trade school or vocational;
Technician level (Junior College);
Professional (University or College).

Too many Chiefs and not enough Indians is not a desirable situation. We need more chainmen and instrument men than we need technical or college men. The chainmen and instrument men should be trained at either the vocational level or by the employer himself. We have found that the better educated men will not stay at the chainman level; he soon departs for greener pastures. If we try to employ only educated people, we find that our labor turnover is much too rapid. We prefer the less educated, more willing worker for these lesser positions.

Chase Ltd., Photo.

PANEL, ACSM PROPERTY SURVEYS DIVISION, MARCH 28, 1963

Left to right: O. R. McElya, Land Surveyor, Dallas, Texas; Charles S. Danner, Land Surveyor, Urbana, Illinois; Llewellyn T. Schofield, Land Surveyor, Framingham, Massachusetts; John E. McIntosh, L. S., Niagara Frontier Land Surveyors Association; Victor H. Ghent, Moderator; Professor Winfield H. Eldridge, University of Illinois; Curtis M. Brown, San Diego, California; and Hugh A. Binyon, St. Petersburg, Florida.

The Chief of Party, our second level of training must have a broader education. He must know trigonometry and other mathematics. He must know how to chain, how to run instruments, how to solve surveying problems, have a knowledge of drafting, and have a broader concept of surveying. The requirements are obviously beyond high schools and the trade schools. We have found that the two year college man or the Junior College man is best suited for this type of work. He is not good enough technically to advance rapidly into higher types of engineering and he is satisfied to remain a reasonably long period of time as a Chief of Party. This is the type of man that the professional surveyor depends upon to take over responsible charge of many phases of a project. I consider them first class technicians. They are the types commonly employed by the engineer on construction projects. And they are the cause for thinking that all surveyors are only technicians.

The universities and colleges today are crowded to capacity, and this is especially true for engineering. It is pointless to expend valuable college space and effort in training technicians that do not have the ability to advance beyond the Chief-of-Party level. But technicians must have some college training. The ideal ground is the Junior College. We have set up a two-year technical course in San Diego at this level which includes the following courses:

1st Semester	Units	2nd Semester	Units
Psychology	3	English	3
Drafting	8	Drafting	8
Phy. Ed.	½	Tech. Science	3
Math. (Alg.)	3	Phy. Ed.	½
Tech. Science	3	Math. (Geometry)	3

3rd Semester	Units	4th Semester	Units
Surveying	8	Surveying	8
English	3	Political Science	3
Phy. Ed.	½	Phy. Ed.	½
Math. (Trig.)	3	Health Ed.	2
		Machine Cal. and Slide rule	3

Admittedly the course is a blind alley. Anyone taking it and wanting to transfer to a major college will find that he has to complete an additional four years to get a degree. But it must be remembered that those taking such a program would be those deficient in their high school work, but acceptable in mathematics and drafting ability. If they show superior ability in such a program, then they would be eligible to enter a four year college.

But how about the bossman, the true professional, the man with the superior ability. Where is he to come from? The Chief of Party is like the driver with tunnel vision. He can see in the direction he is going, but is oblivious to what lies on each side of him. For our profession to advance we need men of superior intelligence, with foresight and imagination. We need university graduates who have the whole picture.

The property line surveyor is licensed in about 75% of the states. His primary function is to serve the public by re-establishing old property lines or setting new lines. The purpose of the law is to protect the public from unqualified surveyors.

In general the land surveyor needs training in:

(1) Mathematics
(2) Drafting and map making skills
(3) Instrumentation (use of transit, tape, level, etc.)
(4) Surveying and geodetic computations
(5) Writing and interpreting descriptions
(6) Law

Most engineering colleges offer training in computations, mapping and instrumentation, but little or nothing in surveying law. A man may be a beautiful technician, a skilled mathematician, and an expert at making measurements, but of what value is his skill it he does, not know where to place a legal property corner? Almost 100% of the fault we find with the men we employ is their ignorance of where to place property corners. The objection is frequently raised that the subject of land law is not engineering. But is that true? Everyone is expected to obey the law and everyone is presumed to know the law. The property surveyor is licensed to set property corners and he is expected to set them in accordance with the correct principles of law. He is not practicing law; he is merely obeying law in the same fashion that you or I do when we obey the speed limit. And if land law is never engineering, why has the engineer from time immemorial had the task of locating right-of-way lines and property lines for his fixed works?

The one thing that elevates the property surveyor above the technician is his knowledge of where to place property corners. Thus, in a given property description there may be conflicts due to senior considerations, intentions of the parties, record monuments, natural or artificial monuments, lines marked and surveyed, distance, area, bearing, possession, mathematical error, magnetic or astronomic bearing or coordinates. There may be the problem of how to distribute accretions and the beds of vacated streets. And then title may be awarded on the basis of possession, rather than upon the existing written deeds.

To my knowledge only two colleges, San Francisco City College and San Diego Junior College, offer special classes in this important phase of the surveyor's education. In fact the scarcity of material on the subject, other than in legal books, prompted me to do extensive research on the subject. Knowing the importance of surveying law, it has always puzzled me as to why so little of it has been offered at the college level.

The civil engineers wish to have all the privileges and rights of the licensed land surveyor, yet too frequently they do not recognize the responsibility of educating themselves for the duties involved. Thus, in the State of California the engineer is exempt from the surveyors act, and the engineers act does not specify that the engineer shall be qualified as a property surveyor. For this reason it has been the custom for only minor questions on surveying to be asked on the civil engineers registration examination.

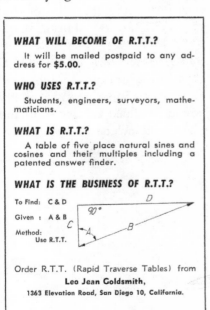

WHAT WILL BECOME OF R.T.T.?

It will be mailed postpaid to any address for **$5.00.**

WHO USES R.T.T.?

Students, engineers, surveyors, mathematicians.

WHAT IS R.T.T.?

A table of five place natural sines and cosines and their multiples including a patented answer finder.

WHAT IS THE BUSINESS OF R.T.T.?

To Find: C & D
Given : A & B
Method:
     Use R.T.T.

Order R.T.T. (Rapid Traverse Tables) from
Leo Jean Goldsmith,
1363 Elevation Road, San Diego 10, California.

At the time the law was passed it was undoubtedly true that most civil engineers had better training in surveying. But today the picture has changed.

The biggest fault with so called land surveying education is that it is often treated as a minor part of another curriculum. The architect takes a few units of surveying. The land planner, the forester, the landscape architect and others likewise receive a minimum of training in what is called surveying. And rapidly joining the ranks of these is the civil engineer. I do not claim this to be right or wrong -- I am merely pointing out a condition that exists. If the civil engineer wants to be considered as the person who designs dams, bridges, sewage treatment works, structures and the like; and he wants to consider surveying as a tool to accomplish that end, the de-emphasis-on surveying is good. And the application of the name "measurements" to what was formerly surveying would be a step in the right direction. The courses presently called surveying and offered to land planners, architects and the like might also be called courses in "measurements." Thus, those taking "measurements" would not be led to believe that they are qualified land surveyors. But if the civil engineer wants to be thought of as competent to do land surveying, the de-emphasis on surveying is bad.

The West is experiencing a development unparalleled at any time in the history of our country. The mass migration of people, among other things, has caused our population to bulge. With expanding population comes land development problems. New roads, new subdivisions, land planning, earthwork, and land measurements are demanding trained men. The new Federal highway program is accelerating the need. The military always wants men in the field of land measurements.

A new era in land measurements is evolving. Aerial photography is eliminating many of the old ground surveying methods. Electronic distance-measuring devices are achieving results unthought of a few years ago. Machines are supplanting many of the slower calculating methods and are making possible improved field methods. New reproduction and mapping methods are evolving. The need for men in the fields of land measurements and mapping is apparent. What are the colleges doing about it?

One solution, as practiced by some of the colleges, is to offer a latitude of choice for the civil engineering student in his junior and senior year. A student might take a predominance of courses in structural, sanitary or hydraulic engineering. To this list would be added an option in land measurement engineering. Such an option would include all of the phases of land development such as:

Property line surveying and law
Highway development
Route surveying
Earthwork and soil testing
Subdivision development
Geodetic surveying
Hydrographic surveying
Mapping and photogrammetry
Land planning and use

The thinking of the average civil engineering student is that he will design building, bridges, dams and large engineering projects. Land measurement and land surveying is often a minor part of his thinking. What we need are men who are specifically trained in the field of land measurements and are trained in how measurements are used. Probably a third of the registered engineers in California make or use land measurements of some type. There is a place in college for the professional surveyor, and it is up to us to find that place.

Only two logical solutions exist. The Colleges should either offer a degree in property surveying or they should offer a degree in civil engineering with an option in land measurement. Present civil engineering courses often include almost all of the training necessary for land surveyors. By merely adding courses in property line law, land use planning, an adequate land surveyor's course can be a part of most engineering colleges.

My conclusion is that property surveying is so closely related to civil engineering that it should not be rejected as a part of engineering. The colleges should take a positive approach to the subject of property surveying and determine how it should fit in; not how it should be de-emphasized. I feel that civil engineering has become so complex that the better solution is to offer options in different fields of engineering and that property line surveying should fit into one of those fields; namely, land measurement engineering.

****

THE SURVEYOR AND THE LAW

EDUCATION REQUIREMENTS
FOR LAND SURVEYORS

MARCH 1964

It is interesting to note the wide variation of the scope of practice permitted surveyors. A few States have no limitations whatsoever (no registration); a few permit the preparation of improvement plans for subdivisions; others permit staking of improvement plans prepared by engineers (but not preparation of plans); and others do not allow the surveyor to either prepare or stake improvement plans. A few years ago (1958) a committee of the Property Surveys Division of the American Congress on Surveying and Mapping presented what they believed to be a good model law. Indiana has recently enacted into law a statute that most nearly approaches the thinking of that committee. According to the Indiana act, the surveyor may prepare improvement plans within subdivisions; he may stake improvements and do other things (this is also true in Virginia and Maryland). Of course, with this privilege much higher knowledge requirements for registration are imposed. The law reads (in part) as follows (63 - 1518):

(d) The term "land surveyor," as used in this act, shall mean a person who is qualified to engage in the practice of land surveying, as herein defined, as attested by his registration as a land surveyor.

(e) The term "practice of land surveying," as used in this act, shall mean the establishment or reestablishment of corners, boundaries, and locations of lots, parcels, tracts or divisions of land, including distances, directions, and acreage, or fractional parts thereof, including, but not limited to, the correct determination and description of the same for any of the following purposes:

(1) To furnish a legal description of any land surveyed to be used in the preparation of deeds of conveyance;

(2) To furnish a legal description of any land surveyed to be used in the platting or subdividing of said land; or

(3) To determine the correct amount of acreage contained in any land surveyed;

(4) To furnish a topographic plat of a lot, parcel, tract or division of land.

(f) The term "board," as used in this act, shall mean the state board of registration for professional engineers and land surveyors.

(g) The term "approved engineering curriculum," shall mean an engineering curriculum of four years or more that has been approved by the board. In approving such engineering curriculum the board may take into consideration the standards of accreditation adopted by the Engineers' Council for Professional Development.

(h) The term "practice of land surveying" shall also include the preparation of a legal description of any tract of land, to be used in the preparation of deeds of conveyance except:

(1) When the description is the same as the one in the deed of conveyance to the current owner, or

(2) When bearings, distances, or measurements are not needed to properly describe the tract being conveyed.

(i) The term "practice of land surveying" as used in this act shall also include, for and within subdivisions being laid out or having been laid out by the land surveyor, the preparation and furnishing of plats, plans, and profiles for roads, storm drainage, sanitary sewer extensions, and the location of residences or dwellings where such work involves the use and application of standards prescribed by local, state, or federal authorities. This shall include the necessary staking and layout work to construct said roads, storm drainage, sanitary sewer extensions or location of residences or dwellings where the plans and profiles were prepared by or under the direction of a land surveyor as defined in this act. This shall not be construed to include the design and construction of sewage disposal stations, lift stations, commercial buildings, pumping stations or bridges or their equivalents.

Chase, Ltd., Photo

ACSM Officers Participating in the 23rd Annual Congress in Washington, D. C.
Left to right, front row: Chairman C. M. Brown, Property Surveys Division; Chairman G. E. Stine, Cartography Division; Chairman M. Laird, Control Surveys Division; Chairman J. C. Kerr, Heart of America Section; Director F. Clemens, representing the St. Louis Section; Secretary W. Le-Compte, representing the Louisiana Section; and *in back row:* Delegate Carl Johnson, representing the Florida Society of Professional Land Surveyors.

(j) The term "practice of land surveying" as used in this act shall also include preliminary surveys for preparation of plans for engineering and building construction projects and the staking out of the same from plans prepared by a registered professional engineer or by a registered architect. This is not to be construed so as to permit the land surveyor to prepare the plans for the construction of engineering projects.

(k) The term "practice of land surveying" shall include all the engineering work incidental to cleaning out, or maintaining existing drainage ditches.

(b) As a professional land surveyor: (Requirements for, 63 - 1528)

(1) Graduation in an approved engineering curriculum of four (4) years or more which includes the fundamentals of land surveying, and a specific record of one (1) year or more of

experience in land surveying work acquired subsequent to graduation, which experience indicates that the applicant is qualified to be placed in responsible charge of land surveying work requiring the exercise of judgment in the application of surveying sciences to the sound solution of land surveying problems, and the successful passing of an examination as provided for in section 14 of this act; or

(2) A specific record of five (5) years or more of civil engineering education and experience in land surveying work, which indicates that the applicant has acquired knowledge and skill and practical experience in land surveying work approximating that required for registration as a professional land surveyor under the provisions of subsection (b) (1) of this section; and the successful passing of an examination as provided for in section 14 of this act.

The key to the knowledge requirements for the land surveyor is then equivalent to that obtained by a person graduating from a four-year civil engineering curriculum *which includes the fundamentals of land surveying.* This law places the responsibility of offering land surveying courses squarely in the lap of Indiana universities, and, in response to the law, Purdue University (Lafayette, Indiana) is now offering land surveying courses within the framework of civil engineering (also photogrammetry, geodesy, and other related courses). It is also offering extension courses to update the education of former graduates and those interested in land surveying subjects.

Surveyors, as a group, have been repeatedly commenting that the colleges should teach land surveying. Is the fault with the laws and not the colleges? If the only prerequisite to taking a land surveyor's examination is a high school education or equivalent, why should the colleges teach land surveying? If surveyors want colleges in other States to offer land surveying courses, should not the registration laws be changed to require the equivalent of a college education? New York State, at the last legislative meeting, raised the requirements to college equivalent. Should not other States follow? What is your opinion?

– CURTIS M. BROWN

124

THE CHALLENGING FUTURE FOR THE LAND SURVEYOR

PRESENTED TO THE PROPERTY SURVEYS DIVISION AT THE 24TH ANNUAL MEETING OF THE AMERICAN CONGRESS ON SURVEYING AND MAPPING (A PANEL DISCUSSION)

1964

The theme of this panel meeting was "The Challenging Future for the Land Surveyor." The first two papers presented at this panel meeting are published in this issue Of SURVEYING AND MAPPING, and the remaining two papers will be published in September. Together, the four papers encompass a sober and thought-provoking view of the profession of land surveying and describe in detail what steps must be taken to assure the continuing growth of this most challenging field. Members of the panel were:

Phillips Bill, R.L.S. & P.E., Moderator
Curtis M. Brown, R.L.S.
Charles S. Danner, R.L.S. & P.E.
Francis H. Moffitt, R.L.S. & P.E.
F. William Pafford, R.L.S.

In introducing Curt, the moderator Phillips Bill honored him with a glowing commentary:

"Presenting the future for us . . . is a man who needs no introduction to any ACSM group. Curtis M. Brown is first and foremost a Licensed Land Surveyor in California. He covers our country pretty well, since he was born in Maine, graduated in civil engineering from the University of California, and practices with the firm of Daniels, Brown, and Hall in San Diego. He is our vice president-elect, past chairman of Property Surveys Division, co-author of the only good texts in our profession in the last 50 years, and currently Visiting Professor in Land Surveying at Purdue University. It gives me a lot of satisfaction to present Curtis M. Brown, who will talk to us on 'Licensing Laws and Land Surveyors' Examinations.'"

[MP NOTE: Curt's speech follows.]

Within the last generation we have witnessed the most rapid advancement in the science of land measurements that has ever occurred in any like period in the history of the world. The more important areas of progress have been in electronic distance measurements, in photogrammetry, in electronic computing, and in the knowledge of the size and shape of the earth, that is, geodesy.

Photogrammetry has supplanted many of the old transit and tape methods. For any large area, distances between control positions are determined electronically; contours are platted from photographs; directions are measured with improved types of theodolites; and trilateralation may someday eliminate part of this step. With the invention of laser beams, it will only be a matter of time until the beams will be adapted to distance measurements. We will probably live to see the day when short distances will be measured accurately and economically with light beams.

In several States, photogrammetry has been used to resurvey land boundaries. Though the cost is as yet excessive for desirable accuracies, this will probably be overcome in the foreseeable future. In a few instances, original property surveys have been made using photogrammetry.

126

The usefulness of the old work horse, the transit and tape, is gradually being reduced in scope. While these instruments probably will never be completely supplanted, their importance will continue to diminish with time.

Many land surveyors have found that they have had to adopt photogrammetry, electronic calculation methods, and electronic measurements in order to survive. Those who fail to use these new tools are apt to find themselves priced out of competitive range.

It can be safely assumed that these new tools are here to stay. With this assumption, let us ask, "How many State boards of registration are increasing the scope of surveyor examinations to include questions in these areas? Are they still confining their questions to the tape, transit, logarithms, and longhand computations? Are the problems restricted to how to solve curves, triangles, closures, and simple elements of star shots? Or have the examination questions been changed to be compatible with existing times and tools?"

The future of any profession is wholly dependent upon the quality of the new men admitted to practice. Are we seeking new, professional surveyors on the basis of what grandpa had to know, or are we seeking them on the basis of what they will have to know to survive in coming years? Are we sticking our heads in the sand and assuming that the profession of land surveying can forever confine itself to horse-and-buggy methods, or are we going to expand the scope of examinations to include new methods?

During recent years I have accumulated a large number of land surveyor's examinations. Many were obtained by writing to the boards of registration and asking for a copy; some boards refused the request. Occasionally copies were given to me with the understanding that they would not be published. In two instances, wherein the board was trying to prevent past examinations from getting into the hands of others, unauthorized copies were readily located. It appears that no matter how good the security methods are, copies do escape.

Registration Laws. The registration laws of each State vary; it is difficult to compare examinations on the basis of subject matter. The laws of Indiana, California, and Virginia will be used to illustrate this point.

Indiana: The Professional Land Surveyor may locate land (resurveys and original surveys), make subdivisions and prepare improvement plans (sewer, water, paving, drainage, etc.), prepare land descriptions, do topographic surveys, do construction staking, do preliminary surveys and plans for engineering work, do engineering work incidental to cleaning out and maintaining existing drainage ditches, do land planning, and other related items.

Because of the right to do improvement plans and minor engineering design, the scope of the Indiana surveyor's examination is beyond that usually found in other States. The requirements for the examinee are: (1) Graduation from an approved civil engineering curriculum of four years or more that includes the fundamentals of land surveying, plus the successful passing of an examination, or (2) a specific record of five years or more of civil engineering education and experience in land surveying work which indicates that the applicant has acquired knowledge, skill, and practical experience in land surveying work approximating that required for registration as a land surveyor under the above section, plus the successful passing of an examination.

California. The surveyor in California may do all of the items permitted in Indiana except that he may not prepare improvement plans. (He may do construction staking from plans prepared by engineers.) In addition, photogrammetry and geodesy are defined as a part of land surveying. California seems to be the only State in which it is mandatory to file records of surveys and place license numbers on all monuments set. Education: minimum requirement is high school graduation.

Virginia. Virginia has two separate examinations. The first tests knowledge of land surveying, and the second tests knowledge necessary for the preparation of improvement plans. A land surveyor may do land surveying work without taking the second test; after passing the second test he may, with some limitations, prepare improvement plans.

Methods of Comparing Examinations. From the above it is obvious that a direct comparison of examinations in different States is not possible. California asks questions on photogrammetry and geodesy and nothing on preparing improvement plans; Indiana, because of its basic civil engineering education requirement, asks questions on friction, heat transfer, entropy, fluid mechanics, kinetics, strength of materials, and other items. Between States there can be a direct comparison of questions pertaining to land location procedures, legal elements of land surveying, mathematics of land surveying, and other related items.

Many indirect methods of comparing questions that are unrelated in subject matter exists. Some of these are:

What is the difficulty of the questions asked?
Do the questions require judgment or mere factual knowledge in the answer?
Does the examination cover a narrow band of knowledge or does it include a sampling of a broad band of knowledge?
Are the questions asked logically? Are they clearly prepared or are they such that they display a lack of knowledge by the person preparing them? These questions will be discussed further.

Objective of a Written Examination. The purpose of any registration act is *to protect the public from the unqualified.* It is certainly not a means of granting to a few an easy means of earning a living to the exclusion of others. As a condition of licensing, the public has a right to expect that those who are licensed are qualified; if they are not qualified, the licensing act merely serves the purpose of deceiving the public.

In the location of land boundaries, the surveyor also locates the boundaries of adjoiners. He is in a quasi-judicial position, in that he is obligated to consider the rights of others, even though they may not pay him a fee. This is the primary basis for limiting the practice of land surveying to a qualified few.

A written examination is for the purpose of testing the capabilities of candidates in given areas; it cannot test capabilities in all areas. Is he honest? Is he ethical? Would he protect the public fairly as compared to his client? The proof of these questions lies in his past behavior. Letters of recommendation and past performances should be inquired into. This topic is not the subject of this paper.

In defining a profession, one of the often cited qualifications is superior knowledge which is used for the benefit of others. The objective of an examination is to test whether a person does in fact have superior knowledge.

Knowledge is difficult to define, but it is more than an accumulation of facts. A surveyor must have a superior knowledge of factual things; he must be able to recall factual things and sort out pertinent information; he must think; he must use logic to come to correct conclusions; and he must effectively communicate his conclusions to others. A surveyor's examination is not the mere process of asking factual questions; it must also test the ability to think, reason, conclude correctly, communicate effectively, and use good judgment.

The objectives of a written question can be classified as follows: (1) testing factual knowledge of surveying (including reading and writing ability, knowledge of the meaning of words, elementary mathematics, tools, and related subjects); (2) testing the application of factual knowledge to surveying problems or questions (this tests the ability to think, use judgment, and come to correct conclusions).

Testing for Factual Knowledge. Factual questions can be classified into the following groups:

a. *Analogy.*
Transit is to angle as tape is to:
1. Slope----. 2. Temperature----. 3 Measurement----. 4. Area----.

b. *Completion.* The Electrotape uses ---------------------- waves.

c. *Cross out.* Cross out the word does not belong to the group:
1. Angle. 2. Direction. 3. Tape. 4. Bearing.

d. *Diagrammatic.* Make a drawing showing how the principal points the compass would appear in the surveyor's compass box.

e. *Enumeration.* List the errors that occur in taping.

f. *Identification.* Place an "A" after those words that pertain to angular measurements; place a "D" after those words that pertain to distance measurements.

Sag----. Catenary----. Refraction----. Deflection of the vertical----. Parallel with----.

g. *Matching.* Match related items in columns A and B by writing the corresponding number in the space provided.

A

1. Temperature above standard
2. Error of closure
3. Cross-sections
4. Leveling
5. Evidence

B

1. Equal sight distances
2. Obliterated corner
3. Summation of latitudes and departures
4. Elongation of tape
5. Cubic yards

h. *Multiple Choice.* Check the word that is not related to traverse error:

Least square adjustment---- Compass rule---- Line of sight---- Closure----.

i. *Sequence.* Number the following items in their order of performed sequence:

Measurements----
Research----
Computations for field closure----
Certificate of survey----

j. *True or False.* George Washington was the first licensed surveyor in the United States.
T _____ F _____

k. *True or false or neither without further data.* Mark a "T" if the answer is true; an "F" if the answer is false; and an "N" if it cannot be answered without further data. A level line at 5000 feet elevation is parallel with a level line at zero feet elevation-----. (A geodetic question, the answer is N).

The following are factual questions found on surveyor examinations that were selected to illustrate a point.

1. The length of your pace may be used for approximate horizontal measurements.
   T _____ F _____

2. The engineer's chain is 100 links long and each link is 0.66 feet long.
   T _____ F _____

3. The coefficient of expansion for an ordinary steel tape is about .0000065
   T _____ F _____

4. The invar steel tape has a larger coefficient of expansion than an ordinary steel tape.
   T _____ F _____

5. An ordinary steel engineer's tape is graduated in feet, tenths of feet, and hundredths feet.
   T _____ F _____

6. A link in the surveyor's chain is 0.66 feet long.
   T _____ F _____

7. A slope of three-quarters to one means that in moving up the slope the vertical distance traversed is three-fourths of the horizontal.
   T _____ F _____

8. Section 18 in a township is generally directly south of Section 12.
   T _____ F _____

9. On a map a full arrow is used to represent the direction of magnetic north.
   T _____ F _____

10. If the half arrow is on the right hand side of the line, then the declination at this location is west.
    T _____ F _____

11. On the compass box used by the surveyor, you will find east and west interchanged from their natural positions.
    T _____ F _____

12. The declination of the magnetic needle when once determined always remains the same value.
    T _____ F _____

13. An error of closure of one part in 500 parts represents a very good traverse.
    T _____ F _____

14. In order to level up (sic) a transit, you use the adjacent leveling screws.
    T _____ F _____

These types of questions are quite appropriate for chainmen, rodmen, and other technicians with limited knowledge and education. But do they have a place in the professional surveyors examination?

Factual information is one of the lower forms of education. True superior education is the ability to *recall factual information* pertaining to a problem, sort out the essential facts by *thinking* and then come to *a correct conclusion.* The ability to parrot factual information without the ability to form conclusions is almost a nullity; parrots can speak but are unable to ask for their dinner.

All of us at one time or another have had employees that could quote the book from one end to the other but who could not put the facts together to solve a problem in a strange situation.

If we are to be a profession, which we claim to be, the object is to discover and license people who, in addition to knowledge of factual information, have the ability to *think* and correctly *reason.* Sixteen hours of examination time is all too short to waste portions of the time on such trivial and meaningless questions as those given above. We are not trying to license technicians; we want people with good judgment. Does this mean that the above outlined methods of testing should not be used?

Some types of factual questions can be used effectively provided that the questions are framed so that the examinee must *think* and use some *reasoning* or *judgment* in selecting the correct answer. A geodetic question illustrating this is:

Circle the statement that is most nearly true:

The shore line of a still body of water forms a level line. (False-only bodies of water at sea level form level lines)

A level line on the earth's surface has a radial center located at the center of the earth. (False)

A level plane of an observer would depart from the earth's surface by about 0.57 foot at the end of one mile.

Refraction in the atmosphere causes a level plane to be distorted. (Not the plane.)

To answer the above question, a person must have a fund of factual geodetic information, he must think, and he must reason as to what is correct. The examinee is apt to say that this is a trick question, but is it? If the examinee *knows his subject* and if he *thinks*, he can answer it correctly. The purpose of the examination is to discover people who can think.

Testing Professional Qualifications. Among the many items of qualifications that professional people should have, the following are often tested on a written examination:

(1) factual land surveying information; (2) mathematical ability; (3) the ability to think; (4) the ability to derive correct conclusions; (5) the ability to use good judgment; (6) the ability to communicate effectively.

Demonstrations of the use of equipment and manual dexterity are seldom tested, though they probably should be. In the test for the United States Mineral Surveyor, the examinee brings his own transit and determines the direction of a given line by solar observation.

In framing questions, the examiner should keep in mind the above objectives. An essay question of this type, "If the surveyor discovers possession not in agreement with the written description, when should he accept the possession as being correct?" requires factual knowledge, good reasoning, and the ability to communicate effectively.

Judgment. The difference between a correct conclusion and good judgment lies in the path taken or method used. In solving a mathematical problem there is usually an easy way and several hard ways; a person using good judgment would take the easy way. In making a topographic map, it would be poor judgment to use ground methods if the job could be accomplished with equal quality at half the cost by aerial methods. Judgment is the ability to select the best approach. It can enter into the solution of mathematical problems or in essay questions.

Ability to communicate effectively. Part of the definition of any profession is that its members have a superior education that *is used for the benefit of others.* If a person is unable to effectively communicate his knowledge to others, he will be unable to benefit others. All of the knowledge in the world will not aid a surveyor on the witness stand if he is unable to communicate effectively to the judge and convince him that his methods are correct. A person can have a superior fund of knowledge, and he can have a superior ability to think, but they are of little value if he is unable to communicate so as to convince others.

Many have argued that the testing of the ability to communicate in all of its forms is not important on a surveyor's examination. Some surveyor examinations ask only mathematical or factual questions that do not require demonstration of writing ability. I cannot agree with this.

Essay and Mathematical Questions. Of all types of questions that may be used to test examinees, essay and mathematical questions are most useful to evaluate thinking, conclusions, logic, effective communication, and judgment----all in one question.

A good mathematical question requires that the examinee have some *factual knowledge* upon which his solution is based; it requires *thinking*, to sort out the essential facts; it requires a *logical* sequence of steps, to arrive at a *conclusion* or final answer; it requires the examinee to *effectively communicate* his thinking to the grader; and it requires the examinee to use good *judgment* in the selection of variables or in the selection of the method of solution. From the standpoint of the person grading an examination, mathematical questions are ideal; they have only one answer or a few variations of that answer; they are easy to grade. The person grading need only memorize one solution with a few minor variations; from then on he does not have to spend much time thinking. It is a routine that is sometimes delegated to clerical help, thus saving grading costs.

Most of the knowledge requirements of the land location surveyor can be classified into the following three categories: (1) the science of measurement; (2) the science of mathematics; (3) boundary law. If the land surveyor is to be tested in all of the areas of required knowledge, it is obvious that questions other than mathematical problems must be asked.

Law regulates human relationships; it never has been and never will be an exact science susceptible of mathematical analysis. It is said that wherever the original surveyor set his original survey monument, that location, as of the date of the deed or as of the moment of filing the map, is conclusive. In trying to discover the original position occupied by the original monument, there may be conflicting evidence on the ground. Jones says it was here. Smith says it was there. An old fence is located in another position. An old survey record of a former surveyor says that it was somewhere else. From all of this conflicting evidence, what is right? One thing is certain, no mathematical problem can be devised to effectively test a person's knowledge in this area: essay questions are best.

In deciding upon the shade of meaning of a word in a deed, the surveyor is confronted with a judgment question requiring a background of factual knowledge. When a function cannot be reduced to numbers, and is relative, a discussion is the only way to test whether the examinee understands the situation or problem.

Essay questions are graded upon the basis of *what is* said and *how* it is said. Knowledge of things without being able to communicate that knowledge to others effectively is only half-knowing. In answering essay questions, or for that matter, any question, the examinee is expected to be *brief, precise, complete, logical, correct,* and display *judgment.* He should not (1) produce a rambling, verbose discussion without any one part being clear;

(2) use too much space devoted to a few unimportant details, the important points being lost in the details; (3) list items without emphasis or plan; (4) introduce an unrelated passage copied from a book; or (5) allow excessive grammatical or spelling errors.

Example of an Essay Question. "Undisturbed found original monuments that are called for in a conveyance or on a map are usually considered as controlling the location of property lines, whether the monuments are located in their record measured position or not. Under certain circumstances, original called for monuments are rejected by the surveyor as not representing the title corners of a client and new monuments are set in another position. What are these circumstances for monuments (1) called for in a metes and bounds description, (2) called for on a subdivision plat, and (3) called for in Federal Government Sectionalized Land notes?"

This question requires factual knowledge in a broad area, it requires thinking, the answer is not found in one place in a text book, and the candidate must communicate his answer in writing.

Admittedly, these questions are difficult to grade. For this reason, they are all too often omitted. Some questions of this type should be on every examination.

Length of Examinations. Most States are giving two-day, 16-hour examinations. The theory is that fundamentals will be asked on the first day and professional questions on the second. After reading the Australian and New Zealand examination in a recent issue of the *Australian Surveyor,* all United States examinations appear to be in the most elementary category; their examination lasted six days of eight hours each. The questions and solutions were published.

As of now, very little, if any, pressure is being exerted to lengthen examination time. In a period of 16 hours it is not possible to include more than a sampling of relatively simple problems. And, where 8 hours of the 16 are spent on testing minor areas of factual knowledge, the scope and difficulty of an examination is further reduced.

SIT Examinations. (Surveyor In Training Examination). The Surveyor in Training Examination has been proposed in several States, but, to my knowledge, it has never been enacted into law. The objective is to permit prospective candidates the privilege of taking a fundamentals test at the technician level. The test would probably consist of factual information and elementary mathematical relationships; it would probably serve the purpose of separating the chief of party from others. In California such a test is given by the joint employer-union committee to determine those qualified to be certified far the chief-of-party rating.

In a few of the States, such as Indiana, a SIT-type examination is given to test a *broad area of knowledge beyond* that given in the usual land surveyors examination; it is nearly or is equivalent to the EIT test. If the land surveyor expects to be permitted to design improvement plans, including water, sewer, paving, drainage, grades, curbs and sidewalks, he must be prepared to be examined in those subjects. In California, where the land surveyor is the only one who can advertise as a photogrammetrist or a geodesist, he must expect to be proficient and tested in those areas.

At the present time, within my knowledge, there are four States that have a definition of land surveying which goes well beyond that of the narrow practice of merely locating and describing land boundaries. In each of those States, the first day of examination is usually devoted to fundamentals, as electricity (for electronic measuring and computing devices), physics, light (refraction, speed, wave lengths, etc.), elasticity (strength of a tape), and many other scientific principles. As the knowledge of land surveying expands, it can be expected that the area of testing will expand.

The concept of dividing the professional examination into two levels, that of testing at the technician level on the first day and the professional level on the second day, is without merit. The question, "Is the examinee being tested for technical or for professional competence?" should set the thought to rest.

The concept of having one day or part of one day of the test with closed books and the second day with open books has same, but not too much, merit.

Open Book vs Closed Book Examinations. The purpose of a closed book examination is to test a person's knowledge of common, well-known laws of science, mathematics, techniques, and other fundamental areas of knowledge that should be recalled purely from memory. If trigonometric functions or other constants are necessary in solutions, they are furnished.

Questions asked when open books are permitted are usually complex; they are designed with the thought that the answer required cannot be copied directly from a book. Such a question as "write a legal description of the property shown on the above drawing," cannot be answered by looking at or reading a book. Requiring an application of knowledge from numerous sources and requiring thinking is the key to composing open book questions.

In closed book examinations, *time* is not an important issue. The examinee either knows the answer to the question, or he cannot answer it. Liberal time can be allotted. But in an open book examination, *time* is a part of the testing tool. If a person is given sufficient time and an open book, he will eventually be able an answer any question. "How do you set the center of section 6?" can be answered by reading from *The Manual of Instructions*; but if time is cut short, the person who must open a book to find the answer will not have time to get complete credit. Open book questions should be regulated to give the examinee sufficient time to look up an occasional function, formula, or odd fact not usually memorized, but not much more.

Closed book examinations are liberal with time, require basic knowledge, and usually test facts the examinee should be expected to know from memory. Open book examinations are designed so that the answers to questions usually require thinking plus the application of knowledge from numerous sources.

Scope of Examinations. The following list has been used by various examiners as a check list for examination questions. This list is only partial where the registration law extends beyond the narrow band of boundary line determination.

The first day consists of: elementary physics; mathematics exclusive of calculus; trigonometric solutions of surveying problems; solution of triangles; properties of circles; intersection of curves; intersection of a curve and straight line; vertical curves; differences in elevation and corrections for earth's curvature; use of rectangular coordinates; use of Lambert or Mercator grids; convergence and observation of the meridians; ratio and proportions; theory of probability and least squares; evaluation of errors; expansion and contraction of solids with change in temperature; Hook's law; properties of lenses; theory of measurements; measurement of distances and differences in elevation; subsurface measurements; measurement of angles and directions; traversing; latitudes and departures; location of points and lines; referencing points; note taking; stadia for distance measurement; use of coordinates; mapping; use of plane table; measurements and calculations for area; uses and adjustments of surveying instruments; hydrographic surveys; subtense bar; three-point problem; radio waves and light waves to measure distances; elementary chemistry; elementary geology (necessary in land planning); construction surveying; magnetometric surveys.

From this list it is obvious that the first day is devoted to *exact* sciences; the element of judgment is usually reserved for questions on the second day test. Each question or instruction given on this portion of the test is usually short; many questions over a broad area are given. It is an objective test requiring thinking.

The second day consists of: Property descriptions; writing descriptions; metes and bounds descriptions; principle of excess and deficiency; subdivision platting; planning; determination of the meridian; relative importance of conflicting elements; problems of boundary retracement; riparian rights; accretion; adverse possession; easements; harmonizing calls; meaning of wording in deeds and descriptions; dedication; liability of surveyors; State and Federal statutes; decisions of State Supreme Courts; sectionalized land system; mining claims; evidence and the law of evidence; professional practices of surveyors; authority, duties and responsibilities of surveyors; ethics; all laws and subject matter peculiar to surveyors in a particular State; State plane coordinates; electronic computers, electronic measurements, geodesy.

This area of the examination extends into inexact sciences; many of the questions are legal elements, a relative science. Often the element of judgment enters and essay questions should be freely used.

Comments on Grading Papers. The grader of examinations has no problem with those candidates who have a high score or a low score; the difficulty is to determine those with minimum qualifications. In considering the question of grading papers, the NCSBEE (National Council of State Board of Engineering Examiners) presented a ten - point grading plan which, with some modifications, can be adapted to the grading of any surveying question. A grading plan that must be adapted to both mathematical and essay problems must be stated in descriptive terms, and the grader must adapt the plan to a particular problem or question. This list is of considerable value because it illustrates the thinking of qualified men. In the following list the word "engineering" was changed to "surveying" and a few minor adjustments were made to better adapt the grading plan to land surveying. The grades extend from 10 (perfect) to zero (no credit).

10. Understands problems and obtains correct solution. Well organized; shows good surveying judgment, and perhaps ingenuity. Demonstrates knowledge of the fundamental principles.

9. Same as 10, but with a more routine approach, displays less judgment. Excessive conservatism in choice of variables, such as allowable errors.

8. Only errors introduced by hastiness; misread tables or minor mathematical errors, or thematic errors. Errors would be caught by routine checking. Results reasonable, though not correct.

7. Shows knowledge of how to obtain solution, but chooses poor approach. Difficult to follow reasoning, in spite of reasonable result. Awkward solution.

6. Same as 7, but with additional difficulty due to numerical mistakes. Problem partially solved or partially answered.

5. Method in error, deviates from intent of problem, but pursuit of erroneous method shows clear thinking and good surveying knowledge.

4. Shows some knowledge of this type of problem, but only vague approach. Probably incomplete solution. Results may be unreasonable, showing this area has been forgotten. Has been more successful in other problems.

3. Approach entirely wrong, results unreasonable, good organization, but misdirected.

2. Does not have good organization to recommend it. A few correct factual statements.

1. Minor factual correctness.

And in all examinations the final grade is influenced by the neatness of the examinee. It must be recognized that he is pressed for time; it cannot be expected that papers shall be letter perfect.

Examinee's Point of View. After taking a long and difficult examination, the examinee is apt to feel that the sole object of the test is to flunk as many as possible; this is far from the truth. Competent, qualified people are always a welcome addition to a profession; without new qualified men, within a few years, the profession would cease to exist. But this does not mean that the test should be so easy that the unqualified may practice. Licensing is a serious step. The State certifies as to the proficiency of the licensee, and the people of the State have a right to expect that all licensees are qualified people. Issuance of licenses to the unqualified only serves to deceive the people; a client is charged for a service that the licensee is unqualified to render.

Failing an unqualified person is doing that person a favor. If a person is licensed to do professional work, and he errs in doing so, he is liable for many years to come. The cost of erroneous work may bring him financial ruin and undue hardship upon the client. It is better to require that the surveyor study more before he commences practice than it is to let him learn by costly mistakes at the expense of an innocent client.

The objective of the examination is to do justice to both the examinee and the public.

Availability of Examinations. California has the best policy with respect to past examinations. Anyone who will supply the cost of reproduction will be furnished a copy. Every examinee may have the benefit of all old examinations. This policy necessitates the making of a new test every year; the tests are quite variable in content. One thing is certain, the examinee never knows what will be asked, but he does know that he must study in a wide area.

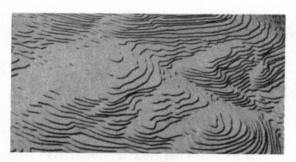

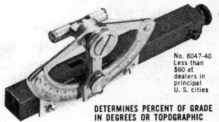

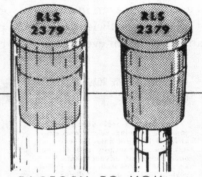

In some States, the examinee is not permitted to take the questions out of the test room, and he is sometimes made to sign a statement that he will not disclose or discuss the contents with anyone. This situation is probably created by a lack of funds to prepare a new set of questions after every examination. But is this really a test at all? Assuming that a person is perfectly honest, all he has to do is go home, sit down, write out all the questions asked, study the subject matter, and on the next test write on the same questions. Why any board of registration makes such a farce out of a surveyor's examination is beyond comprehension. The surveyor's field of practice is sufficiently broad to preclude the necessity of repeating the same question or even the same type of question.

Comments on Examinations. The variation of the subject matter and the quality of the land surveyor's examination is extreme; some tests are difficult while others are ridiculously simple; some tests are broad in scope, others are narrow.

Perhaps the best procedure would be to divide surveyor examinations into three State groups as follows:

These States requiring a broad educational foundation in the sciences plus special knowledge in land surveying, and also testing in any of the following: geodesy, design of improvements, photogrammetry, and land planning.

Those States giving examinations at the professional level but limiting the subject matter to land location procedures, general surveying (including construction staking or limited design of improvements), and land planning.

Those States giving examinations at the technician level and limiting the subject to the practice of locating and describing property (sometimes including planning).

Within the first group are Indiana, Ohio, California, New York, and possibly one or two others. Last year New York passed a new act upgrading the land surveyor qualifications; a copy of the new examination was not reviewed. Not all of these States give tests commensurate with their statutory requirements.

Of the remaining States, less than half of those whose examinations were reviewed gave tests sufficiently difficult to be classified above that of the technician level. Some were of good quality.

Professional standing must be earned; it cannot be attained by self proclamation. The standing of land surveyors in this country must rise or fall with the quality of its members. If the public thinks that land surveyors as a group have superior knowledge, have professional behavior, and deserve to be considered professional people, only then will they be such.

Of all things that will shape the future standing of land surveyors, the quality of new members being admitted to practice is of paramount importance. This can be regulated by critical discrimination in the process of screening candidates and by improving the quality of examinations so that those unqualified will not be permitted to practice.

Those preparing examinations can benefit their profession by composing questions that go beyond the horizon of mere factual knowledge and test candidates ability to think, to use logic and reason, to come to correct conclusions, to demonstrate good judgment, and to effectively communicate all of these to the grader. Tests should be extended into the areas of photogrammetry, electronic measurement, electronic calculations, and some elementary geodesy.

The most severe criticism of examinations is the failure to test newer areas of knowledge and to test beyond the technician level.

Most boards of registration already have the power to determine what the scope of examinations should be. By a mere declaration of policy, better examinations can be given; and, where this is possible, it is hoped the boards will do so.

****

Mountain . . .
Tideland . . .
Rolling Country . . .
City or Town

GEODIMETER IS MASTER OF ANY TERRAIN

The fastest, most accurate way to measure distances . . . anywhere . . . is with a Geodimeter.

Engineers and surveyors throughout the world, using Geodimeters, report unbelievable savings in time and money on both routine and difficult surveys.

Now the Model 4 Geodimeter adds easy portability and low initial cost to well established records of complete reliability and accuracy.

Write for complete data on Geodimeter Systems

The GEODIMETER Co.

Division of
AGA Corp. of America

SOUTH PLAINFIELD
NEW JERSEY

THE FEASIBILITY OF A TECHNOLOGY PROGRAM IN SURVEYING AND MAPPING

BY: CURTIS M. BROWN * AND KENNETH S. CURTIS **

DECEMBER 1965

The papers presented at the ACSM annual meetings have adequately proven the need for surveyor engineer graduates and have dramatically called attention to the deficiencies in surveyor engineer education in the United States. Professor Curtis in a recent paper, *The Case of the Missing Curriculum*, [1] has rather completely discussed the lack of a suitable four-year curriculum in surveying and mapping (geometronics). Professor Arthur J. McNair [2], who recently made a study of the education of surveyor engineers in Europe, forcefully pointed out the disparity between United States surveyor education and that of Europe.

We as surveyors must face up to the fact that surveyor education within the United States is woefully inadequate. Historically, surveyor engineer education has been a part of civil engineering. Quoting from Professor McNair's paper, "In 1937 the average number of required semester hours of surveying courses in civil engineering curricula was 14.3. By 1948, required surveying courses averaged 11.3 semester hours. In 1958, the average was down to 7.7 semester hours. In 1964 the average amount of surveying required in the civil engineering curriculum is estimated to be approximately 5 semester hours."

We should not quarrel with the civil engineer's prerogative to decide for himself what he thinks is proper training for graduates. However, the fact remains that the deletion of surveying courses has created a void in the surveyor engineer education within the United States. Surveyors should not bemoan the loss of standing within the civil engineering department, rather they should apply every effort to answer the question, "Where should surveying education be housed within the colleges of the United States"?

One of the surveyor's areas of educational neglect has been geodesy. The recent accent on space travel created a need for superior students. At Ohio State University, geodesy was given a home in the geology department; today a separate geodetic science department has established itself as the outstanding geodesy school within the United States. Should the surveyors of the United States profit by this example and try to establish a separate four-year surveying school? According to European thinking, this thought must have much merit; practically all major European universities do have separate surveyor colleges. Canada has two such curricula in universities. Could it be that the United States is out of step and the remainder of the world is correct?

Within the last few years, the surveyor has been the subject of a controversy; does he or does he not belong as a part of civil engineering? Even though the civil engineering final viewpoint was that surveying is a part of civil engineering, the offerings of surveying education within civil engineering has and is constantly being decreased. Further, the ECPD accreditation procedures for United States colleges has almost precluded the possibility of an acceptable four-year surveying curriculum being established within the sphere of civil engineering.

In studying the relationship of the surveyor to other engineering disciplines, it can be readily conceded that in some respects the surveyor engineer is most closely related to civil engineering. However, in many other respects he is not. In the ECPD accrediting procedure, which all important universities follow, is the statement:

"Qualitative criteria (of engineering) shall include the following: . . . The extent to which the curriculum develops the distinguishing characteristic of the engineer -- *ability to design*, recognized in its broadest sense by the committee to be the ability to apply creatively scientific principles to design or develop structures, machines, apparatus, or manufacturing processes, or works utilizing them singly or in combination; or to construct or operate the same with full cognizance of their design, and of the limitations of behavior imposed by such operating conditions; all as respects as intended function, economics of operation, and safety to life and property. This definition forms part of the committee's statement, *Differentiation Characteristics of an Engineering Curriculum.*" From this definition, it is obvious that the guidelines of the ECPD accreditation is based upon "the ability to design."

Surveying is more of a science than a design problem. In the determination of a position on the face of the earth or in space, the surveyor uses laws of science and measuring devices to record things as they are; he does not design the position. In preparing maps the cartographer reproduces to a miniature scale the surface of the earth as it exists; he does not design the earth. To be sure, there is some design in surveying and mapping but not nearly to the extent found in designing structures. In general, surveying and mapping has been and probably will be treated as a supporting engineering science that an engineer must acquire to accomplish other more important design ends. From the viewpoint of the civil engineer, this is probably correct; from the viewpoint of the surveyor, it is unacceptable. The modest surveying science education offered does not fill the surveyor's needs. The two-year technical institutes cannot possibly train and educate for professional surveying and mapping either.

The greatest deficiency in the education of the land surveyor is in the area of boundary law and land planning. At Purdue University, a teaching position in this area has been offered. As is the policy of most universities, the qualification established was a Ph.D. and training in land location procedures. As yet, the position has not been filled. Quoting from Professor McNair's paper:

"There is a considerable demand on the part of universities in the United States for men with graduate degree in surveying to enter teaching . . . From the statistics given, it is perfectly obvious that there are not and will not soon be prospective professors produced in the United States with Ph.D. degrees, which is what colleges now demand. The one area of surveying which is in the least tenable position is that of land surveying. There is almost no one taking studies or performing research in land surveying in the United States. Those who receive their education in land surveying in other countries have an extremely difficult time adapting to United States' legal practices, so importing foreigners is not the answer."

Many explanations are presented for this most deplorable situation. The time for offering excuses and explanations has expired; today we are interested in what can be done to correct an unacceptable situation. Our concern should be action, not further discussion. It is obvious that the education of the surveyor is deteriorating while the need is increasing. If the civil engineering department cannot adequately educate the surveyor, is it not logical to try to have a separate surveyor four-year school established? Such a curriculum should include geodesy, cartography, photogrammetry and land surveying. The enclosed chart shows the interrelationship of these disciplines with civil engineering. Time will preclude further discussion of this chart.

In some areas of surveying the fault of educational deficiencies must rest squarely upon the surveyors themselves; this is particularly true with respect to licensed surveyors. Within the United States, there are only four states that have registration requirements equivalent to a college education. Most states require a high school diploma plus passing a written examination. After reading many licensed surveyor examinations, it can only be concluded from their simplicity that the majority of land surveyors do not need a college education to become qualified. Why should the colleges offer training where the practicing surveyors are willing to accept substandard education?

Most state laws should be changed to upgrade the educational requirements; recently this was done in both Indiana and New York. As a result of the Indiana law requiring the land surveyor to have the equivalent education of that obtained by a four-year curriculum in civil engineering with a major in land surveying, Purdue University added a master's program option in land surveying.

In attempting to change a state law to upgrade the educational requirements of the surveyor, a technical difficulty exists; the registration law cannot say that the education shall be equivalent to a four-year college curriculum in land surveying; no such curriculum exists. This is like the old argument - which should be first, the chicken or the egg? If the law is changed, colleges will meet the demand.

In California, the solution to date has been mainly to increase the examination difficulty to that which could be expected of a college graduate in surveying. This procedure is available to many boards of registration under existing state laws; it is hoped that the right will be exercised.

Recently at Purdue University, a School of Technology was created. The feasibility of housing a surveying curriculum within such a school is being studied. If approved, most of the surveying instruction would probably be offered within the civil engineering department. Training in mathematics, cartography, science, etc., would be in other schools.

In general, civil engineering departments will object to granting civil engineering degrees over weighted in surveying subjects, such as geodesy, photogrammetry, cartography and land surveying, at the expense of courses in sanitation, structures, etc. Also, accreditation procedures probably preclude such possibilities. On the other hand, a School of Technology, which is dedicated to the practical and to the application of theory, would appear to be an ideal solution. Surveying is a long and honorable profession for which no man should have to apologize. With the new measuring devices such as the aerial camera, electrotape, tellurometer, and geodimeter; with the new and difficult projects such as mapping the moon; with electronic calculations; with the ever-increasing difficulties of laws regulating boundaries, and with the complexities of land planning, photogrammetry and the geoid, there is ample room for a college curriculum in surveying or geometronics. One man could not master all of these subjects in a lifetime.

Where a school of surveying is housed is immaterial; the establishment of such a curriculum is imperative. The civil engineering departments by their past performance have decreased surveying education to a negligible point; it is not expected that the trend will be reversed. If it is necessary to have a surveying school created to adequately educate surveyors, let us do so.

RECOMMENDATIONS

1. That the ACSM make every effort to encourage the establishment of at least one school of surveying in some university under a separate department.

2. That every state land surveyor organization actively and vigorously attempt to change the legal requirements for surveyor education to *the equivalent education that can be obtained by graduating from a four-year college surveying course.*

APPENDIX

Possible Curriculum in Surveying and Mapping (Geometronics) Technology

Freshman and Sophomore Years:

Common engineering program
Mathematics
Physics
Chemistry
Graphics
Statics and Mechanics

Numeral Analysis and Computers
English and Speech
Basic Engineering Surveying or a Summer Surveying Camp

Junior Year:

Astronomy
Elements of Civil Engineering
    (Routes, Highways, Traffic)
Land Surveying
Cartographic Surveying
    (Topography, Hydrography)
Theory of Errors and Adjustments
Non-technical Elective

Geology
Elements of Municipal Engineering
    (Hydraulics and Sanitary)
Property Law
Photogrammetry
Geodetic Control Surveying
Non-technical Elective

Senior Year:

Airphoto Interpretation
Cartography and Map Projections
City Planning
Advanced Photogrammetry
Engineering & Geodetic Astronomy
Non-technical Elective

Geophysics
Contracts and Specifications
Subdivision Design
Electronic Surveying
Geodesy
Non-technical Elective

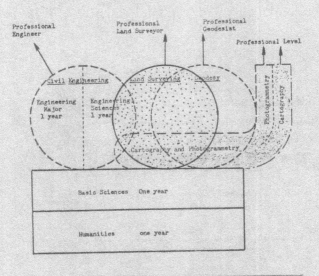

LAND SURVEYOR'S EDUCATIONAL NEEDS AS RELATED TO OTHER PROFESSIONS

* These subjects are listed primarily to show the general content of such a curriculum. Much discussion and consultation would be necessary before a final curriuclum could be decided upon. A program should be designed which would provide education toward a professional career as a land surveyor, surveyor engineer, geodetic surveyor, topographer, hydrographer, photogrammetrist, geodesist, cartographer, control surveyor, or cadastral surveyor.

Presented at the 1964 Regional Convention of the American Congress on Surveying and Mapping, Kansas City, Missouri, September 24-26, 1964.

* President of the American Congress on Surveying and Mapping and Consulting Land Surveyor, San Diego, California.

** Professor, School of Civil Engineering, Purdue University, Lafayette, Indiana.

[1] *Journal of the Surveying and Mapping Division,* A.S.C.E., Paper No. 3963, July 1964, Vol. 90, No. SU2, pp. 27-48.

[2] Presented at the 24th Annual meeting of the American Congress on Surveying and Mapping, Washington, D.C., March 16-19, 1964.

****

1965 Geometronics Institute

A Summer Institute in Geometronics supported by the National Science Foundation was held at Purdue University, Lafayette, Indiana, from June 20 to August 14, 1965. Twenty-six college teachers participated in the institute and came from colleges and universities throughout the United States, with one participant from Canada and one from Mexico. Two additional practicing surveyors attended at their own expense. The purpose of the institute, the third consecutive one supported by N.S.F., was to advance the theoretical training and strengthen the background of surveying and mapping teachers in the areas of geodesy, photogrammetry, electronic surveying, and boundary location. The geodetic surveying course was taught by Professor K. S. Curtis, Purdue University, assisted by Professor L. A. Kivioja and L. M. Ganoung of Purdue. The electronic surveying course was taught by Professor R. C. Gunn, University of Toronto, and the boundary location course by Curtis M. Brown, San Diego, California, president of ACSM. The photogrammetry course was taught by Professor S. A. Veres, Purdue University, assisted by Emil Homick. The airphoto interpretation course was taught by Professor R. D. Miles, Purdue University, assisted by Harold Rib. The eight-week institute featured a series of guest seminar speakers including Eldridge, Konecny, Woodson, Quinn, Laurila, Doyle, Hoffer and Colcord. Professor Curtis served as director of the institute.

1. Robert Larson, Blue Mountain Comm. College, Oreg.
2. Lincoln Ganoung, Purdue University (staff)
3. Emil Homick, Purdue University (staff)
4. Kenneth Lahr, Trinidad State Jr. College, Colo.
5. Richard Ray, Cent. Florida Jr. College
6. Vincent Forss, Lafayette College, Penn.
7. Philip Newlin, University of Arizona
8. Paul Wolf, University of Wisconsin
9. John Hunter, Virginia Polytechnic Institute
10. Al Quinn, Penn. (visiting seminar speaker)
11. Sandor Veres, Purdue University (staff)
12. Lassi Kivioja, Purdue University (staff)
13. John Nutt, University of Pittsburgh
14. Joseph Ricci, Cleveland
15. Mallie Aldred, Middle Georgia College
16. Ronald Rule, U. S. Air Force Academy, Colo.
17. Joseph Gust, Southern Colorado State College
18. Leo Dunham, University of Maine
19. Allen Ellingson, Green Bay School of V & AE, Wis.
20. Walter Hannan, Wisconsin State University
21. Robert Miles, Purdue University (staff)
22. Robert Gunn, University of Toronto (staff)
23. Hector Qutroga-Garza, Tech. Inst. of Monterrey
24. James Root, University of Vermont
25. Robert Johnson, Ferris State College, Mich.
26. Porter McDonnell, Penn. State Univ.—Mont Alto
27. Richard Hauck, Pasadena City College
28. Robert Douglass, Penn. State Univ.—Mont Alto
29. Derle Thorpe, Utah State University
30. Norman Brown, Missouri School of Mines
31. Martin Yez, El Camino College, Calif.
32. John Shuler, North Carolina State University
33. Curtis Brown, San Diego, Calif. (staff)
34. Harold Rib, Purdue University (staff)
35. Kenneth Curtis, Purdue University (staff)
36. James Brower, Wingate College, N. C.

Absent when picture was taken because of illness—Richard Thompson, Ryerson Polytechnical Institute.

COMMENT AND DISCUSSION

EDUCATION FOR SURVEYORS

MARCH 1966

W. G. G. BLAKNEY - The December 1965 issue of SURVEYING AND MAPPING had two articles recommending certain approaches that should insure the proper education of surveyors, an announcement of surveying education offered at Pennsylvania State University and one advertisement of a position of leadership in surveying instruction at Iowa State University.

One can hardly find fault with the editors of SURVEYING AND MAPPING for not giving the problem of surveying education the attention it deserves, but one need only look at the four entries to decide that such a dissimilar array of situations merits more discussion and, better still, action.

The advertisement tells that a person is needed for course leadership in surveying and photogrammetry for a four-year Civil Engineering program and a two-year Construction Technology program. A new first course in photogrammetry and a shifting emphasis of the surveying program are proposed.

Pennsylvania offers two paths to an education in surveying and mapping. One is the four-year Civil Engineering program and the other is a two-year program leading to an Associate Degree, the latter offering 33 hours in subjects related to surveying, the former ten hours related to surveying.

An article by J. E. Colcord of the University of Washington outlines in detail the course offerings within the Civil Engineering Department.

The Bachelor's Degree may be obtained with one course in Geometronics (Surveying). Students particularly interested in this field may take two electives, neither of which contains route or construction surveys. A Master's Degree may be obtained by taking several other surveying courses.

An article by C. M. Brown and K. S. Curtis was a general review of surveying education, with particular attention to the question as to who should teach surveying. By quoting reduced surveying courses in civil engineering departments, inspecting practices in foreign countries and checking guides used for accrediting engineering curricula, an impressive case is made for taking surveying out of engineering. The principal recommendation made is that "ACSM make every effort to encourage the establishment of at least one school in some university under a separate department." In developing this recommendation, it is stated that "the two-year technical institutes cannot possibly train and educate for professional surveying and mapping" and queried "is it not logical to try to have a separate four-year school established"?

Of course, the intent of the two-year courses is to provide good skilled technicians who do not desire to become professional land surveyors, reflecting the recommendation of the ASCE Board of Directors. There is a clear danger here, though; that the requirements for registration in many states is thereby met and that the profession of land surveying will eventually be largely conducted by these people. The other statement concerning separate four-year schools does seem to fly in the face of their observation that Ohio State is administered by a department separate from Civil Engineering.

It would also seem that a four-year program in surveying would leave little in the way of course requirements for an M.Sc. and a Ph.D. degree. This must be true or else Cornell, Princeton, the University of Illinois and the University of California are not giving their Ph.D. candidates the course work they should get. Those that advocate a four-year program while insisting that more Ph.D.'s are needed should offer a tentative curriculum outlining the courses that would occupy seven years of study. Inasmuch as they will likely have to go back to Civil Engineering for many of the problems that motivate surveying, we may as well stay closely associated with that discipline in the first place (Civil Engineering).

There is one other item mentioned of common concern, it being the dearth of instruction in land surveying. It is strange that a Ph.D. is sought by universities to teach boundary law and land surveying when there is likely not a school that would give credit towards a Ph.D. for such a course. Perhaps land planning offers material for credit toward the Ph.D. degree, but then one is back in design work, which is the engineering area being avoided. It may be that there is not as much that can be taught about land surveying at the university as is implied. After the student has been exposed to the "order of calls" and 100 legal precedents, the 101st may well observe yet another combination of points of evidence. Therefore, we have to eventually depend on *judgment* of the surveyor, an item not easily taught in the classroom. It is even difficult to really convey the idea that evidence *could* supersede a system of numbers appearing on a deed.

There may be something in the observation that the United States has almost a unique capacity to react properly to supply and demand. This may suggest that the U. S. system of six universities offering Ph.D. degrees in surveying -- some science or discipline oriented and some engineering or mission oriented -- are closely reflecting the demand for trained personnel.

The other recommendation made in this last article was "that every state land surveyor organization . . . attempt to change the legal requirements for surveyor education to the equivalent education that can be obtained by graduating from a four-year college surveying course." This seems to be oriented in a direction where something should and can be done. Or is it too late now that two-year survey courses are in vogue? It may not be too late; anyway, the public's acceptance of surveyors will likely not be any more enthusiastic than its acceptance of chiropractors until rigid requirements are established by the states for those wishing to offer services to the public. It seems reasonable that four years of college containing one or two courses in surveying plus a written exam should come close to guaranteeing a competence to practice.

In conclusion, it appears that the two-year programs are filling the need for survey technicians and that the schools offering graduate programs are nearly sufficient to fill the need at various professional levels. But it does seem important that the Education Committee of ACSM reach a consensus as to what requirements should be recommended for those making application for registration as land surveyors. That ACSM make those findings known to all registration boards and that ACSM make these views known to all state land surveyor organizations with the recommendation that representation be made to state legislatures for legal adoption.

****

BACHELOR OF SCIENCE DEGREE WITH MAJOR IN SURVEYING AT THE UNIVERSITY OF MINNESOTA

BY CURTIS M. BROWN

SEPTEMBER 1966

PROFESSOR Jesse E. Fant, University of Minnesota, recently pointed out that he has a student majoring in Surveying at the University College of the University of Minnesota. The concept of University College is as follows:

The College has no prescribed curriculum, no requirements regarding a field of concentration, nor stated number of credit hours in a given subject. Courses taken by students may be selected from any of the other colleges and schools if such courses are appropriate to the student's objective and he is eligible to take them. The University College student must satisfy the prerequisites and admission policies that apply for any student in a given course. It is not possible for the College office to answer in terms of specific courses such questions as: "What are the requirements for obtaining a degree through University College"? "What courses or program must I choose in order to be admitted to University College"? Each student follows a program designed to fulfill his particular purposes.

The total number of credits required for a degree is at least equal to the number required in the college in which the student takes the greater part of his work. In no case is the number less than 190 (quarter system). Quality credits are not counted. The grade point average on work done at the University of Minnesota must be at least 2.00 (C) overall and on Upper

Division courses determined separately. Ordinarily approximately one-half of the courses must be of Upper Division level. Often a student will need to take additional Lower Division courses as prerequisites to the work planned in Upper Division courses and sometimes the courses taken previous to admission to University College do not contribute to the objectives in University College; hence, the total number of credit hours will often be considerably more than the minimum required. A degree is not granted merely on the basis of completion of a given number of courses.

The degree earned may be Bachelor of Arts or Bachelor of Science depending on the individual program. No other degrees are granted.

Students who have satisfactorily completed some work at the University of Minnesota may request admission to University College by completing an application form on which they state their objective in college, the courses they have taken, and all the courses they propose to take in earning a degree. In completing this application, they may seek advice from staff members of the University College office regarding particular courses and the best program for their objective. To be admitted, the student must have a definite objective that requires a type of program that may not lead to a degree in another college. The student may, for example, wish to take courses in the School of Business Administration and the Institute of Technology that are not acceptable as a part of the requirements for a degree from the College of Science, Literature and the Arts. A program proposed by the student will be reviewed by members of the University College Committee or other selected staff members. If it is deemed worthy of a degree and permits the student to attain his stated objective, he is admitted to University College.

Ordinarily it will not be necessary to enter University College before the end of the fifth or sixth quarter since basic Lower Division courses in English, mathematics, natural sciences, social sciences, and the humanities, and other courses that will serve as a foundation for almost any later work, may be obtained in one of the colleges accepting freshmen. To be admitted to University College the student must have demonstrated that he can do college work satisfactorily.

University College is not a device whereby students may avoid a particular requirement of one of the other colleges and still retain objectives similar to those of the students in the college from which they transfer or in which they take the majority of their work. It is for those students who know what they want in the college years and cannot attain their objectives through registration in another college. The resources of a great university are available to them through University College.

Under this system, it is possible, and at least one student is doing so, to have a program proposed and approved with a major in Land Surveying. By selecting a "logical sequences of courses," a minor in Land Planning or other related area can also be taken. Here are some of the subjects possible: The usual English, calculus, analytic geometry, chemistry, physics, mechanics, heat and electricity, sound, light, history, etc., and Land Surveying, photogrammetry, Land Planning, Subdivision design, highways and pavements, hydrology, water supply, soil mechanics, graphics, contracts and specifications, geodesy, geometronics, Your Land (titles and legal elements of land location), coordinate surveys, electronic surveys, electronic computations, etc. By such a system, a study in structures can be omitted in favor of more essential needs in related land use subjects such as government and sociology.

The degree granted is not labeled "BS in Land Surveying," but this is a breakthrough in working toward a four-year baccalaureate degree. Professor Fant deserves support in orienting students to the college. Why not a scholarship?

****

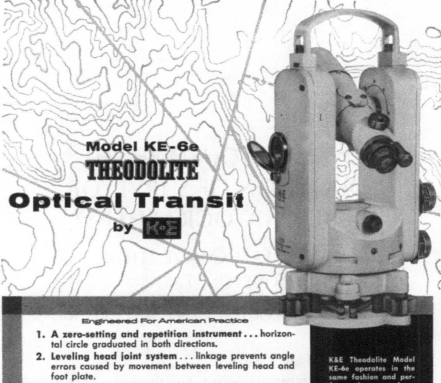

WHAT SHOULD BE THE EDUCATION OF SURVEYORS AND CARTOGRAPHERS?

ASCM FALL CONVENTION HOUSTON, TEXAS

OCTOBER 1966

Anyone can recommend and advise as to how things should be, especially if there are probably many correct answers. For years people have debated, "What is the best method of educating others"? Many say this, and many say that. From the results of tried methods, it can be concluded that there is no one best way. Five hunters taking different paths will flush out far more game than five hunters taking the same path. Lincoln got his education at home; others need to go to college.

Those engaged within the discipline of geometronics come from many paths. Dr. Rolland Hardy in his national report to F. I. G. (published in the ACSM journal, June 1965) points out that within the United States surveying area there are essentially two educational paths: (1) The engineering path. (2) The science path. To this, I would like to add the school of technology, which will be discussed later.

Because surveying was at one time most closely associated with engineering, brief mention of recent developments in engineering education should be presented.

The *"Goals of Engineering Education,"* the preliminary report, was published a few months ago through the efforts of the American Society of Engineering Education. In this report, among other items, it was recommended that the first professional engineering degree be at the master's level. Since the publication of that report, a constant argument on the pros and cons of this and that goal in engineering education has come forth; the very volume and volatility of the arguments prove that few, if any, can convince others what is the correct path for engineering education or even what are the correct aims.

The way-outers envision that ultimately, engineers should be like doctors, they should have four years' training in fundamentals, three years training in engineering subjects and, I suppose, three years' internship. And since those who are pushing the concept seem to be deans of important universities, they may have the power to put the wheels in motion.

The intermediate view expressed by the recent report on "Goals of Engineering Education," that of a master's degree being the first professional degree, is within striking distance, and I believe this will come about in the due course of time whether we like it or not. The American Society of Civil Engineers is strongly behind this move. Unlike doctors, by far the largest percentage of engineers are employees. Whether the employer will be willing to accept this concept remains to be seen.

Many educators believe that engineering and all related subjects to engineering should be based upon a foundation of fundamental sciences, mathematics and humanities, and, as a result, the former teachings of the application of knowledge to devices is being set aside because of time limitations. In large universities, it is true that engineering has become more and more science and humanities oriented and less and less directed towards the application of sciences to industry.

UNI-GRAVER
TRADE MARK

UNI-DOTTER
TRADE MARK

SCRIBING INSTRUMENT
for paint-coated
plates

FOR MAPS ENGRAVED
ON COATED PLASTIC
SHEETS

The UNI-GRAVER employs either needles or flat blades in an interchangeable adapter (Pat. No. 2,735,177, 2,735,178, 2,782,501). Constructed of nickel-plated brass with wrinkled finish, it is fitted with a Bausch & Lomb 2" focal length optic, adjustable at any position.

The manually-operated UNI-DOTTER is designed to mechanically engrave dot symbols, both uniform and clear, for maps engraved on coated plastic sheets. Pat. #2,825,136. It is manufactured of nickel-plated brass with wrinkled finish and mounted on a plastic base.

All Instruments Guaranteed Unconditionally For Workmanship And Materials

See our Catalog for details on the various adaptations of the UNI-GRAVER, the UNI-DOTTER and the fine-line UNI-PENS and for new lowered prices.

UNIVERSAL INSTRUMENT CO. • 3807-11 Bunker Hill Road, Brentwood, Md. • WA 7-8957

Engineering colleges are resisting the tendency to offer numerous undergraduate engineering degree courses. Why should they offer sanitary, highway, hydraulic, structural and other options within civil engineering? Why not have everyone take the same fundamentals and then specialize at the master's level? Why offer a baccalaureate degree in surveying and mapping? Why not an M.S. as thirteen universities are now doing? Thus, specialization is moving to the graduate level.

At one time civil engineering included electrical, chemical, mining and mechanical engineering. Since their departure from civil engineering, some have grown larger in student enrollment than the parent subject. Civil engineering is now broken down into many so-called options. Despite all of the objections and all of the efforts to stop the spreading out of engineering subjects, today we find a wider selection of subjects than at any previous time in the history of education. Ceramic engineers, traffic engineers, transportation engineers, and industrial engineers are a few. My prediction is that despite all of the efforts to stop divergence of engineering in colleges, the process will continue as new needs arise, but the divergence will be at a higher grade level.

Where does this leave surveyors? As yet, within the United States no engineering college has ever offered a 4-year baccalaureate degree in surveying or geometronics. Two science schools have. In Canada, there are three. With this new developing philosophy in engineering education, will the surveyors' chances of inducing a college to offer such a curriculum be improved, or will it be an impossible task?

The decline of surveying in universities is directly attributable to accreditation. Accreditation has done more to stereotype engineering education than anything else; everyone marches to the same tune. Word was released to the accreditation team that surveying education for engineers was to be cut back, and it soon was. We have seen the results.

The variations between different engineering colleges is becoming less and less, and the determination to completely stamp out surveying as a part of engineering seems to be one of the particular objectives of most accreditation committees. ACSM has an education committee attempting to evaluate offerings in surveying and mapping. In a reply from the western university as to whether it was still teaching its four courses in surveying, this was received: "Yes, the courses are still offered and the number of students enrolled last semester were 80, 61, 47, and 23. No curriculum is being planned with emphasis on surveying and mapping. In fact, ECPD accreditation committee last spring requested that credits be reduced. Catalog of 1968 will probably see not over 2 courses in surveying."

The Shortest Distance From The Field To Your Seal On The Plat Is Through Hewlett-Packard Surveying Systems.

Worth Looking Into!

This reflects what has happened and is happening at most civil engineering colleges; surveying has been cut out, not because of a lack of demand, but because of the opinion of accreditation committees.

At the present time accreditation at the master's degree level does not exist, and some engineering colleges, wishing to continue education in the surveying area and realizing the need for education in this area, have offered master's programs. At the present time, 13 universities offer graduate degrees in the general geometronic area and 6 offer doctorate degrees. This is to be applauded - we need such universities to train educators capable of meeting present-day educational standards for professors. However, will such a program meet the needs for educated people in the private practice world of surveying and mapping? The reasons why it will not are obvious. A man who wants to be a surveyor by this program must first have a B.S. degree in engineering with a grade average well above the mean. Following this, he must spend another year to get an M.S. Personally, I have never met such a man in private surveying practice, and I believe it will be quite a few years before I will. The colleges simply do not graduate sufficient numbers to be of any significance to private practice.

Whenever one college deserts an area of need, another soon picks it up. Ohio State University in its department of Geology started a Mapping and Charting Research Laboratory under the direction of George Harding, our eighth president and also one of the founders of ACSM. It was followed by the Department of Geodetic Science within the college of Arts and Science.

The Geography Department of George Washington University, Washington, D.C. in 1959 established the United States' first degree of Bachelor of Science in Cartography. Later this was changed to a Bachelor of Science in Geodetic and Cartographic Science. Any students wanting an education in surveying or photogrammetry should consider these universities.

The science departments have moved into major areas of surveying and they are there to stay. As civil engineering becomes increasingly spread out, that is, requiring more and more studies in areas totally unrelated to specific objectives, more students will be attracted to more direct objectives in the science area.

At Purdue University, and at a few other universities, the need for educated people in a narrower band of knowledge is being recognized. The degree being offered and talked about is not a second-rate degree; it is superior to the education that most of us received at the university some years ago. The distinguishing characteristic is its aim to create a man with a good education in fundamentals channeled into a narrower field of application. Engineering colleges by the present projected aims will be trying to produce fewer but superior graduates with capabilities beyond the so-called technician status of present-day engineering graduates. By its very nature a minimum of six years' college training will be needed; whereas, a technology degree will require four years. In other words, if engineering moves to doctorate or even master's level objectives, the continuing need for 4-year engineering oriented graduates will be met by the school of technology or possibly in the schools of science.

Within this world, we need a lot more Indians than chiefs. We need a few doctorates, more master's degree holders, and many more technologists well trained in fundamentals. At Purdue, the technology concept is well on its way; if I remember correctly, it is the third largest college in this largest of all engineering universities. Other universities are following Purdue's lead. To be sure, the technology graduate will not be tagged with an engineering degree title, but the technology degree will be equivalent to the former 4-year degree you and I got at the university. If the truth were published, I believe that 90% of today's engineering graduates are working at a glorified technician's job, which is classified as professional by self-proclamation. Everyone must start somewhere, certainly not at the top, and only a few make it to the top.

My most serious criticism of the "Goals of Engineering Education" is the inference that a college degree leads automatically to professional standing. Why at the master's level? Why at any level? It is true that superior education in a field of knowledge is one of the requirements for a profession, but nothing in the rulebook says where or how the education shall be obtained. After a person gets his education, how he uses the education, and what his personal behavior is determines whether others will think of him as a professional man or not. Professional standing is something that is earned, and it cannot be bestowed upon a person by an act of the legislature or by the college. You can tell some people by their mortgages and others by their deeds. Many an educated man has fallen

by the wayside in the road towards true professional standing. Sometimes you find them in jail. Many claim professional standing; few have it. Some people grow, others swell. A claim to professional standing solely based upon a certain college degree is a lot of hogwash.

The question was asked whether the new goals of engineering education would improve the chances for a 4-year degree in surveying. My answer is yes, provided it is established in the school of technology or any other school which may or may not be closely related to engineering or may or may not he administered by the engineering department.

Dr. Hardy in his comments on Surveyor Education in the United States expressed an opinion that several colleges in the geometronic area would be established via the science school path as was done at Ohio State. His remarks were:

It becomes clear that for a proper education balance the United States should be graduating nearly 1,700 survey engineers with B.S. degrees each year.

Obviously something is vitally wrong with the United States approach to surveying and mapping education. Unfortunately, in this respect, certain negative results of the proprietary policy of the American Society of Civil Engineers must be reported. The most obvious defect is that in the system sponsored by the American Society of Civil Engineers, one must prepare himself to become a full-fledged civil engineer before he is permitted to become a survey engineer. To many of my European colleagues this approach will seem to be outdated and inefficient. It is. It is like asking a man to become a full-fledged physicist before he is permitted to study for a professional career in chemistry. This is the effect of the dual registration concept that exists nowhere else in the engineering profession. Why this concept should be continued indefinitely in the United States is a mystery that perhaps our civil engineering profession should be asked to explain. It is a historical fact that the civil engineering approach has never, during more than 50 years of experience with land surveyor registration laws, provided enough civil engineers who were simultaneously qualified and interested enough in survey engineering to satisfy the needs of land surveying. If so, there never would have been a need for the apprentice land surveyor system and low registration standards. There is nothing new in the upgraded dual registration concept or in the enrollment figures since 1959 that indicates that any significant source for land surveyors or survey engineers is being developed except by the apprentice system. A crisis of monstrous proportions actually exists. The myth that there is neither necessity or compatibility for both a complete civil engineering approach and an adequate survey engineering approach in the same undergraduate curriculum has persisted too long. The policy of ASCE as stated in 1959 would have been better served if it had held to a view that certain surveying and mapping categories are engineering, rather than to hold that they are civil engineering. The remedy is to simultaneously establish a separate engineering discipline in surveying and mapping at the undergraduate level and to establish survey engineering registration (including land surveying) as a category in the regular engineering registration laws.

In spite of the obviously developing needs for a separate undergraduate discipline in survey engineering, many American engineering educators seem to have a hopeless fear that there is not enough demand or need for surveying and mapping education to justify such programs. Under the current system, this may be true, but here we are obviously witnessing a case of misplaced emphasis. It is not the demand that should be changed but the system. If the system is changed, the demand or interest will respond to changes in the registration laws. One must keep in mind that at least one out of twenty professional engineers will

become a professional geodetic or survey engineer despite all odds against it, i.e., regardless of a lack in his formal preparation. The current cultural development of the United States demands that a significant proportion of engineers and scientists shall be engaged in professional surveying, geodetic, photogrammetric, and cartographic activities. Progress in land use and development demands that these problems should be approached with ever increasing precision and professional attitudes. Students should be made aware of these simple relationships, and hopefully, in the future they will have an opportunity to proceed towards a career in this field through a direct and reasonable approach to survey or geodetic engineering education, as is already possible in geodetic science.

As of now, these remarks of Dr. Hardy, especially those pertaining to "there is something wrong with the system," represents my personal views. I don't care which college surveying is established in, engineering, science, or civil engineering, as long as it is done. But I do not believe that a master's program after a civil engineer's degree will ever meet the surveyor's needs.

Dr. A. J. Brandenberger of Laval University, Quebec, in his paper on the Educational Status of Surveying and Photogrammetry in North America concluded with respect to surveyors:

Based on experience, gained elsewhere, and available information, it can be estimated that, for North America, about 5 per cent is needed on the doctoral level (for university teaching and research), 15 per cent on the master's level (to conduct surveying and mapping projects of an advanced degree of difficulty), 25 per cent to 30 per cent on the bachelor's level (for conventional land and engineering surveying and mapping), 25 per cent to 30 per cent on the technician's level (for routine surveying and mapping work, including work at photogrammetric instruments) and 25 per cent to 30 per cent on the level of auxiliary personnel (draftsmen).

The fact that there is a void in the 25 to 30 per cent bachelor's level in the United States is well recognized. A letter from C. R. Rostron, head of the Department of Engineering Technology, Clark College, Washington, states:

My personal view is that the community colleges and the new four-year engineering technology programs will step into the void left by the engineering schools, since we will always need qualified surveyors and map makers. We hope to attract qualified students to our technology programs and furnish a strong push in this direction.

Engineers have lost a large percentage of the area of land planning to land planners because of failure to supply a sufficient number of graduates to fill the void. Others moved in. Civil engineers are losing the area of land surveying because they are not graduating land surveyors. If it were not for the memory of a few older college graduates who did have surveying training, there would not be a cause for civil engineers claiming land surveying as being a part of civil engineering. Newer graduates are certainly not qualified.

As previously stated, ACSM has a committee that is studying the educational needs of the surveyor. In reality, the study should be for the purpose of forecasting the future needs of surveyors. Forty years ago, it was unlikely that anyone would have predicted that surveyors would have electronic computers, electronic measuring devices and that photogrammetry would develop to its present status. Thus, there is a constant changing need. What you and I consider as essential today may be obsolete tomorrow.

For the surveyor to stay in business today he must have the mobility of the lowly crab; he must be able to move forward, backwards, or sideways with changing conditions.

What the surveyor learns in college today may be insufficient tomorrow. I don't remember studying electronic computers or electronic measuring devices, yet most surveying offices, including mine, use them. How did surveyors pick up knowledge on these subjects? Continuing education is the answer and it is a necessary part of all educational systems. No matter how complete an education a student receives, it can be expected that in a short time it will be partially obsolete. The education committee should not overlook C. E. work, that is continuing education. In reality, this great convention is for the purpose of continuing our education, and the excellent attendance testifies to the need.

The committee on surveying and mapping education has been compiling catalog information on present offerings in colleges. Of course, some of these offerings are not taught.

At universities where civil engineering is offered, 154 offer surveying and 6 do not. Imagine a civil engineer not even exposed to one course in this subject. Six colleges have deteriorated to the point that the subject is not taught. Yet, graduates of these colleges will maintain that they are qualified to do Land Surveys as a right under their so-called "Professional" Engineers license. The average number of surveying units offered per civil engineering college is 8.2. This includes service courses for geologists and others. Required courses for civil engineers averages 5.5 units. From replies to questionnaires sent to colleges, presently taught courses are probably nearer 5 units per college. Within civil engineering colleges 46 offer photogrammetry, 114 do not. The average number of units for those colleges offering photogrammetry is 4.2.

At universities where engineering is offered, but civil engineering is not listed as a separate curriculum, 87 colleges offer surveying at an average rate of 15 units per college. This includes service courses for forestry and agriculture. In these colleges only 5 offer photogrammetry at the rate of 3.2 units per college.

In other departments of the universities, such as Agriculture, Forestry, Geography and Geology, a total of 33 offer surveying at an average rate of 3.2 units. Also, 8 such colleges offer photogrammetry at the average rate of 4.4 units per college.

THE UNIVERSAL STANDARD for accuracy, ruggedness and speed of operation. With readings direct to one second, the instrument is ideal for triangulation and laboratory use. AVAILABLE WITH A COMPLETE RANGE OF ACCESSORIES... Invar Subtense Bar, Diagonal Eyepiece Set, Pentagonal Objective Prism, and Autocollimation Eyepiece.

WILD
HEERBRUGG

WILD T-2
UNIVERSAL THEODOLITE
One of a *complete* line of superb instruments for Surveying, Photogrammetry and Microscopy. *Write for Booklet T-2.*

WILD HEERBRUGG INSTRUMENTS, INC. · PORT WASHINGTON, NEW YORK
In Canada: Wild of Canada Ltd., 157 Maclaren St., Ottawa, Ontario

In the area of cartography, we find 5 engineering colleges offering the subjects at the rate of 2 units per college. There are 112 colleges offering cartography outside of engineering at the average rate of 3.8 units per college. Thus, cartography is not an engineering subject and is taught in other areas. Certain Fundamental conclusions can be drawn from these compiled figures and they are:

(1) There are a lot of elementary surveying courses being offered in the colleges today.

(2) Cartography is being offered outside of engineering schools.

(3) Photogrammetry is offered mostly in the engineering colleges and is about 1/3 as popular as surveying.

(4) Elementary surveying is more frequently offered in the junior colleges than in the civil engineering colleges. Our figures show 187 junior colleges offering surveying at an average rate of 6.2 units per college.

The purpose of this committee is to determine if there is a surveying curriculum offered that would meet the needs of the professional surveyor, photogrammetrist, and cartographer. The above statistics show that there are sufficient offerings in elementary surveying to interest students in further work. If after a person takes elementary surveying, where can he obtain a degree in surveying and mapping?

If he wants a 4-year baccalaureate degree in surveying or in cartography he cannot get it in an engineering college. George Washington University or Ohio State are the best in the United States and they do not offer the courses through engineering colleges. The disadvantage of these colleges is that land surveying is limited in scope and the emphasis is on geodesy and the shape of the earth. In Canada, there is New Brunswick, University of Ontario and Laval, which are excellent. And then there are good offerings in Australia, New Zealand and South Africa.

If a person is willing to settle for a terminal course in surveying, several junior colleges are excellent such as Fullerton Junior College, San Francisco City College, Southern Technical Institute in Georgia, Oregon Junior Technical Institute, and Centralia Junior College in Washington.

Syracuse University Forestry School has a course with emphasis on surveying, and it appears to be a good one. Stephen F. Austin State College is planning a surveying option that will prepare men for Public Surveyor licenses of Texas.

My summary of the present situation is this: The American Society of Civil Engineers has proclaimed surveying to be a part of civil engineering and have stated that there should be a few colleges established with a baccalaureate degree in survey engineering. This has not been done and in my opinion, this will not be accomplished as long as the engineering curriculum is accredited by ECPD. Further, if the Goals of Engineering Education are adopted as proposed, the door for a 4-year surveying baccalaureate degree in engineering colleges will be permanently closed.

The fundamental precept of accreditation of Civil Engineering curriculum is that of "design" or better stated, the application of science to design of things. Surveying and mapping, including geodesy is not the design of maps or the design of the shape of the earth; it is more a study or recording of the shape of things as they exist. You do not design a contour; you measure its position and show its location on a map. When you locate an off-shore drilling rig, you do not design its position, you locate it. For this reason, surveying has been and probably always will be assigned a minor supporting role in engineering curriculum. Measurements are a necessary part of engineering; but only as a science and not as design.

FAMILY!

The "Terra-Fix"

The "Micro-Distancer"

The *"Terra-Fix"* is a short-range system which utilizes the TELLUROMETER micro-wave principles to determine and maintain the position of an unlimited number of small portable receiver units.

The military expects to use the *"Terra-Fix"* to maintain the positions of numerous military units, separated and constantly moving about, in the field.

Three portable transmitters can beam continuously to troops equipped with compact, lightweight remotes. Transmitters are portable by jeep; remotes weigh only 20 lbs. and can be carried by one man in each outfit.

The *"Micro-Distancer"* is the all-purpose TELLUROMETER SYSTEM that proved the practicability of determining geodetic distances by electronic principles. The newest model (the MRA/2) is a precise, rugged instrument which has been widely adopted by private and government surveyors, photogrammetrists, and consulting engineers.

There are more *"Micro-Distancer"* units in field use today than all other electronic systems together, utilizing either micro-waves or light beams. It measures a wide range of distances to accurate specifications, in daylight or dark.

For more information write to:

I do not object to the attitudes of engineering colleges; design subjects and science have grown so complex and require so much time that some subjects must be deleted. Deleting a subject such as surveying does not eliminate the need.

Surveying, mapping, photogrammetry, geodesy and satellite geodesy have become so complex that they deserve a berth of their own. One thing is certain; a man in college would not have sufficient time to do justice to engineering and these subjects at the same time.

From these miscellaneous remarks, my own conclusions as to the direction ACSM should take are these:

1. To recognize that engineering subjects have become so complex that there will not be time nor space to meet surveying needs. We should not complain, we should see what we can do to remedy the situation.

2. The area of geometronics has become so complex that it deserves a separate college ranking. ACSM should go on record as favoring the establishment of a 4-year degree in this area in any college willing to meet the needs in the surveying and mapping area.

****

MEASURES 50 MILES IN FIVE MINUTES!

Cubic Electrotape electronic surveying equipment measures distances from 250 feet to 100 miles in almost the twinkling of an eye. Electrotape accuracy, even under environmental extremes is 1 inch +1 part in 400,000.

PROVED IN USE

Here are two recent examples of Electrotape efficiency. A crew establishing microwave stations along a 1400-mile pipeline for Pacific Gas & Electric used Electrotape to complete the job in two weeks. San Diego County, California, which is larger than the State of Connecticut, is saving years by using Electrotape in an extensive county-wide surveying and aerial mapping program.

Two identical tripod-mounted Electrotape units are used to measure a given distance. As each unit can be operated by one man, surveying crew expenses are minimized. A radio transmitter and receiver, operating on radar frequencies, and ultra-precise phase-measuring equipment, form the heart of the system.

HOW IT WORKS

In simplest terms, Electrotape measures the time it takes for a radio wave to travel from one unit to the other and back again. Since the speed that radio waves travel is known, it is then easy to calculate the distance involved. An Electrotape operator requires no knowledge of electronics, and can learn the basic techniques in only 20 minutes. The equipment is lightweight and may be back-packed over rough terrain. A built-in communications link enables the Electrotape operators to converse, for maximum field efficiency.

Savings made possible by Electrotape can easily pay for equipment cost in less than 1 year.

Write today for your free copy of a booklet on Electrotape, to Dept. SM-100, Industrial Division, Cubic Corp., San Diego 11, California.

cubic CORPORATION

SURVEYOR EDUCATION AND REGISTRATION

MARCH 1967

CURTIS M. BROWN * - I received the following letter from Merritt B. Chalker of Connecticut, a Registered Land Surveyor:

"The ACSM Bulletin No. 20, reporting the observations of President Fennell concerning the August meeting of the Board of Engineering Examiners, was of interest, but points to the need of education, to the Engineering profession and particularly to the examining boards concerning the advancement of surveying education and the decline of opportunity for the same in our accredited engineering institutions."

"Some years ago, my nephew, Robert Gleason, after being employed for two years in my surveying practice, decided to make a career of land surveying. While I was aware that the quickest way to achieve registration as a land surveyor was by graduation from a conventional Civil Engineering course at an accredited college, I also knew that the surveying disciplines in most of such courses had almost reached the vanishing point."

"Largely through my membership in ACSM and the Journal, I decided to advise him to take a conventional course in Engineering for two years and then specialize in Cartography, with a 4-credit course at Yale Engineering Camp in Surveying added for good measure. He received his B.S. in Cartography from George Washington University in 1963."

"He applied for Registration as a Land Surveyor some months ago to our State Board of Registration, but learns that his education is no more acceptable towards registration than if he had no formal education at all."

"This attitude raises considerable question in my mind as to the competency of the examining board, particularly in surveying disciplines."

"Upon graduation he had several offers from government agencies and accepted a position with Naval Oceanography Office, where he has been employed since. I don't feel that the stiff-necked insistence of an Engineering diploma is for the good of the Land Surveying Profession. I am enclosing photographs of his scholastic record, and related material; also reprints of applicable statutes and regulations."

Examination of the courses taken, especially those taken at George Washington University, indicates that Robert Gleason did obtain a better surveying education than that offered in most accredited engineering schools.

The fault lies with our antiquated laws and narrowed attitudes of registration boards. The civil engineering colleges taught at one time surveying, but as of now, in most engineering colleges, this is a thing of the past. Because of their age, members of engineering registration boards did in fact take some training in surveying, and they imagine the same is being given today. A fact far from true.

The worst possible thing that can happen to the surveying profession is for a board to adopt a surveyor educational requirement equivalent to that of an accredited engineering degree. The board, from their Rules and Regulations, have adopted the words "he shall be a graduate of a school or college approved by the board" to mean, he shall have graduated from an accredited engineering college as "compiled annually by the Engineers Council for Professional Development entitled Accredited Curricula leading to first degrees in engineering in the United States."

The Council for Professional Development and accreditation committees is the very one responsible for deletion of surveying from the engineering curriculum. What irony in the situation! It is unfortunate that the board in Connecticut is unwilling to recognize one of the best undergraduate schools in the United States in the area of surveying and mapping. In the graduate schools (Purdue, Illinois, etc.) there are about 11 colleges with an M.S. program that can match George Washington's undergraduate offerings; I know of none equivalent at the undergraduate level.

Connecticut is not the only state with distorted and antiquated ideas on surveyor education. In California when surveying was taught in the civil engineering colleges, civil engineers (as a part of their civil registration) were given the privilege of practicing surveying. Today at a time when California accredited engineering colleges offer about 3 units in "measurements" this same privilege exists. There are about 10,000 engineers "licensed to practice surveying" with about 1/10 of these qualified to do the work.

The situation has come about because we surveyors have allowed it to happen. The only effective remedy for such situations is for surveyors themselves to correct it; no one else will. Is there an effective Connecticut Land Surveyor's organization?

An alternative idea is to set up an accreditation committee within ACSM and then try to get "engineering boards" to recognize their findings. Or would it be better to try for a separate board of registration for surveyors?

* Past President ACSM, Chairman Education Committee.

****

*Because no detail is too small
for Berger Engineering . . .*

THE FIRST ALL NEW PLUMB BOB DESIGN IN DECADES —
Berger twin-point RETRACTA-BOB(T)*

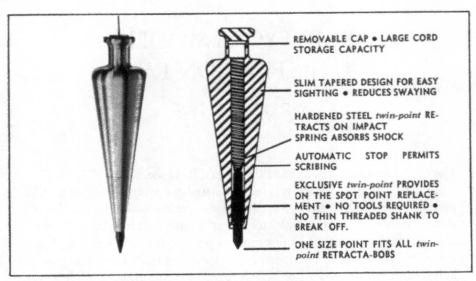

REMOVABLE CAP • LARGE CORD STORAGE CAPACITY

SLIM TAPERED DESIGN FOR EASY SIGHTING • REDUCES SWAYING

HARDENED STEEL *twin-point* RETRACTS ON IMPACT SPRING ABSORBS SHOCK

AUTOMATIC STOP PERMITS SCRIBING

EXCLUSIVE *twin-point* PROVIDES ON THE SPOT POINT REPLACEMENT • NO TOOLS REQUIRED • NO THIN THREADED SHANK TO BREAK OFF.

ONE SIZE POINT FITS ALL *twin-point* RETRACTA-BOBS

*T.M., Pat. Pend.

SURVEYING INSTRUMENTS

Transits

Levels

Alidades

Mining Transits

Theodolites (Geodetic)

Collimators

Astronomical Instruments

Geological Instruments

INSTRUMENTATION AND APPARATUS DIVISION

Precision read-out devices using optical, electronic and photographic means

Precision rotating mechanisms

Precision alignment devices

Circular dividing

Linear dividing

Optical alignment

Designing and manufacturing to order

THE BEST IN SIGHT IS  **BERGER**

Engineering and Surveying Instruments . . . Since 1871

C. L. Berger & Sons, Inc., 43 Williams Street, Boston 19, Massachusetts

SURVEYORS MODEL REGISTRATION LAW
September 1967

Curtis M. Brown * - In 1956 at the annual PSD meeting in Washington a motion was duly made (by me) seconded and passed that PSD of ACSM prepare a Model Registration Law. After some discussion by Gordon E. Ainsworth (then Chairman), Victor Ghent (then Secretary of the Division) and others, it was passed. A few months prior to the next meeting, I was appointed to chair the committee, and it was not until 1958 that general agreement of the committee was reached. By this time, Phil Bill was Chairman of PSD.

The document was ahead of its time. Opinion had not jelled. Brother Barry was soon thereafter actively and forcefully pushing the concept that surveying was civil engineering and ultimately all surveying should be done under the civil engineer's license.

It has been said that no army can stop an idea whose time has come. With the degrading of surveying by the universities, especially by the engineering accreditation teams, it became obvious that it was only a matter of time until licensed surveyors would be forced into defensive activities or extermination. Adoption of the model law is a shift from a defensive position to an offensive position that has long been needed.

In the campaign just passed for the adoption or rejection of the model law, some bitter words were exchanged. The old arguments were revived that surveying should be under the civil engineer's license and that existing land surveyors could not pass a test encompassing all of the things permitted under the model law.

Is land surveying civil engineering? To me the only question is whether civil or other engineers are qualified to do land surveying. Licensing laws are for the protection of the public from the unqualified; they are not a device to give one group an exclusive franchise to make money on surveys.

If engineers are qualified, they should be given every opportunity to prove so by proper examination procedures. They should not be given the privilege by self-proclamation or by tradition. I have been around colleges enough, both as a professor and as an observer, to realize that the substantial majority of civil engineering graduates have little or no training in land surveying. In fact, other colleges (geology, forestry, etc.) have as many or more students taking the subject than do the engineering colleges.

I have no quarrel with the concept of requiring college graduation or equivalent education as a minimum requirement for the practice of land surveying, but I would expect the training to be in the area for which the license is issued. To say that an engineer who has specialized in structural, sanitary, mechanical, electrical, or other branches of engineering is qualified to do land surveying is a mere figment of the imagination. If they are qualified, let them prove it.

The argument that most of the present licensed land surveyors could not pass an examination directed to the subject matter permitted under the new model law is without merit. If you were to ask all of the presently licensed engineers to take the recent engineering examination, most would fail. Knowledge required today is never equivalent to what was required yesterday, nor will it be equivalent to what will be required tomorrow. It is like the old saying, "If you try to do today's job with yesterday's tools, you will be out of business tomorrow." Ninety percent of all scientists who ever lived are alive today; it can only be expected that discovery and advancement will be much more rapid in the future than it was in the past. I can remember when knowledge of electronic distance measurement devices, photogrammetry, and electronic computers was not necessary for surveyors; these methods had not been invented yet. But does this mean that present day surveyors do not need knowledge in these areas? What has been done in the past is immaterial to what will or can be done in the future.

All examinations within a profession should reflect advancements in the areas of knowledge required; adoption of a model law with added requirements can mean only one thing - the examination to follow will be more difficult and more complex. I can well remember my college course in calculus that I had difficulty with; my son took it in high school. One thing is certain about the future: it will be different from the past; i.e., it will be more difficult.

185

It is true that at one time in the past, civil engineers and most other engineers did have good college background in surveying. At that time they did earn the right, as a group, to be considered fairly well trained as surveyors. But you cannot live forever on reputation. What we are concerned with is the "now." The very deficient college education in surveying and the present attitude of the college accreditation teams of "get rid of surveying courses" makes the statement "land surveying is civil engineering" incompatible with reality.

I said I did not care whether land surveyors were classified as engineers or not. It would be wonderful if engineers were qualified land surveyors. But, as a group, they are not. Further, the situation gives no sign of improving. Hence, as of now, I see no other alternative for surveyors than to drop the last rudiments of the myth "surveying is engineering," and adopt the Canadian, Australian, South African, and New Zealand approach wherein surveying is treated as an entity of its own.

* Past President, ACSM.

****

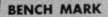

LAND SURVEYOR'S EXAMINATIONS

(PUBLISHED IN 1978 IN THE SURVEYOR'S WORKBOOK WITH ROY MINNICK)

BY CURTIS M. BROWN

CALIFORNIA LICENSED LAND SURVEYOR

Part I

OBJECTIVE OF EXAMINATIONS

SCOPE

Land Surveyors are by reputation and training experts in the science of linear measurements and, among other things, also specialists in determining property boundaries. Since the Land Surveyor cannot qualify himself by self-proclamation, someone must "measure" his qualifications using suitable tests and examinations. Usually this is done under the direction of a Board of Registration.

Edward Thorndike was probably the father, but not the inventor of educational testing methods; he was responsible for many changes that transformed the art of evaluating achievements to the science of measuring them.

Several methods are employed to determine whether an individual meets the minimum qualifications of Land Surveyors. He can be judged by (1) his experience, (2) letters of recommendation from others, (3) demonstration of the use of instruments and, most important, (4) a written examination. The purpose of this treatise is to present methods of gauging the competence of surveyors by written tests.

How to take and how to prepare examinations are like comparing the right and left hand gloves; they are similar but not identical. Few prepare tests; many endure them. For this reason the subject matter is predicated to the examinee whenever it is equally applicable to the taker or maker.

In a test the examinee either follows instructions or answers questions; success or failure depends upon exactly following instructions or answering questions. If the examinee understands why a question is asked and why a particular approach was chosen to determine whether he understands a subject, the examinee is capable of writing .a better answer to the question. Hence, "why the question" and "how to answer it" are stressed.

A written test can be designed to disclose more than mere factual knowledge--for example, judgment, evaluation of skill, reasoning power, writing proficiency and orderly functioning of the mind. Comments will be made on the quality, value, purpose, and methods of preparing questions that call for more than factual knowledge.

A part of this book is devoted to examples; questions are asked and answered; instructions are given and followed. Each problem is selected to illustrate the quality and method of asking questions, and the answering technique to be used.

REGULATING LAWS

Most states have property surveyor's registration laws and passage of a written examination is part of the requirement for licensing. Sometimes an oral examination, including demonstration of usage of instruments is required; only written responses will be included.

The area tested is generally limited by the Land Surveyors Registration law; each examinee should study his individual state law to be certain that he understands the permissible extent and content of the tests. Originally a one-day examination was commonplace; now the two-day test has practically supplanted it. The six-day Australian and New Zealand tests and three-day Virginian tests have been given.

LAND SURVEY EXAMS

In a number of states the first day portion consists of a Surveyor in Training (SIT) examination similar to the EIT section for engineers. Success on the first part usually eliminates the necessity of taking it over again. Failure to pass the (SIT) portion of the examination, even with favorable results on the second day, generally means the examinee must repeat the entire test. A two-day examination with the first day of the SIT variety is assumed herein.

Some states grant the Land Surveyor very broad duties; in others his scope of permissible area of practice is quite limited. In California the surveyor is permitted to do surveys for (1) photogrammetry, (2) geodetic, (3) property, (4) fixed works, (5) land descriptions, and (6) topography. Obviously the California examination covers a much more extensive field than that in a state wherein the Land Surveyor is restricted to property surveying. Photogrammetry, geodesy, and property surveying are specialties within surveying just as hydraulics, structures, and highways are set apart within civil engineering. It is impossible to devise a test that will cover all these areas completely in eight hours time.

The purpose of a test is to prove, as nearly as may be, that the applicant is qualified to perform all the functions permitted by law. Before a license is issued, the applicant must be checked to make certain he is qualified to do all of the things an exclusive franchise demands. Since the field of surveying is broad, and the process of acquiring needed knowledge requires extensive reading, practice, and experience, a long difficult test can be expected.

After taking a lengthy, arduous examination, a person may think that the sole object was to flunk as many as possible. This is far from the truth. Competent, qualified people are always a welcome addition to a profession; without new men, within a few years it would cease to exist. But this does not mean the test should be so easy that an unqualified person might practice. Licensing is a serious step. The state certifies to the proficiency of a licensee and the citizens of every state have a right to expect that all registrants are competent. Issuance of a license to the unqualified serves only to deceive people; a client is charged for a service that the licensee is incapable of rendering.

In reality, failing the unfit is doing those persons a favor. If licensed to do professional work, and they err in doing so, they are liable for many years to come. The cost for erroneous work may bring financial ruin and place undue hardship upon the client. It is better to require that a surveyor study more before he commences practice than to let him learn by costly mistakes after licensing.

THE OBJECTIVE OF AN EXAMINATION IS TO DO JUSTICE TO BOTH THE EXAMINEE AND THE PUBLIC.

EXAM OBJECTIVES

A written examination can serve these useful purposes; test a person's (1) surveying knowledge, (2) reasoning ability and judgment, (3) capacity to comprehend written instructions, (4) aptitude to write, spell, and express himself, (5) mathematical faculty, and (6) scientific knowledge.

A written test is largely impersonal; it does not investigate ethics, honesty, emotions, physical handicaps, and many other things that can be better observed during a personal interview or by considering past behavior. Thus, in addition to a written examination, conferences, letters of recommendation, and demonstrations of the use of equipment are often required.

BOOK LIST

Every person who expects to prepare for a property surveyor's examination must acquire a sizeable library. Many books are available, some of exceptional quality. The book list found in this workbook was selected as a bare minimum to cover the range of necessary knowledge.

In some states, an open book examination is prescribed and a required book list given to each candidate. Normally he is not expected to memorize tables, functions, and odd facts; the book list supplies such needed information. This in no way infers that the questions asked will be limited to the books listed.

EXAM HEADING

Examinations are usually divided into two main headings and several sub-headings. The main headings are: (a) Factual (sometimes called memory). (b) Explanation, or an application of principles or facts.

QUESTION TYPES

Often questions are separated into (1) recognition, (2) recall, (3) evaluation, and (4) application. The lowest level of knowledge is mere recognition of words. Writing or speaking is recall of knowledge and represents its second level. A person who is able to recognize and recall many bits of learning, who is able to evaluate and interpret the recognized and recall items and who can present them in a connected form has elevated himself into the third level. The highest level of all involves application. Surveyors who are able to utilize information acquired from reading or experience and can apply it to the intelligent solution of problems in a different situation have the proper degree of mastery. Surveyors are expected to have attained the fourth level and should be tested at, this level.

FACTUAL QUESTIONS

Factual questions have limited value for the first day of the surveyor's examination; explanation and application queries are better suited to all parts of the test. The latter also requires factual knowledge in order to write a correct answer and thus test several areas. Some of the more common factual types of questions are:

- ANALOGY. Transit is to angle as tape is to:
  1. slope 2. temperature 3. distance 4. area.

- COMPLETION. The electrotape uses _____ waves.

- CROSS OUT. Cross out the word that does not belong to the group:
  1. angle 2. direction 3. tape 4. bearing.

- DIAGRAMMATIC. Make a sketch or drawing showing how the principle points of the compass would appear in the surveyor's compass box.

- ENUMERATION. List the errors that occur when taping.

- IDENTIFICATION. Place an "A" after those words that pertain to angular measurements; place a "D" after those words that pertain to distance measurements.
  Sag _____ Catenary _____ Refraction _____
  Parallel with _____.

- MATCHING. Match related items in columns A and B by writing the corresponding number in the space provided.

A   <u>B</u>

1. Temp. above standard   _____ Cubic yards
2. Leveling   _____ Equal FS and BS.
3. Cross sections   _____ Tape elongation
4. Evidence   _____ Obliterated corners
5. Error of closure   _____ Sum of latitudes and departures.

- MULTIPLE CHOICE Check the word or phrase that is not related to traverse error. Least square adjustment _____ Compass rule _____ Line of sight _____ Closure _____

- SEQUENCE. As pertaining to a property survey, number the following items in their order of performed sequence;
Measurements _____ Research _____
Computations for field closure _____ Certificate of survey _____.

- TRUE OR FALSE. George Washington was the first licensed surveyor in the United States _____T _____F.

- TRUE, FALSE, or NEITHER WITHOUT FURTHER DATA.

Mark a "T" if the answer is true, and "F" if the answer is false, and "N" if the answer requires further data.

A level line at 5000 feet elevation is parallel with a level line at zero elevation _____.
(The answer is N: at the equator the poles, or along a parallel of latitude the answer is true; elsewhere it is false for any level line progressing northerly or southerly).

APPLICATION OF PRINCIPLES

The second class (explanation, or an application of principles or facts) is usually divided into:

(1)   Mathematical and (2) Essay questions.

For general examinations application queries are the essay type, but mathematical problems are more frequently used for surveyors.

CLOSED BOOK vs. OPEN BOOK

The closed book portion of an examination should always be written with simpler questions or directions than is found in an open book test. If trigonometric functions or other constants are necessary, they are customarily supplied with the question asked. The purpose of a closed book examination is to test a person's knowledge of common, well-known laws of science, mathematics, techniques, and other simple areas of knowledge. If asked with an open book, the answer could be readily copied. It is expected that all surveyors have a fund of recognition and recall knowledge that can be brought forth from memory much the same as memorized spelling and reading. If elementary things cannot be readily recalled, how can a person make a proper survey?

If open books are permitted, questions asked are usually more complex and designed to elicit a reply which cannot be copied directly from a book. For example, "Write a legal description of the property shown on the above drawing." cannot be answered by looking at or reading a publication. The response will demonstrate familiarity with mathematics, legal elements of descriptions, description caption and body, spelling, grammar, etc. Requiring an application of knowledge from numerous sources is the key to composing open book questions.

In closed book examinations time is not an important issue. The examinee can or cannot answer a question. A liberal interval can be allotted. But in an open book examination time is part of the testing tool.

Given sufficient time and an open book, a person eventually will be able to fathom any question. "How do you set the center of Section 6?" can be found by reading from THE MANUAL OF INSTRUCTIONS; but if time is short, only known information enters into the reply.

QUESTION PREPARATION

In preparing questions, particular attention should be directed toward balance so they will not be slanted to favor one group. Some surveyors specialize in property surveys; many in highway work; others in geodetic observations and calculations; and still others in photogrammetry. Licensed surveyors are permitted to do many kinds of surveys; if their certification proclaims a proficiency in a branch of surveying, they should be tested to prove that expertise.

As a surveyor's field of practice extends to newer instruments, he must expect an enlarged scope of examinations. Questions have been asked on how to adjust a transit, so why not one on how to repair or adjust an electrotape? How much should the testee know about electronic computers?

QUESTION DISTRIBUTION

If an examination is limited to sixteen hours, it is not possible to devise a written test that will blanket all of the surveyor's required area of knowledge. At best, only a sampling over a wide area can be attained.

In most states the surveyor is given an exclusive franchise to do certain things; in addition he may do many other surveying functions which are not an exclusive prerogative of anyone. Surveyors may be granted the exclusive right to do property surveys, whereas engineers can be accorded the unique privilege to design street grades; and either, or anyone, may have the right to take topography. For those things the surveyor's franchise covers, he must have expert knowledge; every test should be devised so that if the surveyor fails in one of those portions, he should flunk the entire test. To partially accomplish this aim, most examinations require that the candidates pass 70% for each day.

Surveyors need a good technical background in mathematics, sciences, and platting. Office men are best in these subjects. Surveyors should also have a knowledge of the use of instruments. Where the law requires considerable field experience, it may be assumed that the surveyor does have this background.

The second day part is referred to as the professional section of the test; it usually is heavily weighted with questions of statute law, court decisions, professional practice, ethics, judgment, land descriptions, subdivision mapping procedures, planning, photogrammetry, and liability. A good test is designed so that a person who misses a question covering an important area is not likely to get a passing grade. In the public lands areas nothing is more important than proper resurvey procedures for sections--that is, the procedures used in accordance with the Manual applicable at the date of the original survey which is not necessarily the 1947 edition. In those areas at least 30% of the test should be on that subject. Every surveyor does resurveys of subdivisions created under state laws; this phase of the profession should contribute about 30% to the weight of one day of the examination.

JUDGMENT QUESTIONS

Property surveyors must have and display good judgment; some questions are deliberately worded to permit alternate solutions depending upon the circumstances. The answer to such interrogations calls for a display of judgment and a discussion of what is probable and proper. "You find four monuments to represent the corner sought; one might be an original, one was set by the City Engineer, one was set by a known surveyor, and other is weathered by age. What considerations and investigations would you use in deciding upon the proper position to accept?" The answer requires a general discussion of the order of importance of monument evidence, seeking witnesses, seeing the City Engineer's notes, etc., and stating what, in your judgment, is to be done with the evidence.

Judgment questions are easily recognized and may require an essay type answer. Multiple choice questions that necessitate selecting the most nearly correct answer can be designed to test judgment and thinking ability.

Most employers have had experience in hiring extremely well-educated people who can quickly solve any problem reducible to exact scientific laws or numbers, but cannot arrive at a sound conclusion based upon good judgment in the selection of a method or approach to a problem. A person insisting upon the chainmen being within 0.0 feet of a line, yet allowing them to tape without checking elevation errors within the same limits is using poor judgment. A new college graduate is apt to display excellent knowledge but inability to put it to most beneficial use. Triangulation may be employed where direct taping is better; or a level circuit run with a target instead of using a three-wire method.

Judgment is one of the most valuable assets of a surveyor and should be tested. The majority of examinations given in most states are deficient in this regard. Judgment questions are very difficult to grade and for this reason are often omitted.

UNTESTABLE ATTITUDES

Attitudes of persons cannot be directly tested on written examinations; the examinee generally writes what he thinks will produce the most beneficial result. Knowing the science of ethics is not proof that their correct application will be used. Many men profess loudly that they are honest to cover frequent filtching. The science of logic never made a man reason correctly. How can maturity--that is, the ability to see the connection between today's action and tomorrow's results--be tested on paper?

AN EDUCATED PERSON?

In organizing what he observes, an educated person shows his superiority by the (1) variety of concepts he can employ. (2) Number of things he takes into account. (3) Ability to think and conclude.

As an illustration, the distance between Point "A" and Point "B," each located on opposite sides of a lake, is to be determined. A technician who only knows how to pull a tape may wait until the lake freezes so that the distance can be measured directly. A person who knows how to use the transit and tape may (1) lay out a base line and triangulate, or (2) run a random traverse around the lake. A well-educated person would investigate the allowable time and accuracy and then decide which method would most economically give the desired result -- (1) triangulation, (2) stadia, (3) subtense bar, (4) electronic distance measurement, (5) random traverse, (6) directly by stretching a light-weight piano wire across the lake, etc.

An uneducated person (even some technicians) in getting a length with his tape would merely measure the distance and be satisfied. An educated person knows that these things must be taken into account: temperature, sag, levelness (or slope), pull, distance between supports, comparison with a standard, swing of plumb bobs, wind, and straight lines.

Typical questions illustrating knowledge of concepts and things to be considered are:

1. Points "A" and "B" are about 100 feet apart on opposite sides of a lake and 50 feet above its surface. List all of the methods you could use to determine the distance between "A" and "B" and state the approximate accuracy obtainable by each method.

2. In taping from "A" (elevation 100.00 feet) to "B" (elevation

550.00 feet) you are to determine the distance as accurately
as possible. State all the factors you would include.

Every examination has several purposes and perhaps the most important
is the appraisal of the examinee's ability to comprehend, think, evaluate,
and conclude from a body of knowledge.

An educated person possesses and/or can do the following: (1) Possess
an enormous store of factual knowledge. (2) Possess the ability to recall
factual information pertaining to a new situation. (3) The person thinks.
Thinking is a mental activity wherein new relationships between facts or
symbols are brought about by their rearrangement with respect to each
other. After thinking of all the facts and symbols and following the rules
of logic, common sense, and sometimes insight, the result or answer is
deduced, and so (4) the person correctly concludes. Thus, factual knowledge
alone is not proof of being "educated," it is merely one of the many items
possessed by an educated man.

TECHNICAL vs. PROFESSIONAL EXAMINATION

Much confusion exists over the definition of the term "technician." In a
narrow sense it means "those who have superior knowledge in a narrow
band of a total spectrum," as a radio repair technician. It is true that
technicians must have a detailed knowledge of a limited area; but they do
not typically have a total concept.

The American Society for Engineering Education definition of a
surveying technician says: "A surveying technician is one whose education
and experience qualify him to work in the field of surveying technology.
He differs from a craftsman in his knowledge of scientific and surveying
theory and methods and from a surveyor in that he has more specialized
background and use of technical skills to support surveying activities."

Surveying technology is concerned primarily with applying established
scientific and surveying knowledge and methods. Note that the arts of land
surveying (land planning, subdivision layout, interpreting the meaning
of deed words, evaluation of evidence, etc.), are not included in this
definition.

As contrasted with the technician, education of the Licensed Land
Surveyor (as certified or registered by the state) is presumed to include
all of these scientific principles, mathematics and arts in sufficient depth,
and an explanation of them as relevant to surveying processes so that the
surveyor has the ability to apply a series of concepts to a complex problem

and work out a logical and correct solution within the following areas (in some states, although not all, each of the following is within the definition of land surveying): (1) land planning, (2) subdivision preparation, (3) design of utilities, paving, drainage, and minor structures in subdivisions, (4) photogrammetry to determine property lines and topography, (5) resurveys of property, (6) original surveys of property, (7) surveys for construction, (8) hydrographic surveys, (9) cartography (in a limited capacity), and (10) geodesy (limited).

The distinguishing characteristic of the Licensed (Public, Certified, or Registered) Land Surveyor is the talent to adopt a series of concepts to a complex problem and work out a logical and correct solution. This is the area of the examination. All too many examinations are directed toward the technician. It is hoped this will be corrected.

****

<u>Y</u>O<u>U</u>R   <u>N</u>O<u>TE</u>S

****

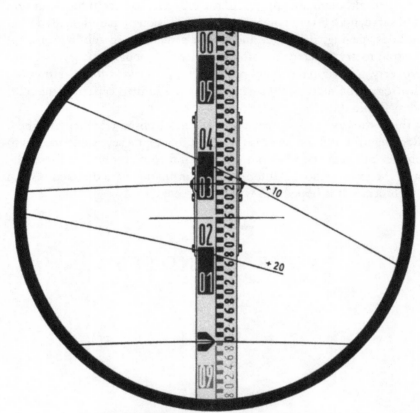

A different slant.

**Two accuracy ranges for distances.
Four accuracy ranges for differences in elevation.
ZEISS Reduction Tacheometer RTa4.**

- Automatically converts slope distance to horizontal distance.
- Gives corrected differences in elevation.
- Short range 6' to 500'.
- Topographic mapping range to 1000'.
- Also functions as optical scale theodolite.

 KEUFFEL & ESSER CO.
20 Whippany Rd., Morristown, N.J. 07960
Manufactured by Zeiss, West Germany.
Sales and service through K&E, U.S.

73 0400

200

Communication via the two-way radio aids the surveyors to train the remote Electrotape units until a "strong" signal is transmitted and received by both units.

Part II

TAKING EXAMINATIONS

PREPARING FOR EXAMINATIONS

It is not possible to explain to someone who has little or no knowledge of surveying how he can pass the registration examination. Suggestions for grade improvement can be helpful, however, to men with experience.

Successfully passing an examination is accomplished only by careful prior preparation. It is assumed that this has been done, and the candidate has looked over past tests. If copies are not available he should talk with others who have recently been through the procedure.

The best approach to an examination is a thorough review. It has been demonstrated frequently that people may forget 50% of what they learn (?) within thirty minutes after they learn it. After a few weeks just the barest outline of what was mastered is remembered. The object of an examination is to check your retention, not to test what you once knew and have now forgotten. Only by reviewing several times can a subject be secured. Many people complain that they knew the material but under the excitement of an examination they could not recall the answers. In reality, they did not go over the essentials a sufficient number of times so that facts could be surfaced at will.

The following chart is an idealized representation of scholastic aptitude (Intelligence Quotient) and achievement of students. In general, the chart is reasonably correct for the majority of people. But there are always many "over-achievers" and "under-achievers"; that is, those who achieve much more and others who accomplish considerably less than their aptitude indicates probable. Motivation accounts for the difference. Some people are lazy, others are not.

SCHOLASTIC APTITUDE

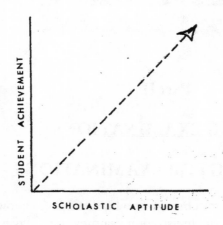

REVIEW

Review is the only way non-dramatic material (not sharp events) can be retained. Certain studies for a specific condition discloses that the percentage of knowledge held as compared to that known at the start was as follows: 1 day, 60%; 2 days, 40%; 3 days, 32%; 4 days, 28%; 5 days, 23%;

10 days, 19%. When there was a review at the end of one day, the material remembered at the end of 10 days was about 30%, an increase of 11%, when no review took place. With reviews at the end of both 1 day and 2 days, the percentage kept at the end of 10 days was about 50%. A schematic chart comparing knowledge retained compared with the number of reviews is shown below.

Remember these very important principles:

1. A ONE-SHOT STUDY SESSION LEADS ONLY TO DISASTER.

2. REVIEWING SHORTLY BEFORE A TEST IS THE BEST REINFORCER OF KNOWLEDGE.

3. AFTER A CERTAIN NUMBER OF REPETITIONS, THE LAW OF DIMINISHING RETURNS TAKES OVER, I.E., THEY NO LONGER ARE PARTICULARLY EFFECTIVE.

Military service research indicates that a person remembers only 10% of what he hears; 50% of what he sees; and 80% of the things done with his hands. A strong indictment of the lecture system! And a recommendation to always study with a pencil at hand for notes and sketches as well as calculations.

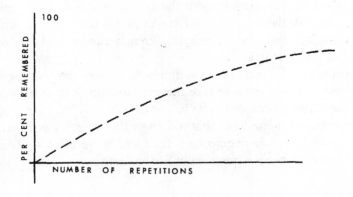

CRAMMING

Normal human beings cannot learn surveying within a few weeks; nor can they acquire sufficient background by a short "cramming" process of review. After a period of intense study there is a span of temporary saturation; the human mind has limitations on how much it can do within a given interval. The principal benefit from a brief last-minute review is the reassurance that you know the subject; it gives confidence and decreases nervousness before a person enters the examination room.

If an examinee has not thoroughly prepared himself before the last night, he will not gain by studying long hours then; the best advice is get a good night's rest. Mental alertness is the most important prerequisite for an exhaustive test.

It has been shown time and again that a ten-minute break after fifty minutes of study increases the percentage of knowledge retained in the next study session. Most colleges and schools (except for lab classes that require physical exercise) have a change of classes and a ten-minute "break" from class to class. Moral: Do not study more than fifty minutes without a ten-minute break; but don't abuse the rule. It has also been shown that excessive excitement can make a person forget what he just learned. Relax and don't seek excitement.

Trying to learn something "new" at the last minute is a waste of time; it is better to review and reinforce "forgotten" knowledge.

ENTERING THE ROOM

Upon entering the examination room the examinee should have pencils, pen, slide rule, calculator, tables and books permitted, colored pencils, triangles, straight edge, scales, compass, French curves, and any other items listed in the instructions.

Nervousness can be expected; usually a little tension sharpens the wits. After working for a few years to take the examination, it is an important challenge. But a person can go too far in nervousness and "go all to pieces." The best prevention is confidence that you know the subject. Examinations should be approached without emotions. The Land Surveyor's test, if failed, can be taken over; it is not a question of life or death.

TIME

The most important element of an examination other than questions, is timing. Based on the weight of questions, an examinee decides how much time to allow for each one, then stays within the limit. This is especially important for essay questions.

READING QUESTIONS

Questions asked in an examination are designed to test a person's knowledge in a given area and to investigate his comprehension of instructions. After a portion of a problem is read, it is poor policy to assume that the remainder of the question will follow the same pattern suggested by the early words. All questions should be read carefully--every word. The answer must be responsive to the query, not to ideas merely suggested. No credit is given for writing about something not asked for. To save time, be certain that the question is understood, then concentrate on that subject alone.

OBJECTIVES ANSWERING QUESTIONS

The examinee is trying to prove he has certain knowledge; can express his comprehension in proper English using correct grammar and spelling; can present his ideas in an orderly and logical fashion; and is capable of good judgment and intelligence in his answers.

In reality, an answer is a report or an exposition. The object of any report is not to show how much can be written on a subject; it is to prove in the simplest and most fundamental terms expressed in logical sequence, that the examinee knows the answer. A report should save the grader's attention by orderly setting forth answers in direct response to the problem stated. A person marking surveyor's examinations is not likely to be an English major; in fact, the reverse is probably nearer the truth. Ordinarily graders do not condone a vulgar display of unusual words calculated to create an impression rather than to orderly convey specific knowledge. Examinees seldom err on that side however; more often they disclose a meager knowledge of writing techniques.

ANSWERING QUESTIONS

Answers to all questions should be brief, precise, complete, and correct without "elucidation" in "ostentatious" language. Graders use cold logic in evaluating responses. Some people can be "snowed" by a deluge of verbosity, but usually not a person marking a test. Remember that he knows more than you do and lengthy, unnecessary explanations are rather boring after grading the 100th paper. Most questions can be answered correctly with a few well-chosen words. Think out what your solution will be, then write it in as few words as possible. But be complete, logical, and correct. Essay questions are graded on the basis of (what) you say and (how) you say it so be sure the subject matter is logically arranged in orderly sequence of thoughts.

In answering any question it is just as important to know what is not called for as to recognize what is. No credit is earned for giving a long dissertation on something not required.

Time spent on such sentences as the following is entirely wasted. "I know all about this question and can write on it for hours, but time is running short and I must stop." If a partial answer was given in the time it took to write that statement some credit would be attained.

(Knowledge of things without being able to communicate it effectively to others is only half-knowing it).

The most common mistakes made in answering essay questions are:

1. A rambling, verbose discussion without any one part being clear.

2. Too much space is devoted to a few unimportant details; the critical points are lost in the maze.

3. Items are listed without emphasis or plan.

4. An unrelated passage is copied out of a book.

A typical complaint, "I did not have sufficient time" is of no avail. Questions are never asked to find out all a person knows about land surveying! They require the examinee to sort out the important from the insignificant in an organized account so that a person with average intelligence and a surveying background can understand the topic even though he has never heard it before.

KEY WORDS

Certain key words often "give" the approach or direction to take for the answer; look for them. As a suggested item of study look up the true meaning of these words: compare, define, list opposites, evaluation, cause and effect, pros and cons, analogy, discuss, series of steps, diagram, and solve.

RECALL vs. RECOGNIZE

Some questions merely require recognition as: Which of the following words mean thus and so? All words are listed; it is not necessary to recall an exact definition--merely recognize the right word or words from the list. In the simpler objective examinations recognition is tested. In more complex ones the clues given must be recognized, rearranged, and the correct answer derived by thinking.

Recall is demanded in most essay questions. A short sentence instructs you to write (muster) all about a given subject. You must assemble in an organized way without examination hints, the facts to be recalled. If the instruction uses such words as "compare," "evaluate," or "cause and effect," thinking may be required. If asked what you would do in a given situation, judgment may enter.

ANSWERS BY REFERENCE

A statement that the answer to this question can be found on page 12 of such and such book will almost always result in a zero. The grader is not interested in what a book says. Does the examinee understand the subject?

RESPONSIVENESS

In an open book examination it is amazing how many attempts are made to get a grade by merely copying a passage out of a well-known text. Rarely does an open book question have an exact answer found in a particular book. Often the passage found only remotely or partially applies to the question. It is far better for the examinee to apply information from several sources and write the answer in his own words. Copying from a book usually displays lack of personal knowledge and mere mimicry; the grader is apt to be quite critical of such material. If the copied answer is only partly responsive to the question, it indicates the examinee does not know the subject and is fishing for a partial mark.

A grader has faith in a person who is direct, concise, to the point, and directly responsive to the question asked. Such a person deserves great credit.

NEATNESS

Graders are only human, and naturally are intolerant of sloppy, unreadable handwriting. To give a passing mark, the grader must be able to interpret what is said. But this does not mean the candidate should spend all of his time preparing a thing of lasting beauty. Neatness without undue loss of time is the best policy. Drawings and diagrams are often the quickest and clearest way to answer questions.

ASSUMPTIONS

It is unfortunate, but true, that questions or instructions are not always clear; without making certain assumptions, perhaps a proper response cannot be made. The following assumptions are recognized:

a) Some type of answer is required. Ninety-nine per cent of the time merely pointing out an ambiguity in a question gives only minor credit. State the inconsistency or deficiency and answer the alternative possibilities, especially the most logical one.

b) In theoretical problems the test tries to extract an answer that illustrates abstract knowledge; such questions are not necessarily practical problems. Do not complain that the situation could not occur in practice; answer the question as given.

c) Frequently data is omitted from a problem; assume that if the data were supplied, they would have no effect. "A tape is found to be 100.01 feet long when compared with a standard. Distance AB was measured with the tape and found to be 1001.03 feet long. What is the correct distance?" No mention is made of pull, sag, alignment, temperature, or wind. In answering, it is assumed that these, if given, would have no effect (in a practical problem they would have an effect).

d) Never make an assumption because it will decrease the length of answer required. An assumption is for a single purpose; to clarify an ambiguity if one exists. If a unique point is stated, a supposition is never proper. Question: "When do you apply proration?" Incorrect assumption: "Since no mention is made of the kind of description, I assume that you mean for sectionalized lands." The answer required includes all circumstances wherein proration is applied, not just in sectionalized land. Such limitations can only result in a poor grade.

COMPLETENESS

Most failures result from incomplete answers. A partial answer gets a partial grade, or none at all. Some of the comments noted for the sample problems illustrate this. A fundamental precept in any examination is that a perfect grade is attained only by a full answer.

CORRECTNESS

Some problems require an unerring answer and nothing short of absolute accuracy will suffice. Various phases of property surveying are applications of "exact sciences." An essential quality of a surveyor is to know when to be "exactly correct" and when tolerances are permissible. A person displays poor judgment if he is more precise than necessary--and incompetence when not as exact as required.

Usually those problems calling for perfection can be detected from the statement. In some cases partial credit is allowed for correct procedure even though the numerical answer is wrong. To give credit for procedure, the grader must be able to clearly and simply follow every step. Shortcuts and unrecorded mental calculations concealing the source of errors lose possible fractional marks.

ANSWER ERRORS

In answering questions a misstatement is apt to be severely graded; a little knowledge is sometimes dangerous. The examinee who makes a misstatement was willing to answer even though he did not know what he was writing about; such men can get clients into trouble. If a point is not attempted, it is assumed, without prejudice, that the examinee did not know the answer; but if the response is wildly wrong, the examinee has proven his incompetency.

ALLOWANCE FOR ERRORS

All examinations allow for errors; no one can be expected to be 100% correct. Most laws set 70% as passing. The grader then marks down from 100% (a perfect answer), and assumes that a 30% margin for errors gives the examinee sufficient "break" for some inadvertent straying. A grader cannot be expected to stretch a point and mark upon the basis of what he imagines the examinee meant. If an answer is not clearly explained and can be taken two or three ways, it is wrong.

ENGLISH

Surveying is a profession; a profound display of incorrect grammar and poor spelling should be down-graded. The surveyor must write reports and speak to the public. Nothing displays a lack of education and destroys confidence quicker than poor English (along with nondescript lettering). This does not imply that surveyors should be outstanding in literary talent--merely a cut above the average.

WEIGHT

The length of answer needed, especially for essay questions, can be judged by the weight of the question. If eight hours represent a weight of 100 and if a question is given a weight of twenty-five, the answer represents two hours of work. "You are requested to survey the land described in the following description. What would be your procedure?" (Weight twenty-five). Obviously a one-page answer would result in little credit--two hours of writing usually fills more pages than this. The answer must describe research, evidence, computations, filing report, and complying with state law.

KNOWLEDGE COMPLETENESS

The mere fact that an examination permits an open book does not mean there will be time to look up answers to questions; usually there is not. A candidate must be thoroughly acquainted with every section of the books taken with him so he can quickly and readily find what is wanted. Open books allow the examinee the privilege of looking up odd facts that have momentarily escaped his memory. Usually questions cannot be answered directly from one page or part of book; knowledge from several sources plus thinking and reasoning lead to a solution. Reliance upon books to find answers will result in failure.

Since books are for reference purposes only, without reasoning they are seldom of benefit. An unprepared person must expect substandard grades because too much time is lost on fishing expeditions through a sea of literature.

TRICK QUESTIONS

A trick question is one designed to deliberately mislead the examinee; they can be quite sneaky. The division line between a trick question and a legitimate question is often a matter of opinion. A person writing an examination will claim the question was designed to test a person's perception or care in noting details. An examinee believes that if every pertinent fact is not properly emphasized, it is a trick question. The field of surveying is broad, the subject diversified and difficult; examiners do not have to resort to undue trickery to determine a person's qualifications.

So-called trick questions are not troublesome if a person knows his subject, and thinks. Surveyors are supposed to reason; such questions are often the only way of finding out how his mind works.

POST-MORTEMS

An examinee with a doubtful passing grade may be called upon for an oral interview during which he will probably be asked questions about his incorrect answers. It is advisable to sit down as soon as possible after an examination and try to recall the questions. Reconstruct them and check your results by authoritative works, for questions that you could not answer.

Some state boards refuse to release examination questions after a test is finished, presumably so the same examination can be given again. Someone will copy the questions and take them away, or will list them after the examination is over--purely from memory. Those who have copies of an old examination then have an advantage. It is strongly recommended that in states where copying test questions is prohibited you immediately rewrite as many questions as is possible from memory after leaving the site. But don't do it in the examination room!

****

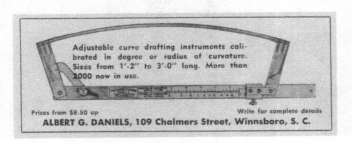

Part III

PREPARING AND GRADING EXAMINATIONS

TEST QUALITIES

Three qualities of a test. The following three items are necessary in a satisfactory measuring test:

1. Validity or truthfulness
2. Reliability or consistency
3. Usability.

These items are defined in the following paragraphs.

VALIDITY

Validity is the degree to which the test measures what is intended. Does it prove that the surveyor is qualified for the profession he is legally entrusted with? Can he measure (linear and angular)? Can he reason? Can he apply science to solve problems? Basically a surveyor's test is an achievement test. Has the surveyor sufficient knowledge to meet minimum requirements? Surveyor examinations are not I. Q. tests (intelligence quotient is the capacity to learn); they investigate what has been learned and the ability to apply that knowledge.

Reliability means consistency of the degree to which a test agrees with itself. This is like measuring with a long tape; the answer will be consistent but not truthful. Reliability is an internal question. Is the test compatible within itself? Validity is an external question: which laws of science prove the answer to be true?

RELIABILITY

Reliability is proven by statistics. If the same test is given to the same people (without intervening study), say a week apart, are the answers identical? A golf player regularly tells everyone he makes 72's, yet he actually shoots 80's. If inconsistent in telling his scores, people are suspicious that the story is not true. Consistency gives the appearance of truth; yet a person can be uniformly wrong all of the time. A test must unfailingly tell the truth.

USABILITY

Usability means practicability. An ideal test may be too difficult to prepare or score. Usability takes into account such items as scoring ease, low grading cost, simple interpretation, mechanical form, and administrative facility.

CONSIDERATIONS IN MAKING UP TESTS

If several parties of equal competence arrive at the same truthful answer, the test is said to be objective. Objective tests depend mostly upon scientific facts. A subjective question is generally answered as a matter of opinion rather than facts. "Are blonds greater lovers than redheads?" The answer to this is usually a guess and such questions are of little value, although interesting to reflect upon.

Objectivity and reliability usually go hand and hand, but this is not necessarily true since on a particular question many answers may be consistently wrong.

As long as validity (measuring what is intended to be evaluated) is not sacrificed, a safe rule is to make tests as objective as possible. Any of the standard types of test questions can be made objective or subjective, depending upon their wording. Thus, essay questions may or may not be objective. "Describe the proper procedure to survey Section 10, Township 12 South, Range 3 East, San Bernardino Meridian as outlined in the Manual of 1973 is fair?" is subjective.

The following should be considered by the person who makes up a test.

ERRORS OF TEST MEASUREMENTS

All measurements are subject to errors; this includes the measurement of knowledge. The person preparing an examination has a difficult task; he must determine the minimum required knowledge of an examinee by a test which has high validity and is consistently truthful, as a minimum cost.

PRELIMINARY DRAFT OF TEST

If at all possible, a preliminary draft of a test should be prepared several months in advance. This permits a critical review for errors and quality.

NUMBER OF QUESTIONS

It is always desirable to include more questions than is needed in the preliminary draft. At a later date some can be eliminated, especially after a "time estimate" is made.

REVISION

After a lapse of time a critical revision should be made by the maker and others with equal knowledge. Ambiguous wording can be then corrected so every question has only one answer.

ORDER OF DIFFICULTY

If possible, easy questions are placed first to give the examinee a morale boost. In a good land surveyor's examination, however, equal points should have commensurate difficulty.

CLARITY OF DIRECTIONS

The least knowledgeable examinee should know what is expected, although he may not be able to provide the solution.

RECOGNITION TESTS

The lowest level of knowledge (mere recognition) is best tested by matching types and multiple choice. The content and form of questions determine the level of knowledge being tested, not their type. Multiple choice questions can be well adapted to testing judgment, evaluation, and thinking, as well as mere recognition of a word.

Since a surveyor's test is supposed to be at the professional level, there is little, if any, need for pure recognition-type queries.

RECALL TESTS

Answers to recall questions must come from past experiences rather than identification of a reply from a series of suggested answers. Many mathematical and physical science questions are pure recall-type. With a little skill, mathematical problems can be designed to include both the elements recall and thinking (or reasoning).

Simple recall tests tend to measure isolated bits of information rather than the interrelationship of numerous facts.

For recall tests to be usable (easy to prepare, understand, and grade) a one-word response is most desirable and it should appear in a single column on the right-hand side of the page. For example,

What is the shape of the earth? (1)_____

What is the elevation datum for topography maps? (2)_____

What is the north star called? (3)_____

What causes steel tapes to elongate? (4)_____

Only one response should be possible for each question. Number (4) above can be answered as "temperature," "pull," and "wear." The same question could be better worded as: "Increased temperature causes a tape to do what? (4)_____."

COMPLETION TESTS

Completion tests are similar to simple recall tests, and unless extreme care is taken in their preparation, they measure rote memory rather than understanding. "When leveling, the formula for the correction of the earth's curvature is _____," can be written from memory, but does the examinee understand what each term means and how to apply the formula?

There are many traps a person preparing completion questions can fall into.

EXAMPLE: Errors in angular measurement are caused by _____.

COMMENT. There are too many possible responses as: vernier calibration, poor targets, heat waves, etc. If asked, this question should be in a different form as, "List the causes of errors in angular measurement." Each completion question should have only one response.

EXAMPLE: When measuring a vertical angle, if the line of sight passes from a hot air mass to a cooler air mass the line of sight is refracted _____.

COMMENT. In this question only "downward" or "upward" are correct.

Specific determiners as "a" or "an" may give unwarranted clues and should be avoided.

EXAMPLE: Distances are measured by a _____.
Distances are measured by an _____.

COMMENT. In the first question "tape" is suggested, whereas "electrotape" is suggested for the second question. In some cases plural and singular verbs or words suggest responses.

EXAMPLE: The three classes of monuments are _____.

Better: Monuments are classified as _____.

COMMENT. An objection to the above is that more than one word is needed. Generally, only a one-word response is desirable (as "artificial" in the following).

EXAMPLE: Monuments made by man are classified as _____.

TRUE-FALSE TESTS

More knowledge from a wider range of subject can be sampled within a given period of time by means of true-false tests than by any other method. Scoring is certain and completely objective.

True-False questions are appropriate to test fragmentary pieces of knowledge such as, "The side line of a street is a record monument." The examinee does not waste time writing; he merely marks an X in the true box. The disadvantage is that the examinee only puts down a cross. Can a person's ability to correctly express himself be tested by a cross? While such questions check comprehension and recall skills, they do not effectively assess writing ability or expression.

Contrary to common opinion, good true-false tests are most difficult to prepare. All too often clues or key words give away a correct response; on the other hand, some statements are too obscure.

Specific determiners of answers that should be avoided are "never," "no," "always," "all," and "none," since these tend to be false. Indicators of true statements are "as a rule," "may," "many," "often," and like items.

Avoid partly true and partly false answers as "Temperature causes tapes to elongate." This is better worded as "Decreased temperature causes tapes to elongate." The first wording should probably be scored as false and the second is definitely false. The first version can be classified as a trick question and is undesirable.

Ambiguous statements that can be interpreted as true with certain assumptions, and as false with others are to be avoided for the reasons already given. Compare these two propositions:

1. Transits are used to measure angles.

2. Angles can be measured with transits.

In the first, the thinker says, "Transits can be used to measure differences in elevation." In that case it would be false. Number (2) question has only one possible interpretation. Usually ambiguous questions penalize the more intelligent rather than the stupid.

Qualitative language such as small, large, old, young, few, etc. lead to ambiguous situations as: "George Washington was the first licensed surveyor in the United States." Another example of a poor question is, "Compensating errors are unimportant." Who can say what it is relative to? Sometimes they are important; at other times they are not.

ESSAY QUESTIONS

Land surveyors must be able to write letters, opinions, and reports. An essay question tests a broad area of knowledge emanating from the brain of the examinee; it searches whether his mental facilities are orderly arranged; and it probes his spelling, grammar, word arrangement, and written expression.

Essay questions are ideal for reviewing judgment or fluency with inexact sciences. A surveyor locating land must evaluate conditions in accordance with the law of evidence; but law is not an exact science. In deciding upon the shade of meaning of a word in a deed, he is confronted with a judgment question. If a function cannot be reduced to numbers, and is relative, discussion is the only way to find out whether the examinee, understands the problem.

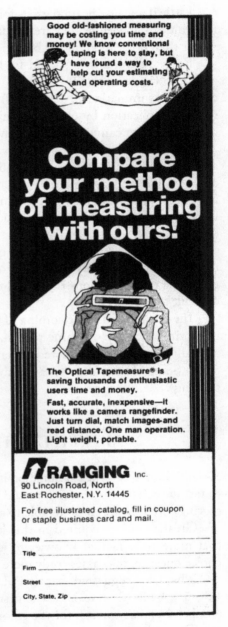

Advantages and disadvantages of essay questions are many. They most effectively measure a person's achievement at the application, interpretation, and evaluation level.

Little if any justification exists for using essay tests to measure recall or recognition knowledge; they are best for scanning functioning of knowledge rather than possession of odd bits and facts.

Essay examinations should be limited to measuring an applicant's ability to (1) describe (2) outline (3) contrast (4) compare (5) discuss (6) explain (7) summarize (8) develop, (9) evaluate and (10) interpret. Emphasis is upon application by use of organization, evaluation, relationship and other skills that cannot be adequately tested by objective questions.

Essay questions are best in two situations: testing (1) journalism and English composition, and (2) advanced subjects wherein evaluation, organization and assimilation of large amounts of material are to be measured for professional people. An individual's ability, upon the higher level, is far better shown by discussion questions than by short objective queries.

Most people know that essay questions are easy to compose; few realize that high-quality ones are extremely difficult to construct. Ease of preparing essay questions is less real than apparent, and they are far more difficult to grade.

The most serious shortcoming of essay tests is the variation of opinion in scoring, even by the same person. Thus a medium-quality paper read after an A+ one may be scored lower than if it is checked following a D effort. Some of these defects can be overcome by a better grading plan (see grading).

MULTIPLE CHOICE TESTS

A multiple-choice-type examination is considered by many as the best form to test judgment, discrimination and understanding. Its usability (ease of scoring) often makes it preferable to an essay pattern.

Greater skill is required in this kind of test than in others to insure that more than factual knowledge is tested. A poorly worded multiple choice question may assess only mere recognition.

It has been suggested that a regular sequence of responses, as 1 − 4 − 2 − 3 − 1 − 4 − 2 − 3 -, etc. is easy to grade. That is, in first question have the number 1 choice correct; for the second problem have item 4 the answer, etc. This order is then repeated throughout the test. Too many students discover such key arrangements so the method must be avoided.

At least four choices should be offered in multiple choice questions. Sometimes it is advisable to require marking the false answer instead of the true response. To test evaluation and judgment the instruction can read, "Mark the most nearly true statement."

A variation on this form is the multiple answer question. In this case five choices are usually given and any one of these may or may not be correct. All may be wrong, or all may be right. This question is weighted five points, one for each choice. If a choice is marked when it shouldn't be, or not marked when it should be, then that decision is marked wrong. The advantages of this type question are (1) easily scored by machine (2) five decisions are required, (3) process of elimination is ruled out since all, none, or a combination may be right, and (4) larger, more complete situations can be created for each problem. A sample series of multiple answer questions are included in the general question section, at the very end. (The preceding paragraph was added by Roy Minnick)

When measuring higher levels of understanding, the choices are very nearly the same, that is, false statements have a degree of untruth difficult to discern. Words having minor or subtle differences are used rather than terms of widely divergent meanings. Compare these words: accretion, alluvion, reliction, and revulsion.

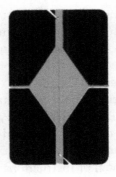

MATCHING TESTS

Matching tests are well adapted for who, what, when, and where types of questions. Thus, an event and a date; an event and a place; or an instrument and a part. They are not well suited to measuring true understanding as compared to rote memory and have a limited use, if any, for testing professional people. It is almost impossible to design a matching test that measures ability to interpret complex relationships.

FRAMING QUESTIONS

No question should suggest its own answer or signal that for a previous query. On open book examinations problems must not give a clue to where the response can be found in the reference work. Nor should the question be one for which the solution can be copied directly from a single quickly found source.

In a closed book examination such instructions as this has been given, "In a sectionalized land state, define the following abbreviations: B, 0, S, R, B, T, 1/4 cor, etc." This kind of question should never be given in an open book examination. A person would get 100% by just copying answers from the "Manual of Instructions for Survey of the Public Lands."

Such questions are factual and do not require the examinee to sort data and come to a correct conclusion. Factual knowledge that a person is "educated." Parrots can speak, but who has ever heard one ask for his dinner when hungry?

"Which state laws must you comply with in filing a record of survey?" can be copied from the statutes; this is a direct approach. An indirect question covering the same subject matter would be, "You are asked to divide a tract of land into two parcels, monument each parcel, and prepare necessary land descriptions. What procedure would you follow after completing the survey and monumenting the property?" The law in this state (California) requires filing a record of survey plat which discloses certain things. The questions did not suggest answers by asking which laws must be complied with; the surveyor should know them. In a closed book examination the direct approach is often used; in an open book test the indirect approach is better.

ESTIMATING ANSWERING TIME

The person framing a question can always answer it faster than can anyone else. If he takes two minutes to read and answer it, a minimum of four minutes should be allowed for others. Estimating completion time requirements demands sound judgment on the part of the examiner; perhaps the best method of obtaining a fair appraisal is to actually try it out on a competent person who is unfamiliar with the questions. Of course the person serving as a prototype must be completely trustworthy; a test in the hands of the examinee insures a 100% grade.

GRADING STANDARDS

The National Council of State Boards of Engineering Examiners (NCEE) published suggested standards for graders of professional engineering examinations. These criteria have been reworded, altered slightly, and predicated to fit the following recommended marking standards for professional surveying examinations.

(1) The most important object in grading examinations is to determine if the candidate has at least the certain minimum surveying qualifications. It is well known that candidates are frequently nervous, and liable to mistakes which would be corrected if more care could be taken. It is a challenge to the grader to decide whether errors arise from haste or incompetency. The grader should tend toward generosity in marking.

Each grader should prepare a complete solution for the problem and a detailed rating plan indicating the principal basis for evaluating an acceptable solution. An outline form is suggested. Alternate logical solutions should be given weight if they are worked out with a professional level approach. A problem, along with a list of penalties for typical errors or omissions that an examinee might make, will assist in the over-all appraisal. The grading schedule should also show what part-score points will be given for inaccurate or only partially worked problem solutions.

A grader should make frequent and readable notations on the examination papers (either on the work or in the margin) to indicate those parts of the solution which are correct or incorrect. Sarcastic or derogatory remarks must be avoided. Comments relative to corrections in calculations are most valuable. If more than one grader reviews a paper, observations must be omitted or placed on separate paper in order to secure independent judgments.

(2) The following paragraphs define the various grades to be given for each problem based on a range of zero to ten. Obviously, judgment of the grader is the ultimate criteria.

10. Understands problem and obtains correct solution. Well organized; shows good surveying judgment, and perhaps ingenuity. Demonstrates knowledge of the fundamental principles.

9. Same as 10, but with a more routine approach, displaying less judgment. Excessive conservatism in choice of variables such as allowable errors.

8. Only errors introduced by hastiness, misread notes, tables, or minor calculation and arithmetic errors which would be caught by routine checking. Results reasonable, though not correct.

7. Displays a knowledge of how to obtain solution but chooses poor approach. Difficult to follow reasoning, in spite of reasonable result. Awkward solution.

6. Same as 7, but with additional difficulty due to numerical mistakes, or grammatical and spelling errors. Partially solved.

5. Method in error, deviates from intent of problem, but pursuit of erroneous method shows clear thinking and good surveying knowledge.

4. Shows some knowledge of this type of problem but only vague approach. Probably incomplete solution. Results may be unreasonable, indicating this area has been forgotten. Has been more successful in other problems.

3. Approach entirely wrong, results unreasonable, good organization, but misdirected.

2.   Does not have good organization to recommend it.

[MP NOTE: There is no item number 1 in the original document.]

Each grader must mark all papers on the same basis, and to the same standard. Consistency of grading is vital to an equitable over-all evaluation of the examination. In general, solutions to problems should approach the quality that could reasonably be expected of a competent, qualified practicing surveyor.

Many problems will be entitled to part credit. Be generous in grading, and give examinees the benefit of the doubt in controversial areas where multi-solutions might apply. Be sure to note constructive comments where possible.

CORRECTION FORMULA FOR GRADING

The obvious defect of alternate-response (true - false, etc.) questions is that a person can guess answers; if he has average luck he can get 50% right. Suppose that it takes 70% to pass a written test, and that of 100 questions the examinee knows 50% of the answers correctly. He then guesses the remaining 50%, and on the average, should get 50% of these right, adding another 25% to his grade. The 50% he knew and the 25% obtained by conjecture is sufficient to pass with a 70% grade. To prevent guessing there must be a penalty for an error equal to the credit allowed for correct answer. The usual custom is to deduct the number of wrongs from rights. Unanswered questions are not subtracted.

In grading true-false questions a master sheet is made with holes cut to match the correct box for true or false. This allows the marker to instantly see which boxes were correctly marked. A clever examinee might "X" both boxes for doubtful questions however; this way no matter which square is masked a correct answer will appear. A grader must always look for double box marks and penalize the examinee heavily for such tactics.

With multiple choice questions having four or more choices it is seldom worthwhile to apply a correction formula, but for two or three choices it is always applied using the form

$$G = C - \frac{W}{n-1} \qquad \text{where}$$

→ G is grade or score for the test corrected for guessing.

→ C is number of correct responses.

→ W is the number of wrong responses.

→ n is number of choices for each item.

For true-false tests *n* is two and the formula reduces to correct minus wrong responses. For three-response questions the formula is number right less one-half the mistaken responses.

At this point, not a great deal more needs to be said and it is time the student try his hand at some practice problems.

****

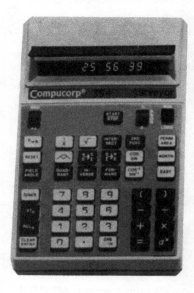

EVIDENCE

THE SURVEYOR AND THE LAW

TIE POINTS

SEPTEMBER 1961

From a local surveyor I received a question concerning the status of tie points and what special value they have as evidence.

My answer is:

Public records are admissible in evidence; there is no trouble introducing evidence of tie point positions. Private records, on the other hand, cannot be introduced as evidence without the author being present (there are some exceptions).

Usually, but not always, the monuments and tie points set by the city engineer or the public surveyor, when performing official duties, is prima facie evidence. At law, prima facie evidence is taken as true until such time as it is proven false. Recorded deeds are prima facie evidence of the contents of writings. The original deed may be produced to refute the contents of the recorded document, but, until it is, the recorded deed is accepted.

Monuments and tie points set by city officials, especially if in connection with their official duties, are often accepted in court as being correct unless proven incorrect. This has advantages and much merit in some instances.

After all of the original monuments of an addition to a city have disappeared and uncertainty exists as to street and property locations, tie points by the city engineer are a welcome sight. And after these have been used a number of years, they become accepted as true. This is one of the methods of establishing boundaries and eventually this gives certainty to locations. Without tie points having prima facie status as evidence, many property lines could not be established without court action.

But tie pointing by the city engineer, improperly done, can cause great harm. In one city in the Imperial Valley the city engineer tie pointed all of the blocks by giving them exactly record measurements, and then placed all of the surplus and deficiency in the streets. Many instances of improper tie pointing are found in the court's records, as at Santa Barbara, Sacramento and Racine (Wis.). The usual objections to improperly set tie points come from surveyors with private records; they know when something is wrong. Prima facie status of evidence (tie points) does not always prevent troubles; but it does, at times, give definiteness to otherwise degenerated situations. Tie points, properly set, represent one of the best methods of giving stability to property location.

– Curtis M. Brown

****

THE SURVEYOR AND THE LAW

LINE TREES

MARCH 1963

When the original section lines of the U. S. sectionalized land system were run, especially in forested areas, it was not uncommon for original surveyors to mark line trees in accordance with the instructions issued by the Surveyor General. The following question was raised by R. E. Schmeling on behalf of the Upper Peninsula Chapter of the Michigan Society of Registered Land Surveyors. "In accordance with the original surveyor's notes, the following original points were found: (1) The NW corner of the section, (2) the north quarter corner of the section, and (3) a line tree located 7.12 chains easterly of the NW section corner and located 9 links north of a straight line connecting the section and quarter corners. The record distance between the section corner and the quarter comer was 40 chains and it was re-measured as 40.13 chains. The line tree was originally reported as being 7.06 chains east of the section corner and it was found to be 7.12 chains easterly (see figure). What effect, if any, does the line tree have on locating the 1/16 corner"?

The 1/16 corner was not originally set; no method other than proportional measurement can be used. The rule for setting the 1/16 corner for most sections of land, is to set the corner half way and on a straight line between the section and quarter corners (there are exceptions to this, but it is assumed that this rule, in the absence of line tree or other line objects, would apply in this case).

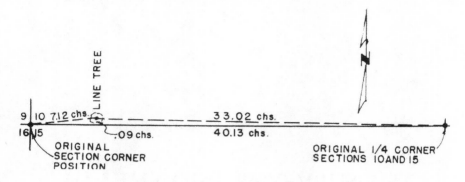

Contrary to locating the 1/16 corner on a straight line is the rule: An original monument, once called for, is unalterable in position except where a superior right is interfered with (senior right, etc.). A line tree is just as much an original monument as is a section or quarter corner. Can we ignore an original monument merely because it is not on a straight line? Do we ignore a quarter corner when it is not on a straight line between section corners? In reading court cases, I have found a number of cases where line trees have been recognized as controlling. Although there are probably a few cases to the contrary, I have never found a case where an original identifiable line tree was not recognized. In a few cases, even blazed trees located on either side of the line have been recognized as controlling direction. The difference between a line tree and a blazed tree off line can be distinguished by the types of markings (see *Evidence and Procedures for Boundary Location,* by Curtis Brown and Winfield Eldridge, John Wiley & Sons, Inc., New York, page 47). Although I am not sure of the Michigan situation and there may be a rule different from the majority opinion (witness the remnant rule in Minnesota), I would use a line tree to control direction until proven otherwise.

In the matter of proration, there is the rule: *Proration may never be applied beyond a found original position.* The only fixed positions with zero error of position are called for objects or monuments in deeds or conveyances (water excepted). Original standard corners (not closing corners), once found undisturbed, are not altered by proration. This holds for all original called for positions. A line tree is declared by the notes to be on the line at a definite distance from other corners. My solution would be to set the 1/16 corner on a straight line between the line tree and the quarter corner at a point proportional distance between the two, that is:

(20.00 x 27.12) - 27.06 from the quarter corner.

This same type of reasoning is applied when prorating from a closing corner. You apply proration from the spot occupied by the closing corner; you do not apply proration from the relocated position on the line closed upon.

This situation verifies the need for laws permitting the surveyor to record evidence. Today, while the line tree is standing, the line is bent; after the tree is destroyed, another surveyor would make it a straight line. If the evidence were recorded in a public place, the later surveyor would also make a bent line. If we do not have all of the evidence upon which a conclusion is based, we make poor decisions.

– CURTIS M. BROWN

****

ERRATA

After commenting on the "Brilliant Boner," * I contributed to a brilliant boner. In the March 1962 issue Of SURVEYING AND MAPPING, "Surveyor and the Law" department, page 120, the mathematical relation should have been:

20.00/32.94 X 33.02 = 20.049

Within one day after the issue came out, four people reminded me of my sin (including Professor Aggeler and one of my employees). At least it is gratifying to know that the column is read.

* SURVEYING AND MAPPING, December 1962, Vol. XXII, No. 4, page 608.

– CURTIS M. BROWN

****

The Surveyor's Notebook

Reporting on Unusual Surveying Problems and Their Solutions

Notekeeper: W. & L. E. Gurley, America's Oldest Engineering Instrument Maker

"A Bit More Mauka ... A Few Feet Makai"

"Surveys in Hawaii introduce many new features to a surveyor trained on the mainland," says Russell Brinker, Head of the Department of Civil Engineering at Virginia Polytechnic Institute.

"**The ancient land system** divided an island roughly into several *mokus* (districts). Each *moku* was split into *ahupua'as*, pie-shaped pieces extending from ocean to mountain top and varying considerably in area.

"Theoretically, each *ahupua'a* contained a *kai* (sea fishery), a stretch of *kula* (upland) and some *kuahiwi* (forest and mountain land). Thus, the ruling chief and his people could get fish, taro and wood from their own land holdings in the Islands.

"**To trace old deeds**, today's surveyor must be able to read descriptions in a 12-letter Hawaiian alphabet. Simple terms like North and South are frequently discarded in favor of visual directions. What, then, could be easier than to send a rodman a bit more *mauka* (mountainward) or a few feet *makai* (oceanward)? Or to tell the chainman to move Diamond Head-way or Punchbowl-way?

"In the mid-'30's, I surveyed small parcels in the Islands for the Government, so that portions could be taken out of rice production. Standard practice was followed the first half day by measuring angles at corners, and lengths along dike sides of the flooded rice

Prof. Russell Brinker (left) instructs students at VPI in the use of the transit. The instrument is one of 25 Gurley transits and levels owned by VPI.

paddies. Since ties between adjacent ownerships and exact areas were not needed, a faster, less accurate method seemed necessary.

"**So we set up** near the estimated center of an individual farm on a paddy bank. Two rodmen started at diagonally-opposite corners and moved clockwise around the field. Stadia distances and azimuths from an arbitrary reference line were read on the two rods in alternate order and recorded.

"As soon as all corners had been sighted, we set up in the next field and repeated the process. Readings were plotted later and areas obtained by planimeter.

Triangulation stations like this are common in Hawaii.

Write for a free copy of "The Surveyor's Notebook."

COMMENT AND DISCUSSION

DECEMBER 1963

The pages of *SURVEYING AND MAPPING* are open to free and temperate discussion of all matters pertaining to the interests of the Congress. It is the purpose of this department to encourage comments on published material or the presentation of new ideas in an informal way.

– Editor

LINE TREES

TED R. MILLER * - Reference is made to the article "Line Trees" by Curtis Brown in the March 1963 journal. I would disagree under the conditions described that an original GLO line tree found between a known section corner and a known 1/4 corner should place a dog-leg in the line connecting the two, and thus placing the 1/16 corner off a straight line.

The controlling points of the original survey were the corners which the original surveyor set and not the path he traveled in determining their location. Otherwise there would not be a straight line in any of the compass-located lines of the original survey between section and quarter corners. Due to man's inability to walk a perfectly straight line when perfectly sober, a compass line inherently wobbles.

Line trees were possibly a required headache for the original surveyor, and their linear location may not have been too closely recorded. I would seriously question prorating the distance from the line tree, thus placing the 1/16 corner other than equidistant between original corner locations. And in direction, who knows how close behind the compassman or the chainmen may have been the axman.

Certainly if either the ¼ corner or particularly the section corner in the case cited, since it was close to the line tree, were lost, then the line tree would be controlling in determining the direction of the straight line and the distance.

* 700 Park Avenue, Charlevoix, Michigan. Registered Land Surveyor (Michigan), and member of the Michigan Society of Registered Land Surveyors and the American Congress on Surveying and Mapping.

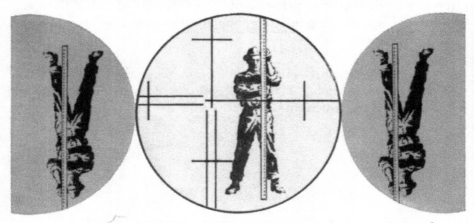

242

IDENTIFYING MONUMENTS

PRESENTED AT THE NEW MEXICO ASSOCIATION OF SURVEYORS AND MAPPERS LAND SURVEYING LEGAL SYMPOSIUM

JANUARY 16-17, 1976

Of the many duties of the land surveyor, one of the most perplexing problems is that of locating original monument positions. The forces of nature along with time destroy most things. Monuments decay or can be disrupted by man's construction activities. All too often the original monument material disappears completely, this necessitating reliance on secondary evidence.

Because of the destruction of physical evidence, in identifying original monument positions we are seldom hunting for the original monument itself; we are seeking an answer to the question, "What spot did the original monument occupy"? The evidence used to prove the former location of an original monument can take many forms. The order of importance of evidence used to identify original monument positions is as follows:

1. If the original physical monument itself can be found and it has not been disturbed, it is conclusive.

2. Accessories to the original monument when found undisturbed prove a former monument's position. If a monument is easily moved and the accessories are not, the accessories might control position in preference to the movable original monument.

3. Surveyor's records of remonumentation of the original monument are next in the order of importance of acceptable evidence.

4. Finding unbiased and reliable witnesses who remember the original monument's location rank next (this includes surveyors).

5. Fences or other line indicators built at the time the original monuments were present, or could be presumed to be present, may be a perpetuation of the original lines marked and surveyed, and as such can control the original monument position.

6. The locations of tie points of public agencies are presumed correct. In the absence of better evidence they control.

7. Reputation and hearsay, as a last resort, sometimes determine original positions.

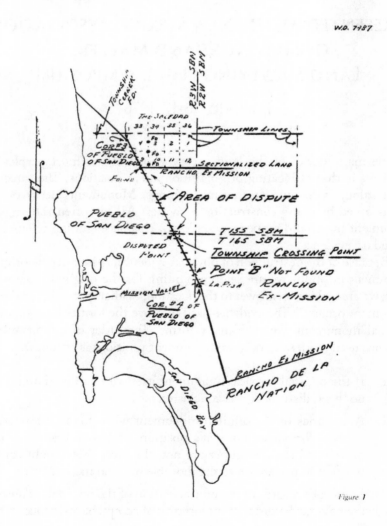

Figure 1

244

Since every survey must start from an existing monument or monuments, in no way can one avoid the necessity of identifying at least two monuments. Even latitude and longitude depends upon two monuments, the earth's axis of rotation and a point in Greenwich, England. Some type of astronomic observation determines bearings, where no basis is specified, and the stars used are monuments.

Since all of you have faced the problem of monument identification and are fairly well acquainted with the process, the usual discussion of each principle in detail will not be made here. The hunt and seek process will be illustrated by an examination of court cases involving a few million dollars.

According to past history, Spanish law permitted Pueblos to acquire 4 square leagues of land. San Diego formed a Pueblo government and in 1845 had one Mr. Fitch, a former sea captain, prepare a map. The crude map indicated points at "The Soledad," a hill above Soledad Canyon; at "La Posa," a pond in Mission Valley; at "Chollas," a dry wash; and along the National Rancho to the south. (See Fig. 1.) After the treaty of Guadalupe Hidalgo in 1848 and after the United States took possession of California, a Commission was set up to determine the valid rights of former Mexican citizens and existing Pueblos.

During the time the commission was holding its hearings, the U.S. Government began surveys. Principal meridians, correction lines, and township lines with set section and quarter corners were run through land grants, including the Pueblo of San Diego.

In 1858, four years after the township line surveys, the Land Commission ordered Hays to make a survey of the San Diego Pueblo grant and part of the instructions were to make ties to the nearest corners on the township lines as those lines were crossed. Although Hays completed the survey in 1858, it was not approved until April 10, 1874.

The survey disclosed that Fitch's map included 11-plus leagues instead of 4 as allowed by Spanish law. Regardless of this, the larger amount was awarded by the commission (48,556.69 acres).

The line from The Soledad (corner 3 of Hays) to Mission Valley (corner 4 of Hays) was 9.75 miles long. At an intermediate point, as Hays crossed the township line, he set an earth mound according to instructions. Later surveys, especially by Fox and Shaw, disclosed that a found monument thought to be set by Hays at or near the township crossing point was about 200 feet westerly of a straight line from The Soledad (corner 3) to the Mission Valley corner 4. Williams in 1917 was ordered by the city to run a straight line from The Soledad to corner 4 and monument it. He found the monument at the township crossing point and measured the deviation from a straight line; it was 213.81 feet westerly. Now there was a dispute as to who owned the area between the two lines. In effect, a sliver of land 9.75 miles long and 213.81 feet wide at its widest point was in question. No structures were erected in this area, since title insurance could not be obtained.

City subdivisions and improvements finally engulfed both sides of this area and a commercial zone was established next to the line. Land values rose to about $65,000 per acre or for the entire disputed area the price tag was a few million.

The State of California Highway Division, wanting to put in a freeway and seeing this clear section of land 9.75 miles long, decided to use the land. To get title they condemned the land, put the money in escrow and, in effect, said, "We do not know whom to pay the money to, but it is in the bank, and the various land owners can bring action to claim it." Since a very sizable sum was involved, numerous parties owning land on each side made claims. There were four attorneys, including the city's attorney, contending for the eastern Williams line and four for the western Shaw line. Four surveyors and engineers testified for the eastern Williams line and two surveyors and an engineer testified for the western Shaw line.

I was interviewed by the city attorney and expressed an opinion that I did not think that the easterly line was correct, so he employed another surveyor. Later the attorneys contending for the western Shaw line employed me. It is my opinion that if you think the side you are asked to work for is wrong, inform them so at the earliest possible date and excuse yourself.

Although there were a lot of side questions in this case, the primary issues as pertaining to surveyors were twofold:

1. Should the land grant line be a straight line from grant corner to grant corner? The Fitch map, used by the Land Commission in their hearings, had a straight line from corner to corner. How could a monument set by Hays at the township line crossing point create a bend in a line that was originally shown as straight?

2. Assuming that a bend in the line at the township crossing point was permissible, is the existing monument at the township crossing point in the same position as that set by Hays in 1858?

246

The first question was largely legal and a question of law; the other surveyors, engineers, and I had little to say about it. My job was to develop evidence that would prove the second point.

The judge, in ruling on the first point, concluded that the Pueblo boundaries as established by the Land Commission were conclusive and no one could go behind their ruling to prove Hays wrong. Since there was a survey, all monuments called for in the field notes were part of the boundaries, including the monument at the township crossing point. What he said, in effect, was that if the monument at the township crossing point could be properly identified and located it marked a point on the line; if it happened to create a crooked line, the line would be crooked.

The proponents of the Williams line, the more easterly line and the more nearly straight line between corners 3 and 4, contended that Hays' crossing point could not be reestablished and, since it is technically a lost monument, a straight line between corners 3 and 4 is, therefore, the true boundary of the Pueblo of San Diego in the area in question. No one questioned the authenticity of corners 3 and 4.

The proponents of the Shaw line or the westerly line had to develop the evidence showing that Hays' 1858 monument did in fact occupy a known location and, if they failed, the corner was then truly lost and, therefore, the Williams line prevailed.

It is interesting to note that when Williams made his 9.75-mile survey in 1917 he failed to make a straight line by about 4 feet. Equipment at that time was inferior to present-day equipment. Occupancy to the Williams line at the date of the trial made it impossible to move the line easterly the necessary 4 feet to make a straight line. A legal right obtained by any of the processes of occupancy always extinguishes written rights.

To develop proof for Hays' monument location: (1) A chain of evidence from 1858 to the present had to be found; (2) evidence of inaccuracy of measurements typical of the era had to be developed to justify a crooked line; and (3) proof was needed that a dirt mound could last 50 to 100 years in the vicinity of the dispute. At the time of the trial, the purported Hays' monument position was in the middle of a paved road and all evidence had been recently destroyed. The added burden was to prove where the purported monument formerly existed about ten years prior to the trial.

All of this was, in simple terms, a research project requiring an enormous amount of time. Fortunately, having worked in the area upon many occasions, I was well acquainted with and had tie-outs to what existed in 1950. When my office made surveys on the west side of the disputed area, we terminated our survey at the Shaw line; when we worked on the east side, we terminated our survey at the Williams line. At no time was I about to "buy" a lawsuit. I just told the adjoiners what the problem was and let them try to make their decisions as to what they wanted to claim. After a few years in the surveying business you learn not to give a client a disputed area; it keeps your pocketbook a little fatter.

The amount of evidence that I amassed filled two file drawers plus a lot of flat file space. The following is a bare outline of the more essential points, given in their historical sequence:

1. Freeman in 1854 ran township lines through the Land Grant. Freeman's notes were placed in evidence.

2. Hays' field notes in 1858 said, "Set post in mound on township line between T15S and T16S, R3W and 33 chains west of corner to sections 1 - 2 - 35 - 36." I presented to the court my copy of the 1855 Manual that explained how mounds and pits had to be constructed at the time. I never got it back. It is still in evidence. The best procedure is to present Xerox copies of the pertinent pages and places the entire book on display for examination only.

3. The adjoining Rancho Mission to the east was surveyed in 1869 by Wheeler. He ran west to the Rancho San Diego boundary line and then southerly along the Rancho San Diego boundary to Hays' township crossing point (he did not say what was found), where

he measured the distance to the section corner common to 1 - 2 - 35 - 36 and recorded it as 33.10 chains. The 0.1 chain difference from Hays' measurement became very significant; if a different distance was measured then both monuments had to exist for the measurement to have been made.

4. The attorney introduced my solar compass for display during the trial and I testified as to the probable accuracy for directional bearings as of Hays' time. I was able to establish the fact that Hays was unlikely to have run a straight line with his equipment. The judge himself looked through the slits for sighting. I also had a 33-foot chain on exhibit. I got these back.

5. In 1885 in the trial of *Luco v. Commercial Bank,* Fox made a partition map of Rancho Mission and filed his survey field notes with the court records. He set several monuments along the Rancho San Diego line, and at the township crossing point he noted an earth mound and post but made no mention as to whether he found or set the mound. He did show a bearing on each side of the monument, and they differed, thus indicating the probability of "found" to justify an angle. In his description of one of the lots in Rancho Mission he wrote, "Thence west one hundred nine chains thirty links to a post marked Lot 38 Cor. #4 on the west line of the Rancho, being a point named in the original field notes of the patent of the Rancho where the Township line between Townships fifteen (15) and sixteen (16) South intersect said West Line." In the forties when I was doing a survey in the area in question I had observed a mound at this location, but the post was missing.

The proponents of the Williams line contended that Fox set this corner at the township line and it was not Hays' original corner. My arguments were threefold: First, as aforesaid, Fox showed an angle point by the change in bearings as he went through the crossing point, thus he had to find the mound to justify his change of direction. Second, we had found an original Fox survey point to the north and that post was on a straight line between corner 3 and the township crossing point. Thirdly, Fox, in his written report to the court, had noted that it was in fact the crossing point.

6. The Williams' proponents introduced in evidence Hays' notes, wherein as he crossed one of the range lines in 1858 he could

not find a nearby section corner. His notes state: ". . . found no mound or post for corner to section 25 – 26 – 30 - 31, supposed to have been destroyed by cattle." Their contention was that if cattle destroyed one corner then it was logical that they would also destroy the township crossing corner. I then pointed out to the court that the corner that Hays could not locate was in a valley where there was plenty of water and where cattle would logically thrive. On the other hand, the corner at the township crossing point was on a mesa with brush, no pasture, and no water. Cattle even in recent times prior to subdivision activities (1940) did not occupy that area.

7. In 1893, Shaw, a city employee, was given the task of running the eastern boundary of the Pueblo of San Diego for the purpose of setting monuments to divide city lands into Pueblo lots. In so doing he found the earth mound at the township crossing with Fox's post in it and noted such in his field books. He ran a straight line from the township crossing corner southerly to the uncontested point in Mission Valley and northerly to the uncontested point at The Soledad. By his bearings there was an angle at the township-crossing mound. He also set numerous points along the line and, in the main, they existed at the time of the court case; however we could not find a statement as to what he set. We did find concrete monuments at all measured places where he indicated a Pueblo lot corner. From Shaw's field notes I was able to plot his entire survey. Admittedly, it was a long and painstaking task; however it paid off. I found that Shaw had located two original township section corner monuments to the west and had tied them out. Furthermore, they were within a few feet of the record (80 chains minus the 33 chains). This added strength to the fact that Shaw had carefully considered other evidence before he accepted the mound with Fox's post in it. Shaw's notes were accepted in evidence even though Shaw was not alive to testify. They had been kept in the city engineer's office. If they had been kept privately, there may have been a problem of getting them accepted in evidence.

8. To the east of Shaw's line were two subdivisions made prior to 1916. Record distances from interior lot monuments terminated in the Shaw line, not that of Williams.

9. In 1916 the power company ran a straight line from corner 3 to

corner 4 and decided on their own that the line must be straight. They then erected a major transmission line along their survey line.

10. In 1917 Williams, another city surveyor, ran a straight line from corner 3 to corner 4, and the city claimed the area between the Shaw and the Williams survey lines, some 123 acres. Williams in running his line tied out all of Shaw's points and set numerous monuments along the new line. At the township crossing point he tied out Fox's mound and post and set a new monument at the township crossing point.

With this evidence we had to convince the judge that there was no gap in the sequence of events and that mounds could last at least as long as the period between our provable survey events. Fortunately for the Shaw proponents, the Williams proponents made a blunder by presenting testimony that one of their surveyors had found the original township corner set by Freeman in 1854 and that it still existed. Why the surveyor looked for a corner that no longer controlled property lines and that existed in the middle of the San Diego Pueblo grant is beyond my comprehension, but he did. I suppose it was surveyor curiosity. Unknown to the Williams proponents, I had found three section and quarter corner mounds set in 1880. They were located just to the northeast in an undisturbed area. In due time a field trip was arranged for the entire court. We went first to the township corner, and the surveyor testified that he had found the monument under a large mountain mahogany, that he had removed the bush and exposed the mound. The mound was obvious, four pits were visible and, upon shaving the surface, the circular stain where the original post existed was clearly visible. This established the fact that if a mound and pits could last from 1854 to 1970 then the mound at the township crossing point could last from 1858 to 1885, the time of the Fox survey.

Next, the court traveled to see the section and quarter corners set in 1880. At the first one, I pointed out the mound and commented that a sandstone marked "1/4" was in the mound several years ago. Someone noted a sandstone lying flat a few yards distant and the judge discovered the "1/4" on the stone. Needless to say, he was elated, and the fact that mounds in this area could last at least 60 years was impressed upon his mind.

At another point at a section corner, the opposing attorneys pointed to several other mounds nearby and wanted to know why this one was different. By scraping the surface, the old pits were faintly visible and also by digging in the center of the mound an iron pipe set by a previous surveyor was uncovered.

To illustrate the errors found in early surveys we resurveyed the north line of Rancho Mission (the adjoining rancho to the east) and found a section corner 200 feet north of the straight Rancho line. It was supposed to be on the line and it was the same corner that the judge had viewed on the field trip. This established proof of large original errors made by early surveyors.

The case went on for more than three months of court time. I was on the stand a total of 11 days in addition to one day in the field. Two days were spent cross-examining me in the matter of basis of bearings.

Perhaps the redeeming feature of the trial was the brilliance of one of the four Shaw attorneys (Mr. Gant) and the intelligence and patience of the judge. Rarely does one find an attorney as well versed in survey matters and a judge who quickly grasps survey situations. At one time in the trial one of the opposing surveyors contended that Shaw did not make a complete circuit and that his survey was dangling in space. Apparently he had not seen all of Shaw's field books. I handed the correct book to Gant, pointed to the page, and with this information he started cross-examination and got the surveyor to admit that Shaw did in fact run a circuit. Pertinent here is the fact that Gant had worked for State Highway crews during his college vacation days and knew how to read notes.

About the author

Curtis M. Brown graduated with honors in engineering from the University of California in 1932. He retired from private practice of land surveyor as partner in the firm of Daniels, Brown and Hall, several years ago, and has been occupied since in research and writing, which includes contributions to a dog show monthly publication, *Kennel Review*, and coauthored a book with his wife entitled *The Art and Science of Judging Dogs*. His wife, Thelma, is a highly qualified dog show judge and has worked shows in Albuquerque, Santa Fe, and El Paso in the Southwestern area. Next winter they are going 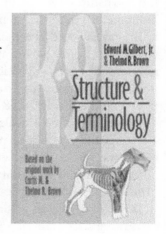 to Australia where Mrs. Brown will judge several shows.

Frequently Curt is called upon as an expert witness in important boundary litigation and is an unpaid consultant to his son, Patrick, a civil engineer with a private surveying practice.

Curt has also been very active in ACSM. He is past chairman of the Land Surveys Division when it was called the Property Surveys Division, was a member of the ACSM Board of Direction, and served as ACSM president in 1965.

He has taught and lectured on the legal aspects of land surveying for many years. Included in this activity are courses at San Diego City College and Purdue University, among others. His book, *Boundary Control and Legal Principles* is well known among land surveyors as is *Evidence and Procedures for Boundary Location*, which he coauthored with the late Winfield H. Eldridge.

Paper presented at the New Mexico Association of Surveyors and Mappers Land Surveying Legal Symposium, Jan. 16 - 17, 1976.

****

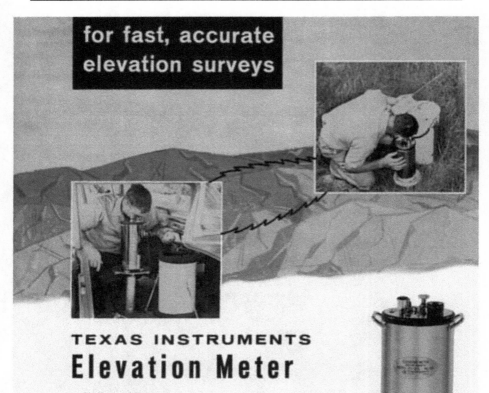

AROUND
THE WORLD

THE SURVEYOR AND THE LAW

LEGAL ELEMENTS OF PROPERTY SURVEYS ARE SIMILAR IN NEW BRUNSWICK AND THE UNITED STATES

JUNE 1964

At the last annual convention of the Massachusetts Association of Land Surveyors and Civil Engineers,* in a discussion with W. F. Roberts, Director of Surveys, Province of New Brunswick, Canada, a comment was made that United States books pertaining to the legal elements of property surveys were recommended reading for those preparing for the New Brunswick land surveyors examination. After reading a few New Brunswick cases, the reason became quite apparent. The laws of both New Brunswick and the United States stem from English common law, and both are identical in many ways. A few examples are given below.

Construed against grantor, except the sovereign -- A grant from the Crown to the subject shall be taken most beneficially for the King and against the party, whereas the grant of the subject is construed most strongly against the grantor. (Wilson v Codyre. 27 NBR 320)

Senior rights -- The true line must be determined by the terms of the earlier grant, regard being first had to the natural boundaries stated in the grant, and, in subordination thereto, to the specified courses and distances, giving preference to the one or the other according to circumstances. (Brevier v Govang, 4 All. 144)

Identification by reference -- Where lands are described by a reference, either expressly or by implication, to a plan, the plan is considered as incorporated with the deed, and the contents and boundaries of the land conveyed, as defined by the plan, are to be taken as part of the description, just as though an extended description to that effect was in words contained in the body of the deed itself. (Grassett v Carter, 10 SCR 105)

Control Monuments- - It is clearly established that in questions of boundary fixed and ascertained objects or monuments or boundary control courses and distances. (Whelply v Lyons 2 Kerr 276)

Control of natural and artificial monuments -- In attempting to ascertain the intentions of parties to a deed, artificial monuments are regarded by the law as evidence of the intentions of the parties, second only in controlling force to that of natural monuments. (Shute v Adney (No. 2) 39 NBR 93)

Control of course and distance -- Where no monuments are called for by the deed, then the courses and distances must prevail. It is a well established principle that extrinsic evidence of monuments found upon the ground, but not referred to in a deed, is not admissible to control the deed. (Landry v Landry, 48 NBR 47, and Montreal Trust v Corey, 18 MPR 427)

Control of artificial stakes on the bank of a river -- If a boundary is described as running to a monument standing on the bank, and thence running by the river or along the river, it does not restrict the grant to the bank of the stream; for the monument in such a case is only referred to as giving the direction of the line to the river, and not as restricting the boundary on the river. (Robinson v White, 42 Main 218)

All of these are, of course, the common law of most States. Those reading United States books on the legal elements of boundary location law will get some ideas on what may happen in situations not yet tried in New Brunswick.

* See SURVEYING AND MAPPING, December 1963, Vol. XXIII, No. 4, p. 638.

– CURTIS M. BROWN

****

COMMENT AND DISCUSSION

DECEMBER 1964

The pages of *SURVEYING AND MAPPING* are open to free and temperate discussion of all matters pertaining to the interests of the Congress. It is the purpose of this department to encourage comments on published material or the presentation of new ideas in an informal way.

– Editor

IDENTIFICATION OF LAND MARKERS

I received a letter from James A. Darling, commenting on *Licensing Laws and Land Surveyors' Examination*, in the June 1964 issue of *SURVEYING AND MAPPING*.

"I noted your statement that California appears to be the only state making it mandatory to file records of surveys and to place license numbers on all monuments set. You might be interested in the attached copy of Chapter 9 of the Government Code of Guam which makes both of such items mandatory here."

The Public Law 6-121 of Guam (Sixth Guam Legislature, Bill 504, enacted July 5, 1962) provides:

"Section 13807. Identification of Land Markers. In addition to the other requirements established by regulations, a permanent land marker shall be set to identify any change of direction of the boundary of any lot, parcel or tract of land, stamped with the letters 'L. S.' and the certificate of registration number of the surveyor setting the marker or, if set by a public officer, stamped with his official title."

I am happy to see other areas requiring identifications on monuments set.

****

REPORT ON F. I. G. MEETING

BY CURTIS M. BROWN

PRESIDENT, AMERICAN CONGRESS ON SURVEYING AND MAPPING

SEPTEMBER 1965

THE PAPERS PRESENTED at the Eleventh International Congress of Surveyors, Rome, Italy, May 25 - June 5, 1965 were many. It is not my intention to review those papers but to comment on general information pertaining to Europe that will probably be of interest to other surveyors, particularly property surveyors.

The Italians are warm people with a great flair for serving excellent dinners, including delightful wine, but their surveyors are different! Rome is a tourist city with many historical places. The Vatican Museum has one of the best art collections in the world, including paintings of maps and men measuring. The meetings were held in EUR (about 15 miles south of the center of Rome in a new section started before the war). Papers being read or discussed were simultaneously translated into four languages (English, French, German, and Italian). As is the usual custom in Italy, three hours were allotted for lunch.

Of particular interest to the property surveyor is the fact that the person who calls himself a "surveyor" in Italy does more house designing and minor architectural work than he does boundary determinations. In an international meeting, it is difficult to adjust your thinking to the definition of terms as used in other areas. It took me several minutes to realize that the Italian paper was in fact a part of a "surveyor's" presentation at this meeting. Odd to say, Italy is not the only country where "surveyors" are building specialists.

When I visited the Royal Institution of Chartered Surveyors in London, I found that there were five areas of practice: (1) Surveyors in general practice (valuation, estate planning, town planning, building surveyors); (2) Quantity surveyors; (3) Agricultural surveyors; (4) Land surveyors; and (5) Mining surveyors. Within England (not Great Britain) property surveyors are rarely found (they exist in former colonies). Appraisers of real estate and evaluators of houses are the most prevalent surveyors. Unlike the situation in Italy, surveyors do not design houses; they merely appraise houses after they are built.

Believe it or not, land in England is not monumented with precise monuments. Surveyors' stakes are not set; drill holes in stones are not used. In England you own what is enclosed; it may be to a hedge line a fence, a wall, or some other object. While this system would probably fail anywhere else in the world, it seems to work in England. Perhaps one of the reasons is that things grow so readily. Abundant water and rapid growth make hedges, trees, and other plants permanent line markers from an airplane, England appears to be indiscriminately divided by crazy quilt patterns of hedges. The ownership of land is registered (not the evidence of title as in the U.S.A.). Areas are determined from Ordnance Survey maps (topographic maps) but location is not precise. For this reason land surveyors, as we think of them, cannot exist because of the lack of economic opportunity.

One of my remarks at a Commission I session, "The location of land is merely the opinion of the surveyor," was immediately challenged by a Nigerian surveyor. It was his view that surveying measurements were exact; hence, the surveyor's location must be exact. Considerable discussion ensued as to legal principles, the control of monuments, and the problem of relocating lost monuments in their original positions from witness evidence. Here is a perfect example of differences in the meanings of terms in different areas of the world. In a few places the land surveyor is the judge, jury, and final authority for land locations; in most areas, he expresses an opinion; and in some areas he is not used at all for boundary determinations.

In the British Empire's former colonies, land surveyors have the important task of locating land. Their work is quite similar to that done by land surveyors in the United States. In many areas land surveyors are licensed, but not in England. The Royal Institution of Chartered Surveyors set their own standards and regulate their members' qualifications. According to law in England anyone can practice surveying, but only chartered surveyors can call themselves chartered surveyors. The society depends upon the quality of its members (not the law) to create the need for their services. The quality requirements are stiff, judging from their examinations.

In many countries (Australia, New Zealand, etc.) the professional society is the sole judge of members' qualifications to do surveying; an examining board created by law and registration by state law do not exist. In California, the civil engineers have been seeking autonomy in registration but have not succeeded.

When stopping in England on the way to the F.I.G. meeting, my concept of time was put in its right proportion. Many of us, including me, are apt to think that the art of writing land descriptions was a relatively recent development. In the British Museum, London, are Babylonian deeds written in cuneiform on clay tablets 4000 or more years ago wherein (1) the land was described by bounds and measurements (linear), (2) the surveyor who surveyed the land was named, (3) the deed was signed, (4) the deed was sealed, (5) a consideration was mentioned, and (6) the deed was witnessed by several persons. From this we can conclude that there was private ownership of land (a practical necessity in irrigated areas), that certain officials were entrusted to make measurements and the principle of the seal and witness was of ancient origin.

In the excavations in Babylonia (Kingdom of Ur and others) the British archaeologists uncovered numerous boundary stones and cuneiform tablets (clay tablets with cuneiform writings) that gave the results of litigation, convincing, commercial agreements, and historical notes. Many of the land descriptions (deeds) had a clay envelope wrapped around the original tablet, and where there was an envelope, the envelope was sealed (an impression seal).

The following notes were taken from museum exhibits.

Cuneiform tablet 26964 was prepared in 1980 B.C., and had this label, "Survey tablet listing the area and dimensions of five fields. The fields being irregular, the area is calculated by reckoning them as forming rectangles or regular figures, and then adding or subtracting from this are such parts of the field as lie outside or inside these lines."

In an old Babylonian lawsuit of 1620 B.C. a judgment in favor of Warad-Sin to recover from the merchant, Idni-Adad, lands formerly belonging to his father was recorded on tablet 92514.

The sale of a date plantation by the four sons of Marduk-stiro to Nabuahheiddina for 22 1/3 mana of silver was recorded on tablet 41399 (559 B.C.).

A 1700 B.C. tablet (131,448) had five seals of five witnesses and was a legal case heard before a judge to determine the division of property between a king and his sister. Could it be that women had rights of land ownership at that time?

Tablet 33236 was an old Babylonian contract tablet with its envelope bearing a duplicate text and the seals of seven witnesses for the sale of a plot of land for 2/3 shekel of silver (1749 B.C.).

A tablet (85194) about 6" x 10" was a collection of mathematical problems, some illustrated by diagrams. Solutions were required to a variety of problems concerning fortifications, siege work, water clocks, conical and cylindrical surfaces, chords of circles, and areas of fields. In each case, the process of solution and the results were given (18th century B.C.).

In the Egyptian collection is shown a Rhind Mathematical Papyrus which contains multiplication and division of fractions and examples illustrating methods of computing the volume and cubic contents of cylinders, measuring the area of a square, a circle, and a triangle, and determining the slope of the sides of a pyramid.

One tablet (4th century B.C.) was a map showing the plan of the city of Tuba and the moat. Perhaps the most interesting exhibits of all were the stone boundary monuments. For the sum of two pounds ($5.80 plus postage) the British Museum will send two volumes entitled *Babylonian Boundary Stones and Memorial Tablets in the British Museum*. If these volumes were reprinted today the cost would be about $25. The price of $5.80 was set in 1912 at the time of printing and will remain the same until the edition is sold out. These volumes would be a valuable addition to any surveyor's library. The exhibited dark limestone boundary monument of Kudurru of Gula-Eresh (size 1'2¼" X 9 ¼" X 5") was completely covered with cuneiform writing and carvings of the gods who were to protect the stone. The condensed translated meaning of the writings was given in the text, as follows:

"Five *gur* of corn-land (not U.S. type corn), one *gan* measured by the great cubit, being reckoned by thirty *Ka* of seed, in the district of Edina, on the bank of the Edina Canal, in the province of Sea Land (that) the prince marked out, adjoining on the upper length, the House of Iddiatu; adjoining on the lower length, the House of Amel-Marduk; on the lower width the province of the Sea Land; and on the upper width the Edina Canal . . . "

So far, this sounds like a bound description of today. Why not "bounded by" instead of "adjoining on the upper length"? The script continued:

"The surveyors of that field; Amurru-belzeri, the administrator; Zakiru, the governor of Edina; and Adad-shum-ibno, the official; measured the field and established it as the property of Bulaeresh."

The surveyor was proclaimed to have measured the land. I doubt if he was called a "surveyor" at that time. The following passage on the same stone indicates thinking on the importance of monuments (this was rewritten slightly to avoid the awkwardness of the literal translation):

"Whenever in times to come, any administrator or official, or adjoiner who shall accept bribes in respect to these lands . . . or shall cause diminution therein, or who shall destroy land - mark or boundary-stone, or shall say, 'It was not measured' . . . because of the evil curses inscribed thereon . . . a man shall have fear . . . to take this stone up, or cast it into the river, or hide it in the earth, or set it in a place where no man can see it . . . may Anu, Enlil, Ea, and Ninmakh, the great gods, curse him with an evil curse that cannot be loosed, may they tear out his foundation, and his seeds may they snatch away . . . etc." Included was the following, "May Nabu, the exalted son, the establisher of the month of the year, shorten his days, so that he may have no posterity!"

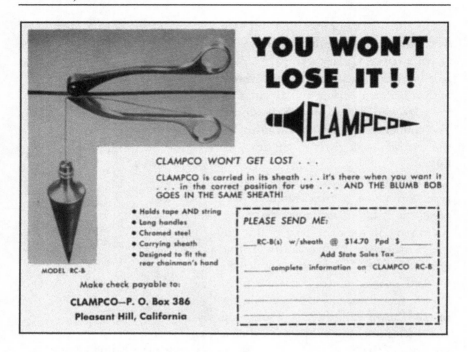
From the necessity of threats and the calling upon the gods for this wrath, it may be concluded that some of the people of 4000 years ago must have been in the habit of switching or moving stones; otherwise, why bother with all the threats? It was also suggested that the stability of the kingdoms was not too good; hence it was better to call upon the gods to protect the stones instead of the king.

Other threats appearing on other stones were: "May Sin, the great lord, with leprosy clothe his body, as with a garment, so that he may dwell by the wall of his city!" "May the lady Gula cause her burden of sickness to come upon him so that while he lives, dark and bright blood he may pass like water!" "And his corpse may she deprive of burial!" "May the great Anu, the great lord, cause him to take a road that is obstructed!" "May Nergal, the lord of spears and bows, break his weapons!" "May Adad, the ruler of heaven and earth, overwhelm his fields, so that there may spring up abundantly weeds in place of green herbs and thorns in place of grain!" "May Nabu, the exalted minister, appoint him days of scarcity and drought as his destiny!" "May all the great gods, whose names are mentioned on this memorial-stone drive him into evil and unhappiness!"

In a number of written deeds and script on stones the sale price mentioned was "manas of silver" or "shekels" and the distances were "great cubit." From found standard weights (on exhibit) as used on balances (they had balances at that time) the Babylonian "mana" was about 1 lb. of silver, and 60 shekels made up a "mana." No Babylonian cubit was on exhibit, but Egyptian "cubit sticks" (1250 B.C.) were 524 mm. in length and were divided into seven palms. The palm was divided into four digits. An Egyptian cubit was not necessarily the same length as a Babylonian cubit.

The British delegation to the XI International Congress of Surveyors was interested in my remarks about their Babylonian boundary stones and indicated that they would try to have them on exhibit at the XII International Congress in London in 1968.

While I was in Rome, I tried to find a Roman milestone (stones set every 1000 paces or 2000 steps of the Roman soldier), but had no luck.

One of the most noticeable things in England was that roads had no standard width; they would suddenly narrow or widen, or they might taper. The same was more or less true of the roads around Rome. Ownership of a cafe in Rome appears to include all of the rights to the sidewalk. Most cafes had numerous tables cluttering up the sidewalks and occasional wooden platforms to set the tables on where the street sloped. People could walk out in the street to get around these obstructions.

In the F.I.G. meeting a great amount of the time was devoted to the problem of re-allotting small fragments of land to form commercially feasible larger parcels. It seems that in many parts of Europe each child inherits part of his parent's land; the slivers and small plots created are not useable. After a period of time whole communities become fragmented to the point that the economy is disrupted. By the process of "putting together many small plots," the European surveyor finds employment.

The moral of this rambling report on the XI International Congress is "Do not expect that in any other part of the world you will find land surveyors performing exactly the same functions as in the United States." But despite this, there are many areas of common interest (often known by another name), especially in the areas of geodesy and the science of measurements.

****

NOW UP TO 3 MILES IN BRIGHTEST SUNSHINE WITH THE MODEL 4D (for daylight) *GEODIMETER®

RANGE: 50 ft. to 3 miles in full daylight; 5-10 miles at dusk; 15-20 miles at night.

LIGHT SOURCE: Mercury Arc Lamp.

ACCURACY: .04 ft. two millionths of the distance.

MEASURING TIME: 5 to 10 minutes; set up time — 5 minutes including pointing. Pointing is now done with a new sighting panel using the Geodimeter's own light for pointing.

For economy, dependability and accuracy . . . . select the AGA Geodimeter.

Write or call today for further details — complete lease and rental service available.

AGA CORPORATION OF AMERICA

P.O. Box 447 • SOUTH PLAINFIELD, N. J.

REPRESENTATIVES

Albinson, Inc., 520 Fourth Ave., S. Minneapolis, Minn. • Baton Rouge Blue Print & Supply Co., 207 St. Ferdinand St., Baton Rouge, La. • E. Phil Harris Co., 5352 First Ave., N., Birmingham, Ala. • Carl Heinrich Co., 711 Concord Ave., Cambridge, Mass. • Miller Blue Print, P.O. Box 1018, 108 East 10th St., Austin, Texas • National Surveying Instruments, Inc., 4050 W. Parker Ave., Chicago, Ill. • Carlos R. Rossi, Inc., Apartado 3547, San Juan 17, Puerto Rico • Seiler Instrument & Mfg. Co., Inc., 1629 Washington Ave., St. Louis, Mo. • Standard Blueprint Co., 1415 Harney St., Omaha, Nebraska • Surveyors Service Co., P.O. Box 905, Costa Mesa, Calif. • Thorpe-Smith, Inc., 308 S. Washington St., Falls Church, Va. • Triangle Blue Print Co., 525 Robertson Ave., Oklahoma City, 314 Cincinnati Ave., Tulsa, Okla.

THE SURVEYOR AND THE LAW

SIMILARITY OF NEW ZEALAND
AND UNITED STATES LAWS

SEPTEMBER 1965

David W. Lambden (with Wilsey, Ham & Blair of San Mateo, Calif.) sent me a book entitled *Summary of the Law Relating to Surveying in New Zealand* (published by the New Zealand Institute of Surveyors, Wellington). The similarity of the New Zealand Laws to those of the United States is obvious.

Within the United States it is a well established fact that old possession can stand as a monument to the original lines as marked and surveyed by the original surveyor. Fences built soon after section lines were run might stand as proof as to where the original lines were run, especially after the destruction of the original monuments.

In the case of the Equitable Building and Investment Co. v. Ross (5 N.Z.L.R., S.C. 229) this principle was at issue and, as quoted from the above book: "It is admitted that the new surveys proceed on no certain basis. Surveying was roughly done in the early days, and has left, it seems, but few monuments, and those of the rudest. In such circumstances, there can really be no better identification of the land to which a grant relates than long and unchallenged occupation by the grantee, and those who claim through him, of an allotment which in position, dimensions and area corresponds in general, though it be somewhat roughly, with the description in the grant. Neither words of a deed, or the lines and figures of a plan, can absolutely speak for themselves. They must, in some way or other, be applied to the ground. Where there are no natural boundaries, and the original survey-marks are gone, and there is no great difference in measurement, a long occupation originally authorized by the proper public authority, and acquiesced in throughout the period by the surrounding owners, is evidence of a convincing nature that the land so occupied is that which the deed conveys."

Within the United States, the general rule is that the person in possession is presumed to be the owner; he can only be ousted by peaceful means or by due process of law. A claimant cannot use force (even though he may have a better title). Quotations from the above book summarize the usual United States and New Zealand law as follows: "Where possession exists the law attaches certain rights to it, such as the right of possession, or the right not to be disturbed except by due process of law. The law presumes that everyone who is in possession is lawfully in possession, and throws upon the man who disputed his right to be in possession the burden of proving a better title. The advantage of this is very great. Possession is thus nine points of the law."

Also, "If his [an owner's] right to possession is infringed, he can re-enter into possession, provided he does so peaceably, or he can bring an action to recover possession against anyone withholding it from him against his will."

In another part of the book it is said, "It is the rule of the Common Law that possession is *prima facie* [true on its face; true until proved otherwise] proof of title."

In New Zealand, as in the United States, proportional measurement is a rule of last resort. Several pages are devoted to Excess and Shortage with final conclusions similar to those presented by me in SURVEYING AND MAPPING, XVIII, No. 4, pp. 455 - 457; XIX, No. 1, PP. 101 - 103; and XIX, No. 3, pp. 595 - 597.

– Curtis M. Brown

****

COMMENT AND DISCUSSION
NEW MEXICO AND SURVEYORS
DECEMBER 1967

CURTIS M. BROWN * - I had the good fortune to be invited to attend the ACSM, New Mexico Section meeting. The cordiality of the group was beyond expectations.

Most of us think of New Mexico as a hot desert area; it just is not so in Albuquerque, a city of about 5000 feet elevation and cool mountain climate.

Some of us are inclined to think of New Mexico as "a developing state," and the surveyors as not being far advanced as pertaining to newer methods. They use photogrammetry and geodimeters, own computers, do scribing and are better qualified than most of us. Since Los Alamos is only a few miles away, this could be predicted; the best scientists in the world are interested in letting work out only to well qualified men. I was impressed by what I saw.

New Mexico Land Surveyors have the usual Rancho Land Grant problems, that is, boundaries that are indefinite and overlap sectionalized land areas. I suppose as long as there are deeds and surveyors there will be evidence evaluation problems. Which monuments? Which word? Which ambiguity? The largeness of land holdings make electronic measurements advantageous.

On Saturday I was taken to the top of a nearby mountain via a tram lift - 4,900 feet up and about 2 miles horizontally. It was one of those almost vertical fault uplift blocks with a steep face and a long slope on the other side. Mr. Koogle had pointed out several of his photogrammetry pre-mark points on the way out. On the last leg of the lift up the cable-suspended tram, I noticed a white pre-mark about 2000 feet up on a cliff and accused Koogle of making a contour map of the mountain. When I looked closer, it said "Welcome Curt." Mr. Elder's son and a member of his survey crew dramatically illustrated rock climbing on a 2000 foot cliff; this is a country where surveyors are men! What a welcome!

The surveyors say they occasionally lose time because of wind but very rarely because of snow. In fact I would like to live there - the pine covered mountains, ski slopes on the nearby high peaks, excellent weather, and friendly people. What more could you ask?

* Past President ACSM.

****

FIG 1968 MEETING

ENGLAND ORDNANCE SURVEYS

THE ordnance survey of Great Britain are among the best examples of surveying and mapping in the world. Recently a request was made

271

to Brigadier R. A. Gardiner, M.B.E. to supply SURVEYING AND MAPPING with a sample sheet; it is reproduced here. Those of you who attend the 1968 F.I.G. Meeting in London will have the opportunity to see these maps.

According to Brigadier Gardiner: Built up areas are mapped at a scale of 1/250 (about 1 inch = 100 feet). Cultivated areas are at 1/2500 (about 1 inch = 200 feet). Mountains and moorland are covered at six inches equals one mile. The entire country was covered at 1/2500 before the beginning of this century, but many of these older maps are out of date, largely due to two world wars. The 1/2500 scale maps are all post war.

England (not necessarily Great Britain) depends upon these maps for evidence in boundary litigation. Property is not sold by metes and bounds descriptions nor by subdivision maps as in the United States. Fences and existing possession are the criteria for limits of ownership rights, and scaling on these maps may be the best available evidence.

– CURTIS M. BROWN

[MP NOTE: Exhibit follows on next page.]

Part of typical ordnance survey map, reduced slightly.   Original scale, 1/1250.

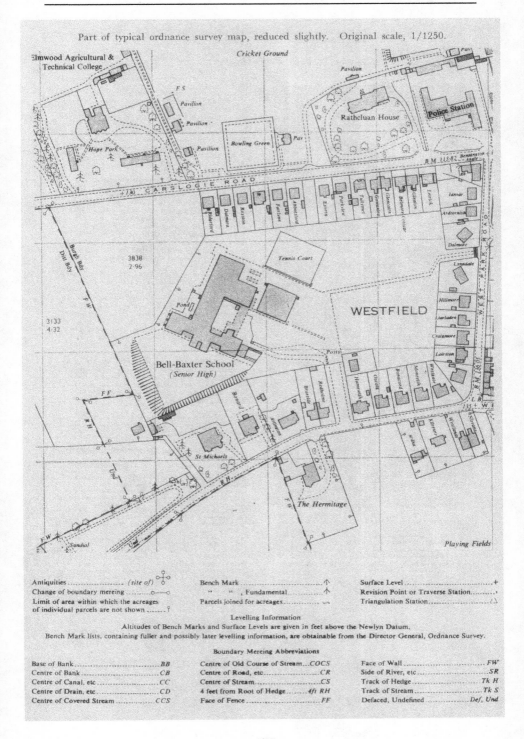

Antiquities .... (site of)
Change of boundary mereing ....o——o
Limit of area within which the acreages
of individual parcels are not shown ....?

Bench Mark ....↑
"   "   , Fundamental ....↑
Parcels joined for acreages ....↶

Surface Level ....+
Revision Point or Traverse Station............,
Triangulation Station ....△

Levelling Information
Altitudes of Bench Marks and Surface Levels are given in feet above the Newlyn Datum.
Bench Mark lists, containing fuller and possibly later levelling information, are obtainable from the Director General, Ordnance Survey.

Boundary Mereing Abbreviations

Base of Bank ....BB	Centre of Old Course of Stream...COCS	Face of Wall ....FW
Centre of Bank ....CB	Centre of Road, etc ....CR	Side of River, etc ....SR
Centre of Canal, etc CC	Centre of Stream ....CS	Track of Hedge ....Tk H
Centre of Drain, etc ....CD	4 feet from Root of Hedge ....4ft RH	Track of Stream ....Tk S
Centre of Covered Stream ....CCS	Face of Fence ....FF	Defaced, Undefined ....Def, Und

273

BOOK REVIEW

DECEMBER 1974

The Land Surveyor and the Law. K. W. Simpson and G. M. J. Sweeney. Printed by: University of Natal, Durban, South Africa, 1973. Hard cover, 297 pp. No price given.

My admiration for a writer goes to the person who takes the scattered knowledge of a field of practice, digests it, and rearranges it in a clear and logical sequence so that a practitioner has a ready reference for correct procedure. In the area of legal elements for land surveyors of South Africa – including professional conduct, conveyancing methods, and the law of boundaries – this text is a must; and for those on the English-derivation countries, it is a valuable reference book. Although South African law is fundamentally Dutch, the law of evidence is definitely English, and the procedure for location boundaries is very similar to that used in the United States. The authors seem to be familiar with the U.S. systems of survey and refer to *Surveying and Mapping,* Clark, Brown, Eldridge, and U.S. court cases. At the end of each chapter there is a bibliography giving proper credit for source information

Three courts exist: (1) the land surveyors field court, (2) a court of arbitration, and (3) the Supreme Court, including all courts of first importance. Matters commence in the surveyors field court. Authority at this point is to obtain agreement and most land survey cases end here. However, if either party disagrees, the matter can be appealed to the courts or sent to arbitration. At arbitration the decision of the arbitrators is final, except for fraud or misconduct.

South Africa registers the owner of the land, not the evidence of ownership as in most of the United States. In land planning the policy of segregating different races territorially for "parallel development" affects regional planning at its roots.

Surveyors are university-trained and registered. A surveyor may not select his location of practice; it is assigned. Further, a surveyor may not move to another district without approval. A surveyor is obligated to live up to written regulations and may be fined for failure to do so. The beacons (monuments) set do not have the registration number of the surveyor attached to the physical object. The survey is "connected" or "unconnected" to the rural "trigonometrical survey" stations. The responsibility for storing field notes as well as "diagrams" is with the surveyor general.

Boundaries are either rectilinear – defined by direction, distance, and mathematically determinate curves – or curvilinear – fluid boundaries, such as rivers and oceans. Along the ocean the upland owner owns to the "high water mark," defined as the "highest line reached by the water of the sea during ordinary storms occurring during the most stormy period of the year, excluding exceptional or abnormal floods."

Apparently, early South African rectilinear surveys were performed as inaccurately as many early surveys of the United States, such as, for example, by using a leather "tape" which was long when wet and short when dry. From the blunders, errors, and neglect of early surveyors evolved many common laws parallel with those of the United States. The intent of the parties to the document, as expressed by writings, controls boundary location, and usually beacons are of first importance to indicate intent.

Those who wish to study the South African system should, in addition to this book, obtain copies of *Land Surveys Act 9 of 1927* and *Regulations* issues by the Survey Regulations Board. From this text, the South African land surveyor's system appears to be superior to that found, if not all, of the states of the United States.

Chapters include: Acquiring Rights in Land, Selecting Positions for New Boundaries, Implementing Contracts and Wills, Marketing and Documenting Boundaries, Restoring Rectilinear Boundary Positions, Relocating Curvilinear Boundary Positions, Partitioning Rights, and Subsurface Rights (Mining).

The book has been reproduced by multicopy procedure from typed pages. It is recommended reading for surveyors, especially those who are seeking new ideas for improving U.S. survey systems.

– CURTIS M. BROWN
Land Surveyor
La Mesa, California

****

BOOK REVIEW

DECEMBER 1974

Legal Aspects of Boundary Surveying as Apply in New South Wales. Frank M. Hallman, LL.B., The Institution of Surveyors, Australia, New South Wales Division, Sydney, 1973, (65 York St., Sydney). Price $10.00 Australian.

This book, written by a man well-versed in surveying and the law of boundaries, covers the subject of boundary surveying completely in eminently readable language. The chapter headings, The Role of the Boundary Surveyor, Boundary Control, Landways, Freehold Estates and Other Interests, New Roads and Subdivisions, The Status of Roads, Consequences of Notation on Plans, Land Titles, Searching, Survey Investigation, and Surveyors and the Law, indicate the extent of contents. In addition, a table of court cases, a table of ordinances and statutes along with a bibliography fill out the needs of the New South Wales surveyor.

Like other English derivatives, such as Canada, South Africa, and the United States, common law is similar. Differences are primarily due to statute laws and historical background. For example, most Crown grants of farmland issued between 1830 and 1844, and many from time-to-time thereafter, contain reservations of all land within 100 ft. of the high-water mark. Also, the doctrine of accretion does not apply to inland lakes.

Commenting on the use of coordinates in land descriptions and the advantages claimed by the proponents, he states: "Such a viewpoint of course overlooks the subordinate parts generally that measurement plays in boundary work. At law it is the evidence of bounds and not that of metes which as a general rule determines the limits of the laterality of a property."

For those who wish to depart from the confines of their own narrow jurisdiction and wish to know how others handle boundary problems, this book is recommended. In New South Wales it is a necessity to know the entire 283 pages.

– CURTIS M. BROWN
Land Surveyor
La Mesa, California

****

BOOK REVIEW

MARCH 1975

Summary of the Law Relating to Land Surveying in New Zealand. E. M. Kelly. Fourth edition, enlarged and revised in 1971 by B. H. Davis. Hard cover, xx + 296 pp. Price not given.

Within its 296 pages this book has a comprehensive treatment of the land laws of New Zealand. Its chapter headings, Introduction to Law, Title to Land, Boundaries and Fences, Subdivision of Land, Town and Country Planning, Roads and Streets, Taking Land for Public Works, Land Settlement, Mining, Maori Land, and General Provisions as to Surveys, adequately describe its contents.

The first chapter, Introduction to Law, provides the surveyor with a short summary of general laws, court systems, and basic land laws. Since both the United States and New Zealand are of English derivation, common laws are similar.

New Zealand is now regulated by the land transfer act of 1952, a Torrens system. Rules of Adverse Possession were abolished and a certificate of title is unassailable except by fraud. Titles adjoining a river are issued without exact location of the center line of the river. River boundaries continue to be migratory as caused by accretion and erosion. The distribution of the ownership of the bed of large lakes is in a state of flux. Islands springing out of the beds of rivers belong to the adjoining land owners and are divided by the median line of the river as is common in the United States.

In subdividing land, before a new plat can be approved and titles issued, a plan must be submitted to the Council, a local governing body, who can 1) refuse approval, 2) require a new plan, 3) require improvements, or 4) approve subject to conditions. The Council may require reserves for recreational purposes or for streets and service lanes. The 1953 Town and Country Planning Act required zoning plans to be prepared for each community.

This book gives the wording of most statutes and the interpretations of the courts with proper legal citations. New Zealand surveyors are indeed fortunate to have such an authoritative work, well written, to help guide them in their practice.

– CURTIS M. BROWN
Land Surveyor
La Mesa, California

THE SURVEYOR AND THE LAW

New York v. Hawaii and Reciprocal Licensing

March 1966

GOOD FORTUNE has taken me to widely separated states just two weeks apart. In Rochester, New York, the snow fell almost continuously and the temperature was at or below zero. How surveys can be made in such conditions amazes me. In Hawaii the sun was bright, the weather warm, the water like a hot bath, the flowers in bloom and the only falling things were coconuts. So I inquired about licensing requirements in Hawaii (not New York). No reciprocal licensing exists and to take the examination you must have proficiency in reading Hawaiian (Polynesian language as recorded by early missionaries and settlers). All early deeds are written in Hawaiian (early means recently by world time scale). Surely this could not be difficult (so I thought) since only 12 letters are used. After a week in Hawaii, the sun, warmth, luxury of laziness and difficulty in pronouncing such words as Mahele, Konohiki, Kuleanas, Ili, Ahupuaa, Kuleana, Pulehunui and Kapiolani, convinced me that Southern California with its simple names like La Jolla, Jamul and Agua Hedionda (stinking water) was preferable; besides it has intermediate temperature.

This points out that the laws and customs of the various states will make it difficult to have reciprocal surveyor registration, especially for states far apart. Examples from Hawaii and New York will further illustrate this point. Most states prorate excess or deficiency among the lots of a given block. In Minnesota (and New Jersey?), if there is an odd shaped lot in the block, the odd shaped lot receives all of the excess or deficiency (called remnant rule).

New York is different. In Mechler v. Dehn, 196NYS460, the disposal of a five-foot deficiency was in question. There were two descriptions, one calling for a plat and the other describing the lot by the same dimensions as given on the plat. The judge specifically called attention to the Minnesota rule (Barrett v. Perkins, 113 Minn. 480) and rejected this remnant rule. Further, he noted that most states used proportional measurement to distribute excess or deficiency among all lots; then he rejected that rule. Quoting from the case, "I do not think we are at liberty to presume that the mere reference to the map in the descriptions that the grantor intended to convey those lots in accordance with the frontage shown on the map, if it was there, or, if not, then in ratable proportion. I am unwilling to carry legal presumptions to any such extent. In my opinion, the mere statement of such a proposition shows its unsoundness." "When the subsequent conveyance of the remaining frontage on Morton Avenue was made, the grantor intended, of course, to convey 100 feet, believing that that frontage remained. But it is equally certain that she could not and did not then intend to convey more than she had. Therefore, she conveyed to defendants' grantor only what was left, or about 95 feet. I do not see that the fact that the lots are shown on a map and their description in the deed made by reference to that map in any degree alters this result. To correct the original mistake by an apportionment of the deficiency would be a purely arbitrary determination by the court, which could in no sense be called judicial."

In New York, if my information is correct (New Yorkers assured me that it was), where there is excess or deficiency in a subdivided block, the order of seniority must be determined to find out who gets the excess or deficiency; it goes to the last buyer!

Hawaii has a "togetherness" history that created many parcels of land simultaneously with equal rights.

To understand Hawaii a little historical background is needed and this is perhaps overly brief. The king (or queen) owned everything, including the subjects' lives. By the mahele, lands went to occupants (30,000 acres), the government (1,500,000 acres), the crown (1,000,000 acres), and the chiefs (1,500,000 acres). As between chiefs the court said (Harris v. Carter, 6 Haw. 195), "Now, although these maheles were executed day after day until the work was completed, it was because it was too great a task to be all completed in one day and they might well have all been dated on one and the same day. It was all one act. None of the maheles by the king to any chief could claim by virtue of its earlier date any priority or superiority of title over the mahele by any chief to the king. The whole work was one scheme; one part was contemporaneous with every other part."

Later cases describe the chief's lands (in re Boundaries of Pulehunni, 4 Haw. 239) as, "With the Hawaiians, from prehistoric times, every portion of the land constituting these Islands was included in some division, larger or smaller, which had a name, and of which the boundaries were known to the people living thereon or in the neighborhood. Some persons were specially taught and made the repositories of this knowledge, and it was carefully delivered from father to son. The divisions of the lands were to a great extent made on rational lines, following a ridge, the bottom of a ravine or depression, but they were often without these and sometimes in disregard of them. Sometimes a stone or rock known to the aboriginal and notable from some tradition, or sacred uses, marks a corner or determines a line. The line of growth of a certain kind of tree, herb or grass, the habitat of a certain kind of bird, sometimes made a division. Through some parts of the country, which must always have been unfrequented by the general population, as thick forests, rough and barren mountain lands, their division lines lay, when they could be traced out by some persons at least in charge of the territory, whose business it was to know them.

"A principle very largely obtaining in these divisions of territory was that a land should run from the sea to the mountains, thus affording to the chief and his people a fishery residence at the warm seaside, together with the products of the high lands, such as fuel, canoe timber, mountain birds, and the right of way to the same, and all the varied products of the intermediate land as might be suitable to the soil and climate of the different altitudes from sea soil to mountainside or top. But this mode of allotment had numerous exceptions. Some of the lands were for some reasons not always understood, and perhaps arbitrary in the beginning, very wide at the top, cutting off a great number of other lands from the mountain; others in like manner wide in the lowlands, cut off land from the sea.

"The contour of lands which have been surveyed and plotted is most irregular. The only general description would be that the lines are not rectilinear, and that there is no preference for right angles. In such ahupuaas are found of from a hundred acres up to thousands, in several instances containing more than one hundred thousand and more than two hundred thousand acres."

Water rights for irrigation is similar to Spanish law in that water can be appropriated. In Peck v. Bailey (8 Haw. 658) is, "There can be no difference of opinion that the complainants were entitled to all the water rights which the lands had by prescription at the date of their title. By the deed, the watercourses were conveyed and a right to the water accustomed to flow in them. The same principle applies to all the lands conveyed by the king, or awarded by the Land Commission. If any of the lands were entitled to water by immemorial usage, this right was included in the conveyance as an appurtenance. An easement appurtenant to land will pass by a grant of the land, without mention being made of the easement or the appurtenances."

At the Minnesota Land Surveyors Association on February 17, 1966, the subject of "Sectionalized Land Procedures" was designed to show the differences in survey procedures used in each state. Ohio differs drastically from Indiana and Illinois; Minnesota varies from each; and California is not the same as any of the others mentioned.

Land surveyors of different states have the science of surveying in common, but not the laws pertaining to land location procedures. It would be difficult to devise a surveyor examination that could be applicable in all states.

– Curtis M. Brown

****

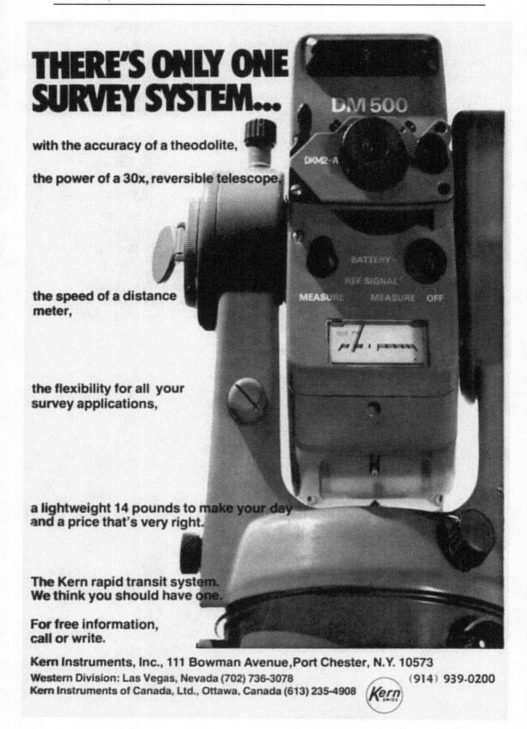

COMMENT AND DISCUSSION

The pages of *SURVEYING AND MAPPING* are open to free and temperate discussion of all matters pertaining to the interests of the Congress. It is the purpose of this department to encourage comments on published material or the presentation of new ideas in an informal way.

– Editor

****

BOOK REVIEW

DECEMBER 1976

Land Law and Registration. S. Rowton Simpson. Cambridge University Press, London, New York. 1976. 726 pp. arranged in one volume consisting of two books. Price $75.00.

This is an authoritative survey of the principles and practices of land registration throughout the world. For those in the United States who are advocating adoption of a Torrens system, this book is a must. Book one pertains to the history, principles, and practices of land registration; book two pertains to the law of registration and particular emphasis on existing laws of Kenya and other nations.

In book 1 a detailed history of deed registration, the advantages of registration, and present practices in Great Britain and Australia (Torrens system) are given, and a lesser space is devoted to other countries. Chapter titles are as follows: Land Rights and Records; Processes of Land Transfer; English Land Law and Registration; English Conveyancing; The Torrens System; Registration of Deeds; The Cadastre and Cadastral Survey; Boundaries and Maps; Objects and Reasons; Obstacles and Objections; Guarantee and Indemnity; Compilation of the Register; Customary Land Tenure and Control of Dealing; Multiple Ownership; Fragmentation, and Consolidation; Horizontal Subdivision; The Process of Systematic Adjudication; Organization and Administration; The Machinery of Registration; Techniques of Cadastral Survey; Registry Procedure; Automation; Appendix A: Land Records of France; Appendix B: Land Records in West Germany; Appendix C: The Computerization of Land

Records and Accounts in Sabah; Appendix D: The Land Data Bank of Sweden.

At the present time no other source covers the subject of land registration as completely as this book. The author is to be congratulated on his thoroughness and clarity of presentation.

– Curtis M. Brown

****

The KERN DKM 1 Theodolite in use during 1948 French Polar Expedition.

KERN DKM1 Theodolite

PRINCIPAL FEATURES:

Simultaneous, eccentricity free reading of diametrically opposed points of both circles to 10 seconds direct and to 1 sec. by interpolation. Average working accuracy 3–4 seconds.

Internally wired for electric illumination.

Maximum compactness and portability. Weight of Instrument 4 lbs.

Ruggedness under all conditions.

New light weight centering tripod.

For Further Details Write For Booklet 154-5

Prompt, Reliable Service
Factory Trained Technicians

KERN INSTRUMENTS, Inc.

Fundamental Surveying Equipment

111 Bowman Avenue, Port Chester, New York

MUSINGS

PLUMB-BOBS

SEPTEMBER 1963

Just because I am writing in these hallowed pages about such plebeian things as plumb bobs, I wouldn't want you to think I am the possessor of a stone (rather than an egg) head. I too have heard about Maser, Laser, Kerr cells, and Astro-gyro, and go through the major survey publications, an earnest seeker after truth. There is an element of compulsion about it, of course. I have the feeling that the youth of the country is being force-fed so much knowledge that, in the words of the Mad Hatter, or some other Carrollian character, I must run at top speed in order to stand still. Academically, that is.

I must say that I am impressed by the erudition of those who write about survey matters. So much so; in fact, that my eyes may be seen to go glassy out of sheer admiration for them. For example, the last few issues of the "Global Surveyor" quarterly (a fictitious publication which I have invented so as not to divulge the actual name) have the following: -

A re-examination of the suitability of cadmium light as a standard of length.

Is surveying a profession or a trade?

The probable incidence of mortality among survey assistants with the use of the death-ray theodolite.

Is surveying a trade or a profession?

Variations in the eccentricity of the geoid arising from the melting of the polar icecap.

Surveying: - Trade or profession?

A new determination of the equatorial bulge.

The surveyor - Tradesman or professional?

Topographic Surveys of the Moon.

The professional surveyor - A tradesman?

Nor are such subjects confined to the magazines. They hold exclusive sway at conventions, and so great is the awe of surveyors for the knowledge displayed by the speakers that the .lecture hall is generally dead silent except for the monotone of the speaker and a certain low, rhythmic sound; no doubt something to do with the air-conditioning. Even the wives of surveyors sit in mute respect, giving every appearance of understanding as much as their husbands do about such cliffhangers as "The Cyclical Nature of the Drift of the Magnetic Pole."

I am particularly impressed by a perusal of the titles of books and articles reputed to be of interest to surveyors, especially those available only in Russian, German, or Hungarian. Certainly, the country need not worry about the erudition of its surveyors. By their books ye shall know them - and by this criterion they are egg-heads of the most perfect ellipticity.

Clearly, one must not be fooled by our professional affinity, when in convention, for Thebar. Beneath our bucolic exteriors there must lurk hordes of scientists.

It is, therefore, with considerable hesitation against such a background that I dare to sing the praises of those lowly toilers in the survey vineyard who are responsible for no technological miracles, who don't know a least square from a Lesser Antille, but to whom we are nonetheless indebted. Let us start by lauding the Californian who recently invented a plumb bob with a retractable cord, at one end of which is a target. The idea is simple, the design rugged, and it will pay for itself by all the fumbling and poor sights it will prevent. While our free-wheeling thoughts may be on the derivation of equations for the index of refraction, many of us must bow to practical considerations and give line. This little gem makes it easier to do just that. Then let us pause for a moment to sing a hosannah for the person who first thought of plastic ribbon in rolls - a development which has altered the whole appearance of surveys. Our lath used to be so well camouflaged that there often had to be a special trip just to show them to the clients. Now our lath, our chaining nails, and the fences near our pipes are fluttering with this bright identification, at what a saving in time and money it would be hard to overestimate.

Next, a peal of the bells for the fellow who realized how handy a twenty-five-foot rod would be, and proceeded to make a telescopic one out of hollow, fiberglass tubing. In the rough California terrain, and at $20 or so an hour per party, or perhaps $2 per turning point, it is easy to calculate that one of these will pay for itself in a week or less, as well as making a wonderful sighting rod and a fast method of getting building ties for a two-man party.

An especially loud flourish of the trumpets for the man who developed *fine, braided, red,* plumb bob cord - thus saving the eyes of surveyors for really beneficial tasks, like watching the girls.

Have you seen the new one-hundred-foot tape in an enclosed reel - it costs $7.00 and makes no pretense of being fantastically accurate, but it does have a beautiful big hook on the end of it, so that one man can get ties and building measurements.

Next, we must send a garland to our benefactor who first thought of surveyor's vests of fluorescent red - thus saving us, if not from death, from pneumonia caused by the draft of near-missing trucks and cars.

For each of the following, an 18-gun salute for their contribution-to Go-Go-Go surveying: -

Paper targets, for lath.
Planed lath (instead of rough).
Staplers for plastic ribbon on lath.
Ink marking pens for lath.
Folding 12' rods, in 4 sections, 3' long, for small cars.
Small brass discs with identifying number, for cementing into pipes.
A ten-second job, which lasts indefinitely.
Hand -levels with a low-power scope built in.

And, finally, three rousing cheers and a tiger for me for suggesting, as I now do, that at the next national convention we have one day for presentation of and discussion about our favorite, surveying time-savers - the ground rule being that we will consider nothing which cannot be immediately comprehended.

Now I must rush off to read a fascinating article about the survey techniques used in building the Great Wall of China. It is written in Mandarin Chinese, with which I am, like most surveyors, familiar. Just say something to me in Mandarin Chinese, if you don't believe me.

– ANDREW GIBSON

Jennings, Halderman & Hood - Santa Ana, California.

COMMENT AND DISCUSSION

December 1963

The pages of SURVEYING AND MAPPING are open to free and temperate discussion of all matters pertaining to the interests of the Congress. It is the purpose of this department to encourage comments on published material or the presentation of new ideas in an informal way.

– EDITOR

PLUMB-BOBS

T. A. SHINN, JR.* - Having just finished reading the article "Plumb-Bobs" by Andrew Gibson in the September 1963 Quarterly, pages 499 - 500; I must agree with Mr. Gibson that all too often our heads are so high in the clouds that we tend to forget our feet should be on the ground to do some practical surveying.

Just a small word on my own background; beside being a land surveyor, (State of California - L. S. No. 2870), I teach first semester surveying at Whittier College, Whittier, California, on the 3-2 program for engineering majors. The first two lectures and field days are taken up with (you guessed it) "Plumb-Bobs" and the other lowly objects of our profession.

I too, like Mr. Gibson, feel a mad desire to rush in and pick up the latest publications, to read all the highly technical treatises, written by men who follow the dinner circuit and who speak at different professional meetings on all kinds of highly technical information.

And then I stop sometimes and say to myself, "Do any of these people ever speak of the common things? Has any equipment been invented lately that will help in the regular daily physical aspects of our profession?" Thanks to Mr. Gibson, I see that someone has come through in the practical field, (the "Plumb-Bob" with the retractable cord. How many times have I stepped on the plumb-bob cord, or have had it catch in the brush, or, pushing through the brush, have had it hang up and burn my neck as it slides around - just about a thousand times or more), with all the other new or near new items listed. Maybe the following story will illustrate how some of us feel.

One man said, "I see they're going to the moon soon. I sure would like to see the moon." The other fellow answered, "The moon! I'd just like to see all of Texas."

So thanks again Mr. Gibson, there's hope for us yet.

* Western Engineering & Construction Co.
11044 East Washington Boulevard, Whittier, California.

****

PLUMB-BOBS

MARCH 1964

CURTIS M. BROWN * - Methinks a hint of a dissatisfied reader emanated from Santa Ana, California, in the September 1963 issue of SURVEYING AND MAPPING. We must admit that the gentleman did get his message across skillfully. He objected without saying he objected. Such literary talent needs further development. Forwarded is a do-it-yourself kit composed of 50 sheets of blank paper and two pencils. I am sure there are others, besides me, that would like to hear further from him.

It is true that there are many technical articles in SURVEYING AND MAPPING, and I believe that the editors will readily admit it. But whose fault is it? Yours and mine. The editors can only publish articles that they receive; they *do not write* articles. All of us enjoy reading about tricky, new developments that simplify work and save time. The plumb-bob mentioned is a good one. But who sends the articles in? Nothing written - nothing published.

W. & L. E. Gurley did put out a notebook disclosing many novel "wrinkles," and it was a success. Many would like to see "Surveyors Tricks" or "Computing Shortcuts" regularly published. Why don't you start it going by jotting down ideas on your "do-it-yourself" kit??

Editor's Note. - We do not look with favor on copy (manuscript, if you will) supplied on blank (unruled) paper and written in pencil. Material sent in for publication should be typed (face and one carbon) if at all possible. Use wide margins, double space everything, and use only one side of each sheet. Paper size should be 8 x 10-1/2 or 8 ½ x 11, and the face copy, at least, should be on heavy (20 lb.) white paper. By "wide margins" we mean at least 1 ¼ inches at both sides and the top. Bottom margin may be as lean as 3/4 inch without causing difficulty.

* 2802 Juan St., San Diego 10, California.

****

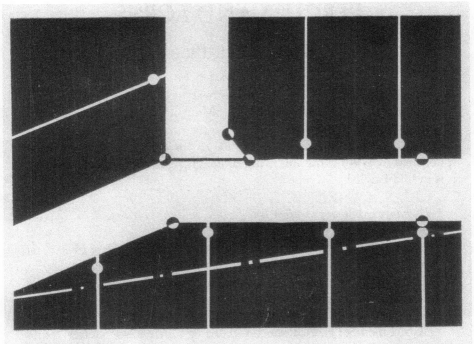

PERCHES AND ACRES
DECEMBER 1966

At times it takes lengthy research to discover an explanation to seemingly unexplainable facts. From Gerald Hyde, Manchester, N. H., was received this information.

In a book entitled *Geodaesia* or *The Art of Surveying* by John Love (published in 1796) is the following (note: change f to s in reading, since it is in Old English):

To change cuftomary meafure into ftatute, and the contrary.

In fome parts of England, for wood-lands, and in moft parts of Ireland, for all forts of land they account 18 feet to a perch, and 160 fuch perches to an acre, which is called cuftomary meafure: whereas our true meafure for land, by act of parliament, is but 160 perches for one acre, at 16 feet and an half to the perch.

ACSM member E. N, Roberts (according to Mr. Hyde's letter) found this to be true in the town of Sutton, New Hampshire, which was originally settled largely by Scotch-Irish.

– Curtis M. Brown

****

POSSESSION

DUTIES AND LIABILITIES OF THE SURVEYOR WHERE LAND IS TRANSFERRED BY UNWRITTEN MEANS

BY CURTIS M. BROWN

DANIELS, BROWN & HALL, SAN DIEGO, CALIF.

DECEMBER 1955

GENERAL

IT IS a well settled principle that land may be transferred by parol means in California, despite the requirement of the State Code that deeds shall be in writing to be valid. Although a person must acquire the *initial* right to a parcel of real property by a written deed, he can gain portions of adjoining land or lose portions of his land by the acts and conduct of himself and his neighbors, or by acts of nature. In other words, the *original* right to land must be based upon a written document; but, after land has been acquired by writing, under certain circumstances it may be added to or subtracted from by parol means, by acts of the adjoiner, or by acts of nature.

SCOPE

It is not the intent to present a detailed analysis of the means by which land might be transferred by unwritten conveyances, but sufficient data will be presented to bring about an intelligent understanding of the following problem confronting the surveyor: Is surveyor permitted to recognize unwritten ownership lines, or must he stake out only that which is written? If he is permitted to recognize unwritten ownership lines, under what circumstances may he do so, and what is his liability?

UNWRITTEN MEANS OF TRANSFERRING TITLE

The more important methods of land conveyancing between adjoining owners without written considerations are:

1. Estoppel,
2. Agreement,
3. Recognition and Acquiescence,
4. Adverse Rights,
5. Statutory Proceedings,
6. Accretion and Erosion, and
7. Escheatment.

Other means such as practical location and private survey are essentially variants or subtypes of the above.

ESTOPPEL

The doctrine of estoppel is based upon the theory that where a party by his acts, declaration, conduct, admissions, or omissions misleads another so that the other is induced to injure himself to the benefit of the person misleading him, the party causing the wrong must suffer the loss and is estopped from revealing otherwise. A party is estopped from telling the truth where he has falsely and deliberately misinformed another so as to cause improvements to be built to his benefit. In California this principle is based upon the Code of Civil Procedure, Section 1962, part 3; "Whenever a party has, by his own declaration, act or omission, intentionally and deliberately led another to believe a particular thing true, and to act upon such belief, he cannot, in any litigation arising out of such declaration, act or omission, be permitted to falsify it."

Four things are essential for the doctrine of estoppel to become effective:

(1) The party being estopped must know the facts.
(2) The party being estopped must intend, or at least act so the other has a right to believe that he intended, that his conduct shall be acted on.
(3) The person claiming estoppel must be ignorant of the facts.
(4) The person claiming estoppel must have relied to his injury on the conduct of the person being estopped.

Estoppel is a denial of the truth and is not looked upon with favor by the courts. All of the above points must be proven conclusively. A hypothetical example of estoppel occurs if Mr. Brown points out to Mr. Smith a line which he knows to be 20 feet from the true line. Mr. Smith not knowing where the true line is, accepts the line pointed out and grades and paves a drive for his benefit. Mr. Brown promptly claims the drive as his own, but is estopped at law from doing so.

AGREEMENT

Boundary lines agreed upon by oral means and by contiguous owners may become the ownership lines if

(1) The true line is unknown,
(2) The line is in dispute, and
(3) The owners agree to accept the line they establish. Where such line agreed upon is built up to and substantial loss would result in a change in position, or where the line is built up to and acquiesced in for the statutory period, the line becomes the true boundary line.

It is certain that adjoining property owners cannot establish a line between their lands by agreement if they know the location of the true line. In such a case a properly written conveyance, based upon a consideration, and containing words of convevancing, must be used.

If the coterminous owners are attempting to establish the true property lines, and they err in establishing the true lines, they are not agreeing to a line but merely establishing what they believe to be the true line. In such case the owners are not denied the right of claiming to their true lines. If a line is capable of being established by a survey, and the parties agree to have the true line established by a survey, and the surveyor errs in the establishment of the true line, the adjoining owners can claim to the true line since no other line than the true line was agreed upon. However, if after the error was discovered there was acquiescence for the statutory time or if there was title by adverse possession, the survey lines would be binding.

In the event that one party misrepresents the lines, or deceives the other, the agreed lines are not binding except on the person misrepresenting the lines. Fraud cannot be the foundation for an agreement. The fact that the lines agreed upon are not the true lines is immaterial to the validity of the agreement; the lines need only to be in dispute and unknown. Owners of adjoining land, or those having vested interests therein, are the only ones who can establish the disputed line by agreement. An agreement between owners, but not including the mortgage holder, is not binding upon the mortgagor.

Parol agreement upon a line is an exception to the rule that all deeds must be in writing to be valid. The idea of a parol agreement is not to convey real property, but to agree to fix the location of that which is already owned and is uncertain. If either party knows the true location of a line, parol agreement fixing another line is void because it amounts to a conveyance by parol means. Where an uncertain line is agreed upon, but at a later date one of the parties finds that the true line could have been ascertained, the line agreed upon cannot be disturbed. In the event that a parol agreement is made and then not followed by acquiescence and possession, the agreement is not binding. Possession need not be physical in the sense of cultivation, but may consist in the erection of monuments or marking the line.

RECOGNITION AND ACQUIESCENCE

Recognition and acquiescence are dependent upon the statute of limitations to become operative. In California a line recognized and acquiesced to for a period of five years may not be disturbed. Civil Code of Procedure, Section 318 states, "No action for the recovery of real property, or for the recovery of the possession thereof, can be maintained, unless it appears that the plaintiff, his ancestor, predecessor, or grantor, was seized or possessed of the property in question, within five years before the commencement of the action." Section 319 of the same code states, "No cause of action, or defense to an action, arising out of the title to real property, or to rents or profits out of the same, can be effectual, unless it appears that the person prosecuting the action, or making the defense, or under whose title the action is prosecuted, or defense is made, or the ancestor, predecessor, or grantor of such person was seized or possessed of the premises in question within five years before the commencement of the act in respect to which such action is prosecuted or defense made."

STATUTORY PROCEEDINGS

Statutory proceedings in California are limited to court actions. In other states, by law, certain officials may establish property lines, and at the expiration of a limited time, if the lines are uncontested, they are conclusive.

ADVERSE RIGHTS

Occupancy of a parcel of land for a period of years, along with certain acts by the possessor, will confer a title against all except the public. In California for any adverse claim to ripen into a fee, the following acts must be complied with continuously for a period of 10 to 20 years:

1. Actual possession,
2. Open and notorious possession,
3. Continuous possession,
4. Hostile possession,
5. Exclusive possession,
6. Under color of title, and
7. All taxes must be paid.

A person claiming adverse possession must have actual possession by such acts as fencing, cultivating, weeding, farming, and improving. A survey, where boundaries are marked, does not indicate actual possession unless the owner follows the survey and improves or cultivates up to the line of the survey.

Possession must be open and notorious such that the owner of the fee title could by occasional visits observe the acts of possession. Possession of the land must be continuous during the statutory period, since any interruption restores the possession to the rightful owner. It is not essential that the same owner be in possession, for tacking on of successive occupants is permitted.

Hostile possession must be against the interests of the fee owner without any admittance on the part of the adverse claimant that the land in question is not his. If at any time the land is rented or leased from the fee owner by the adverse possessor, or if he admits he does not own the land, interruption occurs and the statutory period must start over.

Possession must be exclusive and cannot be shared with the rightful owner, since the owner will never have been deprived of possession. Where by appearance a title exists, yet none actually exists, the term "color of title" is applied. If a subdivision is made and monumented in such a manner as to include a portion of the adjoiner's land, a buyer, buying one of the lots improperly subdivided, would have color of title.

In California taxes must be paid continuously for five years preceding the action for adverse rights based upon a 20-year occupancy. If taxes are paid continuously for a period of ten years, action for adverse rights may he initiated at the end of the ten years.

ACCRETION AND EROSION

Accretion is the process whereby soil is accumulated by imperceptible degrees upon the bank of a body of water. Erosion of land by imperceptible means is the reverse process.

ESCHEATMENT

Escheatment occurs when the state assumes ownership of land due to failure of the former owner to pay taxes, assessments, or the like.

DUTIES OF THE SURVEYOR

The question being considered is: What are the duties and liabilities of the licensed land surveyor in the event fee has passed by unwritten means?

Three of the stated parol means of transferring title can be eliminated from further consideration. Statutory proceedings are certainly not within the scope of the surveyor. Land gained by accretion or lost by erosion is a measurable quantity which, by law, can only be measured by the surveyor. While the division line between properties may be difficult to determine due to ambiguous questions arising when interpreting common laws relating to accretion, the surveyor must make that determination since is the only one authorized by law to make land measurements. The methods used, however are always subject to review by another surveyor or by the courts.

Escheatment is a process of law, vital to the owner and title company, but not within the scope of the surveyor.

The remaining means of transferring title by oral conveyances have one thing in common. Parol evidence under oath must be taken to determine the rights of adjoining land owners. The statutes relating to surveyors in California note that surveyors may take parol evidence by oath where

1. It is necessary to identify or re-establish old, lost, or obliterated corners, or where
2. A monument is in a perishable condition. Nothing permits the taking of parol evidence which will assist in the determination of ownership of land acquired by unwritten means.

The law does not prohibit a surveyor from establishing survey lines or points in accordance with the lines of possession, but if he does, he does so on his own initiative he is assuming the burden of proof. He must prove, even in court if necessary, that the lines of possession are the correct title lines. In view of the fact that such proof requires considerable parol evidence and that the process is complex and expensive, a surveyor cannot afford to take such a risk.

The key to the question regarding the liability of the surveyor in the event he establishes points based upon the lines of possession rests in the instructions given to him by the owner of the property being surveyed. Liability results where the surveyor fails to correctly do the thing that he purports to do. If the owner tells the surveyor to survey his land in accordance with his written deed and the surveyor does precisely that without error, no liability can ensue. If the owner tells the surveyor to survey his land in accordance with the lines of possession regardless of the written title lines and the surveyor does just that, no liability can ensue.

Assuming that a surveyor may mark property in accordance with possession (and there is authority that under certain circumstances a surveyor should so do) what is the effect of such markers and what ethics are involved?

Normally it is assumed by the public - and often by the surveyors themselves - that all property markers found represent points set in accordance with written deed lines. If an owner, whose stakes have been set in accordance with a line of possession, points out to his neighbor a survey marker and states, "This is my property line," deception can occur. The adjoiner assuming that the surveyor may not take over the duties of tile court and that lie may not declare for certain that a line of possession is the true title line without proper court action, is apt to be misled. If the adjoiner discovers the truth, that the markers are merely lines of possession, he will more than likely seriously question the ethics of surveyors. For this reason our office has adopted the policy of seldom marking the lines of possession. When we do, it must be an extremely clear-cut case where we can prove to our own satisfaction, beyond a shadow of doubt, that possession is the only logical answer. Before setting such markers, we make certain that the owner understands the situation; that he has consented to such procedure in writing, or by oral means in the presence of witnesses; and that a plat is sent to him showing the true written deed lines, as well as the lines of possession as staked. By doing this, liability is avoided and the plat cannot be used as a basis to mislead another party, such as a title company insuring title, into believing that the written lines and the lines of possession are in agreement.

Existing California laws make it mandatory that the surveyor shall, when setting stakes not in agreement with the written title, file a record of survey since evidence is found that by reasonable analysis might result in alternate positions of lines or points. Facts of possession and title lines must be clearly shown on the plat.

The opposite situation, where a surveyor marks the written title lines and finds encroachments that might be title lines, does not present potential deception on the part of the surveyor. The surveyor can and should explain to the client that the encroachments might be title lines, and where the encroachments have stood for five years they cannot be disturbed regardless of the written title. In this manner the surveyor is not placed in an unfavorable position to an unknown adjoiner.

Establishing lines based upon possession invites criticism and conflict between surveyors and the public. A surveyor setting markers on the written title line, but out of agreement with another surveyor who has marked the line of possession, makes it appear to the public, and with just cause, that the surveyors do not know what they are doing.

SUMMARY

In order to avoid liability in surveys involving unwritten deeds, a surveyor must be certain that he is following the instructions given him by the owner, or the responsible party requesting the survey. He may stake out written deed lines, or lines of possession, without incurring liability provided he follows exactly and precisely the instructions of the owner. Only by misrepresenting the lines of possession as being the written deed lines, or by misrepresenting the written deed lines as conforming to the lines of possession, can liability ensue. To avoid placing the surveyor in an unfavorable light to the public, marking lines of possession should be avoided excepting where

(1) A court has ruled them to be the true title lines, and excepting where
(2) Extreme extenuating circumstances make the lines of possession the only logical solution. If the line of possession is marked, such fact must be clearly indicated to the client, and it must be shown in relationship to the true written deed lines on a filed record-of-survey plat.

****

THE SURVEYOR AND THE LAW

FENCE LINES AND WRITTEN TITLE LINES

DECEMBER 1959

From Robert D. Hall (Civil Engineering and Land Surveying), 151 E. Hoffman Road, Green Bay, Wisconsin, I received the following hypothetical question:

"Because more than just a few surveyors I have talked with are willing to accept the fence lines as the subdivisional lines prescribed by the U. S. Government, I want to ask for your opinion. Enclosed is a sketch (see accompanying sketch) showing what I might find when I survey for "D" who wants to sell off the south 15 acres of his farm. Please tell me what to do and what to advise Mr. "D" to do to accomplish the sale of his 15 acres. The facts are: Original U. S. Government survey of section 9 was in 1841.

The SW 1/4 was patented to "A" in 1868. In 1869 "A" caused the land to be surveyed into quarters and later fences were erected in accordance with the survey. "B" acquired deed to the SW 1/4 of the SW 1/4 in 1880. "C" acquired SE 1/4 of the SW 1/4 in 1896. "D" acquired the NW 1/4 of the SW 1/4 in 1904. "E" acquired the NE 1/4 of the SW 1/4 in 1908."

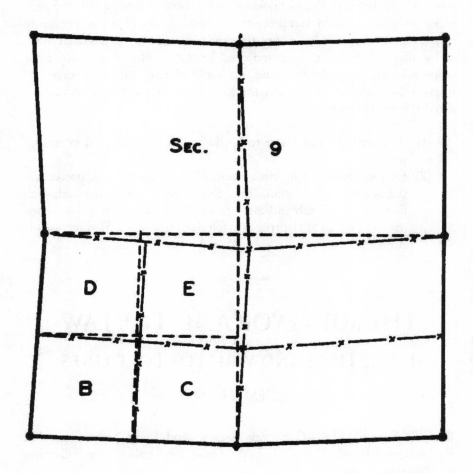

Answer: This question involves three separate and distinct issues: (1) Original survey lines as laid out by the original government surveyor, (2) an improper division of a section some time after the original survey, and (3) the legal acquisition of property by unwritten means. The answer to the problem, in my opinion, is summarized by the following:

Principle: *"The boundaries of the public lands, when approved and accepted are unchangeable, except by resubdivision."* (Restoration of Lost Corners, page 6.)

The first conclusion is that the exterior boundaries of this section must legally be relocated exactly where they were in 1841. It is presumed that the sketch correctly shows these corners and lines as they were originally laid down by the original surveyor.

The words "original survey" need some explanation. Original surveys are made to measure quantities of land prior to conveyancing and have these three characteristics: (1) Monuments are set prior to conveyancing, (2) the survey (which automatically includes monuments set) is called for by the conveyance, and (3) the lines as run by the original surveyor are considered as correct whether in their measured position or not. A resurvey is for the purpose of relocating original survey lines and should never be confused with an original survey.

The original government surveyor seldom ran other than the exterior lines of a section. If the interior lines were run and if the interior survey were called for by the conveyance (patent), these lines as run would be correct where run. But I assume that in this section these interior lines were not run by the government surveyor (this can be checked by reading the original notes). Where the interior lines were not run, the Federal statutes specify the method by which sections shall be divided. This is a Federal law, not a State law. This law is applicable to subdivision of sections for (1) the exterior lines of all patents issued by the Federal government and (2) all subdivisions of sections made while the State was a Territory. After Wisconsin became a State, any further division into parcels (or portions of sections) came under State laws. Common law specifies that when a person sells half of his land he sells half of his area. Federal statutes say that half of a section is determined by connecting opposite quarter corners; hence, half in the case of Federal law does not mean equal area. Most States make an exception to the common law and recognize the Federal statute (connecting opposite corners) as being applicable in the case of sectionalized lands. There are minor exceptions to this. In Wisconsin the law, according to Section 59.62 of the 1951 statutes, is: "When a surveyor is required to subdivide a section or smaller subdivision of land established by the United States Survey, he shall proceed according to the Statutes of the United States and the rules and regulations of the Secretary of the Interior in conformity thereto." Since this is so, then *these lines are unalterable except by resubdivision.*

Principle: *Land lawfully gained by unwritten means extinguishes the old written title, but it does not alter the position of the original survey lines.*

Original survey lines are unalterable, but titles do not have to follow them. Just because there are survey lines does not mean that the survey lines and title lines are coincident. By certain acts of possession, land can be gained or lost by unwritten means. You have indicated that the fences are of exceedingly long standing and that title has probably passed by unwritten means. Let us assume that it has. Owner "D" then has a title, though not necessarily a written title, to all of the land he has enclosed within his fences. He has lost title to land not enclosed. His title "NW 1/4 of the SW 1/4" does not correctly describe his ownership. Paper title and ownership may be identical, but they do not have to be, and in this case they are not. The south 15 acres of the NW 1/4 of the SW 1/4 does not describe the south 15 acres of "D's" ownership. The only way for "D" to clearly convey the south 15 acres of his ownership is by writing a metes and bounds description.

Instances of where possession is out of agreement with paper title lines and where possession has ripened into a fee title are difficult for the surveyor. The surveyor is not qualified, nor is he authorized, to state when possession has changed from an encroachment to a fee title. This is a judicial matter for the courts and the attorneys.

The surveyor is an expert qualified to discover and state what the facts are. He does not try to solve the owner's problem of possession. There is nothing in most laws that prohibits the surveyor from recognizing fences as ownership lines; he does not do so merely because of liability and ethics. When an owner asks a surveyor to survey out the NW 1/4 of the SW 1/4, he wants to know where his paper title lines are. After all, he knows where his fences are; he wants to know whether the fences and the paper title are in agreement. If the surveyor certifies that the fences and the paper title are coincident, and they are not, he is assuming the burden of proof. If owner "D" loses part of his land because of paper title difficulties, he then sues the surveyor.

The surveyor is hired to show the facts as they exist. If he fails to do so and damage results from his failure, he may be liable. Of course, the surveyor in this case will cause some discomfort to "D," but not all surveys are favorable to the client. Owner "D" must solve his own problem. The surveyor can only point out what the problem is. There are many actions at law whereby paper title and possession ownership can be made to coincide. If a title company had knowledge of "D's" situation, they would not insure paper title within the fenced area. Why should they buy a law suit? Prospective owners would probably be reluctant to buy the south 15 acres of "D's" ownership, since they may be buying litigation.

Some surveyors in cases of this type do set markers in the fence corners. This reasoning is often based upon the fact that if people have lived peaceably next to one another for twenty years or more without disturbance, why should trouble be stirred up? This is short sighted.

My opinion is that the owner has hired the surveyor to point out the facts. The surveyor is obligated to discover the correct facts and call them to his client's attention. If his fences encroach on another's paper title lines, such facts should be noted. However, the client should also be told he can lose or gain land by possession and other unwritten means. It should be further pointed out that his fence lines might be ownership lines and that he should see an attorney.

The surveyor should never be a part of a fraud. If he is to describe the south 15 acres of "D's" ownership, he should never do anything that will induce a prospective buyer into thinking that paper title lines and ownership lines are the same. If a surveyor knows that paper title lines and fences are not coincident and he issues a plat showing them to be, he is setting up the conditions for fraud. All the seller has to do is to show the plat and the buyer will jump to a logical erroneous conclusion.

You have noted that in 1869 a survey was made to divide the SW 1/4 and fences were erected on these lines. This survey was not an original survey of the government and it merely purported to locate each quarter of the SW 1/4. Since the surveyor erred, it can be corrected. Age does not make an incorrect survey correct. However, it is apparent that possession has followed these lines and possession has probably ripened into a fee title (unwritten). Such conditions do not give the surveyor the right to hide the true facts from his client, and fail to give him notice that his possession and paper title lines are out of phase.

Fences, at times, are ruled to be monuments as to where the original surveyor ran his original lines. Thus, if an original surveyor surveyed along certain lines, and fences were soon afterward erected along these lines, the fences might be declared as monuments representing where the original surveyor ran his lines. But in this case the original surveyor did not run interior lines, hence the fences cannot possibly be monuments representing where the original surveyor ran his lines. The later surveyor (1869) was not an original surveyor. Any line can be given force by possession, and the courts might rule that the 1869 survey lines are ownership lines, but they should never be given the status of correct sectional subdivision lines.

The Technical Standards for Property Surveys as adopted by the American Congress on Surveying and Mapping state, "Every parcel of land whose boundaries are surveyed by a licensed surveyor should be made conformable with the record title boundaries of such land." So be it.

– Curtis M. Brown

****

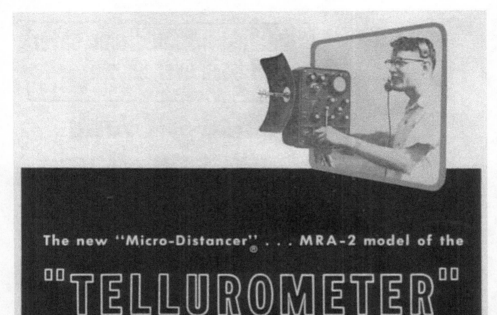

The new "Micro-Distancer"® . . . MRA-2 model of the

"TELLUROMETER"

ELECTRONIC DISTANCE-DETERMINATION SYSTEM

Patents registered in U.S. and Canada. Pending elsewhere.

The "TELLUROMETER" System of distance determination was introduced to the surveying and mapping profession just three years ago. Since then, consulting engineers, photogrammetrists, state and federal agencies and military units have proved the practicability of using micro-waves for precise distance measurement. These pioneering organizations have found, on literally hundreds of projects, that the "TELLUROMETER" technique has saved them time and money, and produced high-accuracy results.

The new Micro-Distancer (Model MRA-2) of the "TELLUROMETER" System incorporates all of the improvements and refinements which, over the past three-year period, have been indicated as desirable by satisfied users all over the world.

Sketch of Abraham Lincoln, the Surveyor, made by Lloyd Ostendorf of Dayton, Ohio, in 1967.

LAND SURVEYOR'S LIABILITY TO UNWRITTEN RIGHTS

BY CURTIS M. BROWN

JUNE 1979

Within the United States, during recent years, vast changes have occurred in the laws regulating social relationships. Of these changes, those regulating liability and those diminishing the rights of private parties to the use of their land are of the greatest interest to land surveyors. Surprisingly, during this time, very few changes have taken place in the laws pertaining to land location procedures as based upon written documents. While new wrinkles have been added here and there, the basics are intact.

Liability for land surveyors has changed dramatically in the past decade. The increased number of lawyers and the inflation in the cost of land are cited as reasons for the problem. The move against professionals generally began in the 60s, when patients began to sue doctors for malpractice. This movement spread to lawyers, engineers, and now to land surveyors.

Today, if people in this country have a mania, it surely must be the desire to sue other people. Juries have been awarding such large claims that it is impossible to predict what the future will hold in cases against land surveyors. One such defense against litigation is to be without money or worldly goods; no lawyer in his right mind would consider taking a case against you. After listening to land surveyors around the country tell me how rough it is to make a living, that might be one of the reasons for the scarcity of suits against land surveyors. In T. S. Madson's new book entitled, *Understanding Your Professional Liability as a Land Surveyor,* he lists 61 cases found after a comprehensive research. It is recommended reading for all surveyors.

Officially, I am retired; however, I am often asked to appear in court cases. Being retired does not mean that you quit work; it merely means that you select *what you* want to do and *when* you do it.

In my early writings, I generally advocated that surveyors should locate land boundaries in accordance with a written deed; all conveyances based upon unwritten rights should be referred to attorneys for resolution. Within recent years there have been cases, and one in particular, wherein surveyors have been held liable for failure to react to a change in ownership created by prolonged possession. The purpose of this paper is to re-examine what a surveyor should do in the event title has been altered by a legal transfer of title by prolonged possession.

Before delving into the question, it should be pointed out that there are two very different types of possession found by the surveyor. One is totally unrelated to the original survey lines; the other is possession, which represents where the original survey monuments were set. Let us suppose that an original surveyor set an original monument to mark a corner; further, a fence was erected at the time the monument existed. Later the monument material disappeared. Now the fence is a monument to where the original monument was located. In this discussion only possession unrelated to original monumental lines and possession out of agreement with written deeds is being considered.

Below is described a case wherein a surveyor located his client's land exactly in accordance with his client's deed, yet found himself in trouble because he failed to take into account the adjoiner's occupancy. The facts are as follows:

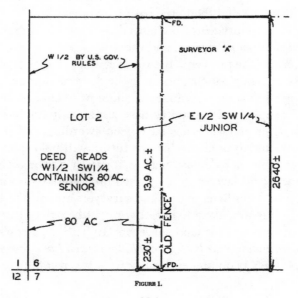

FIGURE 1.

Surveyor "A" was asked to survey the following land: The East Half of the Southwest quarter of Section 6, T - S, R - E, certain Meridian, in accordance with the official government plat thereof. See the attached sketch. The official plat disclosed the said East half as having a full 80.00 acres, whereas the remainder of the SW 1/4 was labeled as Lot 2 with 67 acres. Using the rules given in the booklet, *Restoration of Lost or Obliterated Corners and Subdivision of Sections,* Bureau of Land Management, the surveyor did correctly locate the said E 1/2. There was a little excess, which was properly divided among the parcels. Up to this point, the surveyor did everything exactly correct; he could not be faulted. What happened next did create a problem.

During the course of the survey, Surveyor "A" observed a fence encroaching on his client's deed lines by a little more than 13 acres. At each end of the fence, a surveyor's stake was found (in California a surveyor must put his number on every property stake that he sets), and he was contacted. The adjoiner's deed read as follows: The West half of the SW 1/4 containing 80 acres. Further facts were; the dividing fence was old (more than the statute of limitations of 10 years), the adjoiner was occupying 80 acres, and at one time one party owned all of the SW 1/4 and sold off the W 1/2 containing 80 acres *first.*

On the theory that acreage was subordinate and the client had a written deed to the E 1/2, surveyor "A" monumented the deed as written, disclosed the fence line, and wrote in the gross area, including the approximate 13 acres fenced by the adjoiner. A buyer purchased the land as based upon the acreage figure (per acre purchase price) and a title company insured title on the basis of the survey. When the buyer tried to occupy the land, the adjoiner objected and a lawsuit followed. The court judgment was up to the fence and the Title Company had to pay damages. Following this the Title Company sued the surveyor and won more than $100,000 damages in the lower court. To date the appeal of this case has not been ruled on by the higher court; regardless of how the appeal comes out, Surveyor "A" has lost considerable time and money for legal fees, court costs, travel, expert testimony, etc.

A point to bring out is that the Title Company was acting as a third party; they did not pay the surveyor's original fee for the work. As a matter of law, the surveyor is liable to third parties that have been damaged. *This is a case where the land surveyor correctly located the client's deed lines in accordance with the writings of his client, yet was held liable for failure to recognize the ownership rights of the adjoiner.* The implications suggested by this case deserve further analysis.

I appeared as an expert witness and testified that the surveyor had located the E 1/2 exactly correct in accordance with the government requirements. Also it was my opinion: (1) The title company had all the facts, including the location of the fence, the adjoiner's deed, etc., and (2) they elected to insure the title and collected the fee, not the surveyor; therefore, they should pay the damages. The judge obviously thought otherwise.

With the benefit of 20/20 hindsight, let us look at the case and see what the surveyor could have done, if anything, to have avoided liability or at least have reduced his liability to some degree.

The first question to explore is: What did the client have in mind when he asked the surveyor to locate his boundaries? Was he asking the surveyor to locate his *ownership?* Or just the deed lines? As all surveyors should know, there is a vast difference between ownership and written deed rights. The written deed is merely evidence of ownership, not proof of ownership; title to land can be transferred by unwritten rights. From my experience with clients, very few know that there is a difference between the two; most clients want to know what they own.

One thing is certain: The client is not asking the surveyor to locate his lines of possession; they can see where they exist. *As a minimum, he wants to know if his lines of possession agree with his written title.* If the surveyor has no intention of locating the lines of ownership, that is, he intends only to locate the written deed lines and show possession in relation to the written deed, and if he fails to make the client aware of such fact, the courts will probably find that the surveyor contracted to locate the lines of ownership and hold that the client is entitled to rely on that standard of duty by the surveyor. Seemingly, that is what happened in the above case. While Surveyor "A," in the above case, correctly marked the deed lines, did he inform his client completely about the difference between ownership and deed lines? Did he put on his map, "area claimed by others," or did he put a heavy solid line around the area of confusion, or did he exclude the acreage within the area of confusion from the gross acreage of ownership? By looking at the map, did the client have a right to think he owned the area fenced by others? It is my opinion that if he had done the things suggested by these questions, he probably would have avoided liability.

Within the United States, in most areas, the first right to land must be acquired via writing, however defective. After a written title is obtained, except in Torrens Title areas, imperfections in the writings can be corrected by long possession or the land area can be enlarged or diminished by the acts of adjoining owners. Written title alone is not the only consideration in determining who owns property; actual physical possession of the land can result in the passing of title. In the order of importance of elements determining who has ownership of land, a legally consummated unwritten right ranks higher than a written title (Note: Not so in Torrens Titles).

The second question to explore is: Can a surveyor monument the lines of ownership obtained by unwritten means? To my knowledge, absolutely nothing in the law prevents him from doing so. Clearly, from my conversations with attorneys, this is not an unauthorized practice of law. If the surveyor chooses to claim that a possessor right has ripened into a fee title, he is certainly privileged to do so. The real question is, *What should he do?*

The third question to explore is then: Whenever a surveyor finds possession out of agreement with written title, and he determines that title has or probably has passed due to an unwritten conveyance, what are his obligations and what should he do?

Since the client wants to know if his lines of possession are in agreement with his written title, the surveyor is certainly obligated to report on that. But since most clients think the surveyor is locating ownership lines, the surveyor must *fully* disclose the fact that land can be gained or lost by possession, and if he thinks land has been lost to an adjoiner by some unwritten act, he is obligated to inform his client of such fact. In addition, since the surveyor is liable to all third parties that have a right to rely on the results of the surveyor's findings, the information must be presented in such a manner that no third party can be misinformed. Merely telling the client orally is not sufficient; every document presented must clearly indicate the facts so that no third party can be misled.

In the above case the surveyor was held liable to a third party, the Title Company. If the surveyor had put a heavy border around the disputed area, and if he had clearly marked on his map, "AREA OF DISPUTED TITLE" or "AREA CLAIMED BY OTHERS" he could have saved himself a court trial. In addition, he should not have included the disputed area in the gross acreage of the client; acreage should be sorted into two columns, the first showing what the client owns for certain, and the second showing doubtful areas.

My own policy in handling encroachments has been as follows: First, all adjoiner deeds are read to eliminate the possibility of senior rights. Second, the adjoiners are questioned as to how possession came into being and how long it had been there. If no senior right existed and if the fence were there for a period of time less than the statute of limitations, then the possession would be treated as an encroachment, and stakes would be set in accordance with the written deed. If for any possible reason title could pass because of unwritten considerations, then the area encroached upon would be given a doubtful status. A written report would then be given to the client explaining why ownership is in doubt and a map would be delivered showing the area in question. Admittedly, this solution is not satisfactory to the client; he wants to know what he owns. On the other hand, I was never one willing to assume unnecessary liability. Some time ago I made up my mind that, regardless of how much I knew, there would always be some situation in which it was impossible to find an answer as to who owned what, especially when you take into account what the client is willing to pay. If I were uncertain, I would monument the area the client had for certain, explain the situation, and then let the client decide whether he wanted to go after the doubtful area.

In my own practice, I have at times set monuments in a position that was determined because of long occupancy, and as I reflect on it, in each case the client had color of title, that is, he had a written title that was defective. On its face, the writings appeared to be good, yet in fact they were somehow deficient when you looked up record facts, such as senior rights or the original position of monuments. Two examples that follow illustrate the situation:

A subdivision was made some 50 years ago, and the surveyor measured out 1320 ft. and set a pipe at a corner fence post and wrote "fence corner of long standing." Upon properly breaking down the section, it was discovered that the section was somewhat skewed in the last half mile going into the township line. The subdivision encroached upon the adjoiner's land by about 100 ft. as shown in Figure 2. I was asked to monument the lot in the Northwest corner. Even knowing that the subdivision encroached upon the adjoined, I monumented the lot in accordance with the filed map. It was my opinion that title had passed for the simple reason that the lot owners had paid taxes for more than 50 years with a fence in place; all of the requirements of the law for a possession to change to a fee title had been met. Technically, I was working from a written title, but in fact it was a defective title that depended upon occupancy to ripen into a fee right.

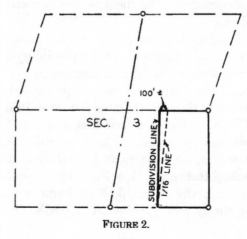

FIGURE 2.

It was my policy that if a subdivision had been made prior to the statute of limitations, and the owner had a fence up for the length of time of the statute of limitations, I would not investigate the correctness of the exterior boundary on the theory that if it were wrong, it did not matter; title had passed by occupancy rights.

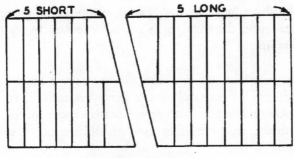

FIGURE 3.

The second situation is shown in Figure 3. The street was the boundary of the City of San Diego and was determined from monuments miles apart. In improving the street and putting in curbs and sidewalks, the city ran the true line; it encroached on the subdivision to the west by about 5 ft. The blocks to the east were 5 ft. too long and those to the west 5-ft. too short. I was asked to monument one of the lots adjacent to the street, and I did so by placing all of the shortage in the last lot. They had lost 5 ft. to the street and I recognized it as such.

Here are two cases in which I reacted to change in title due to possession. In the first one, the party had a written document giving title to land that the adjoiner owned; the second, the lot owner lost land because of continued use by the public. As a summary of the discussion presented, the following is offered:

(1) The surveyor in finding an encroachment on his client's land, must fully inform the client of its significance; further, the information must be presented in such a manner that third parties also understand the significance of any encroachment.

(2) Nothing in the law prevents the surveyor from deciding who has ownership to encroachments, and he may monument ownership lines rather than written title lines.

(3) In some circumstances the surveyor may be justified in monumenting the line that he believes to represent true ownership line. In my experience, this occurs when (1) the client has color of title, (2) the client has paid taxes on the land described with color of title, (3) and the client has had possession by an enclosure for a time more than the statute of limitations. In cases involving adverse relationships (adverse possession), estoppel, or recognition and acquiescence, the surveyor is probably foolish to try to establish ownership.

(4) Since, to avoid liability, the surveyor must fully disclose the significance of encroachments; surveyors must have knowledge of how and when unwritten conveyances occur. It is my recommendation that all surveyors should be required to understand the subject.

A practice that would save the land surveyor harmless is the practice of drafting "Property Line Agreements." This is supported by the policy of the American Congress on Surveying and Mapping that all written deeds should be brought into conformance with the possession of the land. This is accomplished by causing the client and all adjoiners to sign a map stating that they agree that the lines shown thereon are their common property lines. This is a good way to resolve the problem under discussion and all land surveyors should attempt to settle their boundary disputes in this way.

Paper was presented at the NMACSM Legal Seminar in Jan. 1979. Mr. Brown, past president of ACSM and well-known author of a number of books and numerous papers relative to the surveying profession, resides at 5075 Keeney St., La Mesa, Calif. 92041.

****

****

RE: "LAND SURVEYOR'S LIABILITY TO UNWRITTEN RIGHTS" BY CURTIS M. BROWN

PUBLISHED IN 'SURVEYING AND MAPPING,' VOL. XXXIX, NO. 2, JUNE 1979, PP. 119-123

[From: W. G. G. Blakney, Assoc. Professor, Auburn University, Auburn, Ala. 36839] DEAR MR. BROWN: I am pleased by the publication of your paper on "Land Surveyor's Liability" in the June 1979 *Surveying and Mapping*. Though there is much in the paper to cause practicing land surveyors to lose a lot of sleep (the importance of acreage – usually last on the order of calls), it at least puts to rest the oft-heard blunt edict to "survey according to the deed" or the variation that "the surveyor should not practice law." Your clear relating of the court's expectation that the surveyor should pay attention to ownership may lead to a more reasoned use of deed calls and fewer court cases.

But I am confused by your third recommendation for monumenting land by ownership which has "possession for a time more than the statute of limitations." I assumed this would be the statutory time required for adverse possession to take place, but the next sentence indicates this interpretation is wrong. You say "in cases involving adverse relationships (adverse possessions) . . . the surveyor is probably foolish to try to establish ownership."

I would appreciate knowing your meaning of "statute of limitations" if it is something unrelated to adverse possession. Is it the type of statutory period for fences (30 years) mentioned by W. Robillard in that same issue? What is the 10-year statute of limitations you mentioned?

REPLY:

[From: Curtis M. Brown, L.L.S., 5705 Keeney St., La Mesa, Calif. 92041]

DEAR PROF. BLAKNEY: Most unfortunately, the words "adverse possession" means various things in different states. We have two types of cases: (1) those in which the outcome depends upon physical evidence which the surveyor can gather or observe, such as color of title, paying taxes, and provable possession for the period required by law; (2) those cases that depend upon witness evidence, especially where estoppel is involved. One owner claims one thing and the adjoiner claims another; no positive determination is possible. In the first case, I would make a decision; in the second, I would not.

Change the wording to read: "in cases involving adverse relationships . . . to the following, "in cases involving *doubtful* adverse relationships . . . the surveyor is probably foolish to try to establish ownership." This is more specific.

In every state there is a statute of limitations in adverse title cases: the period of time that the land must be held adversely. Statute usually means "enacted by the legislature." However, in the cases of adverse relationships, the time required may come from common law. Limitation is applied against the rightful owner – if he does not eject the adverse claimant within the time allowed by law, he is barred from bringing action. In some southern states this is 5 years; in California (with payment of taxes) it is 10 years. Some states have 15 years, others 20 years. Common law was at first 60 years, then 30, and then taken over by a statute law.

I hope this answers some of your questions.

****

COMMENT AND DISCUSSION

THE GREAT DILEMMA — OR, WHEN IS A FENCE JUST A FENCE?

BY MITCHELL G. WILLIAMS, P.L.S.

MARCH 1980

The pages of SURVEYING AND MAPPING are open to free and temperate discussion of all matters pertaining to the interests of the Congress. It is the purpose of this department to encourage comments on published material or the presentation of new ideas in a formal or informal way. – EDITOR

Mr. Williams, a licensed land surveyor in the State of New York, holds an M.A. degree in anthropology. His mailing address is: 189 Sears Rd., Box 291, West Islip, N.Y. 11795.

ABSTRACT. In much of the surveying literature since the Second World War there has been a confusion between the role of the surveyor and that of the court in the location of boundary lines. This confusion has been recently exemplified in an article by Curtis M. Brown, "Land Surveyor's Liability to Unwritten Rights," in the June 1979 issue of *Surveying and Mapping*. After a brief summary of the history of recorded property transfer and a discussion of the nature of a deed, the duties and obligations of the surveyor as regards boundaries and encroachments are treated in full. There follows a detailed discussion and critique of the aforementioned article by Mr. Brown and the conclusion that the principles enunciated by Brown concerning the role of the surveyor vis-á-vis encroachments are at variance with and contradictory of both legal and historical precedent.

Introduction

"In the case of boundary disputes, they were settled by the competitive marshalling of the oldest inhabitants by the disputants, who would proceed to outswear and out remember each other in great open air oath takings held on the site of the quarrel." [1]

We have come a long way since the early Middle Ages, when the above was a standard method of boundary location - or have we? After 700 years of struggle to ensure that no man could be disenfranchised of real property in secret, without due process of law, there appears to be a trend back to oath-takings and crossbows for property line determinations. Of course, the leaders of this trend do not refer to it explicitly in such terms, and perhaps are not aware of its implications themselves. The approach is presented in the only widely read legal handbook for surveyors, Curtis Brown's companion volumes, *Boundary Control and Legal Principles* and *Evidence and Procedures for Boundary Location*, and more ominously, in the lead article in the June 1979 issue of *Surveying and Mapping*, "Land Surveyor's Liability to Unwritten Rights," by Curtis Brown. The principle enunciated is that of occupation, i.e., the idea that possession of land is sometimes the best evidence for the location of a boundary.

To many readers of this essay, this will seem self-evident, and they may have utilized such a principle in their own work. It is to these readers that I address what follows, for this principle is based on a basic misunderstanding of both the nature of boundary lines and the legal role of the land surveyor.

The Development of Written Transfer

A late medieval manor in England usually consisted of a lord's demesne and outlying lands worked by tenants. [2] These tenants had "rights of common" over the demesne, i.e., they could use specified parts of it for pasture and were responsible for either labor on the demesne for the lord or for a money rent (by the 14th and 15th centuries, most labor services had been commuted into money rents). The growth of a capitalistically-oriented economic system and a shortage of labor resulting from the Black Death created a demand for money among the landholding class, which was also beginning to play a smaller role in the running of the manor, preferring to collect the rents and leave the operation of the farming to a steward or other representative. [3]

Records were important to this system. Rents due, entry fines (an amount to be paid to confirm a hereditary succession, or entry, to a tenure), rights of common, and so on, were simply too complex to remember and often occasioned dispute between tenants. Each manor maintained its own court for the adjudication of property disputes and had a Court Roll in which were entered, usually by a bailiff or stewart, all the tenures, rents, etc., of all the tenants of the lord. Changes in any particulars were noted, and the Court Roll was a kind of incipient deed registry, although only on a local level. [4] However, not all transfers were recorded, and there was a reservoir of "custom," which was unwritten and varied greatly from manor to manor. These customs dealt with land use, rights of pasture, and sometimes rents and fines. The "custom of the manor" was, in essence, the local equivalent of the Common Law. [5]

Such a system was prone to abuse. Recourse in property disputes was to the lord, so that often the tenant was at a severe disadvantage. The recording of deeds was not required, and often ignored. With the great price rise of the 16th century, landlords were hard pressed, and rents rose rapidly. The manor quickly became an investment and a source of income for the nobility, rather than a home and farm to supply their immediate needs. [6] To maximize monetary return, an attempt was made to disenfranchise unproductive tenants and consolidate small, inefficient, personal holdings into large, efficient farms. [7] This attempt, usually referred to as the enclosure movement, continued into the 18th century and effected the change from feudal to capitalistically-organized farming.

Enclosure in this period was for the most part illegal. [8] England was racked during the 16th century by peasant revolts, and there were repeated attempts by the government to stop the nobles' enclosure of their lands, but to little avail. As long as the ownership of land rights was imperfectly recorded in local Court Rolls, it was impossible for the Crown to know who owned what, and consequently manor lords were allowed to disenfranchise tenants almost at will. It was out of this chaotic situation that the idea of mandatory written title developed.

1535 saw the passage, under Henry VIII, of two statutes - that of Uses and that of Enrollments. [9] "Uses" required that for a transfer of title to land to be valid, it had to be accompanied by actual possession and a written deed, and recorded in the proper Court Roll. However, this statute was too easy to circumvent. Since it automatically gave title to the possessor, the courts held that the presence or absence of a recorded deed was really immaterial, since mere possession would establish title. The government accordingly passed the Statute of Enrollments, which ignored possession as a criterion, and simply required that all transfers be written and recorded to be valid. [10]

Of course, agrarian capitalism was established in England despite government and peasant opposition, and the Statutes of Uses and Enrollments were often circumvented by the clever use of loopholes. A public registry of deeds was never established in England and does not exist there today. [11] A secret written transfer of title was little better than an oral one, and the secrecy of land conveyance is one of the drawbacks of the British system. However, when it was transplanted to the American

THE CURT BROWN CHRONICLES

colonies, the system was substantially cleansed of abuses. The Statute of Enrollments was reenacted in all of the colonies. [12] But in the absence of a system of manorial lands and a corresponding lack of manorial courts, the deeds had to be enrolled in a public, central registry, usually at the county level. Thus was established in the United States the current system of recording every transfer of title in a written record filed with the clerk of the county in which the property lies. The colonies accomplished what the mother country is still struggling to do - outlaw the secret conveyance of land and prevent the disenfranchisement of a landowner without due process of law, i.e., a recorded deed.

What Is a Deed?

What exactly is this magical instrument? As it turns out, it is not as foolproof a guard against fraud as was thought. A deed is simply the written statement of the fact that one party granted its right/title/interest to a piece of real property to a second party. It *does not* say that the first party *had* any right/title/interest to grant. It merely states, in effect, that if the first party had such right/title/interest, then he had granted it. As such, a deed is nothing more than *evidence* of title; it is not *proof* of title. [13]

This obviously has important ramifications. Questions of ownership and land rights have always been a fruitful source of litigation, so much so that there have often been attempts to reduce them. The most notable of these, at least in the English-speaking world, is the Torrens System, which registers *title*, rather than deeds. The more common response has been some sort of title insurance, something hardly necessary if a deed was anything more than evidence of title. [14]

All questions of title, unless it has been registered in a Torrens-type system, have to be settled by a court of law. The job has been made easier by the Statute of Frauds (first passed in England in 1672 and repassed in all the states of the Union) which disallows the unwritten transfer of property, so that claimant to title must have written evidence of some sort, such as the color of title required under adverse possession. The courts sometimes will take as evidence unwritten considerations, such as adverse possession and acquiescence, in determining a disputed ownership, but it is the written record that is primary. [15]

The point I wish to make, though, is that "unwritten title" is a misleading phrase. It is actually "unwritten evidence of title," which a court may so consider, and if it decides to accept this unwritten evidence, it ripens into a written title by being recorded in the court's decision and subsequently recorded in the public record. No one has "unwritten title." A court must weigh unwritten evidence, such as long possession, and decide as to its merit. If it is upheld, the claimant acquires a written title to his claim. This cannot occur without due process of law. [16]

Title can only be fixed by court decision. A deed is not proof of title and neither is possession, for no matter how long, until a court has decided that the preponderance of evidence confers title. The complex procedure involved with the initial Torrens registration of a parcel is proof enough that the question of ownership of a piece of real property is not lightly decided.

The Role of the Surveyor

Before the emergence of agrarian capitalism, land parcels tended to be fixed in size and location and demarcated by physical features. England had long been settled and there were no great, open, undeveloped spaces to be subdivided. Deeds in the manorial courts could refer to adjoining owners or topographical features without recourse to measurement because of the physical certainty of the boundary lines. English law recognized, and still does, seven types of boundary: hedges, ditches, walls, fences, roads, streams, and foreshores. All served as barriers to livestock and, as such, constituted boundaries in fact as well as in law. [17]

Enclosure, however, brought great changes to the landscape. Previously disparate parcels were surrounded by a newly constructed hedge or ditch, and the old boundaries were obliterated to aid in farming. Property began to change hands much more rapidly, as land came to be seen as a source of revenue rather than sustenance, and estates were subdivided and combined. There was a need for a profession to record these changes, in the form of maps and geometrical descriptions, because encroachments had become much more common with the destruction of long-standing boundaries and the erection of new ones. [18] Without the evidence of a geometrical description, ownership would become synonymous with occupation and one's boundaries could change overnight by the movement of an extant fence or the construction of a new one. Only geometrical description would give some protection against encroachment.

The old offices of manorial steward and bailiff were transformed into the surveyor, in direct response to this need to define the new fluid boundary lines of the capitalist age. He had to relate the boundary lines on the ground to themselves and to other boundary lines in such a way that they could be replaced if destroyed. Of course, he was not completely successful.

Technological shortcomings crippled the great surveyors of the 16th and 17th centuries, and it was not until the late 18th and 19th centuries that the Ordnance Survey in England and the Public Land System of the United States made real advances in making boundaries self-sufficient, in the sense of allowing their replacements if the physical evidence were destroyed. The process is even now far from complete.

The survey, then, served as further evidence for boundary line location. It did not fix the boundary and was completely independent of ownership. A survey is twice removed from ownership: It is evidence of the location of a piece of property described in a deed which itself is only evidence of ownership. A surveyor who thinks that his location of the bounds of a deed description show his client what the client "owns" is ignorant of the basic precepts of his profession.

> *Except by express statutory authority, (the surveyor cannot) legally determine where the true existing boundary line is. As far as the court is concerned, absent statutory authority, all a surveyor can do is testify as a witness, as to where, in his best judgment, the boundary line is located. . . . The surveyor can, in the absence of statute, play no special role legally in settling a boundary controversy.*[19]

The surveyor gives an opinion. If there are two locations for a boundary line, based on irreconcilable deed calls from one or more deeds, the surveyor is obliged to show either the overlap or the gore, or, if he feels he can make a decision, his survey should clearly state that there is a problem, show what it is, and *then* give his opinion.[20] For that is all he can do. A surveyor cannot anticipate a possible future court decision, because that would involve disenfranchisement without due process. True overlaps and gores can only be resolved by a court. No number of surveys can determine the legally true boundary.

> *Unless the parties have agreed that the surveyor shall make the boundary, or except in the case of a primary government survey, the survey **cannot make the line**. It **merely locates** where the line is.*[21] *[emphasis mine]*

340

When a Fence is Just a Fence

So what happens when you find out that the deed lines run 4 feet outside a party wall and through the neighbor's bathroom, or that there is a fence 100 feet inside the property line you just monumented? This is the great dilemma of land surveying, and its improper resolution has resulted in many incorrect, bad, and fraudulent surveys. The recommendations of Brown, *et al.*, imply that this discrepancy must be due to some "unwritten title," which we have shown to be a fictive concept, and that the surveyor should monument the possession, for otherwise great disruption would result. [22] In light of what is known about the duties and abilities of the surveyor as defined above, such a procedure comes perilously close to depriving someone, either the client or his adjoiner, of real property without the due process of law, not to mention that it oversteps the bounds of a surveyor's job. In addition, to fail to show the discrepancy between the written and unwritten evidence, i.e., the deed and the possession, would mislead the client.

The resolution of the dilemma lies in the realization that when deed lines and possessed lines are contradictory, the issue must move to a higher plane - that of the court. Obviously, there is a discrepancy. Either the deed is mistaken, or the house was actually built on the wrong lot, or someone can claim adverse possession, or there is a second deed that was overlooked in the abstract, etc. These possibilities must be resolved legally, by a court. The Brown solution would result in a kind of "Brownian" motion of property lines. Let surveyor *A* come out and monument your fence. Move your fence 20 feet, rip out all of surveyor *A*'s monuments, wait ten years, hire surveyor *B* to come out and monument your fence, and voila! This process can be repeated innumerable times by all the adjoiners, and soon there will be gunplay in the streets.

It is to be expected that possession occasionally disagrees with record lines. Otherwise there would never be any need for a survey. If possession equals ownership, who needs a map? The idea that possession implies "unwritten title" is an insidious one, because it can, and does, trap the unwary surveyor into accepting lines of occupation over record lines, rather than showing the discrepancy. Of course this is easier and causes fewer problems for the title company, but it is incorrect. Surveying would cease to exist as a profession if it were merely to accept as boundaries what is occupied.

It is instructive to read some legal options of occupation as a determinant of boundary lines:

> *If an owner ignorant of his true boundaries by mistake acquiesces in a line as a boundary, he and his grantees are not thereby precluded from afterwards claiming to the true line and it has been held that one who has no knowledge that his adjoiner encroaches cannot be held to have lost his rights by acquiescence in such occupancy **no matter how long** continued, for one cannot waive or acquiesce in a wrong while ignorant that is acquitted.* [23] *[emphasis mine]*
> *... The mere fact that an owner sets his fence within his boundary lines does not give his adjoiner the right to the land fenced out, for the circumstances must be considered.* [24]

Thus, where there has been no actual agreement between the parties as to the boundary but the parties have merely acquiesced in the situation, even for a long period of time, there would be neither a change of title by adverse possession *nor a practical location of the boundary.* [25] *[emphasis mine]*

> *However, mere license or passive acquiescence in an encroachment will not conclude a party, and the maintenance of a fence for the mutual accommodation of both parties although along a line claimed to by one does not necessarily imply acquiescence, **especially when the true line could be ascertained from the deeds.*** [26] *[emphasis mine]*

Even a court of law will not invariably rule in favor of occupation. It would be foolish for a surveyor to do so.

But what about the so-called doctrine of ancient fences? The question is, what makes a fence ancient? And the answer is, a court! After weighing all evidence of occupation and record lines, the latter supplied by survey, a court may decide that a particular fence is "ancient," and accord it primary weight. "Ancient" does not mean simply old, but legally old enough to control over a document. A surveyor cannot note on his survey, "Ancient fence found and held," without the approval of a legal decision. Sometimes a fence is just a fence.

'Land Surveyors' Liability to Unwritten Rights' - A Reply

The principles presented in Brown's article will be found faulty if examined in the light of the above argument. No one but a court can say that the physical mislocation of a street, as constructed, destroys title to a 5-foot strip of land. One can monument the physical corner, but only if on the face of the finished survey map it is clearly stated that there is an area in dispute, and its extent. To make any pretense that the monuments set by a surveyor show the client "what he owns" is a fraudulent claim. A surveyor's opinion as to ownership is no more valid than a plumber's. The courts only recognize his expertise as to boundary line location and even then only as an expert witness. [27] There is a world of difference between determining the boundaries described in a deed and determining that someone "owns" the land inside or outside these boundaries. The surveyor has no authority to do the latter. It may not be illegal, but then again, it's not illegal for *anyone* to decide who owns a piece of property. However, a court of law will not give any special weight to such an opinion. The absence of a negative sanction, i.e., it's not illegal, does not imply a positive one, i.e., that the surveyor has the authority to determine ownership.

A property owner cannot be deprived of property without due process of law. If a surveyor attempts to decide in the ownership of an area in dispute, he is depriving someone of property. *This* is illegal. The case cited by Brown is a perfect example of the consequences of a surveyor attempting to exceed his legal authority. Let us examine it in some detail. (Particulars are paraphrased from Brown's article.)

A surveyor was asked to survey the easterly half of the southwest quarter of Section 6, T-S, R-E, certain meridian. Apparently the client's description did not contain an acreage figure. On consulting the government plat, it was discovered that the southwest quarter only contained 147 acres, rather than 160, but showed a line dividing it in half in such a way that the eastern half was a full 80 acres and the westerly half was short. In the course of this survey, he found a monumented fence line on a deviate line. The fence and stakes indicated that the *westerly* half had a full 80 acres, while his client's half contained only 67. Upon consulting the surveyor who had set the stakes he was shown a deed describing the westerly half as containing 80 acres. This deed was senior to his client's, the whole southwest quarter having been under single ownership, with the westerly half being sold off first. The surveyor decided that the government line would control the fence, the earlier survey, and a contradictory description in a senior deed, and monumented his client's lot as a full 80 acres. But his survey did not show that there was a deeded overlap between the lots, or that there might be a title problem - he simply showed the deviate fence line.

The first question which leaps to mind is, what does this case have to do with unwritten rights? The senior deed gives written title to the full 80 acres and possessed line, while the junior simply gives it to the easterly half. There is an overlap between the two deeds, and the question of unwritten rights is hardly paramount. The conflicting claims over the central 13 acres exist, even if a field survey had not been done, because the calls of the two deeds and the government plat are patently irreconcilable. The surveyor was not held liable because of any unwritten rights, but precisely because he applied the very principles that Brown espouses in this paper. He anticipated a court of law, deciding that both seniority of description and acreage calls were subordinate to the government survey, i.e., he decided ownership. As Brown points out, nothing in the law prevents him from doing so. But if all of the preceding argument has not convinced anyone that a surveyor in fact cannot decide ownership, perhaps the $100,000 judgment against the surveyor in this case will cause him to examine the case and reconsider the principles involved. The surveyor in this instance abrogated the duty of the court and, in effect, on his own initiative, disenfranchised the owner of the westerly half of 13 acres, not because he was insensitive to unwritten rights but because he took it upon himself to resolve a deed and physical overlap between two parcels, and did not bring the dispute to anyone's attention. "The surveyor cannot legally determine where the true existing boundary line is . . . All a surveyor can do is testify as a witness." (Quoted above.)

Conclusion

At this point the reader is either cheering me on or wishing for a chance to meet me in a dark alley. At the least, I hope I have forced you to think seriously about what exactly the surveyor's job actually is, and I have opened your eyes to some of the fallacies contained in the prevalent advice given to surveyors for locating lines. If I have been too strident in my statements, it is because I am very disturbed to see a statement such as, "Nothing in the law prevents the surveyor from deciding who has ownership to encroachments" [28] in a highly respected journal, particularly when this "principle" is the conclusion drawn from a case where a surveyor was held liable for $100,000 precisely *because* he decided who had ownership to a 13-acre encroachment, and he had guessed wrong.

"He may monument ownership lines rather than written title lines." Who tells him what the ownership lines are? This principle has resulted in near anarchy, at least in the New York metropolitan area, as far as survey lines go. The principle is fallacious. A surveyor can monument anything he wants to - but only his mapping of record and physical lines and their relation to each other is recognized by the courts as his duty. To confuse the deeded lines with possession lines destroys the entire rationale for the profession of land surveying. A survey is only useful to show if there is a discrepancy between deeded boundaries and occupied boundaries. If the two are made synonymous, the survey is superfluous, and we are back in the Middle Ages.

I would like to quote from a letter which appeared in the same issue of *Surveying and Mapping* that contained Brown's article:

1. Fences are fences and boundaries are boundaries and the two are not necessarily the same. . . .
3. Surveyors conduct surveys,
   Attorneys practice law
   Oil and water don't mix.
4. I possess no time machine that permits me to know with certainty the origin of the fences found near, on, or adjacent to that one true dividing line set by statutes. [30]

[MP NOTE: There is no number 2 in the original article.]

For nearly 700 years, there has been a continuous struggle to guarantee legally that a person will not be disenfranchised of real property without due process of law. For most of that time the surveyor has been in the forefront of that struggle.

If he is to maintain his status as an independent professional, he must remain there.

REFERENCES

1. Thompson, F. M. L., *Chartered Surveyors-The Growth of a Profession*, London, (1968), 4.
2. Simpson, S. Rowton, *Land Law and Registration*, Cambridge, (1976), 27.
3. Tawney, R. H., *The Agrarian Problem in the 16th Century*, London, (1912), 52, 211, 310.
4. Kerridge, Eric, *Agrarian Problems in the 16th Century and After*, London, (1969), 24; Scrutton, T. E., *Commons and Common Fields*, New York, (1970), 22.
5. Tawney, *op. cit.*, 125.
6. *Ibid.*, 189.
7. Gonner, E. C. K., *Common Land and Inclosure*, New York, (1966), 315 ff.
8. For a discussion of anti-enclosure legislation, see Geary, Frank, *Land Tenure and Unemployment*, New York, (1969), 53 ff.

9. Pollack, Frederick, *The Land Laws*, London, (1883), 101.

10. For a more complete treatment of the development of English real property law, see Pollack, *ibid., passim.*

11. Simpson, *op. cit., passim.*

12. *Ibid.*, 95-96.

13. *Ibid.*, 15.

14. For a complete discussion of the types of deed and title registration in the English-speaking world, see *ibid., passim.*

15. Grimes, John S., Clark *on Surveying and Boundaries*, 4th ed., New York, (1978), 6.

16. *Ibid.*, 5.

17. Simpson, *op. cit.*, 127.

18. Kerridge, op. *cit.*, 29.

19. Grimes, op. *cit.*, 13.

20. Skelton, Ray Hamilton, *The Legal Elements of Boundaries and Adjacent Properties*, Indianapolis, (1930), 348.

21. Grimes, *op. cit.*, 24.

22. Brown, Curtis M., "Land Surveyors Liability to Unwritten Rights," *Surveying and Mapping*, 39:2 (June 1979), 123.

23. Skelton, *op. cit.*, 368.

24. *Ibid.*, 362.

25. Grimes, *op. cit.*, 632.

26. Skelton, *op. cit.*, 364.

27. Grimes, *op. cit.*, 13.

28. Brown, *op. cit.*, 123.

29. *Ibid.*

30. Robillard, Walter G. "On Comment Re: 'Subdivision of Sections of Rectangular Surveys of the United States' by Lane J. Bouman," *Surveying and Mapping*, 39:2 (June 1979), 163.

[MP NOTE: Reference number 29 was not identified in the original article.]

****

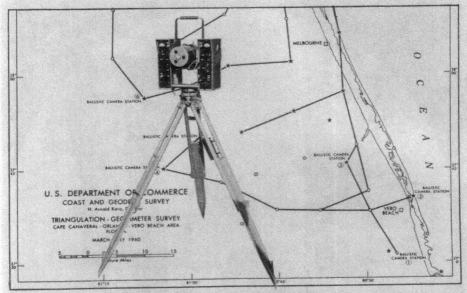

We've been handing you a fast line for years!

That's absolutely right! The Geodimeter® can accurately measure the lines in one day that would take other methods several days. Radial measurements and traverses are so precisely reliable there is no need for time consuming triangulation. Does that sound like a line?
Right again, a very dependable . . . Geodimeter line.

Here are some sound facts and features of the Geodimeter Model 6.
□ Only one instrument and one trained operator necessary in surveying crew. □ Daylight range: 1 — 2 miles, Darkness: 8 —10 miles. □ Average error: 0.03 ft. + 2 millionths of the distance. □ Measuring time 5 to 10 minutes. □ All transistorized . . . reduces power consumption and weight. □ Easily tilted for aiming. □ Digital read-out. □ Built-in 360° horizontal scale. □ Battery operated. □ Lightweight—instrument unit 35 lbs.
There is much more to tell about the Geodimeter . . . for further information and a demonstration, why don't you drop us a fast line.

AGA CORPORATION OF AMERICA

151 New World Way, So. Plainfield, N. J.

FACTORY REPRESENTATIVES: E. Phil Harris Co., 5352 First Ave., N., Birmingham, Ala • **Carl Heinrich Co.**, 711 Concord Ave., Cambridge, Mass. • **Miller Blue Print**, P.O. Box 2065, 108 East 10th St., Austin, Texas • **Seiler Instrument & Mfg. Co.**, 1629 Washington Ave., St. Louis, Mo. • **Surveyors Service Co.**, P.O. Box 1905, Costa Mesa, Calif. • **Thorpe-Smith, Inc.**, 308 S. Washington St., Falls Church, Va. • **Watts Instruments**, 3803 Sullivant Ave., Columbus, Ohio • **Technical Advisors Inc.**, 3911 Newberry St., Wayne, Michigan

FACTORY REPRESENTATIVE: Hans Edvardsson, 6637 S. Arapahoe Drive, Littleton, Colorado

CANADA: AGA Geodimeter® Division of Bravour Electronics Ltd., 178A Queen St., E., Brampton, Ontario
"GEODIMETER" IS A REGISTERED TRADEMARK

347

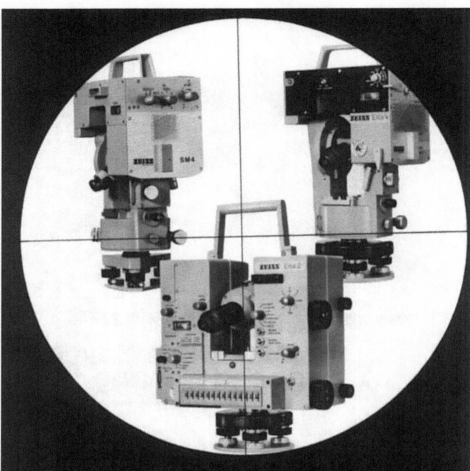

COMMENTS ON 'COMMENT AND DISCUSSION'

[From: Walter S. **Dix, L.L.S., P.E., Secretary Emeritus ACSM]** I am delighted to read the many contributions to "Comment and Discussion" lately in *Surveying and Mapping*. It is a healthy sign. Difference of opinion is the stuff professions are built upon. Professions are not rigid disciplines but are based on bodies of knowledge, experience, interpretation, and ethical judgment. Legal judgments consider facts, findings, conditions, and the influence of preceding judgments, not all of them necessarily right, which can affect a case judgment. Laws have changed over the years in the various states and that too affects judgments. The professional land surveyor in the United States has no legal authority, but as Chief Justice Thomas Cooley of the Supreme Court of Michigan said back in the late 1800s, "Surveyors are not and cannot be judicial officers, but in a great many cases they act in a quasi-judicial capacity with the acquiescence of parties concerned; and it is important for them to know by what rules they are to be guided in the discharge of their judicial functions." Thus the land surveyor performs in an anomalous limbo while striving to match facts and findings on the ground to written prescriptions on paper, to the best of his ability and professional judgment. There are bound to be differences of opinion and the best professional judgment can be overturned in a court of law by a judgment. That is why there are title companies and liability insurance companies. As William C. Wattles always warned "the contrary may be shown." Keep up the comment and discussion in these pages, it is good for the surveying profession.

****

The pages of *Surveying and Mapping* are open to free and temperate discussion of all matters pertaining to the interests of the Congress. It is the purpose of this department to encourage comments on published material or the presentation of new ideas as a formal or informal way. - *Editor*

RE: THE GREAT DILEMMA, OR, WHEN IS A FENCE JUST A FENCE?

BY MITCHELL G. WILLIAMS, R.L.S.

JUNE 1980

Published in *Surveying and Mapping*, under Comment and Discussion, Vol. XL, No. 1, Mar. 1980, pp. 82-87

From: Curtis M. Brown, 5075 Keeney St., La Mesa, Calif. 92041. The article by Mitchell G. Williams in Comment and Discussion in *Surveying and Mapping* entitled "The Great Dilemma, or, When Is a Fence Just a

Fence?" seems to indicate that I advocated fence surveys in my article of June 1979 *Surveying and Mapping* ["Land Surveyor's Liability to Unwritten Rights," pp. 119 -123]; such implosion on his part has no foundation. I believe the message was, "You can get into a libelous situation if you fail to notify your client of the significance of long standing occupancy." This in no way advocates that monuments should be set in every fence line, or that there should be a "Brownian" notion of property lines.

The fact that a surveyor does not have the final say in determining the limits of a property in a resurvey is quite true, but how about an original survey? In litigation did you ever try to claim that an original monument was incorrect? Is it final? One thing is certain, the surveyor has the first say; just try going to court without a report from a surveyor. If there is disagreement, it can go to the trial court, and its findings are final unless appealed to the Appellate Court, and its findings are final unless appealed to the Supreme Court. Who pays the liability for errors? The Appellate Court that was upset by the Supreme Court, or the trial court that was overturned by the Appellate Court, or the attorneys that tried the case and lost? None of these, but if the surveyor made an error, he pays.

If the surveyor is to avoid liability, he must be aware of all of the situations in which liability can occur. He certainly should not allow a client to think that his monuments represent the client's limit of ownership when there is a fence of long standing inside the monumented lines.

In the case cited in my article, the fence was the deciding issue; without it the land in dispute would have gone to the E 1/2. Area (80 acres) is normally subordinate to other considerations. The surveyor of the W 1/2 believed in fences and set his monuments at the end of a fence. The surveyor for the E 1/2 did not believe in fences so he set his monuments in the correct division for the E 1/2 and the W 1/2, and got into trouble. The fence surveyor won.

It is my opinion that most surveyors are incompetent to determine title rights as based upon such legal principles as unwritten agreement, estoppel, recognition, and acquiescence, and most adverse possession cases. If (1) the surveyor sets his monuments in accordance with a written deed, if (2) the monuments are out of agreement with possession, and if (3) there is a chance that the possession could have ripened into a fee right, it is advisable for the surveyor to so inform the client immediately. Once I failed to do so; the next morning the fence was bulldozed out. After the trial, the client put up a brand new costly fence in the same place he had destroyed the old one. How not to make friends and influence people!

I know of no law that says a surveyor must locate boundaries in accordance with a written deed or that he may not locate boundaries in accordance with an unwritten right such as prolonged possession. I think most land surveyors' acts have a void on this subject. As professional land surveyors (so we claim) the courts have bestowed upon us the privilege of liability, and it is this liability that makes me shy away from locating boundaries by some legal principle that I do not feel competent to administer. I sleep better at nights when the matter is referred to an attorney. This in no way bars another surveyor from doing what I refuse to do. Can anyone quote a law that says a surveyor cannot locate boundaries in accordance with an unwritten right principle? While Mr. Williams quotes several persons whose opinion is that a surveyor should not locate land in accordance with an unwritten title transfer (he could have found the same opinion in one of my books), he does not give a legal citation (either common law or statute law) barring a surveyor from doing so. Further, Mr. Williams avoids quotes from those who believe they should pay attention to unwritten title rights *(Liability as a Land Surveyor,* Madsen & Munro, Gainesville, Fla., p. 71, and others).

****

In December 1980, James Williams took issue with Curt's reply. Mr. Williams, licensed by the State of New York to practice the profession of land surveying in 1956, has had, since 1963, a private practice active in the five counties comprising the City of New York and the four neighboring urban and rural counties of Nassau, Suffolk, Westchester, and Putnam. Williams is currently president, Long Island Association of Land Surveyors, Inc. His address is 275 E. Sunrise Hwy., Lindenhurst, N.Y. 11757.

COMMENT AND DISCUSSION

The pages of SURVEYING AND MAPPING are open to free and temperate discussion of all matters pertaining to the interests of the Congress. It is the purpose of this department to encourage comments on published material or the presentation of new ideas in a formal or informal way. – EDITOR

****

THE LAND SURVEYOR'S ROLE IN LAW - IS THERE ANY QUESTION?

BY JAMES E. WILLIAMS

DECEMBER 1980

ABSTRACT. Any apparent confusion as to the legal role of the surveyor in matters of real property boundaries has no basis in fact but is being created by others in an attempt to supply direction to that role.

The article by Curtis M. Brown entitled "Location of Property Lines in Accordance with Possession," and Mr. Brown's reply to "The Great Dilemma, or When Is a Fence Just a Fence"? by Mitchell G. Williams, itself in turn a reply to Mr. Brown's previous article, "Land Surveyor's Liability to Unwritten Rights," all of which appeared in *Surveying and Mapping* during the years 1979 and 1980, require clarification to clear some general misconceptions.

While this paper will address the matters common to all of the aforementioned articles, the specifics of the reply by Williams to the original article by Brown, "Land Surveyor's Liability to Unwritten Rights," will be only touched upon lightly since Brown's reply (*Surveying and Mapping*, March 1980, p. 212) did not properly answer these specifics, but rather restated (albeit in a variant form) the original position of Curtis Brown vis a vis possessory considerations by the land surveyor in determining boundary location.

The treatment of the subject is necessarily cursory due to space considerations; in-depth discussions of all of the ramifications of the surveyor's role in law would fill many more pages but would not be more precise as to basics than the material presented here.

The complete and succinct commentary by Mitchell G. Williams in the March 1980 issue of *Surveying and Mapping*[1] should, in my opinion, have put to rest the fictive concept that there is merit in a land or boundary survey addressing itself to "unwritten rights" in real property law or to "surveys as in possession," to use a quaint term once used and long since repudiated here in "the east" by the legal and land surveying communities. (There are still a few exceptions who cling to this archaic and unacceptable practice, but their maps of purported survey do not dare carry that appellation of derogated practice since such a thing is not, and has not, been acceptable to the legal profession in the Metropolitan New York area for quite some time, say 30 to 40 years.)

I appreciate and value a forum where opinions can be aired and where opinions at variance with available facts can be discussed openly and, through this means, misconceptions, new ideas, opinions, and changes can be brought into focus.

To this end, Brown's "Location of Property Lines in Accordance with Possession - That Is the Question" in the June 1980 issue of *Surveying and Mapping* requires comment.

To myself and my colleagues, there is no such question. Guidelines, statutes, and customary legal criteria are well established, allowing no such question, not even in jest. It is time for the record to be set straight. This can be done by means of a simple analysis and historical litany of the various forces and principles that have led to the current scope of practice legally permitted the land surveyor.

It will become readily apparent as we proceed that statutory law relevant to the surveying of land boundaries, except in a very few specific instances, would be redundant and necessarily limiting of, if not forthrightly in opposition to, existing constitutional precepts. Neither can we ignore the fact that the land surveyor is governed in his actions by the overriding principles of real property law in all of its many ramifications and codifications as statute law.

Not being a student of the law per se, I will not attempt to cite chapter and verse for the multitudinous statutory provisions of the 50 states on the subject at hand but will offer specifics on the overriding principles upon which such law must be based.

Although having a documented genesis in the far reaches of antiquity, our current litany properly begins in the year 1672, when the "Statute of Frauds" [2] was enacted by the English Parliament. According to the 4th edition of Clark-Grimes' *Surveying and Boundaries*, "this statute has been reenacted in one form or another in all of the States of the Union," and its substance is that all conveyances of real property must be in writing. [3]

The only major statute affecting the matter at hand appears to be the 14th amendment to the Constitution of the United States prohibiting action by the states in line with the 5th amendment already prohibiting such action by the federal government. [4]

The very important provisions against deprivation of private property without due process of law are basic in this society and no less binding on the land surveyor in the function of his duties and responsibilities than on any other person or persons.

These two provisions in law, (a) property transfers must be in writing and (b) only a duly constituted court of law may divest an individual of property under definite rules of legal procedure, are apparently the legal authority sought by Brown for the establishment or re-establishment of boundary lines, and they are sufficient in their purpose. All else concerning a surveyor's duties flows from these precepts.

We have never encountered, seen, or heard any legal statement contradicting, contravening, correcting, or in opposition to those fundamental strictures as given above. Even the court cases cited by Brown in his most recent articles confirm these strictures.

The only comprehensive and exhaustive study that has come to hand of the vast body of individual court decisions defining the legal scope of the practice of land surveying is that contained in the opening chapters of the Clark and Grimes volume.

Aside from chapter one of the Clark-Grimes' text, the balance of Clark-Grimes and the substance of *Boundaries and Adjacent Properties* by Ray Hamilton Skelton [5] address the specifies of applying the surveyor's mandate by supplying background in the statutory real property law useful to the practicing land surveyor in the performance of his general obligation. This is accomplished in these volumes by the citation of 780 adjudicated court actions in Clark-Grimes, and 2,130 in the volume by Ray Skelton. Quotes from these volumes hardly constitute mere personal opinion on the part of the authors, where every principle is addressed by means of quotes taken directly from the cited litigation.

Unless, or until changed by statute, the land surveyor's function regarding boundaries is governed by the following legal precepts:

1. Individuals may not be divested of property except by due process of law.

2. Boundaries of written record form the legal basis for the physical existence of such property.

3. Original physical bounds described in the deed and positively identified as such will control.

4. If there was one, the lines laid down by the original surveyor who defined the bounds for the first time and whose description has been incorporated in the deed is the line to be re-established or retraced by the current land surveyor.

Where a boundary has been fixed according to precept no. 2 above, mere "possession" surveys, "mechanical" or property layout exercises from limited, unverified, assumptive physical monumentation do not assure the proper location of a historically defined or current written description of boundary and in more cases than not violate precept no. 1, either by mislocation or deviate configuration of the described bound. In addition, an extant map of survey, unless prepared by the original surveyor who defined the bounds for the first time – or redefined them as part of a court process of redefinition – is not admissible evidence of the location of the record or legal property lines, and its use as a basis for a current survey is thus in violation of precept no. 4.

The vast body of "technical-ese" then, both that of mensuration as an art and a science and the myriad guidelines and court citations for the retracement of lost, obscured, or obliterated lines and corners contained in the literature of the profession, remain merely the tools whereby the land surveyor fulfills his mandatory function as a paralegal entity and unofficial arm of the court in the realization of constitutional and common law guarantees of real property rights of the individual.

A survey or surveyor's work is merely evidence to be weighed by a court under due process as is other evidence relevant to the matters being considered by that court. A land surveyor cannot determine where the legal boundary is to be located except under specific statute or court direction where he is functioning under a different set of rules. The definition of the legality of boundaries is reserved to the court.

A disputed boundary location may only be accommodated in law by a written agreement between the interested parties or settled by court action. In the interests of an amicable settlement and to avoid overburdening the courts a surveyor may supply expert opinion on the matters of physical location to the interested parties to the dispute. The surveyor may also offer the same services to a court or be called upon by the court to supply such service. Possible evidence supplied by the surveyor may include possession lines at variance with written descriptions or deed lines, physical conflict of deed or record descriptions, or ambiguities or insufficiencies of written descriptions which result in an unknown or indeterminate line. In these situations of conflict, the surveyor is only supplying evidence of conflicting rights of the involved parties.

This evidence of a possible conflict of *existing* rights may only be accommodated under law by means of written transfers of all or portions of affected parcels of land by written boundary line agreements between the parties to the dispute, or by court affirmation of such rights by decree. The land surveyor is barred by statute from participating in the determination thereof.

In law, the legal boundary may only be fixed by the parties to the bound as evidenced by the pertinent writings or by the court if deferred thereto by one of those parties. Where then, does this leave the "land surveyor's liability to unwritten rights," or "written title lines," or "ownership lines"? It requires the total denigration of the principle of the statute of frauds and the U.S. Constitution to give credence to an involvement by the land surveyor in and to ownership and/or title to real property.

Such concepts would require that the surveyor subrogate to the legal concept of "ownership" or "title" the location of the legal boundary for which he is actually charged with responsibility under the law.

Even a title insurance company cannot establish "title." They may insure against title defects, but the court is the only legal arbiter and duly constituted authority on "title" and "ownership rights."

It must be self-evident at this point that "ownership" or "title" are legal concepts and are qualities one step removed from the relatively physical quality of boundary.

It is an oversimplification, but perhaps necessary, to state here that something without boundaries (artifacts, such as books, machines, etc.) may be "owned," but there are boundaries without ownership (voting districts, school districts, U.S. Government pier and bulkhead lines, etc.). That these two concepts come together in real property law does not make them synonymous. Only those who have not thought it through for themselves but have depended on long association with the terms or those who have forgotten consider "ownership" and "boundary" as being synonymous.

One, *ownership*, is the sole province of due process. The other, *boundary*, is the consideration of the law based on the evidence of the intentions of the parties to the creation thereof together with the evidence of the physical location by a qualified or otherwise authorized land surveyor.

The determination of ownership and boundary come together only in the law. The surveyor is limited to a consideration of physical determination of boundary and the description thereof.

Even when a surveyor is court-delegated to determine or "run" a boundary as part of a legal proceeding, he is not charged with determining ownership or title; the substance of his charge is physical boundary location and description. Likewise, when the surveyor is charged with furnishing courses and distances (or metes) for a previously unmapped or unsurveyed parcel, his findings or conclusions are not legally recognized descriptions unless or until included in a written deed, and then his work is only evidence in support of that written description. In this light, "ownership lines" are beyond the scope of practice of the land surveyor; "unwritten rights" is a fictitious concept without meaning or substance; "written title lines" is a term best left acknowledged as an unsatisfactory misnomer for "boundary lines" where the land surveyor is concerned.

The case cited by Brown in "Land Surveyor's Liability to Unwritten Rights" [6] is an example of the action of the court in following the principles discussed so far. His statement that, "This is a case where the land surveyor correctly located the client's deed lines in accordance with the writings of his client, yet was held liable for failure to recognize the ownership rights of the adjoiner," [7] is a personal opinion of Brown and does not properly address the questions raised by the case.

Using the guidelines derived from our two basic principles, that of the necessity for written property transfers and of the sanctity of private property rights, it must be obvious that:

1. Since the previous surveyor laid out a subtract within the two parcels apparently held under common ownership by deed, and which subtract bound was accepted as such by the owner of the combined parcels at the time of transfer and likewise by the subsequent purchasers of what became the westerly portion of said tract; the original owner of the combined tracts, by his acts, had now legally divested himself of the westerly 80 acres by both deed and survey, and could not again sell the same property to the client of surveyor "A" and stay within the law.

2. Rather than disclose a possible defect in his client's deed description due to the conflict with the senior deed as monumented on the ground, surveyor "A" prepared his survey according to his client's deed alone, thereby in his own mind and publicly by his acts actually divesting the adjoiner from property legally conveyed to him by the senior or prior deed.

3. It is beyond the scope of practice of a land surveyor to determine which of two apparently conflicting deed lines is the legal ownership line.

4. It *is* the responsibility of the land surveyor, when he cannot satisfy himself as to the commonality of a boundary and harmonize the calls and/or location of the line as evidenced by the supposedly contiguous deeds, to bring the matter to the attention of his client, the owners, or the courts.

358

No, surveyor "A" was not held liable for failure to recognize ownership rights, but was apparently held liable by the court for *usurping the power of the court* by himself determining that his deed, as written, established ownership of the parcel he was given to survey and allowed his client to rely on his act.

In short, surveyor "A" was apparently held liable simply because *he did recognize ownership rights* and proceeded to make his own determination as to those ownership rights by including previously deeded land within the bounds of his current survey without notation as to an apparent conflict of deed or a possible defect in such instrument.

The same charge of liability appears likewise to be the substance of the Oregon case cited by Brown in "Location of Property Lines in Accordance with Possession." This is a situation where not only was there an apparent refusal on the part of the surveyor involved to harmonize common deed intent, but there was disregard on his part of any intent of the deeds whatsoever. In short, he was in effect deciding ownership on the basis of possession and was thus in contravention of all legal authority to the contrary.

These two court cases brought to our attention by Brown follow a common reasoning and conclusion on the part of the courts involved, and we see no cause for concern in the findings of these courts on the part of land surveyors practicing according to legal dictates.

In the quaint wording of title insurance policies currently being written in the northeast, ". . . subject to any state of facts an accurate survey would show . . ." we find a clear statement not only of what is required of the land surveyor but also the use to which his survey is to be put. The survey and the land surveyor exist to show the state the facts and to offer opinion upon the matters of physical boundary. The survey and the land surveyor are not privileged to decide on matters of law.

The technician surveyor, blindly following a metes description of record without recourse to other matters equally as relevant to boundary as the courses and distances given therein, is as reprehensible as a surveyor surveying "as in possession" without recourse to the written record. Neither course of action will necessarily lead to a boundary location in accordance with the law.

The only approach to be taken by a land surveyor in establishing on the ground the intent of written description is the correlation of the pattern of existing physical evidence taken collectively and harmonized with the theoretical and legal deed descriptions of all parties to that bound.

All apparent physical evidence of a boundary - existing maps of survey and field notes; municipal or governmental maps and records; isolated individual surveyor's marks, stakes, or monuments; structures, buildings, physical streets; highway and road construction, parole evidence of presumed competent witnesses, existing physical bounds such as fences, ditches, etc. remains just that, i.e., presumed evidence, until adjudged in totality by the surveyor in the attempt at satisfaction of a relationship in substantial conformance with the original or intended lines as deduced from a construction of the relevant deed descriptions.

It goes without saying that the surveyor in these cases must survey as much of the surrounding and bounding parcels as he feels necessary until he [the surveyor] has satisfied himself in his own mind that all parties to the boundaries of his subject parcel have not been disenfranchised by his actions from lands contained within the bounds set forth in their respective deeds. If he is unable to accomplish such a harmonious and satisfactory boundary location the surveyor must either indicate the nature and extent of the problem and defer to others for consideration and resolvement or he must refuse the job as beyond his capabilities. Anything less is a violation of the public trust invested in the surveyor by all authorities.

Both of the court determinations cited by Brown in his articles of June 1979 and June 1980 appear to be completely in accordance with this tradition and the historicity of American jurisprudence. We do not see any change in the law as evidenced by these cases and wonder why they are being held up to the light in a public forum as anything more than additional citations to be added to the 2,910 already included in the reference volumes noted herein.

Part of the problem at hand may be because it is difficult to comprehend Brown's exact position, relative to the subject matter. If he knows and concurs with the position taken in this article, and we rather think he does, it can only be assumed that the misconceptions created result from the presentation. . . . While Brown's examples and citations of legal proceedings always seem to show the wisdom and correctness of the authorities in any particular context, conclusions are mixed and seem at variance with the proof presented.

The substance of Brown's . . . reply to the article by Williams, published in the March 1980 issue of *Surveying and Mapping*, seems to skirt the issues raised therein and does not come to grips with the substance of the article.

While it is true that there are few specific statute laws governing the means of locating the boundaries of real property, the only one that appears to come close to being a statute is the "Instruction to Surveyors" issued by the U.S. Government for the public lands states by virtue of its inclusion as a required procedure by statutes of at least 12 states [8] the objectives to be accomplished by the land surveyor in his pursuit of his profession are inherent, implicit, and unambiguous in the vast litany of constitutional, common, and case law. Brown is incorrect in asserting that there are no statutes specifically worded directing a surveyor to locate a boundary in accordance with a written deed.

The statutes of 12 states, [9] however, specifically mandate that the current location of a boundary be run conformably to the original survey. Since the calls of an original survey are legally manifest only in a written deed, it would appear to be an unequivocal though unwritten extension of the intent of statute to locate a boundary according to such written deed. These would appear to be so basic to real property law that such a statute mentioned by Brown would be redundant and superfluous in effect.

A background in real property law is absolutely necessary to the proper performance of the land surveyor, as such a background with an attendant understanding of the legal process is the only way the surveyor can fulfill the obligation laid upon the profession.

It should be mentioned that three states - Georgia, Iowa, Oregon - have statutory provisions for possession to be respected *only* in the absence of original marked lines of disputed boundaries arising from conflicting or insufficient deed descriptions. [10]

Since these statutory provisions in law require a basic conflict in written deeds as realized on the ground to be made operative, it does not negate the surveyor's mandate to utilize written deeds as the first evidence and *a priori* base for his subsequent actions.

A written deed with its attendant description as to location and configuration of the subject property is merely a means of locating that property and furnishes evidence to that purpose. Without that written deed, the surveyor has no legal justification for a survey unless he is subdividing an existing tract. If he is subdividing an existing tract he must know where the existing tract boundaries are, which brings us back full circle to the need for a written deed for that tract in order to initiate the subdivision thereof.

A deed description is to be construed in its entirety, and conflicting elements within such an instrument must be explained or dismissed by provable evidence to the contrary. This includes extrinsic evidence such as that provided by accurate survey.

British Admiralty chart of New York harbor (1776) reproduced on Koda-graph Contact Film, Estar Base. Courtesy of The New-York Historical Society.

Surest course to take in drawing reproduction!

Choose from Kodak's great new line—Kodagraph Reproduction Films, Estar Base

There's a selfish reason for making maps and profiles on the new Kodagraph *Estar Base* films: *They're much easier to work with!*

In addition to being as durable and dimensionally stable as any film you can name, Estar Base prints have clean backgrounds, more contrasty images, *and a superior drafting surface on both sides.* You can draw with light strokes . . . use pencils with a wider range of hardnesses. And since there's less abrasive action, pencil points stay sharper longer. Also, detail stays put . . .

is less inclined to smear, can be erased easily. See for yourself. Ask for second originals on Kodagraph Estar Base film.

1. Kodagraph Autopositive Film, Estar Base. First choice for general reproduction work. Gives you same-size *positive* second originals *directly.* Can be handled in room light.

2. Kodagraph Contact Film, Estar Base. Ideal for making same-size reproductions from film or low-cost paper negatives of old or weak line drawings.

3. Kodagraph Projection Film, Estar Base. Gives you sharp and clean results when enlarging microfilm negatives, or reducing large drawings, blueprints, maps.

For free booklet, write to Eastman Kodak Company, Graphic Reproduction Division, Rochester 4, N. Y.

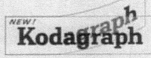

REPRODUCTION FILMS
for best line-for-line reproduction

Since such a deed is merely a paper right without material substance, it only attains its realization when translated to real terms on the ground. Fortunately or unfortunately, according to your viewpoint, the land surveyor is a material part of this process and the only link available to the public and its individual members between the paper and the ground, as well as being the only source of material facts available to the courts to supplement the paper facts already in its possession. This is a real and not a pie–in–the–sky obligation placed on the profession and its members and is not to be subverted to a lesser degree of performance in the interests of economy, low-cost, or marketplace considerations forcing substandard practices. But the latter is the subject of another discourse.

I cannot leave the present discussion without additional comment on Brown's reply (*Surveying and Mapping*, June 1980, pp. 212-213), which bears little relevance to issues raised by Williams. It might be added here that if Brown believes the court to have been in error in deciding on the cited case, he is entitled to that opinion. What he is not entitled to, in my opinion, is to second guess the court by presenting his opinion of what the court would have decided if the facts were different. This is a dangerous procedure as half of all parties to litigation will readily attest.

"He certainly should not allow a client to think that his monuments represent the client's limit of ownership when there is a fence of long standing inside the monument lines." [11]

"He [the surveyor] certainly should not allow a client to think that his monuments represent the client's limit of ownership *under any circumstances*. It is beyond his [the surveyor's] scope of practice."

"In the case cited in my article, the fence was the deciding issue; without it the land in dispute would have gone to the E 1/2." [12]

This is an unwarranted presumption, without merit, as to what a court would do.

"The surveyor of the W 1/2 believed in fences and set his monuments at the end of a fence. The surveyor for the E 1/2 did not believe in fences so he set his monuments in the correct division for the E 1/2 and W 1/2 and got into trouble." [13]

At best this is an oversimplification of the facts at hand; at worst it is presumptive opinion without fact or merit and a disservice to the reader.

"It is my opinion that most surveyors are incompetent to determine title rights as based upon such legal principles as unwritten agreement, estoppel, recognition, and acquiescence, and most adverse possession cases." [14]

This opinion can neither be refuted nor supported and is beneath consideration. It is a fact that surveyors are barred from making just such determinations as beyond their scope of practice. Surveyors attempting to do so will, and have, paid the consequences of such action.

If Brown means to say that surveyors should be cognizant of the legal principles involved in order to furnish proper evidence for use by the court in making a legal determination on these matters, and that he does not believe that most surveyors are competent in that knowledge, he should say so.

"I know of no law that says a surveyor must locate boundaries in accordance with a written deed or that he may not locate boundaries in accordance with an unwritten right such as prolonged possession."

"Can anyone quote a law that says a surveyor cannot locate boundaries in accordance with an unwritten right principle?" [15]

As we are all well aware, a surveyor, no less than any other individual, may do whatever he wants to do, as long as he is willing to assume the liability for his actions, but he would be remiss and somewhat foolish to take the law into his own hands.

There is evidence scattered here and there throughout the three articles under discussion, which indicates that the author may have had more than his share of adverse court decisions, not only during the course of past private practice but also as expert witness in the present. Perhaps beliefs held as to what a surveyor should do under certain circumstances are contrary to the law of the land.

REFERENCES

1. Williams, Mitchell, "The Great Dilemma, or, When Is a Fence Just a Fence"? *Surveying and Mapping*, 40:1 (March 1980), 82-87.

2. *Black's Law Dictionary*, rev. 4th ed. West Publishing Co., (1968), **Statute of Frauds** - This is the common designation of a very celebrated English Statute, (29 Car. II, c.3,) passed in 1677, and which has been adopted in a more or less modified form, in nearly all of the United States. Its chief characteristic is the provision that no suit or action shall be maintained on certain classes of contracts or engagements unless there shall be a note or memorandum thereof in writing signed by the party to be charged or by his authorized agent. Its object was to close the door to the numerous frauds and perjuries. It is more fully named as the "statute of frauds and perjuries." *Smith v. Morton*, 70 Okl. 157, 173, P.520, 521; *Housley*

v. Strawn Merchandise Co., Tex. Com. App., 291 S.W. 864, 867; Goldstein, 92 Conn. 226, 102A, 605, 606.

3. Grimes, John S., ed., *Clark on Surveying and Boundaries*, 4th ed., New York (1978).

4. Article XIV - All persons born or naturalized in the United States, and subject to the jurisdiction thereof, are citizens of the United States and of the State wherein they reside. No State shall make or enforce any law which shall abridge the privileges or immunities of citizens of the United States; nor shall any State deprive any person of life, liberty or property without due process of law; nor deny to any person within its jurisdiction the equal protection of the laws.

   Article V - No person shall be held to answer for a capital, or otherwise infamous crime, unless on a presentment or indictment of a Grand Jury, except in cases arising in the land or naval forces, or in the militia, when in actual service in time of war or public danger; nor shall any person be subject for the same offense to be twice put in jeopardy of life or limb; nor shall be compelled in any criminal case to be a witness against himself, nor be deprived of life, liberty or property, without due process of law; nor shall private property be taken for public use without just compensation.

5. Skelton, Ray Hamilton, *The Legal Elements of Boundaries of Adjacent Properties*, Indianapolis, (1930).

6. Brown, Curtis, "Land Surveyor's Liability to Unwritten Rights," *Surveying and Mapping*, 39:2 (June 1979), 119-123.

7. *Ibid.*, 121.

8. Grimes, John S., *Arizona, Colorado, Idaho, Kansas, Minnesota, Missouri, Nebraska, New Mexico, North Dakota, Oregon, South Dakota, Wyoming–A Treatise on the Law of Surveying and Boundaries*, 4th ed.

9. Grimes, John S., *Arkansas, Delaware, Florida, Georgia, Illinois, Iowa, Louisiana, Michigan, Mississippi, New Mexico, Oklahoma,*

South Dakota-A Treatise on the Law of Surveying & Boundaries, 4th ed.

10. Grimes, John S., *op. cit.*, 965-1024.

11. Brown, Curtis, "Re: The Great Dilemma, or, When Is a Fence Just a Fence"? by Mitchell G. Williams, P.L.S., *Surveying and Mapping*, 40:2 (June 1980), 212.

12. *Ibid.*, 212.

13. *Ibid.*, 212.

14. *Ibid.*, 212.

15. *Ibid.*, 212.

****

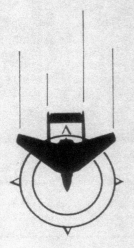

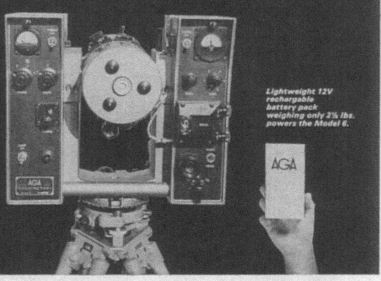

RE: THE GREAT DILEMMA – OR, WHEN IS A FENCE JUST A FENCE?

BY MITCHELL G. WILLIAMS, R.L.S.

DECEMBER 1980

Published in *Surveying and Mapping,* under Comment and Discussion, Vol. XL, No. 1, Mar. 1980, pp. 82-87; response *ibid.,* June 1980, pp. 212-213

A Brief Reply to Curtis M. Brown from Mitchell G. Williams, author: I would like to thank Curtis Brown for his reply to my article, "The Great Dilemma. . . ." [1] Unfortunately, he did not respond to the substance of my complaint, i.e., the conception that a surveyor can determine ownership, save by again insisting, contrary to all the available evidence, that a surveyor may "establish ownership" lines. I will not repeat my earlier argument here, as I have read nothing by Mr. Brown that points up any flaws in it. Regarding my citations from Clark and Skelton, [2] which Mr. Brown refers to as "opinions," the interested reader will find, upon checking the citations, that every quote from those authors is either a *précis* of, or an actual quote from, a court decision. In fact, some of them can be found quoted in Brown's book, *Evidence and Procedures for Boundary Locations.* [3]

However, in a second comment appearing in the same issue as his reply, "Location of Property Lines in Accordance with Possession," [4] Mr. Brown adopts a questionable position concerning the role of the surveyor. He said that, after searching in vain for a "statute" that prevents a surveyor from locating lines according to unwritten lines, a decision handed down by a statutory authority, the Oregon licensing board, was found. In the absence of a statute, I would think that the opinion of a group of men entrusted with the maintenance of the surveying profession would carry a great deal of authority, particularly since property law in this country is primarily common law, based on precedent, rather than statute law, a distinction he seems to find unimportant. In the absence of statute, "custom" is the only thing which can be appealed to and on which a court can base its opinion.

The opinion rendered by the Oregon board is a succinct statement of my argument in my earlier article:

"The duty of a land surveyor is to locate deed lines and notify his client if lines of occupancy differ. Boundary lines should only be established by agreeing owners or the courts. It is not the prerogative of the land surveyor to make this determination. [This surveyor's] reluctance to use the standard procedures prescribed by the Bureau of Land Management Manual leads to great inconsistency in surveys, particularly by surveyors that are apt to follow." [5]

While Mr. Brown finds this position "unfortunate," I argue that the board's conclusion is tautologous. It is no more "unfortunate" than the statement that "the sky is blue or the sky is not blue." It is simply true.

Two property owners dispute the location of their common boundary. They call a surveyor, who proceeds to establish the line to the best of his ability, using all the available physical and written evidence. Now *only* one of two things can happen. The disputants agree that the surveyor is correct, in which case their *mutual agreement*, not the surveyor, has established the line. Both may still feel that the surveyor is wrong and continue to hire surveyors until they find one with whose opinion they agree, or they may take their disagreement to the court for a judge to resolve it, in which case the court establishes the line, using the survey as evidence. There is no other possibility, unfortunate as that might be.

In *summa*, my position can be reduced to three main points:

1. Surveyors cannot establish boundaries without court order or mutual consent of the adjoining owners: ". . . neither his opinion nor his survey can be conclusive upon parties concerned . . ." - Chief Justice Thomas N. Cooley, quoted in Brown, *Evidence and Procedures for Boundary Location*, p. v.

2. Surveyors cannot establish "ownership" of anything - they are merely expert witnesses, supplying evidence of boundary line locations: "Adverse possession may change the title to real property, but it cannot change the location of the quarter-section line." - *Grell v. Ganser*, 255 Wis. 384, quoted in Brown, *Evidence and Procedures for Boundary Location*, p. 162.

3. If possession were synonymous with boundary lines, the surveyor would be an anachronism: Anyone can see where the possessed lines are. This is, in fact, the case in modern England, where the legal doctrine of "general boundaries" has resulted in the near extinction of the property line surveyor.

In my opinion much of the confusion over these issues results from the vague and imprecise usage of terms such as "ownership," "establish," "possession," and "unwritten title" by Mr. Brown. Neglect of the common law, as evinced by searching for statutes, is also contributory. Be that as it may, in my opinion, it is unfortunate that nearly 1,000 years of law and custom, logical arguments, and the opinions of statutory authorities have been ignored in this difference of opinions.

REFERENCES

1. Brown, Curtis M., "Re: The Great Dilemma or When Is a Fence Just a Fence"? by Mitchell G. Williams, R.L.S., *Surveying and Mapping*, 40:2 (June 1980), 212-13.

2. Grimes, John S., *Clark on Surveying and Boundaries*, 4th ed., New York, 1978.

3. Skelton, Roy H., *The Legal Elements of Boundaries and Adjacent Properties*, Indianapolis, 1930.

4. Brown, Curtis M. and Winfield Eldridge, *Evidence and Procedures for Boundary Location*, New York, 1962.

5. Brown, Curtis M., "Location of Property Lines in Accordance with Possession - That Is the Question," *Surveying and Mapping*, 40:2 (June 1980), 215-16.

[**Ed. Note:** The last two comments are by father and son, respectively. Neither knew the other had written.]

****

CLASS OF SERVICE
This is a fast message unless its deferred character is indicated by the proper symbol.

WESTERN UNION
TELEGRAM
W. P. MARSHALL, PRESIDENT

SYMBOLS
DL=Day Letter
NL=Night Letter
LT=International Letter Telegram

1201 (4-60)

The filing time shown in the date line on domestic telegrams is LOCAL TIME at point of origin. Time of receipt is LOCAL TIME at point of destination

HTA009 WB070 =(HT) 255P EST

RX GOVT PD WUX THE WHITE HOUSE WASHINGTON DC 14 103P EST =
BROTHER B AUSTIN BARRY, PRESIDENT AMERICAN CONGRESS ON SURVEYING AND MAPPING REPORT DELIVERY = MAR 14 1962
SHOREHAM HOTEL (CARE ASST MGR ON DUTY)
(FOR IMMEDIATE DELIVERY) =WASHDC =

THE MEETING OF THE AMERICAN CONGRESS ON SURVEYING AND MAPPING AND THE AMERICAN SOCIETY OF PHOTOGRAMMETRY HAS INDEED OCCURRED AT ONE OF THE MOST AUSPICIOUS TIMES IN THEIR HISTORIES. SINCE THE BEGINNINGS OF OUR NATION, THOSE OF YOUR PROFESSIONAL CALLING HAVE CONTRIBUTED IN FULL MEASURE TO ITS OPENING, GROWTH AND DEVELOPMENT. TODAY, OUR HORIZONS HAVE EXTENDED BEYOND THE LIMITS OF THE IMAGINATION OF OUR FORBEARS. THEY WHO FOUNDED OUR NATION INCLUDED IN THEIR NUMBERS MEN WHOSE PROFESSIONAL EFFORTS WERE DEVOTED, AS ARE YOURS, TO THE DESCRIPTION IN EVER-MORE PRECISE TERMS OF THE WORLD ABOUT US. THEN, AS NOW, THIS EFFORT HAS MADE POSSIBLE EVEN FULLER USE OF THE GOD-GIVEN RESOURCES AVAILABLE TO US. I KNOW THAT YOU, WITH THE INSPIRATION WHICH HAS CHARACTERIZED THE WORK OF YOUR PROFESSION, ARE MORE THAN EQUAL TO THE CHALLENGE OF THE FUTURE. AMONG THE GREAT CONTRIBUTIONS ON WHICH ALL OF US COUNT IS YOUR CONTINUED AND VALUED SUPPORT OF THE EDUCATIONAL = DEVELOPMENT OF THOSE WHO WILL FOLLOW YOU. YOUR EFFORTS IN THEIR BEHALF WILL HELP TO ASSURE A FURTHERANCE OF ACHIEVEMENTS THUS FAR REALIZED.

PLEASE ACCEPT MY CONGRATULATIONS FOR WHAT I KNOW HAS BEEN A MOST SUCCESSFUL AND REWARDING CONVENTION CONTRIBUTING TO CONTINUED SCIENTIFIC PROGRESS =

JOHN F KENNEDY. =

THE COMPANY WILL APPRECIATE SUGGESTIONS FROM ITS PATRONS CONCERNING ITS SERVICE

THE LAND SURVEYOR'S QUASI-JUDICIAL RIGHTS AND DUTIES REGARDING BOUNDARY LOCATION

By Kenneth E. Kratz

June 1981

ABSTRACT. In the June 1979 issue of *Surveying and Mapping*, Curtis M. Brown presented a paper entitled "Land Surveyor's Liability to Unwritten Rights." There followed two replies in Comment and Discussion that took exception to this paper. In March 1980 Mitchell G. Williams submitted a paper entitled "The Great Dilemma - or, When is a Fence Just a Fence?" In December 1980 James E. Williams submitted a paper entitled "The Land Surveyor's Role in Law - Is There Any Question?" I am in complete agreement with Curtis M. Brown and therefore must take exception to the positions of Mitchell G. Williams and James E. Williams. This is primarily an attempt to relate this ongoing discussion to everyday real life practice.

If there is uncertainty as to the location of a boundary line, does a land surveyor have a right or duty to decide on a proper location of said boundary? Should this boundary be marked on the ground? In many cases I say, yes, but you better know what you are doing.

The papers submitted to the Comment and Discussion section of *Surveying and Mapping* by Mitchell G. Williams in the March 1980 issue and by James E. Williams in the December issue are obviously well-researched and documented. I have no doubt that they are technically correct; however, I fail to see how they relate to real life practice.

I believe it is the land surveyor's responsibility to decide on a proper location and monument the lines using good judgment. However, as I have already said, you better know what you are doing! As Curtis M. Brown so clearly pointed out, if there is an area within the bounds of a survey that might be claimed by others, this fact must be clearly shown on your map of survey. The land surveyor should keep a detailed written survey analysis that lists the evidence and reasoning used to fix the location of any boundary lines that might be questioned. He must also counsel the client in writing about the area that might be claimed by others and explain some of the options, such as a boundary line agreement, asking a court to quiet title, or building a fence and waiting for time to make the fence the line. The client must be made to understand the risks of putting expensive improvements in an area of disputed ownership before taking steps to clear the title.

It is the surveyor's right and duty to anticipate the court. The theory is that if the surveyor does his work correctly the parties involved will be inclined to accept the line since the court will probably use the same reasoning as the surveyor and therefore arrive at the same location. There is no liability in doing this unless the surveyor is negligent. There still may be a need to clear the adjoining titles by a boundary line agreement, but this will be a lot faster and cheaper than going to court.

It is difficult to cite examples on these pages and include all the detail that might affect a land surveyor's judgment. The example cited by Curtis M. Brown, however, is quite clear. Surveyor "A" was incompetent. He was negligent. He was wrong both because of the fence and the senior rights. He was not held liable because he anticipated the court. He was held liable because he indicated by his map of survey that his client could rely with certainty on his anticipation.

With rare exceptions, attorneys and judges spend a very small percentage of their time dealing with boundary law and, therefore, know little or nothing about it. I do not believe there is a sitting judge within 100 miles of my office either inclined or qualified to hear arguments regarding a boundary dispute. Do you know of any? How many attorneys do you know that are capable of writing a decent metes and bounds description? How many do you know that you would want to go to court within a boundary dispute?

It is a sad but true fact that money makes a difference in our courts. It would be very unusual to find an attorney preparing seriously for a boundary case unless large fees were involved. It would be equally unusual to find a judge who had done research in preparation to hearing arguments on a boundary dispute unless a landmark decision that would make the books was expected. What really happens in most cases is that they go through the motions of a trial for a little while getting the maps in evidence and filling a lot of transcript with people's experience and society membership. Then the judge calls the two opposing attorneys into his chambers and tells them that he has no time to waste on this nonsense. He takes one of the maps in evidence, draws an arbitrary line splitting the difference, and tells the attorneys to get their clients to agree to it. By this time most people have spent so much money in professional fees that they will agree to anything to get it over with. It is a simple matter for a competent land surveyor, who is aware of the aforementioned probabilities, to prepare a map for court that claims twice as much as the client hopes to get, and to show trees, traverse points, or something that can be used to identify the location on the map where you want the judge to draw the line. The judge will then put the line where you wanted it so it can easily be written into the court record. Needless to say, this solution cannot be used in all cases, and you must have some justification for the line you are claiming to. You should also be prepared for the rare possibility that the court will actually rule on which line is legally correct. We all know that some town planning boards are not going to accept a plan without making a major change so they can demonstrate their power and wisdom. A smart surveyor will take a plan that is just the way the client wants it and change it to squeeze in a few more lots or put a dead end street where there should be a through street. This plan is then submitted, and the planning board with its infinite wisdom changes the plan back to its original correct form. If you are going to court, it should be with an attorney that knows the judge as well as you know the planning boards you deal with.

I agree completely with James E. Williams when he says that a land surveyor must have a background in real property law with an attendant understanding of the legal process. I do feel however that textbook knowledge should be tempered with real life experience.

Like snowflakes, no two surveys are ever alike. The land surveyor must make a judgment on how to proceed, using experience and common sense. There are many factors to be considered, such as the value of the land, will improvements be made, are there possible encroachments, is this a boundary dispute or an outgrowth of a fight over kids or dogs, is this a line that must be set in one of two definitive locations, or is it a case of vague or unknown location, and so on.

With the risk and hope of stirring up even more discussion on these issues I will cite some examples from my files. Please try to understand the differences in geographic areas and do not think that a particular example is wrong just because it might not be appropriate for your area of practice at this point in time.

Within the urban sprawl of New York City are many turn-of-the-century subdivision maps. Many of these early maps have large surpluses. One particular map in northern New Jersey shows blocks 500 ft. long comprised of 10 lots, each 50 ft. in width. These blocks are actually 505 ft. long and comprised of 9 lots at 50 ft. and one lot at 55 ft. The 55-ft. lot is where you find it. Every survey on this map is a fence survey and I have done many of them. Never did I worry that a court would come along and relocate these long-standing lines by a proportion method. I knew with absolute certainty that a court was never going to force the change of hundreds of long-standing boundaries, some of which would then run through buildings, just to satisfy a rule. This was not anticipating the court. This was knowing what you are supposed to know if you are in this business. Very few of these old maps had monuments marking the street lines. The streets as laid out and accepted by the public have established location in the same manner of a longstanding fence. They have become a fact of location that can be relied upon.

Mitchell G. Williams asks, "What happens when you find out that the deed line runs 4 ft. outside of a party wall and through the neighbor's bathroom?" I would think that a surveyor seriously intent on doing a survey would proceed to get the facts. Did the deed exist prior to the party wall? How certain is the location of the deed line? What about the adjoining deed? Does it agree with the party wall? Is it senior? How long has the party wall been in existence? Are there yard fences or walls on the extension of the party wall line? If so, how old are they? Once you know the facts you can set markers at an appropriate location and clearly mark your map of survey to indicate any area you feel requires legal remedy.

In the New York City area just about all survey work relating to boundaries is either on or for a major subdivision map. Most deeds simply give a lot and block number on a certain map. Because of the high property values most boundaries have long since been established by good survey description. There is very little chance or incentive to involve oneself in the intrigue of deed versus fence in this "sue crazy" area of high liability. I have been there. I do not argue against a conservative approach in an area of high property values. But what have city surveys got to do with the 80 acres, or was it 67 acres, in question? I am sure that a little historical research will prove that many of today's well-monumented and described deed lines are nothing more than fence or possession lines that time has made fact. How often do you encounter a deed that describes a line established by a court?

I now have a sleepy little practice in upstate New York and will tell you what it is like in another particular geographic area. When the public lands opened up, people started leaving this area and the population is now only half of what it was 100 years ago. When farms and homes are being abandoned people do not spend money for good surveys or competent attorneys.

In 1972 I surveyed a lot in the Village of Westport on Lake Champlain. The deed called for the north part of lot 53 on a map by Ananias Rogers dated July 31, 1802. There was no record of this map in the county offices, but I found the original in the Westport Library. A deed dated October 7, 1817, conveyed all of lot 53 to Zebulon Stoddard. In 1846 Stoddard sold 47 ft. off the south side of lot 53 to Joseph Stacy. In 1847 Joseph Stacy purchased the north half of lot 54, thereby eliminating the line between lots 53 and 54 as a current boundary. The north line of lot 53 was clearly evidenced by an old cedar hedgerow. The old map showed five lots in the block all having a frontage of 1.75 chains for a total block frontage of 577.5 ft. I measured 590.2 ft. A 115.5-ft. lot less 47 ft. leaves a deed width of 68.5 ft. All evidence indicated that the present house existed long before the 47 ft. was sold off. Adding 2.5 ft. for a fair proportion of the surplus for a 71-ft. lot would have been the normal thing to do. The problem was that this still left the old house encroaching to the south by 2.5 ft. I added another 4.5 ft. and monumented a lot 75.5 ft. in width clearing the house by 2.0 ft. on the premise that there was never an intent by Zebulon Stoddard to convey part of his house to Joseph Stacy. I could not have done this in New York City because in the city this problem would not have waited 125 years to surface.

I make decisions daily on when a fence is a fence. A boundary survey of 130 acres was recently completed that included all cases. The current deed for this property called for and described two lots in adjoining tracts as they were originally set out in 1799 and 1812, with two exceptions, exactly as they were sold off in 1850 and 1851. On some sides the existing fence line was monumented and held for line. On some sides a line was blazed and painted through the woods and the relative location of the existing fence was shown on the map of survey. It would be easy to ramble on here filling many pages with the reasoning used in each particular case. I will cite just two lines that have some relevance to the present discussion. The deed south line is the north line of the exception sold off in 1850. This deed has a good metes and bounds description and calls for a line 33.50 chains in length parallel to the lot line and an area of 21 acres more or less. There is a very old straight fence line that is not parallel with the lot line by 52 minutes of angle. There is a 1970 survey of the exception that holds the fence line and indicates an area of 20.92 acres. Who in their right mind would worry about or question the authority of this fence that has been accepted as fact for 130 years? On the west side of this property a fence on a lot line in the tract to the south was continued north across the tract line. The lot lines in these two adjoining tracts are not and were never intended to be on line with each other. This fence, which is over 50 years old, is 60 ft. west of the correct deed and lot line. The deed for the property to the west originally called for this lot line, but a fence survey done in 1948 and recorded in the county records calls the fence the line. The present owners to the west have a deed description taken from this survey and calling for this fence. Here is the key factor, we are talking about a half acre of land with a fair market value of about 100 dollars. I, of course, gave this half acre to my client and put a note on the map of survey explaining why.

This past fall I established the location of and monumented eight corners of mile-square lots in Township No. 4, Old Military Tract, and also blazed and painted 6 mi. of boundary line between these corners. The outside boundary of this township was surveyed in 1794 and the lots are shown on a map dated September 25, 1795. With the exception of two corners on the north line of the township, no evidence, paper or physical, could be found to indicate that any of these corners had ever been set. There is quite a bit of surplus in the township and the nearest existing lot corners were 2 mi. away. There are old iron mines on the property and the local attraction caused the north line of the township to be run in a big curve. As you can imagine from the above facts, I had some latitude and very little liability in locating the lines. The mineral rights on both sides of the lines in question are owned by a third party so the only value to the land is the standing timber. If a court relocated a line after trees were harvested it would be a simple matter to determine and transfer the value of the stumpage so there would not be an injured party. If my locations are reasonable there never will be a judicial review and, in time, these lines will become indisputable fact.

Let us now consider the other extreme: high value property and construction underway or expected. You have been retained to locate and mark the property lines. In this situation you do not want to set any point that could be mistaken for a boundary marker until you are absolutely certain of the proper location. You must guard against the possibility that someone will start construction assuming your mark is the boundary. If you have the slightest doubt as to the location do not set markers before there is a boundary line agreement or court judgment. Do not try to get by by playing it safe, giving the disputed area to the adjoiner. You will only end up in a difficult situation when the adjoiner asks for a certified survey up to this safe line so he can put a building right on the line.

Mitchell G. Williams and James E. Williams are obviously experts in their particular geographic area and anyone planning to practice in that area would do well to study under them. I can only assume that their need to follow liability-proof rules has prevented them from reading Curtis Brown with an open mind.

By now I am sure you realize that I see no "Great Dilemma," unless you are as incompetent as surveyor "A." A fence, or the remains thereof, is simply evidence of the location of a line. The value or weight of this evidence will vary with every situation. If you cannot determine to your satisfaction the correct location of a deed line, then say so. Show the range of possibilities on your survey and tell the client that an agreement line or court settlement is needed. Never certify ownership to anything. A land surveyor should certify to the location and area of a particular parcel described in a recorded deed only. Make sure your client knows that your job is location only and that an attorney or title company will be needed for assurances of ownership.

I have tried to say here with much redundancy precisely what was so perfectly said in one paragraph by Walter S. Dix in "Comments on Comment and Discussion," in the March 1980 issue of *Surveying and Mapping*.

There are fences out there that should be monumented and accepted as fact by land surveyors, regardless of what the deed says. A deed is not proof of location anymore than it is proof of ownership. It has always been my understanding that the judgment needed to know which fence was just a fence was the very thing that made a land surveyor a professional.

Note: Mr. Kratz was licensed to practice land surveying by the State of New Jersey in 1963 and by the State of New York in 1969. He had a private practice in Fair Lawn, N. J., for 5 years prior to moving to Westport, N. Y., in 1970 where he continues in private practice at his office, P. O. Box 97, Elizabethtown, N. Y., 12932.

****

ON: BROWN/WILLIAMS VIEWPOINTS

JUNE 1981

[Refer to: *Surveying and Mapping*, Comment and Discussion, Vol. 40, No. 4, pp. 439-445]

Prof. W. G. G. Blakney, School of Engineering and Engineering Experiment Station, Auburn Univ., Auburn, Ala. 36830. The Brown-Williams debate about how surveyors should place boundary lines is being followed with great interest. The December 1980 issue [of *Surveying and*

Mapping] perhaps contains the last statements on the debate. Since Brown clearly recognizes the court's prerogative of settling ownership boundaries and Williams grudgingly admits there are few statute laws governing the means of locating boundaries, there is more agreement existing than appears at first glance.

It is essentially Brown's idea of recognizing the shades of grey in the law of determining ownership that M. G. Williams must "wish to thrash in a dark alley." Williams must posit in the law a majesty lawyers may be more willing to assign than the public. An author of fiction interpreted American society as being one motivated by rules rather than ethics. Though all generalities fail in a test of specifics, there is a nucleus of truth in the statement. It may be that Williams satisfies the generalization and Brown demonstrates the generalization to be untrue. Williams finds in the law rules of conduct and Brown finds options. Williams doubtlessly is a credit to the surveying profession. He would be a credit as a lawyer to the legal profession. As a chemist, he also would be accomplished, but I suspect he would place a value on the worth of a human in terms of the price of the chemicals contained, and who would dispute such a factual and scientific approach?

The Williams' documented arguments are useful, but if they boil down to the oft-repeated statement that surveyors "must survey according to the deed," then those arguments should not be construed to have "thrashed the idea in a dark alley." C. E. McCall's paper in the December issue "Subdivisions of Land Today" is not the first paper which has quoted Judge Cooley's (Michigan) recognition of the "quasi-judicial capacity of surveyors." That paper reinforces Brown superbly. It should make us share Cooley's concern about surveys made "according to the deed" that "upset a neighborhood." Mr. McCall describes an approach which will serve society well, which will not upset neighborhoods, which will satisfy the law, which will pay attention to exorbitant costs to prove a corner, and not necessarily advocate the line called for by the deed.

Most surveyors are aware of J. E. Williams' reminder that "a surveyor . . . is willing to assume the liability for his actions," or "is foolish to take the law into his own hands." Many surveyors operate in areas where land parcels must be very large to equal the value of small parcels in New York City. The surveys are correspondingly large in size and cost. Citizens in these areas cannot afford the luxury of their legal profession not accepting those things that attorneys in Metropolitan New York do not accept. The Iowa laws quoted by McCall happily and necessarily permit practice that people can afford to purchase. If "surveying according to the deed" ends up costing as much as the land being surveyed, it is time to serve the public by sharing some liability.

****

THE LAND SURVEYOR'S ROLE IN LAW - CONTINUED

BY JAMES E. WILLIAMS

JUNE 1981

The debate appearing in the Comment and Discussion columns of *Surveying and Mapping* over the past year should not be characterized as a debate as to how a surveyor should place boundary lines but is rather a question as to whether a land surveyor in his professional capacity is exempt from ordinary codes of behavior governing all other citizens at large.

It is just this attempt at resolving what has been accurately described as the surveyor's "quandary" that is being attempted in those columns.

The discussion seems to have wandered into the borderlands of philosophy from its pragmatic roots as a question as to how a surveyor should reestablish, reconstruct, or retrace real property boundaries.

Perhaps if the competent parts of the debate were temporarily separated for purposes of discussion, the facts would be more clearly seen in their proper context and the unanimity of theory and practice would emerge in a permanent enlightenment.

For the moment, let us set aside the practical value of a fence post and explore the rationale for the arguments set forth in the response entitled "The Land Surveyor's Role in Law, Is There Any Question?" appearing in the December 1980 issue of *Surveying and Mapping*.

It is not an article of fiction but one of fact that western philosophy of justice rests precisely on the rule of law as its base.

While all of us are assuredly interested in the "shades of grey" in this law, inasmuch as such law has a definite and profound effect on our lives and livelihood; the fact is that the land surveyor is not, no more than is the chemist, and certainly not the lawyer, privileged to decide on matters of law.

This is precisely the point to be made that was attempted in the aforementioned response, said response being very careful to restrain assertions as to matters of law being limited to due process, meaning courts of law (or judge and jury, if you will) or elected legislative bodies.

In the context within which we are dealing, even a lawyer not acting in the capacity of magistrate or legislator is barred by custom, statute, and common law from determining matters of law. He may argue a case as to his beliefs or personal interpretations of law, but if a lawyer could make such a determination there would be simply no need for courts or judges (who may not necessarily be nor are required to be trained lawyers in any circumstance).

How, then, can we maintain that a land surveyor may do what a lawyer cannot?

It is precisely this rule of law as opposed to individual ethical values that distinguishes western and eastern concepts of justice.

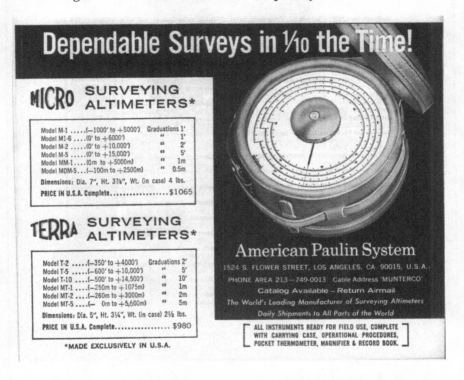

The western concept of justice, including English common law which has been further extended and modified in these United States, arose in the belief that consensus of citizens, both in their legislative configuration as elected representatives of the citizenry and as judge and jury in more localized situations, are more apt to dispense a uniform justice routinely than is a system relying strictly on the personal ethics of an individual.

The Magna Carta, whatever its faults and limitations, established the basis for western law by substituting written guarantees (law) for the personal and variable whims of a sovereign.

Far from being a substitute for ethics, written law is merely another name for the codified collective ethics of a society.

This concept of due process - statutory law by legislative fiat, together with courts working within the limitations of custom and precedent - seems, in the overall scheme of things, workably superior to a system without law where justice is dispensed according to the personal ethics of any one individual at any one time.

While a benevolent despot of high moral character may be more consistently just (witness the reputation of the biblical Solomon) than our own statutory and common law system of justice may at times allow, Solomons are few and far between, and history has mostly proven otherwise.

More often than not, individual or despotic dispensation of justice at the whim of an individual unbound by such statutory or common law leads to the most gross injustices.

We must not confuse lawyers with the law.

The precepts under discussion are *not* a product of the legal profession. Rather, they are rules by which our society through its elected legislatures and courts has decided that all members will adhere.

This has nothing to do with "science" or the scientific approach per se, but rather with established codes of behavior collectively termed the "law of the land."

Perhaps the principles under discussion have been misinterpreted or misunderstood. There is certainly room for judgmental determination of the evidence for a boundary location on the part of the surveyor. In fact, the land surveyor, within the law, comes closest to being permitted to act as a surrogate court in a very narrow sense by utilizing legal procedures of evidence in upholding that law.

There is not only room for such deliberation and ratiocination on the surveyor's part but a mandatory obligation in order for the surveyor to fulfill that role.

The key words in this particular debate are the deduced intent of the deed as written, which certainly does not imply the blind following of a deed description without expert analysis of the literal writings considered together with physical evidence gathered by field survey.

Just as a carpenter exercises personal discretion as to where he places each nail or the length he cuts each board in the construction of a dwelling without altering the shape and configuration of the overall structure or deforming the desires of the architect or owner, so does the land surveyor measure and locate physical boundaries within the defined limits of our legal structure.

This dissertation, while seemingly wandering far afield from the immediate matters at hand, does address questions raised by the exchange of letters in "Comment and Discussion."

I suggest a rereading at this point of my commentary [1] with a view as to what was actually written.

The entire discussion has focused on basic underlying principles, rather than the specifics or "nuts and bolts" of attaining those principles.

There is a small but inherent danger in speaking of such broad general principles to obfuscate the real objectives sought by those principles.

There are actually two separate albeit related arguments. Curtis Brown addressed these broad legal dictates rather than how they were to be achieved and was answered in kind.

The "how to" is where the broad discretion and expertise of the land surveyor enters and is an unending matter of a different nature than that addressed in this "debate."

A major contributor to the "quandary" may lie in the definition of terms. "Intent of the deed as written" is a paraphrase of the implied statement, "intent of the parties to the deed as witnessed by the signed documents executed by them at the time."

It does not mean in any context merely the *intent of the parties to the transaction.*

The law has held that it is impractical to enter into the minds of persons since deceased in order to ascertain their intentions or into anyone's mind at that moment in the past when their intentions were first made manifest. Even live and basically honest persons have been known to change their minds after the fact and with benefit of hindsight.

THE CURT BROWN CHRONICLES

This was precisely the reason the "statute of frauds" was enacted and which also gave rise to a large lawyer class whose duty it was, and still is, to assure that all contractual writings, including deeds, were written to reflect accurately the intentions of the parties at the time of the transaction.

This heavy reliance on the written word as *prima-facie* evidence is the backbone of real property law and is not to be trifled with by anyone, especially not by land surveyors.

Imagine a lawyer arguing that what was written was not what was meant by his client, especially if he or another lawyer had assisted in its preparation and especially if the client is deceased or otherwise absent.

Yet this is precisely what a surveyor is attempting to do when the deed is ignored in favor of a fence or other indication of possession as the intended boundary line, simply because that seems to be what the bounding owners meant by the fact of its mere existence in its present position.

The fact that a fence, or wall, *unmentioned in the deed* may be on or evidence of the very line intended by the parties to that deed is up to the determination of the land surveyor in the "quasi-judicial" function mentioned by Judge Cooley.

The surveyor may not "correct" the line to reflect what he believes to be the intention of the parties or in contravention of a deed description, not by law, not by statute, not by custom, not by any authority, not in the public lands states, not in what once was Colonial America, and certainly not because it is cheaper to the present client for the surveyor to ignore his lawful mandate by not fulfilling his full responsibilities under the law by cutting his work short in line with a limiting fee.

The "quandary" may be because the surveyor is not all that sure of what he is about.

The fence or the stone, or the ditch, or the wall, etc. - may or may not represent the intent of the deed as written and *interpreted* by the surveyor into a reality on the ground.

This is the verity of Judge Cooley's statements, the point at which, after the field exercise or survey has been performed, that the land surveyor exercises his judicial determination as to the validity of the physical evidence in conformance with the intent of the written record.

This principle of law does not contradict Judge Cooley, does not conflict with the opinions of Cleo E. McCall, [2] does not invalidate the "instructions to surveyors" by the federal government and is not in opposition to any state statute as to physical boundary location. Quite the contrary, these authorities are all echoing and reflecting the basic lawful tenets of the profession being pounded to death.

When the surveyor stops to think about it, it must be evident that the originally but erroneously placed quarter section line is *the one intended by deed* and not that of the theoretically perfect quarter section line that was never laid out. This is the rationale behind all of the "instructions to surveyors" about retracing the line as originally laid out so as to "not upset the neighborhood."

This is a "horse of another color" from that of confusing contemporary evidence of a line (shifted from the physical position it occupied at the time of the creation of the boundary) with that original boundary as intended and described by deed.

Judge Cooley's oft-quoted remark is a warning to surveyors not to confuse a theoretical line that was never run out with the actual line that was surveyed, accepted in place, and *incorporated and referred to in deeds of record*.

"Not upsetting the neighborhood" is not a license to accept all contemporary boundary markings. In a neighborhood already "upset" by such shifted lines, accepting such lines as representing the intent of the original parties will only cause great anguish and turmoil when the area of shifted configuration butts up against an area where the original deeded lines are still intact upon the ground.

I dare say there is not a surveyor alive or dead who has not run up against such gores or overlaps at least once during his professional life.

Has anyone wondered at the cause of these gores or overlaps where obviously none was intended by the original parties to the pertinent deeds?

I dare say that indicating where possession varies from the record line so that the affected parties may correct the possession or adjust the deeds is much less unsettling than the legal fees, courtroom time, and anguish created by battling over gores and overlaps; especially when it is considered that most such gores and overlaps were created by surveyors not doing the proper job in the first place. Not only is it less unsettling, it is exactly what the land surveyor is supposed to be doing.

If a surveyor is not going to recognize and ascertain the legal deeded line so as to supply the interested parties with information they are unable to ascertain with their own eyes, the survey and the surveyor are redundant and their services an unnecessary and undue burden on society. (As mentioned elsewhere, this has already happened in "merry old England" where property surveying is all but a dead issue and land surveys as we know them simply do not exist.)

Certain statements about surveying "costs" disturb me greatly. If the land is worth so little that the cost of survey is prohibitive or exceeds the value of the land, **don't have it surveyed.** The solution is just that simple.

The absence of a survey is definitely more desirable than a badly executed, poorly done, inadequate, or illegal survey in any case.

Just because the land surveyor, like the lawyer, the doctor, and the engineer exist to serve a public and private need does not mean they have to be used. This is still supposed to be a free society. But when they are used, the public is entitled to the highest degree of expertise obtainable. I shudder in contemplation of a bargain-basement, cut-rate appendectomy.

A perhaps little known facet of common law as it applies here is " . . . if the description in a deed is such that a surveyor, by applying the rules of surveying, can locate the same, such description is sufficient and the deed will be sustained; otherwise it will be void . . . " [3]

This has interesting ramifications, one of which is the obverse of the implied statement that a deed is void if a competent surveyor cannot locate the property; this obverse being that a deed only has value if a surveyor can locate the described property.

Looked at in this light, the survey and the surveyor are the only instruments available under current law capable of ensuring the physical reality of the paper promise of a deed. This alone should give the *coup de grace* to any belief that a surveyor may ignore instructions in a written deed when physically establishing boundary lines.

This is also a solid base for the establishment of a true profession and professional attitude on the part of the surveyor. A land surveyor may now be seen as something more than just a mensuration technician but more as a professional entity in his own right.

As to the question of the cost of the survey exceeding the value of the land, I have seen almost valueless property appreciate in value many times' more than the cost of the survey which by its very existence created a marketability the property did not have prior to the execution of the survey. (See above, the paper promise of the deed having been proved tangible real estate through the expertise of the land surveyor.)

No one would recommend that someone who cannot afford the price of a car buy half a car or only that portion they can afford, why then do surveyors persist in selling only part of their services or offering or otherwise tailoring their performances to only that portion of their expertise that a client can afford, or more aptly, is willing to pay?

Again, better no survey than one which violates legal dictates of practice.

The client is only being defrauded when the land surveyor takes money for a service the surveyor knows is substandard or deficient for its intended purpose, and the intended purpose of a land survey is to mark on the ground, and/or represent on a map, the limits of real property as defined by the written deed. This function bears little or no relevance to the value of the land per se nor to its geographic location.

If a landowner is truly destitute and a survey is required or necessary, nothing precludes the land surveyor from freely contributing his time and expertise as part of his service to society.

This constant attention to cost above all other considerations is what is really keeping the land surveyor in the merchant or peddlar classification and destroying any and all attempts for the creation of the profession it purports to be.

After all, it is not just the legal profession who must accept the Rule of Law, but the entire body politic, which, unfortunately in the opinion of some, also includes the land surveyor.

If this is a luxury, it is a luxury which can only be afforded by a free people in a democratic society. Think about that.

REFERENCES

1. Williams, James E., "The Land Surveyor's Role in Law - Is There Any Question?" ACSM, Falls Church, Va., *Surveying and Mapping*, XL:4 (1980) 438-444.

2. McCall, Cleo E., "Subdivision of Land Today," ACSM. Falls Church, Va., *Surveying and Mapping*, XL:4 (1980) 415-418.

3. Grimes, John S., *Clark on Surveying and Boundaries*, 4th ed., N.Y., (1978).

Note: Mr. Williams' address is 189 Sears Rd., Box 291, West Islip, L.L, N.Y. 11795.

****

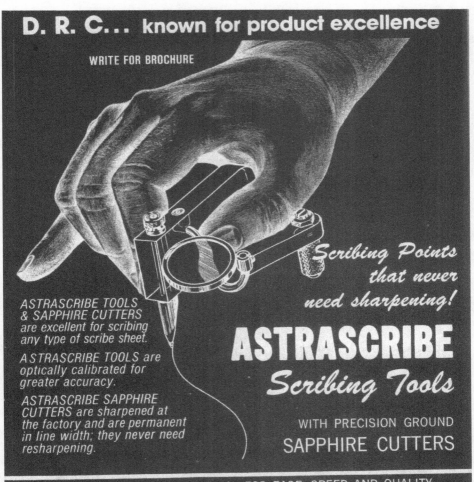

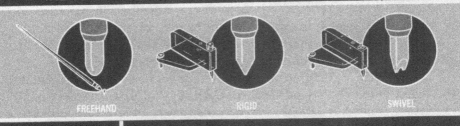

LOCATION OF PROPERTY LINES IN ACCORDANCE WITH POSSESSION – THAT IS THE QUESTION

JUNE 1980

From: Curtis M. Brown, 5075 Keeney St., La Mesa, Calif. 92041. Apparently the land surveyors' hot point of discussion is whether the surveyor can or should locate property lines in accordance with possession, especially if long standing. The following appeared in a recent issue of *The Oregon Surveyor* and pertains to a hearing by the board of registration over revoking a surveyor's certificate. Several charges were presented, among them being "establishment of lines of occupancy and not necessarily deed lines, and surveys not in accordance with the Bureau of Land Management Manual." In the discussion on findings it was stated: "The function of a land surveyor when performing boundary surveys is to establish deed lines, not occupancy lines. If the two differ, the land surveyor should point this out to his client." (This surveyor's) surveys are based on the premise that it is more peaceful in a community to survey the lines of occupancy.

"The board is of the opinion that (this surveyor) was grossly negligent in his failure to comply with provisions of ORP 209.250 (2) with respect to his surveys. Certain declarations were particularly disturbing. An example was his vow that he would never establish a corner by proportionate methods in a developed area. The second was his statement that he doesn't dare to change corners because people have been using them. Another was his announcement that as long as he is county surveyor someone surveying adjoining land had better use his corners because people have been using them." Under the opinion of the board is written, "The duty of a land surveyor is to locate deed lines and notify his client if lines of occupancy differ. Boundary lines should only be established by agreeing owners or the courts. It is not the prerogative of the land surveyor to make this determination. (This surveyor's) reluctance to use the standard procedures prescribed by the Bureau of Land Management Manual leads to great inconsistency in surveys, particularly by surveyors that are apt to follow." [End of quotes.]

The board's opinion that "Boundary lines should only be *established* by agreeing owners or the courts" is unfortunate; in the definition of the land surveyor of Oregon the law says the surveyor "establishes" boundaries. Be that as it may, the reason I was going through Oregon's and other state's statutes was to try and find a law that says a surveyor *must* locate boundaries in accordance with a written deed or written conveyance. The nearest I have come to it is in a state law that authorizes the board to set up rules and regulations as found in Oregon. Here section 672.200 entitled "Grounds for denial of certificate" states: "The board may refuse to issue or renew, or may suspend or revoke a certificate or permit, or reprimand any person holding a certificate or permit: . . . (4) For any violation of the rules of professional conduct prescribed by the board."

Whether it is the right of the board under (4) above to say that a surveyor "must" locate in accordance with the written record or not is questionable. Possibly it can. While it may be the custom among surveyors, as stated by the board, to locate in accordance with the deed, to my knowledge it is not based upon a statute law. I presume that when the board said, "to locate deed lines," they included the effect of (1) senior rights and (2) possession standing as a monument as to where the original surveyor set his monument.

In the above trial for revocation of the surveyor's license, the surveyor's attitude towards "never" establishing a corner by proportionate methods in a developed area is quite unreasonable, but it should also be pointed out that an attitude of "never" using possession to try to determine where the original surveyor was is also unreasonable. In many court trials, possession has been the criterion for establishing where the original "footsteps" were.

Oregon and California are among the recently surveyed states as compared to the eastern seaboard. The eastern surveyor's attitude towards possession is much more liberal than that found in the western states. In the east, original monuments are more frequently lost in antiquity; in the west many of the original monuments are to be found. In the west surveyors tend to forget that proportional measurements as a means of locating property lines is a rule of *last resort;* possession is sometimes (not always) the best indicator of where the original surveyor was. One of the necessary duties of the surveyor is to investigate the cause of possession and why it came into being *before* he resorts to proportionate methods. Sometimes possession should be used and the more ancient the survey the more likelihood that possession will be of greater importance. In law, the usage of *never* usually leads to troubles - law is not an exact science.

****

PROCEDURES

ESTABLISHING A LINE BY THE DOUBLE – LINE METHOD

By Curtis M. Brown

Daniels, Brown & Hall, San Diego, Calif.

September 1955

THE PROBLEM of establishing a true line in hilly country, where points are not intervisible and the distance is not needed, is simplified by using what I call "the double-line method." In figure 1, line 1 and line 2 are run simultaneously as random lines from corner A. The direction of line 1 is run as nearly as possible in the direction desired; this is usually accomplished by using a compass or by guessing. Line 2 is run so as to diverge from line 1 and attain about one hundred feet spread at corner B'. First, the transit is set up at corner A and points 3 and 4 are set. The transitman moves up to point 3, sights back on A, plunges over, and sets point 5. Next he moves over to point 4, sights on A, plunges over, and sets point 6. After moving up to point 5, he sights on point 3 and sets point 7; likewise, he moves over to point 6 and sets point 8. Points 7 and 8 must be adjusted so that they form a straight line with point B. The angle $A8B$ (any angle is satisfactory) and the distances X and Y are measured. Going back to point 4, point 3 is adjusted on line 2 so that line 4–3 is parallel to line 8–7-B.

After measuring the distance K, point 9, a point on the true line, is set by the following proportion:

$$J/K=Y/X$$

$$J=KY/X$$

399

The double-line method is exceedingly handy to use in establishing the center of a section where all other quarter corners are known. Two sets of double lines are run, one set north and south and the other east and west. The center is then set by intersection. Since normally only one quarter is surveyed for a client, the extra work involved in measuring the whole section is avoided.

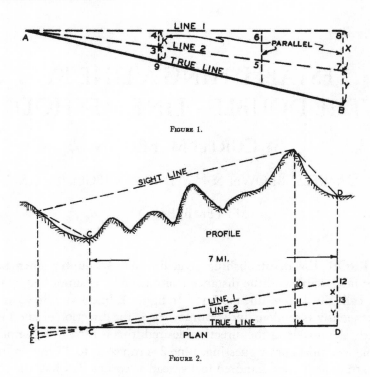

FIGURE 1.

FIGURE 2.

The usefulness of the double-line method is also illustrated in Figure 2, where the distance covered in one day was about 7 miles. Two random flags (designated as *10* and *11*) were set on the peak shown. Lines 1 and 2 were established by setting up on a hill behind corner *C* and setting points *E* and *F* by wiggling in between comer *C* and the two flags on the peak. Next, by setting up on the peak at points *10* and *11*, points *12* and *13* were set by plunging over. After measuring distances *X* and *Y*, point *14* on the true line was set by the above proportion. Returning to points *E* and *F*, the true line at *G* was established by wiggling in between corner *C* and point *14* on the true line. Since the distance was great and the terrain rough with numerous trees and obstructions, we estimated savings of five field days.

****

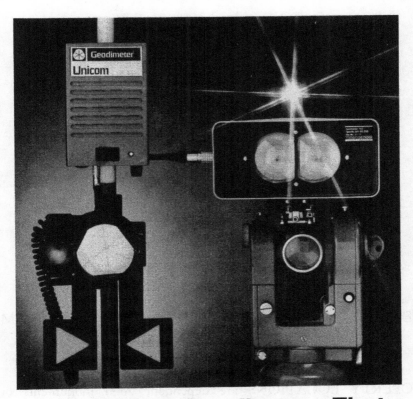

Another Geodimeter First:
The EDM with a Voice

Revolutionary functions in the newest Geodimeter instruments bring unsurpassed productivity to staking-out work and collecting detail.

Unicom
Using the measuring light beam as a carrier, Unicom offers one-way voice communication,

without interference, from operator to reflector rodperson.

Tracklight
Flashing sector light guides rodman quickly on line.

Remote Object Elevation
This optional feature greatly simplifies grade staking or measuring power line sag.

Who Needs a Total Station?

Telescope-mounted, Geodimeter 122 offers horizontal and vertical distance in 0.4 seconds, with no keying in of the vertical angle, plus:

• **Improved accuracy and resolution**
• **Longer range (1.5 miles to single prism)**
• **Automatic data recording**

800-227-1756
(In California 800-772-2664)

UNCERTAINTY OF POSITION AS APPLIED TO PROPERTY SURVEYS

By Curtis M. Brown

Daniels, Brown & Hall
San Diego, California

Presented at the Western Regional Conference, ACSM
Phoenix, Ariz., October 18-21, 1961

PROPERTY LOCATIONS are dependent upon monuments or measurements from monuments. Even when property is described by latitude and longitude, it is always a measurement relative to the poles of the earth and the prime meridian, all being monuments. State Plane Coordinates are relative to monuments set by the Federal Government in their first order triangulation net. Two things contribute to uncertainty of position of property corners or lines: (1) Uncertainty of the position of monuments called for or (2) uncertainty of measurements from monuments.

Uncertainty of original monument positions can arise from (a) inability to identify the monuments called for, (b) destruction of monuments, or (c) disturbance of monuments. Uncertainty of measurements can arise from uncertainties in the original reported measurements and the inability of surveyors to measure without error.

It is a well known fact that all measurements have some error or uncertainty; the only question is the magnitude of error permitted. In ordinary surveys the surveyor works within certain tolerances of uncertainty, and there are many opinions as to what these tolerances should be. Before discussing what the magnitude of uncertainty of position can be for any given situation, it might be well to inquire into who has the authority to declare what is acceptable accuracy.

The Federal Government caused the Public Domain to be presurveyed; that is, the land was monumented and measured prior to issuance of patents. In the survey of a section of land the Government required setting of section and quarter corners and the recordation of measurements between set corners. The closure permitted in a section of land (1/680) is such that an original quarter corner could be set anywhere within a radius of 4 feet and be perfectly acceptable. The expression 2640' plus or minus 4' would be proper to express the acceptable original distance measurement between a section corner and quarter corner.

But let us go one step further; suppose that the quarter corner becomes lost. How is it relocated? The courts tell us that in regular sections it must be located "exactly" half way between section corners; they do not say half way plus or minus 4 feet. This leads to one conclusion with respect to permissible uncertainty of measurements and that is: the permissible uncertainty of measurements allowed when recording the distance between original monuments has no relationship whatsoever to the permissible uncertainty in a resurvey.

In the above example, the Federal Government had absolute authority, as a legislative matter, to specify how the original survey was to be made, and this included specifying the measurement accuracies required. Within a State, new subdivisions may be regulated by law, and, for that matter, any new conveyance may also be regulated. In San Diego, California, even when dividing a parcel into two parcels, the law requires a subdivision map. This leads to the conclusion: the governing agency may by law regulate how land parcels may be divided, and this includes the right to specify permissible measurement uncertainties. The legislative body has the final authority to regulate acceptable accuracies of surveys when creating new conveyances.

But, after a conveyance is made and a question arises as to where or how the described land is located it is a matter of interpreting the conveyance. In matters of interpretation the courts are the final authority, and that authority includes the right to evaluate the accuracy of measurements.

We are faced with two authorities for standards of measurements: (1) legislative and (2) interpretive. The permissible uncertainty of measurements imposed by statute law presents no problems. We can read the law and follow it. We know where we stand.

But in the matter of interpretive accuracies, that is, accuracies imposed by the courts, we have no written standards, nor can anyone other than the courts be the final authority. Surveyor organizations can suggest standards of accuracy, and the courts, at their option, may recognize them for a given situation.

The courts have changing standards of permissible uncertainty of measurements. As previously stated, in regular sections, a lost quarter corner is relocated "exactly" half way between section corners. Since no measurement is exact, what is meant by "exactly half way?" In years gone by, when men used the compass and chain, it would have been indeed difficult to prove an error of 8 feet in a mile. Today it is no problem to measure within one-half foot per mile. In years to come an error of one inch in a mile may be considered excessive.

One thing is certain. For a measurement error to be of significance to the court, someone must be able to prove that the error exists, and he must do that with measuring devices.

The court rule of "exactly half way" can only mean as near as can be measured. Courts cannot impose that which cannot be proved. In a court trial they want measurements as close as is humanly possible.

Each year, with the invention of better measuring devices, the measurement error of locating "exactly half way" is becoming less and less. Court-imposed measurement standards depend upon accuracies attainable at the time of the trial, and they can never be said to be the same from year to year or from trial to trial. They vary with the potential ability of the surveyor to measure accurately and the circumstance of the case.

The courts, in their interpretation of conveyances, have declared that, as between the parties of a conveyance, an undisturbed original monument or any other monument called for by a conveyance and expressing the intent of a conveyance has zero error of position. If we are to have a property that is absolutely certain of location on the earth's surface, it must have its boundaries defined by (1) indestructible, visible, and certain monuments, and (2) the monuments as called for must not interfere with a senior or superior right.

If we were to give several different surveyors the job of setting a point exactly 10,000 feet south of a given position, undoubtedly we would find that the points as set would differ in position within a radius of at least one foot. It is logical to conclude that any point or line whose position is defined by measurements will have uncertainty of location due to the inability of surveyors to measure with absolute accuracy.

The fundamental concept is, then: (1) Properties or points defined by definite monuments have no uncertainty as to position, but they do have uncertainty as to size: (2) properties defined by measurements always have some uncertainty as to location but none as to size.

These simple conclusions are so obvious that we often fail to mention or discuss them. They were presented to clarify the following remarks on "survey accuracy standards," or, as I prefer, "survey uncertainty specifications."

406

We have rules and regulations imposed by legislative bodies as to what measurement uncertainties will be permitted when creating a new subdivision. Most of these use the term "the error of closure cannot be greater than 1/10,000," or some other ratio. Proper analysis will show that an error of closure is never proof of accuracy; errors due to a long tape can never be disclosed by a closure back to the point of beginning. An error of closure merely indicates probable consistency of measurements, not probable accuracy of measurement.

The sum total of error in measurement is never in proportion to the linear distance. Can you measure one inch within 1/10,000? A most difficult thing to do is to set a point at 52 feet within so-called 1/10,000 accuracy. If you want to measure within 1 10,000, the easiest way to do it is merely to increase the distance measured. At five miles it takes little effort to attain the so-called 1/10,000. Many of the errors of measurement are in proportion to the square root of the number of opportunities for error; the further you measure, the less the error ratio.

The greatest factor in new subdivisions, to create certainty of location, is the establishment of monuments. If monuments are located at frequent intervals and in indestructible locations, even moderately accurate measurements will insure reasonable certainty of position. Measurement uncertainties are a function of distance, but certainly not directly proportional to distance. Uncertainty of location is created by original monuments being located too far apart. No matter how good the measurements are, uncertainties in position exist when measurements from distant points are necessary to establish points or lines.

Every original monument found has zero error of position; the certainty of property location is a function of the density of monument control. Requiring excessive accuracy of measurements and no permanent monumentation is futile.

Those of you who have done court work realize the futility of talking in terms of 1/5000 accuracy. The judge certainly will not understand you. All that interests him is how much error can exist at the particular corner. Is it 1 inch, 1 foot, or 10 feet? If you say 1/5000, what is it relative to? Did you measure 30 feet or 10 miles to arrive at the point? The judges want a point set as close as is humanly possible, and he wants to know what the uncertainty is with respect to positive quantities.

In resurveying land for a large commercial building, it is foolish to tell an owner that you located his lines within 1/10,000. As a matter of fact you could have measured from a mile away, and the building could be ½ foot in error. On the other hand, an original monument may only be 6 feet away, and the uncertainty is only 1/8".

A property owner is entitled to know within reasonable limits the probable uncertainty of lines and positions, and this with respect to positive quantities. If measurements are apt to be 2 inches in error, he should be so informed.

In The Netherlands several years ago, I was rather surprised to learn that measurement uncertainty was always expressed as so many centimeters, a higher quantity being allowed for rural areas. Irrespective of distance measured for urban surveys, permissible errors of position are identical.

While we are not as yet prepared to accept this method of expressing uncertainty, in the future, with expansion of the State Plane Coordinate Systems, we may very well come to it. In the meantime, it is my belief that we should change our mode of thinking of uncertainty from that of a nebulous ratio to positive statements of uncertainty in definite units of distance.

The so-called accuracy ratio is never a suitable expression for interpretive surveys, and it is hoped that it will be eliminated from legislative enactments for original surveys.

In new subdivisions the concern should be to require techniques that will insure certainty of remonumentation of lots in their original positions. Since remonumentation will be done by measurements, there will always be some uncertainty in the relocated positions. In residential areas, if lot lines can always be remonumented with an uncertainty not exceeding 2 inches, no great harm would be done. At the most a fence would be in dispute.

In writing specifications for residential subdivision accuracies why not say, "Sufficient permanent monuments shall be set in the streets, two feet below the finished surface, and tied together with U. S. standard units of measurement so that any relocation of any lot will not be uncertain by more than 2 inches." In commercial areas, the uncertainty would have to be not more than a half inch.

Specification that an error may not be more than 1/10,000 specifies nothing. A positional error based upon this can be anything depending upon where measurements commence from. But a specification that no uncertainty greater than 1 inch exists gives positive and certain meaning. It should be used.

In this matter, as of now, many will consider me to be way out in left field, but it is my belief that we will eventually come to this way of thinking and of specifying accuracy of measurement.

****

GRAPHICAL DETERMINATION OF THE STRENGTH OF A TRIANGLE

SEPTEMBER 1964

THE CHART (Figure 1) was prepared to give a graphical solution to the strength of a computation carried through a single triangle. The original purpose was to give the field employees a quick means of determining how precisely they must measure angles in order to prevent the introduction of excessive computation errors.

The graphical presentation can be by several methods. It was felt that the most readily understood chart would be one that gave the angular error that introduced a computation error of 1/10,000.

For example, suppose a triangle, as measured in the field, contained three 60° angles. But unknown to the field man, he measured one angle in error by plus 17.8 seconds and he measured another angle in error by minus 17.8 seconds. The total would be 180°. For these conditions, when calculating the sides opposite the angles in error, a total linear error of 1/10,000 is introduced.

A second example is: A triangle contains 40°, 50°, and 90°. In computing the sides through the 40° and 50° angles, an angular error of more than 10.1 seconds in each of the 40° and 50° angles will introduce a total linear error of more than 1/10,000.

The chart is used as follows: On the right side, the smallest angle used in the computation is located. That line is followed until it intersects the curved line representing the larger angle used in the computation. By following the lines to the left, the number of seconds of error that will introduce a linear error of 1/10,000 is read. The dashed line on the chart indicates that computations carried through 37° and 50° in a triangle can tolerate a 9.4" error per angle without introducing more than 1/10,000 linear error.

This chart analyzes only one item of error, and it should be considered as indicating the precision needed for one item.

This chart need not be limited to 1/10,000 precision, since it is equally applicable for 1/1000 (multiply the allowable seconds of precision error by 10) or for 1/100,000 (divide the allowable seconds of error by 10).

For unfavorable conditions, where computations must be carried through weak triangles, a field man is put on notice as to the precision he must use to restrict angular errors to a predetermined quality. For a 20°,

20°, 140° triangle, where computations are carried through the 20° angles, the field man should use a "seconds" theodolite and close his triangle with less than 3.6 seconds per angle if he is to maintain 1/10,000 computation errors.

The chart was discontinued at 0° 00' 20" error. An error of more than 20" introduces a directional error that is more than 1/10,000; hence, at no time should more than 20" be introduced. In a series of triangles, errors will propagate from one triangle to the next. It is obvious that 1/10,000 for each triangle will not yield 1/10,000 for several triangles.

****

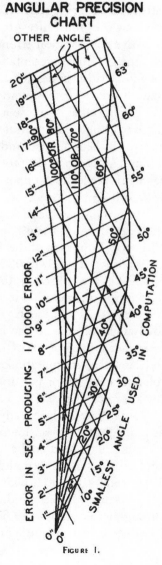

ANGULAR PRECISION CHART

FIGURE 1.

SURVEYING AND MAPPING

CRISSCROSS

JUNE 1960

THE "CRISSCROSS" computation is a time saver. In attempting to determine the history of this useful mathematical tool, I have traced the solution back to at least 1923. H. L. Edwards (Edwards Engineering Company, San Diego, California) states that he and his associates, when working for the Boulevard Land Company, independently developed the formula. He does not know whether others had previously "discovered" the method, but he is sure that their solution was independent of previous writings. It would be interesting to know how many have actually independently "discovered" this process.

To my knowledge, other than in the November 1958 issue of *Civil Engineering* (by John F. Tanner), the crisscross method has not appeared in publication. Since it is a definite timesaver, repetition here is worthwhile for those not acquainted with the procedure.

The crisscross can be used (1) for solving the lengths of two intersecting lines with known bearings or (2) for solving the unknown elements of two lines, one with a known bearing and the other with a known length.

The first solution is:

Given: (1) the difference in coordinates of two points *A* and *B* (See Figures 1A and 1B) and (2) the bearings of two lines, *AC* and *BC*, originating at points *A* and *B*.

Wanted: The length of line *AC* and the length of line *BC*.

Solution: If *N* is the coordinate difference in a north-south direction, *E* is the coordinate difference in an east-west direction, α is the bearing angle for line *AC*, and β is the bearing angle for the line *BC*, then in Figure 1A the length of *AC* is computed as follows:

$$AC = \frac{H}{\sin \Delta}$$
$$H = E \cos \beta - N \sin \beta$$
$$AC = \frac{E \cos \beta - N \sin \beta}{\sin \Delta} \qquad (1)$$

In Figure 1B the length of *BC* is computed as follows:

$$BC = \frac{E \cos \alpha + N \sin \alpha}{\sin \Delta} \qquad (2)$$

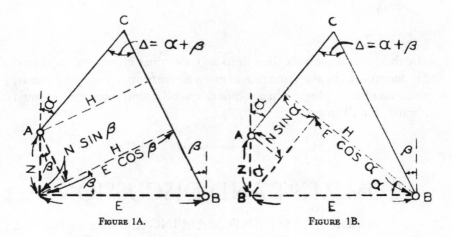

FIGURE 1A.   FIGURE 1B.

Many possible combinations of angles and lines exist. *AC* and *BC* may be in the same quadrants or in opposite quadrants. The delta angle may be more or less than 90°. When solving the problem for all conditions, it will be found that the general equations are:

$$AC = \frac{E \cos \beta \pm N \sin \beta}{\sin \Delta}$$

$$BC = \frac{E \cos \alpha \pm N \sin \alpha}{\sin \Delta}$$

When referring to either Figure 1A or Figure 1B or any other condition, the rule for determining the signs in these general formulas is:

When solving for *AC*, if lines *AB* and *BC* are in the same quadrant (NE, NE; or NE, SW; or NW, SE; or SE, SE) the sign is always minus, but if *AB* and *BC* are in opposite quadrants (NE, NW; or NE, SE; or SE, SW; or SW, NW) the sign is plus.

The reason for the name "crisscross" is obvious. When computing one side, the bearing of the other side is used and vice versa.

The second application of the crisscross is for the curve intersection problem. If *AC* (Figure 1A) is the radius (*R*) of a curve and the direction of *BC* is given, delta can be solved for by:

$$\sin \Delta = \frac{E \cos \beta - N \sin \beta}{R}$$

In the general formula the minus sign becomes either plus or minus and is determined by the same rule as given above (same quadrants, minus; opposite quadrants, plus). When computing subdivision maps, this formula is a "must" for all computers.

****

COMMENT AND DISCUSSION

The pages of SURVEYING AND MAPPING are open to free and temperate discussion of all matters pertaining to the interests of the CONGRESS. It is the purpose of this department to encourage comments on published material or the presentation of new ideas in an informal way. - EDITOR

****

CRISSCROSS

SEPTEMBER 1960

STANLEY M. SHARTLE * - Curtis M. Brown's reiteration (SURVEYING AND MAPPING, June 1960, pages 227-28) of the so-called "crisscross" computation is very worthwhile, but it should be pointed out that there is no dearth of information on the subject. It appeared in J. B. Johnson's *The Theory and Practice of Surveying* (3rd ed., 1887), John Wiley & Sons, page 205 et seq.; W. J. Raymond's *A Text-Book of Plane Surveying* (1st ed., 1896), American Book Co., page 149 et seq.; David Clark's *Plane and Geodetic Surveying for Engineers* (4th ed., 1946), Constable & Co., Ltd., Vol. 1, page 287; and is rejected, as "lacking method" and for being confusing, in A. L. Higgin's *Higher Surveying* (1st ed., 1944), Macmillen & Co., Ltd., page 169. Furthermore, on June 19, 1951, the late Vernon D. George of Silver Spring, Maryland, delivered a paper before the annual meeting of the ACSM entitled "The Intersection Solution" in which he discussed the problem at length and proposed the use of a shortcut form which makes precalculation sketches unnecessary.

Many surveyors are still computing, inversely, the length and bearing of the "closing" line from latitudes and departures between the two points whose coordinates are known, and then solving for the omitted or unknown measurements. A more convenient method is described by Mr. Brown, though it requires the making of sketches or other precomputation constructions to facilitate proper insight. For more than 20 years I have derived the formulas without sketches by forming and solving two simultaneous equations identical with those given by Johnson. The algebraic solution is not difficult, and several of my colleagues have developed the method independently as I did.

* Registered Professional Engineer, 2437 Allison Avenue, Indianapolis 24, Indiana, Staff Engineer, Indiana Toll Road Commission.

415

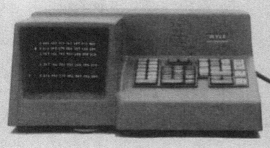
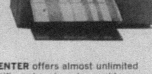

416

ERNEST CHRISBACHER * - In reading over Mr. Brown's article on crisscross computation in the June issue, I was impressed by its similarity to the intersection method used by several surveyors in this area. Charles Kaeffer of Canger Engineering Associates, Fair Lawn, N.J., says that to the best of his knowledge the first practical application of the intersection method was employed by Machael A. Canger while with Frank Harley about thirty years ago.

The intersection computation is based on the solution of simultaneous point-slope equations. The point-slope equation can be expressed as $y - y_1 = m (x - x_1)$, where x,y and x_1, y_1 are the rectangular coordinates of any two points on a line, and m is the slope of the line. Intersection can be used to solve the lengths of two intersecting lines with known bearings by first computing the coordinates of the point of intersection and solving between coordinates to determine the lengths. It has the advantage of offering a check on the bearings when solving between coordinates.

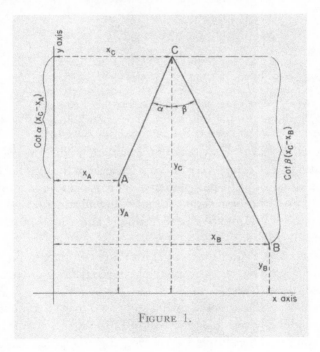

FIGURE 1.

In Figure 1:

Given: (1) The coordinates of two points, A and B, and (2) The bearings of two lines, AC and BC, originating at points A and B respectively.

417

Wanted: (1) The coordinates of point *C*, and (2) the length of lines *AC* and *BC*.

Solution: If α is the bearing angle for *AC*, and β is the bearing angel for *BC*, then the coordinates of point *C* may be computed by solving simultaneous point-slope equations. Cot α is used in place of *m* as the slope of line *AC* and cot β for the slope of the line *BC*.

$$y_c - y_a = \text{Cot } \alpha (x_c - x_a) \tag{1}$$
$$y_c - y_b = \text{Cot } \beta (x_c - x_b) \tag{2}$$

Since x_c and y_c are the only unknowns in equations (1) and (2), cancel out y_c by multiplying equation (1) by minus one; then add the two equations.

$$-y_c + y_a = -\text{Cot } \alpha (x_c) + \text{Cot } \alpha (x_a) \tag{1}$$
$$y_c - y_b = \text{Cot } \beta (x_c) - \text{Cot } \beta (x_b) \tag{2}$$

$$y_a - y_b = (\text{Cot } \beta - \text{Cot } \alpha)(x_c) + \text{Cot } \alpha(x_a) - \text{Cot } \beta(x_b)$$

Solving for x_c, the only unknown—

$$x_c = \frac{y_a - y_b - \text{Cot } \alpha(x_a) + \text{Cot } \beta(x_b)}{\text{Cot } \beta - \text{Cot } \alpha} \tag{3}$$

This equation is very convenient for calculating machine computation of x_c. Substituting the compared value of x_c in either of the original equations enables the value of y_c to be computed. When using equation (3) it is important to use the proper signs for the cotangent functions. Cotangents are always plus for NE and SW bearing angles and always minus for NW and SE bearing angles.

After the *x* and *y* coordinates of point *C* are computed, the lengths of lines *AC* and *BC* can be found by solving between the coordinates of points *A* and *C* and points *B* and *C*.

All possible combinations of intersecting lines may be computed by the use of this method; however, because of the limitations of natural-function tables, accuracy becomes limited as bearing angles approach zero.

* 25 Summit Avenue, Hawthorne, N. J.

****

CRISSCROSS

DECEMBER 1960

JAMES A. H. CHURCH * - While congratulating Curtis M. Brown on his private solution of a very ordinary problem, one doubts its value to the surveyor-in-training and the younger surveyors. It appears to make a special case of a common problem wanting, as presented, progressive checks on computation.

The following is suggested as providing progressive checks and a more rapid solution. The data given, as in Mr. Brown's presentation, are the coordinates of the points A and B and the bearings of the lines AC and BC. We wish to find the lengths of the lines AC and BC.

$$\triangle E = E_a - E_b$$
$$\triangle N = N_a - N_b$$
$$\triangle E \div \triangle N = \tan \text{ bearing } AB$$
$$\triangle E \div \sin \text{ bearing } AB = \text{length } AB$$
$$\triangle N \div \cos \text{ bearing } AB = \text{length } AB \text{ (check)}$$

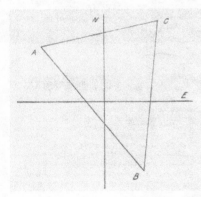

The bearings of all three lines now being known, the three angles of the triangle CBA may be computed from the bearings, and an additional check is obtained when the sum of the three angles equals 180°.

The lengths of the lines AC and BC are then obtained by solving the triangle CBA (using the law of sines) in which all three angles and the length AB are now known.

The computation of the coordinates of the point C from both A and B, using given bearings and computed lengths, furnishes a final check on the validity of the entire computation.

Surely *proof* is the essence of all survey work.

* Nova Scotia Land Survey Institute, Box 58, Lawrencetown, Annapolis County, Nova Scotia.

****

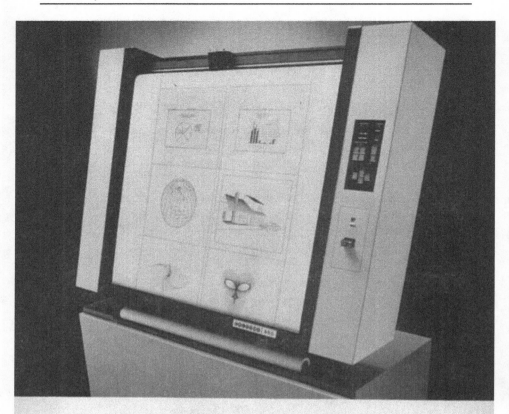

Some artists work faster standing up.

We taught the computer to draw. And from the beginning, we've demanded ever-increasing accuracy—to the point where today, our plotters can draw things that the human would not even attempt.

But in the computer world, time is money. So our *artists* have to perform with remarkable speed.

Last year, we ran an ad where we said that our giant 745 Flatbed Plotter could draw faster than ink flows.

Now we're introducing the 960 Plotter.

It has the fastest *throughput* in the industry.

How fast is fast?

The 960 can draw at a rate up to 30 inches per second.

And from a dead start, it can accelerate to that speed after traveling only 3/10 of an inch.

Less noise. Less space.

The new 960 is extraordinarily quiet. And because it's a vertical plotter, it takes up a lot less space.

Remember, CalComp taught the computer to draw, and our plotter marketing

facilities are unmatched throughout the world.

See our new artist at work. Call or write California Computer Products, Inc., SM-12-75, 2411 West La Palma Avenue, Anaheim, California 92801. Telephone (714) 821-2011.

CALCOMP

THE SURVEYOR AND THE LAW

TEXAS LAW

MARCH 1961

While at the recent Texas Surveyors Association annual meeting and the ACSM Regional Conference, several impressions of Texas law were gained.

In early Texas law (Stafford v King, year 1867, 30 Tex 257) the Hon. George W. Smith wrote, ". . . course and distance are regarded as the most unreliable and generally distance more than course, for the reason that chain-carriers may miscount and report distances inaccurately, by mistake or design. At any rate, they are more liable to err than the compass." And such is the Texas law today. In instructions to the jury the judge states, in suitable court language, "If you are to choose between bearing and distance, bearing is to be considered more certain."

Other than in Texas everyone has parroted the court ruling "distance is more certain than direction." But is it?

In double proportioning (confined almost exclusively to sectionalized lands wherein some corners, when lost, are replaced by double proportion), we must admit that direction is relegated to lesser importance. Within checkerboard subdivisions, block corners could be re-established by double proportion from four found original monuments, but as yet I have not seen it done. Most surveyors use the intersection of straight lines (direction more important).

This poses a question, "Can anyone, other than in double proportioning, think of a situation wherein direction and distance would be in conflict with one another"? If they cannot be in conflict, the argument of which is more important, distance or direction, reduces itself to "which came first, the hen or the egg"? A straight line can be defined in many ways. Essentially they are all variations of (1) defined by monuments and (2) defined by distance and direction (vector quantities). If a line is defined by calling for monuments (along James' land, to an iron pipe, to the ocean, etc.) the monument controls and whatever is in conflict with the call for the monument yields. Bearing and distance are both subordinate, hence neither controls over the other.

Two situations in calls for monuments arise wherein it appears bearing or distance must yield to the other. A call of "North 600 feet to the ocean" goes "North to the ocean whether it is 600 feet or not." A call of "East 100 feet along Main Street" goes "East 100 feet along Main Street whether Main Street is East or N 89° 58' E". In the first instance, it appears that direction is superior to distance; in the second it appears that distance is superior to direction. Actually distance and direction are not in conflict with one another in either case; each is in conflict with a call for a monument. In the first instance 600 feet yields to the call for the ocean, not the call for a bearing. In the second instance the bearing yields to the call for the street line, not the call for a distance.

Vector lines, defined by direction and distance, must have both recited, otherwise the line cannot be located. In such a case, how can bearing be in conflict with distance? What difference does it make if one is said to be superior to the other? As I see it, if the rule of direction being more important than distance is strictly adhered to in Texas, the only difference will be that double proportioning cannot be used. And I don't believe it is. Who in Texas can answer this?

In alienating land, the State of Texas, in general, gave or sold the right to acquire a parcel of land. Land was often surveyed, one piece at a time, as the need arose. In sectionalized land areas, parcels were pre-surveyed prior to land offerings and parcels were acquired in conformity with the survey. In Texas, the land was selected and then surveyed. In Texas this created a sequence of sales with senior rights attaching to other parcels. The problem of senior rights is not unique to Texas; all other States have it. The only difference is that Texas has *more* of it. And, from the size of Texas, they have many more parcels in which this can happen.

Discovery of oil has had a marked influence on the surveyor's status. The value of land in an oil field and the monetary value of every foot of land gained have created a demand for first-grade, top-quality professional surveyors. Oil field surveys often have to be proven in court, and the surveyor who does poor work is in an embarrassing position. After listening and talking to the better surveyors, there is no question in my mind that the better Texas surveyors are among the best.

Public surveyors in Texas were recently registered. The usual problem of the unqualified, grandfathered-in as surveyors, could be discerned. In California, that problem has been largely solved by time; thirty years later few unqualified "grandfathers" have survived.

– Curtis M. Brown

****

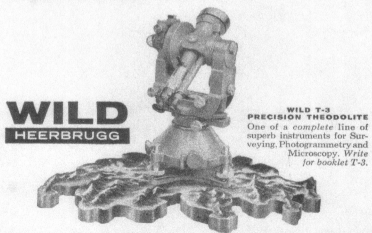

THE PROFESSION, ETHICS, AND STANDARD OF CARE

THE SURVEYOR AND THE LAW

THE SURVEYOR IN COURT

BY CURTIS M. BROWN

DANIELS, BROWN, & HALL
SURVEYORS & ENGINEERS

SAN DIEGO, CALIFORNIA

SEPTEMBER 1958

[NOTE: This paper was presented at the San Joaquin Valley Surveyors Conference held at Fresno State College, Fresno, California, April 4-5, 1958.]

Introduction. The very nature of surveying makes it probable that the property-line surveyor will occasionally be a witness or a litigant in court. When a surveyor is called upon to monument a property line, it may happen that one of the adjoiners will disagree with his monument line location and will refer the matter to the courts. The adjoiner might claim ownership due to a line of possession, or he might claim the surveyor erred. But whatever his claim, the dispute will probably end in court, and the surveyor will be a witness.

Without disagreement, investigation and experiment would cease. The arts and sciences have progressed because people disagreed with the old methods and have advanced new ideas. Not all disagreements are objectionable. Because of disagreement of opinion, the judge of the higher court sometimes reverses the opinion of the judge of the lower court. In fact, many attorneys depend upon differences of opinion for their very livelihood. Disputes have been with people and will continue to be with them. Likewise, it is reasonable to expect that surveyors will occasionally disagree, and litigation will sometimes be created because of such differences of opinion. Honest differences of opinion based upon sound reasoning from the true facts in evidence may be considered as a healthy condition.

The surveyor has many opportunities for errors. He may make a wrong measurement or calculation, and thus be the cause of a costly mistake. Such errors, unless voluntarily settled by the surveyor, usually end in a damage suit.

In some States, such as California, whenever a judge feels that the court needs the services of an expert to aid in interpreting or observing facts, it may appoint an expert on its own motion. Thus, the surveyor, as an expert, might serve the court.

From this discussion, it can be concluded that all actively engaged property-line surveyors must expect, at some time that they will be called upon to appear as a court witness. In this paper, it is presupposed that the surveyor is a witness, not a litigant.

Duties of a Surveyor in Court. In litigation involving land boundaries, the surveyor is a witness, either lay or expert. He has no function other than as a witness describing facts within his perception, or as an expert witness expressing opinions within his special field.

In the practice of surveying, the client asks the surveyor to give him a solution to a particular boundary problem. The surveyor works until he finds a *solution* and presents the results to the client. In a court case, the surveyor is a witness who presents the facts, and the court decrees the solution. Thus, in court cases the surveyor must change his mode of thinking and always remember that it is not he who is solving the problem. He is a witness.

Court Trials. All of the procedures and methods used in court trials, though interesting, are not of vital importance to the surveyor. Since the surveyor is a witness, it is important that he know how to properly conduct himself as a lay or expert witness. And it is important that he know what fees, if any, he is entitled to. These items will be discussed.

Pre-trials. Pre-trials, as practiced in some states, are for the purpose of eliminating unnecessary court time and are an attempt to reach agreement on what are the issues in the case. The attorneys and the judge, in conference, discuss the issues and agree upon which points of evidence will be taken. At this time, the judge or the attorney for either side may ask for an expert witness. Often they are appointed in boundary disputes.

Oath, Questions, and Answers. Prior to testifying, a witness is placed under oath to tell the truth, the whole truth, and nothing but the truth. This does not mean that the witness is to volunteer information and ramble along on any subject that he thinks might have a bearing on the case. He is to answer questions put to him. If the answer to a question result in a half-truth and the witness feels that further information should be given, and yet the information is not called for by the question, he may ask permission of the court to clarify his answer. The reason testimony is, in general, limited to the answering of questions is that the court wants to know in advance whether the subject matter the witness is to talk about is admissible evidence. Also, the opposing side has an opportunity to object if the question asked is improper.

Direct and Cross-examination. The examination of a witness by the party producing him is called the direct examination; the examination of the same witness, upon the same matter, by the adverse party is called the cross-examination. The direct examination must be completed before the cross-examination begins, unless the court otherwise directs. (Sec. 2045, C.C.P.)

[MP NOTE: "Sec. 2045, C.C.P." refers to Section 2045 of the California Code of Civil Procedure. The recitation is a verbatim reading of the code.]

Leading Questions. A question that suggests to the witness the answer which the examining party desires is called a *leading* or *suggestive question.* On a direct examination, leading questions are not allowed, except in the sound discretion of the court, under special circumstances, making it appear that the interests of justice require it. The opposite party may cross-examine the witness as to any facts stated in his direct examination or connected therewith, and in so doing may put leading questions. But if he examines him as to other matters, such examination is to be subject to the same rules as direct examination. (Sec. 2046, C.C.P.)

[MP NOTE: Section 2046 reads as follows: *Leading Question defined. A question which suggests to the witness the answer which the examining party desires, is denominated a leading or suggestive question. On a direct examination, leading questions are not allowed, except in the sound discretion of the court, under special circumstances, making it appear that the interests of justice require it.*]

Hearsay. Evidence not proceeding from the personal knowledge of the witness, but from the mere repetition of what he has heard others say, is called *hearsay evidence.* (*Black's Law Dictionary.* West Publishing Co., St. Paul, Minn.)

Evidence based upon rumor, common talk, or the statement of someone else is hearsay and, with few exceptions, is inadmissible as evidence. In surveying practice, the surveyor often bases his opinions upon hearsay facts, such as a monument found and commonly reported by many as being in a correct position. Obviously a surveyor could not be present in person when all of the original surveys were made; hence his opinion of where property lines belong may be based entirely upon hearsay evidence of where the original surveyor set his monuments.

Expert opinions are admissible even though they may be based upon inadmissible hearsay evidence.

Jury. All questions of fact, where the trial is by jury, are to be decided by the jury, and all evidence thereon is to be addressed to them. (Sec. 2101, C.C.P. Cal.)

[MP NOTE: Section 2101 reads as follows: *Questions of fact, how tried. All questions of fact, where the trial is by jury, are to be decided by the jury, and all evidence thereon is to be addressed to them, except when otherwise provided by this code.*]

A jury trial may be requested by either side. If there is a jury trial, the jury decides questions of fact. If a government section corner is lost and there is a dispute over which of several monuments represents the true corner, the jury would decide which monument represents the true corner. If a fence has been in existence for a period of time and the question arises as to how long the fence has been in existence, the jury would decide. But if there were a question of the legal interpretation of the meaning of a deed term, the judge would decide that.

Not many attorneys care for jury trials in boundary litigations; hence, the judge usually tries both facts and law. In such event, the surveyor testifies to most of the testimony as to the facts concerning boundaries. A surveyor's main duty is to gather facts. He measures distances, angles, and bearings and searches for monuments. Any fact he observes and measures is a fact to which he may testify.

Lay Witness. Lay witnesses are those that may testify to facts within their knowledge and may not state their opinions.

This is the rule. But there are many, many exceptions to the rule. In fact, practically all of the discussion of the rule centers on instances that are exceptions.

Often there is no way of extracting the facts from a lay witness other than by allowing him to express an opinion on things derived from his own perception. A statement that there was an *old* fence between the two properties is an opinion. *Hot* or *cold* may only be an opinion, especially when a person says *how* hot or cold a thing is. The lay witness testifies about subject matter readily understood by the court. Preventing the lay witness from stating opinions, especially on matters regarding which he is not qualified to do so, tends to prevent fraud and perjury and is one of the strongest safeguards of personal rights.

Expert Witness. Generally a witness may testify as an expert witness if he possesses peculiar knowledge, wisdom, or information regarding the subject matter in consideration, said knowledge, wisdom, or information being acquired by study, investigation, observation, practice, or experience. But such knowledge is not of the type that is likely to be possessed by ordinary laymen or inexperienced persons. (King vs. King et al, 161 Miss. 51)

Because of training and experience, many surveyors are qualified to be declared experts by the court. The word "many" instead of the word "all" was used advisedly. Mere licensing is not proof. An expert is one who can demonstrate real knowledge, experience, and wisdom on the point in question.

Because of his special knowledge, the expert is permitted to testify as to conclusions drawn from facts within his field. The expert gives the result of a process of reasoning, which can be mastered only by special training.

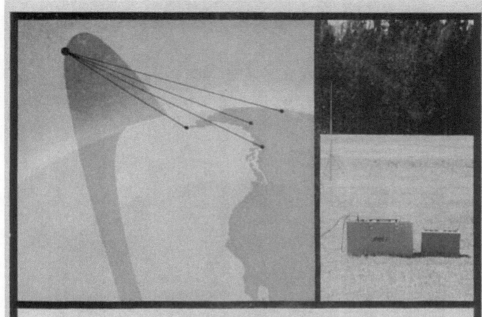

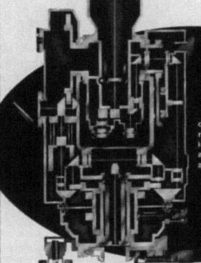

"Whenever it shall be made to appear to any court or judge thereof, either before or during the trial of any action or proceeding, civil or criminal, pending before such court, that expert evidence is, or will be required by the court or any party, to such action or proceeding, such court or judge may, on motion of any party, or on motion of such court or judge, appoint one or more experts to investigate and testify at the trial of such action or proceeding relative to the matter or matters as to which such expert evidence is, or will be required, and such court or judge may fix the compensation of such expert or experts for such services, if any, as such expert or experts may have rendered, in addition to his or their services as a witness or witnesses, at such amount or amounts as to the court or judge may seem reasonable." (Sec. 1871 C.C.P. Calif.)

The practice of the parties hiring their own expert witnesses has been severely criticized. There is an implication of bias towards the party calling the expert, especially when a sizable fee is involved. A precommitment or preconsultation with a party in itself presents the flavor of bias. A party may interview many experts before he can find one that is favorable to his cause, and thus not present a true picture to the court. It is indeed unfortunate that the same brush often tars many. Such ideas are all injustice to the conscientious expert whose only concern is the truth of the principle involved.

Duties of Expert Witness. A summary of the duties demanded of an expert witness is:

a) All questions put to him should be answered clearly and intelligently.

b) He should be absolutely unbiased and honest.

c) He should have real expert knowledge of his particular subject.

d) He should be prepared to discuss the opinions of other authorities and state why he agrees or disagrees with them.

e) His testimony should be limited to things and opinions that he can defend before experts in his particular field.

The opinions of the expert are generally only arguments in behalf of a litigant. Hence, his testimony is often valuable only because of the reasons and facts given to support his conclusions. Rejection of conclusions unsupported by facts or reasons can be expected.

Testimony that cannot be understood by the judge or jury is practically valueless. A statement that "I ran a traverse around the deed and found an error of closure of two feet" is simple to the surveyor but obscure jargon to the average person. It is doubtful if the judge or jury would know that the traverse might be an office calculation and not a field measurement. "Error of closure" certainly needs clarification to most people. A judge became a judge because he was an attorney, not a surveyor. One of the assets of a good expert witness is simple, clear English. Don't try to awe the jury by your ability to "elucidate" by "ostentatious" terminology. Explain by simple terms.

At no time should the surveyor place himself in such a position that he is obligated to take a particular side in his testimony. When the expert is on the stand, he should make every effort to rid himself of any bias or prejudice resulting from who is paying the fee or who has previously consulted with him.

No one can expect to remember in detail all of the facts he is to present without refreshing his memory. Surveyors take field notes and develop evidence in writing. Maps are examined and deeds are read. Prior to taking the stand, the surveyor should re-familiarize himself of all the data; otherwise embarrassment may result from a searching cross-examination. He should be especially prepared to explain the error of the contrary opinion.

Opinion Evidence. As previously stated, the lay witness is limited to testimony concerning facts and may sometimes give opinions on things that are easy for everyone to understand. The expert may give opinions on subjects that are beyond the knowledge of average people. But such right to give opinions is not unlimited.

No witness can give opinions on the *ultimate fact* that is being tried. Permitting an expert to tell the jury what they must decide is usurping their exclusive rights. If the north quarter corner location is in dispute and any one of three stone mounds might be the right one, the surveyor cannot tell the judge or jury which one they should select. He can walk all around the subject and even answer hypothetical questions that almost give direct answers on the solution. He could describe in detail the shape and size of the mounds and describe any special marking found. If leaves were found under one of the mounds, indicating recent construction, such a fact could be emphasized. What was found in other similar locations and whether the original surveyor consistently set a certain type of monument could be discussed. Needless to say, the examining attorney would have to be well versed on the facts observed by the surveyor; otherwise he would not know which questions to ask. The surveyor is more or less limited in his response to the questions asked.

No witness may give his opinion on the questions of law presented. Whether a deed was properly executed or how a deed word should be interpreted are questions of law for the court to decide. The court and attorneys are experts at law, not the surveyors.

No expert opinions may be given to the jury if they are capable of forming their own opinion. The purpose of giving expert opinions is to advise the jury on matters beyond their knowledge, not on matters within their knowledge.

Fortunately, the expert witness does not have to decide when he can or cannot give opinions. The judge will tell him. A question is presented to him, and if the other side objects, the judge will rule on whether the question can be answered.

Hypothetical Questions. A hypothetical question is a question put to an expert witness containing a recital of facts assumed to have been proved or proof of which is offered in the case and requiring the opinion of expert witness thereon.

Hypothetical implies "assumed without proof." Each side thinks or hopes that they can prove certain facts to be true. But neither side can be certain of what the jury will declare to be true. So a hypothetical question such as, "Assuming that this, this, and this are true, could you express an opinion as to whether a person so injured could continue doing surveying work"?, is asked. The facts assumed to be true are the facts presented or to be presented in the case. If the jury finds that the facts are not as assumed, the opinion of the expert is without effect. Several hypothetical questions may be asked by adding extra-assumed facts or subtracting assumptions.

Hypothetical questions are more frequently used for doctors in personal injury cases. Rarely, the surveyor will find such questions presented to him.

Cause and Effect. An expert may testify as to what might have caused a thing; but it is better not to say what did cause it. Thus, a surveyor might testify that measuring from an incorrect monument located five feet from the correct monument might cause the improper location of a fence. He should not say that it was the cause; that is for the jury to decide. To say that a 2" x 2" pine stake located at the property corner would completely disappear in 30 years, due to decomposition, termites, etc., would be improper. To say that at all locations where pine stakes were originally set none were found that were over 30 years old, and those older than 10 years were in a bad state of decomposition, would be proper.

Textbooks. Because the author of a book cannot be cross-examined and the author did not write his book under oath, books are, by common law, excluded as evidence.

In most States, by statute law, the right to use books of science or art and published maps or charts is permitted under limited conditions. In California, section 1936 of the Code of Civil Procedure makes "historical works, books of science or art, and published maps or charts, when made by persons indifferent between the parties . . . prima facie evidence of facts of general notoriety and interest."

From Gallagher vs. Market St. Ry. Co., (67 Cal. 13) is extracted, "Evidence of this sort is confined in a great measure to ancient facts, which do not presuppose better evidence in existence. . . The work of a living author, who is within the reach of the process of the court, can hardly be deemed of this nature. Such evidence is only admissible to prove facts of a general and public nature, and not those which concern individual or mere local communities. Such facts include the meaning of words which may be proved by ordinary dictionaries and authenticated books of general literary history and facts in the exact sciences founded upon conclusions reached from certain and constant data by processes too intricate to be elucidated by witnesses when on examination. Thus, mortality tables for estimating the probable duration of the life of a party at a given age; chronological tables; tables of weights, measures, and currency; annuity tables; interest tables, and the like, are admissible to prove facts of general notoriety and interest in connection with such subject as may be involved in the trial of a cause."

The expert's memory may be refreshed by referring to standard works of his profession, but the books may not be read to the court. The witness may state the reasons for his opinion, even though the reasons were founded on books, as a part of his general knowledge. If a witness bases his opinion upon a book and says so, extracts from the book may be read to contradict him. But, if an expert has testified from his own experience, books may not be received in evidence to show that the authors of books disagree with the opinion of the expert.

Power to Compel Expert to Testify. (2 ALR 1576 annotated, The Lawyers Co-operative Publishing Company, Rochester, N. Y.) The right of an expert to refuse to testify as to matters of opinion, without compensation, is traced back to English common law. In Webb vs. Page (1843) 1 Car. & K (Eng) 23, the right of the expert to demand compensation prior to testifying was upheld.

For the usual witness fee, a lay or expert witness is required to testify to facts seen or observed by him. If a surveyor observes certain facts or sets certain monuments, he may be compelled to testify as to these facts. But, where a party selects an expert to render an opinion on a peculiar subject, the expert can refuse until satisfactory arrangements are made for compensation.

Many jurisdictions hold that an expert must testify to facts within his knowledge even though special study, learning, or skills were required to determine them. In Fonda vs. Bolton (1883) 6 NJLR 240, a civil engineer was denied the right to recover compensation for services as an expert witness. The party who employed him to make a survey called him as an expert. Since he attended court under a subpoena, he was bound to testify as to what he knew, however he acquired the knowledge. In Summers vs. State, (5 Tex. App. 365) a medical expert was compelled to report on the findings of a post mortem examination without extra compensation.

But there is nothing in the law that compels an expert witness to make a free preliminary investigation to prepare himself for expressing an opinion. A surveyor who is asked to perform certain surveys as a preparation for litigation cannot be compelled to do so without compensation. If a deed is presented to a surveyor in court and he is asked where it is located on the ground, the surveyor may refuse to read the document and give an opinion. But if he has already read the document and has already formed an opinion, he probably would be bound to express his opinion.

In United States vs. Cooper, 21 D.C. 491, the court observed that it was an obligation of an expert to serve upon payment of a reasonable fee.

In summary, in many jurisdictions surveyors are bound to testify to the results of surveys performed in the past. They are not bound, without compensation, to express opinions on things that require professional preparation prior to expressing the opinion.

It is interesting to note that an expert witness may not refuse to answer a question on the grounds that it will cause him civil liability. Usually the only grounds for refusal to answer a question are that the answer may cause the witness to self-incriminate himself for a crime. Refusal to answer a question because it may cause embarrassment, disgrace, or monetary loss from civil liability is not an excuse. The privilege of refusal to answer a question applies only to crimes. (CJS Vol. 98, p 98).

Expert Witness Fees. The surveyor's fee for expert testimony is a contractual arrangement between the surveyor and the party engaging him.

The courts cannot compel a person to perform work. If a measurement or observation is required, the right of a litigant to hire an expert is recognized. Before commencing the work, the surveyor should have a clear understanding of what his fee will be. If the work is performed and there is no understanding as to the amount of the fee, the surveyor may be compelled to testify as to what he knows without the benefit of a fee. It is advisable to include within the fee all expenses that will be incurred in court appearances, since a person is compelled to appear in court whether he receives a fee or not. The only collectable part of the contract is the work for preparation to appear in court.

The rule is that a so-called expert witness is not entitled to extra compensation for any testimony, which he may be required to give under an ordinary subpoena of the court. (16 AIR 1462.)

The compensation of an expert witness cannot be dependent upon the outcome of the litigation, since it furnishes a powerful motive for exaggeration, misrepresentation, or suppression.

"We are aware that witnesses who are to be called to give expert testimony which involves the special knowledge and skill of the witnesses, and often requires examination and study upon a particular branch or science, are, from the necessities of the case, justified in demanding and receiving compensation for their time and labor devoted to the investigation of the particular science about which they are to testify; but this practice has been allowed from the necessities of the case, and the inability of courts and juries to determine questions without the benefit of such expert knowledge. Such agreements, however, can never be valid where the amount to be paid is to depend upon the testimony that is to be given, and where the right of compensation depends upon the result of the litigation." (Re Schapiro, 144 App. Div. 1, 128 NY Supp 852.)

Amount of Expert Witness Fee Is Subject to Cross-Examination. Cross-examination may extract from an expert the fact that he is to receive a fee and how much the fee is.

"The amount of an expert's fees, whether stipulated in advance of a trial or determinable in the future, has a direct and vital bearing upon his credibility, interest, bias, or partisanship, and the rule permitting cross-examination with reference thereto should be liberally applied." (33 ALR 2nd 1167, annotation 33 ALR 2nd 1170.)

"An engineer who testified for the petitioner may be asked on cross-examination, if he had not been promised 'considerable money' if the preceding went through, as it is always competent to ask a witness, on cross-examination, by whom he is employed and whether he is paid, in order to show his interest." (West Skokie Drainage District vs. Dawson, 243 111. 175.)

In a park condemnation proceeding, it was error not to allow a question asked of a real estate agent, which had estimated values for the city, as to whether he was interested in the sale of land that would be benefited by the park. (Oakland vs. Adams, 37 Cal. App. 614.)

Survey Must Be Done by Surveyor. The surveyor who testifies in a case must be the one who made the survey. In the case of Hermance vs. Blackburn (206 CA 653) the court notes " . . . it was error to permit a witness to testify that a certain arch protruded over the lot line where said witness testified that the survey was not made by him personally, but by men in his employ."

****

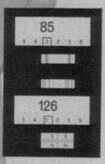

LAND SURVEYORS ETHICS

BY CURTIS M. BROWN

DANIELS, BROWN & HALL

SAN DIEGO, CALIFORNIA

JUNE 1960

CALIFORNIA, like several other states, is preparing a "Manual for Land Surveyors in California." Two years ago, I was appointed to do this project. Certain phases of the manual have been completed, ethics being one of them. This manual is for "Property-Line Surveyors" in its narrow sense. Since surveyors in California may do construction staking (roads, buildings, etc.), take topography, and do other things often referred to as engineering surveying, this code can only be interpreted as applicable to a portion of their practice; i.e., the property-line portion. Although much of it is applicable to "engineering surveys" as classified by the ASCE Task Committee (Brother B. Austin Barry's committee), it would probably have to be enlarged and slightly reworded to include all of these strictly technical surveys.

Because there are so many State surveyor organizations now considering this subject, it is deemed advisable to publish this present thinking on ethics. Perhaps the best book written on ethics is *Legal Ethics* by Henry S. Drinker (Columbia University Press, N.Y.). It is recommended for all ethics committees and, for that matter, anyone else. The Property Surveys Division of the American Congress on Surveying and Mapping has an ethics committee headed by able Victor H. Ghent. This code, proposed for California, does not necessarily reflect the ideas or opinions of that committee and is published merely for the purpose of stimulating thinking. It has not been officially adopted in California.

DEFINITION OF ETHICS

That branch of moral science which treats of the duties which a member of a profession owes to the public, to his professional brethren, and to his client, is ethics.

Ethics is not susceptible to an exact definition. The above definition, adapted from *Bouviers Law Dictionary*, rather clearly expresses the intent and purpose of ethics.

"It is a fact with which everyone is familiar that an individual may strictly observe the laws of the land and yet be an undesirable citizen and a poor neighbor. The idea that each individual can and should establish for himself rules of conduct for such relations as are not covered by law and without reference to the experience or opinions of others seems equally as absurd as would a similar attempt to establish principles of law. Laws must be established by the majority action of a legislative body, and rules of professional conduct must be based on the concurrent opinions of the members of a profession." ("Standards of Professional Relations and Conduct," by Daniel W. Mead, American Society of Civil Engineers). Rules for professional conduct are ethics.

Lord Moulton in an article in the *Atlantic Monthly* (134 Atlantic Monthly 1, 13, 1924) stated, "The real greatness of a nation, its true civilization, is measured by the extent of Obedience to the Unenforceable." Ethics are often unenforceable. True professional stature arises from obedience to the unenforceable.

Rules of ethics, as adopted by any profession, are not intended to particularize; they are general guides of conduct and behavior.

Advocating observances to ethics is not sufficient; the surveyor's personal example is far more potent. It is not sufficient that the surveyor alone feels that he has honesty and integrity; the public, clients, and fellow practitioners must also believe so. The proof of observance of ethics lies in the opinions of others.

If we, as surveyors, are to maintain a respected position as a profession in the community, we must look beyond the club of the law to ethical standards which prohibit the doing of that which the law does not forbid.

THE SURVEYOR'S PROFESSIONAL STATUS

Principle: Professional stature cannot be acquired by self proclamation; others must bestow the title upon the surveyor.

The three professions or learned professions as defined by Webster, are theology, law, and medicine. Definitions of a profession, though not exact, include such phrases as "a group of men," following a "learned art," and as a "public service."

We, as surveyors, know that we are in a profession practiced by a group of highly skilled men pursuing a learned art for the benefit of the public. But we, as professional men, are not the sole judge in this matter; others must also think so. Whether surveying is a profession or not is something that the public bestows upon the surveyor. Fortunately, it is not something that is acquired by self proclamation. If it were otherwise, everyone would soon lay claim and become higher in stature whether qualified or not. The professions that the public recognizes and acclaims as professions, i.e., doctors, attorneys, and clergymen, need not use the title professional doctor, professional attorney, or professional clergyman; everyone knows they are professional. The title was bestowed upon them because of their ethics, behavior, and standing in the community. Friends, business acquaintances, and others will evaluate surveyors by their behavior, technical skills, education, and ethics. Only if they behave and act like professional men will the public bestow upon them the privilege of being professionals.

Surveyors enjoy a personal relationship to the client that is similar to that of the legal and medical professions. The client seeks the services of a surveyor for a personal problem, the surveyor serves the client for a fee and at the same time is obligated to protect certain bona fide rights of others. But, unlike the legal, medical, and theological professions, he is not extended privilege communications. As in law and medicine, the surveyor is often given the exclusive right to perform certain duties, and in exchange for this exclusive right he has obligations to the client, the public, and other surveyors. The differences between the surveying profession and a business are:

(1) A relation with the public as an arbitrator of boundary problems and an obligation to protect the boundary rights of others.

(2) A duty of public service though it may incidentally be a means of earning a fee.

445

(3) The possibility of earning highest eminence without making much money.

(4) A relation to clients in trust.

(5) A relation to other surveyors characterized by fairness.

(6) An unwillingness to use business methods of advertising in self-laudatory language.

(7) Unwillingness to encroach on another surveyor's practice or clients.

SURVEYORS' PRIVILEGES AND OBLIGATIONS

Principle: In exchange for certain exclusive privileges granted by law to the surveyor, he has obligations to the public, the client, and fellow practitioners.

The surveyor and sometimes the engineer, by his license or registration, is given the exclusive privilege to (1) hold himself out as a land surveyor and (2) to monument property lines.

These rights are granted to protect the public from unqualified practitioners. In exchange for these exclusive privileges, the professional surveyor has certain obligations to the public, the client, and colleagues.

The land surveyor has the authority, by law, to monument property lines, but he does not always have the responsibility of perpetuation. In California, a large portion of our lands were divided by one of the finest systems ever devised, i.e., the sectionalized land system. The Federal Government provided the original monumentation, but no provisions were made for the perpetuation of the system. Perpetuation may be accomplished by delegating such responsibility to public office holders or to private land surveyors. In California, each has responsibilities for perpetuation. If in the performance of land surveys, the land surveyor discovers certain facts, such as a material discrepancy from the record (Section 8762 of the Land Surveyors Act), he must file a public record. Thus, there is a perpetuation of records disclosing the location of found monuments and original survey lines.

Filing of public records of re-surveys performed by qualified land surveyors is one of the best methods known for perpetuating surveys. The keeping of secret tie-out records of found original monuments only leads to confusion. If the land surveyor allows the public to delegate to him the exclusive privilege of performing land surveys, he ought to accept the responsibility of devising some system that assures the perpetuation of former surveys. Failure to do so will certainly result in a loss of public respect, and, in some states, just such a thing has happened.

SURVEYORS' OBLIGATIONS TO THE PUBLIC

The surveyor has the following obligations to the public:

(1) to see that the client's boundaries are properly monumented without subtracting from the rights of the adjoiner;

(2) not to stir up boundary disputes;

(3) not to aid in unauthorized surveying practice;

(4) to see that those licensed as surveyors (or as engineers, if engineers are permitted to practice surveying) are properly qualified by character, ability, and training; and

(5) that those who prove unworthy of their privileges have those privileges deprived.

OBLIGATIONS IN MONUMENTING BOUNDARIES

Every boundary survey for a client establishes the boundary of an adjoiner. One of the reasons for giving surveyors the exclusive privilege of marking boundaries is to prevent the unskilled from monumenting lines that encroach on the bona fide rights of an adjoiner. As an obligation to the public, the surveyor should not, in any way, assist a client in acquiring rights to land that are not his to enjoy.

Example 1. - Client "A" asks Surveyor "B" to survey a certain parcel of land by commencing at an existing fence said to be his westerly boundary. The surveyor should refuse. While the surveyor has no liability to the client, since he would be doing as requested, he should decline starting a survey without knowing where the written title lines are. He has an obligation to the public and the adjoiner not to encroach on their rights.

Example 2. - A surveyor is requested to monument a certain property in accordance with a deed known by the surveyor to be defective. If the monuments are set, the client will appear to have land that is not rightfully his. The surveyor should withdraw. He has an obligation to refuse to assist knowingly in morally wrong acts.

STIRRING UP LITIGATIONS

Stirring up litigation, according to common law, is a crime known as maintenance. If the offender in a land boundary case is a surveyor, he is doubly at fault. A surveyor may act as an arbitrator and try to smooth over a difficult boundary situation, but he should not stir up litigation as a solution to the problem, especially where he would collect an expert's fee as part of the litigation.

Because the surveyor is to protect the bona fide rights of the adjoiner, he should not hesitate to point out what the rights of the adjoiner are. If there is long-continued possession and title has probably passed by acts of possession and knowledge of such facts would tend to prevent the client from entering in litigation, the surveyor should not hesitate to disclose such facts. However, the surveyor should also suggest that attorneys are the proper parties to render an opinion on such matters.

AIDING UNAUTHORIZED SURVEYING PRACTICE

No surveyor shall permit his name to be used in aid of, or to make possible, the unauthorized practice of surveying by any agency, personal or corporate. (Adapted from American Bar Association, Canon 47).

What constitutes unauthorized practice of surveying must ultimately be resolved by the courts, and ethics committees should be bound by their findings.

The selling of signatures for a fee, i.e., signing a surveyor's certificate and certifying to the correctness of a survey where the work was not performed by himself, his employees, or his direct subordinates, is the most flagrant violation of the intent of a registration law.

A layman may be hired properly by a surveyor, provided his service does not constitute the practice of surveying and that his compensation is not a proportion of the fee. Having a layman as a partner in charge of a corporation practicing surveying is a violation of ethics.

QUALIFICATION OF SURVEYORS

Every applicant for registration must furnish a list of professional men as references. It is the duty of those replying to the Board of Registration, in response to questions as to a person's qualifications, to disclose all unfavorable as well as favorable qualifications of the applicant. Friendship, family relationships, sympathy, or any other reason should not influence his thinking. Likewise, surveyors and surveyor organizations should not hesitate to comment on the quality of the questions being asked on surveyor examinations.

UNWORTHY SURVEYORS

Occasionally those who are licensed, by their conduct, prove themselves unworthy of licensing and should have their privileges removed. Surveyors are better able than laymen to appraise the qualifications of other surveyors. If a surveyor is frequently negligent in his duties, that fact will be noticed by several surveyors, who, as a group, can prefer charges.

SURVEYORS' OBLIGATIONS TO CLIENTS

The surveyor, when performing a given service for his client, assumes certain ethical obligations in addition to liabilities. But these obligations to the client may not supersede or interfere with the surveyor's obligations to his colleagues or to the public. He should serve his client faithfully, but he should refuse to do that which is illegal, unethical, or violates a duty to others. The surveyor advises his clients as to what is right and proper, and if the client insists otherwise the surveyor should withdraw.

CORRECT SURVEY

Regardless of the fee charged, the surveyor is obligated to perform a correct survey within specified accuracy.

While there are times when the property owner will agree that an inaccurate or approximate property line survey will suffice for his purpose, the surveyor ought not to accept such a commission. Another surveyor, at a later date, discovering the approximate survey monuments, will take a dim view of the surveyor's ability. Future owners, not knowing the circumstances under which the monuments were established, might be misled. Furthermore, approximately located monuments may be the basis for fraud or deceit on the part of the property owner or the client. Most people assume that surveyors' monuments are located correctly; hence the mere finding of an approximate property corner may be the cause of a costly misconception.

SUBCONTRACTING WORK

The property-line surveyor who accepts a commission to do a boundary survey may not, except with the consent and knowledge of the client, subcontract or let another organization perform the work.

Whenever a client employs a surveyor, he has a right to assume that that surveyor will supervise and direct the work. Subcontracting to another, without the knowledge of the client, is a breach of ethics. A client seeks a particular surveyor because he has confidence in him. If he had wanted another surveyor he would have gone to him in the first place.

It is distinctly proper to refer a client to a colleague whenever a surveyor is too busy or does not have the proper knowledge or facilities to handle the job. But the referral should be without any idea of a kickback on a fee.

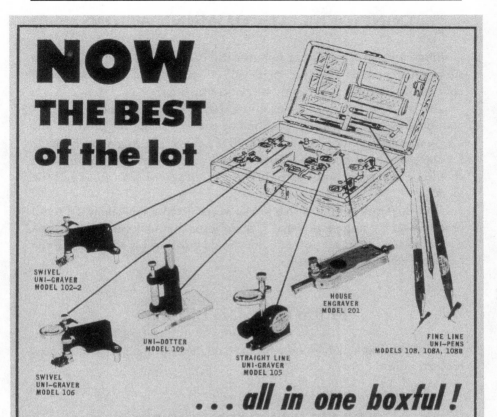

CONFIDENTIAL COMMUNICATIONS

Communications between the surveyor and client are confidential. But the surveyor may not be a party to an illegal act or fraud, and communications concerning illegal acts or frauds are not confidential.

At law, the surveyor is not given the right to withhold privileged communications. But, unless required by law to disclose the business of a client, communications are confidential. If a client is having a survey made for the purpose of building a large commercial center, such information should be kept secret until such time as the client wishes to announce the facts.

But this does not mean that the surveyor is to remain silent if a fraud or illegal act is being perpetrated. The surveyor should never join in nor be a party to any illegal act or fraud, nor should he allow his silence to be the cause of fraud or an illegal act.

PERSONAL INTEREST

The surveyor should not, for his personal gain, take advantage of confidences reposed in him.

REBATES AND DOUBLE FEES

The surveyor shall not accept any remuneration other than his stated charges for services rendered his clients. Accepting a fee from the client and a contractor lends the flavor of collusion. But if the client has full knowledge of such facts, no harm can be done. Fees derived merely because of referral to another are entirely unethical.

The surveyor should never be in a position that, because of remunerations or personal interests, it will interfere with his obligations to his client.

ADJOINING SURVEYS

The surveyor often monuments adjoining properties, but where there is a property line dispute, the surveyor should avoid rendering services for the adjoiner unless he has the consent of his client.

In property disputes, the arguments are usually over encroachments.

A surveyor employed to determine the status of encroachments cannot very well reveal them to a neighbor for another fee. In litigation a surveyor consulted by one party cannot ethically advise the other side, especially if he possesses confidential information. Of course, the surveyor must testify in court to all things truthfully and may not withhold any information he is asked about; but this does not mean that he should have pre-consultations with the opposing side.

CONFLICTING INTERESTS

If a surveyor owns adjoining property, or has an interest in it, he should so inform a prospective client. In the minds of many people is the suspicion that others are always biased towards their own interests. If a surveyor performs a service for such a person without revealing his interest in adjoining property, he may be placed in an embarrassing position if trouble or litigation ensues.

SURVEYORS' OBLIGATIONS TO OTHER SURVEYORS

A profession is partially distinguished by the fairness and courteousness of one practitioner to another and their unwillingness to encroach upon the clients of another. Businesses compete aggressively for competitors' customers; professions do not. A member of a profession values the esteem of his colleagues and the prestige of his calling, especially so the more mature his age. But those who advertise or steal another's customers do not induce cordial reception or pleasant relationship, as it ought to exist, among surveyors. Thus surveyors have obligations to one another.

PROFESSIONAL REPUTATION

The surveyor or engineer does not attempt to injure falsely or maliciously, directly or indirectly, the professional reputation, prospects, or business of another surveyor or engineer.

Confidence in and respect for a profession are gained by praise of one member for another. Constant sniping between professional people can only degrade the profession.

This ethical rule prohibits the engineer or surveyor from "falsely" or "maliciously" harming the reputation of another. This does not prohibit the right of any surveyor to give proper advice to those seeking relief from negligent surveyors. Surveyors should expose, at the proper time and place, dishonest conduct in their profession and should not hesitate to accept employment that will assist a client who has been wronged. But it is distinctly bad taste and ill manners to accept the word of the client without first checking with the colleague. Many times those making the accusations are not entirely unbiased in their presentation of their side of the story.

EMPLOYMENT

It is unprofessional to attempt to supplant another Engineer or Land Surveyor by means prohibited by this code of ethics after definite steps have been taken towards his employment. It is unprofessional to compete with another Engineer or Surveyor for employment on the basis of professional fees, by reducing his usual fees and in this manner attempting to underbid after being informed of the fees named by another.

A surveyor may not properly make a competitive bid for professional service nor may he use decreased fees to entice a client from another. A former employee, who is now starting his own business, may not properly attempt to induce his former employer's clients to turn their accounts over to him, nor should he send announcements of his new office to the clients of his former employer. But he need not refuse employment from them provided he has not either directly or indirectly solicited employment from them.

DISCOVERED ERRORS

In the event a land surveyor discovers an error or disagrees with the work of another land surveyor, it is the duty of that surveyor to inform the other surveyor of such fact.

Surveys are not for the purpose of stirring up arguments and fights between neighbors. If the adjoining property has been surveyed by another surveyor and the two surveys are not in agreement, the matter should be discussed between the surveyors prior to announcing that an error exists. Sometimes evidence found on the first survey may indicate that a different principle should be used in the later survey. Of course, if a surveyor has made a genuine error, other surveyors should not honor the error, but the first surveyor should be given an opportunity to prove the correctness of his survey if he can.

REVIEW OF ANOTHER'S WORK

It is unprofessional to review the work of another Engineer or Land Surveyor for the same client, except with the knowledge or consent of such Engineer or Land Surveyor, or unless the connection of such Engineer or Land Surveyor with the work has been terminated.

Consulting with another's client is considered or appears to be an attempt to supplant the engineer or surveyor. If a request is made to review the work of another, the person making the request should be informed of the ethics involved, and the other surveyor should be promptly notified of the facts. Even in the event that the work of the other surveyor appears to be fraudulent or neglectful, and the other surveyor probably will be charged with misconduct, it is the duty of the surveyor to communicate with the other surveyor and give him the opportunity of reply.

ADVERTISING

It is unprofessional to advertise in self-laudatory language, or in any other manner derogatory to the dignity of the profession.

What is advertising in self-laudatory language is not exactly definable and until surveyors and engineers are more specific, this rule of ethics will have little force. Other professions are more detailed and specific. The sign on an office building (attorneys) is tested by whether the sign is calculated to enable a person looking for a particular lawyer to find him or whether the sign is calculated to attract the attention of persons who might be looking for a lawyer. Canon 27 of the American Bar Association's Professional Ethics states: "It is unprofessional to solicit professional employment by circulars, advertisements, through touters, or by personal communications or interviews not warranted by personal relations. Indirect advertisements for professional employment such as furnishing of inspiring newspaper comments, or procuring his photograph to be published in connection with causes in which the lawyer has been or is engaged or concerning the manner of their conduct, the magnitude of the interest involved, the importance of the lawyer's position, and all other like self-laudation, offend the traditions, and lower the tone of our profession and are reprehensible; but the customary use of simple professional cards is not improper."

DISCREDIT TO THE PROFESSION

It is unprofessional to act in any manner or engage in any practice which will tend to bring discredit on the honor or dignity of the Engineering and or Land Surveying Professions.

A surveyor should not aid a client in perpetrating a fraud nor assist him in an illegal act. He should not, in his personal appearance or manner of conduct before the public or others, bring discredit to himself as a professional man.

FEES

No division of fees for surveying service is proper, except with another surveyor or engineer who by his license is permitted to do land surveying work, based upon a division of service or responsibility. In determining the amount of the fee, it is proper to consider: (1) the time and labor required, the novelty and difficulty of the questions involved, and the skill requisite properly to conduct the survey; (2) the customary charges of the surveyor associations for similar service; (3) the amount of liability involved and the benefits resulting to the client from the services; (4) the contingency or the certainty of the compensation; and (5) the character of the employment, whether casual or for an established and constant client. No one of these considerations in itself is controlling. They are mere guides in ascertaining the real value of the service.

In determining the customary charges of the Surveyors' Associations for similar services, it is proper for a surveyor to consider a schedule of minimum fees adopted by a Surveyors Association, but no surveyor should permit himself to be controlled thereby as his sole guide in determining the amount of his fee.

Minimum fee schedules are a guide and can never be a binding agreement between surveyors. Antitrust laws prohibit such price fixing.

INTERMEDIARIES

The professional services of a surveyor should not be controlled or exploited by any lay agency, personal or corporate, which intervenes between client and surveyor.

****

THE PROFESSIONAL STATUS OF LAND SURVEYORS

BY CURTIS M. BROWN *

MARCH 1961

AT THE present time, the professional status of the land surveyor is the subject of national discussion. Within the next few years the surveyor will be in one of two positions. First, he can have subprofessional standing with low educational requirements and minor areas of practice, or, second, he can bring himself up to the standards of the better professions and assert himself in a larger area of practice. The surveyor cannot afford to stand still. The engineers, land planners, and the like are advancing their stature at a rapid pace, and if they pass the surveyor too far they will supplant him.

All of you are no doubt acquainted with the fact that the original unaccepted report of the American Society of Civil Engineers task committee excluded surveying as a part of civil engineering. The later report, as adopted, included land surveying as a branch of civil engineering. At the recent American Congress on Surveying and Mapping meeting, the ASCE task committee's report, with some modifications to better suit the land surveyor, was adopted by the ACSM status committee.

At the same time the status committee was having its problems resolved, the National Council of State Boards of Engineering Examiner's special committee was meeting to consider a model law (including educational requirements) for surveyors. This meeting was called to coincide with the ACSM meeting so that the two groups could merge ideas. The talks did bring about a unification of many thoughts.

Before pointing out what areas of agreement were achieved at this meeting, a general discussion of the present status of the land surveyor is advisable.

Attaining Professional Stature.

Professional stature cannot be attained by self-proclamation. The lazy say, "give me the prize without the training, the wages without work, the reward without the quest, heaven without probation, a profession's prestige without a profession's skill." If the land surveyor is to have professional standing, that standing must be earned and bestowed upon him by others.

You and I know and believe that land surveying is a profession. But whether it is a profession or not is not our privilege to proclaim; others are the judges. The opinion of learned men and the opinion of the public is the proof.

Fortunately for the world, professional stature is something that must be earned, not merely claimed. If it were otherwise, everyone would soon lay claim to a higher standing, whether qualified or not. Many do attempt to filch good names. The A.F.L. engine operator (dozer operators and the like) inflate their egos by calling themselves "operating engineers." This, of course, proves to them that they are engineers; hence, it is their right to organize all surveyors as a part of the operating engineers union. The boy who carries the stake bag, coats, lunches, and water is certain of his important position in society if he is called an engineering aid rather than a flunky 3rd grade. Mere claiming a good name is not proof that a person has the right to the name. A person's actions, behavior, and conduct are far more potent proof.

The proof of what we are is not what we claim to be. The proof is what others know us to be. We might well ask ourselves, what, on the average, do others think of us?

The professions that you and I and everyone recognize and acclaim as professions, i.e., the doctors, attorneys, and clergy, need not use the title professional doctor, professional attorney, or professional clergy; everyone considers them professional. The title was bestowed upon them because their ethics, behavior, and standing in community. If the land surveyors wish to acquire and maintain a professional reputation, they must earn that right by the average standing, of the majority of all land surveyors.

Definition of a Profession.

I have no intention of trying to pinpoint a definition of what constitutes a profession; even the experts have varied opinions. To make matters worse, there are two definitions - one broad and one restricted. Quotations from a few cases at law will help us understand the meaning.

From *State v. Cohn* (184 LA 53) is quoted, "Very generally the term 'profession' is employed as referring to a calling in which one professes to have acquired some special knowledge, used by way of instructing, guiding, or advising others or of serving them in some art. Formerly theology, law, and medicine were specifically known as 'the professions,' but, as the applications of science and learning are extended to other departments of affairs, other vocations also received the name. The word 'profession' is a practical dealing with affairs as distinguished from mere study or investigation; and an application of such knowledge for others as a vocation, as distinguished from the pursuits for its own purposes."

While research in science is certainly a learned occupation requiring special knowledge, it certainly is not a profession. A profession deals with the affairs of others; it aids others; it does not merely seek knowledge for the sake of gaining knowledge.

From 107 S.W. 555 is quoted, "The word 'profession' in its larger meaning, means occupation, that is, if not industrial, mechanical, agricultural, or the like, to whatever one devotes oneself; the business which one professes to understand and follow. In a restricted sense it only applies to the learned professions."

One last quotation is from *Stiner v. Yelle* (174 Wash 402) and it apparently refers to the higher type of profession. "A 'Profession' is not a money-getting business. It has no element of commercialism in it. True, the professional man seeks to live by what he earns, but his main purpose and desire is to be of service to those who seek his aid and to the community of which he is a necessary part. In some instances, where the recipient is able to respond, seemingly large fees may be paid, but to others unable to pay adequately, or at all, the professional service is usually cheerfully rendered."

From this, it is obvious that in a broad sense "profession" includes many fields such as college professors, engineers, professional boxers, and surveyors, all with varying degrees of qualifications. In a narrow sense there are only three professions, the learned professions of theology, law, and medicine.

Land surveying to me is a profession; my only question is one of classification of standing. I am not so naive as to believe that we, at the present time and in the opinion of others, are anywhere near equal in stature with the three learned professions, but I do believe that by sustained effort we can achieve a standing comparable to the learned professions.

Attributes of a Profession.

Most surveyors have sufficient ego to want to measure up to the three learned professions rather than to measure down to those of doubtful standing whose only claim to fame may be by self proclamation. If the surveyor is to compare with the learned professions, he must approach the attributes of those professions and some of those attributes are:

1. Superior education in a field of knowledge.

2. Service to the public.

3. The possibility of gaining highest eminence without necessarily earning much money.

4. Providing services to those unable to pay.

5. Independent judgment and liability as a result of that judgment.

6. Ethics.

7. If fees are charged those able to pay, fees are dependent upon knowledge rather than labor or product.

Without question, superior education in a field of knowledge is an essential feature of a profession, and there is little question but what a *good* professional land surveyor should have superior knowledge in a specialized field. Some individual land surveyors, by self-effort or by formal training in colleges, are well educated, but, as compared to the learned professions, are surveyors required to have an equivalent amount of knowledge? How many licensed practicing surveyors have the benefit of a college degree as compared to the doctors, attorneys, and clergy? Proof of the simplicity of our knowledge requirements can be had by looking at the past surveyor examinations administered in many states. In a number of states no registration or examination is needed; in others the examination is so simplified that even the flunky, 3rd grade, could make a good showing. No wonder many look askance at our profession. The standing of all surveyors as a professional group will suffer unless we as a whole raise our requirements. Experience is never a complete substitute for education. It augments education, but can never supplant education. Education, of course, can be attained either formally at college or self taught at home. Whichever way it may be gained, there is no reason for allowing a professional surveyor to be registered without having superior knowledge. Without superior knowledge, we have an inferior profession.

Man's knowledge in itself does not make a profession; man must use knowledge to aid, assist, teach, or benefit others. Application of knowledge to the affairs of others is an essential part of the definition of a profession.

The process of acquiring knowledge and the process of application of knowledge are distinctly different. Parrots can memorize a vocabulary of sorts, but who has ever observed a parrot with the ability to tell another of his needs? The knowledge and experience of a professional man combined with his ability to reason and arrive at a solution to a problem is why others seek his advice. The success or failure of each of us is, in a measure, due to our reasoning ability.

In the learned professions the professional man has a call of duty beyond that of a fee. The doctors are obligated to serve the sick regardless of ability to pay; the clergy do not turn away those in trouble; the attorneys defend the criminal. However, it is noted that the doctors and attorneys do charge a fee and those able to pay, must pay. This is as it ought to be.

The land surveyor does not display this type of obligation. It is doubtful if many surveyors would willingly serve those incapable of paying the required fee. Land surveying is not an urgent necessity; if it is not done today, it can be done tomorrow. If a person cannot pay today, his survey can wait until tomorrow. Attorneys more or less adopt this attitude for services in connection with business matters.

The surveyor does have moral obligations to the public and among them is the duty to never subtract from the rights of adjoins. Every boundary survey for a client establishes the boundary of an adjoined. One of the reasons for giving surveyors the exclusive privilege of marking boundaries is to prevent the unskilled from monumenting lines that encroach on the bona fide rights of others. As an obligation to the public, the surveyor should not, in any way, assist a client in acquiring rights to land that are not his to enjoy.

Any surveyor can attain eminence without necessarily earning much money. In your own area, what do other surveyors and the public think of you? Do they consider you ethical? Do they seek you out for advice? Have you contributed anything to the surveying profession, or do you just sit back and let others advance the profession? Is earning a dollar by any means more important than maintaining a principle? Will you sell your signature? Do you aid others in evading the licensing act? Do you degrade your fellow land surveyors? Have you actively pushed the cause of all surveyors or do you selfishly only look out for yourself? Are you active in your professional society? Have you had articles published in a professional surveyor's magazine? Do you serve on committees? Or, do you just sit back on your prerogatives? One of the first duties of a professional man is to advance his profession. These questions serve to evaluate you. It is only by the concerted effort of all, which we as a group will advance to an unquestioned professional stature. In every community we find those that are substandard and those that have attained eminence. Which are you?

Attorneys and doctors charge a fee, which is not dependent upon the physical labor or force applied. Personal knowledge gained through education and experience creates the demand for the service rather than the size of the muscle on the arm. Contracting is for businessmen actively competing on the basis of the lowest cost or the lowest bid. The moment services are based upon the lowest price, a profession has reduced itself to a business. Service based upon superior knowledge is the foundation of the fee of a professional. Are you a member of a profession, or are you a businessman? Many individuals in the matter of fees have attained professional standing. From the complaints I have heard in various meetings, I can only assume that, as a group, on the average, surveyors have not attained professional stature in their methods of charging fees.

Money, in itself, does not enter into the definition of a profession, but it does have a profound influence on what others think of a profession. Members of a group that show by their outward appearances that they are not successful in handling their own financial affairs can hardly instill confidence in the public. A person who uses antiquated equipment and the back room of his house as an office is not likely to contribute to professional standing. Success breeds success. Outward appearances do count. They are a part of the overall picture.

Ethics is that branch of moral science, which treats of the duties that a member of a profession owes to the public, to his professional brethren, and to his client. Without ethics, land surveying can never be a profession.

Everyone is familiar with the fact that an individual may strictly observe the laws of the land and yet be an undesirable citizen and a poor neighbor. Lord Moulton in an article in the Atlantic Monthly (134 Atlantic Monthly 1, 13, 1924) stated, "The real greatness of a nation, its true civilization, is measured by the extent of Obedience to the Unenforceable." Ethics are often unenforceable. True professional stature arises from obedience to the unenforceable.

Advocating observances of ethics is not sufficient; the surveyor's personal example is far more important. It is not sufficient that the surveyor alone feels that he has honesty and integrity; the public, clients, and fellow practitioners must also believe so. The proof of observance of ethics lies in the opinions of others.

If we, as surveyors, are to maintain a respected position as professionals in the community, we must look beyond the club of the law to ethical standards which prohibit the doing of that which the law does not forbid.

What Others Think of Us.

What is the present professional status of a particular surveyor or all land surveyors can only be answered by examining what others think of us. And what others think of us varies considerably depending upon which group or individual you ask. The opinion of the courts is distinctly at contrast with the educators. The layman's opinion is different from that of a non-surveyor engineer.

Courts, in response to liability litigation, have taken a positive stand on the status of all land surveyors. In the eyes of the law the land surveyor is treated with professional respect; he has all the liability accorded a professional man. While from the viewpoint of the pocketbook this privilege of liability does have disadvantages, it is proof, in a backhanded way, that the land surveyor is above the technician level.

The word privilege of liability was used advisedly. Human nature, being what it is, always offers a temptation to meet competition by doing a poorer job for less money. But professional liability is independent of the fee. A person agreeing to do a poorer job for less money carries identical liability to that of a person doing a better job for more money. This is as it ought to be.

Since we, as surveyors, are liable, one of the greatest deterrents to substandard work is this liability. While liability to the individual may be considered a disadvantage, it is an advantage to a profession as a whole. Without liability, I fear that those willing to do poorer work for less money would soon ruin the professional standing of all land surveyors. And so I say, professional liability is a privilege tending to prove the land surveyor's professional standing.

The courts say that we as a group are professional men; but this is not prima facie proof that everyone thinks that each of us is, nor is it proof that we are looked upon with equal standing to the learned professions. If we are to enjoy the standing and dignity afforded professional men, others must know and act as if they believe we are professional men. What do educators think?

Without doubt the educators are the most severe critics of our reputation, and their criticism has justifiable merit. As a whole, and without question, we are not nearly as well educated as is required of the learned professions. We are usually the low men on the totem pole with respect to engineering. Engineering professors, with minor exceptions, are more than likely to refer to the surveyor as a "technician" or sub-professional requiring a small amount of specialized education that can be acquired by the apprentice system. As proof of this, we need only glance at the college engineering curriculum. Surveying, on the average, has been reduced to nothing more than a few hours of fragmentary instructions covering limited phases of the work. Every year additional college summer surveying camps are being abandoned. In short, we are being gradually ousted as a part of engineering education.

In the eyes of the average engineer the average land surveyor is not top-grade "A" quality, and this is probably the result of educational differences. The Professional Engineers Society, with minor exceptions, does not extend surveyors the privilege of membership. Surveyors are looked upon as second grade citizens and assigned to functional groups. Even the American Society of Civil Engineers displayed considerable doubt, to judge by the first report of its task committee. The second report restored the surveyors to membership possibilities. But in their wording for the requirements to advance to the "fellow" grade, they have excluded the surveyor from the possibility of ever achieving this honor. After questioning many engineers of all classifications on this subject, I would say that, on the average, a majority of engineers are more apt to consider land surveyors as technicians rather than as professional men. In a few states, perhaps not exceeding five, surveyors are looked upon with favor.

Within land surveying practice there are many grades of workers. One of our failures, and many engineers' failures, is to properly distinguish between chainmen, draftsmen, technicians, and the professional level. On highway work, the engineer in charge has surveyors who make measurements to determine the shape of the ground. They are merely measuring the ground as it exists and recording the facts as they are. To be sure, the surveyor must have superior ability in knowing how to use instruments and how to make measurements, but this is purely technical. He does not design the road nor does he utilize his measurements. Again, the engineer may tell the surveyor to grade-stake a road in accordance with a given plan. Since no design or judgment is involved, it is a purely technical matter. To the average engineer, the surveyor is a technician who carries out his orders. And often he is just that. But the engineer frequently overlooks the fact that there is a professional land-surveyor level.

Perhaps one of the greatest attributes of a successful practitioner is measured by how well he gets along with others. Knowledge alone does not make a professional man. He must have knowledge and use that knowledge in guiding, teaching, or instructing others, and his success in this depends up how well he can influence others. We have all seen those who have superior knowledge but who are pugnacious, contrary, unyielding, and never wrong. We have all seen those that display the fiery impulse of infuriated calm and those that have the backbone of a wet noodle. Such types seldom succeed as professional men. Often such individuals fail to understand why they cannot get business, and as a final desperate effort they assume that price is the reason and resort to trying to get business by the nonprofessional means of being the low bidder.

The problem of varying ability is common to all professions. Some doctors have good public relations, others do not. This does not explain why one profession is superior to another, it merely explains why some individuals attain greater success than others. To a certain extent all professions are judged by how each individual member gets along with others.

Our Present Shortcomings.

There is no doubt but that land surveying is entitled to professional status of some sort within the broader meaning of the term; the courts indicate such by their decisions. But there is also no doubt that we, on the average, do not measure up to the three learned professions or for that matter, to any of the other better professions.

In the minds of most surveyors, there is no question but that they would like to be looked upon with the same respect, dignity, and standing as the doctor, the attorney, or the clergyman. I have repeatedly heard surveyors compare themselves with doctors. No shortcut to gaining this prestige exists; it must be earned, and as yet, on the average, we have not earned it.

Land surveying can be a profession approaching the level of the learned professions, and whether we wish it to be so or not is ours to decide by group behavior - that is action, not wishful thinking.

Education and knowledge can never be purchased; each individual must acquire these by his own efforts. All the money in the world will not cram knowledge into the heads of those unwilling to learn. It is recognized that all education is not acquired in colleges; but colleges are the major source of education. They are the repository or storage place for accumulated knowledge.

All learned professions have as one characteristic specialized and extensive knowledge in a particular field, and that particular field is offered in the curriculum of many institutes of higher learning. How many colleges offer a degree in land surveying? How many offer a masters degree in geodesy? Colleges simply do not recognize land surveying as a learned profession, and until they do we will not be classified as professionals.

The major deterrent to our becoming a learned profession is our low requirements for the right to practice. So long as we have low admission requirements, we will have low standards of practice and low public opinion. A person must know what is right and wrong before he can practice right. If we are satisfied with our present low professional standing, that of a sub-profession not measuring up to the standards of the better professions, we should do nothing. But if we want to improve our standing, we must raise our standards.

Without ethics, a group of people can never be a profession. Realizing this, most land surveyor groups have adopted some form of ethics; but these ethics are without effective enforcement. The lawyer, for failure to abide by ethics, can be disbarred. The doctor can be removed from the American Medical Association and thus lose hospital practice rights. The clergy can be defrocked. Who has ever heard of a land surveyor being de-licensed for failure to observe ethics? We must seek and find a way to enforce ethics.

An essential part of the definition of a profession is service to others, i.e., knowledge is used to aid and assist fellow men. I presume this means all men. If we are a profession, should we not have free exchange of information between ourselves? How many secretly hoard survey evidence and refuse to allow fellow practitioners the privilege of knowing what formerly existed? Are we a business in this matter or are we a profession? Fortunately, in our area, but not in all of our State, we do have extensive free exchange of information, but from conversations with various surveyors in many areas, I can only assume that this practice is not as widespread as it ought to be.

In California's Owens Valley we have two lakes. One is fresh and trout are in it. Trees spread their branches over it and children play along its shores. A river flows into this lake and out into a second lake. Here in the second lake are no fish and no children's laughter. Travelers choose other routes. Neither man, beast, or fowl will drink of its waters. There is a difference between the two lakes. The first lake receives fresh mountain water. For every drop that flows in another drop flows out. The other lake is shrewder. Every drop it gets, it keeps. The first lake receives and gives, the second lake receives, does not give, and is salted to death. Are we going to be like the first lake and receive and give information, or are we going to be like the second lake and jealously hoard professional information?

Among the many things that would elevate the surveyor to higher stature, perhaps the most important is the word "agreement." All of us have heard the complaint, "it is a notorious fact that no two surveyors are in agreement on the position of a corner." Differences between surveyors are a cause of degradation. We prove by our own survey monuments that we are incompetent, since we cannot all arrive at the same location using the same written deed.

Differences are caused by numerous circumstances, some of which can never be remedied by the surveyor, but in all too numerous instances surveyors cause differences. We, in California, have overcome much of this by certain practices that ought to be a part of all registration acts. Specifically these are:

1. Filing public records of surveys showing all evidence found and all points set.

2. Placing the surveyor's license number on every monument set.

The surveyor is given exclusive privilege to monument property lines, and in exchange for this exclusive privilege he ought to and does have obligations to the public. Original monument evidence should never be the exclusive property of one; it should be the knowledge of all.

Deeds have a chain of title back to their inception. The validity and correctness of a deed is based upon that chain of title. Similarly, monuments should have a continuous chain of history. The original surveyor sets a stone mound for the section corner. Surveyor number two finds a stone mound for the section corner and sets a 2" iron pipe. Surveyor number three finds the 2" pipe and sets reference points 30 feet on each side of a new proposed road. Surveyor number four finds the reference monuments and resets the true section corner in the centerline of the new road. Surveyor number five finds the new monument in the centerline and wants to prove its identity and the correctness of its position. How can he do this without a continuous record of what surveyors numbers 1, 2, 3, and 4 did? The surveyor who discovers and alters evidence has a duty to record and maintain a record of what he did, and unless that record is a public record, it will soon be lost with the death of the surveyor. This is the reason that California has a law that makes it mandatory to file a record of survey under certain circumstances, and these circumstances are:

(a) Material evidence, which in whole or in part does not appear on any map or record previously recorded or filed in the office of the County Recorder, County Clerk, municipal or county surveying department, or in the records of the Bureau of Land Management of the United States.

(b) A material discrepancy with such record.

(c) Evidence that, by reasonable analysis, might result in alternate positions of lines or points.

(d) The establishment of one or more lines not shown on any such map, the positions of which are not ascertainable from an inspection of such map without trigonometric calculations.

On the record of survey must be shown all evidence found and all new points set.

Whenever a monument is discovered it has little value without evidence of its origin. By requiring a license number on every point set by a surveyor, the identity of the point can usually be established by calling the surveyor. This is an incentive to exchange information and maintain liaison between surveyors. If a discrepancy is discovered, the first surveyor can be immediately notified and differences worked out prior to a client's display of a desire for revenge on a hostile neighbor.

Conclusions and Recommendations.

Any single land surveyor can attain outstanding eminence as a professional man. Of necessity, his knowledge would have to be broad enough to include an intimate acquaintance with such related fields as geodesy, photogrammetry, cartography, and land law. His only limitations would be his own desires and his own ability to push his knowledge, his behavior, his conduct, and his ethics to the forefront. A good professional man cannot be a recluse; one of the essential definitions of a professional man is that he serves the public and serves them well.

There are bright spots throughout the United States. Ohio has equal or almost equal knowledge requirements as compared to the civil engineer. California and Massachusetts have good standing, though even here improvements can be made. Minnesota surveyors, by their successful sponsoring of the platting law, have enormously enhanced their professional standing.

Unfortunately, those in the same group are often tarred by the same brush. If most land surveyors throughout the United States are of low professional standing, all will tend to be thought of in the same vein. If we as a group are to be thought of with the dignity and respect that we would like to command, we must all be above reproach. Among the many things that we can do to improve our standing are those areas of tentative agreement reached between the various model-law committees at the ACSM annual meeting and these are:

1. The knowledge or educational requirements of the surveyor should be raised to an equivalent level with that of the civil engineer. This does not mean that both would be given the same examination, nor that both will need to know the same subject matter. It merely means that the surveyor will need to know much more than is being asked of him in present examinations. Ignorance is a voluntary misfortune and should not be tolerated in our profession.

2. Require a minimum of 16 hours of written examination. This would be divided into two parts, one part on fundamentals and one part on professional practice. Passage of the Engineer-in-Training examination of the civil engineer or the passing of the first 8-hour test would entitle a person to take the second half on professional practice of surveyors. I am sure that if a civil engineer can pass the EIT examination he would be qualified in the fundamental mathematics of surveying.

3. The surveyor will be allowed to perform every step in the making of subdivisions. Since this would allow him to design water lines, paving grading, etc., his examination must include these subjects. His scope of examination is increased.

4. Always keep the door open so that it is possible for a man to progress by self-education to the professional level. Formal education in college is merely one of the many ways that a man can acquire an education. A college degree is proof of theoretical training in a given area. The lack of a college degree is certainly not an indication of a man's knowledge. Many have acquired excellent education by their own efforts. After examining present-

day college civil-engineering curricula, I will not hesitate to say that possessing a civil engineering degree is not proof of adequate training in surveying.

5. Require eight years of experience in responsible charge, four years of which may be acquired by an accredited college degree. And that college accreditation implies accreditation in surveying subjects - not thermodynamics, electricity, and the like.

These areas of agreement were attained without a contrary opinion. If these objectives can be put into practice, I am sure the professional tone of all surveying will be on an equivalent standing with that of other learned professions.

The ASCE task committee envisioned that at a future date both the surveyor and engineer would, on the average, have equivalent planes of practice and equivalent professional standing and ideals. At such time, if each professional so desired, it would be possible for reduction to one license. Whether that is advisable or not, we need not concern ourselves; that decision will be made by the next generation.

Most registration acts are only definitions of who may practice surveying; they do not obligate the surveyor to file records of his work nor do they require him to use license numbers on monuments. By adding to most registration laws and requiring surveyors to abide by certain practices, the professional standing can be upgraded.

I have chosen the land surveyors profession because I like it and am proud of it. Although our office does do numerous engineering jobs, I never infer or imply in any way that I am an engineer. I know that we, as land surveyors, should have professional standing, but I also believe that we have not acquired the standing we ought to have. These remarks were designed to point out some of our weaknesses and suggest some remedies.

I started out with a thought and wish to close with the same thought. Professional stature is not gained by self-proclamation. Professional stature must be earned and can only be measured by what others think of us. If you want to find out whether you are a professional man, ask what others think, don't ask yourself. If you want to be a professional man, earn that right.

* Curtis M. Brown is Second Vice Chairman, Property Surveys Division, ACSM; Chairman Legislative Committee, Property Surveys Division: ACSM; a member of the committee of the American Society of Civil Engineers charged with the implementation of its Task Committee's report on "The Status of Surveying and Mapping in the United States";

author of *Boundary Control and Legal Principles*; and a member of the firm of Daniels, Brown and Hall, surveyors and engineers, in San Diego, California. The opinions reflected in this talk, which was given at the Minnesota Land Surveyors Association annual meeting in April 1960, are his own and do not necessarily reflect the official position of the American Congress on Surveying and Mapping.

– Editor

****

THE SURVEYOR AND THE LAW

MARCH 1961

From R. D. Comstock, Registered Engineer and Surveyor, Florida, via Charles A. Whitten and H. Paul Kaufman, comes this question,

"After 49 years of active work in surveying and property improvement I am retiring from practice, and in this connection a question has arisen which is of interest not only to myself but other local surveyors.

"Many of us have carried Errors and Omissions Insurance and the question arises as to the length of time a surveyor is responsible for his work. Is there a statute of limitations for professional men such as surveyors and engineers?"

My own inquiries on this subject are limited to California, but I am sure many of the remarks will be applicable in other places. We must concede that every State has its own regulations and you are bound by them.

(1) Practically all liability items have a statute of limitations.

(2) In California, as in many other States, the statute of limitations with respect to surveys is a given number of years after the discovery of an error.

I think this makes you "forever" liable - that is until death. But another law does give some relief. In California the statute of limitations or occupancy is five years. A person putting up a fence, a building, or the like cannot be ousted once the improvement has been in existence for five years. But if the improvement is removed prior to adverse occupancy rights ripening into a fee title, any new structure must go on the correct line. In effect this means liability is present for five years after improvements are erected.

Also, there is some relief when the property is sold by the client. Although in some States professional men have been held liable for third party actions (the person not paying the fee), it is not universally true. In California real estate has moved so fast that in five years there may be ten new owners. In such a situation the first surveyor would probably be out of the picture.

Most liability insurance covers only "claims arising during the time that the premium is in force." An additional fee is needed to cover cases resulting from surveys made prior to the effective date of the policy. If a person is to stay protected after retirement, he must carry insurance for a period of years after closing shop. In California five years may be adequate. This is a good question to take up with your liability insurance company.

One mode of backsight relief is to practice as a corporation. Here the surveyor is an employee. But I despise the corporation, since the non-register can hide behind the skirts of a corporation and effectively have a surveying practice. If a corporation has 100 percent of its stockholders as registered men, I see no problems, but as yet this is not a requirement in most States.

Perhaps, surveyors from other States would like to comment on this.

– CURTIS M. BROWN

****

COMMENT AND DISCUSSION

JUNE 1961

The pages of SURVEYING AND MAPPING are open to free and temperate discussion of all matters pertaining to the interests of the Congress. It is the purpose of this department to encourage comments on published material or the presentation of new ideas in an informal way.

– Editor

THE PROFESSIONAL STATUS OF LAND SURVEYORS

TRACY B. SLACK * - I write in answer to Curtis M. Brown's article appearing in the March (1960) issue of the *Quarterly Journal of the American Congress on Surveying and Mapping*, "The Professional Status of Land Surveyors."

While I must assume that Mr. Brown's desire is to "Lift up the fallen (or falling)" I am considerably irked by his opening remarks which include: "First, he can have sub-professional standing with low educational requirements and minor areas of practice, or second, he can bring himself up to the standards of the *better professions* (italics mine) and assert himself in a larger area of practice."

In his paragraph which begins, "Without doubt the educators are the most severe critics of our reputation, and their criticism has *justifiable merit*," I say "*Merit* be hanged!" since engineering professors have failed miserably to teach land surveying properly and by contrast have graded land surveying down and sometimes out. Mr. Brown moralizes with regard to low fees on the one hand and working as a public-spirited citizen with less regard to fees on the other.

I deduce from Mr. Brown's reference to a "better profession" an apology for the land surveyor, suggesting that a land surveyor is in some sort of competition with a doctor, lawyer, clergyman, or perhaps a civil engineer!

I do not hold with the idea that the American Society of Civil Engineers is altogether capable of deciding whether land surveying is or is not a branch of civil engineering. Their wavering tactics suggest a fear for the security of their own positions. Their attitude smacks of the old bromides about "being careful of the company you keep," "one cannot be too careful," etc. Another conclusion to be drawn is smugness. A pity.

The engineering schools have little more to offer as "educational requirements" to a student in land surveying than the mechanics they offer the student of civil engineering. During my forty years as a practicing land surveyor (and somewhat of a civil engineer) I have seen but one major effort as *text* for the land surveyor, and that from the pen of Mr. Brown and his co-author Fred H. Landgraf, though I do not take lightly my T. Baker, C. E.'s *Land & Engineering Surveying*, published in London. I gather that a land surveyor would be accepted if he should emerge as somewhat-of-a-civil-engineer, or, in other words, "Can't we dress him up in some sort of way so that he will look good enough not to embarrass the civil engineering profession which has rather hesitantly included land surveying as a branch of civil engineering?"

That "professional stature cannot be attained by self proclamation" is another fallacy. If a land surveyor has a complex about "being left behind," would this not parallel the seeming complex of the dentist who refers to himself as "doctor"? It is true that it is too easy in some states to practice or register as a land surveyor and a great deal of harm is done permanently to both the profession and to land records. I also fail to grasp Mr. Brown's concern as to "What others think of us" since, if we feel secure in our skills and integrity, we have "professional stature."

There are many new, fascinating, mechanical devices -- all the way from photogrammetry to license numbers on monuments -- suggested as ways of improving the *grade* of a land surveyor. I contend that these new and revolutionary methods available to the land surveyor are important mechanical devices, but nevertheless to a great extent as much an affectation as the would-be orator's use of high-flown language, when he would do well to emulate one W. S. Churchill. Contemporaries have been exercising their mechanical skills for years, setting beautifully monumented, exceptionally well closed, and artistically delineated property plans, where property bounds do not now, nor ever did, exist. I still find myself hypnotized by these things.

478

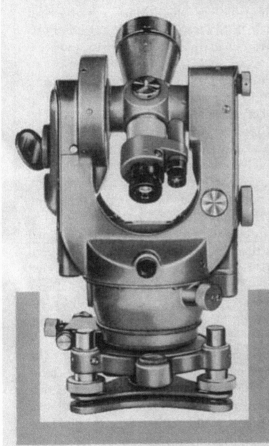

Appropriate to the seeming thread of a combination of sincere alarm, apology, a few homiletics about fees, work for the greater glory -- regardless of fees, ethics, behavior, etc., and a complex about the land surveyor's "professional stature" that runs through Mr. Brown's undoubtedly dedicated article, I am reminded of the saying "He who pleads his own case has a fool for a client" and another about the native of ancient Scotland, a chieftain, who arrived at the banquet late and sat in the nearest chair he could find, whereupon a nervous flunkey whispered "Mr. MacGregor, you're supposed to sit at the *head* of the table," at which MacGregor boomed out "WHEREVER MACGREGOR SITS IS THE HEAD OF THE TABLE!" "Professional stature" is attained through achievement and pride in a demand for one's skills.

I contend that the correction lies not in these window-dressing attempts and homiletics that tend to show a need of pulling ourselves up by our bootstraps, but in the need of real land surveying courses taught by accomplished land surveyors who have no complexes about how they would grade as civil engineers, and these courses augmented by a thorough course in all that a land surveyor (and a civil engineer) should know about real estate law and conveyancing, to be taught by eminent real estate attorneys who, again, have no complexes about real estate law as opposed to more remunerative civil and criminal cases.

I do not prescribe the above through any complex about "professional stature" but to correct the thesis that land surveying is second-rate civil engineering -- that did the practicing land surveyor have degrees in civil engineering there would be no question about his work, regardless of how little he knew about land surveying. Therein lies the whole fallacy, for many civil engineers and land surveyors have a wholesome respect for what they do not know about the other's field. The first-rate land surveyor is a superior person who is ethical and has the intelligence to appreciate the importance of his role as sometimes judge and jury -- acting for both his client and the "adjoiner." So many times not dishonesty but ignorance, that may prevail despite a college degree, can account for much poor handling of boundary or property problems. These are quite distinct from the problems that attend the mechanics of the purely technical questions, which call for more of a "pattern treatment" than the accumulated resourcefulness of an experienced practicing land surveyor. The so-called "woodlot surveyor," whose experience and interpretive abilities are quite superior, is apt to have a complex about these elusive mechanics a little out of his reach, while in reality he should command a wholesome respect for his basic knowledge of land surveying, just as the medical "specialist" who looks down his nose at the "general practitioner" who plugs away at the homely ailments that may be less spectacular but equally vital, so does the land surveyor plug away at the solution of properties problems that are less spectacular and less remunerative than the more purely technical problems that confront the specializing civil engineer.

Excepting forestry schools, which treat the subject earnestly, if inadequately, there do not seem to be any solid courses in land surveying taught anywhere, currently.

With due respect for the need to examine and employ existing and improved land surveying mechanics, I submit there are no more important attributes than that a land surveyor faithfully interpret, faithfully establish or reestablish, and record property monuments without prejudice. An important mechanical feature of land surveying, much neglected, is the establishment of controls, if previously established grids and benches are not economically available.

I have attempted to point out that it is both futile and meaningless to try to equate professions since their importance must derive from a demand and an achievement resulting from the exercise of separate and varying skills. It should be added that the moral and ethical code prescribed by Mr. Brown should be the usual pattern for all men in all endeavor.

* Civil Engineer, Administration, Department of Natural Resources, Commonwealth of Massachusetts; Registered Land Surveyor, Massachusetts and Connecticut; Member, Boston Society of Civil Engineers; and Member, American Congress on Surveying and Mapping. Mr. Slack resides at 177 Montague Road, North Amherst, Massachusetts.

****

COMMENT AND DISCUSSION

DECEMBER 1961

The pages of SURVEYING AND MAPPING are open to free and temperate discussion of all matters pertaining to the interests of the Congress. It is the purpose of this department to encourage comments on published material or the presentation of news ideas in an informal way.

– EDITOR

THE PROFESSIONAL STATUS
OF LAND SURVEYORS

JAY SWEET * -- I have just finished reading the March 1961 issue Of SURVEYING AND MAPPING and would like to comment on the article therein, written by yourself.

First, let me say that I consider your article, under the topic of "The Professional Status of Land Surveyors," the most complete and intelligently written paper on the subject that I have had the privilege of reading. My only comment on this article is in regard to a paragraph stating;

"Money, in itself, does not enter into the definition of a profession, but it does have a profound influence on what others think of a profession. Members of a group that show by their outward appearances that they are not successful in handling their own financial affairs, can hardly instill confidence in the public. A person who uses antiquated equipment and the back room of his house as an office is not likely to contribute to professional standing. Success breeds success. Outward appearances do count. They are part of the overall picture."

What was stated in that paragraph and the manner in which it was stated make it unquestionably true. However, all too many people are ignoring that last sentence. Confidence men and the corporation born of questionable motives (which you so bitterly attack in another article) are quick to recognize these truths and exploit them with deleterious effects on the profession.

The article referred to in the foregoing parenthesis was a reply to a letter from R. D. Comstock of Florida regarding liability insurance. In it you state your feelings and reasons for such, regarding the corporate entity in land surveying. As president and director of a practicing land surveying corporation I feel compelled to come to the defense of the corporate professionals.

Your reasoning that, a non-register can hide behind the skirts of a corporation and effectively have a surveying practice is not a justifiable argument in that there are more opportunities for a non-register to practice under the aegis of an unethical or indifferent license holder than can be found in the loopholes of corporate law. I know of no case where a non-register can practice under a corporation charter that the same condition couldn't be hypothetically manifested in a partnership. On the contrary, in many cases a corporate charter imposes restrictions not affecting partnership or sole proprietorships. Admittedly, my experience and association in corporation matters on a national scale are exceedingly limited, and, as a result, my opinions are based strictly on local observation, and I am ever eager to hear more about these problems both pro and con. You imply that incorporation might be acceptable if 100 per cent of its stockholders are registered men. This is an unreasonable and, in most cases, a crippling condition that defeats the purposes of incorporating. I assume that you mean by 100 per cent of its stockholders you also mean its executives and directors, otherwise what you imply would be meaningless. One of the benefits of a corporation is to bring a diversity of talent into the organization, i.e., engineers, financiers, accountants, attorneys and promoters, etc., in such proportions as to effect a useful and efficient complex.

Sometime ago, an eastern university conducted a study on various levels of success of different professions, and the results seem to prove what has been obvious to many of us. That is, engineers, as a group, are a dismal flop as businessmen. This casts no reflection on the intelligence and the ability of the engineer but rather indicates the limitations of their personalities and emotional makeup. We realize, of course, the ideal professional is a well rounded personality that can do anything, but let us be realistic. Professional men are just like anybody else and nobody is perfect. Therefore, a corporation has a chance to more closely attain the perfection that is being demanded by a society of ever-increasing complexity.

In further defense, let me quote from a paper written by William H. Baker Jr., excerpts of which are published under the topic of "Identification of Title" in the A.C.S.M. Journal mentioned at the opening of this letter. In discussing the relationship between the surveyor and the title insurance company, Mr. Baker ably states, "One of the principal reasons for the growth of title insurance is that the modern investor in mortgages no longer is the local banker who knows the borrower and his father before him, the property and its past history, and the local examiner. The national investor is remote from the scene; deals with cold hard cash; and now wants the indemnity of a financially sound insurance company behind the title. By like token the national investor no longer knows the local surveyor and is unwilling to accept a plat supported only by a local recommendation as to the ability of the surveyor. The investor is insisting upon that survey being supported by the indemnification of a financially sound corporation."

Here, of course, it is understood that the corporation referred to is that of the title insurance company. However, this puts the title insurance company in the position of standing good for the surveyor's blunders and, therefore, it appears obvious that the insurance company would prefer to put their trust in a financially sound organization, which condition cannot always be satisfied by the individual land surveyor as easily as by a corporation.

Finally, let me quote a paragraph from a letter to Engineering News-Record, by E. E. Lyford, Executive Director, Committee on Engineering Laws, New York, N. Y. "For over fifty years, industry has demanded and received their engineering professional services through a corporate form, which industry desires because of its many advantages and the additional protection which industry receives from contracts made with a corporation. Because of this, many fine reputable engineering corporations have been established -- some of them publicly owned and thus unable to change their status and comply with the selfishly drawn proposals of individual engineers who are trying to drive out competition."

I trust the foregoing remarks will be accepted in the spirit of constructive professionalism.

  * Goetech -- Land Surveyors, 3695 American Drive (Granger), Salt Lake City 4, Utah. (An open letter to Curtis M. Brown.)

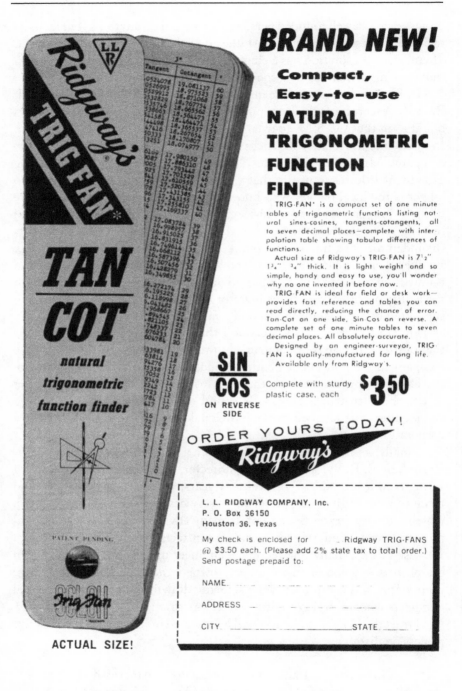

486

PART-TIME SURVEYING PRIVATE PRACTICE

A PANEL DISCUSSION

MARCH 1962

This panel was the feature of the plenary session sponsored by the Property Surveys Division at the Twenty-first Annual Meeting of ACSM on Thursday evening, March 23, 1961. A photograph of the participants will be found on page 183 of the June 1961 issue of SURVEYING AND MAPPING.

– Editor

DISCUSSANTS

Victor H. Ghent, *Moderator*, Chairman of the Ethics Committee of the Property Surveys Division, ACSM; Secretary of the Property Surveys Division; a director of ACSM and a member of the ACSM Executive Committee; Past President of the Virginia Association of Surveyors; in. private practice in northern Virginia.

Curtis M. Brown, Vice Chairman of the Property Surveys Division; Chairman of the Legislative Committee of the Property Surveys Division; Past President of the San Diego Section, California Council of Civil Engineers and Land Surveyors; author of two widely used books; college instructor and speaker; in private practice in San Diego, California.

Morgan E. Kronk, a member of the Ethics Committee, Property Surveys Division; a graduate of Pennsylvania State University; has been employed as a topographic engineer, cartographic engineer, and consulting engineer; now Chief Draftsman for the Peoples Natural Gas Co., Pennsylvania.

Dean C. DeLaMater, Past President of the Michigan Society of Registered Land Surveyors; served in surveying under his father, for the Navy, and for the State of Michigan; in private practice in Cheboygan, Michigan.

H. L. Williams, employed by the City of Jacksonville, Florida, since 1942; is assistant engineer in charge of the Paving Planning Section.

Alonzo L. Cherry, Past President of the Virginia Association of Surveyors; employed by the U. S. Corps of Engineers for 33 years.

Property Surveys Division Panel on "Part Time Land Surveying Private Practice," Thursday evening, March 23, 1961. *Left to right*—Victor H. Ghent, Curtis M. Brown, Morgan E. Kronk, Dean C. DeLaMater, H. L. Williams, and Alonzo L. Cherry.

MR. GHENT - The subject of this panel is a serious matter dealing with professional relationship between surveyors who have full-time private practices and those who have part-time private practices. The problem is very old and is not limited to our profession. We certainly will not solve it at this meeting. It is our hope, however, that the panel talks and the discussion that will undoubtedly follow will enable our Ethics Committee to study the pros and cons and other data on the subject and make such recommendations as are deemed proper, if such be needed, leading to better understanding and relationships among all surveyors. This, of course, will increase the effectiveness of the professional services that we render to the public which we serve.

Prior to introducing the first panel member, I would like to touch on a phase of part-time practice, or "sundowning," as it is often called, which is not covered, I believe, by the other panelists. Many of us grew up in surveying by working for other surveyors in private practice. Quite often we need to supplement our incomes by working part time for other surveyors or even working for other clients. Quite often, too, we are preparing for the day when we will have our own full-time private practice.

It is my opinion that no outside work should be done under these conditions without the consent of the employer. This applies to all employers, whether public or private. It is also my opinion that no work done for another surveyor should be in conflict with your employer or for a client of your employer. You should not work for another surveyor who is considered to be using unethical methods in procuring work, who does inferior work, or who in any manner consistently violates the code of ethics. You should not do any work for a client or another surveyor when that work, under proper conditions, would have been done by your employer. You should not work for another surveyor for lower wages than you are paid by your employer; you should not do work for any client for less than the fees normal for such professional services. You should not undertake any outside work the scope of which is too great for the amount of time that you have readily available, and you should not do so much part-time work as to impair your efficiency.

You should not do work which may, in part, have to be conducted on your employer's time. During my quest of my own private practice, these are the rules under which I attempted to conduct myself. My present partner in private practice was my employer. I am sure that there were times when I tried his patience. However, I am almost positive that nothing I did for another surveyor would have come into our office anyway, and the only "client" jobs that I did were those for friends who spent much time in discussions, which "friends" do not expect to be charged for. Frankly, the overall monetary results were not worth the time and trouble, and I finally gave up all outside work. I would like to sum up this phase of our discussion by noting two things:

first, the problems of an employee under these conditions can become a series of serious ethical burdens and, second, private-practice employers should try to recognize the need to have licensed employees share in the ownership of such private practice, taking into account, of course, the experience and compatibility of the employee.

The subject of this panel discussion has always been "sticky" and is misunderstood on both sides of the fence. I am proud of the quality of the panelists, and I would like to note that all of the employees appearing on this panel do so with the consent of their employers and, in some cases, with their expenses paid by their employers. The talks given by the panelists have been compiled, with their knowledge, into a paper which will be used for handouts after the session is concluded and will be mailed to all surveyor organizations, along with all other PSD papers and reports given during these sessions. We have not attempted in any way to monitor these talks. Neither ACSM nor PSD assumes any responsibility for the opinions expressed herein, but we do hope that these talks and the discussion, which we hope that you will generate, will lead to a better understanding among all surveying and mapping professionals.

CURTIS M. BROWN - The nickname "sundowner" has been used in the surveying profession to indicate undesirable, unethical, hit-and-run, part-time surveyors. It does not have an endearing connotation.

The subject "part-time surveying practice" does not necessarily refer to "undesirable characters," but may include both the desirable and undesirable. The problem of this panel immediately resolves itself into the question of the distinction between desirable and undesirable practitioners.

Fundamentally, there is only one reason to license and give an exclusive franchise to any group, and that is to protect the public. In many states, surveyors have been granted the sole right to monument property lines and justifiably so. For every client's property located, an adjoiner's land or several adjoiners' lands may also be located. The incompetent or the dishonest can cause considerable trouble and anguish to an innocent neighbor. A neutral party, qualified, unbiased, and completely indifferent to temptations, is needed. The surveyor is in a position of trust; he is obligated to correctly locate property lines irrespective of who pays the fees.

In exchange for an exclusive right, the surveyor is obligated to see that those licensed to practice are qualified. The problem related to the part-time practitioner, as I see it, is one of qualifications and one of ethics. We have two types of infringement on surveyors: (1) those with inadequate knowledge posing as qualified surveyors, and (2) those with or without adequate knowledge who filch time, equipment, and office space from an employer to gain a cost advantage.

The law presumes that those licensed are qualified. Unfortunately, we do have many states with substandard requirements for the privilege to practice, but no comment is called for on this. We are not discussing what the surveyors' qualifications should be; we are commenting on "sundowner" encroachments on the private surveyor.

Those with inadequate knowledge and without licenses, whether practicing part time or full time, need to be eliminated. This is a problem common to all professions. It is the fundamental nature of many that they want to have a better stature without earning it. We will always have those who try to move into the fringe area of a profession and attempt to earn money on others' reputations. It is not difficult to rake off a quick profit by doing less work for the same money. In as much as the unqualified and unlicensed are not a problem exclusively applicable to the part-time practitioner, no further comment will be made on this.

The undesirable part-time practitioners are usually those employed in public, semipublic, or other favorable spots who take advantage of their salaried position to reap a dishonest benefit. I would classify dishonest benefits as:

(1) Using an employer's or public body's equipment;

(2) Using an employer's time to do research or mapping;

(3) Using an employer's office to solicit work or to accept work; and

(4) Failure to pay taxes or secure business licenses.

Universities, colleges, county surveyors, city engineers, water districts, and others have surveying equipment. Surveyors using their employer's equipment, especially publicly owned equipment paid for out of tax money, are guilty of theft just as much as though they had taken money. Such competition is ruinous to the private surveyor. Anyone can undercut competition if they have no equipment costs.

We have all seen those in public employment who spend more time doing their own private work than they do tending to the public affairs. This is especially difficult to combat if the boss is in on the deal. Most public agencies have available necessary maps, paid for by the public. It is easy for the part-time public practitioner to sneak a little time to do his research on taxpayer's time. He can also "borrow" the maps for a quick weekend job. It is not doing the job itself that causes complaints; it is the inherent advantages of the public employee that enable him to do part of the work at public expense that causes trouble.

Then we have those who use the public offices to solicit work. It is logical that people would inquire of the university or the city engineer as to how they can get surveys done and as to who does it. Those who are in public employment are expected to refer the matter to those who are qualified; they are not expected to refer the matter to some person who is willing to give them a kickback or to refer the matter to themselves. The public certainly does not erect or rent public buildings for the purpose of furnishing private business offices to employees. This is the basis for most complaints.

Those employed in public field parties have numerous opportunities to contact the public. By using this as a means to solicit business, they take advantages over others. Any private surveyor who could thus eliminate the necessity of an office, telephone, and secretary would eliminate a big share of his costs.

The costs of overhead - that is, bookkeeping for taxes and social security, office rent, secretarial service, and like impositions on the employer, amount to as much as or more than the field work. Public survey employees, including those employed by cities, counties, states, and universities, can escape overhead costs because the public furnishes them a telephone, desk, office space, and even readily available sources of information such as maps. No private surveyor can afford such competition.

We have those who beat the game by not paying taxes. At $25 per city per year, the cost of business licenses soon adds up, especially where there are several cities in the area. If the costs of social security, income taxes, personal taxes, vacations, insurance, and like expenses can be avoided by hiring fellow workers, unfair advantages will result. This, of course, is dangerous to the responsible party, since it can lead to costly liability or even jail terms.

It has been my observation that part-time practitioners are not objectionable so long as they do not take advantage of a salaried position. We do have part-time men, not in favorable business-soliciting spots, who do ethical standard work. But it is also noted that most part-time practitioners are in favorable public employment, where their position is the source of their business. I have never been one to believe that it was the intent of the public to furnish office space to employees for private use.

I see no objection to part-time practitioners who maintain offices, who do not take advantage of a public position to solicit business, who pay all costs, and who do not cheat on their full-time employer. I have seen practitioners who have kept their public positions completely separate from private business, but they are the exception rather than the rule.

****

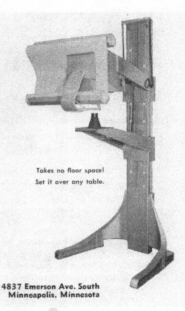

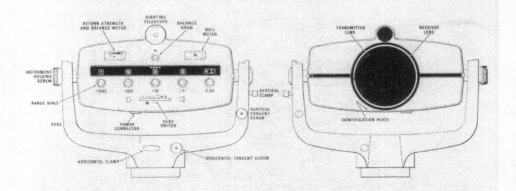
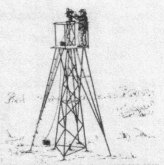
494

PROFESSIONAL PRACTICE

NATIONAL REPORT TO F.I.G. COMMISSION I ELEVENTH INTERNATIONAL CONGRESS OF SURVEYORS

ROME, ITALY

MAY 25 - JUNE 5, 1965

BY CURTIS M. BROWN

A REPORT from the American Congress on Surveying and Mapping on the status of the profession within the United States of America is difficult to understand without a brief explanation of overlapping jurisdictions.

Within the United States of America there are 50 states; each may regulate licensing of cadastral (land) surveyors independently of the others. In addition, the Federal Government regulates surveyors who work within its sphere of authority.

As a result of each state having independent jurisdiction over registered cadastral surveyors, registration laws and the rights to practice are variable; some states have no regulatory laws, while others have stringent registration requirements. The boundaries of states often act as barriers to those in private practice. If the surveyor wants to practice in another state, he must pass an examination as prescribed by that state. Some examinations, in states with lower survey standards, are quite easy; others, in states where standards for surveys are professionally higher, are difficult.

The Federal Government, except for the U. S. Mineral Surveyors, does not register surveyors. For example, those working for a Federal agency such as the Coast and Geodetic Survey are classified by position, but, since they are not registered by examination and by law, their classification or title does not go with them upon resignation of their civil service positions. However, a good number of Federal surveyors and engineers do hold their own individual professional licenses.

Throughout the years the survey agencies of the United States government have maintained positions of high respect and professional reputation nationally and internationally. Some differences exist in evaluation of the professional and ethical standing of the cadastral (land) surveyors of various parts of the United States of America, which are created primarily by the numerous differing state laws regulating surveyors; it is probably true that no two states of the United States of America have exactly the same registration and practice laws, especially for surveying.

As an example of variation, one state requires the examinee to have a high school (no college) diploma, another requires a 4-year college degree in civil engineering. In many states the cadastral (land) surveyor may only locate land boundaries and the civil engineers are responsible for the design of all street improvements such as sewers, water, drainage, etc. In other states, the cadastral surveyor may design improvements. If 50 different laws specify requirements for registration as a land surveyor, what standard should the National Society use? This presents a major problem to the American Congress on Surveying and Mapping in the classification of its members.

With this introduction to the regulatory differences governing surveying practices within the United States of America, it can be readily understood that no specific statement can be made as to the status of private land surveyor practice or as to the ethics of the practitioner without specific reference to an area or particular state.

During the last 15 to 20 years, cadastral engineers, or land surveyors, as they are more commonly called, have organized professional societies within their local states, or have reactivated dormant groups, to advance themselves professionally. The pattern of organization has been somewhat heterogeneous. Some organizations limit membership to only those in private land surveying practice, such as licensed surveyors; others admit anyone with an interest in any branch of surveying and mapping, including those in related fields or interests. Outstanding leadership on behalf of the professional land surveyor has come from California, Florida, Minnesota, Texas, Virginia, Massachusetts, and New York, with varying support from a few other states. Truly professional standing has been attained by the members of professional surveyor organizations in several states of the United States of America. In a few states even a beginning cannot be claimed.

During the years since American Congress on Surveying and Mapping Past President George C. Bestor's report to the 9th Federation Internationale des Geometres Conference, the private surveyor in the United States of America has steadily improved in professional standing. Several states have enacted laws requiring a college degree as a condition of taking the surveyor registration examination; several new organizations of land surveyors in other states have been organized; eleven universities now offer master's degrees in geometronics, the science of surveying; new registration laws have been enacted; and membership in surveyor organizations throughout the United States of America has increased.

The American Congress on Surveying and Mapping (ACSM) is the National Society that represents the surveyors of the United States. If surveyors of the United States of America are to attain uniformity of practice and professional standing of equal merit, a major part of the accomplishment will be done through the efforts and effectiveness of the American Congress on Surveying and Mapping.

****

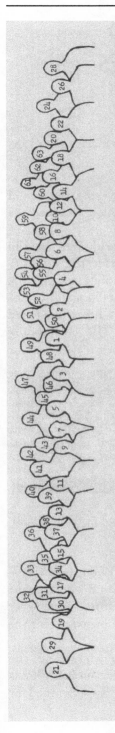

F.I.G. Delegates and Meetings Officials, South Court, U. S. Department of State, Washington, D. C., 1963.

(Background statue by F. M. Fredericks depicts mystery of the universe.)

1. AIREA Representative, B. T. Barnard, USA; 2. ACSM President, W. S. Dix, USA; FIG President, Dr. Neumaier, Austria; FIG President-elect, E. De Biagi, Italy; 5. FIG Vice President, Hollhuber, Austria; T. J. Blachut, Canada; 7. Miss Hollhuber, Austria; 8. Prof. Peevski, Bulgaria; 9. G. K. Emminizer, Jr., USA; 10. P. Oryshkewych, USA; 11. H. Ahrens, Germany; 12. E. V. Harboe, Denmark; 13. R. Meyer, Germany; 14. Prof. Sztompke, Poland; 15. M. Naceur, Morocco; 16. W. B. Williams, USA; 17. R. Steel, Great Britain; 18. Dr. Brunner, Germany; 19. P. Deluz, Switzerland; 20. W. V. Blackie, Canada; 21. B. F. Cooke, USA; 22. Dr. Ewald, Germany; 24. Cyril Barsky, USA; 26. G. Burette, Belgium; 28. W. G. Burrow, USA; 29. Dr. Gigas, Germany; 30. Prof. Delbard, France; 31. Brother Barry, USA; 32. B. Burroughs, USA; 33. H. Topp, Germany; 34. R. Perrin, France; 35. C. D. Pilcher, Great Britain; 37. Dr. Fantini, Italy; 38. G. C. Bestor, USA; 39. FIG Secretary-General Barvir, Austria; 40. E. Spinelli, Italy; 41. FIG Treasurer Kamenik, Austria; 42. D. Calzolari, Italy; 43. Dr. Meelker, Netherlands; 44. Prof. Marstboom, Belgium; 45. J. M. McAlinden, USA; 46. M. Christensen, USA; 47. Lt. Col. Colvocoresses, USA; 48. Prof. Witt, Netherlands; 49. G. DeBoeck, Belgium; 50. Dr. Draheim, Germany; 51. FIG Vice President Chiaramello, Italy; 52. ACSM Vice President Griffith, USA; 53. C. M. Brown, USA; 54. R. E. Clarke, Liberia; 55. B. J. Collins, Great Britain; 56. Prof. Joncas, Canada; 57. A. F. Striker, USA; 58. M. Dancose, Canada; 59. R. DeCeuster, Belgium; 60. W. R. Kahl, USA; 61. W. I. Schachterle, USA; 62. D. D. Dickson, USA; and 63. G. E. Pearcey, USA.

SPECIAL AWARD TO
WILLIAM C. WATTLES

JUNE 1965

[MP NOTE: The award was presented by Curt in his capacity as ACSM Vice President.]

Within the United States there are many land surveyors, but few, if any, have attained the stature and professional recognition accorded the man we are to honor today.

Throughout his lifetime of 84 years he has been keenly interested in land title work and has become known among surveyors as the authority on land titles. He graduated from the Colorado School of Mines in 1903. He was formerly chief engineer for Title Insurance Trust Company of Los Angeles, having joined that organization in 1916. He is a registered civil engineer and licensed land surveyor of California. His outstanding contribution is his book "Land Survey Descriptions."

He was three times the vice president of the American Congress on Surveying and Mapping and by his own choice declined the nomination for president.

Some years ago, when I was starting in the land surveying business, Czerny Anderson gave me a lot of notes on land title interpretations, which I did not at the time realize were recorded from lectures given by the California

Chase, Ltd., Photo.

ACSM Vice President Curtis M. Brown, left, presents the ACSM Quarter Century Citation awarded to William C. Wattles to his son Gurdon Wattles.

gentleman we honor today. His teachings predate most of our practices.

A measure of a man's standing can be judged from how others regard him. Although I have heard a few people disagree with him, I have never known his writings to be ignored; thus, others have acknowledged him as being the authority.

When a man becomes well educated in an area of knowledge, the courts frequently call upon him for testimony. Mr. Wattles probably holds the all-time record for surveyors; he was examined and cross-examined for 46 days in the Richfield Oil Company case.

Although he is "retired" from the business world, he is active. Just two years ago he gave several hour-long lectures to the Florida Land Surveyors. The University of California employed him to conduct a class in the San Francisco area; he commuted by airplane between Los Angeles and San Francisco. In this world very few people attain this distinction in their late seventies.

Win Eldridge's *Bibliography* indicates he has published five articles in SURVEYING AND MAPPING, and one in the *Proceedings* of the A.S.C.E.

This being the 25th anniversary of the American Congress on Surveying and Mapping, we wish to honor one of the greats of the quarter century, Mr. William C. Wattles.

William C. Wattles, being unable to attend the meeting, the actual physical presentation of the award was made to his son, Gurdon H. Wattles, who accepted the award on behalf of his father.

[MP NOTE: Czerny Anderson was a prominent San Diego Land Surveyor who had made several contributions to ACSM publications over the years.]

The wording of the citation is as follows:

AMERICAN CONGRESS ON SURVEYING AND MAPPING QUARTER CENTURY CITATION 1941-1965. WILLIAM C. WATTLES FOR OUTSTANDING AND UNSELFISH PROFESSIONAL CONTRIBUTION IN THE PUBLIC INTEREST IN THE FIELD OF LAND-TITLE AND PROPERTY-LINE SURVEYS. ACSM 25TH NATIONAL CONGRESS. PRESENTED APRIL 1, 1965, WASHINGTON. D. C.

****

AN ACKNOWLEDGEMENT

JUNE 1965

WILLIAM C. WATTLES * - To you and through you to the officers and members of ACSM, my thanks and deep appreciation for the high honor and recognition given me at the 25th Anniversary Convention, and evidenced by the beautiful Plaque and Honorary Membership Certificate; they are and will be held as symbolic of a height in my career.

Although regretful, I was unable to attend, your acceptance of my son's presence as my proxy was a fine gesture of understanding for which additional thanks.

I was truly sorry to miss the Convention and the association with my many friends in the "bull sessions." Correspondence is a poor substitute for personal contact.

ACSM in principles and activities has been and will be close in my ideal for advancement in the Land Survey Profession; may it ever prosper. Be assured, my services to ACSM will be available at any time as far as I am able to function.

* 1653 Santa Barbara Ave., Glendale, California 91208 – a letter to the Executive Secretary, ACSM.

****

SURVEYOR REGISTRATION IN NEW ZEALAND

MARCH 1966

A. H. BOGLE * - In your issue of September 1965, you have a "Report on F.I.G. Meeting" by Mr. Curtis M. Brown. On page 406, his second paragraph down, he has made a note as follows:

"In many countries (Australia, New Zealand etc.) the professional Society is the sole judge of members' qualifications to do surveying; an examining board created by law and registration by state law do not exist."

That statement is incorrect. The facts are as set out below:

The early surveyors operating in New Zealand either held a certificate as an authorized Surveyor, issued by the Surveyor General of the Colony, or a Certificate of Competency from the Board Examiners constituted under the Land Act 1892.

The New Zealand Institute of Surveyors and Board of Examiners Act, which became law in 1900, was "An Act to provide for the Formation of an Institute of Surveyors in the Colony of New Zealand, and for the Incorporation thereof, and to constitute a Board of Examiners of Surveyors."

Clause 11 of the 1900 Act states that the Governor General may appoint four persons who together with the Surveyor General shall be a Board to be called "The Surveyors Board," with the Surveyor General as Chairman ex officio. Of the other four members, two are to be nominated by the Council of the Institute and two by the Minister of Lands.

In 1908 a further Act consolidated Enactments of the General Assembly relating to the Institute of Surveyors, and again in 1928, a Surveyors Registration Act was "to make Better Provision with respect to the Examination and Registration of Surveyors and the Practice of the Profession of Surveying."

The current Act governing our professional activities is the Surveyors Act 1938. This Act provides that a student who has served professionally under Articles for four years and has passed the necessary written papers, practical test plans, and oral examination of the Survey Board is issued with a Certificate of Competency and is then entitled to apply to the Board for a Certificate of Registration as a surveyor, subject to certain routine conditions. With this in hand he may then apply to the Institute of Surveyors for an annual practicing certificate, on receipt of which he automatically becomes a member of the Institute, whether or not he applies for such membership.

Reply by CURTIS M. BROWN, President, ACSM - Obviously, I was wrong and should have used "England." Thanks for the correction.

* Editor, New Zealand Surveyor.

****

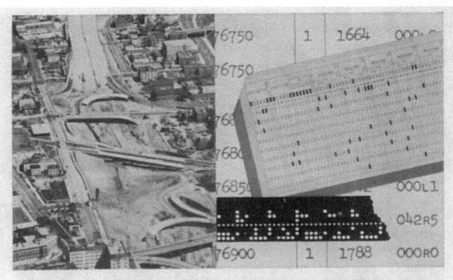

New Fairchild Service provides cross section and profile data in DIGITAL FORM *automatically!*

- Saves time and money in highway and railroad location design and construction.
- Equals or exceeds field accuracy of estimating cut and fill.
- Reduces chance of human error.
- Re-cross sectioning at periodic intervals gives engineer check on progress of earthmoving; provides basis for paying contractor.

The recorded terrain output data is automatically typed and simultaneously produced on punched cards. Punched paper tape output is also available.

Free brochure! Phone, wire or write your nearest Fairchild office.

🗲AIRCHILD
AERIAL SURVEYS, INC.

DECEMBER 1965

In the August 12, 1965 issue of *Engineering News-Record* there appeared an article entitled "Surveyor Was Practicing Law" by I. Vernon Werbin. After reading the court report re Maynard H. Welch, 185 A 2nd 458, Supreme Court of Vermont, my abstract is:

A client went to an attorney concerning subdividing his land and was advised to have a surveyor first survey the land and prepare descriptions.

The surveyor (there are no examinations for surveyors in Vermont, thus, there are no published standards to determine qualifications, other than self proclamation) made the surveys in 1962, prepared the descriptions, set the descriptions on conveyance forms, and stated that "There would be no need for the parties in interest to obtain further services of an attorney with respect to the drafting and execution of the necessary instruments of conveyance." The surveyor advised the client of the type of estate and the manner of holding the same. For the survey, drafting, deeds, supervising and execution, delivery, and recording he received $65 (prices are low in Vermont).

Quoting from the case:

"In general, one is deemed to be practicing law whenever he furnishes to another advice or service under circumstances which imply the possession and use of legal knowledge and skill . . . . Practice of law includes the giving of legal advice and council and the preparation of legal instruments and contracts of which legal rights are secured."

"The protection of the unauthorized practice of law is a matter of public policy in all of the United States. This policy rests upon the necessity of protecting the public rather than the lawyer . . . Such unauthorized practice of law is a criminal contempt of this court."

It has been my opinion that the surveyor must obey the law as it exists (everyone is presumed to know the law) and to obey the law a surveyor must know what the law is, but this never gives him the right to prepare conveyances. In most states the surveyor is granted the privilege of preparing property descriptions (as in California), but, to my knowledge, no state grants him the privilege of placing the description on a conveyance form. Ask your attorney!

– CURTIS M. BROWN

****

ACSM MODEL REGISTRATION LAW FOR LAND SURVEYORS

JUNE 1967

AN ACT to regulate the Practice of Land Surveying; providing for the registration of qualified persons as Licensed Land Surveyors, defining the terms "Licensed [2] Land Surveyor," "Subordinate," and "Practice of Land Surveying," creating a State Board of Registration for Licensed Land Surveyors and providing for the appointment of its members; fixing their powers and duties; setting forth the minimum qualifications and other requirements for registration; establishing fees with expiration and renewal requirements; imposing certain duties upon the State and political subdivisions thereof in connection with land surveying and providing for the enforcement of this Act and penalties for its violation.

SECTION 1. PRACTICE OF LAND SURVEYING DECLARED TO BE SUBJECT TO REGULATIONS.

Be it enacted by the ---------- of the State of ----------------------- that it is a matter of public interest and concern that only qualified persons be permitted to engage in the *Practice of Land Surveying* and in order to safeguard life, health and property, and to promote the public welfare, any person in either public or private capacity practicing or offering to practice land surveying shall hereafter be required to submit evidence that he is of good moral character and qualified so to practice and shall be registered and licensed as hereinafter provided; and it shall be unlawful for any person to practice or offer to practice land surveying in this State, as defined in the provisions of this Act, or to use in connection with his name or otherwise assume, use or advertise any title or description tending to convey the impression that he is a Licensed [2] Land Surveyor or land surveyor, unless such person is duly registered and licensed or exempt under the provisions of this Act. All provisions of this Act renting to the Practice of Land Surveying shall be construed in accordance with this declaration of policy.

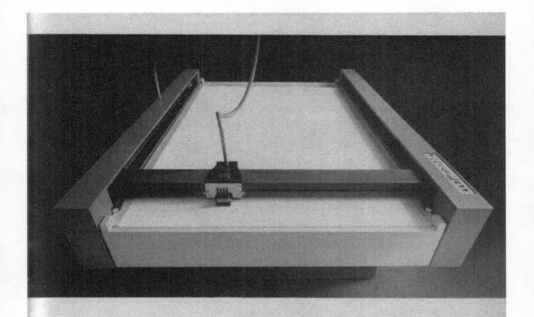

It draws faster than ink flows.

We call it the 748. It's big. And it's fast.

Its 4 inking pens move at speeds over 40 inches a second. That's faster than ink flows, so we had to figure out a pressure inking system that lets the ink catch up to the pens.

If you make integrated circuits or maps, or if you have precision drafting needs, this is the new tool.

The 748's plotting area is 48" x 82". It can scribe coated materials and cut strippable film. At peak speeds!

The quality of its line is not impaired by its incredible speed. And like all CalComp flatbed plotters, the new 748 offers easy-to-use software for most computers.

We service it in 29 countries. But the way we've made it, you won't be calling us very often.

Do call us to see it.

Our number is (714) 821-2011. Or write California Computer Products, Inc., SV-M3-74, 2411 West La Palma Avenue, Anaheim, California 92801.

CALCOMP

SECTION 2. DEFINITIONS AS USED IN THIS ACT.

(A) The term *Surveyor* as used in this Act shall mean a Licensed [2] Land Surveyor as hereinafter defined.

(B) The terms *Licensed [2] Land Surveyor* means an individual who is qualified to practice land surveying as hereinafter defined, as attested by his registration in this State as a Licensed Land Surveyor.

(C) The term *subordinate* means a person who is directly supervised by a Licensed Land Surveyor and who assists a Licensed Land Surveyor in the Practice of Land Surveying.

(D) The term *responsible charge* means a position that requires initiative, skill and independent judgment. This term excludes chain-man, rodman, instrument man, transitman (unless acting as Chief of Party), ordinary draftsman and others doing routine work.

(E) The term *Practice of Land Surveying,* within the meaning and intent of this act, includes the following.

    (1) The location, relocation, establishment, reestablishment or retracement of any property line or boundary of any parcel of land or of any road or utility right-of-way, easement or alignment.

    (2) The performance of any survey for the subdivision or resubdivision of any tract of land.

    (3) By the use of the principles of land surveying, the determination of the position of any monument or reference point which marks a property line boundary or corner, or setting, resetting or replacing any such monument or reference point.

    (4) The determination of the configuration or contour of the earth's surface or the position of fixed objects thereon or related thereto, by means of measuring lines and angles, and applying the principles of mathematics, photogrammetry or other measurement methods.

    (5) Geodetic or cadastral surveying, underground surveying and hydrographic surveying.

    (6) Procuring or offering to procure land surveying work for himself or others.

    (7) Managing or conducting as manager, proprietor, or agent, any place of business from which land surveying work is solicited, performed, or practiced.

(8) Preparing subdivision planning maps.

(9) Determining the grades and elevations of roads in conjunction with subdivisions or divisions of land.

(10) Providing for small drainage structures and waste water removal in conjunction with subdivisions or divisions of land.

(11) The preparation of drawings showing any of the above.

(F) The term *Board* means the State Board of Registration for Licensed Land Surveyors provided for in this Act.

SECTION 3. BOARD OF REGISTRATION: APPOINTMENT OF MEMBERS; QUALIFICATIONS; TERMS; REMOVAL OF MEMBERS.

A State Board of Registration for Licensed Land Surveyors is hereby created whose duty it shall be to administer the provisions of this Act. The Board shall consist of five Licensed Land Surveyors, each of whom shall be appointed by the Governor. Each shall be a citizen of the United States and resident of this State, shall have been engaged in the Practice of Land Surveying and a Licensed Land Surveyor for at least twelve years, and shall have been in a responsible charge of land surveying work for at least five years. The members of the first Board shall be appointed within ninety days after the passage of this Act; one member for one year, two members for two years, two members for three years, or until their successors are duly appointed and qualified. Every member of the Board shall receive a certificate of his appointment from the Governor and before beginning his term of office shall file with the Secretary of State his written oath or affirmation for the faithful discharge of his official duty. On the expiration of the term of any member, the Governor shall appoint for a term of three years a Licensed Land Surveyor having the above qualifications, to take the place of the member whose term on the said Board is about to expire. Each member shall hold office until the expiration of said term for which such main-her is appointed or until a successor shall have been duly appointed and shall have qualified. The Governor may remove any member of the Board for official misconduct, incompetency, neglect of duty, gross immorality, or for any other sufficient cause, in the manner prescribed by law. A member of the Board may serve only two full consecutive terms.

Vacancies in the membership of the Board shall be filled for the unexpired term by appointment by the Governor.

SECTION 4. COMPENSATION AND EXPENSES OF BOARD MEMBERS.

Each member of the Board shall be entitled to receive a reasonable per diem compensation for his services when actually attending to the work of the Board or any of its committees and for the time spent in necessary travel; and, in addition thereto, shall be reimbursed for all actual traveling, incidental, or clerical expenses necessarily incurred in carrying out the provisions of this Act.

SECTION 5. ORGANIZATION AND MEETINGS OF THE BOARD.

The Board shall hold a meeting within thirty days after its members are first appointed, and thereafter shall hold at least two regular meetings each year. Special meetings shall be held at such time as the bylaws of the Board may provide. The Board shall elect annually the following officers: a Chairman and a Vice Chairman who must be members of the Board, and a secretary who may or may not be a member of the Board. A quorum of the Board shall consist of not less than three members. The Board shall have an official seal, which shall be affixed to every certificate issued by the Board and to such other documents as may be appropriate. The chairman shall preside over Board meetings, or in his absence, the vice chairman shall preside.

SECTION 6. GENERAL POWERS OF THE BOARD.

(A) BYLAWS. The Board shall have the power to adopt or amend all bylaws and rules of procedure, not inconsistent with the constitution and laws of this State or this Act, which may be reasonably necessary for the performance of its duties.

(B) REGISTRATION OF LICENSED LAND SURVEYORS. The following shall be considered as minimum evidence satisfactory to the Board that the applicant is qualified for registration as a Licensed Land Surveyor.

510

(1) The applicant shall be a citizen of the United States.

(2) The applicant shall have passed a written or a written and oral examination unless he is exempted as provided in (4) below.

(3) The educational qualifications and experience in land surveying which the applicant shall possess shall not be less than the following prescribed minima: (a) Eight years of experience of which three years must be in a responsible position as a subordinate to a Licensed Land Surveyor, or a land surveyor exempt from registration by Section 8A and 8B. (b) Graduation from an approved four-year college course in Land Surveying or other approved curriculum, or proportionate credit for lesser time, may be substituted for four years of non-responsible experience.

(4) The Board may register without examination anyone who meets the requirements of this Act and who files an application on or before ...., 19... showing that he has been satisfactorily and legally Practicing Land Surveying.

(C) APPLICATIONS: REGISTRATION FEES: CERTIFICATES OF REGISTRATION. Applications for registration shall be on forms prescribed and furnished by the Board, shall contain statements made under oath showing the applicant's citizenship, education, and detailed summary of his technical work, and shall contain the names of not less than four references of whom at least three shall be licensed Land Surveyors having personal knowledge of his land surveying experience and moral and ethical qualifications. The registration fee for land surveyors shall be --- ------ dollars ($--------), --------- dollars ($--------) of which shall accompany the application, and the remaining ------------- dollars ($-------) to be paid before the issuance of the certificate. Should the Board deny the issuance of a certificate of registration to any applicant, the initial fee shall be retained as an application fee.

(D) EXAMINATIONS. The Board shall prescribe the scope, manner, time, and place for the examinations for applicants for registration as Licensed Land Surveyors. Such examinations, not to exceed three days duration, shall be written, or written and oral, at the discretion of the Board, and with or without instruments. The methods and types of examination shall be provided in the procedures and rules of administration of the Board. At least one examination per year must be given.

(E) EXPIRATION AND RENEWALS. The annual [3] renewal fee shall be determined by the Board but shall not exceed ----------- --- dollars ($-------) and shall be due the --------- day of ------- ---- each year. [4] It shall be the duty of the Secretary of the Board to notify every person registered under this Act by mail at his last known address at least --------- month(s) in advance of the due date. Registration shall be suspended ------------ months after the due date if the renewal fee has not then yet been paid. Said suspension shall be lifted at any time up to ---------- months after the due date on payment of a fee of ---------- dollars ($--------) in addition to the required renewal fee. Thereafter the suspended certificate may not be renewed except by the unanimous consent of the Board and on payment of both the above fees.

(F) RECEIPTS AND DISBURSEMENTS. The Secretary of the Board shall receive and account for all moneys derived under the provisions of this Act, and shall deposit the same in a fund with a bank or other financial institution approved by the Board where such moneys shall be kept and shall be paid out only by the signatures of the Chairman, or in the absence of the Chairman, the Vice Chairman, and the Secretary of the Board. The Secretary of the Board shall give a surety bond in such sum as the Board may determine the premium to be regarded as a necessary expense of the Board and shall be paid out of the fund. The Secretary of the Board shall receive such salary as the Board may determine in addition to the compensation and expenses hereinbefore provided for members of the Board. The Board may employ such clerical or other assistants as are necessary for the proper performance of its work, and may make expenditures from this fund for any purpose which, in the opinion of the Board, is necessary for the proper performance of its duties under this Act.

(G) ROSTER. A roster showing the names and addresses of all Licensed Land Surveyors shall be published by the Board during the month of ------------- each year. Copies of this roster shall be mailed to each person so registered, placed on file with the Secretary of State, and with the County ---------------- of each county, and furnished to the public at such price per copy as the Board may fix.

(H) RECORDS AND REPORTS.

    (1) The Board shall keep a record of its proceedings and a register for applications for registration, which register shall show (a) the name, age, and residence of each applicant; (b) the date of application; (c) the place of business of such applicant; (d) his educational and other qualifications; (e) type of examination required; (f) whether the applicant was rejected; (g) whether a certificate of registration was granted; (h) the date of the action of the Board; and (i) such other information as may be deemed necessary by the Board.

    (2) The minutes of Board meetings shall be *prima facie* evidence of the proceedings of the Board set forth therein, and a transcript thereof, duly certified by the Secretary of the Board under seal, shall be admissible in evidence with the same force and effect as if the original were produced.

    (3) Annually as of the end of the fiscal year, the Board shall submit to the Governor (or Secretary of State) a report of its transactions of the preceding year, and shall also transmit to him a complete statement of the receipts and expenditures of the Board, attested by affidavits of its Chairman and Secretary.

(I) REVOCATIONS. The Board shall have the power to suspend or revoke the certificate of registration of any person registered hereunder who is found guilty of any fraud or deceit in securing a certificate of registration, or of frequent or continued or serious negligence, incompetence, or misconduct. Proceedings for the suspension or revocation of a certificate of registration shall include a hearing. The time and place of the hearing shall be made known to the accused person by registered mail, and at the hearing the accused shall have the right to be present in person or represented by legal counsel or both. The Board, for reasons it may deem sufficient, may re-issue a certificate of registration to any person whose certificate has been suspended or revoked, providing three or snore members of the Board vote in favor of such re-issuance.

SECTION 7. VIOLATIONS AND PENALTIES.

Any person who shall practice or offer to practice land surveying in this State in violation of this Act; or who shall attempt to use as his own the certificate of registration or number of another; or who shall give false or forged evidence to the Board, or to any member thereof, in obtaining or attempting to obtain a certificate of registration; or who shall falsely impersonate any other registrant of like or different name; or who shall attempt to use an expired or revoked certificate of registration, or the number therefrom; or who, by verbal claim, by sign, advertisement, letterhead, card, or in any other way represents himself to be a Licensed Land Surveyor, when in fact he is not registered under the provisions of this Act; or who through the use of any title including the word "Land Surveyor" or words of like import, or by any other title, implies that he is a Licensed Land Surveyor, when in fact he is not registered under the provisions of this Act; or who signs as a Licensed Land Surveyor any map, plat or surveying report, when in fact he is not registered under the provisions of this Act; or who shall violate any of the provisions of this Act shall be guilty of a misdemeanor, and shall, upon conviction, be sentenced to pay a fine of not less than one hundred dollars ($100.00), nor more than five hundred dollars ($500.00), or suffer imprisonment not to exceed three months, or by both fine and imprisonment.

SECTION 8. EXEMPTIONS.

No person shall hereafter practice or offer to practice Land Surveying unless such person has been registered under the provisions of this Act, excepting

(A) A subordinate practicing under direct supervision of a Licensed Land Surveyor.

(B) Officers and employees of the United States of America, practicing solely as such officers or employees.

SECTION 9. FORM OF ORGANIZATION FOR PRACTICE.

Licensed Land Surveyors may practice under this Act as individuals or partners, but not as corporations.

SECTION 10. SEPARABILITY.

If any provisions of this law or of any rule, regulation or order thereunder or the application of such provision to any person or circumstance shall be held invalid, the remainder of this law and the application of such provision of this law or of such rule, regulation or order to persons or circumstances, other than those as to which it is held invalid, shall not be affected thereby.

SECTION 11. REPEAL OF CONFLICTING LEGISLATION.

All laws or parts of laws and regulations promulgated thereunder in conflict with the provisions of this Act shall be, and the same hereby are, repealed.

[2] In lieu of "Licensed" (in connection with "Land Surveyor") any of the following alternates may be used throughout the Act: "Registered," "Public," or "Certified."

[3] or "biennial."

[4] or "biennium."

****

[MP NOTE: There is no number 1 in the original document.]

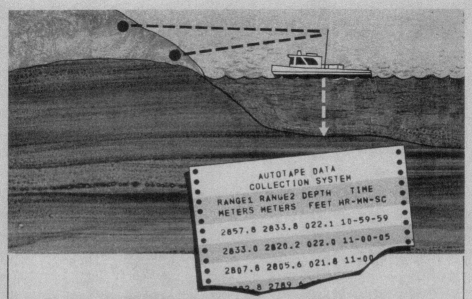

AUTOTAPE DATA
COLLECTION SYSTEM
RANGE1 RANGE2 DEPTH TIME
METERS METERS FEET HR-MN-SC

2857.8 2833.8 022.1 10-59-59

2833.0 2820.2 022.0 11-00-05

2807.8 2805.6 021.8 11-00

2.8 2789.6

Automate offshore surveys with a complete Autotape system for positioning, sounding, and data recording.

Now, from Cubic, a total system, customized to meet your exact survey boat application. It provides Autotape's precision electronic positioning of the vessel, records ranges, depths and time — even makes point-to-point plots.

The Autotape automatically reads out two ranges per second, positioning the boat with precision microwave techniques. Accuracies of 0.5 meters + 1:100,000 can be achieved at distances up to 60 miles. The Autotape is coupled with a digital depth sounder, a digital real-time clock, and a complete recording system. All data is recorded on magnetic tape or punched paper tape and can be printed out in easy-to-read tabular form.

For a complete system, add the Autotape Position Plotter which automatically plots the track of the vessel from the Autotape ranges. A pre-plot track can be used with a local grid or coordinate alignment with the desired track. For details, write Cubic Corporation, Dept. H-171, Electronic Surveying Division, 9233 Balboa, San Diego, Calif. 92123 or phone collect (714) 277-6780.

CUBIC CORPORATION **ELECTRONIC SURVEYING DIVISION**

SURVEYORS SERVICE TO SOCIETY

BY CURTIS M. BROWN [1]

LICENSED LAND SURVEYOR, SAN DIEGO CALIFORNIA

SEPTEMBER 1971

An address presented in theme of convention to the Fourth Annual Convention of the Arkansas Association of Registered Land Surveyors and the Arkansas Section of the American Congress on Surveying and Mapping, Hot Springs, Arkansas, April 15 - 17, 1971. The Speaker was introduced by ACSM's former Executive Secretary Earle J. Fennell.

TECHNICALLY, I have retired. From a practical point of view, I am still a land surveyor. Although my introduction may have given the impression that I spent more time in the office than in the field, it is not true. By far, the majority of my time was spent packing a transit, chaining lines, and brush cutting. Like most backwoods people, I was not very fond of running a large office. I believe I retired early to get rid of administration problems.

Recently I was asked, "What one thing, above all others, does the land surveyor offer?" My answer is *knowledge*. Many people can measure; few have sufficient knowledge to know where and what to measure.

In 1933 when I graduated from college, I had what was considered an excellent education. Photogrammetry was barely mentioned. I was not exposed to matrix problems. Of course, we used logs to solve all of our problems. Hand crank calculators were the best available. Unknown and uninvented were the electronic-measuring devices and electronic computers.

We were taught that the atom was the smallest particle. Protons were unknown. By today's academic standards we were undereducated in the sciences and overeducated in how to do its subjects. The one redeeming feature of the time was that students were taught how to use instruments.

Things change. I recently took time to study some of my old records in retrospect. I found sheet after sheet of traverse computations with sine, cosine, bearing, distance, latitude, departure, double meridian distances and area all neatly tabulated by hand. Out of curiosity, I took one complex traverse, ran it through my electronic computer and found that I could do the job in one - tenth of the time shown on my old time sheets.

Some years ago we "brushed" a line one-mile long and measured it all in two days with three men. A short time ago we remeasured the same line with modern equipment and knowledge and found that it could be done in one-half hour with two men. We also found a small error in our original work.

The moral to this story is that if *we try to do today's job with yesterday's knowledge, we will be out of business tomorrow.*

It is my opinion that the half-life of my college education was ten years; that is, half of what I learned in science and engineering was obsolete or insufficient ten years later. No man in business can afford to stand still; he either gains knowledge by continual study or he falls to the wayside. Ignorance is voluntary misfortune.

My father was a surveyor; he almost graduated from grammar school in the late 1800s. His quest for knowledge began in a strange way. He was a chainman on a railroad gang. He also loved to hunt. His prized possession was a red-ticked hound of considerable tracking ability. The hound, called "Red," always followed dad wherever he went. In those days in California, most quarter and section corners were redwood posts. It was not long before the hound found out what my dad was looking for; the dog would quarter ahead, find the post, and, like all good hounds, leave a moist spot and *bugle* "tree." Soon the Brown family prospered; the business of locating section corners by contract flourished. We graduated from beans to white rice and cake. But our good fortune vanished, when I, in my youthful ignorance, taught old "Red" to retrieve sticks. Nothing could break him of the habit of bringing the section posts back to the master. In one contract where dad was supposed to locate all of the posts in a township, he arrived early, set up camp and bedded down for the night. In the morning, when he woke up, at the foot of his cot were all of the section posts; old "Red" had retrieved them all during the night. Dad was like the grain of wheat that got reaped. He had found a gimmick that worked for a while, but in the long run real knowledge was needed to stay in business. It was then that dad decided that he had to take some correspondence courses to learn how to survey. I have always admired him for completing an ICS course in surveying. Man should be like the lowly crab; he should be able to move backward, forward, or sideways. If things change, as they have in the last decade, man should move with the changes. If newer knowledge is needed, surveyors should acquire it. My dad taught me one thing: Never hunt for a corner in the township where old "Red" retrieved. Knowledge of the past history of an area plus modern knowledge of surveying are the tools of the surveyor.

Within the United States, surveyors have been able to convince the legislators that registration benefits the public. At no time has the object been to give the surveyor an exclusive franchise for the purpose of earning more money. The state has been willing to legislate registration laws on the condition that the public be protected from the incompetent and the unscrupulous. In exchange for this exclusive franchise, surveyors have public obligations. It is not unreasonable that the public should expect surveyors to devise systems whereby the certainty of property line location is assured. The public should look upon the surveyor as a fair and impartial person who places boundaries where they belong, regardless of who he is working for. Two surveyors, each contending for a different location for the same point, can only cause degradation of standing.

If surveyor organizations continually fight for legislation that benefits their selfish interests and increases their prospect of financial gain, it can be expected that the public will contemplate rejection of the surveyors' exclusive rights. We, as surveyors, must not view things in the light of what would be most beneficial to us; we must think in terms of what is beneficial to the public. We must grow, not swell. Of course, we must be able to make a living - otherwise the system would not endure - but at the same time money cannot be the major point of interest.

With these thoughts in mind, what can we do that will benefit the public and yet at the same time, if possible, be of benefit to surveyors?

In the matter of locating boundaries, to me, there is nothing more important than preservation of evidence. Examinations for registration prove a surveyor's competency to make measurements; they prove a person's proficiency in mathematics. Letters from qualified people may prove the examinee's integrity and honesty. But this alone is not sufficient; a surveyor must understand the laws of evidence. Every boundary survey must start from a point on the surface of the earth, and the validity of that starting point is dependent upon evidence.

The law is exact and specific: Wherever the original surveyor set his original monument, that spot is the correct location for that corner. If we are to preserve that original position, we must have a continuous chain of records from the time of the original setting of the monument to the present. The original surveyor may have set a wooden stake that was later replaced by an iron pipe. At a later date the iron pipe may have been removed by highway construction and new reference points set. Who can prove what happened without a continuous chain of records stating what was done? Without question, more property line disputes arise from loss of evidence than from any other cause. The surveyor locating property lines from incomplete evidence can find himself paying out large sums for erroneous monumentation.

Mutual interest of both the public and the surveyor demands that evidence of monument positions be filed as public records. This produces harmony and exchange of knowledge between surveyors.

Two requirements in California that insure a better system of maintaining orderly boundary locations are: (1) license numbers permanently attached to all set monuments, and (2) the filing of plats disclosing evidence found.

Contrary to the thinking of some, these provisions of the law have proved to be of far greater benefit to the surveyor than they have been a detriment. Quite often in my former office we got referral work merely because the adjoiner identified my license number on a property corner. The major benefit from the usage of numbers on monuments is the free exchange of information. A proper location for a corner can only be determined after an evaluation of all the evidence. By the time the second surveyor arrives on the scene, part of the evidence that the first surveyor observed may be gone. If the first surveyor is identifiable by a license number on his

monuments, a telephone call usually brings a satisfactory explanation of differences in location.

The old concept that the surveyor's records are his personal secret - not to be disclosed to anyone - is gradually dying out. In California's Owens Valley we have two lakes. One is fresh and trout are in it. Trees spread their branches over it and children play along its shores. A river flows into this lake and out to a second lake. Here, in the second lake, are no fish and no children's laughter. Travelers choose other routes. Neither man, beast nor fowl will drink of its waters. There is a difference between the two lakes. The first lake receives fresh mountain water. For every drop that flows in, another drop flows out. The other lake is shrewder. Every drop it gets, it keeps. The first lake receives and gives, the second lake receives, does not give, and is salted to death. Are we going to be like the first lake and receive and give information, or are we going to be like the second lake and jealously hoard professional information?

For states westerly of the original states, the United States devised a rather effective system of surveys. The more important feature was the setting of monuments prior to the sale of land. Accurate notes were kept exactly describing each monument set. In addition, bearing objects and trees were called for to aid in identification in the event of destruction of the monument itself. The system was turned over to the states, and no provision was made for preservation of monument positions. Today, out of the millions of monuments and markers originally set, precious few are left. We, as surveyors, are constantly discovering evidence of old corners or witnesses to old corners. What happens to our records? After we die are they lost forever? The number of states that provide a place for the surveyor to publicly record discovered monument evidence is few indeed; only one state makes it mandatory.

The law of every state should provide a place for the filing of surveyor evidence records and, under certain circumstances, it should be mandatory for the surveyors to file their records.

In some cities and counties the surveyors are surprised to find that no one will accept their plat records. The Forestry Department of the U.S. Government has been instrumental in trying to get laws passed to provide public depositories for their records. The acts in Minnesota, Wisconsin, and Montana probably had their inception from foresters engaged in public land surveys.

Knowledge is a useful tool, and it is of value only when it is used. In the business world, if you cannot convince others that they should pay you to raise your knowledge, you may never have the opportunity. The fundamental precept of all human relationships is that it is not sufficient to be right, you must also persuade. An idea that must be acted upon by others is useless until such time as others can be persuaded to act upon it. That is the art of letting others do what you want done. A man may be a veritable Encyclopedia Britannica so far as his store of knowledge is concerned, but all of his mental efforts will be of no avail unless he can convey to others what he knows and thinks.

At one time I asked a friend what on earth ever made him move so far out into the country. His reply was, "One of the best real estate salesman in the business."

The accepted method of soliciting professional work is a vigorous campaign of presenting yourself in a dignified manner to the public. It is not a passive effort. The people you meet, the services you render, your talks before groups, your personal display of wisdom, your friendliness and desire to serve others, your personal appearance, your ability to write, all direct attention to you. The opinion formed by others is the key to your success. If you have done a good job, both in technical skills and selling, others will seek you or will give you referrals.

Within the last 10 to 15 years, engineers, surveyors, and many others have been doing a lot of soul searching. It seems that everyone wants to have a magic name attached to their particular service. Some have been exceptionally vocal in proclaiming themselves as professional people. We have all kinds of so-called professions: professional boxers, professional baseball players, professional real estate brokers, and the oldest profession. Even proclaiming yourself as being a professional man has its dangers. One time in riding down an elevator with my wife, a shapely thing got on at the 10th floor, gave me that sexy look and said, "Mr. Brown I haven't seen you recently." My wife's frozen glare could have stopped a clock. After Blondie got off at the third floor my wife asked, "What was that"? I said, "Just someone I met in a professional matter." My wife asked, "Whose profession, yours or hers"?

I have not yet heard a doctor, attorney, priest, or professor saying I am a professional attorney, doctor, or professor. Everyone knows they are. It is a failing of people that they want the title without the effort, the degree without the education, heaven without probation. People usually get what they earn.

No one acquires standing by self-proclamation. Because of behavior, knowledge, integrity, ethics, skill and service to others, people have acclaimed doctors as belonging to the professions. It is others who bestowed the title upon them. If surveyors behave and act like professional men over a long period of time, then and only then will the public and their peers recognize them as such. It is the total picture of an individual that determines his standing; surveyors cannot be biased towards their own interests.

What is the future of land surveying? It is whatever you make it. You are the ones who are carrying the ball. You can tell some people by their mortgages, others by their deeds. As Shakespeare once said,

Men at some times are masters of their fates.
The fault, dear Brutus, is not in our stars
But in ourselves, that we are underlings.

People are of three types: those that watch things happen; those that don't know things are happening; and those that make things happen. Are we going to be underlings or are we going to make things happen?

For thousands of years surveying has depended upon its members as individuals for those creative achievements of mind that have guided it along the path of professionalism. When an idea comes, where does it originate? From the crowd? *Never.* The individual? Always. It is he and he alone who transmits ideas to his fellowmen. Wisdom and virtue cannot be forced from a crowd. There is no such thing as general intelligence. There is only individual intelligence communicating ideas to individual intelligences. There is no such thing as group professionalism; there is only a composite of individual professional standings.

One thing is certain, if we are going to acquire a standing or position in society, we must earn it individually by our own efforts. No man can acquire honesty by merely saying, "I am honest." No man can acquire respect by saying, "I should be respected." No man can acquire an education by merely saying, "I am educated." Our individual actions, effort, and behavior are the proof of what we are. The sum total of all our individual actions is proof of what we are as a composite group, and the composite group is no better than the individuals. I hope that each of you, as an individual becomes recognized as a professional man, then all of us as a group will be acclaimed as a profession.

Editor's note: If readers accept Curt Brown's story of "Old Red" without further "evidence" which C. M. B. emphatically avers is all important to conclusive judgments, perhaps they'll lend an ear to this tale which hearkens back to planetable and transit stadia surveys when in the dire straits of the great economic depression of the late 1920s and early 1930s we trained "pointers" to stand *tail erect at point,* and with their tails painted in alternate red and white stripes we could take stadia shots on them as they ranged over the terrain. - W. S. Dix

[1] Curtis M. Brown is a licensed land surveyor in California, author of "Boundary Control and Legal Principles" and co-author with the late Winfield Eldridge of "Evidence and Procedures for Boundary Location." An honor graduate of the University of California, he is a visiting professor at Purdue University, President of the land surveying firm Daniels, Brown & Hall, and a Past President of ACSM, a practicing land surveyor, and a foremost authority on land surveying in the United States.

[MP NOTE: W. S. Dix (Walter S. Dix) was ACSM President from 1962-1963 as well as one of the organization's most active members.]

****

PRORATION

THE SURVEYOR AND THE LAW

DECEMBER 1958

Dear Mr. Brown:

Will you comment on how to apply proration and on when proration is applicable and when it is not?

(Signed) E. L. M.

The definition of proration is simple; the difficulty is in knowing when to apply it. Below are a number of principles with brief explanations. It must be understood that any principle is merely a rule of construction or presumption that is subordinate to senior rights and subordinate to the intentions of the parties. Proportionate measurement is a means of distributing any surplus or deficiency that exists between related, found monuments or related, established points.

Definition of proportionate measurement

"A proportionate measurement is one that gives concordant relation between all parts of the line, i.e., the new values given to the several parts, as determined by the remeasurement, shall bear the same relation to the record lengths as the new measurement of the whole line bears to that record." (Section 364, *Manual of Surveying Instructions*, Bureau of Land Management, 1947.)

In the above definition, "of the line" infers a line run by the *same surveyor* or a line resulting from the same map or plat or from simultaneous conveyances. When locating a lot within a subdivision and applying this principle of proration, proration does not extend beyond the boundaries of that subdivision.

Proration does not apply where senior rights exist.

If a person has conveyed part of his property to another, he cannot at a later date convey it to someone else. The first deed gets all that is coming to it and the seller owns *all of the remainder*. If a person owns a remainder, no excess or deficiency exists. A remainder does not have a definite size; it is more or less in character. A person may have more or less land than he expects, but, so long as he has a remainder, the unexpected quantity of land, be it large or small, is all his. It is not divided among several owners.

The key to understanding when proration is applicable and when it is not are the words "time" and "creation." If parcels are *created* in sequence with a lapse of *time* between them, senior rights exist and proration does not apply. For example, if Brown sells a parcel to Jones and at a later time sells another to Smith, Jones has senior rights over either Smith or Brown's remainder. Smith is senior to Brown (the seller must deliver all that he has sold, hence the seller is junior to the buyer), but junior to Jones. Brown is junior to both Smith and Jones. Where such junior and senior deeds exist, any measurement that differs from the record measurement is applied to the particular property to which it is applicable, and this is usually determined by senior rights. It is not divided among all the properties.

But what about subdivision maps where lots are sold in sequence and proration is applied? The word "created" is the key to the difference. Metes and bounds descriptions are usually *created* with a lapse of *time* between each creation and hence are *created in sequence*. Lots in a subdivision map are all *created* at the same *moment of time* (when the map is filed or accepted) even though the lots are sold in sequence. Lots created simultaneously cannot have one lot with greater rights than another, hence senior rights do not exist because no *lapse of time* exists between *creation of parcels.*

Sometimes measurement index is mistaken for proration. If a survey is called for in a particular metes and bounds description and it is discovered that the original surveyor used a chain which was consistently long or short, in order to follow the footsteps of the original surveyor a consistently long or short chain is used. This is not an adjustment between several ownerships or lots, but is an adjustment that applies to one ownership. Strictly speaking this is not proration but is an application of the index-error principle.

Proration is applied whenever the intent of the original owner indicates that he created several parcels simultaneously with equal rights and there is no one parcel designated to receive a remainder.

Simultaneous descriptions are as follows:

(1) Wills and gifts wherein none of the heirs or benefactors are designated to receive a remainder.

(2) Lots in subdivisions wherein a map is filed with a governing body and no lots are sold prior to filing the map or prior to staking.

(3) Lots in any subdivision wherein it is impossible to distinguish an intent to give senior rights to buyers in sequence.

(4) Court proceedings in partition wherein each litigant is given a proportionate share of the whole, and no one is designated to receive the remainder.

(5) Metes and bounds descriptions that are created simultaneously, and no one is designated to receive a remainder.

To illustrate when proration is applied, the following hypothetical situations are used.

Mr. Smith decides that he is going to sell several parcels of land in accordance with the wishes of the buyers. The first buyer takes the east 60 feet; the second buyer takes the west 50 feet; the third buyer takes the 80 feet immediately west of the first buyer, and the fourth buyer takes the remainder. With the fourth sale Mr. Smith files a map (under old laws any map was filed by presentation of filing fees, and in some areas this is still done) showing all four of the parcels with lot numbers. In this case, there has been a *creation of parcels in sequence;* hence, proration does not apply and senior rights exist in spite of the fact that there is a filed map.

Again, Mr. Smith decides to sell off parcels of land, has a plat prepared, proceeds to sell parcels in accordance with the plat, and gives each buyer a copy of the plat. In most states this procedure is now illegal (plats must be filed with a governing body), but in the past this was commonly done. In this instance proration applies, since each lot was created prior to the sale of any one lot and since the map was a consideration of each sale.

Again, Mr. Smith decides to sell off parcels of land and has a plat prepared. He then conveys each parcel by a metes and bounds description without any reference to the plat, although the parcels agree in size and shape with the plat. Proration does not apply since the buyers have no knowledge of the map nor is the map mentioned as a consideration of the deed. Each parcel has a described perimeter that cannot be construed to be a proportional part of a whole. Even if the seller intended each lot to be a proportional part of a map, the buyer could not be held to the secret intentions of the seller; the intentions must be in writing.

Again Mr. Smith decides that he will sell several parcels, has a map prepared, files the map with a governing agency, and sells lots by lot and block numbers. Proration applies since a person buying one lot is buying a proportionate part of a block and there is no way of distinguishing a senior intent or a remainder.

Mr. Smith decides to give each of his three friends one-third of his land. He has metes and bounds descriptions prepared (perimeter descriptions) that gives each an equal amount. He presents all three deeds at substantially the same time. If a deficiency or surplus is discovered, each is entitled to a share, since the intent was to create three parcels of equal size. Proration applies.

But there are certain rules about proration that limit its application.

Proration is not applied beyond an undisturbed original monument that is considered as part of the deeds.

Where there is a survey called for and the original surveyor marks the position of lots, the lots are unchangeable except by resubdivision or proof of fraud. Proration is not used to alter the original location of the original lots but is used to prorate discrepancies found to exist between original monuments.

Proration is not used to distribute an error that can be proved to exist in one place.

Proration is for the purpose of disposing of discrepancies, the location of which cannot be fixed. It presupposes the idea that each owner has an equal right to any surplus or deficiency. Where an error is proved to exist in one place, the presumption that each owner has equal rights is overcome and the error is placed where it occurs.

Proration, as a means of distributing discrepancies, is a rule of last resort.

Only when the idea of equal rights to land is conveyed is proration applied. If it is possible to distinguish a person with prior rights, proration is not used. Proration may be used to re-establish a lost corner, but only after every means has been exhausted to determine the actual original location of the corner. The courts have gone so far as to state that in many instances old, existing fences and lines of occupancy are better evidence of where the original lines were located than is proration or measurements from distant points. If fences show where the original lines were located, proration cannot be used to alter the original lines. Thus, only after other considerations have been eliminated is proration applied. It is a rule of last resort used to distribute unaccountable discrepancies.

Proration cannot alter rights obtained by unwritten means.

If land is gained by occupancy, agreement, or other unwritten means, proration cannot alter these rights. The old lines are extinguished and new title lines exist.

Proration is applied to proportional conveyances under State laws, but not always under Federal sectionalized land law.

A proportional conveyance, such as the North half of Lot 12, receives a proportionate part of the whole area by common law. For sectionalized land Federal Statute law defines proportional conveyances (North 1/2 of the NW 1/4 of Section 7) in such a manner that a proportional part of the area is *not* conveyed.

These are my ideas on the subject, as based upon my reading. Perhaps some of you disagree or would like to add to the above by sending your comments to the editor.

– Curtis M. Brown

EDITOR'S NOTE. - Further explanation is given in Mr. Brown's recent book, "Boundary Control and Legal Principles." (Reviewed, SURVEYING AND MAPPING, October-December 1957, Vol. XVII, No. 4, pages 435 - 436.)

****

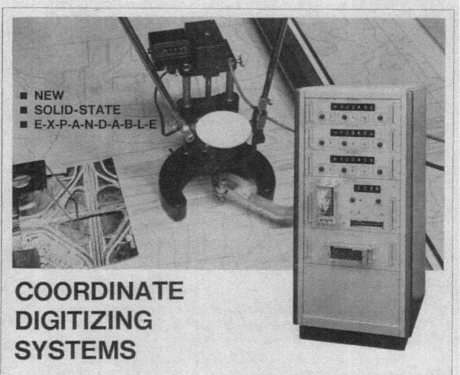

THE SURVEYOR AND THE LAW

MORE ON PROPORTIONATE MEASUREMENT

MARCH 1959

One of the longest trials involving land boundaries has finally appeared in print (Nov. 28, 1958, Advanced California Appellate Reports, Bancroft Whitney Company, page 54). After about 340 days, and about 38,000 typed pages later, a verdict was reached. William Wattles (a former vice president of ACSM) was cross-examined for some 46 days. An official copy of the transcript cost some $6,000.

Of course, the land was valuable. Oil was discovered. Chandler (*Chandler et al v. Hibberd et al*) was the owner of the south half of Section 25 (leased to the Superior Oil Company). Section 36, lying immediately south of Section 25, was owned by Hibberd and leased to the Richfield Oil Company. The dispute arose over the location of the common line between Sections 25 and 36, Township 10 North, Range 27 West, San Bernardino Meridian.

To avoid using such words as plaintiff, defendant, appellants, respondents, etc., in this summary,

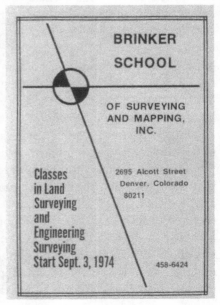

BRINKER
SCHOOL

OF SURVEYING
AND MAPPING,
INC.

Classes
in Land
Surveying
and
Engineering
Surveying
Start Sept. 3, 1974

2695 Alcott Street
Denver, Colorado
80211

458-6424

the word "Superior" will be used to include all owners and interested parties in Section 25 and "Richfield" will be used to include all parties interested in Section 36.

Superior claimed that the line between Sections 25 and 36 had to be located by proportionate measurements. Richfield claimed that the line was fixed by an old fence (acquiescence, agreement or adverse possession). The original section corners were either lost or obliterated. It was stipulated that the court was to determine the true location of the common line between Sections 25 and 36 whether the fence constituted the original ownership line or not.

The lower court declared that the fence *did* constitute the true ownership line and declared that the true original section line was north (at a specified place) of the fence line. The court rejected proportionate measurement in this case. Upon appeal to a higher court (Appellate), the higher court declared that the fence line *did not* constitute an agreed property line and that the true section line, as determined by the lower court, must be used. Since this section line was north of the fence, Richfield obtained more land than they contended to be theirs.

Two items are of interest to surveyors. (1) Why was proportionate measurement rejected? (2) What was it that determined the section line when the original corners were absent from view? As of secondary interest, why did the lower court accept a fence and the upper court reject it?

The fence erected between the two properties was the result of a survey, was for the purpose of a cattle enclosure, and was erected by a leasee. The owner of Section 25, at the time of the erection of the fence, wrote a letter (1938) to the owner of Section 36 to the effect that he would not object to the erection of the fence "as long as he did not make a boundary line between the two properties." For this reason, the upper court reasoned that the fence was not an agreed boundary nor was it acquiesced in. Since the upper court did not accept the fence, the original location of the section line between Sections 25 and 36 became the division line.

Proportional Measurement. Superior contended that the corners common to Sections 25 and 36 were lost and that proportionate measurement was the only means that could be used to restore them. Their contention was that the court must accept measurements between a corner a mile north of the disputed line and a corner a mile south of the disputed line and then reset the "lost" corner by proportionate methods. When doing this a 660-foot shortage existed; hence, Sections 36 and 25 would each be 330 feet short. Of course, this contention is perfectly valid providing (1) the missing corner is in fact lost and (2) providing the corners from which the measurements are made are in fact the original corners.

An examination of the evidence presented indicates that the corners one mile north of the disputed corners were questionable. The surveyor for Superior accepted an old fence line as being the north line of Section 25. The authenticity of the original corners along this line was never proven. To further complicate things, the corners located in more than a mile to the north of the disputed line fell within the limits of Cuyama Rancho and were never set. "The court found that they (corners along the north line of Section 25) were not actually relocations of corners or corner accessories of the original (Glover) survey and that they are not located in the position of Glover's corners or accessories." There being no north line established for Section 25, the shortage in boundaries disappears and with it the sole basis for relocation of the corners of the South line of Section 25 by proportionate means.

Upon commenting on the proportionate method, the following points were brought out. Proportionate measurement "must not be resorted to unless all other prescribed methods fail" (*Verdi Development Co. v. Dono - Han Mining Co.*, 296 P 2nd 429). Proportionate measurement is not used "if the line can be retraced as it was established in the field" (*County of Yolo v. Nolan*, 77 P 1006). "If the exact spot (for a corner) cannot be found, it (the court) must, if possible, decide from the data appearing in evidence its (the corner) approximate position, and the proportionate method is to be used only when no other reasonable method is possible and it must be so used that it does not contradict or conflict with the official data that are not impeached, and which, when not impeached, confine the actual position within certain limits." (*Weaver v. Howatt*, 161 Cal 77). "The law is well established that the obliteration of a monument made in a survey does not destroy such survey nor justify a court in disregarding it where enough data remain to locate the place occupied by the monument by reference to natural objects referred to in the survey. Nor does such obliteration justify the adoption of the proportionate method of locating a common corner as a lost corner, where the field-notes refer to certain natural objects which can be found along the line mentioned so as to approximately locate it." (*Hammond Lumber Co. v. Haw*, 274 P 386).

The court found that the corners were obliterated, not lost. In deciding where to locate the obliterated corner, the court examined (by field trips) the topography and other evidence to be found in the field and compared the topography and evidence with the original field notes. J. R. Glover, a United States Deputy Surveyor, made the original controlling survey in 1881 and 1883. The terrain was rough. The marks set by Glover to monument the corners of Section 25 were not found.

The southwest and southeast corners of Section 36 were found and were not in dispute. The rerunning of the westerly line of this section illustrates the court's processes of relocating the obliterated corners. The call of Glover's notes is "Ascend. 31.00 (chains) Top of spur, bears East and West, descend." The court found this spur at a distance of 31.26 chains with certainty. The next note states, "67.57 Cross gulch 10 links wide, course Northwest and ascend." The gulch was found identifiable with certainty, but it was found to be 73.20 chains north of the southwest corner instead of 67.57 chains. The next call was "70.00 Top of spur, bears Northwest and Southeast and descend. 80.00 set post for corner." There was an ascent to the spur and a descent to the corner. If proportionate measurements were used, the proportionate point would fall on the ascent to the spur instead of on the descent from it. The court found that the most certain location for the section corner was 12.43 chains north of the gulch and on the descent as called for in the field notes. This made the section line 85.63 chains long. Superior had contended there was a shortage of five chains; the court concluded that there was an overage of 5.63 chains.

The east boundary of Section 36 did not have many natural monuments. The east boundary, being a township line, was retraced twice by early deputy surveyors and found by them to be as originally reported (or very nearly so). Certain "descents" and "enter rolling land" were identified closely in

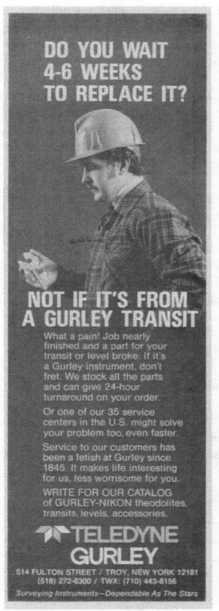
accordance with the original notes. Since the terrain was consistent with the notes, the court ruled that the proper location of the corner was 80.12 chains (at N 00° 06' 20" W) from the southeast corner of Section 36 as called for in the original notes. The bearing was arrived at by means not clear in the report.

The following points, as quoted from previous court cases, were brought out. "It is not the province of the Court to determine where the corner should have been fixed. This is not an action to vacate the government survey. It must be assumed that the line was measured and the monuments set. Their positions, as set, fix the rights of the parties, regardless of the inaccuracy of the measurements and the errors in distance found in the field-notes. The trial court must ascertain, as near as may be, where this monument was set by the government surveyor." (*Weaver v. Howatt*, 161 Cal. 77). On page 86 of this same case is stated, "It is for the trial court, upon all the evidence, to fix the place at a point where it will best accord with the natural objects described in the field notes as being about it, and found to exist on the ground, and which is least inconsistent with the distances mentioned in the notes and plat." And in 171 Cal 302 is, "The court is bound to assume that the line was run on the ground and that the post was set in a mound of stones at a place fixed for the common corner of the four sections as the field notes show. All trace of that monument has disappeared, and the exact place where it was erected cannot now be identified. But under the above rules these circumstances do not destroy the survey nor justify the court in disregarding it, when enough can be ascertained therefrom and identified on the ground to approximately locate the corner. The court, under the above authorities, and in obedience to the former decision of this court, could not do otherwise than it did, that is, fix the corner 'at a point where it will best agree with the natural objects described in the field notes as being about it, and found to exist on the ground and which is least inconsistent with the distances mentioned in the notes and plat.' The government owned the land, caused the survey to be made, and sold the land by reference thereto. Purchasers must abide by the results regardless of the lack of rectangular shape of the subdivisions so made."

Comments on the case. In this case proportionate measurement was rejected for the obvious reason that the original location of corners from which proportionate measurement could have been made were never proven. If the location of the corners north of the obliterated corners could have been identified beyond a shadow of doubt, would the outcome have been the same? I am inclined to think that it would.

Proportionate measurement, as clearly brought out, is a "rule of last resort." All other means must be proven inapplicable before resorting to proportionate measurement. "In the absence of senior rights, excess and deficiency found to exist between original monuments are distributed among the lots in proportion to the original record measurement of the lots. This is a principle of last resort." (*Boundary Control and Legal Principles*, by Curtis M. Brown).

When the public lands were surveyed, field notes were kept. The terrain, natural monuments accessories, and like objects called for in the original government field notes make it improbable that proportionate measurement will be used to restore corners in sectionalized lands. But in the case of private surveys, such as a local subdivision done by a local surveyor, field notes are usually not available. Without field notes to identify natural objects, the usage of proportionate measurement, as a last resort, is much more frequent. The number of times that proportionate measurement may be used increases with a decrease in knowledge of what the original surveyor did. Proportionate measurement is a means of disposing of errors the location of which cannot be explained, and, with meager original survey notes, many errors cannot be explained.

The method used by the court to locate lost corners by identifiable natural objects is following well-established principles. Quoting from *Boundary Control and Legal Principles*: Section 171. "The boundaries of the public lands, when approved and accepted, are unchangeable, except by re-subdivision." Section 172. "The original township, section, and quarter-section corners must stand as the true corners which they were intended to represent, whether in the place shown by the field notes or not." Section 177. "The plat and all the original field notes become a part of the grant." Section 184. "Where the direction of a line can be determined from the mean position of line trees or blaze markers, the direction so established will be controlling where the corner monument is lost. Sometimes a stream or canyon crossing becomes controlling, especially where the crossing is close to a corner."

When making a survey, it is often a temptation for the surveyor to "bury" discrepancies by proportionate means rather than diligently spend the time to discover the cause of the discrepancy. Proportionate measurement should not be used except as a last resort.

– Curtis M. Brown

****

SEPTEMBER 1959

I received the following letter from William C. Wattles, one of the surveyors in the Superior - Richfield case (See SURVEYING AND MAPPING, March 1959, Vol. XIX, No. 1, pages 101-103). Apparently there was adequate foundation for the possibility of using double proportioning; however, the court chose to use topography in preference to double proportioning. Unfortunately court reports only publish the winning side of a case, and such information as given by Mr. Wattles generally is not available.

Dear Curt:

I read with interest your review and comments on the Chandler-Hibberd (Superior-Richfield) case Appellate decision. You did a good job of quoting and commenting. There is one item apparently which you overlooked or were unaware of.

The first three lines on page 102 of your article in SURVEYING AND MAPPING (March 1959) read – "the corners located more than a mile to the north of the disputed line fell within the limits of the Cuyama Rancho and were never set." This is incorrect.

The history of the Cuyama Rancho in brief is this. Shortly after the

Commission for operation of the Treaty of Guadalupe was created, a petition for patent for the Cuyama was filed. After some time of consideration the petition was denied, and the land became Public Land. In 1854 surveyor Norris was authorized to survey the area and did so, covering T. 10 N., R. 26 & 27 W., and other land in the area. In so doing he surveyed and monumented in T. 10 N., R. 27 W., only sections between the south line of Sections 1 to 6 and north line of Sections 19 to 25, stating in his field notes that the latter line was run as a Township offset line. His field notes for both Townships give considerable topography.

In 1872 the petition for Patent of the Rancho was revived and granted. So, in 1872 surveyor Harris was ordered to survey the boundaries of the Rancho. This he did, tying specifically by recital of lines and monuments found to section lines of Norris, as far as the south boundary of the Rancho survey was concerned. The Rancho was patented and map recorded.

In 1881 & 1883, surveyor Glover was authorized to complete the survey of the T. 10 N., R. 27 W., and other land in the area. His field notes show he followed the south ranch line, finding the original corners set (or, rather, discovered) by Harris at the angle points of the Ranch boundary.

So we have a continuous location and positioning of the south Ranch line from original sectioning, through patent, and boundary sectionizing.

There is considerable information, some of it evidential, that the fence line purported to be the south Ranch boundary was set some 10 chains south of the patent boundary and partially monumented, due either to design to get more ranch area or to faulty location of purported corners of sections of the Glover survey.

In Thomasson's and my run of the lines, we picked up some dozen original corners or bearing tree positions or reliable replacement monuments in Ranges 26 to 27; also some 20 excellent "topo" ties, which gave corner positions of great strength. The record distances were exceptionally close to the re-measurement, and the bearings were also within limits. The total of our findings gave a clear indication that the fence line purported to be the ranch line was incorrect. It was the only thing out of gear in the whole area, except a couple of bearing trees, which were proven to be unassociated with proper section corners.

I thought this might clear you from any misconception as to location. Incidentally, the substance of the above notations was presented to the court as testimony, so there was judicial notice to warrant the decision in these respects as to the location of north line Section 36 (the disputed line).

Cordially, WM. C. WATTLES

****

544

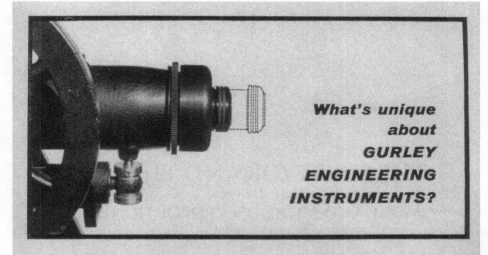

THE SURVEYOR AND THE LAW

MORE AND MORE ON PROPORTIONING

SEPTEMBER 1959

The property surveyor frequently finds situations that are not discussed or explained by standard textbooks. It is these perplexing problems and their solutions that stimulate thinking and prevent our profession from reaching the doldrums. Even simple problems sometimes require careful consideration. Below are two familiar sectionalized land problems that, to my knowledge, still have the last word to be said on them. Both are lost corner-proportioning problems.

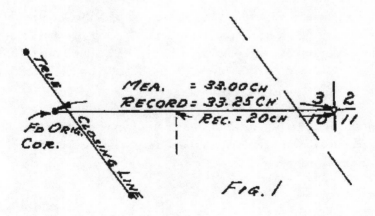

In Figure 1, the closing corner and the section corner are both found.

By rerunning the Rancho grant line it is found that the closing corner was set one chain within the Rancho grant. The original recorded distance to the closing corner was 33.25 chains, and the recent measure to the found original corner was 33 chains.

Problem: Where do you set the 1/16 corner which was originally shown as being 20 chains from the section corner? Two solutions exist, and these are:

(1) 20/33.25 x 33 = 19.85 chains.

(2) 20/33.25 x 32 = 19.25 chains.

The closing corner must, of course, be moved to the line closed upon (the Rancho line). The actual length of the line is then only 32 chains instead of 33.25, as originally recorded or 33.00 chains as recently measured. The 1/16 corner, never having been set originally, is always set by proportionate measurement between the corners to the east and west. But do you proportion from the grant line or from the original stone as set?

My contention has always been that since the original surveyor set a monument and recorded a certain distance to that particular monument, the recent surveyor should proportion from the found position of that original stone. After he has done this, he relocates the closing corner on the true line closed on. In this illustration, the fractional parcel to the west would receive the major portion of the shortage. The proportional measure would be

13.25/33.25 x 33 = 13.15 chains.

From this would be subtracted one chain, hence the western parcel suffers a loss of 1.10 chains, while the eastern parcel suffers only a loss of 0.15 chain. This is just. The fractional parcel was original given land that the government did not own, hence it must suffer that loss.

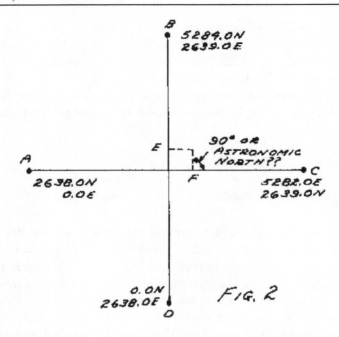

In one instance in California, closing corners were set more than 1,200 feet into a land grant (El Cajon). Obviously, it would be impossible to prorate other than from the original corners. All of certain fractional parcels were found to be wholly within the Rancho. Since the government did not own the land, title could not pass. This would be equivalent to finding the true grant line in the position of the dashed line in Figure 1. If the true grant line were discovered in this position, it is obvious that the 1/16 corner could not be prorated.

A second problem involves double proportioning. Suppose that the four quarter corners are found as shown in Figure 2 and that the record distances were each a half mile. The rule calls for a re-measurement from *A* to *C* and set a point halfway (*F*). Next, measure from *B* to *D* and set point *E* halfway. From point *E* a line is run east or west, and from point *F* a line is run north or south. What is meant by north and east? Do you run astronomic north and east, or do you run at 90° to the lines *AC* and *BD*? The problem of double proportioning is simplified if east and north mean due east and due north. The coordinates of the true corner would be

(5284.0 N - 0.0 N) /2 = 2642.0 N, and
(5282.0 E - 0.0 E) /2 = 2641.0 E.

Obviously, considerably more calculation is required if east and north are interpreted to mean at 90° to the lines. Correspondence with the Bureau of Land Management indicates that they interpret the east and north to be astronomic and the method of computing coordinates as illustrated is correct.

Some of the record-of-survey checking departments (Los Angeles) insist that 90° to the lines is proper, others (San Diego) insist that astronomic east and north is correct. In most instances, the differences will be negligible. However, occasionally when lines deviate substantially from north or east, significant differences arise. I will take the Bureau of Land Management's letter as final (astronomic directions) until they indicate a change of thought.

****

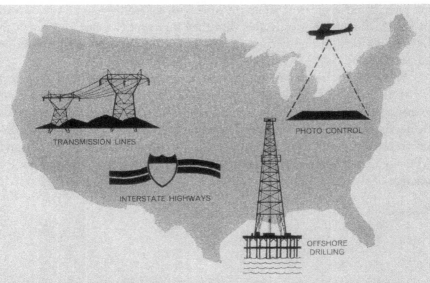

Electrotape cuts survey costs everywhere it's used!

THE SURVEYOR AND THE LAW

REMNANT RULE AND PRORATION

SEPTEMBER 1960

Dear Mr. Brown:

At the Minnesota Land Surveyors meeting in April [1960] will you comment on the Barrett Perkins case (113 Minn 480)?
(signed) HAROLD HOFSTRAND

DISCUSSION:

Below are shown the essential data of Hughes' Addition to the City of St. Paul. The significant facts are:

(1) Lot 22 scales 50 feet, more or less, but not 75.38 feet as indicated.

(2) The block, when measured, is 25 feet short.

(3) The court ruled that Lot 22 must take all of the shortage merely because it was irregularly dimensioned, or more specifically, it was a remnant.

Court cases should be viewed with caution. Each case is judged on its own merits. A case that is similar, yet has one point of difference, may end up with opposite results. The Barrett-Perkins case, like all other court cases, cannot be taken at its face value and extended to all other cases which by outward appearances seem to be similar.

If we are to believe the Barrett-Perkins case, which I do not, the remnant rule may be applied in Minnesota. However, the case does not spell out when the rule may or may not be applied. To apply the remnant rule, according to this case, two elements must be present and a third one is implied. First, there must be regular sequence of lots with uniform width, said width usually being in even feet. Second, there must be only one-odd shaped or one irregularly dimensioned lot at the end of the block. The theory is that if the subdivider had known that there was a different block length he would have given it to the end lot, hence excess or deficiency should be given to that end lot. The implied third element, slighted, but there, is a mistake.

This remnant rule has obvious shortcomings. It is never proper to conjecture on what a man would have done had he known differently; what he did is what counts. The remnant rule is based upon a possibility, not a probability. Very few jurisdictions accept it, and I am in complete agreement that it should not be used.

Why should a fully dimensioned lot be reduced in size merely because it is off shaped?

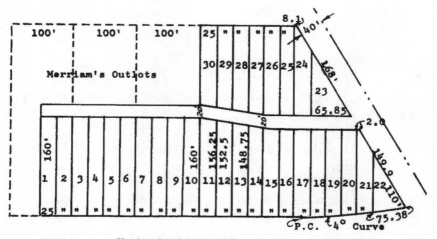

Hughes' Midway Add.

The remnant rule is like color of title in that by outward appearances it seems to be good, but actually it is not. There are numerous circumstances whereby the end lot in a block is given all the surplus or deficiency, but the reason for giving the end lot the surplus or deficiency, in my opinion, should never be attributed to the remnant rule. While the verdict in the Barrett-Perkins case was just and correct, the wording of the opinion of the judge was unfortunate.

Before going into an analysis of this case, I would like to remind you of three legal principles that all of us recognize as being correct.

First, I think that you will all agree that once a surveyor sets an original monument or line and conveyances are made calling for that monument or line, the line is fixed in position and can only be changed by resubdivision. While it is true that title lines may be altered by unwritten rights or by written conveyances, original lines, except for resubdivision or where a senior right is interfered with, are unalterable.

Second, if the original surveyor makes a mistake in recording his measurements and monuments are in conflict with his record distances, the monuments control. What the surveyor set upon the ground is proof of what he did; what he records is merely an aid to find what the surveyor did on the ground. A mistake in recording measurements does not serve as an excuse to change monument positions. If a surveyor makes a mistake in a particular lot, that mistake is left in that particular lot. To bring this principle of mistake into operation there must be sufficient evidence to show that there was a mistake and also there must be sufficient evidence to prove where the mistake belongs. A mistake, the location of which cannot be fixed, must be disposed of and proration is often applied, but a mistake that can be localized is never prorated.

Third, proration is a rule of last resort. If there is proof of where excess or deficiency belongs, then that discrepancy is placed where it occurs. If someone is designated to receive a remainder, then proration cannot apply. Proration is a means of disposing of errors, the positions of which cannot be fixed. It is not a means of distributing a discrepancy that can be proven to exist in one spot.

Below are a series of actual circumstances that illustrate the shortcomings of the remnant rule and also illustrate the above points.

In Figure 1 is a condition to be found along the Rancho El Cajon land grant line. It can be proven by existing monuments that the government surveyor, for some unexplainable reason, did overlap the true grant line by some 1,200 feet. In such a situation, the 1/16 corners, or, as they are sometimes called in Wisconsin, 1/8 corners, should never have been penalized by prorating from the true grant line. Corners are prorated from the location as monumented by the government, then the area lost by overlap is subtracted. The 1,200 feet of deficiency is not prorated. By appearance, the remnant rule seems to apply in this circumstance, but obviously the reason for giving the deficiency to the odd lottings is because of a mistake and not because of the remnant rule.

Figure 3 illustrates this same point. Part of the Bay of San Diego was subdivided. Since title to land below the mean high tide line could not be conveyed, part of Lots 'F' and 'G' could not exist. Lot 'F' was fixed in position and cannot be enlarged by proration. All the deficiency in this block was caused by a mistake (the mistake of subdividing San Diego Bay) and that mistake belongs in Lots 'F' and 'G.' The deficiency of some 4.5 feet is certainly not prorated. Here again the remnant rule seems to be applicable, but in reality it is not. A mistake caused the trouble.

Figure 2 shows a condition found to exist between San Diego and former East San Diego. The boundary between the two cities was formed by a Spanish Land Grant line. When surveying blocks within the subdivision of City Heights, all blocks except those adjoining the land grant line are found to be of record measurement; those adjoining the land grant line are 4.8 feet long. In the University Heights subdivision, all blocks except those adjoining the land grant boundary are of record measurement; those adjoining the boundary are 4.8 feet short. The implication of the evidence is obvious. After the subdivisions were filed and of record, the City of San Diego improved, paved, and tie pointed Boundary Street. At the time they did this, they located the true land grant line some 4.8 feet westerly of the old line. The surveyors for the subdivisions were definitely wrong. Unfortunately, this took 4.8 feet away from one side of Boundary Street and gave it to the other side. In such a situation, proration from the new street line cannot apply. The lots that had their land taken away by the City must suffer the loss. Proration only applies from the original position of lots, never from a new position gained by occupancy. The remnant rule appears to be proper in this circumstance, but the real reason is adverse occupancy. While adverse occupancy can alter title lines, it can never alter original survey lines.

Figure 4 shows a situation almost identical to that found in the Barrett-Perkins case. Lot 'D' has a dimension of 66.58 feet on the map, yet it scales 96 feet. A mathematical closure of the data shown on the original map reveals that the lot will not close by 30 feet east and west. The 66.58 feet is proven to be a mistake and should be 96.58 feet. Only a fool would try to argue that the 30 feet of excess must be prorated among all the lots. The intent from scaling the drawing and the intent as disclosed by a mathematical closure was to make Lot D 96.56 feet. Mistakes are placed where they occur and in this case, it is in Lot 'D.' The excess of 30 feet is not prorated. The reason for doing so is not because of the remnant rule

- both ends of the block are remnants. The reason is because of a mistake in Lot 'D.'

To me, the Barrett-Perkins case is an identical situation. If all of you will scale the east-west dimension of Lot 22 on the map before you, you will find it to be 50 feet. To show the absurdity of the lower court's contention that the length of Lot 22 was 75.38 feet, scale off on the southerly line of Lot 22, 75 feet from the southeast corner. You will find that it falls exactly on the lot line between Lots 21 and 20. Next draw a straight line connecting this point and the most northerly corner of Lot 22 as plotted. You have a diagonal line completely out of agreement with the original subdivider's intent.

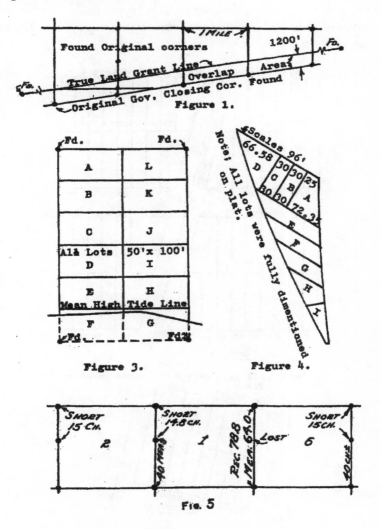

Figure 1.

Figure 3.

Figure 4.

Fig. 5

A mistake was made on the map and it is placed where it occurs, namely in Lot 22. The fact that the block is almost 25 feet short also proves this. The original subdivider made a mistake by the width of a 25-foot lot.

I am in complete agreement with the court in the final outcome of its verdict, but I do not agree with the reasoning, i.e., the application of the remnant rule. The judge noted that there was a mistake and said so; he should have stopped right there.

The syllabus in a court case is the opinion of the reporter or abstractor of the case. In this syllabus the abstractor indicates that a mistake is the cause of the trouble and because of this mistake the deficiency must fall in Lot 22. The judge in his analysis accented the idea of the last lot being a remnant, hence, so he says, the mistake is to be put in the last lot because it is a remnant. If he had said that the deficiency belongs in Lot 22 because of a mistake, he would have been on firm ground.

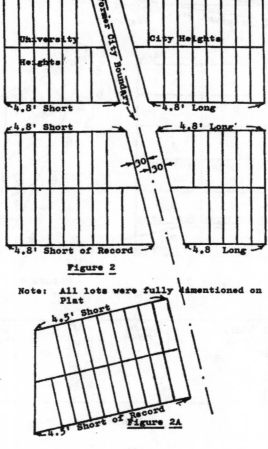

Figure 2

Note: All lots were fully dimentioned on Plat

Figure 2A

The remnant rule of giving surplus or deficiency to the last lot merely because it is irregular in dimension is without reason. In one block along the City of San Diego boundary line the situation is shown in Figure 2A. As pointed out, the reason for the shortage indicated is that 4.5 feet was taken from Lots 10 and 11 when Boundary Street was improved. According to the remnant rule, every lot would be shifted 4.5 feet westerly and the shortage given to Lots 1 and 20. In such a situation the remnant rule can never apply! The deficiency must be placed where it occurs, namely in Lots 10 and 11. This is exactly the reverse of the remnant rule.

The judge in the Barrett-Perkins case did render the correct decision, but I can hardly believe that he meant his decision to apply to every case wherein a dimensioned irregular lot exists at the end of a block. The more logical view of his opinion is, "Where there is a remnant lot and the evidence supports the idea that the remnant should receive all the excess or deficiency, then place it there. But if the evidence shows that the remnant lot was to receive its full measure, it is entitled to an equal share of surplus or deficiency." Viewing his decision in this light it makes sense. You will note that one of the closing statements of the judge was, "The rule furnishes a definite and safe method and guide for *mistakes* of this type."

At law, every case is judged on its own merits, and this case justified his opinion. Another one might not. To illustrate the proof of this we need only to refer to sectionalized lands. The most northerly and most westerly tiers of lottings in a township are remnants; they are what is left over. Yet the judges have uniformly refused to apply the remnant rule even in extreme cases when justice would be better served by doing so. In the case of Goroski v Tawncy, 121 Minn 189 the evidence was as shown in Figure 5.

Three section lines proved that the original surveyor had, in fact, set the 1/4 corner very close to 40 chains from the section corner and that very large deficiencies existed in the closing half mile. What would be more logical than to apply the Barrett-Perkins idea in relocating the lost 1/4 corner between Sections 1 and 6 and thus place the entire remnant mistake of 15.39 chains where it logically belongs: in the last half mile? But, did the court do this? Despite all the evidence that a mistake should belong in the last half mile and despite the remnant rule, the lost corner position was determined by proration. The remnant rule does not apply to sectionalized lands, yet if the law were consistent with the Barrett-Perkins case, it would. This merely points to the fact that Minnesota law can frown upon the remnant rule.

While it is true that in most instances where there is a remnant, the remnant rule does appear to apply, it is also true that in most instances there is another more logical rule for giving the deficiency to the end lot; i.e., the rule of a mistake.

In most blocks with small measurement errors, we adjust our chain to the original length of the original surveyor's chain and no problem ensues. This is the measurement index principle. But where there is a large discrepancy, the chances are that a blunder was made and the entire mistake belongs where the blunder occurred.

A far better rule than the remnant rule is: "Seek the cause of surplus or deficiency, and if a mistake can be found, place the mistake where it occurs."

****

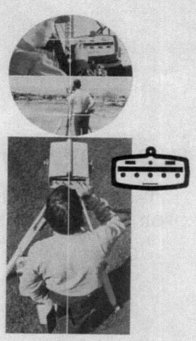

THE SURVEYOR AND THE LAW

PASSING CALLS AND
PROPORTIONAL MEASUREMENTS

CURTIS M. BROWN

SEPTEMBER 1962

Questions concerning proper procedures to be followed in locating property boundaries will be answered to the best of our ability in this department. Contributions suitable for publication in this department – covering special legal problems or the results of court cases – are requested. Communications should be addressed to Harold R. Brooks, Chairman, Publications Committee, ACSM, Coast and Geodetic Survey, Washington 25, D.C.

Frequently, questions as to how to do legal research are asked. It can be done with a good law library, some time, and knowledge of legal notations. In general, law books, such as *Corpus Juris Secundum*, under the headings "boundaries," "waters," or "deeds" may be found references sufficient for several years of study and reading.

William Wattles, in his numerous talks, has frequently referred to Weaver v. Howatt, a classic case contrasting proportional measurement as opposed to passing calls and other physical objects called for in the original, government, sectionalized-land notes. This case is further proof of the statement that "proportional measurement is used as a last resort."

The legal notation is Weaver v. Howatt, 161 Cal 78. In California Supreme Court reports, within volume 161, on page 78 is found a summary of this 1911 case. To illustrate court cases, parts are quoted below. The first part of the report is known as the syllabus and represents the opinion of the court reporter; it is a summary of the law. The second portion of the report contains the summary of facts in the case and arguments as to why the case was decided as it was. Opposition arguments are often omitted. The note "Shaw, J." means that this opinion was written by Judge Shaw.

Reading only one case can lead to serious errors of opinion; a later case may reverse the early one. Also, a small difference in evidence may lead to a different outcome. While one specific case is of interest and is fun to read, the old adage "a little knowledge is a dangerous thing" may be applicable. Final opinion on what to do for any set of survey facts must come from extensive knowledge of survey location procedures as used under many circumstances. In fact, many people refuse to quote cases because there is danger of erroneous interpretation.

J. H. G. WEAVER et al., Respondents, v. THEODORE H. HOWATT, Appellant.

Public Lands - Official Survey - Lost Monuments - Location of Boundaries - Proportional Sub-division. - In a controversy involving the adjustment of the boundary lines of United States sections and sectional subdivisions, and in which the place where the original monuments were set cannot be located on the ground, and the objects referred to in the record of the official survey furnish no means of finding the actual location of the original lines or corners, it is proper to resort to the proportional method of subdivision.

Id. - Field Notes and Plat of Survey – Re-Establishment of Lines as Originally Located - Such method should not be followed where there are data in the maps and field notes constituting the official survey, which, in connection with the evidence as to the present condition and position of the natural objects referred to therein, renders it possible to re-establish the actual position of the controvert lines as originally located.

Id. - Map and Field - Notes Part of Description in Patent. - The maps and field-notes of the survey, embodied in a United States patent to land, constitute a part of the description.

Id. - Monuments Control Courses and Distances. - The monuments and natural objects referred to in such survey, so far as they can be located, are controlling, and usually prevail over courses and distances.

Id. - Fixing Common Sectional Corner - Errors in Field-Notes and Plat - Approximate Position as Determined by Field Notes - Proportionate Subdivision when inapplicable. - In such a controversy, when it becomes necessary to fix the common corner of four adjoining sections, the monument of which has become lost, the court, notwithstanding errors in the field notes and plat rendering it impossible to locate the exact spot fixed by the official survey, is not justified in fixing the corner at a point determined by a theoretical subdivision of the common boundary line, if the field-notes and plat contain ample data to show that it was not fixed by the official survey at or near the place selected by the court. It is not the province of the court to determine where the corner should have been fixed, and, if the exact spot cannot be found, it must, if possible, decide from such data its approximate position.

Id. - Proportionate Subdivision When Applicable - Location Within Defined Limits. - The proportional method of subdivision is to be used only when no other reasonable method is possible, and it must be so used that it does not contradict or conflict with the official data that are not impeached, and which, if not impeached, confine the actual position within certain limits. The application of the proportional method must, in that case, be also confined to the same limits.

Id. - Duty of Court to Fix Controvert Point to Conform to Natural Objects. - Under such circumstances, it is for the trial court, upon all the evidence, to fix the place where it will best accord with the natural objects described in the field notes as being about it, and found to exist on the ground, and which is least inconsistent with the distances mentioned in the notes and plat.

Id. - Distances May Control Under Certain Circumstances. - The circumstances may be such that distances control, especially where the natural objects do not definitely fix the place, but leave it to be fixed within certain limits.

APPEAL from a judgment of the Superior Court of Humboldt County. Clifton H. Connick, Judge.

The facts are stated in the opinion of the court.

G. W. Hunter, and Denver Sevier, for Appellant.

B. W. Wilson, J. H. G. Weaver, and W. F. Clyborne, for Respondents.

SHAW, J. - This is an appeal from a judgment in favor of plaintiffs.

In form the action is to quiet title to land, but the sole object of the suit is to determine the location of the boundary line between the lands of plaintiffs and the lands of the defendant.

All the lands are situated in township two, south, range three, east, Humboldt base and meridian. The plaintiffs own the north half of the northeast quarter of section 11, and the northwest quarter of the northwest quarter of section 12. The latter adjoins the eastern end of the first tract. The defendant owns the southwest quarter of the southwest quarter of section 1 and the adjoining southeast quarter of the southeast quarter of section 2. The north line of sections 11 and 12 forms the north line of plaintiff's land. The same line, being also the south line of sections 1 and 2, forms the south line of the defendant's land. The location of this common boundary is the point in dispute. The location claimed by plaintiffs is, according to the findings of the court, several chains north of its position as claimed by the defendant. A tract ten chains wide, north and south, and about forty chains long, or the full extent of defendant's two tracts, east and west, comprises the disputed territory.

The location of this common section line was fixed by the official survey of the United States from whom both parties derive title. The court found that the monuments set by the United States surveyors at the common corner of sections 1, 2, 11, and 12, to show the position of this line, have disappeared and that the original location thereof could not be ascertained. The same finding was made as to the quarter section corners on the line dividing sections 1 and 12 from sections 2 and 11. The north common corner of sections 1 and 2 and the south common corner of sections 11 and 12 were accurately ascertained and located by the government monuments there set. No attempt was made to locate the position of the east and west line in question by reference to monuments set elsewhere thereon, for instance, at the northeast corner of section 12 on the range line, or at the northwest corner of section 11. It was apparently agreed that those corners could not be found. The court found, in effect, that the north and south line actually run by the government surveyors between the common corner of sections 11, 12, 13, and 14 and the common corner of sections 1, 2, 35, and 36 cannot be retraced, found, or located on the ground by any of the monuments set thereon or by any of the natural objects mentioned in the field notes, and that the distances therein given between the natural objects mentioned are not accurate. Having decided that it was impossible to find the actual position of the monument set at the common corner of sections 1, 2, 11, and 12 or the positions of the monuments set at the quarter section corners on this north and south section line, the court concluded that they were "lost corners" and that it must remeasure the whole line, divide it into four equal parts and set monuments accordingly without regard to the government survey. This was done and the portions falling to plaintiffs and defendant, respectively, by this method were adjudged to them, the result being to take from defendant a large part of the land he claims.

The propriety of this mode of adjusting boundary lines of United States sections and sectional subdivisions, in a case where the places where the original monuments were set cannot be located on the ground, and the objects referred to in the record of the official survey furnish no means of finding the actual location of the original lines or corners is not seriously disputed. The defendant's claim is that this is not such a case and that there were data in the notes and maps from which the court could have and should have found and declared the actual position or location of the line in controversy. If this is true, of course the rule for re-establishing lost corners or lines does not apply. (Yolo Co. v. Nolan, 144 Cal. 448). The decision of the case, therefore, depends on the question whether from the records of the official survey, that is the maps and field notes, and the evidence as to the present conditions and positions of natural objects the position of the line can be lawfully located and should be fixed at a point more favorable to defendant.

The line upon which the chief dispute arises is the line dividing sections 1 and 12 from sections 2 and 11. S. W. Foreman ran the section lines of the official survey in July 1875. In running the line, he began at the south common corner of sections 11 and 12 and ran north to the township line. The following is a copy of his field-notes of the survey of that line.

"North bet. secs. 11, 12, Var. 18° 30' E.

40.00 – Old 1/4 sec. post 4 ft. long and 4 in. dia., stone mound made mound 4-1/2 ft. at base and 2 ft. high for 1/4 sec. cor. No trees near. Brushy.

"55.00 – Begin steep descent.

"80.00 – Old sec. cor. post 4 ft. long and 4 in. square and made mound 4-1/2 ft. at base and 2 ft. high, with pits 18 x 18 x 12 in. for the cor. to secs. 1, 2, 11, 12. No trees near.
Land hilly, N.W. slope.
Soil 2d rate.
Timber, fir, oak, redwood & Madrone.
Brush some and chaparral.
"North on a random line bet. secs. 1, 2,
Va. 18° 30' E.

"11.85 – A creek 20 lks. wide runs N.W.

"13.00 – Enter bottom land bears E. & W.

"20.60 – To a point 10 links E. of old meander post on left bank of Eel River bet. secs. 1, 2, from which post I run a base West 300 lks. to a point from which the old meander post on right bank of Eel River on line bet. secs. 1, 2, bears N 19 1/4° E which gives 8.59 chs. for the distance across the river, to which add 20.60 chs. the distance S. of river gives.

"29.19 – To a point 10 lks. E. of old meander post on right bank of river.

"40.00 – Set temporary 1/4 sec. cor.

"80.50 – Intersect the N. Bdy. of Tp. 40 lks E. of the cor. to secs. 1, 2, 35, 36, which cor. agrees with the notes furnished by the office and from which I run S 0°17' E on a true line bet. secs. 1, 2.

"40.50 – Set a 1/4 sec. post 4 ft. long and 4 in. dia. in old stone mound made 4 – 1/2 ft. at base and 2 ft. high. No trees near.

"51.31 – Old meander post 4 ft. long and 4 in. dia. in a mound 4 ft. at base and 2 ft. high with pits 18 x 18 x 12 in. and from which old bearing tree an alder 10 in. diam. bears N 18° W, 86 lks. dist.

"59.90 – Old meander post on left bank of Eel River on line bet. secs. 1, 2, with mound and pits.

"80.50 – The cor. to secs. 1, 2, 11, 12.
Land broken, hill slopes N. & S. to River.
Soil 2d & 3d rate.
Timber, oaks, fir, redwood and madrone."

The distances given in these notes as those at which the natural objects were reached are all found to be inaccurate.

The effect of the judgment of the court dividing the common line of the four sections arbitrarily into four equal parts, regardless of the natural objects referred to in the field notes, is to place the section corner, locating the line dividing plaintiff's land from that of the defendant, at a point in the "bottom land" noted on the plat, 13.09 chains south of Eel River and in the midst of a thick forest of large redwood trees.

We do not think the evidence justifies such wholesale disregard of the official survey. While it is true that the errors in the field notes and plat make it impossible to locate the exact spot fixed by the official survey as the common corner of sections 1, 2, 11, and 12, in the absence of the monument set to mark it, yet there is ample evidence to show that it was not fixed at or near the place selected by the court, upon its theoretical subdivision of the line. It is not the province of the court to determine where the corner should have been fixed. This is not an action to vacate the government survey. It must be assumed that the line was measured and the monuments set. Their positions, as set, fix the rights of the parties, regardless of the inaccuracy of the measurements and the errors in distance found in the field notes. The trial court must ascertain, as near as may be, where this monument was set by the government surveyor. If the exact spot cannot be found, it must, if possible, decide from the data appearing in evidence its approximate position. The proportional method is to be used only when no other reasonable method is possible and it must be so used that it does not contradict or conflict with the official data that are not impeached, and which, when not impeached, confine the actual position within certain limits. The application of the proportional method must, in that case, be also confined to the same limits.

The country between the corner of sections 11, 12, 13, and 14, and the place of "steep descent," and also between Eel River and the north township boundary is very hilly and rough. It is stated in the evidence, without contradiction, that the discrepancies in distance between the official survey and the private survey, between these points, 1.10 chains in the first instance and 2.33 chains in the other, are not an unusual difference between successive surveys over such ground. The distance to the place where the steep descent begins was, therefore, stated in the field notes with substantial accuracy. The field notes state that at the common corner there are no trees near. That the soil there is second or third rate, that the land is hilly, that it is on a northwest slope, and that what timber there is near consists of fir, oak, redwood, madrone, and brush or chaparral. They also show that the government surveyor in his progress north arrived at the corner post and monument before he entered the "bottom land." The distance given is apparently wrong, but the natural object, the bottom land, is there and the field notes describe it as having been encountered after passing north of that corner. The court fixed the corner not on the slope before reaching the bottom land, nor where the land is hilly, but nearly ten chains into the bottom land, and on practically level land; not in the second, or third-rate soil, but on first class rich soil; not where the timber is fir, oak, redwood, madrone, brush, and chaparral, as is the case on the slope, but in the midst of a thick forest which is all redwood. It is obvious from these facts that the original corner is not near the place fixed by the judgment. Furthermore, the field-notes show that the line between sections 1 and 2 was established by surveying two lines: (1) A random line run north to the township line at a point 10 links, or less than 7 feet, east of the old township monument set as the section corner and (2) By a true line run south from that monument to the south section corner stated to be 20.60 chains south of Eel River. The true line was, of course, the line officially established. The notes of this survey of the true line show that the surveyor again found the meander posts on Eel River at the same distance from the township line as before and again found the south corner, here involved, at the same distance from the river as before, and again noted that it was situated on hilly land, on a slope, in second and third-rate soil, that the timber about it was oak, fir, redwood, and madrone, and that it was 20.60 chains south of Eel River.

These natural objects and conditions still exist, and they are all found a considerable distance south of and not at the place in the redwood forest selected by the court. They indubitably show that the court's location is wrong and that the true corner must be located farther south, where it is not in a redwood forest, nor in first-rate soil, nor in distinctly "bottom land." The distance of 20.60 chains from the corner to the river may be incorrect. Under the rule established, it must give way, as evidence of location, to the natural objects mentioned in the field notes as descriptive of true location, so far as the two conflict. They do describe the actual location with some certainty and within ascertainable limits. The false calls and inaccurate measurements being rejected, those objects referred to which are found to exist must control, so far as they point to or circumscribe the location. The case is, in this respect, very like Chapman v. Polack, 70 Cal. 487, where a similar conclusion was reached. We cannot determine the place. It is for the trial court, upon all the evidence, to fix the place at a point where it will best accord with the natural objects described in the field notes as being about it and found to exist on the ground and which is least inconsistent with the distances mentioned in the notes and plat. It may be that, under all the circumstances, the distance of 20.60 chains, measured from the south bank of Eel River and noted on the plat, affords the most reliable means of ascertaining the approximate position, but as upon a new trial there may be different evidence, we lay down no rule to that effect. Circumstances may be such that distances control, especially where the natural objects do not definitely fix the place, but leave it to be fixed within certain limits.

The judgment is reversed.

Angellotti, J., and Sloss, J., concurred.

The old rule "proportional measurement may not be extended beyond a fixed original position" is applied here. Ordinarily, proportional measurement is used to dispose of small errors whose position cannot be fixed. Large errors or blunders are usually left where they can be proven to exist. The surveyor's problem is to prove facts - this elevates him out of the doldrums of a technician.

Is land surveying an art or a science? It includes both. Measuration is an exact science; law never was and never will be. The land surveyor, when locating boundaries, must obey the rules of law as they exist, and since they are not exact, land surveying can never be an exact science. The case above is ample proof; the Supreme Court recognized the fact that the "exact" corner location could not be determined but charged the lower court to do the best it could on an approximate basis.

This is the "exact point" where those accustomed to doing engineering get into trouble; they have sufficient training to know that measuration is an exact science, but they have insufficient knowledge to realize that all aspects of land surveying are not regulated by an exact science. More disagreements arise from improper application of the rules of evidence than from any other source. Many an accusation that the other surveyor made a "bull" in his measurements is not the result of a measurement error at all; it is a difference of opinion as to where the measurements should have started from or when "proportional measurements" should have been used.

****

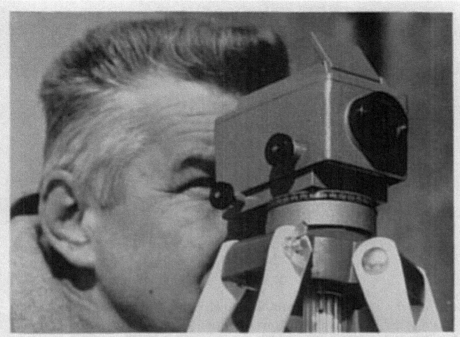

THE SURVEYOR AND THE LAW
PRORATION AND DELAYED STAKING
SEPTEMBER 1963

In a letter from Roy L. McCuistion, Jr., the validity of proration and the control of original monument positions as applied to delayed staking projects is questioned. In California, in some counties, the law requires that the surveyor must place a note on his subdivision map stating, "I will set monuments (of a given size and kind) at all lot corners, angle points, and change of direction within 30 days after the installation of all improvements." This delayed staking provision applies to interior stakes and not boundary stakes. All boundary corners must be set prior to filing of the map. After placing the note on the map, the map is filed, and the lots are sold prior to setting interior stakes.

To illustrate the question, the following hypothetical situation will be assumed. Mr. Jones buys Lot 2, Block 2, Hillview Acres. Two months after he buys the lot, the surveyor, in accordance with his agreement, sets the lot corners; but in so doing he makes an error of 2.00 feet. Does the stakes bind Mr. Jones or can he claim that he bought by the measurements on the map?

To my knowledge, this question has not been tried by the courts, but it is an ideal speculative question. In California, the first thing to note is that the law requires posting of bond by the sub-divider guaranteeing final lot staking. If errors were discovered prior to the release of the bond, the chances are that the surveyor would have to correct erroneous stakes and probably would be responsible for any damages.

After the bond is released and the public agency has, in effect, admitted that the surveyor has complied with the law, are the owners then bound by the surveyor's monuments even though set incorrectly? When Mr. Jones purchased his lot, he accepted title as Lot 2, Block 2 according to the plat. The plat stated that delayed staking would be done, and the purchaser of the lot agreed in writing to accept title in accordance with those conditions. In effect, the purchaser agreed in advance that the surveyor would locate his lot. After the surveyor did locate the lot, should not Mr. Jones be held to that location? Suppose that the neighbor, in good faith, builds a concrete - block wall right on the monumented line but 2.00 feet in error by measurements. Is the neighbor to blame and should he move his wall? Probably not. If parties agree to a future event, and the item is done, the parties have a reasonable time to object or accept the event. Silence over a period of time indicates acceptance.

Until such time as the courts rule upon delayed staking, I have adopted the following (it can be wrong, but I will use it until proved otherwise): If there have been no improvements and no one will be harmed by correcting an error, I call the original surveyor and come to an agreement as to what should be done. Usually the stakes are moved to the correct measured position. But, if someone has acted in good faith and has erected improvements, the monuments, to me, are fixed in position and cannot be altered irrespective of measurement errors. Of course, any monument that can be proved to have been moved or disturbed would be an exception.

The second part of the question asked is, "If you find a stake out of measured position in a delayed staking project, can you use it for prorating in another corner"? Normally, proration cannot extend beyond an original monument position, and unless there were unusual circumstances, I would use this rule. Once delayed stakes are set and accepted (by silence or by a period of time), they are the original stakes called for. But, if the results of proration are impossible or ridiculous, I would hesitate to use the rule.

Maybe, at some future date, a trial will settle the issue.

– Curtis M. Brown

****

THE SURVEYOR AND THE LAW

PROPORTIONATE MEASUREMENT
FOR LOTS IN SECTIONS

JUNE 1965

In Bozeman, Montana, at the annual meeting of the Montana Association of Registered Land Surveyors (MARLS-same abbreviation as used in at least one other State) an interesting discussion followed this legal problem:

Given: Lot 1 of Section 7 as shown in Figure 1.

Question: What constitutes the East 1/2 of Lot 1?

Conveyancing Situation: The U.S.A. recently granted to a citizen the East 1/2 of Lot 1 and retained the West 1/2 (Note: This was a mistake to grant the East 1/2 without a supplemental plat; however, it was done). All of Lot 1 was owned by the U.S.A. prior to conveyancing.

Discussion of Principles Involved: Whenever lands pass into private ownership, the State automatically assumes jurisdiction. The deed was formulated while the Federal Government had jurisdiction, and the West 1/2 still belongs to the government. It is probable that the Bureau of Land Management rules would prevail since it would be under Federal jurisdiction.

In accordance with the rules for cabin sites (where five-acre parcels can be sold), and in accordance with the representative from the Bureau of Land Management at the meeting (also in accordance with my opinion) the East 1/2 would get ten chains proportional measurement and the West 1/2 would get the remainder by proportional measurement. In Figure 1 the East 1/2 would be entitled to 10/21 times the present measurement from A to B and the West 1/2 would be entitled to 11/21 times the present measurement from A to B. Likewise, if Lot 1 were originally only 19 chains, the East 1/2 would be entitled to 10/19 of the measured distance from A to B.

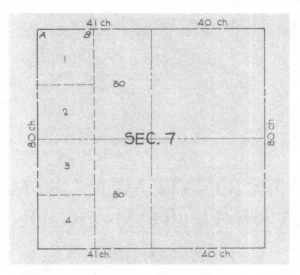

FIG. 1: Where is the E 1/2 of Lot 1 of Sec. 7?

Some of the surveyors felt that the East 1/2 was entitled to 1/2 the area of Lot 1. This could very well be true provided that the land was conveyed entirely under State jurisdiction at the time of the conveyancing and provided that the State of Montana did not have at the time of the conveyancing a statute requiring Federal procedure to be followed. The common law of practically all States is that 1/2 of a whole is 1/2 of the area. This is, of course, voided whenever a statute states the contrary.

Generally speaking, a conveyance is interpreted in favor of the grantee, but this rule is not generally applicable as against the interest of the public. In Figure 1, it cannot be argued that the East 1/2 should be in favor of the grantee since the grantor was the government.

In determining equal areas for the East 1/2 and the West 1/2 by a State rule, the north and south line would not be split into equal linear measurements. If Lot 1 were trapezoidal in character, the linear dimensions could be greater on the East 1/2 than on the West 1/2 or the reverse.

For this situation, I know of no court case or Federal statute that directly approves placing 10 chains proportional measurement in the East 1/2. The Bureau of Land Management does have the right to formulate rules and regulations so as to put statute law into effect.

– CURTIS M. BROWN

****

PROPORTIONATE MEASUREMENTS A PANEL PRESENTATION

MARCH, 1968

The following . . . papers constitute a Panel on Proportionate Measurements presented at the ACSM, General Session conducted by the Land Surveys Division on March 11, 1968, at the 28th Annual Meeting of the American Congress on Surveying and Mapping at the Washington Hilton Hotel in Washington, D. C. ACSM Past President Curtis M. Brown presided. - Editor

INTRODUCTION

BY CURTIS M. BROWN

PAST PRESIDENT ACSM

CONSULTING LAND SURVEYOR, SAN DIEGO, CALIFORNIA

LAND SURVEYORS are expert measurers. Most surveyors can agree upon the distance between two monuments. Disagreement usually stems from an argument over where an original monument position was, or over the application of a correct legal principle.

Land surveying can never be said to be an exact science since the locations of property corners and lines are dependent upon law, and law is not an exact science. Among the many argumentative rules applicable to land surveying are, the numerous rules for proportionate measurements. This panel consists of nine papers on this subject.

Surveyors from most states do recognize proportionate measurements as having a valid application under certain circumstances that may vary from state to state. Our purpose here is to find out what these circumstances are and what variations exist from state to state.

Before proceeding, further, a clear definition should be made of the words *measurement index* and *proportionate measurement*. A measurement index is the result of an error on the part of the original surveyor wherein he used a tape too long or too short. Thus, within the area of a given original survey, measurements are consistently long or consistently short by a ratable amount. All of Horton's Addition to the City of San Diego is consistently one-half foot long for a 300-foot block, or 0.17 foot per hundred feet. This is typical of a measurement index.

One type of proportionate measurement as used by surveyors is justified by the existence of a measurement index, but there are other types of proportionate measurements that are not dependent upon a consistent index error. An example is a will wherein three parcels were granted to three sons, the westerly 500 feet to one, the easterly 1000 feet to another, and the middle 750 feet to another. During a survey it was discovered that only 2050 feet of land existed instead of 2250 as supposed. In most states each son would receive his proportionate share of the whole, and each would share a proportionate part of the 200-foot shortage. Since the will was constructed without benefit of a survey or measurement, there could be no error attributable to an index of measurement.

Accretions along streams and along the ocean are divided among riparian owners in some ratable manner such as by the proportion of the new shore line to the old shore line. In this situation, obviously, there is no error involved; it is merely a question of how to divide lands resulting from growth. Measurement index is a measure of a consistent error on the part of a given surveyor, whereas an application of proportionate measurement may or may not be related to an original measurement error.

A proposed definition of proportionate measurement is:

As used by land surveyors, proportionate measurement is the process of dividing existing surplus or deficiency of land among two or more parties by a mathematical proportion that is based upon a court precedent.

Within this definition, excess or deficiency could be proportioned by area or lineal measurement; the origin of the excess or deficiency is immaterial, and opinion is eliminated since the process is dependent upon a court precedent.

Measurement index is one of many justifications for using proportionate measurement and can be classified as one of several criteria for developing a proportionate formula.

In developing a mathematical formula for a method of distributing surplus or deficiency, two items are always implied: (1) An original record quantity and (2) a recently measured quantity which differs from the record quantity. Usually the original quantity resulted from an original measurement, though not always. In the case of accretions there may be a recent measurement to determine where the old shore line "originally existed as of the date of the original conveyance and also a recent measurement to determine the position of the new shore line. The ratable proportion is then based upon two recent measurements.

Except in the case of accretions, in the application of proportionate measurement there is often an *implication of error;* that is, the originally reported quantity is larger or smaller than the actual quantity. In the rules that determine whether proportionate measurement should or should not apply, the distinction between "error" and "blunder" is necessary. For this panel the usual surveyor's meaning is adopted; that is, an error is of small magnitude and results from the inability to measure exactly. When evaluating the word "error," it must be related to the time of the measurement. In 1800, at the time the compass was used and directional accuracy was to the nearest 1/2 degree, the word error implied a much larger magnitude than that implied today. The word "blunder" is a mistake; i.e., writing 1012 instead of 1021, or dropping one chain length in 80 chains.

In defining rules as to when proportionate measurement may or may not be applied in accordance with some court precedent, the following items need to be considered:

A. Is proportionate measurement applicable to

 1. Errors?

 2. Blunders?

 3. Protracted lots?

 4. Accretions?

 5. Restoration of lost corners?

 6. Senior rights?

 7. Linear measurements?

 8. Area measurements?

B. Is proportionate measurement different under Federal rule than under state rules?

C. For the same circumstances, does the method of applying or not applying proportionate measurement vary from state to state?

Most proportionate measurements arise from situations wherein a whole is divided into proportionate parts and no part is designated to receive a remainder. Thus, a rectangular block is divided into two tiers of 6 lots, 50 x 100 feet each, and only block corners are monumented. Later measurements disclosed the fact that the block as measured between monuments is 300.60 feet long instead of 300 feet. Since no one lot can be designated to receive the 0.60 foot surplus, it is divided among all of the lots. Some conveyances are automatically proportionate parts of a whole by their very nature, i.e., the east 1/2 of Lot 10 and the west 1/2 of Lot 10.

Many proportional measurement problems arise from protracted lots or parcels. In the sectionalized land system, the smallest parcel surveyed and monumented was usually the section. Portions or sections were created by protraction, that is, the portions were plotted, on the township plat but were never surveyed. An example is the Northwest Quarter of the Northwest. Quarter of Section 6.

When a subdivision is created under state laws, lots are often indicated by protraction. Thus, an owner may have fifty blocks platted, surveyed, and monumented on the ground. On the same map he may have 12 lots protracted on each block, that is, the lots are shown on the map but none were individually surveyed or monumented.

Whenever the lots or parcels are created by protraction the following is implied: (1) Several lots or parcels are created on paper at the same time (that is at the moment the map is recorded or approved). (2) The lots or parcels were not originally monumented. (3) The lots or parcels are sold by reference to the lot or parcel designation of the map. Examples of protracted lots or parcels are: Lot 1, Block 2, Black Acres. The Northwest Quarter of the Northeast Quarter of Section 10, Township 15 South, Range 2 East, San Bernardino Meridian. This would exclude the situation wherein lots are created by protraction and later sold in sequence by metes and bounds descriptions as is so often done in New York.

[MP NOTE: In the ensuing eight papers of this Panel, the respective authors discussed proportionate measurement as it is practiced within specific states.]

****

PUBLIC LANDS

COMMENT AND DISCUSSION

LAND BOUNDARIES

JUNE 1960

L. W. MAHONE * - In the December 1959 issue of SURVEYING AND MAPPING, on pages 495 - 497, Curtis Brown discusses a problem in land boundaries which arose in Wisconsin. As might be expected, he has definitely and correctly stated the technical aspects of the situation, and yet the discussion leaves me somewhat disturbed.

Any discussion of this type is always hampered because *all* the facts seem never to be set forth. It does seem definite that in 1869 the section was divided into quarter sections and fences marking these boundaries were built and these fences have been accepted ever since. Mr. Brown infers that these fences *probably* have become the property lines. Court decisions in the middle West would indicate this to be true. If these are property boundaries, the only usable section center is the fence intersection. A technically correct section center would be of no actual value.

There could be a question as to whether the center of the section *was* incorrectly located. Certainly, the procedure mentioned by Mr. Brown is usually the correct one, but in the earlier instructions, some peculiarities crept in. The sketch indicates that the surveyor found the center of the E - W and N - S dimensions. I have heard of this being done, but done, I believe, in error. However, I have not seen all the early instructions in Wisconsin, and I doubt if Mr. Brown has.

On page 107 of "Public Land Surveys" by L. O. Stewart, it is mentioned that the Surveyor General at St. Louis in 1856 said the center of a section lay midway on the line connecting E - W quarter corners. Some such erroneous instruction *could* have prevailed in Wisconsin for a while.

Even if the survey were erroneously made, it probably was an "honest error" and has been accepted for many years. Mr. Brown says: "Since the surveyor erred, it can be corrected. Age does not make an incorrect survey correct." Once again, we have a matter of interpretation. Technically a correction is possible; practically, correction is not possible here.

Reference is made to the rather well-known "The Judicial Functions of Surveyors," by Justice Cooley of the Michigan Supreme Court. He says in part: "Of course nothing in what has been said can require a surveyor to conceal his own judgment or to report the facts one way when he believes them to be another. He has no right to mislead, and he may rightfully express his opinion that an original monument was at one place, when at the same time he is satisfied that acquiescence has fixed the right of the parties as if it were at another. But, he would do mischief if he were to attempt to 'establish' monuments which he knew would *tend to disturb settled rights.*"

In making hundreds of property surveys in northern Iowa, I have run into many similar problems. Any attempt to correct the multitude of past mistakes would result in utter confusion.

* Professor, Department of Civil Engineering University of Arkansas, Fayetteville, Arkansas.

****

THE SURVEYOR AND THE LAW
SECTIONALIZED LAND SURVEYS IN THE NORTHWEST TERRITORY
SEPTEMBER 1964

Surveyors who practice in the rectangular land survey area of the West are apt to think that the 1947 *Manual of Instructions for the Survey of the United States* is the guide for the resurveyed or subdivision of all sections; this thought is far from true. Procedures for re-surveys in the early sectionalized land states, such as the Northwest Territory (Ohio, Indiana, Illinois, and Michigan) and Louisiana, have many differences created by early federal statutes. Another erroneous thought that can easily arise in the minds of eastern surveyors who look at plats showing the Public Land States is that all of the West was surveyed into sections. Much of California and some of the other western states were surveyed under Spanish and Mexican laws; and many land grants do exist.

Figure 1. Ohio Sectionalized Land Surveys

The evolution of the early rectangular system is best illustrated by a series of drawings (Figures 1 to 7). In each figure the solid lines represent the lines actually run on the ground; the dotted lines represent not surveyed protraction lines as provided for by law. The dots represent corner monuments as required by law.

Figure 1 shows some of the sectionalized areas surveyed in Ohio, including the five-mile townships. Figures 2 and 3 are schematic plats of The Seven Ranges as provided for in the Continental Congress Ordinance of 1785.

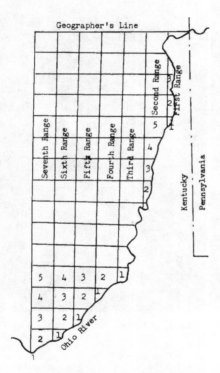

Figure 2. ---- The Seven Ranges. Townships are shown.

The exterior lines of blocks of land six miles by six miles were surveyed and mileposts set (no other corners). Interior lots (the word "section" was not used until 1796) were determined by protraction; that is, the lines were not surveyed on the ground. Every other township was sold entire; the remainder could be sold in units of not less than a lot (one square mile). The word "township," indicating a block of land six miles by six miles, and the word "range," indicating a tier of townships, were apparently adopted from the New England area wherein townships and ranges were a common term used on town plats.

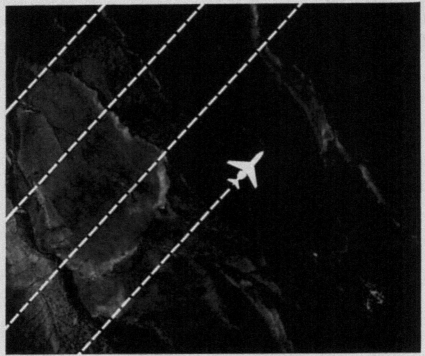

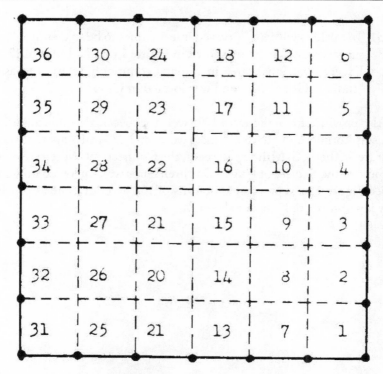

Figure 3. ---- Numbering of sections protracted in the townships
of the Seven Ranges. Dots indicate where original corners
were set. Sections under this act were called "lots."

Lot (section) 16 was reserved for schools, and it has been ever since.
Only part of the land authorized by the act of 1785 was surveyed; surveys
of the area ceased after 1788.

The Act of May 18, 1796 revived the sectionalized land system and
required:

(1) All township lines monumented every mile (no quarter corners).

(2) *Every other* township to be surveyed by lines run two miles apart
     in each direction (Figure 4).

(3) Corners set within alternate townships as shown in Figure 4.

(4) Numbering of sections (the term "lot" was dropped) to be as shown
     in Figure 4.

(5) Townships with un-surveyed interior lines to be sold entire. Lands surveyed by this act are shown in Figure 1 (marked "Act of 1796"). Except for a small area in Indiana commonly referred to as the "Indiana Gore," this land was located in Ohio.

Also provided for in the act of 1796 were the so-called 5-mile townships. Township corners and quarter corners were set 2-1/2 miles apart as shown in Figure 5. The U. S. Military Reserve, the Connecticut Western Reserve, and some of the Society of United Brethren lands were surveyed under this act (see Figure 1) and protracted in units of 100 acres or more as provided for by law (protracted lots not shown).

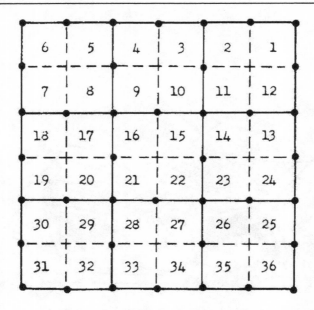

Figure 4. ---- Sections of land surveyed in accordance with the Act of 1796. Dots represent original corners to be set. Every other township had only the exterior township lines run.

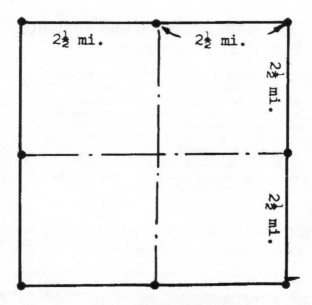

Figure 5. Ohio 5 - mile townships. Dots represent original corners.

590

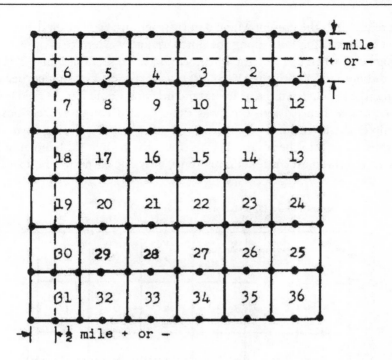

Figure 6. Act of May 10, 1800, provided for setting the north and south quarter corners and placing surplus or deficiency in the north and west rows of the section. Dots represent original corners.

The Act of May 10, 1800 provided for placing *errors and convergence* (this was the first act providing for convergence of the meridians) in the north and west tiers of sections; it provided for the setting of quarter comers on the north and south sides of sections, as shown in Figure 6. For the first time land could be sold in half sections.

The Act of March 26, 1804 provided for selling lands in quarter sections.

The Act of February 11, 1805, was the last significant change in the statutes regulating how lands should be surveyed. Most changes after that date resulted from changes in survey instructions issued by the surveyors general. Except for the "gore of Indiana" and a few other small areas, Indiana, Illinois, and Michigan were most commonly surveyed in accordance with the instructions of Mansfield and Tiffin; Figure 7 shows the usual pattern of double corners resulting.

Most interior sections of townships were surveyed in a manner similar to that required in the present Manual of Instructions; significant differences arose in the closing lines along the northern and western tiers of sections. In Figure 7, when running the line north between sections 1 and 2, if the line did not fall in with the existing standard corner, a closing corner was set and the falling from the nearest standard corner noted in the field book. Two corners then existed. One was the standard comer for sections 35 and 36 of the township to the north; the other was the closing corner for sections 1 and 2 to the south. If, by chance, the corner did happen to fall in with the standard corner (a rare event), only one corner would exist.

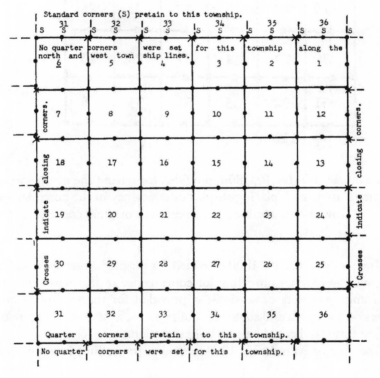

Figure 7. Double corners permitted in the Indiana, Illinois, and Michigan by the instructions of Mansfield and Tiffin (1803 to about 1843). Dots indicate original standard corners set; crosses indicate original closing corners.

In running the closing line for the western tier of sections, according to the instructions, closing corners could be set whenever the line as run failed to fall in with the existing standard corner. In all townships there could be 5 sets of double corners on the north and west sides. In subdividing the township to the south and east of the one shown in Figure 7, closing corners could be set on the south and east township lines; thus, double corners could and do exist on any side of a township. Double corners rarely existed at township corners.

This brings up the question, what is the significance of the quarter corners along the township lines? Double quarter corners were not originally set. Section 2 of Figure 7 shows a closing section corner for the northeast and northwest corner of the section. Is the existing quarter corner between sections 2 and 35 the north quarter corner of section 2? The answer is no. The north quarter corner of section 2 was not set; the existing corner is the south quarter corner of section 35. There should be a jog at the quarter corner the same (average) as is shown at the northeast and the northwest corners of section 2. For a given township, the quarter corners set on the south and east township lines pertain to that township; the quarter corners set on the north and west township lines pertain to the next townships to the north and west respectively. Because Louisiana and a few nearby southern states had surveys made shortly after 1805, it is probable that they have similar, double-corner problems.

In Indiana two correction lines exist, 90 and 96 miles apart. The convergence of the meridians in this distance is quite considerable and large deficiencies do occur.

Since double corners often occur on township lines, there are jogs in fence lines every 6 miles. When flying over in an airplane, it is easy to be fooled; the jogs are not correction lines. In the far West, correction lines are usually 24 miles apart; jogs rarely occur elsewhere.

The moral to this discussion is simple. Land surveyors who practice in one sectionalized land state are not necessarily qualified to practice in another; they must become acquainted with local problems.

– CURTIS M. BROWN

REFERENCES

Public Land Surveys, Lowell O. Stewart, Collegiate Press, Ames, Iowa.

American Rectangular Land Survey System, William D. Pattison, University of Chicago, Research Paper No. 50 (copies are available at $3.00).

Federal Statutes.

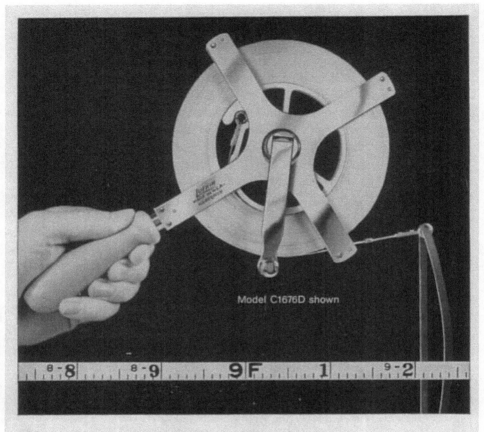

Model C1676D shown

FOR PIN-POINT ACCURACY AT A GLANCE
CHOOSE THE TAPE WITH GRADUATIONS
AT ANY READING (It's a LUFKIN, of course)

Just as the entire family of Lufkin products has become the standard of accuracy wherever measurements must be "on the button", so this popular model has earned particular acceptance with the surveying profession.

It's Lufkin's dependable "Western" Chrome Clad steel tape, available in either 100-or 200-foot lengths. Graduated throughout, this model's jet black markings stand out boldly against the glare-free, chrome-white finish — proven to resist abrasion, heat, rust and corrosion. Bright red handle protects against loss.

Choose any Lufkin tape and you know you're right; choose the "Western" and you're *on the button!*

YOU'RE RIGHT WITH **LUFKIN**

THE LUFKIN RULE COMPANY/Saginaw, Michigan

SECTIONALIZED LAND SURVEYS IN THE NORTHWEST TERRITORY

MARCH 1965

RICHARD R. MAYER * - Curtis Brown's explanation of cadastral surveys in the Northwest Territory should enlighten both the "public land" surveyor (for whom everything is true and square) and the "colonial" surveyor who finds things quite the contrary.

Several years ago the writer was commissioned to prepare base maps covering most of Ohio and on which these various systems were compiled in their proper geographic relationships. Although exasperating, the task was most interesting, and one can see on one sheet the various, independent, rectangular systems as they were tried and developed from area to area - including five-mile-square townships containing over 100 "sections," varying orientations, radial subdivisions of a township, and, of course, standard townships.

While prepared specifically for a group of geologists (whose need for an over-all picture is understandable) I believe the maps are still available from Nelson Rudd, Consulting Geologist, Mt. Vernon, III. They cover Ohio at 1/62, - 500, in six sheets, and might be quite interesting to anyone wishing to look further into the question.

* Surveyor-Engineer, 418 Adams St., Fort Atkinson, Wisconsin 53538.

****

THE SURVEYOR AND THE LAW

THE ONE EIGHTH CORNER

SEPTEMBER 1964

Those residing in sectionalized land states are quite familiar with 1/4 and 1/16 corners. In the older sectionalized land states, such as Indiana and Illinois, the term 1/8 corner is found in old court cases.

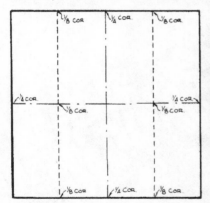

By the Continental Congress Ordinance of 1785 the smallest parcel created was a lot of one-mile square (not a section); every other township was sold in its entirety. Later acts provide that the least sale should be one section, then one-half section, then one-quarter section, then one-half quarter section (80 acres), then one-quarter section, and then in recent times cabin sites of 5 acres. During the time land was sold in half quarter sections (1820 to 1832) the land divisions were as shown in the diagram. Since the section was divided into 8 parts, the corners of the parts became known as 1/8 corners. Today these corners are known as 1/16 corners. Even in areas where the term 1/8 corner could be meaningful, the term is seldom heard.

– CURTIS M. BROWN

****

597

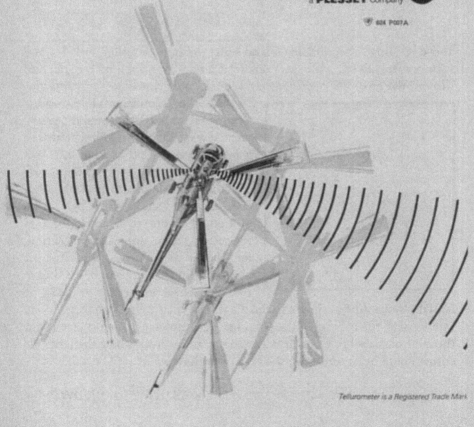

THE SURVEYOR AND THE LAW

RESTORATION OF LOST OR OBLITERATED CORNERS IN THE SECTIONALIZED LAND AREAS OF PARTS OF OHIO, INDIANA, ILLINOIS, AND MICHIGAN

DECEMBER 1965

The pamphlet entitled *Restoration of Lost or Obliterated Corners and Subdivision of Sections* published by the Bureau of Land Management, Department of the Interior, 1963, is of considerable aid to the land surveyor. It does not explain several local situations found in Ohio, Indiana, Illinois, and Michigan. In the words of the B. L. M. Director, "The pamphlet does not cover controversial questions or exceptional situations." These are intentional omissions.

After a state joined the Union, the jurisdiction over private lands passed from the Federal Government to the state. While the laws for resurveys in each state should be the same, they are not. In Missouri, a statute law was passed stating exactly how lands should be resurveyed and how sections should be cut up; the law differs in some respects from the procedure outlined in the above pamphlet. In Missouri, the surveyor must realize that court cases will be tried in the state courts and these courts have the final jurisdiction.

In the older sectionalized land areas such as Indiana and Illinois, where double and triple corners were common on every township line (See *Surveying and Mapping*, September 1964, Vol. XXIV, No. 3, pp. 491 - 494, "Surveyor and the Law"), a special explanation is needed.

The first pamphlet entitled *Restoration of Lost and Obliterated Corners* was published in 1883. There were previous publications (two to four pages) in November 1879 and May 3, 1881. The four-page pamphlet published in 1879 contained a statement that is completely at variance with the 1883 pamphlet and with present practice. It is: "Missing section corners in the interior of townships should be re-established at proportional distance between the nearest existing original corners north and south of the missing corner." In the March 1883 pamphlet, this was changed to the double proportionate method, and this has been used ever since. It is probable that a court case in the intervening time changed thinking. The explanation of double proportionate measurement (the process of double proportion was not given the name "double proportionate measurement" until a later date) was poorly explained at that time but quite recognizable as the method clearly explained in the recent pamphlet.

In the 1883 pamphlet, single proportionate measurement was recognized for restoring lost quarter corners and all corners on the township line except for township corners where double proportionate measurement was used.

The most important part of the 1883 pamphlet pertained to re-establishment of lost double and triple corners along township lines (See above reference for origin of these corners). Since this information is no longer available to surveyors of Indiana, Illinois, and Michigan areas, it is reproduced as written.

8. *Where double corners were originally established, one of which is standing, to re-establish the other* -- It being remembered that the corners established when the exterior township lines were run along to the sections in the townships north and west of those lines, the surveyor must first determine beyond a doubt to which sections the existing corner belongs. This may be done by testing the courses and distances to witness trees or other objects noted in the original field notes of survey and by re-measuring distances to known corners. Having determined to which township the existing corner belongs, the missing corner may be re-established in line north or south of the existing corner, as the case may be, at the distance stated in the field notes of the original survey, by proportionate measurement, and tested by re-measurement to the opposite corresponding corner of the section to which the missing section corner belongs. These double corners being generally not more than a few chains apart, the distance between them can be more accurately laid off, and it is considered preferable to first establish the missing corner as above and check upon the corresponding interior corner than to reverse the proceedings, since the result obtained is every way more accurate and satisfactory.

9.   *Where double corners were originally established, and both are missing, to re-establish the one established when the township line was run.* -- The surveyor will connect the nearest known corners on the township line, by a right line, being careful to distinguish the section from the closing corners, and re-establish the missing corner at the point indicated by the field notes of the original survey, by proportionate measurement. The corner thus restored will be common to two sections either north or west of the township boundary, and the section north or west, as the case may be, should be carefully retraced; thus checking upon the re-established corner and testing the accuracy of the result. It cannot be too much impressed upon the surveyor, that any measurements to objects on line noted in the original survey are means of determining and testing the correctness of the operation.

10.   *Where double corners were originally established and both are missing, to re-establish the one established when the township was subdivided.* -- The corner to be re-established being common to two sections south or east of the township line, the section line closing on the missing section corner should be first retraced to an intersection with the township line in the manner previously indicated and a temporary corner established at the point of intersection. The township line will, of course, have been previously carefully retraced in accordance with the requirements of the original field notes of survey and marked in such a manner as to be readily identified when reaching the same with the retraced section line. The location of the temporary corner planted at the point of intersection will then be carefully tested and verified by remeasurements to noted objects and known corners on the township line, as noted in the original field notes of survey, and the necessary corrections made in such relocation. A permanent corner will then be erected at the correct location on the township line, properly marked and witnessed, and recorded for future requirements.

11.   *Where triple corners were originally established on range lines, one or two of which have become obliterated, to re-establish either of them.* -- It will be borne in mind that only two corners were established as actual corners of sections, those established on the range line not corresponding with the subdivisional survey east or west of said range line. The surveyor will, therefore, first proceed to identify the existing corner or corners, as the case may be, and then reestablish the missing corner or corners in line north or south, according to the distances stated in the original field notes of survey in the manner indicated for

the re-establishment of double corners, and testing the accuracy of the result obtained, as hereinbefore directed in other cases. If, however, the distances between the triple corners are not stated in the original field notes of survey, as is frequently the case in the returns of older surveys, the range line should be first carefully retraced and marked in a manner sufficiently clear to admit of easy identification upon reaching same during the subsequent proceedings. The section lines closing upon the missing corners must then be retraced in accordance with the original field notes of survey, in the manner previously indicated and directed, and the corners re-established in the manner directed in the case of double corners. The surveyor cannot be too careful, in the matter of retracement, in following closely all the recorded indications of the original line, and nothing, however slight, should be neglected to insure the correctness of the retracement of the original line; since there is no other check upon the accuracy of the re-establishment of the missing corners, unless the entire corresponding section lines are remeasured by proportional measurement, and the result checked by a recalculation of the areas as originally returned, which, at best, is but a very poor check, because the areas expressed upon many plats of the older surveys are erroneously stated on the face of the plats or have been carelessly calculated.

12. *Where triple corners were originally established on range lines, all of which are missing, to re-establish same.* -- These corners should be re-established in accordance with the foregoing directions, commencing with the corner originally established when the range line was run, establishing the same in accordance with previously given directions for restoring section and quarter section corners; that is to say, by re-measuring between the nearest known corners on said township line and re-establishing the same by proportionate measurement. The two remaining will then be re-established in conformity with the general rules for re-establishment of double corners

It is to be observed that in most of the country wherein double and triple corners exist, the area is agricultural land. There will be very few lost original positions since possession in agricultural land will usually stand as a monument to where the original lines were marked and surveyed.

The area west of the Mississippi was, in general, surveyed at a later date, so double and triple corners did not exist except on correction lines. It is quite noticeable that the above principles are quite similar to those used for restoring lost corners on correction lines.

Quarter corners immediately south of any correction line were rarely (almost never) set. Where double corners were set in the early sectionalized land states, the quarter corners along township lines only applied to one township (See above reference for explanation. Thus, if there were double corners, the existing quarter corner was not the north quarter corner of sections 1, 2, 3, 4, 5, and 6 and the existing quarter corner was not the westerly quarter corner of sections 6, 7, 18, 19, 30 and 31. To set these missing corners the pamphlet states that the local surveyor should:

6. *Re-establishment of quarter section corners on township boundaries.* -- Only one set of quarter section corners are actually marked in the field on township lines, and they are established at the time when the township exteriors are run. When double section corners are found, the quarter section corners are considered generally as standing midway between the corners of their respective sections and, when required to be established or re-established, as the case may be, they should be generally so placed, but great care should be exercised not to mistake the corners of one section for those of another. After determining the proper section corners marking the line upon which the missing quarter section corner is to be re-established and measuring said line, the missing quarter section corner will be re-established in accordance with the requirements of the original field notes of survey by proportionate measurement between the section corners marking the line.

Where there are double sets of section corners on township and range lines, and the quarter section corners for sections south of the township or east of the range lines are required to be established in the field, the said quarter section corners should be so placed as to suit the calculation of areas of the quarter sections adjoining the township boundaries as expected upon the official township plat, adopting proportionate measurements when the present measurements of the north and west boundaries of the section differ from the original measurements.

This all points to the fact that the rules for the survey of public lands as described in the 1947 Manual and in the pamphlet, *Restoration of Lost or Obliterated Corners and Subdivision of Sections,* do not always apply to older surveys.

– Curtis M. Brown

****

THE SURVEYOR AND THE LAW
DECEMBER 1966

While in Wisconsin, I spent considerable time discussing how to properly set the center of sections. As everyone knows, under Federal rule the only correct method is to connect opposite quarter corners by straight lines. William T. Wambach dug up this 1862 statute of Wisconsin (Ch. 120, Section 4): "Whenever a surveyor is required to make a subdivision of a section, as determined by the United States survey, except where the section is fractional, *he shall establish* the interior quarter section corner therefore, at a point which *is the same distance from the east quarter section corner that it is from the west quarter section corner, and the same distance from the north quarter section corner that it is from the south quarter section corner.*"

According to Mr. Wambach's letter most of this law was repealed in 1867 and the law became: "Whenever a surveyor is required to subdivide a section or smaller subdivision of land established by the United States Survey, he shall proceed according to the Statutes of the United States and the rules and regulations made by the Secretary of the Interior in conformity thereto."

How many centers of sections were set between 1862 and 1867 by county surveyors? If they were set at that time, can they be changed? This further points to the necessity of understanding local laws by a surveyor. It is difficult for a surveyor in one state to practice in another.

– Curtis M. Brown

****

Cubic DM-20 Electrotape system quickly pinpoints location of off-shore installation.

ELECTROTAPE WORKS WHERE CHAIN AND TAPE WON'T:

The new, lightweight, all-transistorized version of Cubic Electrotape, Model DM-20, marks a major breakthrough in the art of surveying. Electrotape eliminates time-consuming chain and tape work, and lets even unskilled operators measure distances from 150 feet to 40 miles in just a few minutes per set-up. Easily operable by one man, the DM-20 weighs only 25 pounds. Its accuracy is 1 centimeter plus 3 parts per million, and the front panel readout is directly in centimeters, eliminating scope or meter interpretations. The DM-20 operates day and night, in any weather, with a built-in radio-telephone permitting communication between operators at all times. A single tripod-mounted unit incorporates the recessed parabolic antenna, regulated power supply, compact battery, and electronic circuits. Write for descriptive literature to Dept. SM-102, Industrial Division, Cubic Corporation, San Diego 11, California.

cubic CORPORATION

INDUSTRIAL DIVISION
SAN DIEGO 11, CALIFORNIA

[MP NOTE] In December 1981, an article appeared in the ACSM *Surveying and Mapping* journal. It generated an unprecedented response and produced a series of articles that extended over several years. The debate was contentious and resulted in considerable and exhaustive discussion.

****

SUBDIVISION OF A SECTION

BY JOHN G. MCENTYRE, PH.D., L.S., P.E.

DECEMBER 1981

Certain articles which I have read in recent months and opinions which I have heard at various meetings motivated me to write this paper. I wish to bring attention to a situation in which I believe that surveyors are obtaining what often is the correct answer for a boundary location but justifying it with the wrong reason.

Prescribed Procedures for Subdividing a Section

The problem involves the location of a boundary line which is also the center line of a section or a quarter-section. The Act of 1805 stipulated that the subdivision of a section was to be accomplished by running straight lines from established corners to opposite corners. Thus, the center lines of the section are obtained by joining opposite quarter corners and the interior boundaries of the quarter sections formed are portions of these lines. The center of a section is the intersection of these lines and is a quarter corner common to the NE 1/4, NW 1/4, SW 1/4, and SE 1/4. The General Land Office (GLO) and its successor, the Bureau of Land Management (BLM), has perpetuated this procedure as their policy. Of course it is often accepted that individual state statutes and common law of the individual states prevail in the states involved after title to a piece of land is granted by the United States. It is interesting to note, however, that in his paper, "The Judicial Functions of Surveyors," that Thomas M. Cooley states the contrary (italics added by author for emphasis):

3. No statute can confer upon a county surveyor the power to "establish" corners, and thereby bind the parties concerned. Nor is this a question

merely of conflict between State and Federal law; it is a question of property right. The *original surveys must govern*, and the *laws under which they were made govern*, because the land was bought in reference to them; and *any legislation*, whether *state or federal that should have the effect to change these, would be inoperative*, because of the disturbance to vested rights.

The GLO Circular "Restoration of Lost and Obliterated Corners," issued March 13, 1883, stated that the Acts of May 24, 1824, and April 5, 1832, "provided that corners and contents of half quarters and quarter-quarter sections should be ascertained as nearly as possible in the manner and on the principles prescribed in the Act of Congress approved February 11, 1805." It further stated:

From the foregoing synopsis of Congressional Legislation it is evident
- ....

3d. The quarter-quarter corners not established by the Government surveyors must be planted equidistant and on line between the quarter section and section corners.

Furthermore, the GLO publication, "Restoration of Lost or Obliterated Corners" issued June 1, 1909, states relative to the subdivision of sections into quarter-quarters:

Preliminary to the subdivision of quarter sections, the quarter-quarter corners will be established at points midway between the section and quarter-section corners, and between quarter corners and the center of the section, except on the last half mile of the line closing on the north or west boundaries of a township, where they should be placed at 20 chains, proportionate measurement, to the north or west of the quarter section corner.

The quarter-quarter section corners having been established as directed above, the subdivision lines of the quarter section will be run straight between opposite quarter-quarter section corners on the quarter-section boundaries. The intersection of the lines thus run will determine the place for the corner common to the four quarter-quarter sections.

The *Manual of Surveying Instructions* 1973, published by BLM in section 3-89, calls for the same procedure to subdivide a quarter section as the Restoration publication issued by GLO in June 1909. The intent of the Act of 1805 relative to subdivision of a section is that the outside corners of the parcel (section, quarter section, quarter-quarter section) to be subdivided were to be determined and the dividing lines placed by joining opposite subdivision corners. The center of the parcel to be divided is the intersection of these lines.

Controlling Factors for Parcel Corners

In any state where state laws or common law do not prescribe otherwise and where the original government surveyor did not set any interior subdivision corners, the record center lines of a section should be established by joining opposite quarter corners. Also, in these states the record center lines for quarter sections should be set by joining opposite quarter-quarter corners. If the quarter-quarter corners on the outside boundaries were not set by the original public land surveyor they should be set by proper proportionate measurement on the quarter section boundary. All these procedures ignore such items as fence lines and establish the position of *record* corners and *record* lines. The key word is "record." This is the proper location of the record corners and lines. The actual *title* lines may be different. It is the difference between the meaning of the words "record" and "title" which is the key to this discussion. The position of "title" corners will be discussed later in this paper.

All surveyors know that the intent of the original surveyor controls the location of corners. All surveyors know that found monuments, if set by the original surveyor or proven to be in the position established by him, control the location of a corner, even prevailing over directions and distances in the written description. If the original public land surveyor did not set a monument in the field, such as the center quarter corner of a section or the north quarter-quarter corner of the NE 1/4 of a section, then the original plat, along with the prescribed GLO and BLM procedures to subdivide a section, control the location of the subdivision corners and lines of a section. Any later surveys attempting to establish these corners must stand on their own merit and are subordinate to original corners as established by the original plat. An Alabama case states this principle. The opinion in *Upton v. Reid*, 265 2d, 644 includes the following wording (all italics added by the author to emphasize key points):

The suit arose over a disputed boundary line separating plaintiffs' forty acres on the west from the forty on the east on which the defendant had authority to cut timber. The plaintiffs derived title from their father and it was their contention on trial that, regardless of where the true line dividing these two forties was, their said ancestor and the owner of the forty on the east had agreed to a survey made by one Morton in 1931 as the division line between the properties.

FAIRCHILD first with RADAN® 500

Doppler radar navigational system for aerial geodetic and survey purposes!

Only RADAN 500 combines the proven features of military-type Doppler systems with the latest advances in the state of the art.

This newest Fairchild navigational aid is the most modern Doppler radar equipment available. With it precision flight paths can be flown over any terrain without photos, maps, or ground stations of any kind. Since much of the cost of surveying lies in obtaining photography or establishing ground stations for accurate flight path control, the RADAN 500 dramatically reduces survey costs. Actual flying can get underway faster and surveys are completed sooner.

This new Fairchild service is available for geophysical and photomapping projects anywhere in the world. For complete information write or TWX:

WHAT IS DOPPLER?

The RADAN 500 Doppler radar automatically and continuously determines ground speed and drift angle of the aircraft. From this information an electronic "brain" in the aircraft computes its exact position, enabling the pilot to fly precise flight paths over desert, jungle, ice or any featureless terrain without ground control of any kind.

FAIRCHILD AERIAL SURVEYS, INC., Los Angeles, Calif., 224 East 11th Street · Offices in: New York · Chicago · Boston · Birmingham · Houston · Brussels · Istanbul · Vancouver, B.C. · Toronto · Guatemala City · Caracas · Bogota · Lima · La Paz · Rio de Janeiro · Buenos Aires · Santiago

The defendants could have so framed their complaint as to bring into issue the question of an agreed boundary line between the two properties, but did not do so. The complaint limited recovery to timber cut by defendant on the NW 1/4 of the NE 1/4 of said section. *The question then was not one of location of a boundary line between the properties as determined by the acts of the parties,* as was discussed in the Bledsoe and other cases, supra, *but rather one of location of the dividing line between the NW1/4 of the NE1/4 and the NE1/4 of the NE1/4 of the sections; that is, the location of the subdivision line between the two forties according to the government survey* setting up the section lines, corners, etc. *This conclusion is attained* from such cases as Alford v. Rodgers, 242 Ala. 370, 6 So. 2d 409, holding to the effect *that no act of the parties can relocate the section line as established by the government survey* and other cases as Oliver v. Oliver, supra, and Edwards v. Smith, 240 Ala. 397,199 So. 811 *making the same principle applicable to the interior subdivision lines of a government surveyed section.*

The last cited case has this pertinent observation: *"These interior subdivision lines, not surveyed or marked in the government survey, are none the less certain in legal contemplation. They are fixed and determinable by a subdivision of the section, using the four corners of the section shown on the official field notes."*

(The author is indebted to Professor David R. Knowles, University of Arkansas, for the preceding citation reference. Professor Knowles cited this case in his paper, "Subdivision of a Section as Ruled by the Courts.")

Possible "Chaos" of Preceding Determination of Record Lines

It should be evident from the preceding sections and the discussion quoted from the *Upton v. Reid* case (supra) that the proper procedure to locate "record" corners and lines is the procedure prescribed by GLO and BLM for the subdivision of a section. "Title" lines or ownership lines could differ from the "record" corner lines. The *Upton v. Reid* case (supra) contemplated this aspect when it stated: "The defendants could have so framed their complaint as to bring into issue the question of an agreed boundary line . . ." It is the author's opinion that they were calling attention to the fact that their decision would have been that the "title" line would have been the line to which they cut timber.

The responsibility of a professional surveyor in a state that does not have statute law or common law contrary to established procedures promulgated by GLO and BLM is (1) to locate the record subdivision lines of a section, (2) to determine ownership lines and their history, and (3) to advise his client as to the weight-of-authority in the type of instance involved. He should then advise him to consult with his adjoiner and agree on a boundary line. If they accept the record line the present public land description is correct. If they desire to use some line other than the record subdivision line of the section, such as an ownership line (fence line), then they should draw up a new description, reference it to the record corners, monument the new title corners, and record this information.

This solution places collateral evidence, such as fence lines, fence corner posts, and roads in the proper perspective: (1) They may be accepted as evidence of an obliterated corner monument *set* by the original surveyor or (2) they can be used as evidence of title lines gained by unwritten rights (agreement, acquiescence, estoppel, adverse possession). It goes without saying that they cannot be used as evidence of a position of a corner that was not set on the original survey, such as a center quarter corner or the north quarter corner of a NE 1/4.

There is no doubt that many center quarter corners and center lines of sections and quarter-quarter sections were originally established by adjoining farmers who "eyed" in their lines and placed fence lines accordingly. These lines will probably attain the status of title lines but would not be considered as record center lines of a section, thus making a farce of the prescribed procedures to subdivide a section. If a surveyor in the past, possibly not knowledgeable in the prescribed procedures to subdivide a section, ran a fence line survey of a center line of a section or quarter section to locate the boundaries of a client and the line is accepted by the adjoiners for many years, the title line located by him, as suggested in this article, would probably be the incorrectly located line. Chaos is not created in boundary lines in the area. Also the dignity of being a properly executed survey is not given to the incorrect survey. This concept of using old established fence lines and roads as record subdivision line of a section could and will be used by surveyors to excuse improper or incomplete fence line surveys done in the past or even in the future.

This proper recognition of record lines and possible title line does not result in chaos. On the contrary it lends credibility to collateral evidence when it is valid and preserves the dignity of procedures prescribed by GLO and BLM. Where common law or statute law has not negated this procedure, it should be used.

Summary

In states where the subdivision of a section is not prescribed by statute law or common law by contrary procedures, the record center lines of a section should be located by joining opposite quarter corners. The record center of a section should be established at the intersection of the lines joining opposite quarter corners. The record center lines of quarter-quarter sections should be located by joining opposite quarter-quarter corners. The record center quarter-quarter corner of a quarter section at the intersection should be established at the intersection of the lines joining opposite quarter-quarter corners. If record quarter-quarter corners were not set by the original public land surveyor on the outside boundaries of a section they should be established by proper proportionate measurement procedures between related corners. As mentioned earlier in this paper Justice Cooley in his article, "The Judicial Function of Surveyors," stated that this procedure could govern in a state that had a statute negating it.

Collateral evidence, such as fence lines, roads, and corner posts may only be used to reestablish corners set by the original surveyor and should not be used to establish record subdivision lines of a section and corners not set in the field by the original public land surveyor. "These interior subdivision lines, not surveyed or marked in the government survey, are none less certain in legal contemplation. They are fixed and determinable by a subdivision of a section, using the four corners of the section shown on the official field notes." *(Upton v. Reid, supra)* Thus, collateral evidence can be used to establish boundary lines which in the opinion of the owners are their title boundaries. Hopefully, with adequate research by the surveyor and productive consultation with his client, and possibly the attorney of his client, most of the cases of difference between record boundaries and title boundaries will not result in litigation.

It is my opinion, therefore, that those who use collateral evidence to establish subdivision lines of public land sections and corners not established in the field by the original public land surveyor are using the wrong procedure to arrive at what often is the correct title line. They are using collateral evidence to establish record lines which are legally established by the original plat and have not been set in the field, thus their location cannot be established by such collateral evidence. They should research and evaluate this collateral evidence to see if it would determine title boundaries. If it does they arrive at the same solution for the position of the boundary lines but are not using the proper reason for accepting it as such. Using the wrong reason to justify what might be a correct solution of a title line has a very bad possible consequence. It could result in a fence line being used as a title boundary when the record subdivision line of the section as described on the original plat is the correct title boundary.

Let's not introduce chaos into the subdivision of a section after such an excellent system has been designed by those very capable surveyors and congressmen who preceded us. Let us follow the intent as set forth by Congressional Acts and further established by procedures prescribed by the General Land Office and the Bureau of Land Management.

Professor McEntyre is a professor of land surveying at Purdue University, West Lafayette, Ind. 47907.

****

****

COMMENT AND DISCUSSION

MARCH 1982

The pages of SURVEYING AND MAPPING are open to free and temperate discussion of all matters pertaining to the interests of the Congress. It is the purpose of this department to encourage comments on published material or the presentation of new ideas in a formal or informal way. - Editor.

Center of Section Revisited

From Dexter M. Brinker, P.E., L.S., 6547 Otis St., Arvada, Colo. 80003: Professor McEntyre has done a good job of taking the lid off a can of worms that troubles most land surveyors in the "G.L.O." states [see "Subdivision of a Section," *Surveying and Mapping*, 41:4, Dec. 1981, pp. 385-388]; however I believe he has raised more questions than he has answered. In my opinion, several of the conclusions reached or inferred are totally unworkable.

I will agree that (at least in many respects) the Public Land Survey System was, and still is, an "excellent" system. However, it had, and still has, several extremely serious weaknesses. Two of these are

1. No provision was made to maintain and preserve the original corner monuments, and

2. While a method was specified for the subdivision of sections, no standards were established for these subsequent surveys, including positional tolerances for the aliquot corners so established.

It seems very likely that many of the public land states created the office of County Surveyor to perform the first function and quite possibly to conduct, or at least supervise or review, all subsequent surveys in the county, at least those of an aliquot nature. Unfortunately, for reasons too numerous to mention here, the office has been ineffective in most states.

One of the significant features of the Public Land Survey System is that it allows original monumentation to control over official distances and directions. Hence, a section line officially reported as running north 80 chains with a quarter section corner set at 40 chains and on line may be found to have a considerable "dog-leg" in it. In many cases neither "half" of such line runs north, and the two parts are neither 40 chains long nor equal to each other. Yet we must accept these corners as found, provided, of course, that we feel they are original and unmoved, or are in the same location as the original corners. Does it then make any sense to "nit-pick" the location of a center quarter corner and allow *no* positional tolerance whatsoever? I think not! More attention should be paid to the phrase "as nearly as possible" when used by the early instruction writers to describe various required survey operations. Apparently they realized that all measurements are approximate and a straight line exists in theory only.

Professor McEntyre says that accepting a farmer's eye-ball line as a record line makes a "farce" of the public land survey methods. Not so! At least four factors indicate otherwise:

1. The Public Land Survey instructions did not specify who could or could not subdivide a section. (Perhaps the designers of the system hoped that a public official such as the County Surveyor would fill the gap.)

2. Until about 1919 (and much later in many states) there was no such thing as statutory recognition of "professional" surveyors.

3. A farmer (or anyone for that matter) equipped only with three makeshift range poles could run a "reasonably straight" line between two recognizable monuments, even over difficult terrain. In many cases, especially with favorable terrain, such lines might be far straighter than numerous acceptable and unchallenged section lines established by the original surveys.

4. Not even the best surveyor can produce a "truly straight line." Hence the concept of "tolerance" is implied even if not defined.

This is not to condone the practice of making "fence line surveys" with little or no research, by assuming that an existing fence line is automatically both a record line and a title line. But there are many times when fences (or roads) are the best available evidence as to where the original corners were. In fact, when we evaluate fences or roads on or near the center lines of sections, we should consider the possibility that these improvements may be better evidence of the location of original quarter corners than current survey monuments which may have been set using improper restoration procedures!

The answer to the problem of properly locating aliquot lines (record lines, if you prefer) is not, in my opinion, to follow blindly a set of incomplete rules, nor to rely solely on the interpretations of lawyers or judges, many if not most of whom don't understand the problems of physical measurement and who have no more ability to evaluate boundary evidence than surveyors have. It seems to me that the answer is for every state surveyor society to get involved in *completing the rules* through state and, if necessary, federal legislation, so that once a subdivisional corner is set with *acceptable tolerance,* properly monumented, and made a part of the public record, that corner will have the same "majesty of the brass cap" as is enjoyed by corners set in original surveys by G.L.O. or B.L.M., and subsequent surveyors will be obliged to accept and use it. In other words, let's make the system work. Lines determined in this fashion will indeed be "record" lines. Obviously it will be helpful to have some legal guidelines to help us evaluate existing evidence on or near aliquot lines, but that poses no insurmountable problem, nor does the need to specify an "acceptable tolerance."

It is my firm belief that surveying will never attain the status of a true profession as long as we are willing to work as technicians and turn all our difficult problems over to engineers, lawyers, or the courts for decision.

****

COMMENT AND DISCUSSION

JUNE 1983

The pages of SURVEYING AND MAPPING are open to free and temperate discussion of all matters pertaining to the interests of the Congress. It is the purpose of this department to encourage comments on published material or the presentation of new ideas in a formal or informal way. - EDITOR.

Re: "Subdivision of a Section," by John G. McEntyre Published in Surveying and Mapping, Vol. 41, No. 4, pp. 385-388.

From: Leonard E. Lampert, R.L.S. (S-129), 220 Greenbriar Ave., Park Ridge, Stevens Point, Wis. 54481. Professor McEntyre's fine article was well rebutted by Dexter M. Brinker in Surveying and Mapping, Vol. 42, No. 1, Mar. 1982, p. 73. This is a further elaboration on the subject.

Neither article recognized two conditions, demanding consideration, which exist in the subdivision of a section. The section not previously subdivided can be treated precisely as indicated by Professor McEntyre. Those sections are a distinct minority. The section which has been previously subdivided requires following the footsteps of the previous subdivider if the chaos Professor McEntyre refers to is to be avoided. Setting up the record lines in those sections so they disagree with the title lines is a disservice to the public, the profession of land surveying, and introduces conflict.

Let us examine what Chief Justice Cooley said about this in this paper, *The Judicial Functions of Surveyors.*

"It is often the case when one or more corners are found to be extinct, all parties concerned have acquiesced in lines which were traced by the guidance of some other corner or landmark, which may or may not have been trustworthy; but to bring those lines into discredit when the people concerned do not question them, not only breeds trouble in the neighborhood, but it must often subject the surveyor himself to annoyance and perhaps discredit, since in a legal controversy the law as well as common sense must declare that a supposed boundary line long acquiesced in is better evidence of where the real line should be than any survey made after the original monuments have disappeared." (*Stewart v Carleton*, 31 Mich. Reports, 270; *Diehl v Zauger*, 39 Mich. Reports, 601)

Now let us delve deeper into the sections which have previously been subdivided since these are far and away the greater number of sections encountered in the rectangular land states. If the surveyor cannot follow his predecessor he must establish his own control and go back to the principal meridian and base line and proceed to lay out the base for the record lines - **Talk about chaos!**

In almost every midwestern metropolitan area you will find a p.i. at each 1/16 corner (a dogleg, as Dexter Brinker refers to it). This is a clear indication that the subdivision of the section did not create the straight lines the system dictated. To lay out the record lines now would accomplish the "mischief" to which Justice Cooley referred in his paper. To attempt to lay out the record lines as opposed to the title lines is for all practical purposes impossible. If it were, thousands of adjustments would be required in order to resolve the instances in which the record and title or occupancy do not agree. Subdivisions, streets, buildings, and other improvements would have to be moved. The litigation resulting would be endless.

The prime requisite for the surveyor is the exercise of independent judgment. No manual ever written can possibly cover every conceivable condition which may arise. I agree wholeheartedly that in boundary disputes the surveyor should point out the legal problems in a written report. (It is desirable to furnish the client an extra copy for his legal counsel.)

When a survey is completed, the monuments placed, descriptions written, conveyances made, and the abutting landowners agree upon the lines they can be overturned only by a court. The *Manual of Instructions for the Survey of the Public Lands* has consistently provided for the preservation of bona fide rights of landowners. The chapter on resurveys contains countless illustrations of this policy including the following: "Once it is accepted a local point of control has all the authority and significance of an identified original corner."

Professor McEntyre's article could encourage the inexperienced surveyor to fail to follow the footsteps of the predecessor and set up conflicting record and title lines. If the preceding surveyor is not followed, the following surveyor by upsetting his predecessor's work, and the neighborhood as well, is usurping the functions of a court. I find Ned Elder's statement, "an area is not to be set into an uproar by a surveyor in order to correct an error . . ." particularly refreshing and significant.

Justice Cooley was keenly aware of the consequences of such activity on the part of surveyors and he spelled out the interest of the public in the eight paragraphs of his paper which precede the discussion of meander lines. His remarks on the duty and authority of the surveyor are as appropriate today as if he were alive and speaking to us. His paper emphasizes the vagary of the theory versus the common sense approach.

John S. Grimes in *Clark on Surveying and Boundaries,* in discussing the surveyor's function, states, "It is not the surveyor's responsibility to set up new lines except where he is surveying heretofore unplatted land or subdividing a new tract. Where title to land has been established under a previous survey, the surveyor's duty is to solely locate the lines of the original survey. He cannot establish a new corner, nor can he even correct surveys of earlier surveyors. He must track the footsteps of the first."

Francis Hodgman in his *Manual of Land Surveying* (1891-1913) in section 2 of chapter XII Miscellaneous, points out the authority of the surveyor is quite limited and that he has "no more authority than other men to determine boundaries, of their own motion . . . ." "Surveyors may or may not have in certain cases means of judgment not possessed by others, but the law cannot and does not make them arbiters of private rights." His manual further states, "New surveys disturbing old boundaries are not to be encouraged."

Brown and Eldridge in *Evidence and Procedures for Boundary Location* in section 17-12 discuss the surveyor's obligation to the public "not to stir up boundary disputes." In section 17-15, "Provoking litigation, according to common law, is a crime known as maintenance." A. C. Mulford in his manual, *Boundaries and Landmarks*, quotes from John Wait's *The Law of Operations Preliminary to Construction in Engineering and Architecture:* "The highest and best evidence of the location of a tract of land is that furnished by the monuments found on the ground and which have been made for that particular tract. The line originally run, fixed, and marked is the true boundary line that will control irrespective of any mistakes or errors in running and marking the line. The marks on the ground of an old survey, indicating the lines originally run are the best evidence of the location of the survey . . . ."

Chaos will indeed be created by the refusal to accept the preceding surveyor's work. The difference between theory and common sense is apparent. Dexter Brinker pointed out the failure of the rectangular system to preserve the original corners was accompanied by no specific assignment for the subdivision of the section. To set up a conflict between record and title inciting litigation is certainly not in the public interest.

****

Not just in the dream stage . . . Not just a prototype model

. . . *But*

PROVEN IN THE FIELD

The "Tellurometer" is the *only* electronic distance-determination system that has been tested and proven practical in the field. After two years of hard use on all kinds of terrain and under all kinds of climatic conditions, it has won the endorsement of photogrammetrists, consultants, state and federal mapping agencies.

SPEED

Two men (one with transmitter, another with receiver) can measure any distance from 500 ft. to 40 mi. in 10 minutes, plus only 10 minutes required to unpack and mount instrument on common tripod.

Proven in the field

ACCURACY

Tellurometers produce accuracies of 1 part in 300,000 ± 2 inches (or better, by individual calibration). Users obtain 3rd order results on lines 500 to 1,500 ft; 2nd order—1,500 ft. to 1 mi.; and 1st order—1 to 40 mi.

Proven in the field

ECONOMY

Federal agencies, state highway engineers and private firms report 40% savings in costs of establishing horizontal controls. Users frequently report jobs completed in half the normal time required.

Proven in the field

When you buy an electronic distance-determination system

Buy Experience

TELLUROMETER, INC., 224 Dupont Circle Bldg., Washington 6, D.C. "Micro-Distancer"

DECEMBER 1983

Re: "The Retracement" and Comment "Re: 'Subdivision of a Section,'" by Leonard E. Lampert Published in Surveying and Mapping, Vol. 40 No. 3, September 1980, pp. 315-323; and Vol. 43, No. 2, June 1983, pp. 223-224, respectively

From: Anthony B. Kiedrowski, R.L.S., P.E., President, Kiedrowski Engineering, Inc., 4340 80ᵗʰ Street, South (Kellner), Wisconsin Rapids, Wis. 54494. I had hoped surveyors would see the fallacy in Mr. Lampert's philosophy as he explained it in the 1980 article by saying, "In summation, the surveyor should follow the steps of the preceding surveyor, be he the original surveyor *or a later surveyor.* However, it keeps getting attention with another boost from Mr. Lampert himself in the June 1983 issue of *Surveying and Mapping.*

Now what Justice Cooley and Ned Elder and John Grimes and Francis Hodgman have said about new surveys upsetting old surveys does indeed have an element of truth. But let's be careful how we apply it to a particular situation. Some surveyors are using this idea as a cover-up for surveys poorly done. If we follow Mr. Lampert's philosophy to its logical conclusion, surveyors would then become a group who are continually covering each other to the detriment of a landowner who may suffer substantial damages because of an erroneously placed monument.

Let me give an example. A couple of years ago, I did a survey for a client whose land was bordered on one side by a section line. It was necessary to have a particular section corner and quarter corner. Some 1940 surveys had called for stones at these corners. However, about 1970, the County Surveyor came along and set new cast iron monuments at these corners without looking for the stones. Both corners were in a blacktop road. We excavated with a backhoe and quite easily recovered both stone monuments. This was disturbing to several surveyors in the area since about 20 surveys had already been done from the new cast iron monuments.

So whose neighborhood should we not disturb? The new surveys in the area, or the old possession lines which are in harmony with the stone monuments? Am I to lie to my client and tell him he has encroachment problems when I know that he doesn't?

You see, the problem comes from the careless way some surveyors reestablish government corners. Except for New England and Texas, practically the whole country has been conveyed at one time or another with descriptions based on the government corners. One quarter corner affects 32 forties and probably all the parcels therein. That's a lot of neighborhood that can get upset by just one monument if it gets reset in the wrong place. I'd want to be very careful *which* preceding surveyor's footsteps I'm going to follow.

There is a myth that is often quoted in support of the Lampert philosophy. That is, that once a survey is done and monumented and recorded, and conveyances are signed and delivered and recorded, that survey is sacred. A grantor can only convey that which he owns. If a survey erroneously includes a chunk of the adjoining property, that conveyance does not make the survey correct. It makes no sense to take a known erroneous survey, particularly a recent one, and proceed from there just because a conveyance has been made.

****

DECEMBER 1983

From: Carlisle Madson, L.S., 209 Shady Oak Rd., Hopkins, Minn. 55343, and Alver R. Freeman, L.S., 8315 Dupont Avenue South, Bloomington, Minn. 55420. We are in full agreement with the well written article by Professor McEntyre. We do not agree with the rebuttal by Leonard E. Lampert, appearing in *Surveying and Mapping. Vol.* 43, No. 2, pp. 223-224. Our reply to Mr. Lampert follows:

Setting up the record land lines in conformance with the 1805 Act of Congress in previously subdivided sections, even though they disagree with the occupation lines, is not a disservice to the public. The surveyor's role is that of a fact-finder. It is his obligation to determine if there is a difference between the occupation and record lines. The client does not ask the surveyor to locate his lines of occupation; he can see these lines where they exist. What the client really wants to know is if his lines of occupation agree with his deed of record. And, bear in mind, the surveyor's responsibility extends beyond his immediate client to third parties who rely on his survey when purchasing land or insuring title.

In the PLS states a court action is usually necessary to obtain a marketable title to lands occupied under an unwritten right. It is extremely difficult to determine whether an unwritten

right has ripened into a fee right. This probably accounts for the prudent land surveyor's reluctance to assume the liability for making a decision regarding ownership of disputed areas claimed by others. The surveyor must recognize that the situation is a legal matter; and the surveyor should recommend that the client seek legal counsel if he wishes to gain a marketable title to land he occupies beyond his written title, or if he wishes to protect the land in his written title occupied by others.

When the earliest settlers acquired a patent from the federal government, they acquired title to a specific tract of land as depicted on the GLO plat. The boundaries of the title conveyed were those recited in the writings in the patent, and these were to be determined on the ground by surveys that complied with the rules laid down in the Act of 1805. This system of subdivision provided simplicity, was easy to apply, was designed to keep order upon the land, and minimized questions of title.

State legislation *can not* contravene Federal Statues or Acts of Congress, neither could the GLO. The GLO - as well as some state legislators - has attempted at various times, either by design or by misinformation, to contravene the Act of Congress of February 11, 1805, relative to the establishment of the Legal Center of Section. The legislators in Iowa, Minnesota, Wisconsin (and perhaps several other states) have been guilty of passing legislation which resulted in advancing erroneous methods for establishing the center of section. Wisconsin, for example, was blessed with two wrong methods in a 14-year period (1843 to 1867) before their legislation was changed to agree with the federal rules. In Wisconsin the problem of the center of section is now resolved by statute law. [1] Minnesota legislation promoted erroneous center of section locations for a span of 28 years, 1875 to 1903. However, the rules for the subdivision of sections are based on federal laws and regulations - a state statute which controverts the federal laws and regulations would be *VOID* and *SHOULD NOT* be followed. [2] What a pity it is that the 19th-century surveyors did not understand and abide by this simple truth. There was, perhaps, some justification, based on lack of communication, for the early surveyors to plead ignorance of the law; but surely, it is not a valid plea today.

REFERENCES

1. General Laws of Wisconsin 1867, Chapter 169, §§1, 2, and 3.
2. *Clark on Surveying and Boundaries*, 4th ed., §189, pp. 189-190.

On page 78 of their book entitled *Fading Footsteps,* T. S. Madson and Louis N. A. Seeman have a crystal clear explanation of the Legal Center of Section as a record monument. With the kind permission of the authors, we quote the following two paragraphs.

"Another example of a *record monument* is the *center quarter-section corner* of a section of land in the public land system. The reason that this point is a *record monument* is because the eight exterior corners of the section were established by the placement of the monuments at their positions by the original surveyor and because the location of the center quarter-section corner is clearly defined in the 1973 *Manual of Surveying Instructions for the Survey of the Public Lands of the United States, p.* 89, §3-95, as follows: 'The position of the center quarter-section corner is at the intersection of the centerlines unless previously marked.'

"This position, therein, is determined by running straight lines between opposing quarter-section corners. The intersection of these two straight lines is the *record monument* for the center quarter-section corner. An interesting and little-understood relationship is that, since the *Manual of Instruction* addresses the breakdown of a land section into its aliquot parts from the exterior monuments, all of these aliquot corners must, of necessity, be record monuments and precise of location. Persons who foolishly argue otherwise fail to understand the true meaning of the survey and conveyancing of the public lands of the United States."

The "unless previously marked" in the last sentence of the first paragraph means unless marked by the original government surveyors prior to acceptance of the plat by the General Land Office.

In dealing with the public land survey, it is important to remember that the first dependent resurveyor to set foot on the position of the center of section is not the "original" surveyor. The "original" surveyor, as far as the corners of the aliquot parts of the section are concerned, is the person or persons who set the exterior corners of the section before GLO acceptance of the township plat. The corners set by a dependent resurveyor are, at best, common report monuments and lack any real authority. It is the *original* corners, set by the *original* surveyor, that are considered "sacred." Since all the aliquot parts of a section are fixed by law - and precise of location - any resurvey of the section must recognize all parts of an *original* survey. The chronology, the dates and sequence of events, is most important in the survey and subdivision of a section. If the monuments came before the GLO plat - then the monuments control. However, if the GLO plat came before the monuments - then the GLO plat controls. Now, an erroneous corner set by a resurveyor for the center may ripen into a title corner or ownership corner, but it cannot correctly be said to be the center quarter-section corner or the Legal Center of Section!

By calling the record lines and the occupation lines one and the same - when in fact they are not the same - promotes future litigation. The great sin of the occupation-line surveyor lies not in calling the occupation line the ownership line, which he does in nearly every case; he damages the world by calling the occupation line the record line. And finally, since when is it a "disservice to the public" to observe the law of the State of Wisconsin?

****

COMMENT AND DISCUSSION
JUNE 1984

The pages of SURVEYING AND MAPPING are open to free and temperate discussion of all matters pertaining to the interests of the Congress. It is the purpose of this department to encourage comments on published material or the presentation of new ideas in a formal or informal way. - EDITOR.

Re: "Subdivision of a Section," by John G. McEntyre
Published in *Surveying and Mapping* Vol. 41, No. 4, pp. 385-388

* Emphasis by italicizing words and phrases has been supplied by the author in citations throughout the comments on and discussion of the subject of subdivision of sections.

From: Doyle G. Abrahamson, P.L.S., Surveying Coordinator, Merrick & Company, P.O. Box 22026, (10855 E. Bethany Dr., Aurora, CO 80014), Denver, CO 80222. Since being published, Professor McEntyre's article on the subdivision of a section has had many responses, both pro and con. I think it is good for the surveying profession to start discussing our surveying problems amongst ourselves and try to solve some of our most basic surveying problems.

Professor McEntyre states: "We should not introduce 'chaos' into the subdivision of a section." All chaos can be eliminated, if our Congressional Acts and the procedures prescribed by the General Land Office (GLO) and the Bureau of Land Management (BLM), are not taken out of context. First, there is no Congressional Act or interpretation of a Congressional Act by GLO or BLM which will allow one to subdivide a section by any other means than by *surveying* it out on the ground.

The Act of February 11, 1805, is entitled "An Act Concerning the Mode of *Surveying* [emphasis supplied] the Public Lands of the United States." Section 2 of this Act states in part:

. . . the *corners** of half and *quarter sections*, not marked on said surveys, shall be placed, as *nearly as possible*, equidistant from those two corners which stand on the same line. . .

. . . and the boundary lines, which shall not have been actually run, and marked aforesaid, shall be ascertained, by *running* straight lines from the established corners to the opposite corresponding corners; . . .

The Act of April 5, 1832, in addressing the lines of division of Half-Quarter Sections, states that subdivisional corners shall be located "*as nearly as may be.*" This Act states in part:

. . . And the corners and contents of Quarter-Quarter Sections, which may thereafter be sold, shall be ascertained *as nearly as may be*, in the manner, and on the principles, directed and prescribed by the second section of an Act entitled "An Act Concerning the Mode of Surveying the Public Lands of the United States," passed on the eleventh day of February, eighteen hundred and five; . . .

As one can see by our Congressional Acts, the only procedure mentioned to subdivide a section, is by field surveying and to locate the corners "as nearly as may be" or "as nearly as possible."

Mr. McEntyre states that the "record center of a section should be established at the intersection of the lines joining opposite quarter corners." In our Congressional Acts, the only thing of *record* is the surveying procedure to be used to subdivide a section. It is clear that aliquot corners of a section were to be surveyed in and that they were not to be theoretical corners, because they cannot be theoretical corners if, by our Congressional Act, they are only to be located "as nearly as may be" or "as nearly as possible."

In reviewing the procedures prescribed by GLO and BLM, it is clear that they are talking about subdividing a section by survey also. At this time, I think it important to consider the *Manual of Surveying Instructions*, 1973, U.S. Department of the Interior, Bureau of Land Management, hereinafter called the *Manual*, in its full context and not to take one sentence, one paragraph, or one chapter statement out of context.

Chapter 3 of the *Manual* is entitled, "The System of Rectangular Surveys." In subparagraph 76 of Chapter 3, the *Manual* states in part:

. . . The local surveyor is employed as an expert to identify lands which have passed into private ownership . . . . The work usually includes the subdivision of the section into the fractional parts shown upon the approved plat. *In this capacity the local surveyor is performing a function contemplated by law.*

Now, if, in fact, the interior aliquot corners of a section are theoretical corners, as suggested by Professor McEntyre, then when a client comes to us to break down and monument the interior corners of a section, we should tell him that the interior corners are theoretical corners and we cannot monument said corners. Any monument set by you or anyone else might be close, and even though the corner designation is stamped on the face of the monument, it really is not the corner. No one upon the face of this earth can tell you exactly where a theoretical corner is or to where one owns. The state statutes of Colorado (38-52-101 (7)) require that a private surveyor set the same type of monuments as the BLM, said monument to be marked as specified in Chapter IV of the *Manual* for all interior corners of a section. We also have to file a corner recordation on said monument (38-53-103). If an interior aliquot section corner was, in fact, a theoretical corner, then we could not locate it to monument it, and therefore, we could not file a corner recordation on it, either. But that is something we do not have to worry about because there is not a scintilla of evidence in our Congressional Acts, or procedures in the *Manual*, to support such a finding.

In further quoting from the *Manual* in regard to the subdivision of a section, subparagraphs 3-77 through 3-84 deal with subdivision by Protraction. Subparagraph 3-85 is entitled "Subdivision by Survey." Subparagraph 3-86 is entitled "Order of Procedure in Survey," and the last sentence of the subparagraph states:

The following methods should be employed:

The following subparagraph 3-87, which is entitled "Subdivision of Sections into Quarter Sections" states:

. . . To subdivide a section into Quarter-Sections, run straight lines from the established Quarter-Section corners to the opposite Quarter-Section corners. The point of intersection of the lines thus run will be the corner common to the several Quarter-Sections, or the legal center of the section. . . .

Chapter 3, Subsection 124, puts accuracies on what the Acts of legislature meant when they stated that subdivision corners should be located "as nearly as possible" or "as nearly as may be." Subsection 124 states:

The "limit of closure" set for the public land surveys may now be expressed by the fraction 1/905, provided that the limit of closure in neither latitude nor departure exceeds 1/1280.

Keep in mind that the subdivision of a section, as mentioned in the Congressional Acts and BLM *Manuals,* discusses procedures to be used in field surveying in the aliquot corners of a section. The Colorado State Board of Registration for Professional Engineers and Land Surveyors in a letter dated May 9, 1979, stated:

The Board does consider the B.L.M. Manual, 1973, 3-124, applicable for closures for the re-establishment of public land survey monuments.

These accuracies may have been raised in different states by their state laws.

By reading our Congressional Acts and the *Manual* in their entirety, it makes what seems to be a difficult task, very simple and practical.

Professor McEntyre states:

. . . the center lines of the section are obtained by joining opposite Quarter corners and the interior boundaries of the Quarter Sections formed are portions of these lines. . . . the Bureau of Land Management has perpetuated this procedure as their policy . . .

Professor McEntyre does not state his source of information, but in a memorandum of the Bureau of Land Management, dated May 8, 1981, on the subject of Acceptance and Rejection Statements in Field Notes, from the Chief, Cadastral Survey Examination and Approval Staff, to the Chief, Division of Survey and Mapping (D410), it is clear that the position of the BLM on this subject is quite to the contrary. The above-referenced memorandum had this to say:

Collateral evidence may consist of, but is not limited to, fence corners, road intersections and private survey monuments established in good faith and by legally accepted practice . . . When collateral evidence is accepted for the position of a corner which was not established during the course of the original survey or a subsequent Public Land Survey System survey, an acceptance statement is absolutely necessary . . . Where 1/16, 1/64, or other corner position were never monumented by county or private surveyors, the description may be completed by the statement, "and is accepted as a careful and faithful determination of the position of the corner."

If a monument is set for an aliquot corner of a section, using the practices, procedures, and accuracies that were acceptable at the time the monument was set, then it is the legal aliquot corner and should be accepted as such today.

There is a lot of talk about professionalism in surveying. However, I find it hard to be called a true professional when you can go to an interior aliquot corner of a section and discover five monuments in a 0.3 ft. circle. I have photographs of this particular case. In another case, I set a 2-1/2 x 30 in. monument at a 1/16th corner and came back a year later to find that another surveyor had put another chiseled cross on the top of a monument 0.025 ft. away from mine. *That's chaos!*

If the Congressional Acts and the *Manual* had intended that the interior aliquot corners of a normal section be, in fact, theoretical corners, then we, as surveyors, should not be addressing this subject because the section has already been subdivided with theoretical corners and none of us is capable of setting a theoretical corner. If that is the case, we should advise our clients that the monument we set is an "approximate" monument and that it cannot be used as a boundary monument. Professor McEntyre suggested that if a discrepancy was found between the theoretical corner and the land use or other found monument, then he should advise his client to talk to the adjoiner and agree on a boundary line. This would surely create *chaos*, because if you are talking about the distance between the found monument and the theoretical corner, that distance cannot be determined and would be a different value for every different surveyor who surveys to the corner. Some distances may be close, but none would clear up the title unless one would say something like: that portion of the SE 1/4 lying westerly of the found monuments. But we do not have to worry about this because in reading our Congressional Acts and the BLM *Manual* in full context, it is clear that the interior aliquot corners *are not theoretical* corners.

In reviewing court cases on this subject, most cases deal with procedures and not accuracies. In some cases, it would appear that the courts are talking about theoretical corners, but then they go on to say that "just as the center of section 34 can be and was later correctly established upon the ground" *(Mathews, et al. v. Parker,* 299 P. 354). In *Rodenbaugh v. Egy* (128 P. 381), the Kansas Supreme Court said, "It does not appear, nor is it seriously contended, that the surveyor or the Court erred in determining the true division line between the NW 1/4 and the NE 1/4 of Section 30." In the Montana Supreme Court case of *Vaught v. McClymond* (155 P. 2d. 612) the court, in establishing the true boundary line between the Northwest Quarter and the Southwest Quarter had this to say: "We have concluded to remand the cause to have another survey made, either by a surveyor or surveyors to be agreed upon by the parties, or by a surveyor or surveyors whom the District Court may see fit to appoint." These cases were all talking about procedures to be used in conducting a survey and, in all cases, the court's opinion was that a surveyor could locate the aliquot corners. I find no reference that the interior aliquot section corners are, in fact, theoretical corners, which are not locatable by a surveyor.

630

THE COMPLETE SURVEY SYSTEM— WILD

MEASURES DISTANCES FROM 1 TO 2000 METERS WITHIN 1 CM ACCURACY. MEASURES ANGLES WITH YOUR CHOICE OF THEODOLITES. BOTH IN ONE COMPACT, EASY TO USE, PORTABLE UNIT.

This is the second generation DI-10 Distomat Infra-red Distancer, with all the versatility, reliability and service of the nearly 2000 older models now in world-wide use.

Improvements? *Double the range.* Thin, flexible cables. Electronic damping. Measuring time, 15 seconds. Available with, or retrofitted to T-1A, T-16 or T-2 theodolites.

Write or call for more information, delivery and leasing arrangements.

WILD HEERBRUGG INSTRUMENTS, INC.
FARMINGDALE, NEW YORK 11735
(516) 293-7400

WILD OF CANADA, LTD., 881 LADY ELLEN PLACE, OTTAWA, 3 ONTARIO
WILD OF MEXICO, SA, LONDRES 256, MEXICO 6, D. F.

In order to keep this paper as short as possible, I could not quote the Congressional Acts in their full context, or to elaborate much on the *Manual*. If one wants to understand more clearly the laws and procedures governing the subdivision of a section, I would suggest getting the full context of our Congressional Acts, reading the *Manual* from the front cover to the back cover, and researching court cases that deal with the subdivision of a section.

****

SEPTEMBER 1984

Re: "Subdivision of a Section," by John G. McEntyre; and Comment on (Abrahamson)

Published in Vol. 41, No. 4, Dec. 1981, pp. pp. 385-388, and Vol. 44, No. 2, June 1984, pp. 141-143, respectively

From: Richard J. Mitchell, 255 Portofino Way, Slip A-9, Redondo Beach, California 90277 [Division Engineer, Survey Division, Los Angeles County, California (ret.)]. It would appear to the writer that both Professor McEntyre and Mr. Abrahamson have missed a couple of significant points in their consideration of the acceptance and/or restoration of public land survey corners whether they be interior corners or exterior corners.

First, if the land on both sides of the line being run has not yet passed from federal ownership to private ownership then the lines are, and can only be, where the Bureau of Land Management says they are. There is no other authority! If the land on either (or both) sides of the line has been patented out (passed into private ownership), then the line is fixed in location as of the date of the patent. It remains only to recover it or to reestablish it *as it existed on that date*. Subsequent surveys by either the United States or by private practitioners or by local governments cannot change the location. In this case it behooves the surveyor making the recovery survey to give attention only to marks (or direct perpetuation of marks) that *existed on that date*. "Marks," of course, include monuments, accessories to monuments, witness monuments, line trees, bearing trees, brush cuttings, fences, and all of the other physical evidence of where the line was *on that date*. We should not have to note that the recovery survey will also show the location of all encroachments, gaps not of record, and all monuments found, even those that show a location other than that which existed at the *date of the original patent*. Parole evidence (oral testimony) will be accepted only to help establish the location of the line (or a corner on that line) as of the date of patent - no other has meaning. Nor does the advice, coercion, threats, letters, protestations, or other acts of any adjoiner, whether private or federal, have any bearing on the location of the line.

If the line (or corner) must be restored by proportionate methods, i.e., if no direct evidence of its location can be found, then only corners that existed on *the date of patent* may be used as a basis for the proportional restoration.

Now, lest it be said that this writer has lost touch with reality, let us acknowledge that the cost of the survey may well exceed the value of the land. In this case, the surveyor may be well advised to change his hat and offer his services as an arbitrator to establish, not the line of the patent but a line that can be accepted by the adjoiners in lieu of the line of the patent.

The *second* major point that both Mr. Abrahamson and Professor McEntyre seem to have missed concerns the matter of multiple monuments at a point such as a center of section. (We assume that the center in question was not established by the United States prior to the patent and that the full section was returned in the survey on which the patent was based.) We present here three questions to be asked: (1) (As suggested by Mr. Abrahamson,) was the first of the found monuments established by an actual field survey running of the lines between the identified opposite quarter corners using equipment and care appropriate to the date of the running? (2) Have any of the found monuments been used as a basis for occupation or do any of them support an occupation of any of the quarter sections? (3) Barring an occupation of any of the quarters, has the value of the land increased to an extent that would warrant a more precise running of the lines?

In this case we take a stand somewhat between that of Mr. Abrahamson and that of Professor McEntyre.

We strongly object to nitpicking but abhor carelessness. The *true* center is at a theoretical intersection of two straight lines defined by the quarter corners; however, reality supports Mr. Abrahamson's contention that if the lines are run with an accuracy consistent with the value of the land and especially if an occupation based on that running follows the running, then the monument thus established should be accepted by subsequent surveyors. To do otherwise casts a shadow on the professional stature of the surveyor. If, however, no reliance has been placed on the monument set and if land values make the differences significant, then we *might* advocate the setting of a new corner. We would have strong objections to rejecting a monument set within 0.30 ft. of where we believe the true corner to be (as was described in the published paper) and can only laugh at the punch mark 0.02 ft. from the monument center.

Specific examples of each of the points we have made above can be found in the records of Los Angeles County, an area of generally high professional standards and of very high land values.

We add two more points for consideration: (1) California law requires that a record-of-survey be filed when a material discrepancy with the existing record is discovered and that a corner record be filed when a Public Land Survey corner is recovered. If this law were rigidly adhered to in all areas (California included), many of the problems addressed would not exist. (2) The authority of the County Surveyor is that granted to him by the public trust (and the trust of his professional colleagues) and not to any authority granted by law. This we have accepted as a responsibility and have been honored by it.

****

SEPTEMBER 1984

Re: "The Retracement"; Comment re: "The Retracement" and Comment Re: 'Subdivision of a Section,'"; Comments on (Kiedrowski) and (Madson and Freeman)

Published in Vol. 40, No. 3, Sept. 1980, pp. 315-323; Vol. 43, No. 2, June 1983, pp. 223-224; Vol. 43, No. 4, Dec. 1983, pp. 410-413, respectively

From: Leonard L. Lampert, P.E., R.L.S., 220 Greenbriar Avenue, Park Ridge, Stevens Point, Wisconsin 54481.

Re: Kiedrowski Comment

The writer of this comment seems to be undecided as to whether to agree with my comments. It should be pointed out here that, if a surveyor is unable to accept the preceding surveyor's work, then he should proceed to make his own independent check of the meridian and the base line to satisfy himself on their correct positions prior to making any survey.

The rebuttal by Mr. Kiedrowski to the Lampert paper and subsequent comment uses an example with which I am familiar. The comments did not include the outcome nor the result of this finding of the old stone monuments, which if used would upset or overturn 23 surveys of record. As a matter of fact, of the record surveys, 11, including the first to use the cast iron monuments set by the county surveyor, were made by Mr. Kiedrowski. Twelve were made by other surveyors.

The controversy over the proper corner location was aired at a meeting of the Central Wisconsin Chapter of the Wisconsin Society of Land Surveyors at Wisconsin Rapids on August 16, 1979. This meeting was attended by the chairman of the County Board and the corporation counsel. As a result of this meeting the chairman of the county board requested an opinion by the Wood County Surveyor. This four-page opinion, dated August 28, 1979, presents the history of the corners in question. It also pointed up a lack of proof that the stones were the original 1851 corners. The field notes stated *wood posts* were placed in the original government survey. The county surveyor stated in his report that the cast iron monuments set by the county should control and continue to be used. The Kiedrowski rebuttal appears to present a different opinion. It freely admits reserving decision properly assigned to the courts.

handy
to
have
along...

the
BRUNTON
POCKET TRANSIT
that is!

Yes, it's handy to have along...
for use as a compass, transit, level, plumb,
alidade and clinometer. Write for Booklet.

*Brunton is a registered trademark of

WM. AINSWORTH & SONS, INC.
2151 LAWRENCE STREET · DENVER 5, COLORADO

Re: Madson and Freeman Comments

This rebuttal is a classic example of the difference between theory and common sense. (John McEntyre is a good friend who, I am certain, would strongly defend my right to disagree, as likewise I would defend his.)

In the rebuttal by Madson and Freeman the *occupation lines referred to are in fact title lines.* The weaknesses of the 1805 Act of Congress are spelled out very well in Dexter Brinker's rebuttal in *Surveying and Mapping* (Vol. 42, No. 1, Mar. 1982, p. 73). To repeat, "no provision was made to maintain and preserve the original monuments." In addition, no criteria was established fixing the responsibility or qualifications for subdivision of the section.

Consider the many mid-western metropolitan centers where a "dog-leg" or point of intersection occurs at all 1/16 corners on the quarter lines subdividing the section. These breaks in the quarter line are plainly visible to anyone who cares to look. To set up now the record line - a straight line between opposite quarter corners is indeed a disservice! The buildings, streets, subdivision, and utilities which follow the previously subdivided line will not move. The prudent surveyor will not attempt to upset the existing improvements by setting forth difference between record and title lines.

The client employs a surveyor to locate and mark the boundary of his property and to provide him with the best available evidence on the ground. The client does not need or want involvement in litigation and he certainly does not want a report that will inform him the record line is in one location and the title line in another. The experienced surveyor will not set up a different center of section from that previously monumented in the original subdivision which would move streets, utilities, buildings, and other improvements simply because it does not conform strictly to statutes or rules. Common sense controls - not theory!

Based upon a considerable number of court appearances as an expert witness I have observed the courts to follow consistently this doctrine. In my experience several of these cases were appealed to and decided by the Wisconsin Supreme Court.

Another aspect entering into the establishment of the previously subdivided section is error tolerance. Errors were permitted at the time the section was subdivided. Note the phrase "as nearly as possible." Setting up conflicting positions for the center of section, which would result from a difference between record and title lines cannot be in the public interest - *since when is inciting litigation the function of a surveyor?* Even if such an attempt were made no court would sanction it. The underlying viewpoint of Justice Cooley's paper is that common sense must be applied by the courts and by the surveyor.

When a section has not been previously subdivided, theory will apply, and the center can be set at the intersection of straight lines from opposite quarter corners. However, these sections are few in number. The majority of sections have been subdivided and in these common sense *must* apply. The footsteps of the preceding surveyor must be followed. This is the only realistic position possible.

REFERENCES

Brinker, Dexter M., "Comment and Discussion," *Surveying and Mapping*, Vol. 42, No. 1, Mar. 1982, pp. 73-74.

Lampert, Leonard L., "Comment and Discussion," *Surveying and Mapping*, Vol. XXXIX, No. 4, Dec. 1979, pp. 363-365.

Lampert, Leonard L., "Comment and Discussion," *Surveying and Mapping*, Vol. 43, No. 2, June 1983, pp. 223-224.

McEntyre, John G., "Subdivision of a Section," *Surveying and Mapping*, Vol. 41, No. 4, Dec. 1981, pp. 385-388.

Wambach, Wm. T., "Comment and Discussion," *Surveying and Mapping*, Vol. XXXIX, No. 4, Dec. 1979, pp. 361-362.

U.S. Department of the Interior, Bureau of Land Management, *Manual of Instructions for the Survey of the Public Lands of the United States*, Technical Bulletin 6, GPO, 1973.

****

DECEMBER 1984

[**Ed. Note:** There have been a number of comments and discussions submitted for publication in this section since author McEntyre's article appeared in the December 1981 issue of *Surveying and Mapping*. Some of the viewpoints were not only stated once, but were reiterated, elaborated on, and rebutted. Of course, that is just what this section of the Journal is meant to provide a forum, a sounding board, an opportunity to present ideas to professional peers, pros and cons affecting the disciplines represented by ACSM and the association itself, and, last but not least, discussion of papers presented in the publication. It is now felt by this editor that, unless there are new ideas to present, discussion of the paper, "Subdivision of a Section," and of subsequent comments and discussions should be brought to a close. Further comments or discussion on this specific topic, involving this particular paper, will be refereed by at least three professional peers not involved in the discussion for decision as to publication.

Here follows author McEntyre's final comments and remarks of Freeman and Madson directed to a recent rebuttal.]

AUTHOR SPEAKS TO COMMENTS ON PAPER, "SUBDIVISION OF A SECTION"

From: John G. McEntyre, Ph.D., L.S., P.E., Professor of Land Surveying and Head, Surveying and Mapping Area, School of Civil Engineering, Purdue University, West Lafayette, Indiana 47907. To the editor: My article "Subdivision of a Section" was published in the December 1981 issue of *Surveying and Mapping*, Vol. 41, No. 4, pp. 385-388. It inspired a few comments which were subsequently published. Carlisle Madson and Alver Freeman wrote a discussion in support of my original article which appeared in the December 1983 issue of the Journal (Vol. 43, No. 4, pp. 411-413). After the publication of this discussion I saw no need for me to write a discussion.

Doyle Abrahamson wrote comments concerning the original article which were published in the June 1984 issue (Vol. 44, No. 2, pp. 142-144). The ideas which were expressed by Abrahamson must be answered. Therefore, a discussion written by me is enclosed in this letter. It is requested that it be published in the appropriate section of the Journal as soon as possible. This discussion represents the closing comments by the original author. In my judgment nothing can be gained by further discussions. Professionals who read their journals have adequate discussion to read in the four separate issues (five when my discussion is published) relative to the topic "Subdivision of a Section." You are referred to the first and last paragraphs in my enclosed discussion for ideas expressed relative to this concept.

I appreciate ACSM publishing my original article, which I hoped and was relatively sure would develop discussion. Your practice of publishing discussions in the Journal is an example of good professional practice and is to be commended.

I wish you continued success in future publications.

[Ed. Note: There have been a number of comments and discussions for publication in this section since author McEntyre's article appeared in the December 1981 issue of *Surveying and Mapping*. Some of the viewpoints were not only stated once, but were reiterated, elaborated on, and rebutted. Of course, that is just what this section of the Journal is meant to provide — a forum, a sounding board, an opportunity to present ideas to professional peers, pros and cons affecting the disciplines represented by ACSM and the association itself, and, last but not least, discussion of papers presented in the publication. It is now felt by this editor that, unless there are new ideas to present, discussion of the paper, "Subdivision of a Section," and of subsequent comments and discussions should be brought to a close. Further comments or discussion on this specific topic, involving this particular paper, will be referred to at least three professional peers not involved in the discussion for decision as to publication.

Here follows author McEntyre's final comments and remarks of Freeman and Madson directed to a recent rebuttal.]

SUBDIVISION OF A SECTION

When I wrote my article "Subdivision of a Section" which was published in the December 1981 issue of *Surveying and Mapping* it was my intention not to write a discussion of the comments which would be published about the article. My intent at that time was to write a clear and concise explanation of the proper procedure to subdivide a section. In my opinion the original paper accomplished this goal. After a few discussions were published I did consider writing comments relative to them. However, the December 1983 issue included a discussion by Carlisle Madson and Alver Freeman, which supported the concepts in my original paper. This discussion summarized the proper procedure to subdivide a section and was a better defense of my original article than I could have written. At that time I felt that the original paper had been the motivation for several discussions by dedicated professional surveyors and was an excellent contribution to the reference material for professional surveyors. There seemed no need to write more.

The comments by Doyle G. Abrahamson in the June 1984 issue of *Surveying and Mapping* must be answered. Surveying colleagues contacted me and recommended that I respond to it. It is difficult to compose an answer to this discussion by Abrahamson since illogical interpretations and incorrect concepts are threaded throughout his discussion.

Abrahamson's comments will be answered by first discussing the two items which he constantly repeated in his writings. These topics are: (1) The correct procedure to subdivide a section is by field surveying ("surveying it out on the ground") to locate the corners "as nearly as may be" and (2) the terminology "theoretical corner" which would necessitate our advising our clients that the monument we set is an "approximate" monument and cannot be used as a boundary monument. This presentation will then be concluded with six concepts related to public land surveying which negate the conclusions made by Abrahamson.

The center of a section is a point that is capable of being mathematically ascertained after the positions of the original quarter corners have been determined. The brilliant and practical professionals who designed our public land procedures, and those who followed them and refined these procedures, were too knowledgeable and experienced to require that the lines between opposite quarter corners be determined by field surveying. When they stated, ". . . shall be ascertained *by running* straight lines from established corners to the opposite corresponding . . ." (emphasis added by author) they were not requiring that the straight line be determined by field procedures. The data for these called-for straight lines could already be mathematically determined and were to be "run" then in the field. This would be consistent with this wording. Any practicing surveyor knows the difficulty, and virtual impossibility, of running a straight line directly in the field. All kinds of obstacles, such as hedgerows, trees, swamps, creeks, and rivers necessitate the use of offsets or traverses to determine the position of a straight line. When these procedures are necessary the straight line established is a mathematically determined line derived from a mathematical solution. One might interject here, "Why not eliminate a lot of this procedure to determine a line by field surveying combined with mathematical analysis, and calculate the position of the line from the known position of the quarter corners?" It is obvious that most intersections determined by field procedures are mathematically determined from the field data obtained from procedures required by field conditions. By necessity and practicality, in all the history of surveying, a large percentage of surveys involved random lines, offset lines, and traverse lines (which represent mathematical solutions of straight lines). The practical men who designed our public land procedures did not intend to tie the surveyor to the often inaccurate "running in the field" procedure to determine the intersection of two straight lines. This is merely a less accurate mechanical solution of a mathematical procedure. These men must be given credit for this practical knowledge and it should be realized that they were not requiring the use of field procedures when they called for "running" straight lines. The field position of these lines could be determined by "running" according to data already mathematically determined. Certainly, they did not intend, when the subdivision procedure was originally specified, to require the determination of the center of the section by locating the position by field surveying with the compass and chain. The proposition that lines and their intersections are to be determined by field surveying is a critical mistake in the writings by Abrahamson. It is an interpretation which must be negated.

Relative to "theoretical corners" (all corners are "theoretical"), it is recognized that the exact position of a corner ("theoretical position") can never be determined. We all realize that there is an error in every corner position that is monumented by a surveyor. Abrahamson states, "If a monument is set for an aliquot corner of a section, using the practices, procedures, and accuracies that were acceptable at the time the monument was set, then it is the legal aliquot corner and should be accepted today."

This rationalizing to accept an incorrect corner position is incorrect and is practically impossible to apply. Who is going to be the authority that determines that a monument was set in a careful and faithful manner? Who will decide that acceptable procedures, principles, and accuracies were used in setting the monument? These decisions fall far beyond the normal research expected of a prudent surveyor. Acceptable accuracies at the time of the survey is difficult, if not impossible to determine. One must also realize that acceptable accuracies were those acceptable by the individual surveyors and varied from locale to locale. Furthermore, acceptable procedures can only be determined by reviewing the field notes of the surveyor and most field notes of earlier surveys are impossible to find. This, therefore, is an inappropriate procedure which is practically impossible.

In conclusion, I wish to recite some truths, accepted by many responsible professional surveyors and which I believe are self-evident. They represent not only my thoughts but principles borrowed from the writings of Curtis M. Brown, Gurdon Wattles, and Ted Madson. They also incorporate the principles expressed to me by respected colleagues. Following is the statement of these principles.

1. In the practice of land surveying, we must deal with two basic kinds of monuments. First is the well-known physical monument which needs no further explanation. A second, and more subtle, type of monument is the record monument. An example of this kind of monument is "the point of intersection of the west line of Roe with the north line of Doe." This point, although not located by a physical monument on the ground, is just as certain and definite as though it were a brass disc in a concrete marker set on the point. It can be located. It exists in one place and one place only on the face of the earth. It is definite, and finally, it is unambiguous.

2. The legal center of section, or center quarter-section corner, is another example of a record monument. The reason that it is a record monument is because the eight exterior corners of the section were established by the placement of monuments at their positions by the original surveyor, and because the location of the legal center of section is clearly defined in the February 11, 1805,

Act of Congress, in all the corner Restoration Circulars and in U.S. Manuals of Instructions since 1881. The 1973 Manual of Instruction at page 89, Section 3-95, states: "The position for the center quarter-section corner is at the intersection of the center lines unless previously marked." (Unless previously marked refers to monuments set by the "original" government surveyor who did, in some instances, place monuments at aliquot corners prior to the acceptance of the township plat.)

3. The center of section is determined by running straight lines between opposite quarter-section corners; the intersection of these two straight lines is the record monument for the center quarter-section corner. An interesting and little-understood relationship is that, since the Manuals of Instructions address the breakdown of a section into its aliquot parts from the exterior monuments, all of the aliquot corners must, of necessity, be record monuments and precise of location. People who argue otherwise fail to understand the true meaning of the survey and conveyancing of our public lands.

4. The argument for calling the occupation corner the center quarter-section corner is, at best, short-sighted. As early as 1857, and perhaps before, this same argument was common among surveyors. In 1859, Abraham Lincoln addressed the problem and stated clearly that the center quarter-section corner is at the intersection of two straight lines connecting opposite quarter-section corners, unless set by the "original" government surveyors prior to acceptance of the plat by the General Land Office.

5. In an original survey, not only are the monuments set by the "original" surveyor considered sacred, but also all the aliquot parts are fixed by law. Any resurvey, therefore, must recognize all parts of an original survey. Furthermore, the first dependent resurveyor to set foot on the position of the center quarter-section corner is not the "original" surveyor referred to here. The "original" surveyor, as far as the corners of the aliquot parts of a section are concerned, are the surveyors who set the exterior corners of the section prior to the time the township plat was accepted. Aliquot corners monumented by surveyors after the original surveyors must stand on their own merit. These are not original corners and hence are not the true corner by law. These monuments may be the "first" monuments set

in an attempt to establish the corner. They have the same status as a monument set to mark a corner called for in a deed written years before the survey was performed.

6. The great sin of the occupation line surveyor lies not in calling the occupation line the property line, which he certainly does in nearly every case. He damages the world by calling the occupation line the line of the aliquot part of the section.

This discussion represents my last writing endeavor on the topic "Subdivision of a Section," It is my opinion that my original article "Subdivision of a Section," which appeared in the December 1981 issue of *Surveying and Mapping*, Vol. 41, No. 4, pp. 385-388, presented a concise and clear discussion on the proper procedure to subdivide a section. The discussion written by Carlisle Madson and Alver Freeman in the December 1983 issue of *Surveying and Mapping*, Vol. 43, No. 4, pp. 411-313, supported and justified the procedures in my original paper better than I could. This discussion reinforces my original article. These writings by Madson, Freeman, and myself set forth the proper procedures and defend them completely. They are excellent reference material concerning the subdivision of a section. Nothing can be gained by writing more.

****

COMMENTS RE: LAMPERT REBUTTAL TO MADSON & FREEMAN ON "SUBDIVISION OF A SECTION"

DECEMBER 1984

Published in Vol. 44, No. 3, Sept. 1984, p. 287

From: Alver R. Freeman, L.S., 8315 Dupont Ave. So., Bloomington, Minnesota 55420 (Hennepin County Surveyor, Hennepin County, Minnesota, (ret.)) and Carlisle Madson, L.S., 209 Shady Oak Rd., Hopkins, Minnesota 55343 (Vice President, Schoell & Madson, Inc., Hopkins, Minnesota (ret.), Carver County Surveyor, Carver County, Minnesota). In his discussion and comments, Mr. Lampert refers to his method of subdividing a section as *common sense* - our method as *theory*. We contend that the "legal center of section" is not a position based on *theory* - but a position based upon federal law adopted by the State of Wisconsin.

The surveyor is a fact finder. He should not try to solve the owner's problem of possession. The surveyor is neither qualified nor authorized to determine when possession, not in agreement with the record, has ripened into a fee title.

A stubborn resistance to authority and a disregard of rule is one of the less admirable traits of any of our surveyors. They want to do things their way regardless of how wrong it may be. For example, Mr. Lampert suggests adoption of *double standards* as the panacea for section subdivisions, and then has the temerity to call it *common sense*. He would have us believe we should follow the rules and establish the "legal center of section" provided no occupation exists within a section. But, if occupation exists in a section - no matter how erroneous - forget the legal center! Accept the occupation and blindly go along with it - all in the name of *common sense*. Now, that's a fallacious approach to land surveying, a recalcitrant approach.

It seems as if we ploughed this ground before, but it still appears to be fallow. In Wisconsin the law is: "When a surveyor is required to subdivide a section (or smaller subdivision) established by the USPLS, he shall proceed according to the Statutes of the United States and the appropriate rules and regulations of the Secretary of the Interior." Since this is so, then the subdivision lines are unalterable except by resubdivision.

Pause now, and consider the following five items, peruse them, if you will.

1. Land lawfully gained by unwritten means extinguishes the old written title, but it *does not* alter the position of the record lines (the lines of the aliquot parts of the section). Weight of authority.

2. Record lines are unalterable. Weight of authority. But, occupation and title lines do not have to follow the record lines. Just because there are record lines does not mean that the record lines, occupation lines, and title lines are congruent.

3. Unless the preceding surveyor was the *original* surveyor, his footsteps may not be the ones to follow. The *original* surveyor, as far as the lines of the aliquot parts of a section are concerned, is the person who set the exterior corners of the section. If the section was subdivided by someone other than the *original* surveyor, it

merely purports to locate the aliquot parts. Mind you, if the survey is erroneous, it can be corrected - age does not make an incorrect survey correct!

4. The surveyor is employed to show the facts as they exist. If the surveyor fails to do the thing that he purports to do correctly, and damage results from his failure, he may be liable. Our opinion is that the owner has hired the surveyor to point out the facts. The surveyor is obligated to discover the facts and call them to his client's attention. True, the client may neither want involvement in litigation nor desire a report that tells him the record line is in one location and the occupation line in another, but, if those are the facts, as they exist, the surveyor *must* point them out to his client or lose all credibility as a professional.

5. The surveyor should never, never be part of a fraud. If he knows that record lines and occupation lines are not identical and he issues a plat of survey showing them to be identical, he is establishing the conditions for fraud. And, in today's litigious society he may rue the day sooner than he expects.

We agree the courts are prone to grant title to longstanding occupation lines which are not in harmony with record lines. But how, in heavens name, can the court make such a decision unless the surveyor is competent enough, experienced enough, and honest enough to demonstrate to the court that the occupation lines and record lines are not coincident? If possession has followed occupation lines for a long period of time, possession has probably ripened into an unwritten fee title; however, such conditions do not give the surveyor the right to hide the true facts from his client or the court. The surveyor is honor bound to give his client notice when his occupation lines and record lines are not in harmony.

We also agree that Justice Cooley's paper admonishes the land surveyor to use common sense; however, the reader should remember that Justice Cooley's paper was concerned with the restoration of corners set in the PLS - not with the subdivision of sections.

We said it before, it is worth repeating, and we close with it: "The great sin of the fence line surveyor lies not in calling the occupation line the ownership line, which he does in nearly every case. He damages the world by calling the occupation line the record line or deed line."

****

RE: "SUBDIVISION OF A SECTION"

BY JOHN G. MCENTYRE AND
SUBSEQUENT COMMENTS

MARCH 1985

Published in Vol. 41, No. 4, 1981 ; Vol. 44, Nos. 2 and 4, 1984, respectively

[Ed. note: The following comment, according to the editorial policy stated concerning this particular article, has undergone peer review and has been recommended for publication. It is felt that the insight of Curtis M. Brown is germane to further understanding.

From: Curtis M. Brown, L. S., 5075 Keeney St., La Mesa, California 92041. After reading John McEntyre's article (Vol. 41, No, 4, 1981) and the reply by Doyle Abrahamson (Vol. 44, No. 2, June 1984) and comments (Vol. 44, No. 4, December 1984) pertaining to how to run the centerline of a section, the following is offered.

The Manual of Instructions for the Survey of the Public Lands of the United States is a guide for U. S. A. surveyors and applies to "how USA surveyors made original surveys as of the date of the Manual"; it may or may not apply to how to re-survey between private holdings within a state. In a resurvey the courts all recognize the control of original monumentation, but when it comes to how to reestablish a lost corner or how to set a corner that was not set originally, some state court opinions, differing from the Manual, are enforced. In fact it is possible (but has not occurred) to have 51 opinions (each state court and the Federal Government). As an example, in most states a lost section corner is re-established by double proportionate measure. In Missouri, in those cases involving private parties, the same corner is set by the intersection of straight lines as determined from the nearest found corner on each side of the lost corner, and this has been approved by the courts. The Manual is not followed, nor must it always be followed.

Merely because something is stated in the Manual does not mean that it is applicable to a resurvey under state jurisdiction. Even the U. S. A. surveyors do not always follow the Manual's instructions or statute law. I am yet to see a federal crew use a 2-pole chain to establish the center of a section, yet it is required by law. In Alaska, section and township corners have been set by intersection of lines of sight, using aircraft and dropping a can of paint to mark the spot. In one township, corners were reset using photogrammetry. The Federal Government can order its surveyors to resurvey or make original surveys in any manner they wish, and if they want to have their crews run lines on the ground between opposite quarter corners, that is their privilege, but this does not mean that state courts will require the same procedure to establish the center of a section in cases under their jurisdiction.

The Manual says that an original quarter corner can be set with an error of 1/905 or within 2.9 ft. of its true position. In every court case that I have been in, and in every case that I have read, a lost 1/4 corner must be relocated "exactly" halfway between section corners (as close as can be measured at the time of the recent measurement, not as of the time of the original measurement). No such thing as setting the corner per Manual within plus or minus 2.9 ft. exists. The state courts, wherein the Federal Government is not involved, can adopt any method they want to re-establish a lost corner or to set a corner which was not set originally; and they do not have to follow the procedure set out in the Manual, even though it is often done. In locating the center of a section, in no case have I found a court accepting a procedure wherein the corner can be within 2.9 ft. of its true position. It is set at the point of intersection, nowhere else. The location of boundaries between individuals in a state is determined by **state law**, not federal law or the Manual.

While all states do now recognize that the center of a section, which was divided into quarters by the Federal Government, is to be located by connecting opposite quarter corners, it is not true that all states require the centerlines be run on the ground. Only in those states, which have adopted a law requiring the Manual to be followed, is this true. In some instances by state court rule, where a party patents an entire section and sells the west half, he is selling the west half by area; the centerline located by Manual method does not apply! The same rule by area has been applied where half of a quarter has been sold.

My advice to land surveyors is not the same as advocated by Abrahamson: Understand that portion of the Manual that is applicable in your state; treat the rest as interesting reading. Also remember that those surveys made prior to 1851 **had no Manual in force.** How can a later Manual be used as a foundation for surveys made previous to the Manual, especially in Indiana where McEntyre lives? The argument that the centerlines should be run on the ground in Indiana is ridiculous. Of far more importance to the surveyor is understanding the pamphlet "Restoration of Lost or Obliterated Corners

& Subdivision of Sections." This pamphlet is fairly well in agreement with what the various state courts have approved. However, even parts of this are not applicable in all states (Missouri and some surveys made prior to 1851).

By the Manual, distance measuring devices are not mentioned for use in a resurvey. Fortunately, most state courts that had a Manual in force at the time of the original survey do not care what system is used to make measurements. All that is needed is a certified accurate measurement by an acceptable device. There are a few places where, if you are going to court, you should run the center lines of sections on the ground (in states that have adopted by law the procedures used in the Manual). Unless the state laws or state courts have specified how measurements must be made, use any accurate measuring method applicable to the problem in hand.

McEntyre's article was well written and, in my opinion, accurate. I well remember years ago when I first read the Manual and believed it to be entirely applicable to surveys of sections; how wrong I was. Only parts are applicable.

****

COMMENT AND DISCUSSION

SEPTEMBER 1986

The pages of *Surveying and Mapping* are open to free and temperate discussion of all matters pertaining to the interests of the Congress. It is the purpose of this segment of the *Journal* to encourage comments on published material or the presentation of new ideas in a formal or informal manner.

Published articles in *Surveying and Mapping* are open for subsequent discussion in the two issues following the issue in which the original article appeared. - EDITORIAL REVIEW BOARD AND EDITOR

Response to –
Comments on Paper, "Subdivision of a Section," from John G. McEntyre. Comments re: Lampert Rebuttal to Madson and Freeman on "Subdivision of a Section," from Alver R. Freeman and Carlisle Madson, both published in *Surveying and Mapping*, Vol. 44, No. 4, Dec. 1984, pp. 386-390, and Curtis M. Brown Comments, published in *Surveying and Mapping*, Vol. 45, No. 1, Mar. 1985, pp. 67- 68.

From: Doyle G. Abrahamson, P.L.S., M.S., Merrick & Company, Engineers and Architects, P.O. Box 22026, Denver, Colorado 80222; Leonard L. Lampert, P.E., L.S., Lampert, Lee & Associates, 10968 Hwy. 54 East, Wisconsin Rapids, Wisconsin 54494; Dexter Brinker, P.E., P.L.S., Brinker Surveying Seminars, 6547 Otis Street, Arvada, Colorado 80003.

[Ed. Note: The following comment has been reviewed and explicitly approved for publication by the Editorial Review Board.]

Appropriate procedures for the subdivision of Public Land Survey (PLS) sections deserve all the attention they have recently received in *Surveying and Mapping*. It is essential that the center of section have only one position. Thus, it is in the interest of the land survey profession to clear up some of the misconceptions which have arisen.

The profession will have a diminished role in the real property area if the theoretical intersection of straight lines connecting opposite corresponding quarter corners is accepted as the controlling position when relocating a previously established center of section. It is our contention that once the center of section has been established in a competent survey using procedures outlined in the Act of February 11, 1805, entitled "An Act Concerning the Mode of Surveying the Public Lands of the United States" and appropriate GLO (General Land Office) and BLM (Bureau of Land Management) survey manuals, the monument set to mark the center of section or reliable collateral evidence controls the location of future land conveyances in the section. The theoretical line intersection position would not be controlling if in conflict with the competently established monument position.

The points Professor McEntyre makes and outlines carefully in his rebuttal are not supported by authority. In other words, the principles he sets forth are his personal opinions. The same can be said for the Madson and Freeman answer. The effect of those opinions on the practicing land surveyor, especially the person in private practice and in particular the inexperienced surveyor, causes considerable concern. We have reviewed thousands of surveys, most of them recorded documents, and to the best of our knowledge have yet to see one in which the record line is shown in one location and the title line in another. Even with a positional tolerance of 0.05 ft., it is likely that less than one percent of existing center quarter corners are in their correct "theoretical" positions.

The recognized authorities all appear to agree upon the role of a surveyor. If the theoretical corner philosophy is followed, the surveyor is unable to mark the deed description upon the ground and is unable to prepare a map indicating its position for delivery to the client. He is instead required to show a theoretical position and indicate only a paper solution - a solution which is not reproducible on the ground.

The subdivision of a section is intended to be by actual field survey. Error tolerances were written into the regulations to provide for the running of lines in the field. Error tolerances in the written instructions to surveyors only make sense if the intent is to set the center of section and then use the established point from that time onward. A theoretical position has no error. In fact, the only way a section can be subdivided for any practical purpose is by survey. It is reasonable to assume that the designers of the rectangular system intended the subdivision of sections to follow the same scheme as the primary PLS framework; i.e., prior survey, adequate monuments, public records, monuments controlling once set, and collateral evidence to be properly evaluated when restoring obliterated corners.

The surveyor must of necessity follow the work that preceded him. Indeed, if he could not, it would become necessary for him to retrace the base line and principal meridian and establish their reliability before he could use them. To disregard the monumented subdivision of a section simply because the lines of the subdivision are not precisely straight lines between opposite quarter corners is not possible. To do so would create endless litigation in most of our midwestern municipalities. The surveyor can in no manner avoid an obligation to protect the bona fide rights of the public (property owners). When deeds have been written and conveyances made based upon monuments set by previous surveyors, the monuments are a condition of the conveyance and title has passed to that particular parcel. The rights of the property owner cannot be violated by some surveyor who does not follow the first surveyor as long as the first surveyor who initially monumented the center of section used acceptable practices and accuracies. In evaluating the reasonableness of that first surveyor's work, bear in mind that the first surveyor was probably not a professional surveyor by modern standards.

The claim has been made in past articles and comments that a surveyor has no authority to make decisions as to interpretations of the proper survey procedures as outlined in the controlling survey manuals. The claim has been made that the only answers a surveyor has authority to make are mathematical solutions. We respond with a quote from the first paragraph of Justice Cooley's famous paper entitled "Judicial Functions of a Surveyor." "When a man has had training in one of the exact sciences, where every problem within its purview is supposed to be susceptible of accurate solution, he is likely to be not a little impatient when he is told that, under some circumstances, he must recognize inaccuracies, and govern his actions by facts which lead him away from the results which, theoretically, he ought to reach. Observation warrants us in saying that this remark may frequently be made of surveyors."

There also appears to be a misunderstanding of the difference between a monument and a corner, as they relate to the Public Land Survey System. For instance, McEntyre makes reference to record monuments as being points of intersection. The 1973 *Manual (Manual of Instructions*, published by BLM), in definitions of words used in the Public Land Survey System, at 5-4, states that a corner is a point determined by the surveying process, and a monument is the object or physical structure which marks the corner point. It is clear that when the 1973 *Manual*, discusses corners and monuments it is referring to points established by the surveying process. It is most important to read the 1973 *Manual* in its entirety.

Dr. McEntyre states, "any practicing surveyor knows the difficulty, and virtual impossibility, of running a straight line directly in the field." How true! Most quarter section corners are theoretically on a straight line and halfway between section corners per the original plat, yet the monuments are not. If we can live with this deviation from theory, why impose zero tolerance on the center of section monument? In addition, in evaluating evidence near the center of a section which appears to be in conflict with existing quarter corners on the section lines, the surveyor should consider that it may be the quarter corners that have been restored in an inappropriate manner.

When the 1973 *Manual of Instructions,* by the United States Bureau of Land Management, was prepared, they addressed this particular problem in Chapter 2 of the *Manual.* Chapter 2 is entitled "Methods of Survey." In this chapter they state some of the acceptable procedures for surveying a line which cannot be surveyed directly because of rough terrain. Section 2-5 of the 1973 *Manual* states a line can be traversed where the terrain is too precipitous for chaining, as long as traversing is kept to a minimum. Section 2-6 of the 1973 *Manual* states triangulation may be used in measuring a distance across water or over precipitous slopes. It is very clear that when the 1973 *Manual* states that one should run a straight line, one can traverse or triangulate to get around obstacles that may prevent the physical running of a straight line. It is very important when one reads the 1973 *Manual* to read the *Manual* from the front cover to the back cover, so the intent of the *Manual* is clearly understood and not taken out of context.

Dr. McEntyre also makes the following statement "The proposition that lines and their intersections are to be determined by field surveying is a critical mistake in the writings by Abrahamson. It is an interpretation which must be negated." In an attempt to negate Abrahamson's documented citation of authority, Dr. McEntyre was unable to come up with a single documented citation opposing Abrahamson's 15 fully documented citations regarding the subdivision of a regular section. Dr. McEntyre's only citation made reference to a partial section. That citation is to Section 3-95 of the 1973 *Manual,* which falls under the heading "Survey of Parts of Sections." Because the citation refers to subdivision by "survey," it more strongly supports Abrahamson's position than his.

In response to Brown's comments, initially it would appear that he is in agreement with McEntyre's position. After carefully reviewing his comments, however, it is apparent that if Brown had thoroughly understood Abrahamson's comments, he would be supporting a different position. Brown recognizes that a surveyor can establish a center quarter corner by survey when he states ". . . a surveyor can use any accurate measuring methods applicable to the problem in hand." Brown does not say so, but we are assuming when he uses this statement that if he came back to a center quarter corner established the previous day and did the same survey over again, he would not set another monument because he missed the monument he set the previous day by a small amount.

Brown misinterpreted Abrahamson's comments when he stated that

Abrahamson's position was that one could set the center quarter corner anywhere within 2.9 ft. and call it the center quarter corner. In establishing and monumenting the center quarter corner for the first time, a surveyor *must* establish the center quarter corner at the intersection of straight lines as surveyed upon the ground according to his measurements. Surveyors can be "exactly" correct in following a procedure, but a surveyor is never "exactly" correct in making a measurement. The courts were not saying or even addressing the issue of what tolerance had to be achieved when setting the monument. They were addressing only a procedure to be used in the field to reestablish the lost corner. Brown's reference to the "Restoration" pamphlet provides little enlightenment. While it covers some general principles about collateral evidence along section lines, it carefully avoids any discussion of tolerances for interior aliquot corners, either found or set. Once the lost corner has been properly reestablished using an "exactly" correct procedure, it remains only to test that it falls within acceptable tolerances. Abrahamson is not advocating a procedure that would originally establish the center quarter corner at a position other than the intersection of surveyed straight lines. The positional tolerance is to be used when testing an already established monument set by others to see if it falls within acceptable tolerances. It is basic knowledge that any monument set will vary from its theoretically computed position. It is impossible to measure anything perfectly since there is always some greater refinement in measurement that may be made.

Brown, in his comments, refers to a theoretical corner at times. However, he contradicts himself when he states that one can establish a center quarter corner by using an accurate measuring method applicable to the problem. If the legally controlling position of the center quarter corner is a theoretical location only, then we as surveyors should not be addressing this subject because none of us can monument a theoretical corner.

If a section cannot be subdivided by survey then a lot of surveyors are going to be seeking other employment. If a surveyor cannot mark the boundaries of a client's property, who would want to engage his services and what function would he perform?

Our advice to other surveying practitioners is to use with caution journal articles based on personal opinions unless substantially supported by statutory law, common law, or uniformly accepted practices of the profession if not previously addressed by statutory or common law. The surveyor should obtain full copies of all references cited in a journal article and make his own decisions on the proper procedures to be followed if he is still in doubt.

We hope that this response to the above-mentioned papers will clear up the misinterpretation which some surveyors obviously have concerning the controlling rules and principles to be followed in locating the corners of previously subdivided regular sections and regular sections that have never been subdivided.

Summary of Published Comments in 'Surveying and Mapping' re: the McEntyre Article

Dec. 1981   pp. 385-388   Original article by McEntyre

Responses

Mar. 1982	pp. 73-74	Brinker
June 1983	pp. 223-244	Lampert
Dec. 1983	pp. 410-411	Kiedrowski
Dec. 1983	pp. 411-413	C. Madson and Freeman
June 1984	pp. 142-144	Abrahamson
Sept. 1984	pp. 285-286	Mitchell
Sept. 1984	pp. 286-288	Lampert
Dec. 1984	pp. 386-389	McEntyre
Dec. 1984	pp. 389-390	C. Madson and Freeman
Dec. 1984	p. 386	Editor's Note *
Mar. 1985	pp. 67-68	Brown
Mar. 1985	p. 67	Editor's Note **

* Note states all further comments will undergo peer review before publication.

** Note states that Brown comments had undergone peer review and had been recommended for publication.

****

STREETS AND HIGHWAYS

THE SURVEYOR AND THE LAW
VACATED STREETS AND LOT CORNERS
SEPTEMBER 1964

Within the United States, the commonly accepted rule is that whenever a lot is created by platting, a given corner of a lot will remain fixed in position until such time as the land is re-subdivided; vacation of a street will not alter the original lot-corner position. Within the state of Indiana, according to the rule laid down in *Jacqua v. Heston*, 81 Ind. App. 142, and the original lot corner changes position after a street has been vacated.

Figure 1 shows the conditions as they existed after 32 feet of Bridge Street was vacated. Following the vacation, a parcel was sold: "Parts of Lots 113 and 114 in South Portland Add'n to the City of Portland, Indiana, described as follows: Beginning at the Southwest Corner of said Lot 114 and running thence North 44'; thence East 132'; thence South 44' to the south line of Lot 113; thence West along the South line of lots 113 and 114 to the place of beginning." All of Lot 113, at a later date, was sold to another party.

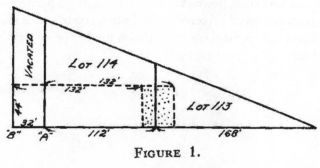

FIGURE 1.

659

Dispute: Does the deed commence at the southwest corner of Lot 113 as originally plotted (point A) or at the Southwest comer of the 32-foot strip of vacated street (point B)?

In this case the court cites paragraph 8912 Burns 1914, Acts 1907 p. 617, now Burns 1950 Replacement 48 - 905, which reads: "When any platted property shall have been vacated, the descriptions of the several lots and parcels thereof shall be preserved as in the plat set forth, to which the proportionate part of any street or alley, or part thereof, vacated shall be added according to law, * * *." unless the owners in writing agree otherwise.

Indiana court rule: Commence at B. "When a portion of Bridge Street was vacated, the boundary lines of lot 114 as originally designated on the recorded plat, were readjusted by sheer force of law so as to include the vacated portion of the street. In other words, that when a portion of the street was vacated, then, by operation of law, the Southwest corner of lot 114 was fixed at a point 32' west of the corner, as shown by the original lines of the recorded plat. The foregoing contention is prima facie valid."

The reason for the rule coming into being in Indiana apparently was a result of the unusual wording of the statute law above cited: "* * * to which the proportionate part * * * * vacated shall be added according to law, * *". The court reasoned that, according to this statute, any vacated portion automatically became a portion of the lot; other states do not have this statute.

Whether the surveyors think that the above decision is right or wrong is not theirs to say; in Indiana it is the law. At least, within Indiana, if it is desired to start a description from point A of Figure 1, care must be used as for example: "Beginning at the southwest corner of lot 114 as it existed prior to the vacation of any portion of Bridge Street."

I believe that most surveyors, including myself, would have reasoned this way: The deed says, "to the South line of lot 113" and "west along the South line of lots 113 and 114," therefore, a portion of lot 113 must have been conveyed. If a portion of lot 113 was conveyed, then the deed must have commenced at point A. (If it starts at B no portion of lot 113 could have been conveyed.) According to Indiana courts, this reasoning is wrong; it is generally right elsewhere. This is further proof that law is not an exact science.

– Curtis M. Brown

****

LIGHTWEIGHT
FLUORESCENT RANGE POLE

NEW
for the Progressive
Engineer and Surveyor

- New and lightweight, a 1¼" diameter Range Pole which can be seen from a much greater distance, due to vinyl material in black and daylight fluorescent arc yellow fabricated on the metal core.

- Rugged and chip-proof because of its impregnated color . . . always retaining its brilliant lustre

section of range pole
shows lightweight construction

- Write for full details: includes color combinations and lengths available as well as price list

NEW FLUORESCENT PLUMB BOB TARGETS

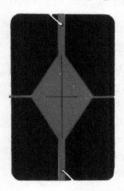

- 4 x 2½" laminated vinyl target in black and translucent daylight fluorescent arc yellow

- Special construction insures color that will never become dull or wear off . . . made to last indefinitely

- $1.50 each . . . mailed postpaid anywhere in the United States and Canada . . . please enclose check or money order

C. & R. Manufacturing Company
P. O. BOX 610 - MONROVIA, CALIFORNIA

Manufacturers of Modern Fluorescent Survey Equipment

THE SURVEYOR AND THE LAW

SEPTEMBER 1966

The following letter from W. G. G. Blakney, Associate Professor of Civil Engineering at Auburn University, Auburn, Alabama, was referred to several members of the Property Surveys Division for comment. Discussions were offered by Curtis M. Brown, Past President, ACSM, and Past Chairman, PSD; James A. Thigpenn III, Chairman, PSD; A. Phillips Bill, Vice President, ACSM, and Past Chairman, PSD; and Elmer J. Peterson, Past Chairman, PSD. These discussions follow the basic letter. Further comments, adding pertinent additional information, are welcomed from readers of SURVEYING AND MAPPING.

W. G. G. BLAKNEY - I wonder if "The Surveyor and the Law" portion of the ACSM publication SURVEYING AND MAPPING could respond to the situation outlined in the following paragraphs.

One of the most recently published textbooks on surveying has listed several of the more important principles for the legal interpretation of deed descriptions. One of these has to do with ownership of land adjacent to highways. It states "land described as being bounded by a highway or street conveys ownership to the center of the highway or street. Any variation from this interpretation must be explicitly stated in the description."

I have somehow come to believe that this was not the principle observed, believing that ownership would have been to the edge of a supposed right-of-way, until such time a right-of-way is proved not to exist. I have also come to believe that a statute of limitation works against private ownership of highways, so that a person must reaffirm the fact that he and not the public has claim to the land used as a highway. These seemed logical expectations, especially when one considers the fact that street and highway widening programs are such that it cannot be assumed that the existing centerline of a highway coincides with the historic centerline. In the absence of complete records of highway development, the surveyor is more likely to be able to conduct a successful search for evidence at the right-of-way. Also, the surveyor is able to mark his survey in the most efficient manner.

Legal interpretations are sometimes surprising but reasonable when explanations are given. If this were reasonable, I would appreciate knowing the significance of this interpretation. I feel sure other ACSM members will find a discussion of this subject to be of interest.

CURTIS M. BROWN - Several factors are involved that are not directly asked but simply implied by the question. The common law principle stated "land described as being bounded by a highway or street conveys ownership to the center of the highway or street" is a presumption with certain definite limitations.

Limitation 1. No effective statute law states the contrary. Ohio has a statute law that says, in effect, that any offer of a street to the public is an offer of the fee rights to the bed of the street. The state acquires the entire rights (not merely an easement right), and upon the abandonment or vacation of the easement, all rights revert (revive is a better word) to, the state. Most states, in acquiring "freeway" or "throughway" rights-of-way, now condemn a "fee" for the bed, not an easement.

In Alabama, it is my understanding that a statute law does exist stating, "acknowledgment and recording of such plat or map shall be held in law and equity to be a conveyance in fee simple of streets, alleys, or public grounds." But the Supreme Court of Alabama has declared that in view of common law and other state laws, the statute means that the subdivision only gives an "easement to the state" and "fee title" is retained by the adjoiner. The statute is not effective because of court opinion.

Limitation 2. At the time of the sale of the land adjoining the highway, the seller did, in fact, own the bed of the highway. If the seller did not own the bed, obviously he could not convey it to another.

Limitation 3. The fee title goes to the centerline (subject to an easement) provided the seller owns on both sides of the street as of the day of the sale.

Example: Plotting land in a subdivision and creating lots on both sides of the street. If at the time of the sale the owner had part of the street, he conveys to the limit of his ownership, which may be more or less than up to the centerline. In some cases, all of the street may be conveyed subject to an easement.

Limitation 4. The laws of the land *as of the date of the deed apply.* Example: Roads created under Dutch rule in New York reserved the fee to the bed in the crown. Conveyances adjoining such roads can never convey a fee to the bed of the road.

Limitation 5. Court interpretation in different states rarely gives variation to these rules.

Limitation 6. All rights to the bed of a street are interpreted "as of the date of the deed." Later events, such as widening of the street, do not alter the centerline as of the date of the deed.

To prevent the fee in a street from passing, words of exclusion must be used such as, "along the side line of the street," "excluding the street," etc. Why is this so? Easements are generally given free to the public or are condemned. If they are given free, the courts assume that the minimum title was intended or a mere easement right was given. If the right-of-way is condemned there is an unwilling giver; rights are taken by force. In this event, the law usually allows taking minimum needs. The fee is not needed; only a right-of-way is needed. For freeways, access rights are taken; hence it is necessary to take the fee rights as well as an easement right. Most states have laws allowing "fee" condemnation for freeways.

Upon the sale of property it is generally assumed that the seller intended to sell all of his land and not retain a small amount of land in a road that he could not use. If it were otherwise, who would pay for the improvements in the street? Would the adjoined pay to improve the land that someone else owns? It is a practical necessity to presume that the adjoiner automatically takes to the centerline (or to the limits of a given ownership) to prevent many fragments of unsold land to exist. A presumption can be overcome by contrary facts; hence the rule is merely a presumption.

Further information on this subject can be found in Chapter 6. *Boundary Control and Legal Principles*, CURTIS M. BROWN, John Wiley and Sons, Inc., New York.

JAMES A. THIGPENN III - Although, as suggested by Professor

Blakney, a discussion of the legal aspects of property rights where lands adjoin a street or highway may be of considerable interest to all of our members, it must be recognized that the guidelines stated in a textbook must necessarily follow the general rules, and a further enlargement of the statements to which he referred, whether added to the text of such book or contained within a resume in the ACSM JOURNAL, would not fully satisfy the need of Professor Blakney. The fact will still remain, he is more in need of information relating to the Alabama statutes and local case laws than he is of such a general discussion. General discussions, such as found in the textbooks, to which, no doubt, he referred, are intended primarily to serve as a pattern for study and not for particulars of local laws or customs.

Alabama laws are not as different, in this matter, as Professor Blakney's letter would seem to suggest. Title usually carries to the center of streets, except where restricted by specific calls. In *Tuskegee Land Company v. Birmingham Realty Company, 161 Ala. 542, 49 So. 378 (1909),* it was held that a conveyance to the "side," "margin," or "edge" of the street restricted title to the side of the highway. However, in *Brewer v. Avinger, 208 Ala. 411, 94 So. 590,* it was said that where a deed describes land as bounded on an alley or street the grantee's title extends to the centerline of the alley or street, but unless reference is made in the deed to an alley or street in the description (as by incorporation of a survey or map therein) there is no authority for the proposition that the grantee acquires such an interest in fee.

The general rule appears to be related to the common law of England under which it was held that, unless a reservation was made, land bounding on a highway, water course, or a street conveyed title to the center thereof, and that the owner has a right to all above and underground except only the right of passage for the King and his people. In Alabama, as well as in most other jurisdictions, the common law has played an important role in court opinions. For example, in *Real Estate Handbook, Land Laws of Alabama,* page 175, the following is stated: "Title 56, Section 14, Code of Alabama of 1940 says that the acknowledgment and recording of such plat or map shall be held in law and equity to be a conveyance in fee simple of streets, alleys, or public grounds. However, the Supreme Court has held that, construed in the light of common law and the presumption that the Legislature did not intend to make any implied change in the law, the statute means that the owner retains the fee to the center of the streets or alleys shown on the plat, subject to the public easement." *(Cloverdale Homes v. Town of Cloverdale, 182 Ala. 419, 62 So. 712; Smith v. Birmingham Realty Co., 208 Ala. 114, 94 So. 117).*

It is unlikely that every factor affecting the status of ownership of lands included within the rights-of-way of streets and highways has been covered by statutes or court opinion in any state. A very comprehensive paper, "Florida Conveyances and Monuments of Appreciable Width," prepared by a senior graduate student during the 1965 Advanced Real Property Seminar offered at the College of Law, University of Florida, which included a study of many of the reported cases, still required some reference to court cases in other states. Therefore, it is reasonable to assume that a discussion in the JOURNAL, although not slanted for a particular state, could serve to introduce a résumé of pertinent factors that would be of value, as a guide to Land Surveyors in every region. However, to merely enlarge on the general rules given in the textbooks, without preparing an extensive treatment of the subject, could create an enlargement of the deception already created in such textbooks. In my opinion, we should either develop a proper treatise, or merely pass on such information as included in this letter relating to the State of Alabama directly to Professor Blakney.

A. PHILLIPS BILL - The letter from W. G. G. Blakney, Associate Professor at Auburn University, dealing with the fee ownership of highways, streets, and other ways raises several interesting questions which, I am afraid, have, at best, very insular answers. For example, here in New England the neighboring states of Massachusetts and New York have diametrically opposite legal positions in this matter. I am sure that publication of Professor Blakney's letter, with an accompanying request for comment, would generate a most valuable discussion.

ELMER J. PETERSON - This subject matter could be easily set down in volume by someone who is well familiar with the laws relative to highways and their properties. I am not one of those qualified, but I will attempt to set down some of the ramifications that I have run into during the last twenty years. I don't think, however, that there is anything very new or different than what Professor Blakney implied in his letter.

I think we are all familiar with the fact that if we go back to pre-war conditions, and beyond that, we find that right-of-way for roads and highways were normally acquired by easement and the centerline was normally what it said, in that it was actually the center line of the highway. It was also the usual manner in cases involving the abandonment or vacation of roads such as those in that they would revert to the original owner of the land.

Many things have changed, however, during the last decade,

particularly in all areas adjacent to metropolitan areas where many more roads, highways and streets have been constructed. This, of course, also includes all other types of construction such as freeways, state highways, even limited access county roads, etc.

In metropolitan areas, many counties have turned over to townships and villages excess mileage of county roads which they no longer wish to claim and maintain. Most of these, of course, were acquired by the county either through usage under statutory permission or by easement from property owners. This, then, doesn't constitute much of a problem in case the village or township vacates the road in that it would normally go back to the original owner providing the original owner no longer is in existence.

We have of late however, come into a vast, new area involving this entire matter of acquiring and abandoning or vacating roads and highways. Much of the rights-of-way acquired now a day by states and counties are bought in fee and they can do with the land as they please. Turn backs, however can cause a lot of legal entanglements. Suppose the state turns over to a county the right-of-way of a state highway acquired under fee and the county in turn decided to vacate. Let us also say that the highway is of recent vintage, but because of rerouting and new planning and other things that can cause such changes, it became necessary to vacate by the county. Because the state held the land in fee, it would be necessary then that the county would have to have the title cleared before any transferring could be accomplished. If the adjacent land owner petitioned to purchase to centerline of right-of-way, who then would get the money if the title had not been cleared? Would it be the county or would it be the state?

We know now that in many instances it is very difficult to make a re-survey of the centerline of a limited access highway or, as more commonly known, a double-lane highway because in reality it is not a centerline, it is a survey line. The surveyor can in most instances, of course, make a survey on offset, but sometimes this is extremely difficult. We also know that, because of the irregularity in many instances of the right-of-way line of a highway such as this, the survey also becomes difficult in nature. One of the major factors in building a highway now is the fact that the acquisition of the right-of-way is sometimes in excess of the actual cost of construction, depending upon the value of land. There will be few instances of a vacation relating to a highway such as this after construction, but there are many instances where land has been acquired at a high price by the state and a small part of it or in some instances a considerable part of it may never be used in that, after purchase, a rerouting came into being and then the land as such is owned by the state. In many instances, land may be held by the state for a long time because of the high cost of acquisition, and because of rerouting of the highway the land left as useless for highway purpose may have also lost a considerable amount of its original value. It is almost certain that in many states, and probably in most states, this would require an act of the legislature to allow the state to sell this land back to the original owner or to anyone else who applied to purchase same.

Most problems dealing with rights-of-way now, other than the older highways and roads not engendered with complexities, becomes a matter for the attorneys. Attorneys in state departments who deal with problems such as this must also be learned in the law that pertains to all the ramifications and complex problems that are involved in any negotiation of rights-of-way, whether it is for acquisition or for vacation.

To go back to the original question, I don't know of any method, at least here in this area of the country, where it is necessary to reaffirm the fact that a person has a claim to the land used as a highway rather than the public. When we speak of the old methods, it was nearly always the rule to quitclaim or grant an easement to the center of the road if it were situated on a section or property line. This, of course, would be altered if it ran across someone else's property and then this person would hold fee and would again acquire ownership if and when it were vacated. If we again come back to our present-day system, we know that there are many areas even in the construction of freeways where surveys are not as complete and exact as they should be. One reason for this is that it is almost impossible to acquire the services of county surveyors in many areas in order to use their assistance in establishing section lines and section corners that would assist the state in tying in their right-of-way lines.

The last paragraph says that legal interpretations are sometimes surprising, but reasonable when explanations are given. This is quite often true, but one also finds that legal interpretations relative to the many areas involved in acquisition and construction of new highways are sometimes just as surprising. This is because of the laws of the states involved, which have not upgraded their statutes to deal with the complexities at hand.

****

ACSM President Brown extends a welcome to those attending the ACSM Awards Luncheon. Seated at the head table are: (left to right) Secretary Dix, Mr. and Mrs. Rappleye, Stuart A. Boyles, President and Mrs. Brown, President-Elect and Mrs. Fennell, and Mr. and Mrs. Erwin Shalowitz.

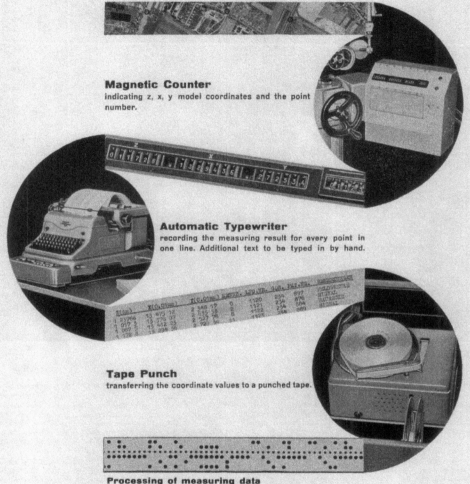

INDEX

126, 128, 129, 147, 148, 149, 150,
151, 157, 166, 167, 168, 170, 171,
172, 173, 175, 176, 181, 184, 185,
186, 190, 460, 473, 478, 480, 496
Civil Engineering 15, 29, 101, 152, 153,
156, 157, 176, 180, 315, 412, 638,
662
Clark 102, 172, 275, 346, 354, 355, 365,
369, 371, 390, 619, 624
closure 13, 106, 131, 132, 133, 193, 404,
407, 436, 554, 629
color of title 328, 330, 331, 337, 552
convergence 139, 593
conveyance 105, 121, 137, 281, 283, 317,
327, 336, 393, 404, 405, 505, 535,
573, 576, 623, 653, 663, 665
Cooley 349, 370, 381, 387, 388, 582,
606, 612, 618, 619, 622, 636, 645,
653
County Surveyor 614, 615, 622, 634,
635, 643
Court of Appeals 87
curriculum 17, 117, 121, 122, 123, 128,
147, 148, 149, 150, 151, 157, 160,
166, 171, 173, 175, 176, 181, 467,
469, 511
curvature 106, 139, 219

D

deed 9, 12, 91, 92, 93, 94, 95, 100, 101,
102, 103, 104, 105, 112, 121, 136,
158, 198, 221, 233, 258, 263, 269,
281, 283, 286, 316, 324, 325, 326,
327, 331, 334, 335, 336, 337, 338,
339, 341, 343, 346, 351, 355, 356,
357, 358, 359, 360, 361, 363, 364,
369, 376, 377, 380, 381, 386, 387,
388, 389, 390, 392, 393, 431, 436,
437, 439, 448, 470, 532, 534, 572,
623, 643, 645, 652, 660, 662, 664,
665
Deed 13, 91, 337
Deeds 91, 103, 286, 338, 470
description 12, 28, 93, 99, 100, 101, 102,
104, 105, 106, 117, 121, 135, 137,
138, 194, 249, 258, 265, 269, 281,
282, 318, 338, 339, 343, 344, 355,

356, 357, 358, 359, 361, 374, 376,
377, 386, 387, 389, 505, 506, 532,
533, 561, 608, 611, 629, 652, 660,
662, 665
Dix 8, 14, 349, 380, 526, 527
double corners 593, 600, 601, 602, 603
Drafting 114, 116
Due 92, 240

E

earthquake 80, 81, 82
easement 12, 51, 283, 508, 663, 664,
665, 666, 667, 668
education xvii, 3, 16, 29, 114, 117, 123,
128, 129, 133, 135, 147, 148, 149,
150, 151, 156, 157, 158, 164, 165,
166, 167, 168, 169, 170, 171, 173,
180, 181, 185, 186, 198, 445, 463,
465, 467, 469, 472, 511, 519, 521,
525, 526
Education 6, 17, 29, 113, 120, 129, 159,
164, 165, 169, 170, 176, 198, 464,
468
Eldridge 14, 15, 16, 28, 236, 253, 275,
371, 527, 620
electrotape 151, 192, 195, 219
encroachment 318, 327, 329, 338, 342,
344, 622
Enrollments 336
estoppel 330, 332, 351, 363, 611
ethics xx, 7, 140, 191, 195, 197, 318,
381, 383, 385, 443, 444, 445, 448,
449, 450, 454, 456, 461, 465, 466,
469, 471, 480, 489, 490, 496, 525
evidence 26, 28, 81, 82, 93, 94, 136, 140,
158, 196, 198, 221, 233, 234, 237,
243, 244, 247, 248, 249, 250, 251,
258, 262, 263, 270, 272, 275, 277,
326, 331, 335, 337, 338, 339, 341,
342, 356, 357, 358, 359, 361, 364,
369, 370, 374, 375, 377, 378, 380,
386, 387, 388, 428, 430, 431, 435,
436, 438, 456, 469, 470, 471, 506,
510, 513, 514, 522, 523, 524, 526,
535, 539, 541, 553, 554, 557, 561,
562, 564, 566, 567, 568, 611, 612,
615, 616, 618, 620, 628, 629, 632,

APPENDIX

THE JUDICIAL FUNCTION OF SURVEYORS [1]

BY THOMAS M. COOLEY

CHIEF JUSTICE, SUPREME COURT OF MICHIGAN, 1864-1885

When a man has had a training in one of the exact sciences, where every problem within its purview is supposed to be susceptible of accurate solution, he is likely to be not a little impatient when he is told that, under some circumstances, he must recognize inaccuracies, and govern his action by facts which lead him away from the results which theoretically he ought to reach. Observation warrants us in saying that this remark may frequently be made of surveyors.

In the State of Michigan, all our lands are supposed to have been surveyed once or more, and permanent monuments fixed to determine the boundaries of those who should become proprietors. The United States, as original owner, caused them all to be surveyed once by sworn officers, and as the plan of subdivision was simple, and was uniform over a large extent of territory, there should have been, with due care, few or no mistakes; and long rows of monuments should have been perfect guides to the place of any one that chanced to be missing. The truth, unfortunately, is that the lines were very carelessly run, the monuments inaccurately placed; and, as the recorded witnesses to these were many times wanting in permanency, it is often the case that when the monument was not correctly placed, it is impossible to determine by the record, with the aid of anything on the ground, where it was located. The incorrect record of course becomes worse than useless when the witnesses it refers to have disappeared.

It is, perhaps, generally supposed that our town plats were more accurately surveyed, as indeed they should have been, for in general there can have been no difficulty in making them sufficiently perfect for all practical purposes. Many of them, however, were laid out in the woods; some of them by proprietors themselves, without either chain or compass, and some by imperfectly trained surveyors, who, when land was cheap, did not appreciate the importance of having correct lines to determine boundaries when land should have become dear. The fact probably is that town surveys are quite as inaccurate as those made under authority of the general government.

RECOVERING LOST CORNERS

It is now upwards of fifty years since a major part of the public surveys in what is now the State of Michigan were made under authority of the United States. Of the lands south of Lansing, it is now forty years since the major part were sold, and the work of improvement begun. A generation has passed away since they were converted into cultivated farms, and few if any of the original corner and quarter stakes now remain.

The corner and quarter stakes were often nothing but green sticks driven into the ground. Stones might be put around or over these if they were handy, but often they were not, and the witness trees must be relied upon after the stake was gone. Too often the first settlers were careless in fixing their lines with accuracy while monuments remained, and an irregular brush fence, or something equally untrustworthy, may have been relied upon to keep in mind where the blazed line once was. A fire running through this might sweep it away, and if nothing was substituted in its place, the adjoining proprietors might in a few years be found disputing over their lines, and perhaps rushing into litigation, as soon as they had occasion to cultivate the land along the boundary.

If now the disputing parties call in a surveyor, it is not likely that any one summoned would doubt or question that his duty was to find, if possible, the place of the original stakes which determined the boundary line between the proprietors. However erroneous may have been the original survey, the monuments that were set must nevertheless govern, even though the effect be to make one half-quarter section ninety acres and the one adjoining seventy; for parties buy or are supposed to buy in reference to these monuments, and are entitled to what is within their lines and no more, be it more or less. While the witness trees remain, there can generally be no difficulty in determining the locality of the stakes.

When the witness trees are gone, so that there is no longer record evidence of the monuments, it is remarkable how many there are who mistake altogether the duty that now devolves upon the surveyor. It is by no means uncommon that we find men, whose theoretical education is thought to make them experts, who think that when the monuments are gone, the only thing to be done is to place new monuments where the old ones should have been, and would have been if placed correctly. This is a serious mistake. The problem is now the same that it was before: To ascertain by the best lights of which the case admits, where the original lines were. The mistake above alluded to, is supposed to have found expression in our legislation; though it is possible that the real intent of the act to which we shall refer is not what is commonly supposed.

An act passed in 1869, Complied Laws 593, amending the laws respecting the duties and powers of county surveyors, after providing for the case of corners which can be identified by the original field notes or other unquestionable testimony, directs as follows:

"*Second.* Extinct interior section corners must be reestablished at the intersection of two right lines joining the nearest known points on the original section lines east and west and north and south of it.

Third. Any extinct quarter-section corner, except on fractional lines, must be established equidistant and in a right line between the section corners; in all other cases at its proportionate distance between the nearest original corners on the same line. The corners thus determined the surveyors are required to perpetuate by noting bearing trees when timber is near."

To estimate properly this legislation, we must start with the admitted and unquestionable fact that each purchaser from government bought such land as was within the original boundaries, and questionably owned it up to the time when the monuments became extinct. If the monument was set for an interior section corner, but did not happen to be at the intersection of two right lines joining the nearest known points east and west and north and south of it it nevertheless determined the extent of his possessions, and he gained or lost according as the mistake did or did not favor him.

EXTINCT CORNERS

It will probably be admitted that no man loses title to his land or any part thereof merely because the evidences become lost or uncertain. It may become more difficult for him to establish it as against an adverse claimant, but theoretically the right remains; and it remains a potential fact so long as he can present better evidence than any other person. And it may often happen that notwithstanding the loss of all trace of a section corner or quarter stake, there will still be evidence from which any surveyor will be able to determine with almost absolute certainty where the original boundary was between the government subdivisions.

There are two senses in which the word extinct may be used in this connection: one is the sense of physical disappearance: The other the sense of loss of all reliable evidence. If the statute speaks of extinct corners in the former sense, it is plain that the serious mistake was made in supposing that surveyors could be clothed with authority to establish new corners by an arbitrary rule in such cases. As well might the statute declare that if a man loses his deed, he shall lose his land altogether.

But if by extinct corner is meant one in respect to the actual location of which all reliable evidence is lost, then the following remarks are pertinent.

1. There would undoubtedly be presumption in such a case that the corner was correctly fixed by the government surveyor where the field notes indicated it to be.

2. But this is only a presumption, and may be overcome by any satisfactory evidence showing that in fact it was placed elsewhere.

3. No statute can confer upon a county surveyor the power to establish corners, and thereby bind the parties concerned. Nor is this a question merely of conflict between State and Federal law; it is a question of property right. The original surveys must govern, and the laws under which they are made govern, because the land was bought in reference to them; and any legislation, whether State or Federal, that should have the effect to change these, would be inoperative, because of the disturbance to vested rights.

4. In any case of disputed lines, unless the parties concerned settle the controversy by agreement, the determination of it is necessarily a judicial act, and it must proceed upon evidence, and give a full opportunity for a hearing. No arbitrary rules of survey or of evidence can be laid down whereby it can be adjudged.

THE FACTS OF POSSESSION

The general duty of a surveyor in such a case is plain enough. He is not to assume that the monument is lost until after he has thoroughly sifted the evidence and found himself unable to trace it. Even then he should hesitate long before doing anything to the disturbance of settled possessions. Occupation, especially if long continued, often affords very satisfactory evidence of the original boundary when no other is attainable; and the surveyor should inquire when it originated, how, and why the lines were then located as they were, and whether a claim of the title has always accompanied the possession, and give all the facts due force as evidence. Unfortunately, it is known that the surveyors sometimes, in supposed obedience to the state statute, disregard all evidences of occupation and claim of title, and plunge whole neighborhoods into quarrels and litigation by assuming to establish corners at points with which the previous occupation cannot harmonize. It is often the case when one or more corners are found to be extinct, all parties concerned have acquiesced in the lines which were traced by the guidance of some other corner or landmark, which may or may not have been trustworthy; but to bring these lines into discredit when the people concerned do not question them not only breeds trouble in the neighborhood, but it must often subject the surveyor himself to annoyance and perhaps discredit, since in a legal controversy the law as well as common sense must declare that the supposed boundary long acquiesced in is better evidence of where the real line should be than any survey made after the original monuments have disappeared. (*Stewart v. Carelton, 31* Mich. Reports, 270; *Diehl v. Zanger, 39* (Mich. Reports, 601) And county surveyors, no more than any others, can conclude parties by their surveys.

The mischief's of overlooking the facts of possession most often appear in cities and villages. In towns the block and lot stakes soon disappear; there are no witness trees, and no monuments to govern except such as have been put in their places, or where their places were supposed to be. The streets are likely to be soon marked off by fences, and the lots in a block will be measured off from these, without looking farther. Now it may perhaps be known in a particular case that a certain monument still remaining was the starting point in the original survey of the town plat; or a surveyor settling in the town may take some central point as the point of departure in his surveys, and assuming the original plat to be accurate, he will then undertake to find all streets and all lots by course and distance according to the plat, measuring and estimating from his point of departure. This procedure might unsettle every line and every monument existing by acquiescence in the town; it would be very likely to change the lines of streets, and raise controversies everywhere. Yet this is what is sometimes done; the surveyor himself being the first person to raise the disturbing questions.

Suppose, for example, a particular village street has been located by acquiescence and used for many years, and the proprietors in a certain block have laid off their lots in reference to this practical location. Two lot owners quarrel, and one of them calls in a surveyor, that he may make sure his neighbor shall not get an inch of land from him. This surveyor undertakes to make his survey accurate, whether the original was so or not, and the first result is, he notifies the lot owners that there is error in the street line, and that all fences should be moved, say one foot to the east. Perhaps he goes on to drive stakes through the block according to this conclusion. Of course, if he is right in doing this, all lines in the village will be unsettled; but we will limit our attention to the single block. It is not likely that the lot owners generally will allow the new survey to unsettle their possessions, but there is always a probability of finding someone disposed to do so. We shall then have a lawsuit; and with what result?

FIXING LINES BY ACQUIESCENCE

It is a common error that lines do not become fixed by acquiescence in a less time than twenty years. In fact, by statute, road lines may become conclusively fixed in ten years; and there is no particular time that shall be required to conclude private owners, where it appears that they have accepted a particular line as their boundary, and all concerned have cultivated and claimed up to it. Public policy requires that such lines be not lightly disturbed, or disturbed at all after the lapse of any considerable time. The litigant, therefore, who in such a case pins his faith on the surveyor is likely to suffer for his reliance and the surveyor himself to be mortified by a result that seems to impeach his judgment.

Of course, nothing in what has been said can require a surveyor to conceal his own judgment, or to report the facts one way when he believes them to be another. He has no right to mislead, and he may rightfully express his opinion that an original monument was at one place, when at the same time he is satisfied that acquiescence has fixed the rights of parties as if it were at another. But he would do mischief if he were to attempt to establish monuments which he knew would tend to disturb settled rights; the farthest he has a right to go, as an officer of the law, is to express his opinion where the monument should be, at the same time that he imparts the information to those who employ him, and who might otherwise be misled, that the same authority that makes him an officer and entrusts him to make surveys, also allows parties to settle their own boundary lines, and considers acquiescence in a particular line or monument, for any considerable period, as strong if not conclusive evidence of such settlement. The peace of the community absolutely requires this rule. It is not long since, that in one of the leading cities of the State an attempt was made to move houses two or three rods into a street, on the ground that a survey under which the street had been located for many years, had been found in a more recent survey to be erroneous.

THE DUTY OF THE SURVEYOR

From the foregoing it will appear that the duty of the surveyor where boundaries are in dispute must be varied by the circumstances.

1. He is to search for original monuments, or for the places where they were originally located, and allow these to control if he finds them, unless he has reason to believe that agreements of the parties, express or implied, have rendered them unimportant. By monuments in the case of government surveys we mean of course the corner and quarter stakes: blazed lines or marked trees on the lines are not monuments: they are merely guides or finger posts, if we may use the expression, to inform us with more or less accuracy where the monuments may be found.

2. If the original monuments are no longer discoverable, the question of location becomes one of evidence merely. It is merely idle for any State statute to direct a surveyor to locate or establish a corner, as the place of the original monument, according to some inflexible rule. The surveyor, on the other hand, must inquire into all the facts; giving due prominence to the acts of parties concerned, and always keeping in mind, first, that neither his opinion nor his survey can be conclusive upon parties concerned; and, second, that courts and juries may be required to follow after the surveyor over the same ground, and that it is exceedingly desirable that he govern his action by the same lights and the same rules that will govern theirs.

It is always possible when corners are extinct that the surveyor may usefully act as a mediator between parties, and assist in preventing legal controversies by settling doubtful lines. Unless he is made for this purpose an arbitrator by legal submission, the parties, of course, even if they consent to follow his judgment, cannot on the basis of mere consent, be compelled to do so; but if he brings about an agreement, and they carry it into effect by actually conforming their occupation to his lines, the action will conclude them. Of course, it is desirable that all such agreements be reduced to writing; but this is not absolutely indispensable if they are carried into effect without.

685

MEANDER LINES

The subject to which allusion will now be made is taken up with some reluctance, because it is believed the general rules are familiar. Nevertheless it is often found that surveyors misapprehend them, or err in their application, and as other interesting topics are somewhat connected with this, a little time devoted to it will probably not be altogether lost. The subject is that of meander lines. These are lines traced along the shores of lakes, ponds and considerable rivers as the measures of quantity when sections are made fractional by such waters. These have determined the price to be paid when government lands were bought, and perhaps the impression still lingers in some minds that the meander lines are boundary lines, and all in front of them remains unsold. Of course this is erroneous. There was never any doubt that, except on the large navigable rivers, the boundary of the owners of the banks is the middle line of the river; and while some courts have held that this was the rule on all fresh-water streams, large and small, others have held to the doctrine that the title to the bed of the stream below low-water mark is in the State, while conceding to the owners of the banks all riparian rights. The practical difference is not very important. In this State the rule that the center line is the boundary line is applied to all our great rivers, including the Detroit, varied somewhat by the circumstance of there being a distinct channel for navigation in some cases with the stream in the main shallow, and also sometimes by the existence of islands.

The troublesome questions for surveyors present themselves when the boundary line between two contiguous estates is to be continued from the meander line to the center line of the river. Of course the original survey supposes that each purchaser of land on the stream has a water front of the length shown by the field notes; and it is presumable that he bought this particular land because of that fact. In many cases it now happens that the meander line is left some distance from the shore by the gradual change of course of the stream, or diminution of the flow of water. Now the dividing line between two government subdivisions might strike the meander line at right angles, or obliquely; and , in some cases, if it were continued in the same direction to the center line of the river, might cut off from the water one of the subdivisions entirely, or at least cut it off from any privilege of navigation, or other valuable use of the water, while the other might have a water front much greater than the length of a line crossing it at right angles to its side lines. The effect might be that of two government subdivisions of equal size and cost, one would be of great value as water front property, and the other comparatively valueless. A rule which would produce this result would not be just, and it has not been recognized in the law.

Nevertheless it is not easy to determine what ought to be the correct rule for every case. If the river has a straight course, or one nearly so, every man's equities will be preserved by this rule: Extend the line of division between the two parcels from the meander line to the centerline of the river, as nearly as possible at right angles to the general course of the river at that point. This will preserve to each man the water front which the field notes indicated, except as changes in the water may have affected it, and the only inconvenience will be that the division line between different subdivisions is likely to be more or less deflected where it strikes the meander line.

This is the legal rule, and is not limited to government surveys, but applies as well to water lots which appear as such on town plats. (*Bay City Gas Light Co. v. The Industrial Works*, 28 Mich. Reports, 182.) It often happens, therefore, that the lines of city lots bounded on navigable streams are deflected as they strike the bank, or the line where the bank was when the town was first laid out.

IRREGULAR WATERCOURSES

When the stream is very crooked, and especially if there are short bends, so that the foregoing rule is incapable of strict application, it is sometimes very difficult to determine what shall be done; and in many cases the surveyor may be under the necessity of working out a rule for himself. Of course his action cannot be conclusive; but if he adopts one that follows as nearly as the circumstances will admit, the general rule above indicated, so as the divide as near as may be the bed of the stream among the adjoining owners in proportion to their lines upon the shore, his division, being that of an expert, made upon the ground, and with all available lights, is likely to be adopted as law for the case. Judicial decisions, into which the surveyor would find it prudent to look under such circumstances, will throw light upon his duties and may constitute a sufficient guide when peculiar cases arise. Each riparian lot owner ought to have a line on the legal boundary, namely, the centerline of the stream, proportioned to the length of his line on the shore, and the problem in each case is, how this is to be given him. Alluvion, when a river imperceptibly changes its course, will be apportioned by the same rules.

The existence of islands in a stream when the middle line constitutes a boundary, will not affect the apportionment unless the islands were surveyed out as government subdivisions in the original admeasurement. Wherever that was the case, the purchaser of the island divides the bed of the stream on each side of the owner of the bank, and his rights also extend above and below the solid ground, and are limited by the peculiarities of the bed and the channel. If an island was not surveyed as a government subdivision previous to the sale of the bank, it is of course impossible to do this for the purposes of government sale afterward for the reason that the rights of the bank owners are fixed by their purchase: when making that, they have a right to understand that all land between the meander lines, not separately surveyed and sold, will pass with the shore in the government sale; and having this right, anything which their purchase would include under it cannot afterward be taken from them. It is believed, however, that the federal courts would not recognize the applicability of this rule to large navigable rivers, such as those uniting the great lakes.

On all the little lakes of the State which are mere expansions near their mouths of the rivers passing through them - such as the Muskegon, Pere Marquette, and Manistee - the same rule of bed ownership has been judicially applied that is applied to the rivers themselves; and the division lines are extended under the water in the same way. (*Rice v. Ruddiman*, 10 Mich., 125.) If such a lake were circular, the lines would converge to the center; if oblong or irregular, there might be a line in the middle on which they would terminate, whose course would bear some relation to that of the shore. But it can seldom be important to follow the division line very far under the water, since all private rights are subject to the public rights of navigation and other use, and any private use of the lands inconsistent with these would be a nuisance, and punishable as such. It is sometimes important, however, to run the lines out for considerable distance, in order to determine where one may lawfully moor vessels or rafts, for the winter, or cut ice. The ice crop that forms over a man's land of course belongs to him. (*Lorman v. Benson*, 8 Mich., 18; *People's Ice Co. v. Steamer Excelsior*, recently decided.)

MEANDER LINES AND RIPARIAN RIGHTS

What is said above will show how unfounded is the notion, which is sometimes advanced, that a riparian proprietor on a meandered river may lawfully raise the water in the stream without liability to the proprietors above, provided he does not raise it so that it overflows the meander line. The real fact is that the meander line has nothing to do with such a case, and an action will lie whenever he sets back the water upon the proprietor above, whether the overflow be below the meander lines or above them. As regards the lakes and ponds of the State, one may easily raise questions that it would be impossible for him to settle. Let us suggest a few questions, some of which are easily answered, and some not:

1. To whom belongs the land under these bodies of water, where they are not mere expansions of a stream flowing through them?

2. What public rights exist in them?

3. If there are islands in them which were not surveyed out and sold by the United States, can this be done now?

Others will be suggested by the answers given to these. It seems obvious that the rules of private ownership which are applied to rivers cannot be applied to the great lakes. Perhaps it should be held that the boundary is at low water mark, but improvements beyond this would only become unlawful when they became nuisances. Islands in the great lakes would belong to the United States until sold, and might be surveyed and measured for sale at any time. The right to take fish in the lakes, or to cut ice, is public like the right of navigation, but is to be exercised in such manner as not to interfere with the rights of shore owners. But so far as these public rights can be the subject of ownership, they belong to the State, not to the United States; and so, it is believed, does the bed of a lake also. (*Pollard v. Hagan*, 3 Howard's U. S. Reports.) But such rights are not considered proper subjects of sale, but like the right to make use of the public highways, they are held in trust by the State for all the people.

What is said of the large lakes may perhaps be said also of the interior lakes of the State; such, for example, as Houghton, Higgins, Cheboygan, Burt's, Mullet, Whitmore, and many others. But there are many little lakes or ponds which are gradually disappearing, and the shore proprietorship advances *pari passu* as the waters recede. If these are of any considerable size - say, even a mile across - there may be questions of conflicting rights which no adjudication hitherto made could settle. Let any surveyor, for example, take the case of a pond of irregular form, occupying a mile square or more of territory, and undertake to determine the rights of the shore proprietors to its bed when it shall totally disappear, and he will find he is in the midst of problems such as probably he has never grappled with, or reflected upon before. But the general rules for the extension of shore lines, which have already been laid down, should govern such cases, or at least should serve as guides in their settlement.

Where a pond is so small as to be included within the lines of a private purchase from the government, it is not believed the public have any rights in it whatever. Where it is not so included, it is believed they have rights of fishery, rights to take ice and water, and rights of navigation for business and pleasure. This is the common belief, and probably the just one. Shore rights must not be so exercised as to disturb these, and the States may pass legislation to preserve these little bodies of water as permanent places of resort for the pleasure and recreation of the people, and there ought to be such legislation.

If the State should be recognized as owner of the beds of these small lakes and ponds, it would not be owner for the purpose of selling. It would be owner only as trustee for the public use; and a sale would be inconsistent with the right of the bank owners to make use of the water in its natural condition in connection with their estates. Some of them might be made salable lands by draining; but the State could not drain, even for this purpose, against the will of the shore owners, unless their rights were appropriated and paid for.

Upon many questions that might arise between the State as owner of the bed of a little lake and the shore owners, it would be presumptuous to express an opinion now, and fortunately the occasion does not require it.

QUASI - JUDICIAL CAPACITY OF SURVEYORS

I have thus indicated a few of the questions with which surveyors may now and then have the occasion to deal, and to which they should bring good sense and sound judgment. Surveyors are not and cannot be judicial officers, but in a great many cases they act in quasi-judicial capacity with the acquiescence of parties concerned; and it is important for them to know by what rules they are to be guided in the discharge of their judicial functions. What I have said cannot contribute much to their enlightenment, but I trust will not be wholly without value.

[1] The text is of a talk by Justice Thomas M. Cooley which he delivered at the second meeting of the Michigan Association of Surveyors and Civil Engineers at Lansing, Michigan, between January 11 - 13, 1881.

Printed in the USA
CPSIA information can be obtained
at www.ICGtesting.com
LVHW091531100124
768636LV00032B/1139/J